DRAMA ON STAGE

DRAMA ON STAGE

Second Edition

Randolph Goodman

Brooklyn College
City University of New York
Adjunct Professor in Playwriting, Columbia University

Holt, Rinehart and Winston

New York   Chicago   San Francisco   Atlanta   Dallas
Montreal   Toronto

COVER: Pablo Picasso, *Harlequin*. Oil on canvas. 32⅝ by 24¼ inches. Signed and dated (lower left): *Picasso 1901*. The Metropolitan Museum of Art, Gift of Mr. and Mrs. John L. Loeb, 1960.

LIBRARY OF CONGRESS CATALOGING IN PUBLICATION DATA
GOODMAN, RANDOLPH G.
    DRAMA ON STAGE.
    1. DRAMA—COLLECTIONS. 2. THEATER—
HISTORY—ADDRESSES, ESSAYS, LECTURES.
3. DRAMA—HISTORY AND CRITICISM—ADDRESSES,
ESSAYS, LECTURES. I. TITLE
PN6112.G64 1978   792   77-16442

ISBN 0-03-020326-0

Copyright Acknowledgments

Medea translated into English by Frederic Prokosch. Copyright 1947 by Frederic Prokosch and reprinted with his permission.

Excerpts from *Medea* by Robinson Jeffers. Copyright 1946 by Robinson Jeffers. Reprinted by permission of New Directions Publishing Corporation.

"Send in the Clowns." Reprinted with permission of Macmillan Publishing Co., Inc. from *Sondheim & Co.* by Craig Zadan. Copyright © 1974 by Craig Zadan.

A Funny Thing Happened on the Way to the Forum by Burt Shevelove, Larry Gelbart, and Stephen Sondheim. Copyright © 1963, by Burt Shevelove, Larry Gelbart, and Stephen Sondheim. Lyrics from musical compositions (except "The House of Marcus Lycus"), copyright © 1962 by Stephen Sondheim. "The House of Marcus Lycus" copyright © 1963 by Stephen Sondheim. Reprinted by permission of Dodd, Mead and Company, Inc.

The Misanthrope by Molière, translated into English by Richard Wilbur. Copyright © 1954, 1955, by Richard Wilbur. Reprinted by permission of Harcourt Brace Jovanovich, Inc.

In memory of
Philip, Bertha, and Harvey

Preface

Drama on Stage, Second Edition, retains five of the six plays from its First Edition and adds six others. The plays in the First Edition tended to put a rather heavy emphasis on serious, even tragic, themes. The new material demonstrates that laughter has also played an important part in the history of the drama. In addition to the injection of humor, I have kept in mind the interest of contemporary students by translating the text of the medieval morality play *Everyman* into modern English for easier comprehension and greater appreciation.

The history of dramatic literature is comparatively rich. We can read plays written in a wide variety of styles for every important period during the past twenty-five hundred years. Our records of theatrical productions, on the other hand, are relatively poor because of the transitory nature of the theater's physical properties. Costumes, scenery, and furnishings have decayed, disappeared, or been destroyed; even stone playhouses have been torn down or have crumbled away. And what of the actors' performances? Powerful though they may be in execution, concluded and applauded they are no more than an insubstantial memory.

Articulate spectators, critics, and members of the theatrical profession have left eyewitness reports, the best of which provide us with vivid images of outstanding productions and performances; many of these reports have been made more graphic by the inclusion of sketches, engravings, and photographs. But it is absolutely impossible to re-create a play merely by the use of words and pictures (even *moving* pictures), because the minimum basic requisites for living theater are flesh-and-blood actors confronting flesh-and-blood audiences. And all professional playwrights have written for the living theater! A play is born in a manuscript and buried in a printed text; it knows life, like a human being, only in the bright world of action.

Molière was well aware of this fact. With a genius for both dramatic literature and theatrical production, he directed the following words to the readers of the published version of his play *Love Is the Best Doctor:* "There is no need to tell you that many things depend entirely on the manner of the performance. Every one knows well enough that plays are written only to be acted; and I advise no one to read this unless he has the faculty, while doing so, of catching the meaning of the business of the stage."

It is the aim of this book to help the reader catch "the meaning of the business of the stage." This is not an easy assignment. A play is a complex and difficult form of art. As presented in the theater, it is, in fact, a synthesis of all the other arts. The story unfolds in poetry or prose; the action is expressed by voice, gesture, and movement; the scenery involves painting, architecture, and lighting; music and dancing are often integral elements of the work.

If the reader is to keep all of these elements in mind while attention is fixed on the text of the play, he or .she must have some preparation and assistance; must be aware of the theatrical conditions under which each work was originally performed, as well as of the varying conditions affecting its later productions. It is especially useful to be acquainted with the individual, and often conflicting, points of view and practices of the playwright's corps of collaborators—the actors, directors, scene and costume designers, lighting and sound technicians, musicians, dancers, stage managers, and stagehands—whose job it is, collectively, to turn a verbal plan into a viable production.

The interviews with artists and technicians that introduce each of the plays in this volume are intended to stimulate the imagination of the reader and to familiarize him with the procedures of the best professional theater craftsmen. Those that appeared in the First Edition remain as originally written to preserve their flavor, though the persons themselves—and the tenses—may no longer be present. How enlightening it would be if we had Euripides' comments concerning the composition of *Medea* as we have Duerrenmatt's remarks on *The Visit*; and how helpful to an actor if he were able to compare Burbage's interpretation of the character of Macbeth with Olivier's or Eric Porter's! The collection and preservation of such revelations as these is the task of the theater historian.

My intention in preparing the First Edition was to offer a significant play for each important period of the drama; but a mere half dozen works, it was clear, could not possibly represent the rich dramatic literature of the Western world. There was no representative play for the Roman period, for the eighteenth or nineteenth century, or for the avant-garde theater of today. I have tried to rectify that situation by adding to the present edition a modern musical comedy based on the plays of Plautus, a farce by Richard Brinsley Sheridan (suggestive of *The Recruiting Officer,* George Farquhar's Restoration comedy), a problem play with contemporary overtones by Henrik Ibsen, and a brief and innovative work by Samuel Beckett. Read chronologically, the plays provide, in condensed form, a history of Western drama. Secondly, each play selected has had numerous and significant productions, particularly during recent years, so that the artists involved have been available for interview.

It is the author's hope that this book will provide at least a clue to the meaning of the business of the theater, and that it will, in any case, arouse the reader's interest in drama on stage.

I take special pleasure in expressing my gratitude to those individuals and institutions without whose generous cooperation this book could not have been written. My thanks go first to the professional theater people, mentioned by name in the text, who took time out of busy schedules to talk with me about their work. I am indebted, in addition, to the following:

In New York: To George Freedley, Curator, and to Elizabeth P. Barrett and Paul Myers of the Theater Collection of the New York Public Library, to the staff of the Photographic Division of the Library, and to Gabriel C. Austin of its Information Service; to Anne Minor of the Cultural Division of the French Embassy and to Daisy J. Lebel of its Library; to the French Institute; to Lisa Basch of the Photographic Services at Columbia University; and to the Austrian, British, French, German, Netherlands, and Swiss information offices.

In New Haven: To Professor Alois M. Nagler of Yale; and to Mary Grahn of the library at the Yale Drama School.

In London: To the British Museum; to the Library of the University of London; to George Nash of the Enthoven Collection, Victoria and Albert Museum; to Sybil Rosenfeld, Phyllis Hartnoll, Ifan Kyrle Fletcher, and David Magarshack.

In Stratford-on-Avon: To the Shakespeare Memorial Library.

In Paris: To the Bibliothèque Nationale; to André Veinstein of the Bibliothèque de l'Arsenal.

In Vienna: To Professor Heinz Kindermann of the University of Vienna; to Gerda Doublier of the Library of the Institut für Theaterwissenschaft.

In Salzburg: To the Festival Information Office.

In Berlin: To Hugo Fetting of the Deutsche Akademie der Künste (*Theatergeschichte*); to the Schillertheater Clipping Files.

In Copenhagen: To the Drama Collection of the Library of the University of Copenhagen.

In Stockholm: To Professor Agne Beijer, Dr. Gustaf Hilleström, Alf Sjöberg, and Per Sjöstrand; to Dr. Karl-Ragnar Gierow, director of the Royal Dramatic Theater; and to the Library of the University of Stockholm.

In Oslo: To Knut Hergel, director of the Oslo National Theater: to Lita Prahl and Christian Stenersen; and to Carl Frederick Engelstad and his family.

In Geneva: To François Simon and Georges Descombes.

In Zürich: To Dr. Kurt Hirschfeld and Ruth Bossard of the Schauspielhaus; to Peter Schifferli of Die Arche Verlag; and to Dr. Elisabeth Brock-Sulzer.

In Spoleto: To the Festival Information Office.

In Rome: To John L. Brown, cultural attaché to the American Embassy; to Dr. Giordano Falzoni of the Cultural Division of the American Embassy; to Maria Theresa de Ruette Scalero of the Library of the United States Information Service; and to Franco Zeffirelli.

Finally, it remains for me to acknowledge my obligations to Robin Leigh III, who started me on the adventure of this book; to Professor M. C. Kuner, who proffered wise advice during the writing process; to Dr. Margarete Bieber, my teacher and friend, who kindly consented to read the chapter on Greek theater; to Professor Otto Reinert, of the University of Washington, who read the entire book in manuscript and offered innumerable and invaluable suggestions; to the Alexander family, Ron Gaskell, and Bernard Michal, dear and helpful friends in London and Paris; and to Jordan Hott, Mrs. Eva Baratta, and Mrs. Evelyn B. Pearlman, who assisted me in the preparation of the manuscript.

In enlarging the text, I have obviously incurred additional obligations. I want to express my gratitude to Paul Myers and the staff of the New York Public Library and Museum of the Performing Arts at Lincoln Center; to Mrs. Lena Daun, of the Swedish Information Service; to Pamela Jordan, of the Yale Drama Library; to April Koral and Richard Sasanow, resourceful envoys to the Enthoven Collection of the Victoria and Albert Museum, London; to Frederic Proud for material relating to his Soho Poly (London) production of *St. Patrick's Day*; to Alan Schneider for the generous loan of material relating to Samuel Beckett and to *Krapp's Last Tape*; to Professor Charles R. Sleeth, for providing many valuable emendations to my translation of *Everyman*; to Professors Robert L. Antrim, James Hooks, and Howard Scammon, for reading the new material and offering helpful suggestions; to David Stark for his photographic expertise; to Professor M. C. Kuner, for her insightful comments and supportive discussions; to Professor Leif Sjöberg and Valborg Anderson for material on *The Ghost Sonata*; to David M. Glixon and Ruth Chapman, skillful and perceptive editors; and to the editorial staff at Holt, Rinehart and Winston, which has proved most helpful in every way. To those whose names I may inadvertently have omitted, I offer thanks and apologies in equal measure.

R. G.

New York
January 1978

Contents

xi

Macbeth

WILLIAM SHAKESPEARE

The Misanthrope

MOLIERE

St. Patrick's Day

RICHARD BRINSLEY SHERIDAN

An Enemy of the People

HENRIK IBSEN

The Ghost Sonata
AUGUST STRINDBERG

Cat on a Hot Tin Roof
TENNESSEE WILLIAMS

The Visit
FRIEDRICH DUERRENMATT

Krapp's Last Tape
SAMUEL BECKETT

(*Above*) The theater at Epidaurus, Greece, dating from the fourth century B.C. Used today as it was in ancient times, the theater seats about 14,000 people. Performances in antiquity, we are told, ran from sunrise to sunset. (D. A. Harissiadis)

DIE MEDEA-VASE IN MUNCHEN

(*Left*) *The Revenge of Medea*, depicted on a vase of the early fourth century, B.C., from Canosa, Italy, now in Munich. In this version, later than Euripides', the death of the princess was reported to the audience by a messenger. Medea escaped in a dragon-drawn chariot that was moved by "the machine." (From A. Furtwängler and K. Reichhold, *Griechische Vasenmalerei*, 1904–1909)

Medea

~~~~~~~~~~~~~~~~~~ EURIPIDES

Introduction

Euripides, the son of Mnesarchides, was born in the vicinity of Athens some time between 485 and 480 B.C., presented his first set of tragedies in 455, and won his first victory in 441. He won only four prizes during his lifetime, though another was awarded him posthumously; this is a very unusual record for a man who wrote about eighty-eight plays (twenty-two sets of four) and who was compared even while he lived with Aeschylus and Sophocles. The reason why the judges ignored him is clear: Euripides did not cater to the prejudices of the Athenian crowd.

He did not approve of its superstitions and follies, its social injustices or its moral standards; he objected to its cynicism and its neglect of that human value which he considered highest—love of one's fellow man. And so he dared to write about the decay of the state religion, the disintegration of family life because of the subjection of women, the demoralizing effect of Athenian aggression carried on in the name of democracy, and the false distinction which was made between freeman and slave. His sympathy was reserved for ordinary human beings, including peasants, aliens, and slaves, his scorn for evil-doers and tyrants whether they were men or gods. In fact, he brought the gods, as well as the ancient heroes and heroines, down to the level of the common man, and represented all "not as they ought to be, but as they are." To Euripides the traditional legends implied that the morality of the gods was lower than that of good men.

Such views were revolutionary and objectionable enough, but to make things worse Euripides began to tamper with the very structure of tragedy itself. Greek tragedy, it must be remembered, was nothing like modern drama, for it was not a secular art but a religious one. It was not written primarily to provide entertainment, although that was expected, but to furnish religious instruction and moral inspiration, to effect a purging of the psyche, a catharsis. Even Greek comedy had a ritualistic basis and a didactic purpose.

The modern dramatist may write on any subject he cares to and present it in any form that strikes his fancy, but the Athenian playwright was more or less constrained to select his material from Greek history or legend and to present it in a well-established and highly conventional form. The play had to be written in verse and was accompanied throughout by music; it had to have a chorus, it could use no more than three actors; no violent action could be shown upon the

1

stage, but a messenger might report it; and, finally, a crane-like machine might deposit a god (*deus ex machina*), or several gods, upon the stage, either during or more often at the end of the play, in order to show how the deities were involved in man's life and often settled man's problems. There was even a strict prescription for the use of the verse: The Chorus sang an ode as it entered at the beginning, and as it left at the end of the play; it also sang an ode between each of the five dramatic episodes into which the play was divided. The episodes themselves were written mainly in two kinds of verse, satirical (usually iambic) and lyric, resembling somewhat the recitatives and arias in a modern opera. This traditional and unrealistic form of drama was ideally suited to the mystical visions of Aeschylus and the idealistic views of Sophocles, but it could not properly accommodate the rationalistic and satirical concepts of Euripides. The young playwright, therefore, made a number of changes in the accepted form of tragedy, and earned as a result the general censure of his contemporaries.

Because he wrote plays in which theme and plot were usually more important than character, Euripides introduced long prologues and epilogues which served to announce his thesis, to suggest a pattern for the various episodes, or to supply a moral. He did not hesitate to alter or curtail the use of the Chorus. Aeschylus and Sophocles had written about public conflicts and so a Chorus of Theban Elders might very well take part in the action; but Euripides was concerned about private discords between husband and wife (Jason-Medea) or father and son (Theseus-Hippolytus) and in these a chorus would have little place. The Chorus often actually got in the way of the action, and so we find Euripides apologizing for its presence and limiting its use. Occasionally he brought them on, as a sort of entr'acte, to sing an irrelevant ode between episodes. Euripides also introduced innovations in the musical accompaniment. We do not know exactly what effect was produced, but apparently instead of singing one syllable to a note, so that the meaning of each word would be clear to the audience, the syllables and words were trilled and repeated until they became incomprehensible, as is so much of modern grand opera. Euripides, generally speaking, threw all "classic restraint" to the winds; nor did he write about the fall of a good person brought about by a flaw in his character. The people he chose to write about were driven by sexual passion, anger, revenge, or a desire for power.

The cavalier manner in which the playwright distorted or summarily dismissed the basic elements of tragedy as later enumerated in the *Poetics* makes it impossible for us to classify Euripides' plays as Aristotelian tragedies; not one of his plays, in fact, exactly fits the definition. After careful analysis, we are obliged to refer to them simply as dramas, comedy-dramas, melodramas, romances, and fantasies, while some even approach musical comedy. It is no wonder then that conservative audiences objected, that judges demurred, and that, throughout his life, Euripides was the butt of serious critics and comic poets alike.

In 408 B.C., Euripides left Athens, a voluntary exile because of the ill-will of his fellow citizens, and went to live at the court of Archelaus in Macedonia. He died in exile at the age of 78, in about the year 406, and was buried at Arethusa.

If Euripides was not sufficiently appreciated in his own day, he has been amply vindicated since, for nineteen of his plays are extant, more than double the number of those of all his rivals put together. His *Medea* (431 B.C.) took only third prize, but the plays that placed first and second that year are unknown. As the creator of love-drama, moreover, Euripides was the forefather of Greek New Comedy and of Roman and modern drama as well. He introduced to the stage many forms of intrigue, adventure, and suspense, as well as recognition scenes and psychological probing which have all found their way into the plays that grace our stages and motion picture and television screens. He became the most influential and highly imitated of all the Greek playwrights, and the one whose plays have been most frequently and consistently revived and adapted down to our own time.

In writing the *Medea* Euripides was dealing with one of his favorite myths, one he used as the basis for three separate plays. The love affair between Jason and Medea held strong appeal for the dramatist, for it was a romance fraught with tensions and conflicts.

When Jason claimed the throne of Iolcus, which rightfully belonged to him, his traitorous uncle, Pelias, who occupied it, agreed to give it up on condition that Jason fetch the Golden Fleece from Colchis. Pelias assigned this impossible task believing that the young man would fail in the enterprise and would meet his death at the hands of the barbarians who dwelt in that distant land. Jason coolly set about building the Argo, the first Greek ship, and sailed for Colchis, where at the royal court, he met Medea, a wild, passionate girl who fell deeply in love with him. Medea was the daughter of the king; the grand-daughter of Helios, the sun god; and the niece of Circe, the enchantress; from these forebears she had inherited great powers, both natural and supernatural, and she did not hesitate to put them all at the disposal of the man she loved. She cruelly deceived her father and made it possible for Jason to seize the Golden Fleece; then she boarded the Argo with her lover and fled her own country. Pursued by her brother, Absyrtos, she slew him brutally without any qualms. When they reached Thessaly, Jason and Medea discovered that Pelias had no intentions of giving up the throne, whereupon Medea tricked the king's daughters into causing their father's death. Jason, fearing vengeance, renounced his claim to the throne, hoping, perhaps, to sit upon a richer throne elsewhere. Banished from his own land, Jason took Medea and their two sons to Corinth where the family was granted sanctuary. It seemed as if they would be able to live in peace now; but Creon, the king, having no male heir, was looking about for a mate for his daughter, Glauce, and decided that Jason would be ideal. The king informed Jason that if he agreed to marry the princess, he would be named successor to the throne. Since Medea was an alien, her marriage to Jason was not legally recognized in any Greek city, and her children were considered illegitimate. From a legal point of view, therefore, there was nothing to prevent Jason from leaving Medea to marry Glauce, which is exactly what he did, without informing his wife.

Euripides' play opens shortly after Medea learns that her husband has deserted her. She is in a torment of humiliation and despair, and has become ill and

emotionally upset planning revenge. Her Nurse's lament, which serves as a prologue to the play, informs us of the sacrifices that Medea has made in the past
for the man who has just left her; we are again reminded of these sacrifices when
Medea reproaches and reviles Jason; and we hear of them for the third time from
Jason's own lips at the very end of the play. This last touch is a beautiful piece
of irony, since Jason clearly remembers his wife's crimes but conveniently forgets
that she committed them for his sake. Euripides, however, will allow neither
Medea nor the audience to forget that there was strong motivation—even justification, perhaps—for the horrible crimes about to be perpetrated. In Medea love
is as ruthless, as brutal, and as destructive a force as hate. Appalling and terrible
as she is, Medea is still understandable and real. Where once she dared anything
to bring Jason pleasure, she now fears nothing to give him pain.

It is difficult to sympathize with her, but we are forced to admit that Medea
was a loyal and devoted wife, who would stop at nothing to advance her husband's welfare. It is Jason who has failed in devotion and fidelity and who, instead of being grateful for the aid his wife has given him, defends himself against
her recriminations with insolent and specious arguments. He tells her that it was
for her good and for the best interest of their sons that he has married Glauce;
he offers her money and letters of introduction to his friends in foreign cities, for
she is about to be cast out of Corinth; and he insists that he has adequately
repaid her for her services by bringing her from barbarous Asia to civilized
Greece. Here Euripides achieves another brilliant piece of irony in making Jason
sound like the president of the chamber of commerce congratulating a refugee on
reaching God's own country.

But Medea is not so easily taken in; she has dealt with cleverer men than Jason;
she has outsmarted princes and kings. She can bend any man to her will because
she uses the proper psychological approach to each one. When Creon orders her
out of the country at once, she manages by a subtle appeal to his kindness to get
one day's grace, which is all she needs to effect her revenge; when Aegeus, the
Athenian king, tells her that he is unhappy because he is childless, she sees at
once a way to blast Jason's happiness, and in exchange for Aegeus' vow to protect
her in his city she promises to cure his sterility. On Jason she practices the greatest
deceit and for him she reserves the cruelest punishment, for she not only wrecks
his hope of inheriting Creon's throne, but destroys all his loved ones in the
bargain.

The manner in which Medea makes her escape from Corinth—in a dragon-
drawn chariot sent to her by her grandfather, Helios—has met with the severe
disapproval of many critics as an unwarranted intrusion of the supernatural. It
certainly would have been easier for the playwright and more credible to the
audience simply to have announced Medea's departure, but to a showman and
poet of Euripides' caliber the present ending presented at least three distinct
advantages: first, it is extremely theatrical and spectacular; then, it better explains
how Medea managed to deposit her children's bodies at the temple of Hera at
Acrocorinth where, in the dramatist's time, there was a cult involving these
children; finally, it was a symbolic means of vindicating Medea, for it was the

sun—emblem of reason—that sent the chariot which enabled her to effect her escape.

It is possible to read many themes into the play, but the significance of this work is greater than the sum of all of them. We are shown, for instance, the unfair treatment accorded aliens in Greece; the eternal battle of the sexes; and, most terrifying of all, the oppressed striking back to achieve not justice but revenge.

The odes sung by the Chorus in this play are more closely related to the subject matter of the drama than is generally the case in Euripides. Hearing Medea lament, the Chorus of Corinthian Women enters and in the first ode (called the parados) offers sympathy and cautions her to practice restraint. The next time they sing they mention that the old order is changing: women used to be accused of faithlessness, but now the men have grown deceitful, and Medea has been deserted in a foreign land. After the scene in which Medea hurls her scathing denunciations at Jason, the Chorus again suggests restraint and expresses pity because Medea has no friend to help her; at this point Aegeus, king of Athens, who is passing through Corinth on a journey, meets Medea and promises to give her sanctuary, unaware of the crimes she is planning. Here the Chorus sings an ode in praise of Athens, which must have delighted the audience, although it is not entirely relevant to the action. The Chorus itself wonders how such a sacred city can give protection to a murderess, and begs Medea not to destroy her sons. Here we see the awkwardness of the Chorus in Euripidean drama: All the women in Corinth know that Medea plans to murder her children, but they do not inform Jason, nor do anything else about it, except to advise Medea against it. After Medea sends her children to Glauce with the poisoned gifts, the Chorus expresses sorrow at the fact that the boys will be accomplices in their mother's crime, and weeps again because Medea intends to slay them. When the boys return, Medea, torn between her love for them and her determination to kill them, leads them resolutely into the house, while the Chorus laments that children bring only endless cares. As the women hear the cries issuing from indoors, but are prevented from entering, they pray to heaven to stay Medea's hand. At the end of the play, the Chorus sings a final song (the exodos); here the poet expresses his view of life in words which appear almost verbatim at the conclusion of four of his other plays. Euripides' outlook is not a cheerful one; he stresses the uncertainties of life and points out that those things we count on do not come to pass, while the things we do not dream of are bound to happen. Perhaps because such a viewpoint is based upon feelings of insecurity and anxiety, it has found ready acceptance throughout the ages and is widely held today, as the plays of Tennessee Williams (pp. 489–491) and many others clearly show.

PRODUCTION IN THE THEATER OF DIONYSUS

The Great Dionysia was an important fertility festival celebrated in Athens in honor of the god Dionysus Eleuthereus. This god was introduced into the city by the tyrant Pisistratus in the sixth century B.C. from the village of Eleutherae. First one temple, then another was built in honor of the god on the southern slope of the Acropolis; beside these temples, on holy ground, the Theater of Dionysus began to take shape and grow until the stage-building hid the temples from the view of the audience, but the drama always retained its religious function.

The Great Dionysia was celebrated each year about the end of March when the skies are clear and the air is warm, for the spring comes early in Greece. As part of the festival, lyric choruses performed, and tragedies and comedies were produced in the Theater of Dionysus. As in most Greek festivals, the presentation of plays took the form of a competition.

The chief religious magistrate of the city, who was in charge of the festival, selected three dramatic poets and three choregoi, rich men who were compelled to finance the plays, to compete. In order to enter the contest, each dramatic poet had to submit a group of four plays, called a tetralogy, consisting of three tragedies (which might or might not be related to each other in subject matter) and a satyr-play, a drama in a lighter vein. The playwright chosen to compete trained his own chorus, directed his play, and served also as costume and scene designer, choreographer, and composer. The choregoi functioned as producers; each one was assigned a poet and had to pay all the expenses involved in putting on that poet's plays. They paid the salaries of the members of the chorus and of the flute-player, and supplied the costumes and scenery. The play might succeed or fail depending upon the generosity or stinginess of the choregos.

Elaborate precautions were taken to insure fairness in the selection of the five judges who awarded first, second, and third prizes to the playwrights at the end of the contest. The verdicts were generally just, but despite all precautions judges were sometimes bribed or influenced. The victorious poet was proclaimed by the herald and was crowned in the theater with a crown of ivy; his choregos also received a crown and a tripod to commemorate the occasion. Plays which failed were often revised by the author and reproduced at less important festivals.

The order of events at the Great Dionysia was roughly as follows: On the day before the festival the audience gathered in the theater to hear the announcement of the names of the plays, playwrights, and leading actors who were to take part. This served in lieu of the printed program. On this day, too, the statue of Dionysus Eleuthereus was paraded in the theater, hymns were sung, and sacrifices offered. The first day of the actual festival started with another procession in which phalloi were carried, then sacrifices were made to the god, and the choregoi appeared in colorful and lavish robes. In the evening a lively performance was put on by revelers who sometimes disguised themselves as animals; this was called a *komos,* the root of the word *comedy.* The next three or four days were taken up from dawn till dusk with the presentation of the plays. On the final day of the festival, a special assembly was held in the theater. This assembly inquired into the conduct of the officials and heard all complaints concerning misconduct or injuries connected with the festival.

The Great Dionysia became increasingly important during the Golden Age of Greece not only because of the performances of dramatic contests, but because it was open to the whole Hellenic world and served as an advertisement of Athenian wealth, power, and public spirit, as well as of her artistic and literary leadership. Surplus revenues were displayed in the theater; the sons of veterans were paraded and rewarded; foreign ambassadors attended; prisoners were released on bail; no legal action could be taken; and it was a general holiday.

The Theater

The Theater of Dionysus grew up functionally out of the needs of the people and the contours of the land. Beside the temple on the southern slope of the Acropolis, a large, circular area was leveled off to make a place for the performance of ritualistic dances. The orchestron, or dancing place, consequently, is the oldest element of the theater. Worshipers at first stood around the circle to watch the performers, then moved up the slope to get a better view; there they stood or sat. By the beginning of the fifth century B.C., rows of wooden benches had not only been built up the mountainside but had fanned out in semicircular shape around the northern side of the orchestron. The auditorium, or hearing place, was thus the second element of the theater to appear. The *skene*, or scene-building, which developed into the raised stage, came last. The ritual dances became more pantomimic and dramatic; then actors separated themselves from the chorus and began to speak or chant lines impersonating various characters; soon a need was felt for a scene-building and dressing-rooms, which led to the erection of the *skene*, a wooden structure put up on the southern side of the orchestron facing the auditorium. The three component parts of the theater never achieved complete architectural unity during the fifth century, but improvements were made in each part from year to year: the dancing place was paved and drained; the wooden benches gave way to tiers of stone seats; and the *skene* was replaced each year by a more elaborate one especially designed to improve the stage picture.

The Actors

Thespis is credited with being the first actor; he won that distinction by stepping out of the chorus and assuming a dramatic role. Down to the time of Aeschylus, there appears to have been but one actor in a play and that actor was the poet himself. Aeschylus introduced the second actor. Sophocles took no part in the performance but introduced the third actor; thereafter only three actors were permitted to appear but each played several roles. By the middle of the fifth century the actors were chosen along with the plays and choregoi by the chief magistrate; the three best actors were assigned one each to each of the tragic poets. We know the names of some of the actors of this period; outstanding among them were Kleandros, Mynniskos, Kallipides, Tlepolemos, and probably Kephisophon. Only men were permitted to take part in the performances, as was true later in the Elizabethan and Japanese theaters.

The various parts in the plays were distributed among the three actors, who changed roles by changing masks, costumes, and voice. Children appeared in many of Euripides' plays but they did not speak. In the *Medea*, the parts might very well have been distributed as follows: 1st Actor—Medea; 2nd Actor—Nurse, Jason, Creon; 3rd Actor—Tutor, Aegeus, Messenger; the lines of the children, coming from off-stage, might have been spoken by adult actors.

The actors used words, gestures, and bodily movements. There were three kinds of speech: 1. Speech unaccompanied by music, in dialogue or monologue, which was in iambic trimeters, considered the rhythm closest to prose speech; 2. Speech accompanied by a musical instrument (the flute) called recitative and written in tetrameters and iambics inserted in the midst of lyric systems; and 3. Songs, in lyrics with music.

If the chorus danced while the actors spoke or sang, the flute must have accompanied both. A lyre was used sometimes, as were rattles and various other noisemakers.

The actors' voices were considered very important. The acoustics were good in the theaters, but actors had to speak clearly and correctly. The style of speaking was oratorical, occasionally realistic; vocal tricks, such as imitations of animal cries, bird calls, and other sound effects were also used.

Facial expressions were unalterable because of the masks which the actors wore, but gestures and movements were free in other respects—embracing, kneeling, crawling, and so on. As time went on this freedom grew. The dignified old actor, Mynniskos, nicknamed a younger actor, Kallipides, "The Monkey," because of his excessive use of gesture. In Old Comedy every sort of gesture and movement was used, unrestrained by costume or a sense of delicacy.

The Chorus

The entire performance had originally been put on by the chorus, and the chorus played a part in all Greek drama. In the early plays of Aeschylus it fills the major role, but after the introduction of the second and third actors its importance decreases. It was Agathon, a contemporary of Euripides, who is said to have introduced choral passages that could be transferred from one play to another, as they were merely incidental to the action.

There were twelve men in the chorus of Aeschylus; fifteen in the choruses of Sophocles and Euripides. The members of the chorus were masked, and wore costumes indicative of the characters portrayed. In the *Medea* they represented Corinthian women. The tragic chorus performed in rectangular formation: there were three rows, five men in a row. The leader of the chorus was the choragus. Some of the members of the chorus were said to be mute, that is, they took no vocal part in the action but merely danced. The flute-player entered and left with the chorus.

When the chorus took part in the dialogue, the leader spoke for the entire group; the odes and other choral passages were sung or spoken in unison by full or semichorus.

All dancing was considered mimetic and freely employed expressive and rhythmical gestures. The hands especially were used very pantomimically, and the gestures were intimately associated with the words from moment to moment. After a while the postures and attitudes came to be standardized and named.

The playwrights invented many dances for the chorus; Sophocles and Euripides had themselves been dancers. Various types of dances were done, some slow, some rapid, and some seductive. It is believed that the chorus danced as it sang; or that one part of the chorus danced, while the other part sang. In comedy the dancing was unrestrained, consisting of leaps and kicks, or was obscene, as in the *kordax*, a form of strip-tease sometimes done by an old woman (a man in disguise, of course).

Costumes

The most characteristic aspect of the actors' costumes was the masks. It is believed that masks had their origin in the rites connected with Dionysiac worship. Masks were obligatory for those who took part in the Dionysiac *Komos*, and in the satyr-dances. The chorus from which Thespis detached himself probably was masked, and the actor continued to wear a mask though it probably differed from the others. Thespis is said to have disguised his face originally with white lead, then with leaves, and then with plain linen masks. After that the playwright Choerilus improved the masks and robes, and Phrynichus introduced feminine masks. Later writers of tragedy made further alterations, adapting the masks to the personalities of the characters represented by the actors. It was Aeschylus who first used brightly colored and terrifying masks.

The dresses worn in tragedy were designed to make the characters look more noble, regal, and dignified; the long gowns reached to the ankles, and the sleeves covered the arms to the wrists. The fabrics were rich and highly ornamented and decorated. The chorus was dressed according to its supposed nationality or occupation. Individual characters were also specially dressed, in mourning, for instance, or in rags. Euripides was criticized by Aristophanes for permitting his heroes and heroines to appear in tatters.

Tragic actors wore soft shoes that went up high on the leg; these were called the *kothurnos*. It was not until the Hellenistic period that the soles were made several inches thick; and in the Roman theater the leading actor had thicker soles than the others, the added height showing his greater importance.

The costumes in Old Comedy were more varied and more indecent in order to induce laughter; actors had heavily padded bodies, and very short chitons with exaggerated phalloi showing; on their feet they wore soft, sloppy socks. Their masks were often caricatures of actual celebrities.

Scenery

The *skene*, or stage-building, in front of which the plays were performed generally represented the façade of a palace, a temple, or a house, since these were the locales most frequently called for in the tragedies. As the *skene* was re-erected each year, various improvements and additions were made in its structure. Side wings, called *paraskenia*, as well as platforms and levels, appeared from time to time to intimate the nature of the building which the *skene* was supposed to represent. There were passageways, called *paradoi*, to the right and left of the *skene*, used not only by the spectators for entering and leaving the theater, but also for the entrances and exits of the actors and the chorus. There were additional entrances and exits for the actors in the *skene* itself, for the building had three front doors—a very large center one, and a smaller one on each side of it.

The outdoor theater put a severe limitation upon the playwrights in the choice of scenes which could be convincingly shown as taking place in front of a house, temple, or palace, or in some other open-air setting; it was not possible to present interior scenes realistically. But a mechanical device was introduced during the fifth century which helped partially to overcome the difficulty; it was a platform on wheels, called an *eccyclema*, which was rolled out of the *skene* and on which was represented an action that was supposed to be taking place indoors.

Several other mechanical devices were put to use during the dramatic action. A sort of crane, or derrick, "the machine," lifted a god over the stage-building and brought him down into the midst of the action. When a playwright could not work out his plot, he might bring in a god to wind the play up. This mechanical solution of the problem came to be known as the *deus ex machina* (the god from the machine), a phrase still in use among drama critics. Euripides employed "the machine" frequently; in the *Medea,* for instance, it was by means of this device that the heroine could appear in her chariot on the roof of the *skene* at the end of the play.

Another mechanical apparatus was the *periaktos*, a three-sided prism on each side of which were painted pictures or symbols showing the time or place of the action. There were two *periaktoi,* one on each side of the *skene;* a change of scene could be indicated simply by revolving them.

Painted back-cloths or screens, easily removable, might also have been used during the performance to indicate changes of locale, but positive proof of this is lacking. We do know, however, that many plays called for scene changes both during the action and between separate works. In the bill of plays by Euripides that included the *Medea,* for instance, some scene changes must have been made, for the *Medea* takes place before a palace, the *Philoctetes* requires a mountain and cave, the *Dictys* probably required a house, while the satyr-play, the *Harvesters,* suggests a field or country region.

The one permanent element in the scenery was the altar situated in the very center of the dancing place. This was not a stage property but a real religious altar, connected with the temples which still stood behind the *skene,* and was part of the sacred ground on which the theater had been erected. Many playwrights took advantage of the presence of the altar, and in their temple scenes required the actors to make use of it.

Music

A great deal of music was used in the drama but not much is known about it because so little of it is extant. It appears to have been very complicated; in addition to being written in modes (varying intervals between notes), it could have diatonic, chromatic, or enharmonic form, and could be sung or played in a number of keys (absolute pitch could be varied). The modes were connected with the emotions: Dorian was considered majestic; Mixolydian, pathetic; Phrygian, sensuous or excited. Aristotle approved of the use of Hypodorian and Hypophrygian modes by the actors when realistic action was called for. The Phrygian mode was considered overemotional; one scrap of this type survives for a passage of Euripides' *Orestes*, lines 338-344.

At first the music was subordinate to the words, but later on, it became more elaborate and florid—a single syllable set to several notes—until the words were unintelligible. Instrumental music apart from words was seldom used, except in special cases in comedy, such as the song of the nightingale imitated in the *Birds* and the twanging of a lyre in the *Frogs*. The coryphaeus (leader of the chorus) gave the chorus the first note.

The Audience

The seating capacity of the great theater of Dionysus in Athens has been estimated to be somewhere between 14,000 and 17,000. Men, women, and children attended. We do not know the price of a seat in the fifth century (in the fourth, it was two obols), but Pericles decreed that those who could not afford to buy a ticket were to be given the money from the theoric fund (a surplus in the treasury). Pericles might have been attempting to win the favor of the people, but the struggle for tickets was so violent and the buying up of seats such an abuse, that the poor only got a chance to attend the theater through the theoric fund. The distribution was not made in cash but in the form of free tickets given out by the authorities of each deme, and only full citizens were entitled to a share.

An official called the Superintendent of Buildings (or Seller of Seats) was in charge of the theater; his salary was paid by the State and it was his duty to see that the theater was kept in good repair and that the seats were properly assigned. Admission to the theater was by ticket or token. Tokens were made of bronze, ivory, bone, lead, clay, and terra cotta. Those of bronze, ivory, and bone were probably for the upper classes, the occupants of the first rows; those of lead, clay, and terra cotta were inexpensive and might have served for most of the audience.

Seats of honor were given by the State to certain priests, officials, and foreign ambassadors. Sixty seats in the front row are inscribed with names of important people for whom the seats were reserved. The center seat in the front row—later a large, elaborately carved, thronelike chair of white marble—was occupied by the priest of Dionysus Eleuthereus; and two seats were provided for priests of Dionysus Melpomenus, for this god was worshiped by the Artists of Dionysus, the actors' union.

Women were seated separately from men, and courtesans apart from other women. The women were placed at a distance from the orchestron. Foreign men and foreign women were seated separately at the extreme left or right of the theater.

The theater was divided into thirteen wedge-shaped blocks; each tribe (there were ten tribes in the fifth century) had its own block of seats and on their tokens were stamped the letter indicating the block and a symbol of the tribe.

Since the performances went on from dawn till dusk, the audience brought refreshments: food, wine, dried fruits, and candy. These items may also have been
sold in the theater. Food was thrown at unpopular actors. The audience had few
comforts, but cushions were put on the stone seats.

The audience was very noisy—applauding, hissing, and kicking with their heels
—but they could also be extremely attentive. Arguments and fights often developed; and special officials were there to keep order.

Contrary to common belief, not all members of the audience knew the stories of
the plays; only the more intellectual ones did. But the audiences were critical:
they hissed a line in praise of money and applauded some verses in praise of
freedom. They were particularly sensitive to anything that appealed to, or con-
flicted with, their moral and political sentiments; their point of view was highly
utilitarian. Their ability to follow devotedly day after day three great tragedies,
and to enjoy the wit of Aristophanes, shows that they had a high degree of
awareness.

THE PRODUCTION RECORD

Euripides' *Medea* received its first performance at the Dionysiac festival in
Athens in 431 B.C. Although it won only third prize, the play became so popular
and was performed so frequently that its lines were known throughout the
ancient world. Many playwrights, both Greek and Roman, borrowed the story
from Euripides.

In A.D. 60 Seneca, basing his work on Euripides' play, wrote a *Medea* that
lacked the emotional and psychological power of the Greek play, but served
nevertheless as a model for many neoclassical playwrights. Seneca departed from
Euripides by making Jason a sympathetic character; he also heightened the
spectacle and horror by having Medea kill one child on stage and the other on
the roof, possibly even flinging their bodies down, in full view of Jason and the
audience.

Corneille, whose version of *Medea* appeared in 1634, had two great actors at
his disposal for the leading roles: Montdory, the star of the Théatre Marais, and
La Villiers, the leading lady, who detested her colleague heartily and as a result
gave a very convincing performance as Medea. Corneille based his play on
Seneca's version but did not hesitate to rewrite it completely. He omitted the
chorus, cut the monologues, built up the dialogues and made them less mechanical, and added several complexities to the plot. Since Montdory was the star, his
role was enlarged to more than six times the original length, which made Jason
almost as important as Medea. There were many other changes, including
Aegeus' unreciprocated love for Creusa (Glauce), and the final suicide of Jason.
This treatment was well-suited to the tastes of Corneille's audience and proved
to be an enormous success.

There have been many *Medeas* in America in original form and in adaptation. Maxwell Anderson's *The Wingless Victory* (1937) is an interesting treatment

of the story which did not succeed in the theater. Medea here became the African princess, Oparre, who saved the life of a Yankee sea captain and returned with him to New England where, her common-law marriage repudiated, she was estranged and abandoned and slew her children in revenge. In 1946, Jean Anouilh adapted and modernized the play, making Medea a foul-mouthed Russian gypsy, who finally burned to death in her own caravan.

Robinson Jeffers' poetic adaptation of the *Medea* was written at the request of, and dedicated to, Judith Anderson. The play opened in New York on October 20, 1947, and closed on May 15, 1948, after a run of 214 performances. Most of the alterations made in the play were done for the purpose of building up the star's part: Medea's speeches were lengthened; Jason became more insignificant; three women served in place of a chorus; all the supernatural elements were removed from the story, thus highlighting Medea's psychological power; and Medea was given the final lines; she, rather than the poet, has the last word. Miss Anderson's interpretation of the role was as perceptive as it was passionate, and for her efforts she won the Drama League Award for the best acting of the year. Miss Anderson toured with the play almost continuously for the next eight years. During the week of October 12, 1959, a television version of *Medea* was presented for seven performances on Channel 13, WNTA-TV, New York. This was a slightly cut version (air time: 1 hour, 53 minutes, 25 seconds) of the Robinson Jeffers' adaptation with Judith Anderson giving her usual electrifying performance; the star was strongly supported by Aline McMahon as the Nurse and Morris Carnovsky as Creon. The play was produced by David Susskind and Lewis Freedman and directed by Jose Quintero and Wesley Kenney. Note that when *Medea* was produced outdoors in the Theater of Dionysus in Athens it was accounted a play of cosmological and sociocultural scope; later, when it was mounted behind the proscenium arch of an indoor theater, it seemed to be a work of lesser import, dealing merely with the wrath of a vengeful woman; confined to a television screen in a private living-room, its meaning was correspondingly reduced, the play providing the viewer mainly with a magnificent display of virtuoso acting.

This brief notice has of necessity been forced to omit mention of innumerable performances and productions of the *Medea*, both in its original form and in more or less free adaptations, in the two thousand five hundred years of its history, a history which has at the moment no foreseeable end.

BROADWAY PRODUCER
An Interview with Robert Whitehead

Robert Whitehead, one of the busiest and most successful of the theatrical producers on Broadway, is soft-spoken and genial. "He is a man of great singleness of purpose," says Brooks Atkinson, recently retired drama critic for the *New York Times*. "He has taste, skill, and imagination, and he loves the theater as one of the public arts."

Whitehead was born in Montreal, Canada, in 1916. As a child, he took part in living-room theatricals with his cousin, Hume Cronyn, and became dedicated to the stage for life. He arrived in New York at the age of twenty looking for work as an actor, but jobs were not easy to find. He enrolled for a two-year course in acting at the New York School of the Theater (now defunct), studied privately with the well-known coach Benno Schneider, spent a summer with the Barter Theater in Virginia, and found occasional work in New York as a stage-manager or player of "bit" parts.

After his service in World War II Whitehead returned to New York, eager to get back into the theater. The sort of parts he was able to get made acting less and less satisfying, and he began to cast about for another sphere of activity in the theater, possibly producing.

While he was appearing with Bert Lahr in a summer stock version of *Burlesque*, Whitehead met Harold Hecht, who was later to become a film producer. During their conversation, Hecht suggested that Whitehead take a look at Robinson Jeffers' version of *Medea*, a play that the Theatre Guild had had under option but had recently dropped from its schedule. Jeffers' adaptation had been published and Whitehead got hold of a copy. Although he had not been thinking of doing a Greek tragedy, he saw immediately that the play had great theatricality and, in its own terms and with the right cast, would be highly "actable"; it impressed him as being a psychological drama dealing with modern problems. Whitehead decided that he would "go out on a limb and try to put on the show."

Since the Jeffers' play had been written for, and dedicated to, Judith Anderson, Whitehead got in touch with the actress, who lives on the West Coast, and offered her the role, which she eagerly accepted. Then Whitehead took a quick trip to the Coast to talk with Robinson Jeffers. As an unknown and inexperienced producer, he was not sure that Jeffers would consent to his doing the play, but the author agreed. Whitehead explains this by saying, "Jeffers had waited five years to have the *Medea* produced. Four producers had held options on the script, and had given them up. I got the play because nobody else wanted it at that moment; if I'd had any competitors, I'd have lost out." Final business arrangements for the production were handled by the author's agent in New York.

Whitehead had in the meantime acquired as partner Oliver Rea, whom he had met in the army, and who, like himself, was interested in starting a theater with "lofty standards." The two men formed a company, estimated that they would need about $75,000 to do the play, and went about raising the money. Rea was responsible for bringing in two-thirds of it; Whitehead contributed five thousand dollars of his own; and a former actress by the name of Terry Fay, at present Whitehead's casting director, helped to gather money among small investors, such as waiters, secretaries, and switchboard operators. The reaction of a business man, to whom the script had been sent when he expressed an interest in a possible investment in the production, was typical of many received by the producers. The man returned the play, saying, "I think it is beautiful. In fact, so much so that I had my wife read it to me twice. But I don't think you can find an audience for it." Whitehead's puzzled comment was, "I am not sure what made him feel he was in any way more sensitive than an average audience." It took a full year to raise the complete production cost, but the play turned out to be one of the major successes of the season and paid off its backers in seven weeks.

The next task was to find a director able to handle a serious verse drama. There were very few to choose from on Broadway, and these were either not interested in or not available for *Medea*. While watching a performance of *The Importance of Being Earnest* starring the English actor-director John Gielgud, Whitehead was forcibly struck by the star's brilliance and versatility; he was just as expert in handling Wilde's farce as he had been in mounting Shakespearean tragedy. Whitehead went backstage to talk to Gielgud and later sent him a copy of *Medea*. Gielgud liked the script but was planning on returning to England to do a play by Terence Rattigan, and so he rejected Whitehead's offer. The young producer felt that he had reached a dead end, that he would never get the play on. Then, unexpectedly, Gielgud phoned, announced that he had decided to remain in New York, and offered to direct *Medea*.

Gielgud, Whitehead, and Rea spent the summer of 1947 casting the play, keeping in constant touch with Miss Anderson by long-distance telephone. Whitehead soon learned that he had a strong-willed star to deal with, for her intense and definite opinions concerning every aspect of the production caused innumerable and sharp disagreements. One of the most heated arose over the casting of the part of Jason. It was impossible to select a leading man who would satisfy everyone. There is not enough "meat" in the part to interest an important actor, and one of lesser ability or stature would not have Miss Anderson's approval. Rehearsals were scheduled to start in three days and still the cast lacked a Jason. Miss Anderson arrived in New York and was asked to attend a meeting at which Tibor Serly's incidental music for the production was to be discussed; this discussion deteriorated at once into a wrangle as to who would play Jason. Miss Anderson urged Gielgud to undertake the role himself. Whitehead objected because he wanted the director to concentrate on directing and not be distracted by having to double as an actor; Gielgud objected because he felt that he was wrong for the part, never having portrayed what he called a "Butch-type"; but Miss Anderson kept insisting that since she had once seen fit to play Gertrude to Mr. Gielgud's Hamlet, there was no reason why he should not play Jason to her Medea. Nothing was decided finally at that meeting, but a day or so later Gielgud and Whitehead were walking along Madison Avenue, and the producer was startled to hear his director soliloquizing: "There's no reason to refuse to play Jason because I've never played such a part. After all, this would be a good time to try it. Besides, the part's been turned down by so many that I might as well do it. And, furthermore, I'll be starting work on *Crime and Punishment* in six weeks, so I won't have to stick with it too long." Little by little, Gielgud sold himself the idea.

In agreeing to play the part of Jason, Gielgud simultaneously solved two other problems for the producer. As a beginner in the field, Whitehead was having trouble booking a theater for his play, but with the names of two stars—Judith

(*Above*) A ballet version of *Medea*, choreographed by Birgit Cullberg for the New York City ballet to music by Béla Bartók. The dancers are Violette Verdy, Jacques d'Amboise, and Melissa Hayden. (Martha Swope) (*Left*) An eighteenth-century production of *Medea*. Mlle Clairon played Medea in contemporary dress; Lekain, as Jason, wore the costume *à la Romaine*. (Bibliothèque Nationale)

Anderson and John Gielgud—on the marquee, he was able to get a theater at once. Gielgud's connections with the production as actor-director also attracted investors who put enough money into the show to bring the total up to $75,000, the amount needed to open.

It was Whitehead's function as producer to engage the scene and costume designers; he employed Ben Edwards, who was young, new, and talented, to do the sets and David Ffolkes, a seasoned and expert theatrical artist, for the costumes. Then endless discussions with the star began: the costume designer was replaced, but Edwards' set remained.

Whitehead is enormously sensitive to the turbulent moods of the theater and on many occasions has demonstrated a remarkable skill for tactfulness. He is not, however, infallible in his dealings. His most notable failure, as he is the first to admit, occurred with Judith Anderson. When Whitehead attempted to suggest to Miss Anderson that she curb some of her exuberant dramatics during her performance, the actress became enraged; and when it came time to seek a replacement for Gielgud who was leaving the cast, the fireworks started again. The result was that for a considerable portion of the run of the play, star and producer were not on speaking terms; they communicated only through an intermediary. Whitehead has, nevertheless, the greatest respect for Miss Anderson as an artist, and realizes now that she was often right in her suggestions and that he was young and headstrong; he has mellowed a great deal since then.

During the very first tryout of the play at the McCarter Theater, in Princeton, New Jersey, Whitehead left the theater in the midst of the performance and actually hid in the bushes. "The play didn't come up to my expectations," he explains. "I thought it was way off base . . . a mess." Later, when more and more people congratulated him, and the box-office returns echoed their opinions, he realized that the play was a great success. "Then I began to feel like a fraud . . . as if I'd fooled everybody . . . because the actual production never comes up to the ideal conception of it. I've had that feeling many times . . . after every success, in fact . . . as if I'd got away with something."

The stage set for a twentieth-century German production at the Rheinisches Landestheater, Neuss. (German Information Center)

Medea was on the road for two and a half weeks; the text was cut in a few places, but not much else was done to the script; its entire running time was a little over an hour and a half. The play had a starkness that had appealed to Whitehead from the beginning, and there was a definite growth in the characters and increasing tension in the situations. Jeffers had done a masterly adaptation in investing an ancient Greek play with a quality and a tempo that were especially American and contemporary. *Medea* played to full houses on Broadway for seven months, and then toured the country. It was mounted in London by Gielgud, who also played Jason to Eileen Herlie's Medea; the British critics did not take kindly to the play and it closed after three months.·

"The success of *Medea* started me on the road to production," says Whitehead. "If the play had failed, I'd probably have gone back to acting."

It is almost impossible to define the job of the producer because it has no limits; the producer must be able to function on every level of the production whenever and wherever his services are needed. Although his job differs with each production, he must constantly and resolutely bolster the weak elements without impeding the strong. A few of the things that a producer must know are how to select a script, how to choose collaborating artists (director, actors, designers), how to finance the play, how to negotiate with the unions (actors', stagehands', musicians'), how to book a theater, when to bring the play in, and how to attract audiences through public relations. All of these skills, naturally, come with experience, are learned by trial and error; but even the most adept and gifted producer is called upon to handle so many details that he can very easily go astray among them and neglect the most important thing—the play itself. The producer's primary concern, always, is to understand precisely what the author is trying to say and precisely what effect the director wants the production to achieve, and to attempt to bring these two factors together in a way that will be best for the play. Whitehead says, "It's a colossal job of diplomacy. You are dealing with creative and artistic people all the time and the idea is to get the job done with the least amount of unnecessary emotion. Everything is fine so long as you are producing winners (the plays I liked best somehow seemed to do best), but if you make too many mistakes, you lose your backers, and you're out of the producing business."

GIELGUD REHEARSES *Medea**
By Virginia Stevens

The start of the rehearsals for John Gielgud's production of Robinson Jeffers' *Medea* was an occasion of many firsts. It was the premiere of the American poet's free adaptation of the Euripides classic which he wrote expressly for Judith Anderson; it was John Gielgud's first production of a Greek classic; and it was his and Judith Anderson's first appearance in a Greek drama. . . .

* From *Theatre Arts Magazine*, November, 1947, pp. 31-34. Reprinted by permission.

In the house on East Thirty-Eighth Street which serves the youthful producing firm of Whitehead and Rea as headquarters, the cast assembled for the first time on a stifling hot day in September. In a small library on the second floor, before a card table which had been set out for him, John Gielgud sat, promptbook in hand, while the actors gathered in a semicircle about him: Judith Anderson, Albert Hecht (Creon), John Straub (Aegeus), Richard Hylton, Kathryn Grill, Leone Wilson, Grace Mills.

On the mantelpiece in the library stood Ben Edwards' detailed model of the set—the pillared façade of Medea's house with the long steps, a garden at the side, the sea in the background.

The reading began, and the imminence for us today of Robinson Jeffers' version of the prodigious tragedy of passion and revenge was quickly evident. Medea's exile in a strange land, her loneliness and isolation among the alien Greeks, Jason's ruthless drive for power, even the hideous denouement—all are familiarly paralleled in the world we know; indeed we have known even larger, more hideous tragedies. Expanding, vitalizing the text, Gielgud's direction gives the flesh-and-blood reality of today to these legendary people.

The first day every actor was stopped in his reading while his character was described by the director in a few telling phrases. "The tutor is a meek man with a servant's habitual respect." The three actresses representing Chorus, who had been chosen for contrast of body and voice, were immediately personalized. Gielgud did not hesitate to give the actors his own interpretations and in his illumination of the roles the richly dramatic elements of the play were revealed. But when he finished he would tell the actor, "Do what is natural to you." To demonstrate is his own quick, instinctive method of directing. He is first the actor.

No false note escaped his sensitive ear. The actors on this first day had an understandable tendency to read their lines as poetry. He let nothing pass. "Pay no attention to the punctuation. That's one way writers torment actors. It's the meaning you must observe."

He stressed contrast. "You must look for the opposite colors. In a strong person like Creon, for example, find the tenderness. There's too much Goering now. Don't ever be obvious." Again and again he emphasized, "Think out the meanings. The reading will depend on thought and motive."

The youngest member of the cast delivered a full performance, muscles tensed, body quivering. Gielgud's lean face looked quietly amused. Slender and small, Judith Anderson sat utterly relaxed, her black tortoise-shell glasses perched now on her nose, now shoved up on her forehead in a quick little gesture as she turned to the director. "I'd like to get that all in one breath. What do you think, John?" It was startling to hear the passionate speeches, the deep resonant voice coming from the small, quiet figure in the modern easy-chair.

Perspiration was running off the actors' faces. Not a breath of air stirred. There was a break for ice water. Walking over to the model of the set, I saw that little chessmen indicated the actors' positions. "Do you work out all the business beforehand?" I asked Gielgud.

"In no cut-and-dried sense," he answered, "but I have a definite plan even if it's only something to break away from. It's important for the actors to feel that you know precisely what is to be done."

The reading proceeded. With his perfect sense of timing, his unfailing ear for the right emphasis, Gielgud orchestrated the voices, suggested readings for variety and contrast—but never without motivation. He directs with a strong musical sense. "This whole passage is like a song. Diminuendo here, soaring there."

On the second day the play was broken down into scenes, each one taken separately. This day was utterly different from the first. There was complete informality, a gaiety which no doubt the subtle director had created for the relaxation of his cast. (Until the fifth day of rehearsal is passed and his contract thus assured, it is hard for an actor not to work with tension.) Gielgud himself was full of bubbling humor; his ideas poured forth in a stream.

"We must try to marry the two methods, Shakespeare and realism," he pointed out to the actors. "The emotions come out of reality, but in physical terms—in gesture and movement—it is a heightened reality. This is Bach, played with a grand simplicity."

He began to give them the atmosphere. "Here in this first scene there is sun-shine and the feeling of the sea, the archaic life. No atom bomb, no noises of today, but the laughter of children, the soft air, light and peace, the beauty of living among simple real people—the whole quality of this first mood is in utter contrast to Medea."

An actress read:

> Never pray for death, never pray for death,
> He is here all too soon.

"Why does she say this?" he interrupted. "Perhaps her own child died last year. It must have some such strong personal meaning for you. Each thought must be clear. The image must come into your brain just a second before you speak—as it would in real life. It is the way all actors must work on Shakespeare. So much of good acting is knowing when and how to pause. You must time to the split second."

With vivid similes and paraphrases he goaded their imagination. "Here she turns on him like a cobra." "His words are like detectives tracking her down."

With constant change of tempo and key he thrust monotony out. Medea talks to the women of childbirth. They huddle together, soft and intimate in shared experience:

> It is easier to stand in battle three times, in the front
> line, in the stabbing fury, than to bear one child.

But an instant later she has broken the mood completely with her dark hints of revenge.

Gielgud was quick this day to compliment an actor for a correct reading. "Actors are very easily hurt," he explained later. "I should say the ideal approach to them is ruthlessness combined with politeness. (As an actor I'm not very touchy. I like to be told about mannerisms.) But it all depends on the actor. You must study your cast and know how to handle each one.

"You see, an actor's perceptions are delicate and complex," he continued, slumping down in the chair, his long legs swinging over the side. "With one set of feelings he is creating the emotions of the character, he is listening as if he had never before heard the questions and replies of the other actors, as if his own words were new to his ear. At the same time another set of nerves is reacting to the audience, tightening the reins if they are not attentive. Yet it's fatal to become too conscious of an audience. That's when they begin to encourage you in your worst effects. By their quick response to broad effects an audience will tempt you to indulge in cheaper things but you must never allow them to dictate to you."

On the third day there was much excitement among the cast, for Gielgud had agreed to play Jason. This time he put the play on its feet. He was everywhere suggesting movement and gestures. Like the chessmen he had been experimenting with on his model stage, the actors now seemed merely his puppets.

He talked to them of costumes. "We must begin to use the long draped skirts, the flowing sleeves as quickly as possible," he told the women. "Flowing sleeves and drapes will suggest many effective gestures to you. Ellen Terry always wore her dresses longer in front so she could catch up the folds. I remember the unutterably graceful gestures she had!"

The fourth day the actors had taken his suggestions to themselves, they were making them their own. They were no longer puppets.

Judith Anderson would do nothing that did not seem to her to coincide with the thought and feeling of a scene. There is an encounter, for example, between Medea and Aegeus. Having been banished from Corinth by Creon, father of Jason's bride, Medea throws herself on the mercy of Aegeus of Athens. She promises him the use of her occult power if he will help her. Aegeus has just come from the Delphic Oracle. He longs for a son and Medea promises him fulfillment:

> I should need peace and a free mind
> While I prepared the medicines to make you well.

Gielgud suggested that Aegeus rise in his eagerness:

> You'll have them,
> you'll have them, Medea.

"No, no, it isn't right," Judith Anderson said. "The movement makes too much of this. Medea wants to get through with this deal and get on to what is really filling her mind." They tried it her way: a simple pledge with hands, as Aegeus kept his sitting position. Now it was a lesser thing. Gielgud agreed.

Even in the small room, as they worked one could begin to see a suggestion of form, of the pose and movement, the style that was being slowly created.

Whenever Judith Anderson read, the extraordinary power and credibility of her tortured Medea came clear. Her readings indicated long study. "I understand her in modern terms, as modern as I can," the actress told me after the rehearsal. "The words are so beautiful, they speak for themselves. I can forget them and work for the reality of the emotion . . . I see her as the great barbarian, purely animal, all her reactions fiercely primitive in contrast to the smooth and cultured Greeks. I love the part because it is such a challenge. Lady Macbeth with her few telling scenes is simple compared to Medea who must sustain this play."

"What did you mean when you told the actors to marry Shakespeare and realism in this play?" I asked John Gielgud.

"All those—like Laurence Olivier, Maurice Evans and myself—who have successfully produced the classics for modern audiences have found a half-way ground. We must raise young actors to a broader style and the traditional actors must be brought down to a more realistic level. The people in these great plays have the same fundamental emotional reactions that we do, the psychology of emotion is the same. But if one is at all atavistic it is facinating to step into another time. I think an audience should be excited and held by *Medea*. I want them to take out of the theater a feeling of splendor and pity and terror."

On the sixth day the rehearsals moved to the theater. Against the blank walls of the stage, in the bizarre light of rehearsal spots, the figures of the actors took on dramatic dimension. Occasionally a scene came alive. But in the main the actors struggled to coordinate words and movement in the larger space.

Gielgud's tall thin figure strode down the aisle from the back of the theater, leaped on the stage to demonstrate a walk, a gesture. "Simpler. Make it simpler. You're doing too much." Quickly he seized the right movement, the effective grouping. He was continually aware of the stage picture.

And when he stepped in to play Jason, with penetrating and quick intelligence he set the key of the rehearsals; the actors were on their toes to match him.

A scene between Jason and Medea began to suggest the power of the play. Jason has come to chide Medea for her anger, to reason with her. . . . In the rebuke his movement is toward her but her furious reaction drives him back. (The bodies of these two obeyed their thought like well-drilled soldiers while their voices registered every nuance. Their skills were beautifully matched.)

Now she comes to him, dominating him with her passionate reproof, vividly recalling the crimes she has committed for him. Her voice is low in pleading, velvet in remembered tenderness, tense in the moment's pain:

> The world is a little closed to me, ah?
> By the things I have done for you.

But Jason recovers his poise. He will not be moved.

> I see, Medea,
> You have been a very careful merchant of benefits.

He can even tear at her pride.

> As to those acts of service you so loudly boast—whom
> do I thank for them? I thank divine Venus, the goddess

Who makes girls fall in love. You did them because you
had to do them; Venus compelled you; I enjoyed her favor.

In a frenzy of wild fury, Medea drives him from her. . . .

The two actors let the emotions design the movement. At the end of the scene
Medea has won the encounter and stands alone, high on the steps of her house, a
terrible figure of fury.

From here on the pace quickened, culminating in the opening in Princeton.
But the pattern had been set early: the "splendor and pity and terror" of the stars'
acting and the director's conception was all there in that first week as this
modern retelling of the ancient tragedy unfolded under their expert hands.

The Scenery
An Interview with Ben Edwards

As a friend of the producers, Whitehead and Rea, Ben Edwards had an opportunity to see the script of Robinson Jeffers' *Medea* before the play had actually
been bought for production. Edwards was impressed by the work and was delighted when he was offered the opportunity to design the set.

His first task was to read and reread the play until he was thoroughly familiar
with the characters, their motivations and their relationships; with the country,
its people and its customs; and with the immediate locale—Medea's palace—in
all its spatial and temporal dimensions.

It was necessary for the designer to find a unifying concept, a single point of
view for the production; conferences with the producers, the director, and the
star began. The play calls for just one set—Medea's palace. It was Gielgud's idea
that the architectural style of this building should be in keeping with the primitive emotions of the barbarian princess who inhabited it. It was not to have the
subtle lines and gleaming whiteness of a palace of the Periclean age, but was to
be heavy and archaic, hinting of Mycenaean or Cretan origins.

In Edwards' final design, there were five rough-hewn steps leading up to a large
central door, and the palace itself appeared to be situated high up on the rocky
coast, allowing a view of the sea and of the distant mountains beyond it. In so
placing the palace, Edwards had two things in mind. First, he wished to re-create
for modern audiences the feelings of the ancient spectators in the Theater of
Dionysus in Athens, who had only to raise their eyes and look above and beyond
the *skene* to see the actual mountains and sea in the distance; secondly, he wanted
the location of the palace to provide a physical expression of the theme and mood
of the play. Here was a marriage that had gone on the rocks, and a home now
standing empty of love and hollow on barren and precipitous ground.

Edwards had an even more subtle idea for heightening the tension of the play
in visual terms; he attempted to make the playing areas as straitened and confined as were the souls of the protagonists. He did this by changing the position
of the set during the play. For the first act, the façade of the palace stood at an

angle to the footlights, allowing the audience a glimpse past the building to the open sea, the sea across which Jason had brought his bride to Corinth; but for the second act, the palace was turned so that it stood parallel to the footlights and the entire building was moved downstage, thus not only cutting off the view and any apparent means of escape, but also giving the impression that Medea was hemmed in and trapped. "Even if an audience is not consciously aware of an altered perspective," Edwards states, "the psychological effect of such a shift of scenery upon the emotional responses of the spectators is unmistakable."

A further assault was made upon the audience's sensibilities by the lighting and costume designers, who worked in close creative collaboration with the scene designer. Peggy Clark, who was responsible for the play's lighting plan, accentuated the coldness and starkness of the palace and of Medea's face by eliminating from her spectrum all the warm colors and using white and steel-blue light exclusively. The achievement of such a symbolic effect by the arbitrary control of light was denied Euripides, for his play was illuminated solely by the brilliant sunlight of Greece. In costumes, too, a symbolism was devised in keeping with the somberness of the play's theme, though contrary to historical accuracy. Euripides' actors wore rich and elaborate gowns in bright and gleaming colors, and such gowns were at first designed for the Jeffers production; then Castillo, Miss Anderson's designer, redid the costumes entirely in grays and black—except for the glistening panoplies of the soldiers—and thus achieved a funereal and muted mood, and an artistic truth greater than the actual.

The technical procedure followed by the scene designer begins with his drawing of sketches embodying his ideas for the set. After the sketches have been approved, the designer makes a miniature model of the set and proceeds to draw detailed construction plans and blueprints from which the builders must be able to construct scenery that will not only stand up and look as sturdy as it is supposed to, but will also support and withstand the life lived in it: the beating of Medea's fists and head against the door and its frames, and the stamping of her feet as she races up and down the steps.

The scenery for *Medea* was built at the Turner Studios in Fort Lee, New Jersey. On several occasions the members of the cast went to the studios and rehearsed on the set while it was under construction to make sure that the acting areas were right and comfortable. Edwards worked in particularly close collaboration with Judith Anderson on the design of the palace steps, for they were meant to represent irregular blocks of stone—some thick, some thin, some narrow, and some wide. It was absolutely necessary that she be able to manage them easily, for she played most of her scenes on these steps.

During the play's tryout period at the McCarter Theater, in Princeton, New Jersey, Edwards worked on such details as checking properties, testing lights against the paint of the scenery, observing the scene-shift, and making sure that every aspect of the physical production worked smoothly. Edwards works at this refining process, as do most other designers, until the curtain goes up at the play's official opening, and sometimes it is necessary for him to make changes during the run of the play.

In the early stages of the production, Edwards sent his sketches to Robinson Jeffers in order to get the poet's reaction to the proposed scenery. In his letter of response, Jeffers told Edwards that he was particularly pleased with the "fiery sky" that was to appear during the final moments of the play. He had called for just such a sky in his script. During the rehearsal period, however, the hot sky was washed out by the lighting designer along with even mildly lukewarm colors, as has already been noted. After seeing the play at its premiere in New York, Jeffers commented especially to Edwards on the absence of the "fiery sky," which apparently disappointed him; he thought, nevertheless, that the scenery was "beautiful and impressive."

THE COSTUMES
An Interview with Antonio del Castillo

The costumes for Judith Anderson, as well as for the other members of the cast of *Medea*, were originally designed in chiffon and brocades in brilliant colors with heavy incrustations of gold. The keynote of these gowns was lavishness and high style, but Miss Anderson disliked their formality and stiffness. The star decided to go for advice to Antonio del Castillo, who had previously designed gowns for her. He advised her to get rid of the chiffon and to use flannel or gray wool, the actual fabrics worn by the primitive Greeks. Miss Anderson agreed, and Castillo molded the cloth to her body. He explained that as she perspired it would cling to her contours more and more and increase in naturalness and beauty. She had to wear these heavy clothes at rehearsals in order to get used to them and to start to make them adhere to her body.

It was at the first performance of the play in Princeton that Castillo saw the gold and brocaded gowns on all the other actors and realized that the entire cast would have to be recostumed. By the time the play reached the Locust Theater in Philadelphia, early in its out-of-town tour, Castillo had arranged with an American designer, Helene Pons, to assist him in replacing the costumes. Miss Pons set up her workshop in the basement of the theater, while Castillo himself draped the cloth on the actors, cut it, pinned it, and basted it by hand with leather thongs. Then he would rush up to the auditorium to see the actor make his entrance on stage in the newly created costume, and dash back to the basement to go on with the clothes for the other actors.

He improvised as he went along. The three women who represented the chorus were on stage practically throughout the play, and yet they had been dressed in brilliant and eye-catching gowns; Castillo felt that since they were almost never absent from the scene, they should not be so "aggressive to the eye," and therefore clothed them in dresses that blended with the scenery and caused them to intrude less into the dramatic action.

The task of recostuming the cast was completed by the end of the week in Philadelphia. In addition to making all the clothes, Castillo made the wigs for

The Robert Whitehead production of Robinson Jeffers' adaptation of *Medea*. Judith Anderson is seated on the palace steps at John Gielgud's feet. The entire play was performed in front of this primitive façade. (Somoroff)

Medea's women attendants, dexterously, with his own hands, creating them out of skeins of ordinary knitting wool.

The gowns, which had never been sewn, but had been pinned or basted with leather thongs, served the members of the cast for the entire run of the play. It is interesting to note that Castillo's method was very close to the original Greek way of making clothes; they were hand-sewn or pinned, and combined a respect for the fabric with a feeling for the beauty of the drapery.

ᖇᖇᖇᖇ *Medea*

TRANSLATED BY FREDERIC PROKOSCH

CHARACTERS

MEDEA	ATTENDANT
JASON	NURSE
KREON	AEGEUS
MEDEA'S CHILDREN	A MESSENGER
CHORUS OF CORINTHIAN WOMEN	

Scene: Corinth, before the house of Medea.

(*The* NURSE *enters from the house.*)

Nurse. Oh how I wish that famous ship,
The Argo, had never made its way through
The blue Symplegades to the land of Colchis!
How I wish the pine tree had never been felled
In the glades of Pelion, and never 5
Been hewn into oars for the heroes
Who went to fetch the Golden Fleece
For Pelias! For then my mistress, Medea,
Would never have sailed to the towers
Of the land of Iolcos, her heart on fire 10
With love for Jason! Nor would she
Ever have beguiled the daughters
Of Pelias into slaying their father,
Nor have come to live in Corinth with her
Husband and children. For a long time 15
She found favor with the people here
In the land of exile; and she did
All things in complete accord with Jason;
And indeed it is this—when a woman
Stands loyally by a man—which brings 20
To men the only sure savlation. But now
Their love has fallen into decay; and
There's hatred everywhere. For Jason
Has betrayed his children and my mistress;
He has taken a royal bride to his bed, 25
The daughter of Kreon, who is the ruler
Of this land. And poor Medea, scorned
And deserted, can do nothing but appeal
To the vows they made to one another, 29
And remind him of the eternal pledge

They made with their right hands
  clasped.
And she calls upon the gods to wit-
  ness
How Jason is repaying her for her
  love.
She lies half famished; her body is
  bowed
Utterly with grief, wasting away the
  whole   35
Day long. So it has been since she
Learned that he has betrayed her.
Never stirring an eye, never lifting
Her gaze from the ground; and when
  her friends
Speak to her in warning she no more
  listens   40
Than a rock listens, or the surging
  sea wave.
Only now and then she turns her
  snowy neck
And quietly laments, and utters her
  father's
Name, and the name of her land and
  home,
Which she deserted when she fol-
  lowed   45
The man who now brings her such
  dishonor.
Pitiful woman! She has learned at
  last
Through all her sufferings how lucky
Are those who have never lost their
Native land. She has come to feel   50
A hatred for her children, and no
  longer
Wants to see them. Indeed, I fear
She may be moving toward some
  dreadful
Plan; for her heart is violent.   54
She will never submit to this cruel
Treatment. I know her well: her
  anger
Is great; and I know that any man
Who makes an enemy of her

Will have it hard . . . Look;
Here come the children; they have
  been playing.   60
Little they know of their mother's
  misery; little
The hearts of the young can guess of
  sorrow!

(*The* ATTENDANT *brings in* MEDEA'S
children.)

Attendant. Why are you standing here,
  in front of the gates?
You've been maid for so many years
  to my mistress;   64
Why have you left her alone, then,
Only to stand outside the gates and
  lament?
Nurse. Listen, old man, who watch over
  Jason's
Sons! It's a sad, sad thing for faithful
Servants like us to see our master's
Fortunes meet with disaster; it stirs
Us to the heart. I am so lost in grief,
Now, that a longing came over me
  to step   72
Outside the gates, and tell the whole
  wide
World and the heavens of my mis-
  tress's sorrows!
Attendant. Poor lady! Hasn't she ceased
  her weeping yet?   75
Nurse. Ceased? Far from it! This is
  only
The beginning; there is far more to
  come.
Attendant. Poor, foolish lady; though I
  shouldn't call her that;
But how little she knows of this latest
  trouble!   79
Nurse. What do you mean, old man?
Come! Don't be afraid to tell me!
Attendant. Nothing at all; I should
  never have mentioned it.
Nurse. No, no; by your wise old beard
  I beg you,

Don't hide anything from your fellow
servant!
Tell me; and, if you wish, I'll keep it
secret.   85
Attendant. Well, as I was passing the
usual place
Where the old men sit playing
draughts,
Down by the holy fountain of Pirene,
I happened to overhear one of them
saying
That Kreon, king of the land, intends
to send   90
These children, and their mother
from Corinth,
Far away into exile. But whether it
was
The truth he was speaking, I do not
know;
I hope and pray it wasn't the truth.
Nurse. And will Jason allow this thing
to happen to his sons,   95
Even though he is on bad terms with
their mother?
Attendant. Old ties give way to new
ones; and his
Love for this family of ours is dying
away.
Nurse. Oh, it looks dark indeed for us;
New sorrows are being added to old
ones,   100
Even before the old ones have faded!
Attendant. Be still, be still; don't whis-
per a word of it.
This isn't the proper time to tell our
mistress.
Nurse. O little children,
Do you hear how your father feels
toward you?   105
May evil befall him!
But no; he is still my master. Yet how
cruelly
He has betrayed his dear ones!
Attendant. And which of us has not
done the same?

Haven't you learned long ago, my
dear,   110
How each man loves himself far more
Than his neighbor? Some, perhaps,
From honest motives; some for pri-
vate gain.
So you see how Jason deserts his
children   114
For the pleasure of his new bride.
Nurse. Go back into the house, chil-
dren;
All will be well. Try to keep them
Out of the way, old man; keep them
far
From their mother as long as she
feels
This desperate anger. I have already
seen   120
The fire in her eyes as she watched
Them, almost as though she were
wishing
Them harm. I am sure her anger
Won't end till she has found a victim.
Let's hope the victim will be   125
An enemy, and not a friend!

(*Within the house.*)
Medea. Lost, oh lost! I am lost
In my sufferings. I wish, oh I wish
That I could die. . . .
Nurse. My dear children, what did I tell
you?   130
Your mother's mind is filled with the
wildest
Fancies; her heart is wild with an-
ger!
Run quickly back into the house.
Keep out of her sight. Do not
Go near her. Beware of the wild-
ness   135
And bitterness of her heart!
Go, quickly, quickly!
I can feel that her fury will rise
And redouble! I can hear   139
In that cry the rising thunderstorm,

I can feel the approach of thunder
  and lightning!
Oh what will she do, in the pride
And torment of her soul? What
Evil thing will she do?

(*The* ATTENDANT *takes the children
into the house.*)
(*Within.*)

Medea. Oh, I have suffered   145
And suffered enough for all these
  tears!
I call destruction upon you, all, all
  of you,
Sons of a doomed mother, and the
  father too!
May ruin fall on the entire house!
Nurse. I am full of pity,   150
Full of deep pity for you! Yet why
Do the children share their father's
  crime?
Why should you hate them? O my
  poor children,
I fear some outrage will befall you!
Yes, strange and terrible is the temper
  of princes.   155
There is none they need to obey;
There is none that can check them:
There is nothing to control
The madness of their mood.
How much better off are the rest of
  us   160
Who've been taught to live equally
With our neighbors! All I wish
Is to grow old quietly, not in pride,
But only in humble security.
It's the moderate thing that always
  sounds   165
Best to our ears; and indeed it is
The moderate thing that is best in
  practice.
For power grows beyond control;
Power brings comfort to no man.
And I say, the greater the power, the
  greater   170
The ruin when it finally falls.

(*Enter the* CHORUS *of Corinthian
women. The following lines are
chanted.*)

Chorus. I heard the voice,
I heard the loud lament
Of the pitiful lady from Colchis:
Oh tell me, mother, is she still   175
Unquiet? As I stood
By the house with the double gates
I heard the sound of weeping from
  within.
I grieve for the sorrow of this family
Which I have come to love.   180
Nurse. There is no family left; it has
  gone,
It has gone forever. The master now
Has a royal bride in the bed beside
  him,
And our mistress is withering away
In her chamber, and finds no sol-
  ace   185
Or warmth in words
That friends can utter.

(*Within.*)

Medea. Oh how I wish that a stroke of
  lightning
Would fall from heaven and shatter
  my head!
Why should I live any longer?   190
Death would bring release; in death
I could leave behind me the horror
  of living.
Chorus. Did you hear, almighty Zeus?
O earth, O heaven, did you hear
The cry of woe this woman has ut-
  tered?   195
Oh why, poor lady, should you long
For that unutterable haven of rest?
Death only can bring it; and death
  comes only too soon!
No, no, there is no need to pray for
  death.
And if your man is drawn   200
To a new love, remember,

Such things occur often; do not feel
hurt.
For God will be your ultimate friend
the judge
In this as in all matters.
So do not mourn too much,   205
Do not waste away in sorrow
For the loss of the one you loved!

(*Within.*)

Medea. Great Themis, O lady Artemis,
look down
On all I am suffering; and suffering
in spite
Of all the vows my husband made
me.   210
I pray that I may some day see
Him and his bride brought down to
ruin
And their palace ruined for all the
wrong
They dared to do me without cause.
O my own father, my own coun-
try,   215
Shameful it was of me to leave you,
And to have killed my brother be-
fore I left you!

Nurse. Do you hear what she says? Do
you hear
How loudly she cries to Themis, the
goddess of promises,
And to Zeus, whom men think of as
the Emperor of Vows?   220
One thing I know. It is no small
thing
That draws such anger from our mistress!

Chorus. Let her come forth and see us,
Let her listen to our words of warn-
ing,
Let her lay aside the rage and vio-
lence of her heart;   225
Never shall I refuse to help my
friends,
Never shall they turn to me in vain.

Go, go, and bring her from the house
That we may see her; speak kindly
to her!
Hurry, before she does some violent
thing.   230
I feel her passion rising to a new
pitch.

Nurse. Yes; I shall go; but I deeply
doubt
Whether I can persuade my mistress.
Still, I shall gladly go and try;
Though she glares upon her servants,
those   235
That approach and dare to speak to
her,
With the fiery look of a lioness with
cubs!
You would be right, I think,
If you called both ignorant
And trivial those poets of old who
wrote   240
Their songs for festivities and ban-
quets,
Graceful and pleasant sounds for
men
Who lived in gaiety and leisure.
For none of them learned a way
For the song or the musicians   245
To still man's suffering. And suffering
it is
From which all killing springs, and
all calamity
Which falls on the homes of men.
Yet it would be a blessing, surely,
If songs could heal the wounds which
sorrow   250
Inflicts on men! What good is music
And singing at an idle banquet? It
seems to me
That men who are sitting at the ban-
quet table
Have pleasure enough already . . .

(*The* Nurse *goes into the house.*)

Chorus. I heard a cry that was heavy
and sick with sorrow.   255

Loud in her bitterness she cries
On the man who betrayed her mar-
    riage bed!
Full of her wrongs she cries
To the gods, to Themis, to the bride
    of Zeus,
To the Keeper of Vows, who brought
    her away   260
To the shores of Greece which face
    the shores of Asia,
Through the straits at night to the
    gateway opening
On the unlimited salty sea.

(*Toward the end of this song*, MEDEA
enters from the house.)

Medea. Ladies of Corinth, I have come
    forth   264
From my house, lest you should feel
Bitterness toward me; for I know that
    men
Often acquire a bad name for their
    pride—
Not only the pride they show in pub-
    lic,
But also the pride of retirement;
    those who
Live in solitude, as I do, are fre-
    quently   270
Thought to be proud. For there is no
    justice
In the view one man takes of an-
    other,
Often hating him before he has suf-
    fered
Wrong, hating him even before he
    has seen
His true character. Therefore a for-
    eigner   275
Above all should fit into the ways of
    a city.
Not even a native citizen, I think,
    should risk
Offending his neighbors by rudeness
    or pride.

But this new thing has fallen upon
    me
So unexpectedly, my strength is
    broken.   280
O my friends, my life is shattered;
My heart no longer longs for the
    blessings
Of life, but only for death! There was
One man through whom I came to
    see   284
The world's whole beauty: and that
Was my husband; and he has turned
    out
Utterly evil. O women, of all crea-
    tures
That live and reflect, certainly it is
    we
Who are the most luckless. First of
    all,
We pay a great price to purchase a
    husband;   290
And thus submit our bodies to a
    perpetual
Tyrant. And everything depends on
    whether
Our choice is good or bad—for di-
    vorce
Is not an honorable thing, and we
    may not
Refuse to be married. And then a
    wife is   295
Plunged into a way of life and be-
    havior
Entirely new to her, and must learn
What she never learned at home—
She must learn by a kind of subtle
Intuition how to manage the man
    who   300
Lies beside her. And if we have the
    luck
To handle all these things with tact
And success, and if the husband is
    willing
To live at our side without resent-
    ment,   304

Then life can become happy indeed.
But if not, I'd rather be dead.
A man who is disgusted with what he
Finds at home, goes forth to put an end
To his boredom, and turns to a friend
Or companion of his own age; while we   310
At home continue to think of him,
And of him only. And yet people
Say that we live in security at home,
While the men go forth to war.
How wrong they are! Listen: 315
I'd rather be sent three times over
To the battlefront than give
Birth to a single child. Still,
My friends, I realize that all this applies   319
Not to you but to me; you after all
Have a city of your own, and a family
Home, and a certain pleasure in life,
And the company of your friends. But
I am utterly lonely, an exile, cast off
By my own husband—nothing but a captive   325
Brought here from a foreign land—without
A mother or brother, without a single
Kinsman who can give me refuge in this sea
Of disaster. Therefore, my ladies, I ask   329
Only one thing of you: promise me
Silence. If I can find some way, some
Cunning scheme of revenge against my
Husband for all that he has done to me,
And against the man who gave away his
Daughter, and against the daughter who   335

Is now my husband's wife; then please
Be silent. For though a woman is
Timid in everything else, and weak, and
Terrified at the sight of a sword: still,
When things go wrong in this thing of love,   340
No heart is so fearless as a woman's;
No heart is so filled with the thought of blood.

Choragus. Yes; I promise this. You will be right,
Medea, in avenging yourself on   344
Your husband. It does not surprise
Me to see you lost in despair . . .
But look!
I see Kreon, our king, approaching:
He will have some news to tell us.

(*Enter* Kreon, *with his following.*)

Kreon. Listen to me, Medea! You, with your angry looks
And all that bitterness against your husband: 350
I order you to leave my kingdom! I order you
To go with both your children into exile,
And immediately. This is my decree. And I
Will not return to my house until I have
Hurled you beyond the borders of my kingdom.   355

Medea. Oh, now I am lost indeed! This is the end
Of all things for me! Now my enemies
Are bearing down on me in all their force;
And I have no refuge left in this hour of ruin.
And yet, let me ask you this one thing, Kreon: 360

Why is it, Kreon, you are sending me
　　away?
Kreon. I am afraid of you. I need no
　　longer pretend
　　Otherwise. I am afraid you will do
　　my daughter
　　Some mortal harm. And I have many
　　reasons
　　For being afraid of this. You are a
　　cunning   365
　　Woman, Medea, expert in all kinds
　　of magic,
　　So I hear. And you are enraged by
　　the loss
　　Of your husband's love. I have also
　　heard
　　Them say that you are planning some
　　kind
　　Of mischief against Jason and the
　　bride,   370
　　And the bride's father, myself, as
　　well.
　　It is against these things I take pre-
　　cautions.
　　I tell you, Medea, I'd rather incur
　　your hatred now
　　Than be soft-hearted and later learn
　　to regret it.   374
Medea. This is not the first time, Kreon!
　　Many times before has this strange
　　reputation
　　Done me harm. A sensible man
　　should
　　Never nowadays bring up his chil-
　　dren
　　To be too clever or exceptional. For
　　one thing,   379
　　These talents never bring them profit;
　　For another, they end by bringing
　　envy
　　And hatred from others. If you pre-
　　sent
　　New ideas to a group of fools, they'll
　　think you

Ignorant as well as idle. And if your
　　fame
　　Should come to exceed the estab-
　　lished reputations,   385
　　They'll hate you for it. This has been
　　My own experience. Some think me
　　clever,
　　And resent it; some think me not
　　So very clever after all, and disap-
　　prove.   389
　　And you, Kreon, are somehow afraid
　　That I may do something to harm
　　you.
　　But you need not worry. It isn't for
　　someone
　　Like me to quarrel with kings. After
　　all,
　　Why should I? You haven't harmed
　　me.
　　You've allowed your daughter to
　　marry   395
　　As you saw fit. I hate my husband,
　　certainly;
　　But as for you, I feel you have acted
　　Reasonably enough. I don't grudge
　　you
　　Your good fortune. I wish you luck
　　With your daughter's marriage,
　　Kreon,   400
　　But beg you only, let me live on in
　　this
　　Land. I have been wronged, but I
　　shall remain
　　Quiet, and submit to those above me.
Kreon. Your words are gentle enough,
　　Medea.   404
　　Yet in my heart I can't help dreading
　　That you are planning some evil;
　　And I trust you now even less than
　　before.
　　It is easier to deal with a quick-
　　tempered
　　Man or woman than with one who is
　　subtle

And soft-spoken. No. You must go at
   once.   410
Make no more speeches. It is settled.
You are my enemy, and there is
   nothing
You can do to prolong your stay in
   my country.
Medea. I implore you! By your knees,
   by your newly wed daughter!
Kreon. You are wasting your words. You
   will never persuade me.   415
Medea. Then you'll drive me out with-
   out listening to my prayers?
Kreon. I shall; for I love my own family
   more than you.
Medea. O my country! How my heart
   goes back to you now!
Kreon. I, too, love my country above all
   things, except my children.
Medea. How cruelly passionate love
   can deal with men!   420
Kreon. And yet, it all depends on the
   luck men have.
Medea. O Zeus, never forget the man
   who caused this!
Kreon. Go now; go. Spare me this use-
   less trouble.
Medea. No trouble, no pain, nothing
   has been spared me!
Kreon. Soon one of my men shall lead
   you away by force.   425
Medea. Not that, Kreon, not that! I beg
   you, Kreon.
Kreon. It seems you insist on creating
   a disturbance.
Medea. I will go. I will go. That is not
   what I intended.
Kreon. Why all this commotion, then?
   What is it you want?
Medea. Let me stay here just a single
   day longer,   430
   Kreon. Let me stay and think over
      where
   I shall go in exile, and how I shall
      find

A living for my children, for whom
   their father
Has completely failed to provide.
   Take pity
On them, Kreon! You too have chil-
   dren   435
Of your own; you too must have a
   soft place
In your heart for them. What hap-
   pens to me now
No longer matters; I only grieve
For the suffering that will come to
   my children.
Kreon. I am not a cruel man, Medea. I
   have often made   440
Blunders, out of sheer compassion.
   Even now
I feel I am making a mistake. All the
   same,
Have it your own way. But let me
   warn you! If
Tomorrow at sunrise still finds you
   and your
Children within the frontiers of my
   land,   445
You shall die for it. That is my ver-
   dict;
It is final. So stay this one day
Longer, if you must. One day is
Not enough to bring disaster.   449

(*Exit* KREON *with his following.*)

Choragus. Pitiful woman! Oh we pity
   The sorrows you suffer!
   Where will you turn now? Who can
      help you?
   What home remains, what land
   Is left to save you from destruction?
   O Medea, you have been hurled by
      heaven   455
Into an ocean of despair.
Medea. Everything has gone wrong.
   None can deny it.
   But not quite everything is lost; don't

Give up hope, my friends! There still are　459
Troubles in store for the young bride,
And for the bridegroom too. Do you think
I would have fawned on that old man without
Some plan and purpose? Certainly not.
I would never have touched him
With my hands. But now, although he　465
Could have crushed all my plans by instant
Exile, he has made a fatal error;
He has given me one day's reprieve.
One day in which I can bring death
To the three creatures that I loathe:
The father, the bride, my husband.
There are many manners of death.
Which I might use; I don't quite know yet
Which to try. Shall I set fire
To the bridal mansion? Or shall I sharpen　475
A sword and steal into the chamber
To the wedding bed and plunge it
Into their hearts? One thing
Stands in my way. If I am caught
Making my way into the bridal room　480
On such an errand, I shall surely
Be put to death, and my foes will end
By triumphing over me. Better to take
The shortest way, the way I am best trained in:
Better to bring them down with poison.　485
That I will do, then. And after that?
Suppose them dead. What city will take me in then?
What friend will offer me shelter in his land,
And safety, and a home? None.

Then best to wait a little longer;　490
Perhaps some sure defense will appear,
And I can set about this murder
In stealth and stillness. And if no help
Should come from fate, and even if death
Is certain, still I can take at last　495
The sword in my own hand and go forth
Boldly to the crime, and kill. Yes,
By that dark Queen whom I revere above　498
All others, and whom I now invoke
To help me, by Hecate who dwells
In my most secret chamber: I swear
No man shall injure me and not regret it.
I will turn their marriage into sorrow
And anguish! Go now, go forward to this
Dangerous deed! The time has come for courage.　505
Remember the suffering they caused you! Never
Shall you be mocked because of this wedding
Of Jason's, you who are sprung from a noble
Father and whose grandfather was the Sun-God
Himself! You have the skill; what is more,　510
You are a woman: and it's always a woman
Who is incapable of a noble deed,
Yet expert in every kind of mischief!
(Strophe 1)
Chorus. The sacred rivers are flowing back to their sources!
The order of the world is being reversed!　515
Now it is men who have grown deceitful,

Men who have broken their sacred
vows.
The name of woman shall rise to
favor
Again; and women once again
Shall rise and regain their honor:
never   520
Again shall ill be said of women!
                    (Antistrophe 1)
Those poets of old shall cease at last
To sing of our faithlessness. Never
On us did Phoebus, the god of music,
Lavish the talents of the lyre,   525
Else I should long ago have sung
A song of rebuttal to the race
Of men: for the years have many
things
To tell of them as well as of us!
                    (Strophe 2)

You sailed away from your father's
dwelling   530
With your heart on fire, Medea! And
you passed
Between the rocky gates of the seas;
And now you sleep on a foreign
shore,
In a lonely bed: now you are driven
Forth, and far away from the land
Once more you go in exile and dis-
honor!   536
                    (Antistrophe 2)
Gone is the dignity of vows,
Gone from great Hellas the sense of
honor.
It has flown and vanished in the
skies.   539
And now no father's dwelling house
Stands as a refuge from this storm!
Now another princess lies
In the bed which once was yours,
and rules your home!

(*As the* Chorus *approaches the end
of the song,* Jason *enters.*)

Jason. This is not the first time I have
noticed
How difficult it is to deal with a vio-
lent temper.   545
Ah, Medea, if you had patiently ac-
cepted
The will of our ruler, you might have
stayed on
Quietly in this land and this house.
But now your pointless complaints
Are driving you into exile. Not that
I   550
Minded them myself; I didn't mind
it at all
When you called Jason an evil man.
But,
Considering your references to the
King
Himself, you may count yourself
lucky
That your punishment is exile. Per-
sonally,   555
I have always done my best to calm
The King's anger, and would have
liked
To see you stay on here. But you
refused
To give up this sort of folly, and kept
on
Slandering him; with the result that
you   560
Are facing banishment. Nevertheless,
In spite of your behavior, I feel in-
clined
To do you a favor; I have come to
make
Some sort of provision for you and
the children,
My dear, so that you won't be pen-
niless   565
When you are in exile; for I know
that exile
Will not be easy. And even though
you hate me,

Medea, my thoughts of you will continue
To be friendly as always.
Medea. You filthy coward!   570
That is the only name I can find for you,
You and your utter lack of manliness!
And now you, who are the worst of my enemies,
Now you too have chosen to come to me! No!   574
It isn't courage which brings you,
Nor recklessness in facing the friends
You have injured; it is worse than that,
It is the worst of all human vices:
Shamelessness. Still, you did well to come to me,
For now I can ease my heart by reviling you: 580
And perhaps you too will suffer as you listen.
Let me begin, then, at the very beginning.
I saved your life; every Greek who
Sailed with you on the Argo knows
I saved you, when you were sent to tame   585
The fire-breathing bulls and to yoke them,
And to sow the deadly fields. Yes,
And I killed the many-folded serpent
Who lay guarding the Golden Fleece,
Forever wakeful, coil upon coil. 590
And I raised a beacon of light
To bring you to safety. Freely
I deserted my own father and my own home;
And followed you to Iolcos, to the hills   594
Of Pelion: and all this time my love
Was stronger than my reason. And I brought
Death to Pelias by his own daughters'

Hands; I utterly destroyed the household.
All of these things I did for you,
Traitor! And you forsook me, and took   600
Another wife, even though I had borne
Your children. Had you been childless,
One might have pardoned your wish
For a second wedding. But now
All my faith in your vows has vanished.   605
I do not know whether you imagine
That the gods by whom you swore
Have disappeared or that new rules
Are now in vogue in such matters;
For you must be aware that you have   610
Broken your vows to me. Oh this poor
Right hand, which you so often pressed!
These knees, which you so often
Used to embrace! And all in vain,
For it was an evil man   615
That touched me! How wildly
All my hopes have fallen through! . . .
Come, Jason, I shall speak to you quite frankly,
As though we still were friends. Can I possibly
Expect any kindness from someone like you?   620
Still, let us assume that I can:
It will only make you appear
Still more ignoble. Very well.
Where shall I go? Home to my father?
Home to him and the land I betrayed   625
When I followed you? Or back
To the pitiful daughters of Pelias?
What a fine welcome they would give me,

Who arranged the death of their own
    father!
So this is how it now stands with
    me.   630
I am loathed by my friends at home;
And for your sake I made enemies
Of others whom I need never have
Harmed. And now, to reward me
For all this, look, look,   635
How doubly happy you've made me
Among the women of Hellas! Look
What a fine, trustworthy husband
I have had in you! And now
I am to be cast forth into exile,   640
In utter misery, alone with my chil-
    dren
And without a single friend! Oh,
This will be a shameful shadow upon
    you,
As you lie in your wedding bed! That
Your own children, and their mother,
Who saved your life, should go   646
Wandering around the world like
    beggars! . . .
O Zeus, why have you given us a
    way to tell
True gold from the counterfeit, but
    no way,
No emblem branded on a man's
    body whereby   650
We can tell the true man from the
    false?
Choragus. Dreadful is the anger,
    And past all healing,
    When lovers in fury
    Turn against each other!   655
Jason. The time has come, it seems,
    When I must speak, and speak well,
And like a good helmsman
Reef up my sail and weather   659
The tempest of your tongue . . .
And since you dwell so heavily
On all the favors you did me,
Medea, I am certain that I owe
The safety of my voyage to Aphrodite

Alone among gods and men. Not
    that I   665
Doubt your skill; but all the same,
I prefer not to dwell on this notion
That love, with all its irresistible
Power, compelled you to save my
    life.
I don't think we need go into de-
    tails.   670
I admit that you meant well,
And did your best. But when it comes'
To this matter of my safety, let me
Point out that you got rather more
Than you gave. First of all,   675
Instead of living in a barbaric land,
You've come to Greece and enjoyed
Contact with a country where justice
And law prevail, and not brute force;
And what is more, the Greeks
    thought   680
Rather highly of you. You even
Acquired a certain fame here. Where-
    as,
If you had stayed on in that outer
Fringe of the world, your name
Would now be quite unknown.
    Frankly,   685
I'd rather have real fame and distinc-
    tion
Than mighty stores of gold in my
    halls
Or the talent to sing more sweetly
Than Orpheus. That is my answer
To your version of all my labors;
    remember,   690
It was you who brought up this
    matter.
As for your bitter attack on my
    marriage
With the princess, I think I can prove
First of all that it was a shrewd
    move;   694
Secondly, a thoroughly sober one;
And finally, that I did it in your
    interest

And that of your children . . . Wait!
Please remain calm . . . Since I had
  come
From Iolcos involved in every kind
  of trouble,   699
And an exile, what could be luckier
For me than marriage with the king's
Own daughter? It was not—since it
  is
This that seems to rankle in you—
It was not that I grew weary
Of going to bed with you, and be-
  gan   705
To look around for a new wife. Nor
Was it that I was anxious
To have more children. The two
We have are quite enough;   709
I don't complain. No, it was this,
First of all: that we might live
In comfort, and not in poverty.
Believe me, I have learned how
A man's friends desert him
The moment he is penniless . . .
  And then   715
I wanted to bring up my sons
In a manner worthy of my position; I
Even hoped that by having more
  sons,
Who would live as brothers to yours,
We might draw the entire family   720
Into harmony, and all be happy. You
Yourself need no more children;
But I would do well to help
The sons I have through the sons
I hope to have. Do you disagree   725
With all this? You would agree
If it weren't for this matter of love
Which rankles in you. But you women
Have developed such curious no-
  tions:
You think that all is well   730
As long as your life at night
Runs smoothly. But if something
Happens which upsets your way of
  love,

Then all that you once found lovely
And desirable you now find hate-
  ful.   735
Believe me, it would have been better
Far if men could have thought up
Some other way of producing chil-
  dren,
And done away with women; then
No evil would ever have come to
  men.   740
Choragus. O Jason, you have given this
  speech
Of yours a convincing enough air;
  and
Yet I somehow feel, though perhaps I
Shouldn't say so, that you have acted
Wickedly in betraying your wife.
Medea. I suppose I am different in
  many   746
Ways from most people, for I feel
That the worst punishment should
Fall on the man who speaks
Brilliantly for an evil cause,   750
The man who knows he can make
An evil thing sound plausible
And who dares to do so. And still,
Such a man isn't really so very
  wise   754
After all. Listen, Jason. You need
Not bring forth these clever phrases
And specious arguments; for a single
Word from me will destroy you.
  Consider:
Had you not been a coward, Jason,
  you   759
Would have spoken frankly to me
First, and not concealed your wed-
  ding
Plans from the one who loved you.
Jason. And you, no doubt, would have
  Done all you could to help
Me, if I had spoken of this   765
Matter: you, who even now cannot
Control the rage in your heart.

Medea. It wasn't this that restrained
you.
No. It was that you thought it might
Not be altogether proper, as you grew
Older, to have a foreign wife.   771
Jason. You may be quite sure of one
thing,
Medea. It was not because of any
Woman that I made this royal   774
Marriage. It was as I said before:
Because I wanted security for you,
And also to be the father
Of royal children bound by blood
To our two children: a thing which
Would have brought welfare to all of
us.   780
Medea. I don't want the kind of welfare
That is brought by suffering. I
Don't want the kind of safety
Which ends in sorrow.   784
Jason. Reflect on that opinion, Medea;
It will make you wiser. Don't
Search for sorrow in prosperity.
Don't keep looking for pain
In a piece of good luck.   789
Medea. Go on; mock me. You at least
Have a home to turn to. But I
Am going into exile, and alone.
Jason. It was you who made this choice;
There is no one else to blame.
Medea. How so? By marrying and de-
serting you?   795
Jason. You called down an evil curse
on the royal house.
Medea. I have brought a curse to your
own house too, I think.
Jason. Well, I don't propose to go
Into this any further. But if
You'd like to take along some   800
Of my money into exile, please
Say so. I am prepared to be
Generous on this point, and even
To give you letters to friends of mine
Abroad who will treat you well. It
would   805

Be madness for you to refuse this
offer.
It will be to your own gain,
Medea, if you give up your anger.
Medea. I will never accept favors
From friends of yours; and I'll   810
Accept nothing from you, so please
Don't offer it. Gifts from a coward
Bring luck to no one.
Jason. Very well then. I call upon
The gods to witness that I   815
Have tried in every way to help
You and the children. It is
You who refuse my offers. It
Is you who are stubbornly rejecting
Your friends. And for this,   820
Medea, you will surely suffer.
Medea. Please go! I can see you are
Longing to be with your new
Sweetheart. Aren't you lingering 824
Too long outside her bedroom? Go,
And taste the joys of your wedding.
Go, and God help you; you may end
By regretting this kind of wedding!
(JASON *goes out.*)

(Strophe 1)
Chorus. When love has passed its
limits
It brings no longer good: 830
It brings no peace or comfort to any
soul.
Yet while she still moves mildly there
is no fire
So sweet as that which is lit by the
goddess of love.
Oh never, upon me, Cypris,   834
Send forth from your golden bow
The unerring arrow poisoned with
desire!

(Antistrophe 1)
Let my heart be temperate: for
that
Is the wisest gift of the gods.
Let not that terrible goddess drive

Me to jealousy or rage! Oh let me
never   840
Be one of those who incessantly are
driven
To some new, forbidden longing!
Let her guide us gently toward the
man we choose;
Let her bless our beds with repose.

(Strophe 2)
O my country, my own home   845
Let me never leave my city,
Let me never lose my way
In that dark and pitiless life
Where each new day brings sorrow!
O, let me first succumb   850
To death, yes, let me die
Before I suffer the hopeless
Grief of the loss of a home!

(Antistrophe 2)
I have seen it with my own eyes,
I have heard my own heart tell me:
There is no city, no,   856
No friend who will give you pity
In the hour of your deepest woe.
O, let him perish in darkness
Who is faithless to his friends   860
And lets his heart stay frozen!
Let no such man be my friend!

(MEDEA *has been sitting in despair
on the stairway during this song.*
AEGEUS *enters.*)

Aegeus. Joy to you, Medea! This is the
best
Kind of greeting between old friends!
Medea. And joy to you, Aegeus, son
Of Pandion, king of Athens!   866
How does it happen that you
Have set foot in this country?
Aegeus. I have come from the ancient
oracles of Phoebus.
Medea. And why did you visit that
great center of prophecy?   870
Aegeus. I went to ask how I might
bring fertility to my seed.

Medea. Tell me, has your life been
childless hitherto?
Aegeus. Some divine visitation, I think,
has made me childless.
Medea. Have you a wife, or not?
Aegeus. I have, Medea.   875
Medea. And what did Phoebus tell you
about begetting children?
Aegeus. Words far too subtle for any
man to understand.
Medea. Is it proper for you to tell me
what he said?
Aegeus. Certainly; what I need is cleverness like yours.
Medea. Then what were the God's
words? Tell me, if I may hear
them.   880
Aegeus. That I shouldn't loosen the
hanging neck of the wine skin . . .
Medea. Till when? What must you do
first? Where must you go?
Aegeus. Till I have returned again to
my native home.
Medea. Then why have you come sailing to this land?
Aegeus. There is a man called Pittheus,
who is King of Troezen.   885
Medea. A son of Pelops, so they say,
and a man of piety.
Aegeus. I want to discuss this oracle of
the God with him.
Medea. He is a man full of skill and
experience in these matters.
Aegeus. As well as the dearest of my
old spear-bearing friends.
Medea. Good luck to you then! And
success to your wishes!   890
Aegeus. But why do you look so pale
and woebegone?
Medea. O Aegeus, my husband has
turned out to be the vilest of men!
Aegeus. What do you mean? Tell me
what has made you so unhappy.
Medea. Jason is wronging me, and utterly without provocation.

Aegeus. What has he done? Tell me
  more clearly, Medea.   895
Medea. He has taken another wife to
  take my place.
Aegeus. Does he really dare to do such
  a cruel thing!
Medea. He does indeed! He loved me
  once, but no longer.
Aegeus. Has he fallen in love? Has he
  wearied of your bed?
Medea. Ah, he's a great lover! But never
  true to his love. . . .   900
Aegeus. Let him go, then, if he is really
  as bad as you say.
Medea. He's in love with the idea of
  marrying royalty.
Aegeus. And who is the father of this
  princess? Please go on.
Medea. Her father is Kreon, King of
  Corinth.
Aegeus. Indeed, Medea, I understand
  your grief.   905
Medea. I am lost. And there is more: I
  am being banished!
Aegeus. Banished? By whom? This is
  something new you tell me.
Medea. Kreon is driving me from Cor-
  inth into banishment.
Aegeus. Does Jason consent? This is a
  contemptible thing.   909
Medea. Not in so many words, but he
  Has not really opposed it.
  O Aegeus, I beg you, I
  Implore you, by your beard
  And by your knees, I beseech you,
  Have pity on me! Have pity   915
  On a friend who is in trouble!
  Don't let me wander about
  In exile! Let me come
  To your land of Athens, let me   919
  Find refuge in your halls! And there,
  With heaven's consent, you may find
  Your love grow fertile and be
  Blessed with children, and your life
  At last end happily. You don't   924

  Know, Aegeus, how good your luck
  Has been, for I shall end
  Your sterility; I shall bring
  Power to your seed; for I know
  Of drugs that can do this.
Aegeus. There are many reasons, my
  dear   930
  Lady, why I should like to do
  This for you: first, for the sake
  Of the children you promise me
  (For in that matter, frankly,
  I'm at my wits' end). But   935
  Let me state my position. If
  You arrive in Athens, I shall
  Stand by you as I am bound
  To do. But I must warn you
  First, my friend: I won't agree   940
  To take you with me. If you
  Arrive at my halls of your own
  Accord, you shall live there in safety;
  I shan't surrender you to anyone.
  But you yourself must manage   945
  Your escape from this land, for
  I have no wish to incur ill
  Will among my friends here.
Medea. Very well. So be it. Make me a
  formal
  Pledge on this, and I shall be satis-
  fied.   950
Aegeus. Do you distrust me? What is
  it that troubles you?
Medea. I trust you, yes. But the house
  Of Pelias and Kreon as well,
  Both detest me. If you are bound
  To me by an oath, then,   955
  When they come to drag me
  Away from your country, I know
  You will remain true to your
  Vow and stand by me. Whereas,
  If it's only a promise, you might   960
  Not be in a position to resist
  Their demands; for I am weak,
  And they have both money and
  A royal house to help them.

Aegeus. You show considerable fore-
    sight   965
In these matters, I must say. Still,
If you insist, I shan't refuse you.
From my own point of view, too,
It might be just as well to have 969
An excuse like this oath to present
To your enemies . . . Now name
    your gods.
Medea. Swear by the plain of Earth.
And by my father's father Helios,
The Sun God, and in one sweeping
Phrase by the whole host of the
    gods. . . .   975
Aegeus. Swear to do what or not to do
    what?
Tell me.
Medea. Swear that you will never cast
Me from your land, nor ever,
As long as you live, allow   980
An enemy of mine to carry me away.
Aegeus. I swear by the Earth,
And by the holy light of Helios
The Sun God, and by the entire
Host of the gods, that I will   985
Abide by the terms you have just
    made.
Medea. Very well. And if you should
    fail,
What curse are you willing to incur?
Aegeus. Whatever happens to such as
    disregard the gods.
Medea. Go in peace, Aegeus. All is
    well,   990
Now; I shall arrive in your city
As soon as I possibly can—after
I have done what I must do,
And accomplished what I desire.

(AEGEUS *goes out.*)

Choragus. May Hermes, the God of
    Travelers,   995
Go with you on your way, Aegeus,
And bring you safely home!
And may you find the thing you have
    been seeking

For so long; you seem to be a gener-
    ous man.   999
Medea. O Zeus, and Justice who are
The child of Zeus, and light
Of the Sun God! Now, my friends,
Has come the hour of my triumph.
Now I have started on the road;
Now I know that I shall bring   1005
Revenge on the ones I hate. For
At the very moment that my doom
Looked darkest of all, this man
Aegeus appeared, like a harbor for
    all
My hopes; and to him I can   1010
Fasten the cable of my ship
When I come to the town and for-
    tress
Of Pallas Athene. And now let me
Tell you of all my plans. Listen;
They will not be idle words,   1015
Or pleasant. I shall send
A servant to Jason and ask
For an interview, and when he
Comes, I shall be soft and concil-
    iatory;   1019
I shall tell him that I've thought
Better of it; that I agree; that
Even the treacherous marriage
With the princess, which he is
Celebrating, strikes me as sensible,
And all for the best. However,   1025
I shall beg him to let the children
Stay on here: not that I'd dream
Of leaving my babies to be
Insulted in a land that loathes
Me; but purely as a stratagem;   1030
And I shall kill the king's
Own daughter. For I shall
Send them with gifts in their
Little hands, to be offered
To the bride to preserve   1035
Them from banishment; a finely
Woven dress and a golden diadem.
And if she takes these things and
Wears them on her body, she,

And whoever touches her, will   1040
Die in anguish; for I shall
Rub these things with deadly
Poison. That will be that;
But it is the next thing I   1044
Must do which sets me weeping.
For I will kill my own
Children! My own dear children,
Whom none shall take from me.
And when I have brought ruin
On the house of Jason, I shall   1050
Flee from the land and flee
From the murder of my children;
For it will be a terrible deed
To do! It isn't easy, my friends,
To bear the insults of one's   1055
Enemies. And so it shall be.
For what have I left in life?
I have no land, no home,
No harbor to protect me.
What a fool I was to leave   1060
My father's house, to put
My faith in the words
Of a Greek! And for this
He will pay the penalty,
So help me God. Never   1065
Again will he see his sons
Alive; never will he have a son
By this new bride. For she
Is doomed to die, and die
Hideously from the power   1070
Of my poison. Let no man
Think I am a feeble, frail-hearted
Woman who sits with folded
Hands: no, let them know me
For the opposite of that—one   1075
Who knows how to hurt her
Enemies and help her friends.
It is lives like this that
Are longest remembered!
Choragus. Since you have told us all
    your plans,   1080
Let me say this to you:
Do not do this thing!
Medea. There is nothing else I can do.

It is forgivable that you should
Say this: but remember, you   1085
Have not suffered as I have!
Choragus. Woman, can you really bring
    yourself
To destroy your own flesh and blood?
Medea. I can; for in that way   1089
I can hurt my husband most cruelly.
Choragus. And yourself as well! You
    will be
The most miserable of women.
Medea. Then I will; no matter.
No word of warning now can stop
    me!

(*The* Nurse *enters;* Medea *turns to
her.*)
Go and tell Jason to come to me.
And remember, I send you   1096
On a mission of great secrecy. Say
Nothing of the plans I have
Prepared; don't say a word, if
You are loyal to your mistress   1100
And loyal to the race of woman!
             (Strophe 1)
Chorus. Oh listen! We know of a land
Where dwell the sons of Erechtheus,
Fed on the food of wisdom, and
    blessed with the blood of gods,
Raised on a soil still holy and still
    unconquered; and there   1105
Moving amid that glittering air
    where the legends
Say that lovely Harmonia, the
    golden-haired,
Brought forth the Sacred Nine, the
    Pierian Muses!

           (Antistrophe 1)
And where they say that Cypris,
The divine one, sailed to draw the
Water out of the wandering stream of
    Cephisus, and the gentle   1111
Winds passed over the land: and
    over her glittering

Head the long, sweet-scented rose wreaths
Were wound by the Loves, who sit by Wisdom's side
And in all virtuous deeds are the friends of mortals.

(Strophe 2)
Then how can this city. O how   1115
Can these scared streams which welcome
Only the ones they love,
O tell, how can they welcome
You who are evil? You   1119
Who are killing your sons? O think
Of the sons you plan to slay,
Of the blood you plan to shed!
We beg, we implore you, Medea:
Do not murder your sons!

(Antistrophe 2)
Oh where can your hand or your heart,   1125
Medea, find the hardness
To do this frightful thing
Against your sons? O how
Can you look on them and yet
Not weep, Medea? How   1130
Can you still resolve to slay them?
Ah, when they fall at your feet
For mercy, you will not be able
To dip your hand in their blood!

(JASON *enters.*)
Jason. I have come at your bidding,
Medea. For although you are   1136
Full of hatred for me, this small
Favor I will grant you; I will
Listen to you, my lady, and hear
What new favor you are asking.
Medea. Jason, I beg your forgiveness for what   1141
I have said! Surely you can afford
To forgive my bad temper; after all,
There has been much love between us!   1144

I have reasoned with myself and
Reproached myself. "Poor fool," I said,
"Why am I so distraught? Why am I
So bitter against all good advice,
Why am I so angry at the rulers
Of this country, and my husband
As well, who does the best he can   1151
For me in marrying a royal princess,
And in having royal children, who
Will be brothers to my own? Why not   1154
Stop complaining? What is wrong
With me, when the gods are being
So generous? Don't I have my
Children to consider? Don't I realize
That we are exiles after all, and in need   1159
Of friends?" . . . And when I had
Thought all this over, Jason, I saw
How foolish I'd been, and how silly
My anger. So now I agree with you.
I think you are well advised in
Taking this new wife; and I was mad.   1165
I should have helped you in your plans, I
Should have helped arrange the wedding.
I should have stood by the wedding
Bed and been happy to wait   1169
On your bride. But we women are—
Well, I shan't say entirely
Worthless; but we are what we
Are. And you men shouldn't stoop
To our level; you shouldn't reply
To our folly with folly. I give in.
I admit I was wrong.   1176
I have thought better of it all. . . .

(*She turns toward the house.*)
Come, come, my children, come
Out from the house, come
And greet your father and then   1180

Say goodbye to him. Give up
Your anger, as your mother does;
Be friends with him again,
Be reconciled!

(*The* ATTENDANT *enters with the children.*)

Medea. We have made peace now;
Our bitterness is gone. Take   1186
His right hand . . . O God:
I can't help thinking of the things
That lie dark and hidden
In the future! . . . My children,
Hold out your arms—the way   1191
One holds them in farewell after
A long, long life . . . I am close
To tears, my children! I am
Full of fear! I have ended   1195
My quarrel with your father at last,
And look! My eyes are full of tears.

Choragus. And our eyes too
Are filling with tears. O,
Do not let disasters worse   1200
Than the present descend on you!

Jason. I approve of your conduct,
Medea; not that I blame you
For anything in the past. It is
Natural for a woman to be   1205
Furious with her husband when he
Begins to have other affairs. But
Now your heart has grown more sensible,
And your mind is changed for the better;   1209
You are behaving like a woman
Of sense. And of you, my sons,
Your father will take good care,
And make full provision,
With the help of God. And I
Trust that in due time you   1215
With your brothers will be among
The leading men in Corinth. All
You need to do is grow up,
My sons; and as for your future,
You may leave it safely   1220

In the hands of your father,
And of those among the gods
Who love him. I want to see
You when you've grown to be
Men, tall and strong, towering   1225
Over my enemies! . . . Medea, why
Are your eyes wet with tears?
Why are your cheeks so pale? Why
Are you turning away? Don't these
Happy words of mine make you
    happy?

Medea. It is nothing. I was only thinking about these children.   1231

Jason. Take heart, then. I shall look after them well.

Medea. I will, Jason. It is not that I
don't trust you.
Women are weak; and tears come
easily to them.

Jason. But why should you feel disturbed about the children?   1235

Medea. I gave birth to them, Jason.
And when
You prayed that they might live long,
My heart filled with sorrow to think
That all these things must happen.
Well now; I have told you some of
    the things   1240
I called you here to tell you; now
Let me tell you the rest. Since
The ruler of this land has resolved
To banish me, and since I am
Considered an enemy, I know   1245
It will be best for me not to stand
In your way, or in the way of the
    king,
By living here. I am going forth
From this land into exile. But these
Children—O let them feel that you
Are protecting them, and beg   1251
Of Kreon not to banish them!

Jason. I doubt whether I can persuade
him; still, I will try.

Medea. Or at least ask your wife
To beg her father to do this,   1255

And give the children reprieve from
exile.
Jason. I will try; and with her I think
I shall succeed.
Medea. She's a woman, after all;
And like all other women.   1259
And I will help you in this matter;
I will send the children to her
With gifts far more exquisite,
I am sure, than any now to be
Found among men—a finely woven
Dress and a diadem of chased gold.
There; let one of the servants   1266
Go and bring me these lovely orna-
ments.

(*One of the* ATTENDANTS *goes into
the house.*)

And she'll be happy not in one way,
But a thousand! With so splendid
A man as you to share her bed,   1270
And with this marvelous gown
As well, which once the Sun-God
Helios
Himself, my father's father, gave his
descendants.

(*The* ATTENDANT *returns with the
poisoned dress and diadem.*)

There, my children, take these wed-
ding   1274
Presents in your hands and take
Them as an offering to the royal
Princess, the lucky bride;
Give them to her; they are
Not gifts to be scorned.   1279
Jason. But why do you give them away
So rashly, Medea? Do you think
The royal palace is lacking
In dresses, or in gold? Keep them.
Don't give them away. If my wife
Really loves me, I am sure she   1285
Values me more highly than gold.
Medea. No, don't say that, Jason.
For I have heard it said
That gifts can persuade even   1289

The gods; and men are governed
More by gold than by words! Luck
Has fallen on your bride, and
The gods have blessed her fortune.
She is young: she's a princess.
Yet I'd give not only gold   1295
But my life to save my children
From exile. Enter that rich palace
Together, children, and pray
To your father's new bride; pray
To my mistress, and beg her   1300
To save you from banishment. Pre-
sent
This garment to her; and above
All let her take the gift from you
With her own hands. Go; don't
linger.   1304
And may you succeed, and bring
Back to your mother the good
News for which she longs!

(*Exit* JASON, *the* ATTENDANT, *and the
children bearing the poisoned gifts.*)

(Strophe 1)
Chorus. No hope now remains for the
children's lives!
No, none. Even now they are moving
toward death;
The luckless bride will accept the
gown that will kill her,   1310
And take the golden crown, and hold
it
In her hand, and over her golden
head will
Lift the garment of Hell!

(Antistrophe 1)
The grace and glitter of gold will en-
chant her:
She will put on the golden robe and
wear   1315
The golden crown: and deck herself
as the bride
Of death. And thus, pitiful girl,
Will fall in the trap; will fall and
perish.

She will never escape!   1319

(Strophe 2)

You likewise, O miserable groom,
Who planned a royal wedding cere-
mony,
Do not see the doom you are bringing
Upon your sons; and the terrible
death
Now lying in wait for your bride.
Pity   1324
Upon you! O, how you are fallen!

(Antistrophe 2)

And I weep for you too, Medea,
O mother who are killing your sons,
Killing in revenge for the loss
Of your love: you whom your lover
Jason   1329
Now has deserted and betrayed
To love and marry another mistress!

(*Enter* ATTENDANT *with the children.*)

Attendant. My lady, your children are
reprieved
From exile. The royal bride was
Delighted to receive your gifts
With her own hands. And there   1335
Is peace between her and your chil-
dren . . .
Medea! Why are you so distraught
At this lucky moment? Why are you
Turning your head away? Are you
not   1339
Happy to hear this news, my lady?
Medea. Oh, I am lost!
Attendant. That cry does not suit the
news I have brought you, surely!
Medea. I am lost! I am lost!
Attendant. Have I told you of some
disaster, without knowing it?
Was I wrong in thinking that my
news was good?   1345
Medea. You have said what you have
said:
I do not wish to blame you.

Attendant. Then why are you so dis-
turbed? Why are you weeping?
Medea. Oh, my old friend, I can't help
weeping.
It was I, it was I and the gods,   1350
Who planned these things so badly.
Attendant. Take heart, Medea. Your
sons will bring
You back to your home some day.
Medea. And I'll bring others back to
their homes,
Long before that happens!   1355
Attendant. And often before this,
mothers have been
Parted from their sons. Bear your
troubles,
Medea, as all mortals must bear
them.
Medea. I will, I will. Go back into the
house;
And plan your daily work for the
children.   1360

(*The* ATTENDANT *goes into the house,
and* MEDEA *turns to her children.*)

Medea. O my children, my children,
You will still have a city,
You will still have a home
Where you can dwell forever, far
Away from me, far forever   1365
From your mother! But I am
Doomed to go in exile to another
Land, before I can see you
Grow up and be happy, before
I can take pride in you, before   137c
I can wait on your brides and
Make your marriage beds, or hold
The torch at your wedding
Ceremony! What a victim I am
Of my own self-will! It was   1375
All in vain, my children, that I
Reared you! It was all in vain
That I grew weary and worn,
And suffered the anguish and pangs
Of childbirth! Oh pity me! Once

I had great hopes for you; I   1381
Had hopes that you'd look after
Me in my old age, and that you'd
Lovingly deck my body with your
    own hands
When I died, as all men hope   1385
And desire. But now my lovely
Dreams are over. I shall love
You both. I shall spend my life
In grief and solitude. And never
Again will you see your mother
With your own dear eyes; now   1391
You will pass into another
Kind of life. Ah, my dear children,
Why do you look at me like this?
Why are you smiling your sweet
Little smiles at me? O children,
What can I do? My heart gives   1397
Way when I see the joy
Shining in my children's eyes.
O women, I cannot do it! . . .   1400
Farewell to all my plans!
I will take my babies away with me
From this land. Why should I hurt
Their father by hurting them? Why
Should I hurt myself doubly? No:
I cannot do it. I shall say   1406
Good-bye to my plans . . . And
    yet—
O, what is wrong with me? Am I
Willing to see my enemies go   1409
Unpunished? Am I willing to be
Insulted and laughed at? I shall
Follow this thing to the end.
How weak I am! How weak to let
My heart be touched by these soft
Sentiments! Go back into the
    house,   1415
My children . . . And if anyone
Prefers not to witness my sacrifice,
Let him do as he wishes! My poor
Heart, have pity on them, let them
Go, the little children! They'll bring
Cheer to you, if you let them   1421
Live with you in exile! . . . No,

By all the avenging Furies,
This shall not be! Never shall I
Surrender my children to the inso-
    lence   1425
And mockery of my enemies! It is
Settled. I have made my decision.
And since they must die, it is
Their mother who must kill them.
Now there is no escape for the
    young   1430
Bride! Already the crown is on
Her head; already the dress is
Hanging from her body; the royal
Bride, the princess is dying! This
I know. And now—since I   1435
Am about to follow a dreadful
Path, and am sending them
On a path still more terrible—
I will simply say this: 1439
I want to speak to my children.

(*She calls and the children come
back; she takes them in her arms.*)

Come, come, give me your hands,
My babies, let your mother kiss
You both. O dear little hands,
Dear little lips: how I have   1444
Loved them! How fresh and young
Your eyes look! How straight
You stand! I wish you joy
With all my heart; but not here;
Not in this land. All that you   1449
Had here your father has stolen
From you. . . . How good it is
To hold you, to feel your soft
Young cheeks, the warm young
Sweetness of your breath. . . . Go
    now;   1454
Leave me. I cannot look at you
Any longer . . . I am overcome. . . .

(*The children go into the house
again.*)

Now at last I understand the full
Evil of what I have planned.
At last I see how my passion   1459

Is stronger than my reason: passion,
Which brings the worst of woes to
  mortal man.

(*She goes out at the right, toward
the palace.*)

Choragus. Many a time before
I have gone through subtler rea-
  soning,
Many times I have faced graver ques-
  tioning
Than any woman should ever have to
  face: 1465
But we women have a goddess to
  help us, too,
And lead us into wisdom.
Not all of us; perhaps not many;
But some women there are who are
  capable of wisdom.
And I say this: that those who have
  never 1470
Known the fullness of life and never
  had children,
Are happier far than those who are
  parents.
For the childless, who never dis-
  cover whether
Their children grow up to be a cause
  for joy or for pain,
Are spared many troubles: 1475
While those who know in their houses
The sweet presence of children—
We have seen how their lives are
  wasted by worry.
First they fret about how they shall
  raise them
Properly; and then how to leave
  them enough 1480
Money to live on; and then they con-
  tinue
To worry about whether all this labor
Has gone into children that will turn
  out well
Or turn out ill: and the question re-
  mains unanswered. 1484

And let me tell of one more trouble,
The last of all, and common to all
  mortals:
For suppose you have found enough
For them to live on, and suppose
You have seen them grow up and
  turn out well;
Still, if fate so decrees it, Death 1490
Will come and tear away your chil-
  dren!
What use is it, then, that the gods
For the sake of children
Should pile on us mortals,
After all other griefs, 1495
This grief for lost children? This
  grief
Greater by far than any?

(MEDEA *comes out of the house.*)

Medea. I have been waiting in sus-
  pense,
Ladies; I have waited long to learn
How things will happen . . . Look!
I see one of Jason's 1501
Servants coming toward us; he is
Panting; and the bearer of news,
I think; of bad news . . .

(*A* MESSENGER *rushes in.*)

Messenger. Fly, Medea, fly! 1505
You have done a terrible thing, a
  thing
Breaking all human laws: fly,
Take a ship for the seas,
Or a chariot for the plains!

Medea. Why? What reason have you
  for asking me to fly? 1510

Messenger. She lies dead! The royal
  princess
And her father Kreon too!
They have died: they have
Been slain by your poisons!

Medea. You bring me blessed news!
  Now 1515
And from now on I count you
Among my friends, my benefactors!

Messenger. What! Are you insane? Are
    you mad,
  Medea? You have done an outrage
  To the royal house: Does it make
    you   1520
  Happy to hear it? Can you hear
  Of this dreadful thing without hor-
    ror?
Medea. I too have words to say in
    reply
  To yours. Do not be impatient,
  My friend. Tell me: how did   1525
  They die? You will make me doubly
  Happy if you say they died in an-
    guish!
Messenger. When those two children,
    your own babies,
  Medea, came with their father and
    entered
  The palace of the bride, it gave   1530
  Joy to all of us, the servants
  Who have suffered with you; for in-
    stantly
  All through the house we whispered
  That you had made up your quarrel
  With your husband. One of us
    kissed   1535
  Your children's hands, and another
  Their golden hair, and I myself was
    so
  Overjoyed that I followed them in
    person
  To the women's chambers. And there
    stood   1539
  Our mistress, whom we now serve
  Instead of you; and she kept her eyes
    fixed
  Longingly on Jason. When she
    caught
  Sight of your children, she covered
    up
  Her eyes, and her face grew pale,
    and she   1544
  Turned away, filled with petulance

At their coming. But your husband
    tried
  To soothe the bride's ill humor,
  And said: "Do not look so unkindly
  At your friends! Do not feel angry:
  Turn your head to me once more,
    and   1550
  Think of your husband's friends
  As your own friends! Accept these
    gifts,
  And do this for my sake: beg
  Of your father not to let these chil-
    dren   1554
  Be exiled!" And then, when she saw
  The dress, she grew mild and
    yielded,
  And gave in to her husband. And be-
    fore
  The father and the children had gone
  Far from her rooms, she took   1559
  The gorgeous robe and put it on;
  And she put the golden crown on her
    curly
  Head, and arranged her hair in the
    shining
  Mirror, smiling as she saw herself
    reflected.
  And then she rose from her chair
  And walked across the room, step-
    ping   1565
  Softly and delicately on her small
  White feet, filled with delight at the
    gift,
  And glancing again and again at
    the delicate
  Turn of her ankles. And after that
  It was a thing of horror we saw.
  For suddenly her face changed its
    color,   1571
  And she staggered back, and began
  To tremble as she ran, and reached
  A chair just as she was about
  To fall to the ground. An old   1575
  Woman servant, thinking no doubt
    that this

Was some kind of seizure, a fit
Sent by Pan, or some other god,
Cried out a prayer: and then, as
she   1579
Prayed, she saw the flakes of foam
Flow from her mouth, and her eye-
balls
Rolling, and the blood fade from
her face.
And then it was a different prayer
She uttered, a terrible scream, and
one   1584
Of the women ran to the house
Of the King, and another to the
newly
Wedded groom to tell him what had
Happened to the bride; and the
whole
House echoed as they ran to and fro.
Let me tell you, time enough for a
man   1590
To walk two hundred yards passed
Before the poor lady awoke from
her trance,
With a dreadful scream, and
opened
Her eyes again. A twofold torment
was
Creeping over her. The golden
diadem   1595
On her head was sending forth a
violent
Stream of flame, and the finely
Woven dress which your children
gave
Her was beginning to eat into the
poor   1599
Girl's snowy soft flesh. And she
Leapt from her chair, all on fire,
And started to run, shaking her
head
To and fro, trying to shake off
The diadem; but the gold still
Clung firmly, and as she shook her
hair   1605

The fire blazed forth with double
fury.
And then she sank to the ground,
helpless.
Overcome; and past all recognition
Except to the eye of a father—
For her eyes had lost their nor-
mal   1610
Expression, and the familiar look
Had fled from her face, and from
the top
Of her head a mingled stream
Of blood and fire was pouring. And
It was like the drops   1615
Falling from the bark of a pine
Tree when the flesh dropped away
From her bones, torn loose
By the secret fangs of the poison.
And terror kept all of us   1620
From touching the corpse; for we
Were warned by what had hap-
pened.
But then her poor father who knew
Nothing of her death, came sud-
denly   1624
Into the house and stumbled over
Her body, and cried out as he
folded
His arms about her and kissed her,
And said: "O my child, my poor
child,
Which of the gods has so cruelly
Killed you? Who has robbed me of
you,   1630
Who am old and close to the grave?
O
My child let me die with you!" And
he
Grew silent and tried to rise to his
Feet again, but found himself
Fastened to the finely spun dress,
Like vine clinging to a laurel   1636
Bough, and there was a fearful
Struggle. And still he tried to lift

His knees, and she writhed and
  clung
To him; and as he tugged, he   1640
Tore the withered flesh from
His bones. And at last he could
No longer master the pain, and
Surrendered, and gave up the ghost.
So there they are lying together:
And it is a sight to send us weep-
  ing. . . .   1646
As for you, Medea, I will say
Nothing of your own problems: you
Yourself must discover an escape
From punishment. I think, and I
  have   1650
Always thought, the life of men
Is a shadow; and I say without
Fear that those who are wisest
  among
All men, and probe most deeply
Into the cause of things—they are
The ones who suffer most deeply!
  For,   1656
Believe me, no man among mortals
  is happy;
If wealth comes to a man, he may
  be
Luckier than the rest; but happy—
  never.

(*Exit* Messenger.)

Choragus. It seems that heaven has
  sent, today,   1660
A heavy load of evils upon Jason;
And he deserves them. Alas, poor
  girl,
Poor daughter of Kreon! I pity you
And your anguish; and now you are
Gone, all because of your wedding
  with Jason: 1665
Gone away to the halls of Hades!
Medea. Women, the deed shall be
  done! Swiftly
I will go and kill my children,
And then leave the land: and not

Delay nor let them be killed by
A crueler hand. For die they   1671
Must in any case: and if
They must be slain, it is I,
Their mother who gave them life,
Who must slay them! O my heart,
My heart, arm yourself in steel!
Do not shrink back from this hid-
  eous   1677
Thing which has to be done! Come,
My hand, and seize the sword, take
  it
And step forward to the place
  where   1680
My life's true sorrow begins! Do not
Be a coward . . . do not think
Of the children, and how dear
They are to you who are their
  mother!   1684
For one brief day, Medea, forget
Your children; and then forever
After you may mourn; for though
You will kill them, they were dear
  to you,
Very dear . . . I am a miserable
  woman!

(*With a cry* Medea *rushes into the
house.*)

(Strophe)
Chorus. O Earth, and the all-bright-
  ening   1690
Beam of the Sun, look, look
Upon this lost one, shine upon
This pitiful woman before she raises
Her hand in murder against her
  sons!
For lo! these are the offspring   1695
Of thine own golden seed, and I fear
That divine blood may now be shed
  by men!
O Light flung forth by Zeus,
O heavenly Light,
Hold back her hand,   1700
  Restrain her, and drive out

This dark demoniac fury from the
house!

(*Antistrophe*)

Was it all in vain, Medea,
What you suffered in bearing your
sons?
Was it utterly in vain   1705
You bore the babes you loved, after
you left
Behind you that dark passage
through the straits
And past the perilous rocks, the
blue Symplegades?
Wretched woman, how has it hap-
pened   1709
That your soul is torn by anger
And darkened by the shadow of
death?
Heavy will be the price
To pay for kindred blood staining
the earth!
Heavy the woe sent down by
heaven
On the house of the killer for such
a crime!   1715

(*A cry is heard from the children
within.*)

Choragus. Listen! Do you hear? Do
you hear the children crying?
Hate-hardened heart! O woman
born for evil!

(*Crying within.*)

1st Son. What can I do? How can I
run from mother's hands?

(*Crying within.*)

2nd Son. I don't know! We are lost,
we are lost, brother!

Choragus. Shall I enter the house? Oh
surely   1720
I must help! I must save these children from murder!

(*Within.*)

1st Son. Help, in the name of heaven!
We need your help!

(*Within.*)

2nd Son. Now, now it's coming closer!
The sword is falling!

Choragus. Oh, you must be made of
stone or steel,
To kill the fruit of your womb   1725
With your own hands, unhappy
woman!
I have heard of only one,
Of all the women who ever lived,
who laid
Her hand upon her children: it was
Ino,
Who was driven insane by the
Gods   1730
When the wife of Zeus sent her
wandering from her home.
And wild with grief at killing her
children,
She flung herself from the sea-bat-
tered cliff
And plunged into the sea, and in
the sea   1734
Rejoined her two dead children.
Can anything so dreadful ever hap-
pen again?
Woe flows forth from the bed of a
woman
Whom fate has touched with trou-
ble!
Great is the grief that they have
brought on men!

(*Enter* JASON *with his attendants.*)

Jason. Ladies, you have been sitting
near   1740
This house! Tell me! Is Medea, is
The woman who did this frightful
Thing, still in the house? Or has she
Fled already? O believe me, she'll
have
To hide deep under the earth, or
fly   1745
On wings through the sky, if she
Hopes to escape the vengeance

Of the royal house! Does she dream,
After killing the ruler of the land,
    that
She herself can escape from these
    halls   1750
Unpunished? But I am thinking of
    her
Far less than of her children; for
    she
Herself will duly suffer at the hands
Of those she wronged. Ladies, I have
Come to save the lives of my   1755
Boys, lest the royal house should
Harm them in revenge for this
Vile thing done by their mother.
Choragus. O Jason, you do not yet
    know
The full depth of your misery,
    or   1760
You would not have spoken those
    words!
Jason. What do you mean? Is she
    planning to kill me also?
Choragus. Your boys are dead; dead
    at their mother's hand.
Jason. What have you said, woman?
    You are destroying me!
Choragus. You may be sure of this:
    your children are dead.   1765
Jason. Oh where did she kill them?
    Was it here, or in the house?
Choragus. Open the doors, and you
    will see their murdered bodies!
Jason. Open the doors! Unlock the
    bolts! Undo
The fastenings! And let me see this
    twofold
Horror! Let me see my murdered
    boys!   1770
Let me look on her whom I shall
    kill in vengeance!

(*His attendants rush to the door.*
MEDEA *appears above the house in
a chariot drawn by dragons. The
dead children are at her side.*)

Medea. Why do you batter at the
    doors?
Why do you shake these bolts,
In quest of the dead and their
Murderess? You may cease your
    trouble,   1775
Jason; and if there is anything you
Want to say, then say it! Never
Again shall you lay your hand on
    me;
So swift is the chariot which my
Father's father gave me, the Sun
    God   1780
Helios, to save me from my foes!
Jason. Horrible woman! Now you are
    utterly
Loathed by the gods, and by me,
    and
By all mankind. You had the heart
To stab your children; you,   1785
Their own mother, and to leave me
Childless; you have done these fearful
Things, and still you dare to gaze
As ever at the sun and the earth! O
I wish you were dead! Now at
    last   1790
I see clearly what I did not see
On the day I brought you, loaded
With doom, from your barbarous
    home
To live in Hellas—a traitress
To your father and your native
    land.   1795
On me too the gods have hurled
The curse which has haunted you.
    For
You killed your own brother at his
Fireside, and then came aboard our
Beautiful ship the Argo. And that
Was how it started. And then you
Married me, and slept with me, and
Out of your passion bore me chil-
    dren;   1803
And now, out of your passion, you
    have

Killed them. There are no women in all
Of Greece who would dare to do this. And
Yet I passed them over, and chose you
Instead; and chose to marry my own
Doom! I married not a woman,
But a monster, wilder of heart than
Scylla in the Tyrrhenian Sea!   1811
But even if I hurled a thousand
Insults at you, Medea, I know
I could not wound you: your heart
Is so hard, so utterly hard. Go,
You wicked sorceress; I see   1816
The stains of your children's blood
Upon you! Go; all that is left
To me now is to mourn. I shall never   1819
Lie beside my newly wedded love;
I shall never have my sons, whom
I bred and brought up, alive
Beside me to say a last farewell!
I have lost them forever,
And my life is ended.   1825
Medea. O Jason, to these words of yours
I could make a long reply; but
Zeus, the father, himself well knows
All that I did for you, and what
You did to me. Destiny has   1830
Refused to let you scorn my love,
And lead a life of pleasure,
And mock at me; nor were the royal
Princess and the matchmaker
Kreon destined to drive me into exile,   1835
And then go untormented! Call me
A monster if you wish; call me
The Scylla in the Tyrrhenian Sea.
For now I have torn your heart:
And this indeed was destined, Jason!   1840
Jason. You too must feel the pain; you will share my grief, Medea.

Medea. Yes; but the pain is milder, since you cannot mock me!
Jason. O my sons, it was an unspeakable mother who bore you!
Medea. O my sons, it was really your father who destroyed you!
Jason. But I tell you: it was not my hand that slew them!   1845
Medea. No; but your insolence, and your new wedding slew them!
Jason. And you thought this wedding cause enough to kill them?
Medea. And you think the anguish of love is trifling for a woman?
Jason. Yes, if her heart is sound: but yours makes all things evil.   1849
Medea. Your sons are dead, Jason! Does it hurt you when I say this?
Jason. They will live on, Medea, by bringing suffering on you.
Medea. The gods are well aware who caused all this suffering.
Jason. Yes, the gods are well aware. They know your brutal heart.
Medea. You too are brutal. And I am sick of your bitter words!
Jason. And I am sick of yours. Oh Medea, it will be easy to leave you.   1855
Medea. Easy! Yes! And for me too! What, then, do you want?
Jason. Give me those bodies to bury, and to mourn.
Medea. Never! I will bury them myself.
I will take them myself to Hera's
Temple, which hangs over the Cape,
Where none of their enemies can
Insult them, and where none can defile   1862
Their graves! And in this land
Of Corinth I shall ordain a holy
Feast and sacrifice, forever after,
To atone for this guilt of killing.
And I shall go myself to Athens,

To live in the House of Aegeus,
The son of Pandion. And I predict
That you, as you deserve, will
    die   1870
Without honor; and your head
    crushed
By a beam of the shattered Argo;
And then you will know the bitter
End of all my love for you!

Jason. May the avenging fury of our
    sons   1875
Destroy you! May Justice destroy
You, and repay blood with blood!

Medea. What god, what heavenly
    power
Would listen to you? To a breaker
Of oaths? To a betrayer of love?

Jason. Oh, you are vile! You sorceress!
    Murderess!   1881

Medea. Go to your house. Go, and bury
    your bride.

Jason. Yes, I shall go; and mourn for
    my murdered sons.

Medea. Wait; do not weep yet, Jason!
    Wait till age has sharpened your
    grief!

Jason. Oh my sons, whom I loved! My
    sons!   1885

Medea. It was I, not you, who truly
    loved them.

Jason. You say you loved them; yet you
    killed them.

Medea. Yes. I killed them to make you
    suffer.

Jason. Medea, I only long to kiss them
    one last time.

Medea. Now, now, you long to kiss
    them!   1890
    Now you long to say farewell:

But before, you cast them from you!

Jason. Medea, I beg you, let me touch
    the little bodies of my boys! 1894

Medea. No. Never. You speak in vain.

Jason. O Zeus, high in your heaven,
    Have you heard these words?
    Have you heard this unutterable
    Cruelty? Have you heard this
    Woman, this monster, this murder-
    ess?   1900
And now I shall do the only
Thing I still can do! Yes!
I shall cry, I shall cry
Aloud to heaven, and call on
The gods to witness how you   1905
Killed my sons, and refused
To let me kiss them farewell,
Or touch them, or give them burial!
Oh, I'd rather never have seen them
    live,   1909
Than have seen them slaughtered so!

(*The chariot carries* MEDEA *away.*)

Choragus. Many, many are the things
    That Zeus determines, high on the
        Olympian throne;
    Many the things beyond men's un-
        derstanding
    That the gods achieve, and bring to
        pass.
    Many the things we think will hap-
        pen,   1915
    Yet never happen.
    And many the things we thought
        could never be,
    Yet the gods contrive.
    Such things have happened on this
        day,
    And in this place!   1920

Pseudolus / A Funny Thing Happened on the Way to the Forum

~~~~~~~~~~~~~~~~~~~~~~~~~~~ PLAUTUS/SHEVELOVE, GELBART, AND SONDHEIM

INTRODUCTION

Titus Maccius Plautus, who lived from about 254 to 184 B.C., was a native of the Umbrian town of Sarsina in Northern Italy and the most important writer of Roman comedy. He is said to have engaged in various occupations and to have had several rises and falls in fortune before settling down rather late in life to playwriting. It is believed that he served as a soldier in the Roman legions, became a merchant, went bankrupt, turned miller and baker's assistant, then actor.

He probably appeared as a member of a theatrical troupe in the rowdy, slapstick farces that originated in Atella in rural Campania and that dealt mostly with life in the country, as several of their titles suggest: *Daddy the Farmer, The Yokel, The Cowherd.* The characters in these plays were stock figures who wore identifiable masks: Maccus the stupid clown, Bucco the glutton and braggart, Pappus the foolish old man, and Dossenus the clever conniver. These plays drew laughs with their improvised jokes and tricks, and their obscene language and gestures. Men played the parts of women, and all the actors appeared barefoot. Plautus is believed to have derived two of his names from characters in these plays: Maccus and Plotus (flatfoot); hence, Titus Clown Flatfoot would come to mind when people spoke of Titus Maccius Plautus. But the playwright borrowed more than his name from the Atellana, for though the farces retained their popularity long after the introduction of literary comedy, Plautus managed to work into his plays many of their characters, plots, and comic devices.

When Plautus began to write at about the age of fifty, the soldiers of the Roman Republic were conquering Greek territory and Roman writers were "annexing" Greek literature. The decline of Greek civilization brought about the end of the Old Comedy of Aristophanes, with its great themes and grandiose conception of the world, and produced the more limited New Comedy of Diphilus, Philemon, and Menander, whose plays reflected the life of the rich Athenian citizen and his almost total involvement with domestic and romantic problems. They are comedies of manners written with skill and polish. Menander's plays actually show the influence of Euripides in their dramatic action and psychological probing, and are marked by unusual refinement in the treatment of character.

Plautus, who is credited with having written about one hundred and thirty plays, twenty of which survive, took his plots and characters from Greek New Comedy. All his plays are set in Athens or other Greek cities and his actors wore the Greek *pallium*, or cloak, instead of the Roman toga, which gave the name *palliata* to his comedies. Under the Greek cloak, however, were Roman citizens discussing local customs and habits and actual events of the day in colloquial Latin. Aware of the taste of Roman audiences for broad, fast-moving comedy, Plautus coarsened and enlivened the Greek originals and, like other contemporary playwrights, resorted to the process known as *contaminatio*, which meant helping himself to choice bits and pieces from more than one Greek play in order to construct one Latin play. This patchwork often produced the impression of careless workmanship, but Plautus was less interested in achieving perfect structure than in raising laughter in the audience.

The plot of the average Plautine play—which is divided into the conventional five acts—is an intricate network of intrigue and deception, laced with jests and sight gags, songs and dances. The plays are basically domestic comedies in a variety of guises: mothers and fathers, sons, daughters, and slaves are continually involved in tangled love affairs, misunderstandings, mistaken identities, and lucky discoveries or carefully planned tricks, which clear up the problems and provide a happy ending. Although the plays' prologues describe a good deal of the action and often foreshadow the outcome, there are always suspense, surprise, and an ironic note at the conclusion, but no special emphasis on moral or theme.

Since the characters in Plautus' plays have to serve the needs of the stereotyped plots, they are neither deeply nor subtly motivated. They represent instead a wide spectrum of stock figures. Among the men there are three main types: the young lover, the old man, and the slave. The female characters fall into four groups: the matron, the courtesan, the housemaid, and the virgin. The characters who unfailingly provide much of the laughter, however, are the coarse and ignorant professional types: the moneylenders, the cooks, the slavedealers, the bragging soldiers, and the parasites. These, and the tricky slaves, lent themselves best to farcical treatment and caricature and were especially dear to Plautus. And yet several of the plays achieve unity and coherence largely because of the strength of the central character, such as Euclio, the miser, in *The Pot of Gold (Aulularia)*; Pyrgopolynices in *The Braggart Warrior (Miles Gloriosus)*; and Pseudolus, the wheeling-and-dealing slave, in the play named for him.

The language in Plautus' plays is fast, funny, and verbose. It is based on the everyday speech of the educated Roman of the time as well as on the slang of the slave quarters, but it is not completely realistic since it contains colorful metaphors, alliteration, assonance, malapropisms, and words coined by the playwright. Plautus was careful to provide language suitable for each character: when refined, elevated speech was called for he was capable of supplying it, but his specialty was the coarse abuse, obscene humor, and comical expressions of the uneducated. Exaggerations, puns, double meanings, repetition, irony—in fact, every type of verbal jest—were exploited by him for the amusement of his audiences.

Like all the Greek and Roman dramas known to us, Plautus' plays were written in verse, but they contained a greater variety of meters than those of any other playwright. In certain scenes the dialogue was spoken, in others it was chanted or spoken to music; there were also songs, closely related to the plot, sung by one, two, or three actors; but there was no chorus. One method of dating the plays is by the amount of music they contain; in the "early" works there are only a few songs, while the "later" plays contain a great deal of music, and many songs and dances. The combination of song, dance, and comedy is thought to have originated in the Atellan farces; it is a formula which may very well account for the great popularity of the old farces, of Plautus' plays, and of our own musical comedies.

Besides those mentioned above, his best-known and most frequently produced and imitated plays are the *Amphitryon, Casina, The Twin Menaechmi, Mercator* (The Merchant), *Mostellaria* (The Haunted House), and *Rudens* (The Rope). Plautus' influence on European and American drama has been enormous. His stock characters were transformed into Harlequin, Columbine, and Pantaloon for the Italian comedy of improvisation, the *commedia dell'arte*; and his tricky slaves were renamed Mascarille and Scapin by Molière, who also reworked *The Pot of Gold* into *L'Avare (The Miser)*. In Shakespeare's brilliant adaptations, *The Twin Menaechmi* became *The Comedy of Errors;* the hero of *The Braggart Warrior,* Falstaff; and *Rudens*, with its storm and shipwreck, part of *The Tempest.* A host of other playwrights in various countries have been indebted to Plautus for characters, situations, lines of dialogue, and complete plots.

In the present century, audiences have applauded Jean Giraudoux's *Amphitryon 38,* which by the French playwright's count was the thirty-eighth reworking of Plautus' *Amphitryon,* the original bedroom farce in which Jupiter seduces a chaste woman by assuming the guise of her husband. Rodgers and Hart's successful musical comedy, *The Boys from Syracuse,* was adapted from *The Twin Menaechmi* via *The Comedy of Errors;* and *A Funny Thing Happened on the Way to the Forum,* a frothy concoction by Burt Shevelove, Larry Gelbart, and Stephen Sondheim, was based mainly on the *Pseudolus,* with choice bits from several other Plautine plays whipped up in the soufflé

The *Pseudolus* is one of the two plays of Plautus for which we know the actual date of production; according to the official record it was presented in April, 191 B.C., at a religious festival, the Ludi Megalenses, along with special games in honor of the Magna Mater (Great Mother), to whom a temple was being dedicated.

The play is made up of familiar elements: A young man is in love with a virgin who is being held in the house of a pimp. The girl was bought by a soldier for twenty minae, fifteen of which he paid before going off to fight. He left a token identifying himself and arranged for the pimp to hand over the girl to anyone who paid the balance of the money and showed a similar token. Pseudolus, the young man's clever slave, manages by trickery to get hold of the token and the necessary sum of money, deceive the pimp, and get the girl for his master.

The play is fast-moving and consistently funny but presents two difficulties in the plot. The young man's father has a friend who, it appears, will be involved in the intrigue; but he vanishes after the first act, never to be heard of again. The second difficulty is more serious: Pseudolus promises to trick the hero's father as well as the pimp, but the play contains no tricking of the father. If Plautus composed the *Pseudolus* by the process of *contaminatio*, that is, by combining two Greek originals—one of which dealt with the tricking of a pimp, the other with the swindling of a father—he probably counted on the complexity of the plot as well as the speed of the action to keep the audience from noticing the careless linkage. The spectators, at any rate, were less interested in the convolutions of the plot than in the jokes, the songs, and the dances.

The *Pseudolus* apparently continued to please in the theatre, for we learn that in the first century A.D. the great comic actor Roscius appeared in the rôle of the pimp rather than in that of the clever slave. Such serious critics as Horace and Quintillian, who wrote long after the death of Plautus and probably based their judgments on the scripts of his plays, objected to the obscenity and the complexity of his style, and were as condescending to his work as are many critics of musical comedy today.

PRODUCTION IN THE ROMAN THEATER

Roman drama, like its Greek predecessor, began in primitive religious rites and crude comedy. Between the sixth and fourth centuries B.C., a variety of entertainers converged on Rome to take part in a ritual that would ward off a plague. Musicians and dancers came south from Etruria; comedians, who specialized in crude verse plays consisting of improvised jokes and personal satire, came west from Latium; and the troupes of actors who appeared in the coarse Atellan farces came north from Campania. These entertainers performed at religious ceremonies, funeral games, athletic contests, and at the numerous festivals held during the year in honor of various gods and goddesses.

Early in the third century B.C., Livius Andronicus, an educated citizen of the Greek city of Tarentum, was taken prisoner by the Romans. A slave at first, he was later freed, became a teacher, and the earliest known translator from Greek to Latin. From 240 to 207 B.C. he put into Latin the tragedies of Sophocles and Euripides as well as Greek New Comedies. These works provided inspiration and source material for Roman playwrights. Plautus, a contemporary of Livius Andronicus, drew freely on them for his rowdy farces; and Terence, two generations later, tapping the same source, produced comedies of greater refinement. More than a century and a half after that, Seneca (5 B.C.-65 A.D.), the last important Roman playwright, composed ten tragedies which kept the dramatic and theatrical forms of his Greek models, even including the chorus, but adapted the borrowed material to the Roman character. Seneca's plays are of special interest in the history of the drama because of their powerful influence on the playwrights of the Renaissance. Shakespeare and his contemporaries are known to have read, admired, and imitated the plays of Seneca.

Occasions for the performance of both tragedies and comedies were the old religious festivals, or *ludi* (games). Celebrated in honor of Magna Mater, Jupiter, Venus Victoria, and other divinities, they consisted of such athletic events as boxing, wrestling, and racing; of gladiatorial bouts; and of the presentation of plays. At the end of the third century B.C. a total of about twelve days was allotted during the festivals for the production of plays; this increased gradually until by the fourth century A.D. one hundred and seventy-five days were given over each year to the festivals, on one hundred of which plays were performed.

A play reached the stage in Plautus' day by a complicated series of arrangements. An appropriation of money was made by the Roman senate to officials delegated to supervise the production of plays at the public games. If the sum allotted was not sufficient, the deficit might be made up by the officials themselves as they were wealthy men, like the Greek *choragoi* (producers). Since admission to the games was free to the public, there was no income from that source.

The officials made a contract with an acting company to produce the play. The money paid to the manager of the company, who was usually the chief actor, had to cover payment to the playwright and the actors, and to take care of all production costs. The actor-manager bought the play from the poet, cast it, and arranged for rehearsals. He also hired the musicians, costumes, masks, and stage properties. The playwright sold his play outright and had no control over its production. The manager assumed the entire risk. If the play succeeded, he would be called on again by the public officials, as would the playwright; if it failed, it was the manager's loss. It is obvious that although the production of a play was considered a social and religious enterprise, it had its highly commercial aspects.

But religious rites were never omitted whether or not they continued to have meaning. Roman theatrical presentations were regularly preceded by a sacred procession. The parade included the prominent youth of the city, the actors, dancers, and musicians, persons carrying incense and perfumes and precious objects from the temple treasuries, and finally the gods, represented by statues or other symbols borne on special wagons. The procession ended with a sacrifice preceding the plays. In the theater there was an altar or a group of altars at which the soothsayer officiated; special chairs were carried into the orchestra for the comfort of the god who was presumed to be present in spirit. On the chairs were cushions, and symbols of the gods. These pagan rites continued, it is thought, as long as the theaters existed, and were responsible in part for the closing of the theaters by the Christians.

From the second century A.D. onward, Roman games and plays spread throughout the Empire. The better class of drama persisted, but entertainment in general degenerated into sensational amusements for the common people. The Atellan farce was revived in cruder form; pantomime and ballet, in which women appeared, became popular; there were aquacades and mock naval battles; and finally bloody and brutal exhibitions were offered in the theaters and amphi-

Remains of the Roman theater at Lyons (Lugdunum), built about the first century A.D. It seated over ten thousand spectators. (Library and Museum of the Performing Arts, Lincoln Center)

theaters, during which slaves, prisoners of war, criminals, animals, and Christian martyrs had to fight for their lives or be defenselessly slaughtered.

In the sixth century A.D. the Emperor Justinian of Byzantium and his queen Theodora, who had been a strip-tease artist, embraced Christianity and ordered the closing of all places of public entertainment in their realm. This marked the end of public theater and drama until their revival in the medieval period.

The Theater

The Roman theater started very modestly with a portable stage of simple design, which could be used out of doors in a variety of locales. It was a low platform with a narrow wooden floor, backed by painted boards above which was a small gable or overhang suggesting a roof. A short flight of steps led up from the ground to the front of the stage. This practical scaffold arrangement was brought to Rome by the actors of the Atellan farces and could be set up in market places, temples, or on hillsides, where spectators could stand or sit. Later, as in Greece, wooden benches were provided for the audience.

This temporary wooden structure, much elaborated, became the model for the Plautine stage. The platform on which the comic actors performed was very long

A model of the Lyons theater, exhibited in Frankfurt-am-Main in 1937, showing the *scaenae frons* decorated with niches and pilasters, the doors to three houses, and, downstage, a trench for the curtain. The Roman theater building was an architectural unit. (Library and Museum of the Performing Arts, Lincoln Center)

and narrow (said to be as much as sixty yards) and usually represented a city street. All the action took place on the street; there were no indoor scenes. The extreme length of the stage made it possible for characters to indulge in asides and soliloquies, to hold conversations as though they could not be overheard, and to pretend not to see other characters on the stage. The background was painted to represent one, two, or three houses with practical doors opening onto the street. The doors were framed with columns, excellent for eavesdropping; and the houses frequently had an upper storey with windows. Actors made entrances and exits through the house doors, and also from the right and left wings. According to convention, if the character entered from the audience's right he was supposed to be coming from the forum or the country; if from the left, from the harbor.

A temporary wooden stage of this nature could be erected in the Circus Flaminius or the Circus Maximus on the days scheduled for scenic plays and removed on those days set aside for the circus games. In those great amphitheaters the seats for the audience were permanent; but when the stage was erected in the forum or other open place, temporary bleachers had to be put up.

In 179 B.C. an attempt was made to construct a permanent theater of stone but it did not reach completion. Twenty-five years later, in 154 B.C., another effort was made to build a stone theater but that plan fell through as well; the opponents in the senate at that time issued a decree that as seats were harmful to public morals, they should not be provided in any theaters!

Pompey built the first permanent stone theater in 55 B.C. A second magnificent house was erected by Lucius Cornelius Balbus in the Campus Martius in 13 B.C.; and two years later, the Theater of Marcellus, larger and more elaborate than the others, which had been begun by Caesar, was completed by Augustus.

The structure of the permanent theaters demonstrated how superior Rome was to Greece in the art of organization and the practical aspects of architecture. The Greeks had never unified the three elements of their theater: the auditorium, the orchestron (dancing place), and the scene building. The Romans, however, managed to combine these elements to form an architectural whole. They built their theaters on level ground as well as on hillsides, and raised the structure to a height of two or three storeys. They eliminated the orchestron and joined the auditorium to the scene building. The stage itself was high and narrow, and the background was a permanent architectural façade fitted out with three doorways, innumerable pilasters and free-standing columns, niches, and statues, all highly ornamented, painted in bright colors, or gilded. A curtain was lowered into a slot in the stage floor at the beginning of the play, and raised when the play was over; at a later time, it was raised and lowered in the manner familiar to us. Backstage were the dressing rooms for the actors.

In spite of the fact that it held thousands of spectators, this was not a democratic but a class theater, separated into galleries and special sections for the various ranks of society. Boxes and seats in the front rows of the orchestra were set aside for senators, public officials, and distinguished citizens. The public did not even have to mingle when entering or leaving the theatre, as special doors and stairways led to the segregated tiers. The theater had a roof over the top row of seats but otherwise was open to the sky. During the Empire, colorful awnings were drawn across the opening on very hot days and the auditorium was sprayed with perfume.

Roman theater architecture, though ornate, was highly practical and exerted a strong influence on the design of theaters from the Renaissance to modern times.

The Actors

From the Etruscan word *ister*, for performer, Roman actors came to be called *histriones*, which has given us the adjective histrionic. The Roman actor had to learn to sing, to dance, to declaim, to mime, and to master the art of gesticulation. A wide variety of gestures, many of them obscene, accompanied the dialogue in place of facial expressions, which were hidden by masks. For the strenuous requirements of the rôles in farce and comedy, the actor often trained like an athlete. Some characters in important rôles like Phronesium, the young virgin in the *Pseudolus*, spoke no lines and were called "mutes."

The acting of tragedy, particularly in the early days of the Republic, required a more dignified and declamatory style, and more restrained gestures and movement, which came across as stiff, strained, and unnatural. There is some doubt as to whether Seneca's tragedies were ever produced in a public theater. Since many Senecan scenes are more narrative than dramatic, it is very likely that they were presented at court as play-readings for the entertainment of the Emperor Nero. Roman audiences, at any rate, were not partial to tragedy.

The fact that all the actors wore masks and spoke or declaimed their lines to the accompaniment of flute music makes it clear that Roman acting was not realistic as we understand the word. In order to make their voices carry to the farthest seats in the theater, the actors stood well to the front of the stage, facing and addressing the audience almost as frequently as they did the other players. These stylized techniques—particularly the rhythmical declamation of lines while the flute player stepped up now to one, now to another, to accompany each actor in turn—make it difficult for us to imagine what Roman acting was like.

The acting troupes, which were made up of freedmen, aliens, and slaves, consisted of five or six players, who, by doubling, were able to present a play with as many as fourteen characters. Each troupe tried to attract the most proficient actors, as there was keen competition among the different companies, and they vied for prizes sometimes by unfair means. They supported claques and were known to attempt to bribe the officials.

For just one period in Roman drama, in the third and second centuries B.C., the preeminence of the actor was challenged by the playwright. Plautus was not only popular but wealthy, and Terence, for his play *The Eunuch*, was paid the unprecedented sum of eight thousand sesterces. It is interesting to note the opinions of these writers concerning actors. Plautus said that bad acting could spoil a good play, while Terence believed that good acting might give a bad play undeserved success.

The Age of the Performer returned toward the end of the first century B.C., with the Empire. Such stars as Roscius, who played in both comedy and tragedy, and earned half a million sesterces annually by his acting, was a teacher of his art and wrote a book about it. His contemporary and close rival was Aesopus, an actor of tragedy, who left a fortune of twenty million sesterces.

In the final days of Imperial Rome, women were admitted to the stage. They appeared in mimes, short plays about common people; and in pantomimes, movement and gesture with musical accompaniment, on subjects of a licentious nature. Actors, male and female, vied with each other in demonstrations of sensuality.

Costumes and Masks

The Romans classified their drama according to the characteristic dress worn by the actors. The main categories were the Fabula Palliata (imitation Greek comedy in Greek costume), the Fabula Togata (comedy about Romans in everyday dress), and the Fabula Praetexta (Roman history or legend in patrician costume), as well as tragedy.

Along with the plots and characters of Greek New Comedy, the Roman playwrights adopted Greek costumes, as the name Fabula Palliata tells us. The pallium worn by men and the palla worn by women were the Greek himation, draped in various ways. This was a long outer garment under which was worn a short tunic. The chlamys was a cloak worn by young men in the military, by parasites and travelers, and by slaves when they were sent on errands. Women wore the long tunic, as did dignified old men. The footwear in comedy was a slipper or sock. The head was usually uncovered but a traveler would wear a flat, wide-brimmed hat called a petasos. Different classes were distinguished by their hand properties: a soldier by a sword, a cook by a spoon or pot, a slave dealer by a moneybag and straight staff. Wigs were worn and probably attached to the mask —white for old men, black for young men, and red for slaves. The masks, which all actors wore, covered the entire head and indicated the character of the wearer. Pollux listed forty-four different personality masks for comedy, but they can be divided into two broad classes—the grotesque, big-mouthed type for slaves, parasites, old men, and comic characters, and the natural masks for young men and women.

The Fabula Togata, played in ordinary Roman dress, usually dealt with the humble life of workers and poor people who lived in small private houses (*tabernae*) in country towns, and hence was sometimes called Fabula Tabernaria. In addition to the toga, the actor wore the Roman tunic, cloak, and sandals. The masks were similar to those worn in the Fabula Palliata—ugly caricatures for the comic characters and attractive features for the young people.

The Fabula Praetexta, named for the toga of the patricians which was ornamented with purple stripes, was a patriotic chronicle play that took as its subject old Roman history or legend. It resembled Roman tragedy in many respects, being melodramatic, bombastic, and flamboyant in its character portrayal. These exaggerations also appeared in the costumes and masks of both Fabula Pratexta and tragedy. The togas and mantles were rich, colorful, and ornately embroidered, and draped with great care. The entire figure was lengthened as the actor wore the cothurnus (a high boot with thick soles) and, above the mask, a tall hairdress, called an onkos. The soles of the cothurni, which in the classical Greek period had been flat, were built up more and more with thick blocks as time went on, the extra height supposedly suggesting the greater importance of the actor or the character. The bodies of the actors were padded so that they would not appear to be too thin; this resulted in their seeming to be inflated, like the rhetorical style of the play. Roman tragic masks had wide openings for the mouth and eyes, and luxuriantly curled and twisted locks of hair and beards for the men. The women's masks often showed expressions of pain or terror; the hair, simply arranged, was bound with a fillet.

In the plays and spectacles of the late Roman Empire, the costumes became scantier, and masks were not always worn. The actors in the mimes, little dialogued comedies, played in everyday Roman dress and wore no masks; while the pantomime artists, who were considered shameless, presented legendary tales and strip-tease acts in seductive movements and gestures to the accompaniment of music, wearing flimsy costumes and masks with closed lips. For the ballets, aquacades, and mock naval battles the performers wore no masks. The dancers, who represented Venus, Cupid, and the Graces, were slightly veiled; the swimmers appeared in brief bras and bikinis; and the young men and women who contended with each other in miniature ships performed in total nudity.

Although it is difficult for us to conceive of a performance in which all the actors are masked, the use of masks had distinct advantages. It allowed a small company of actors to represent a great number of characters; the minor parts could be as well performed as the leading rôles; the exaggerated features made it possible for the spectators even at a distance to recognize the characters; the appearance of the character could be made to correspond to the description provided by the playwright; men could play women's parts; and the identity of the actor could be concealed. The great Roscius, who squinted, was grateful for masks. In such plays of Plautus as *The Twin Menaechmi* and the *Amphitryon*, where there are identical twins and characters who appear in the guise of others, masks would be extremely useful.

Music and Dance

Very little is known about Roman music except that it was widely used, as was the dance, in all theatrical performances from the most primitive times to the end of the Empire.

In the plays of Plautus there is a much larger proportion of song and dance than seems to have been present in the Greek comedies he imitated. Modern conjecture about where and when music was used in his plays is based upon the meters of the verse. Plautus' lines display greater metrical variety than those of any other Roman writer. It is believed that the lines in iambic meter were spoken with no musical accompaniment, but the verses written in trochaics, anapests, and a host of other meters were either chanted or sung to the music of the flute. By this method of evaluation, there are more than sixty songs in the plays of Plautus, an average of about three a play. Add to these the numerous lines that are supposed to have been chanted, and the effect of the plays must have been something like that of musical comedy. The lyrics of the songs are unrhymed but they are closely related to character and to plot. In a serenade sung in the *Curculio* there are references to "foreign dancers" and their leaping and springing. Music for a dramatic performance was supplied by a player of the double-pipe; whether he was the composer of the music is not known. The names of two such musicians have come down to us: Marcipor, the slave of Oppius; and Flaccus, the slave of Claudius.

There are very few songs in the plays of Terence as he felt that they were not suitable for his style of "serious" comedy. Seneca and the other writers of tragedy, on the other hand, used the music of flute players in imitation of the practice of the Greeks.

In the pantomimes and the other entertainments of the late Empire, the dances became wild, frivolous, and lascivious; and noisy orchestras, made up of such instruments as flutes, lyres, trumpets, tambourines, cymbals, clappers, and rattles, provided the music.

Because of his dedication to comedy, music, and dance, Plautus is praised in an epitaph which states that the chief mourners at his grave are Laughter and Rhythm.

The Audience

In Rome all classes of society went to the theater, but as the composition of the population changed, as a result of the Roman conquests and the influx of foreign-speaking peoples, the character of the audience and their taste in entertainment changed accordingly.

Down to the end of the fourth century B.C., the spectators who enjoyed the Atellan farces and the simple mimes were for the most part hard-working free-men, unsophisticated, and semiliterate. In the third century B.C., following the military victories over the Greeks, the effect of Greek-Hellenistic culture was beginning to be felt in Italy. Highly cultivated and educated Romans were using Greek slaves as tutors and sending their sons to Greek cities and thus becoming familiar with the Greek language and literature. These aristocrats encouraged Roman writers to imitate the plays of the Greek comic and tragic playwrights, and became prominent members of the audience in the second century B.C., when the spectators in general were more literate and sophisticated. The middle class was growing in wealth and power and responded to the comedies of Plautus, Caecilius, and Terence, and the tragedies of Ennius, Pacuvius, and Accius.

Admission to the theater was free, so along with the dignified senators and magistrates, for whom special seats were provided, went the unruly populace—gossiping women, bawling infants, harlots, and slaves. Members of the claques led the applause, and quarrels often broke out during the performance. Ushers moved around among the spectators to keep order. In the prologues to several plays, the writer urges the audience to be quiet and to give his work a fair hearing. As many events of the festival were presented simultaneously, the members of the audience who grew bored with the play could get up and go out to watch a company of tight-rope walkers, a boxing match, or a gladiatorial combat. No food was sold inside the theater, but outside there were vendors of all sorts of refreshments that lured the hungry and thirsty. Still at this time it was possible to hold the attention of large audiences with plays of literary merit. A century later, in the last days of the Republic, revivals of the Roman "classics" played to dwindling numbers.

In the first century A.D., the enormous slave population that had been brought to Rome by force during the Punic Wars was winning its freedom and creating the new proletarian citizenry that had to be amused at festival seasons. These spectators found the tragedies and comedies tedious; they barely understood the language. They much preferred the farces, pantomimes, ballets, and aquacades, which were mostly non-verbal.

To enter the magnificent theaters built in Imperial Rome, the polyglot audience was given tickets—round or square tokens made of bone or ivory—with an engraved picture on one side, and the seat location on the other. In these beautiful theaters, and in the amphitheaters, the entertainment became more and more degenerate to please the taste of the audience. For a long time the Romans had been offering only lip-service to religion. Growing ever more materialistic, prosperous, and skeptical, they had given their hearts completely to conquest and commerce and, in theatrical performances, sought titillation and release in sexual exhibitions and bloody spectacles.

A MODERN MUSICAL VERSION

No presentation of the *Pseudolus* of Plautus in a literal translation can begin to suggest to a modern audience what it was that aroused the enthusiastic response of the Roman playgoer. But such a work as *A Funny Thing Happened on the Way to the Forum,* which is based on the *Pseudolus*—with interpolated material from half a dozen other Plautine plays, in a sort of super-*contaminatio*—has roused modern audiences to the pitch of a Roman holiday.

The idea for *A Funny Thing* originated with Burt Shevelove, an accomplished writer, director, and producer, who, while a student at the Yale Drama School, wrote and produced a musical called *When in Rome,* which was based on several of Plautus' plays. In 1958 Shevelove, who had worked in television with Larry Gelbart, another successful writer of comedy, collaborated with him on the book of *A Funny Thing.* Stephen Sondheim, composer-lyricist, became the third member of the team and created the music and lyrics for the show.

To turn the *Pseudolus* into a modern musical comedy, Shevelove and Gelbart used the basic outline of the original plot: a clever slave gets a young girl for his master by tricking a pimp; also retained was the Greek name Pseudolus for the crafty slave. The other characters from the original play were rechristened: Hero, the young lover; Senex, his old father; Erronius, the father's friend; Lycus, the pimp; Philia, the virgin; and an assortment of humorous appellations for the courtesans and slaves. To this group, Shevelove and Gelbart added the swaggering soldier from the *Miles Gloriosus;* the domineering mother and the male slave disguised as a bride from the *Casina;* the old man who avoids his "haunted" house from the *Mostellaria;* and the slave girl who turns out to be a freeborn virgin from any number of Plautus' plays. The idea of a slave who wins his freedom by his cleverness serves as the premise for *A Funny Thing* and derives from *The Twin Menaechmi.*

From these diverse materials, Shevelove and Gelbart wove a seamless, flawless fabric. The play is fast, funny, and faithful to the spirit of Plautine comedy, a mixture of farce, vaudeville, and burlesque, in which character counts for little, while plot, dialogue, rowdy action, song, and dance mean everything. Hilarious as the text is, it is imperative that the reader imagine the doubletakes, the pratfalls, the wild grimaces, the grotesque gestures, the shouting, whining, and wailing, and the furious cavorting of the actors that add to the excitement and humor of the play in performance.

For *A Funny Thing,* Stephen Sondheim created sassy, satirical lyrics that not only match the verve and humor of the dialogue but provide elements essential to the Plautine plot. Equivalent to the ancient prologue, which tells the audience what the play is about and how it will all come out, is the opening song, "Comedy Tonight." Hero's lament, "Love I Hear," perfectly expresses with a humorous twist the exaggerated complaint of the lovesick Plautine swain. Hysterium's hysterical rendition of "I'm Calm" represents Plautus the vaudevillian; and "Bring Me My Bride" has the characteristic arrogance and swagger of the braggart warrior. Regarding his music for the play, Sondheim feels that his score and the libretto do not "go together." In an interview with Max Wilk, he said, "The libretto is truly low comedy—literate and polished, but very low comedy. Very traditional. . . . But my score for the show was essentially intellectual—it doesn't mesh with the low vaudeville comedy." Despite his reservations, Sondheim's music for *A Funny Thing* is lively and serviceable.

Although Plautus set the actions of his plays in Athens and dressed his characters in the everyday garb of Greek citizens and slaves, Shevelove and Gelbart chose to use Rome as the locale for *A Funny Thing* with the populace wearing appropriate Roman dress. This conception was executed by the British scene and costume designer Tony Walton, who created for the modern proscenium stage a workable reproduction of the Roman platform stage, and costumes that seemed to be sly caricatures of the originals. On the stage are shown three houses, with alleys between them, facing a street that leads off in one direction to the harbor and in the opposite direction to the forum and the country. The houses have practical doors and windows and ample acting areas around and between them to allow for the furious action. The characters are dressed in simulated Roman fashion, the cut, color, and texture of the fabrics slightly laugh-provoking; the slaves are in short tunics with long-sleeved undergarments, the citizens in togas, the women in flowing mantles, the soldiers in the uniform of the Roman legionnaire, and the courtesans in variations played on bra and G-string. The performers wore no masks.

The troupe of comedians assembled to perform *A Funny Thing* did not need masks, for the grotesque expressions of such experienced farceurs as Zero Mostel, David Burns, Jack Gilford, Raymond Walburn, John Carradine, Phil Silvers, and Larry Blyden would have won applause in the Atellan farces. The secret of farcical acting lies in timing and technique, the perfect control of body and voice which enables the performer to produce surprising effects that startle and delight an audience. This is probably the most demanding style of acting, for the performer must have unlimited resources of energy and vitality and total control of movement, gesture, voice, and facial expression, for split-second reactions and, in musicals, to the precise beat of the music. Such precision creates the impression of mechanistic behavior and puppetry, but beneath it the actor must preserve a sense of reality and of truth to nature if he is to stir the audience's imagination to recognition and response, as did the comic clowns in *A Funny Thing Happened on the Way to the Forum.*

SEND IN THE CLOWNS*
By Craig Zadan

Back to work on *A Funny Thing Happened on the Way to the Forum* after his six-month break to do *Gypsy*, Sondheim found confusion rampant.

Leland Hayward, who was initially interested in producing it, dropped out and David Merrick picked up the option. By this time, Phil Silvers, for whom the musical was written, read the first act and said he didn't want to do it because it was "old shtick," not realizing that that was precisely the show's intention. Then Jerome Robbins withdrew from the project, mostly because Robbins and Merrick had gotten along so badly on *Gypsy*. Joshua Logan then agreed to direct but pulled out when the authors would not agree to rewrite the book to his taste.

Merrick drew up a new list of directors for the writing triumvirate to consider —all of whom they turned down. Finally, Sondheim and Flora Roberts [Sondheim's agent] met with Merrick.

"Steve was very frightened of him," Flora Roberts relates. "But we explained to Merrick that we wanted to put the show in a drawer and let it sit because we didn't know what to do with it. So we returned his $4,000 option payment and that was that . . . until five months later when Jerry [Robbins] came back and said, 'I can't forget that show. Why don't we ask Hal Prince to do it.' Meanwhile, Hal agreed to produce it, Jerry took a vacation in Paris, hadn't signed his contract, and upon returning, said that he'd changed his mind *again*."

David Merrick's telling of the story is somewhat different: "When they came to me asking for their show back, it seemed that they felt the only way they could get Jerry was if Hal Prince and Bobby Griffith produced it. And I released it to them on this promise: that if Jerry didn't do it, they'd bring it back to me. They said they would and it was all a gentleman's agreement. And lo and behold, Jerry wasn't doing it and George Abbott, whom I had wanted all along, was. Somewhere, I have a letter from Steve apologizing and saying that he owed me a big favor. So that's where we stand, although I don't expect the favor to ever be paid off."

"I had always wanted to do *Forum*," admits Prince. "I had the same conviction about it that I had with *West Side [Story]* but my partner Bobby Griffith wasn't crazy about it. Finally, he did agree to do it with me, but then he died. I had no shows running on Broadway for the first time since we started in '54, and here it was '61 and I had just had two failures and no partner. It was a very lonely time, but I decided to produce the show by myself. To give you an example of how unattractive it was to people, we gave it to the Theatre Guild, and not only did we *not* get the subscription, but they didn't even approve it for consideration. They thought it was confusing and unfunny. Somehow at the piano and on paper it was a show that, to put it mildly, was attractive to a minimal number of people."

"It was difficult to explain to people what the intention of the show was," Burt

---

* From *Sondheim & Co.* by Craig Zadan, Copyright © 1974 by Craig Zadan; reprinted with permission of Macmillan Publishing Co. Inc.

Shevelove says. "People are oriented by the shows they've seen before. They said, 'There's only room for one or two dances in it and you don't care anything about the kids.' And we said, 'You're not *supposed* to care anything about the kids.' Also, one set of costumes didn't strike them as a musical. Our reason for putting it on was an affectionate one. Low comedy and farce in America are rarely done and are rarely successful."

After Harold Prince released to the press that Milton Berle would be coming to Broadway as the star of his new musical comedy (in the role originally written for Silvers), Berle, afraid that many of his best lines might be cut during the numerous revisions of the libretto, insisted that script approval be included in his contract. Prince refused and Berle withdrew.

Zero Mostel, who had made a big name for himself in the artistically successful *Ulysses in Nighttown* and *Rhinoceros*, was next offered the role, and unimpressed, passed it up.

Mostel: "I read it and I didn't like it . . . so I turned it down. Then Hal Prince went to my wife and asked why I wouldn't do it and she came to me and said, 'I hear you turned down *Forum*.' And I said, 'Oh, yes, I forgot to tell you.' And she said, 'If you don't take it, I'm going to stab you. . . .' So I said, 'All right, but this is the last time I'm gonna do something for money for you! Next time I'm gonna do what *I* wanna do!'"

Shevelove: "We weren't completely satisfied with Zero. . . . I don't think any of us were. Anybody can be as difficult as he likes, commensurate with his talent."

Gelbart: "Zero is a giant. He's a giant talent . . . and a giant pain in the ass. But there are very few leading men—and leading men, in the conventional sense, are immediately snatched up for pictures. The theater keeps getting robbed of that kind of guy, but Zero has no major movie career so he can afford to return to the theater."

At long last, with George Abbott set to direct, with Mostel, Jack Gilford, and David Burns signed to head the cast, and with Harold Prince producing, the show began to piece together. "We spent a long time on the plot," Shevelove says. "Although it's really a series of interconnected incidents, one incident has to start before the incident before it can be solved. You have to work it out almost on graph paper so you know what's going on."

"*Forum* is not generally recognized as being experimental," Sondheim says, "but I find it very experimental. *Forum* is a direct antithesis of the Rodgers and Hammerstein school. The songs could be removed from the show and it wouldn't make any difference. . . ."

"Except one," Shevelove disagrees. "Without the songs, the show would become relentless. It would exhaust you and you wouldn't get any breathers, any savoring of certain moments. 'Everybody Ought to Have a Maid' is a chance to stop running in and out of doors and conniving. When Steve first started, he only wanted to write songs integrated into the show that would advance the plot and increase your knowledge of the characters. I tried to tell him that the songs don't have to do that. Plays have breathers, too, and in *Forum* the songs can be respites. Sometimes they can serve as background for the comedy, like the wailing during the funeral sequence. Although it has funny lines in it, it also has, during that song, a funny situation. Will that body remain there when they sing 'Bring on the fire!'? So the song enhances that. If it were done without music, it wouldn't have been as effective. You can enhance a play a lot of ways and one of the most delightful is with music.

"In writing the book, we selected the characters from Plautus's plays and created a plot. The only thing extremely un-Roman was making a big thing out of the slave wanting to be free. Although slaves in Roman comedies wanted to be free, it was a very casual thing. But to give it some vague relevance to our times, we made *Forum* about a slave who would do *anything* to be free. It gives an overall thing to all the connecting incidents because they are all basically dependent on the fact that he has to buy his freedom."

"I think," Sondheim says, "that the book is vastly underrated. It's brilliantly constructed. We worked on the show over a period of four years. It took Larry and Burt eleven complete and distinct separate drafts, and everybody thinks that it was whipped up over a weekend because it plays so easily. The plotting is intricate, the dialogue is never anachronistic, and there are only two or three jokes—the rest is comic situation. It's almost like a senior thesis on two thousand years of comedy with an intricate, Swiss watch-like farce plot. The style of the dialogue is very elegant . . . the phrasings and grace of that dialogue are better than most of the writing of the musical or nonmusical theater of the last twenty years. It's almost a foolproof piece—it can be done by any high school class or a group of vaudevillians and the play holds up."

Sondheim also notes that the writing of the score for the show was his own rebellion against all his years with Oscar Hammerstein, suddenly finding that there were ways to write shows outside the Rodgers and Hammerstein tradition. He found it most difficult since he had been trained to use songs solely for dramatic purposes, unlike other songwriters who received their training in revue or nightclub work in which a song must be its own entity without having to relate to anything around it.

"I felt then," Shevelove admits, "but less strongly about it now, that the score should have been brasher, more songs of the style of 'Everybody Ought to Have a Maid.' There was too much intellectuality in the show. But, again, it was his first time writing music and lyrics for a Broadway show and your tendency is to show all your skills. *Forum* should have tapped one part of Steve. He was trying desperately to show that he was not just a tunesmith. The songs should have been brassier—from the school of Irving Berlin, as some of them turned out to be."

Sondheim himself says today that a month before the show went into rehearsal, he played the score for playwright and friend James Goldman, who immediately pointed out the incongruities between book and score. But as one member of the production put it, it was the sophistication of the score that brought the show up to a higher level than that required for a farce musical.

Under George Abbott's direction, *A Funny Thing Happened on the Way to the Forum* went into rehearsal and opened in New Haven to disastrous reviews.

Gelbart: "The show didn't work because by the time we had opened, we had put it through a strainer and taken out a lot of complications in the plot, subplot, sub-subplot, as George Abbott suggested. But upon seeing it we realized we had done it a great deal of damage because a lot of fun was in the organized confusion. So we put it all back—and probably a little more.

Prince: "It was very unpleasant on the road. Steve felt unduly pressured. There was a lot of talk about how the book and score didn't mix. The one thing that I quarreled with was the casting of the ingenue and juvenile. Both of them, Karen Black and Pat Fox, *were* replaced, but *not* by people I would have cast. Somewhere earlier I had brought in a girl and boy, namely Barbara Harris and Joel Grey, and I was laughed out of that audition. The point that I was trying to make was that the two young people should have been terribly comic. I still think I was right and if I was doing the show today, that's the way I'd do it. They would probably still fight me, but I'd win. Let's put it this way, in those days they were happy with me just as a producer. And I think I was a good one. The trouble we went through was appalling when we got to Washington."

Richard Coe in *The Washington Post* greeted the show with great reservation: "It's not a bad idea to have an intimate musical from an old Roman farce, but a good deal more steam will be needed to reassure you that you haven't wandered into amateur night."

"We played one matinee to fifty people," Prince says. "The main review said to close the show, and I think my biggest contribution to the show was that I was very sure about it. When the whole world's falling apart, you should have *somebody* who's sure. I never doubted for one minute that the show would be a smash in New York. The problems all were with the authors—they weren't getting along very well at that point. Steve needed somebody else to tell him what to do. Namely, Jerry Robbins."

The very same Mr. Robbins who intended to direct the show from its conception was called down to Washington as play doctor. And the problem proved to be basic.

"We had a perfectly charming opening," Sondheim says. "It was a vaudeville-style number called 'Love Is in the Air,' and about a month before rehearsals I had wanted to change it because Burt, Larry, and I began to realize that it was the wrong number. So I wrote another song called 'Invocation,' which really told the audience what the show was all about. But George Abbott wouldn't have it because he wanted something he could hum, and he didn't think the new song was hummable, and he said that you *have* to start a show with a hummable song. This hummable song cost us $100,000 out of town—that's how much we lost. The first thing Jerry did when he came in was to tell us to change the opening number, to tell the audience what the evening is about because the show is perfectly terrific but they don't know what it's about until it's too late. . . . They don't know that it's low comedy, they think it's going to be a rather charming, delicate evening and certainly won't be ready to laugh at Davey Burns. Well, the minute Abbott heard that, he suddenly agreed. I played Jerry 'Invocation' and he old me that was what the tone of the song should be but that I should write another number, one that Abbott would like. So one weekend in Washington I wrote 'Comedy Tonight.' Jerry staged it over the next week (along with restaging several other musical numbers in the show and reblocking the end chase scene). 'Comedy Tonight' played the first preview in New York and it not only brought down the house, but the entire show was clearly a hit . . . and it was all a matter of the opening number . . . and all a matter of George Abbott not being able to hum."

Forum's triumphant Broadway opening on May 8, 1962, did not register immediately at the box office, and the Prince office was worried for the first eight weeks of its run, until it began to sell out. Another boost came when *Forum* won a slew of Tony Awards, including Best Musical. Stephen Sondheim, however, was not even *nominated* for either his music or his lyrics.

Sondheim: "The reviews were generally excellent, but they did tend to describe it as a 'romp.' You'd think that Walter Kerr, who taught drama, would have understood it. He had a good time but he didn't really understand what was going on. As far as Zero was concerned, he was wonderful on the road, but the minute he got to New York and became a star from the reviews, he would begin doing things like announcing the results of the heavyweight fight from the stage . . . wish everyone a happy Halloween . . . imitate the other actors. He did that in *Fiddler*, too, which was even less seemly. At least *Forum* seemed to be this loose farce so that, as obnoxious as the ad-libbing was, the audience could take it, but when you do it on a piece like *Fiddler*, it really wrecks it."

Mostel: "There's a kind of silliness in the theater about what one contributes to a show. The producer obviously contributes the money; the bookwriter, the book; the composer, the music; the lyricist, the lyrics; but the actor contributes nothing at all? The theory that it's strong material . . . I'm not a modest fellow about those things. I contribute a great deal. And they always manage to hang you for having an interpretation. Why must it be dull as shit? I don't think theater should be like that. Isn't that where your imagination should flower? But the producer, the director, the authors, all go on their vacations and they come back well tanned and I'm pale from playing the show, and they say, 'It's altered a great deal since opening night.' But I'm not the actor who can do it in a monotone all the time. Suppose you have a bellyache, can't you use it when you're on the stage? Don't you use what you have? Guys who call it shtick give me a pain in the ass. If you have the premise that a guy wants to be free, no matter what crazy things you do on the stage, as long as you feel that it's keeping with that premise, it should be accepted by the audience."

Eleven years later, Mostel opened for a limited engagement, re-creating his role of Pseudolus for the Guber and Gross music fairs, and his stage antics seemed only to have heightened.

"He told some Watergate jokes," Shevelove says angrily. "In the original, at least, Zero stuck to the lines. He did outrageous things, but at least he interpreted the script and played it. You see, the play was written broadly enough to leave the clowning to the actors so they don't feel tied in. It's written in cartoon, two-dimensional style; then the players bring humanity to it, some sort of warmth, some sort of emotion. But I do like the actors to stick to the lines as they are written. When I saw the show in the 'round' recently with Zero, I was horrified. There's a line, and it may be my favorite line in the show. It's when he's looking for a body and says, 'I know Gusto, the body snatcher. He owes me a favor.' I just think it's comic that a body snatcher would owe you a favor. Zero changed it and said, 'I know Gusto, the body snatcher. He owes me a snatch.' Now that's dirty. That's a little child sitting at the table saying cocky, cocky, doodie, doodie, and that's not funny. Most of the laughs that you get when you're doing low comedy are things like, 'She's back!' It's not a funny line, but in its context it's funny. There was a line where he says, 'You go and hide behind that clump of myrrh,' and the girl says, 'Will you call me when the captain comes?' and he says, 'Don't we always?' Because she's been called about eleven times. That other night, she said, 'Will you call me when the captain comes?' and Zero said, 'I'll knock on your clump three times.' *That's* perversity."

The motion picture version of *Forum* was a terrible failure both financially and artistically. Directed by Richard Lester (who directed the Beatles in *A Hard Day's Night*, and the recent version of *The Three Musketeers*), the film was produced for United Artists Pictures.

"In casting Phil Silvers in the role of Lycus," Gelbart says, "they felt they needed to build up the part for him so that it would be as big as Zero's. So they began to invent new story points and lots of twists. *Forum* is a very finely put together Chinese puzzle, and if you change one piece you have to account for about fifty more pieces behind it. They cut a lot of the musical numbers and they lost any continuity of style.

"The next problem was that they asked Zero who he would like to direct it and he gave the producer a list of five: Charles Chaplin, Orson Welles, Mike Nichols, Richard Lester, or Seth Holt. He got Richard Lester, who makes films in which the camera never stops. *Forum* is essentially a very literary piece of work and there arose a great contrast in approach of styles, which developed into an enormous power struggle between Lester and Mel Frank, who was coauthor of the screenplay and producer of the film, to the point where Frank was literally not allowed on the set lest he incur Lester's displeasure. Well, it's pretty hard to be funny with all that unfunny stuff happening behind and around the camera. I think the work shows it. Any film in which Buster Keaton is an embarrassment says a lot for how unfunny it is."

Even Mostel became disenchanted with his choice of Lester as director. "The stupid damned thing of Hollywood is to open up a film!" Mostel bellows. "The great thing about the piece on the stage was that it was one set, sixteen characters, three houses, and you did it very simply. You go to the movie and there's horses, zebras, peacocks . . . , your father's moustache, orphans, winos, donkeys. . . . "

"I went to the opening of the film in London," Gelbart winces. "It was like being hit by a truck that backed up and ran over you again. It was one of the most painful evenings of my life."

In 1972, following a highly successful revival of *Forum*, directed by Burt Shevelove at the Ahmanson Theatre in Los Angeles, starring Phil Silvers, Larry Blyden, and Nancy Walker, Blyden decided to acquire the sets and costumes and bring the production to New York.

"Steve wrote a new song for Nancy called 'Farewell' for the West Coast revival," says Blyden, "and we kept it in, although Nancy didn't come to New York with the rest of us. She lives in California, and her family is out there and hers was the smallest part in the show. But she *was* marvelous."

Also added to the score was "Echo Song," a number that was deleted in New Haven from the original Broadway production. And on the way to New York this time around, "Pretty Little Picture" was dropped when Phil Silvers couldn't perform it.

The show was most welcome in revival (this time with Silvers playing the role that was written for him) and received even better reviews than when it opened originally.

Clive Barnes in *The New York Times* led the jubilation: "Everyone ought to have a favorite Broadway musical. Personally, my favorite for ten years has been *A Funny Thing Happened on the Way to the Forum*. Last night *A Funny Thing* happened once again, and I fell in love with it as desperately as ever. This is the funniest, bawdiest and most enchanting Broadway musical that Plautus, with a little help from Stephen Sondheim, Burt Shevelove and Larry Gelbart, ever wrote. . . . Mr. Sondheim's music is original and charming, with considerable musical subtlety but a regard for down-to-earth show-biz vigor that is precisely what is needed. And, as always, his lyrics are a joy to listen for. The American theater has not had a lyricist like this since [Lorenz] Hart or [Cole] Porter."

"People said a decade ago that the score of *Forum* was tuneless," remarks Shevelove, "and it came out in the light of today as very melodic. Some of the same critics reversed what they said. Now the music makes more sense. Steve is a child of his times, and in expressing himself, he is not being derivative, as most composers are. You see, the critics and audiences were startled originally that a play following Rodgers and Hammerstein and all their descendants could be written so abstractly as *Forum*. But when they came to see it again, they didn't mind the abstraction because they knew what to expect. Audiences go to the theater preconditioned. They didn't laugh at the lyrics originally, mainly because of the music. Most of the time when you write a comic song you put it to a very simple melody so that the lyrics shine out. Well, Steve's music is a little tricky. Today, we hear the music more easily because our ears have changed and the lyrics seem much funnier when the music is easier to comprehend."

Though the revival of *Forum* won two Tony Awards—Best Actor in a Musical (Phil Silvers) and Best Supporting Actor in a Musical (Larry Blyden), business did not stay on an even keel. But just as it appeared to be holding its own, Phil Silvers suffered a stroke, and the show immediately closed after only 156 performances and a loss of its entire $280,000 investment.

A year and a half later, however, with Phil Silvers back in good health, a production of *Forum* starring Silvers toured the British provinces with a stopover in London scheduled upon the availability of a West End theater. (In England, *Bilko* was being rerun and Silvers was very popular.)

"We were very pleased to have *Forum* back," Shevelove says. "We wanted to do it again to give the younger generation, who weren't old enough to see it the first time, a chance to go today."

A Funny Thing Happened
on the Way to the Forum

A musical comedy based on the Pseudolus and other plays of Titus Maccius Plautus. Book by Burt Shevelove and Larry Gelbart, with music and lyrics by Stephen Sondheim. First presented by Harold Prince at the Alvin Theatre, New York, on May 8, 1962.

CAST OF CHARACTERS

PROLOGUS (an actor)	*Zero Mostel*
THE PROTEANS	*Eddie Phillips, George Reeder, David Evans*
SENEX (an old man)	*David Burns*
DOMINA (his wife)	*Ruth Kobart*
HERO (his son)	*Brian Davies*
HYSTERIUM (slave to Senex and Domina)	*Jack Gilford*
LYCUS (a buyer and seller of courtesans)	*John Carradine*
PSEUDOLUS (slave to Hero)	*Zero Mostel*
TINTINABULA (a courtesan)	*Roberta Keith*
PANACEA (a courtesan)	*Lucienne Bridou*
THE GEMINAE (courtesans)	*Lisa James, Judy Alexander*
VIBRATA (a courtesan)	*Myrna White*
GYMNASIA (a courtesan)	*Gloria Kristy*
PHILIA (a virgin)	*Preshy Marker*
ERRONIUS (an old man)	*Raymond Walburn*
MILES GLORIOSUS (a warrior)	*Ronald Holgate*

The time is two hundred years before the Christian era, a day in spring.
The place is a street in Rome in front of the houses of Erronius, Senex, and Lycus.
The action is continuous, with a single intermission.

AUTHORS' NOTE: *This is a scenario for vaudevillians. There are many details omitted from the script. They are part of any comedian's bag of tricks. The double take, the mad walk, the sighs, the smirks, the stammerings. All these and more are intended to be supplied by the actor and, hopefully, the reader.*

ACT I

(PROLOGUS *enters through curtain and salutes the audience.*)

Prologus. Playgoers, I bid you welcome. The theatre is a temple, and we are here to worship the gods of comedy and tragedy. Tonight I am pleased to announce a comedy. We shall employ every device we know in our desire to divert you.

(*During this scene,* PROLOGUS *and the three* PROTEANS *do various bits of pantomine and general clowning.*)

Prologus. (*Gestures to the orchestra, sings:*)

Something familiar,
Something peculiar,
Something for everyone—a comedy tonight!
Something appealing,
Something appalling,
Something for everyone—a comedy tonight!
Nothing with kings,
Nothing with crowns,
Bring on the lovers, liars, and clowns.
Old situations,
New complications,
Nothing portentous or polite;
Tragedy tomorrow,
Comedy tonight!
Something familiar,
Something peculiar,
Something for everyone—a comedy tonight!
Something appealing,
Something appalling,
Something for everyone—a comedy tonight!
Proteans. Tragedy tomorrow—

Prologus. Comedy tonight!
Something convulsive,
Something repulsive,
Something for everyone—
All. A comedy tonight!
Prologus. Something esthetic,
Proteans. Something frenetic,
Prologus. Something for everyone—
All. A comedy tonight!
Proteans. Nothing with gods,
Nothing with fate.
Prologus. Weighty affairs will just have to wait.
Proteans. Nothing that's formal,
Prologus. Nothing that's normal,
All. No recitations to recite!
Open up the curtain—
Comedy tonight!

(*The curtains part to reveal a street in Rome, with three houses set well back. On the Right is the house of* ERRONIUS; *in the Center, the house of* SENEX, *with a curtain in front of it, hiding it from the audience; on the Left, is the house of* LYCUS.)

Prologus. (*Speaks.*) It all takes place on a street in Rome, around and about these three houses. First, the house of Erronius, a befuddled old man abroad now in search of his children, stolen in infancy by pirates. (*Sings:*)
Something for everyone—a comedy tonight!

(*The* PROTEANS *appear in the upper window of* ERRONIUS' *house and pantomine.*)

Something erratic,
Something dramatic,
Something for everyone—a comedy tonight!

Frenzy and frolic,
Strictly symbolic,
Something for everyone—a comedy
  tonight!

(*Speaks, indicating* LYCUS' *house.*)
Second, the house of Lycus, a buyer
and seller of the flesh of beautiful
women. That's for those of you who
have absolutely no interest in pirates.
(*Sings:*)
Something for everyone—a comedy
  tonight!

(*Speaks.*) Raise the curtain! (*The
curtain in front of* SENEX's *house
drops into the floor.*) And finally, the
house of SENEX, who lives here with
his wife and son. Also in this house
lives Pseudolus, slave to the son.
Pseudolus is probably my favorite
character in the piece. A role of enormous variety and nuance, and played
by an actor of such . . . let me put it
this way . . . I play the part. (*Sings:*)
Anything you ask for—comedy tonight!

(*The* PROTEANS *enter and approach*
PROLOGUS.)

And these are the Proteans, only three,
yet they do the work of thirty. They
are difficult to recognize in the many
parts they play. Watch them closely.
(PROTEANS *appear in and out of*
SENEX's *house in assorted costumes.*)
A proud Roman. A patrician Roman.
A pretty Roman. A Roman slave. A
Roman soldier.

(PROTEAN *appears with crude wooden
ladder.*)

A Roman ladder.

(PROTEAN *enters, juggling.*)

Tremendous skill.

(*He juggles badly.* PROTEAN *enters.*)

Incredible versatility!

(*He fumbles in changing wigs.* PRO-
TEAN *enters with gong.*)

And, above all, dignity!

(*He strikes gong, his skirt falls.*)

And now, the entire company!

(*The* COMPANY *enters from* SENEX's
house and forms a line downstage.)

All. (Sing:) Something familiar,
  Something peculiar,
  Something for everybody—comedy
    tonight!
Stage Right. Something that's gaudy,
Stage Left. Something that's bawdy,
Prologus. Something for everybawdy—
All. Comedy tonight!
Miles Gloriosus. Nothing that's grim,
Domina. Nothing that's Greek,
Prologus. (*Indicating* GYMNASIA.) She
  plays Medea later this week.
Stage Right. Stunning surprises,
Stage Left. Cunning disguises,
All. Hundreds of actors out of sight!
Erronius. Pantaloons and tunics,
Senex. Courtesans and eunuchs,
Domina. Funerals and chases,
Lycus. Baritones and basses,
Philia. Panderers,
Hero. Philanderers,
Hysterium. Cupidity,
Miles. Timidity,
Lycus. Mistakes,
Erronius. Fakes,
Philia. Rhymes,
Domina. Mimes,
Prologus. Tumblers, grumblers, fum-
  blers, bumblers,
All. No royal curse,
  No Trojan horse,
  And a happy ending, of course!
  Goodness and badness,
  Man in his madness,

This time it all turns out all right!
Tragedy tomorrow!
Comedy tonight!

(*All exit, except* PROLOGUS. *He addresses the heavens.*)

Prologus. Oh, Thespis, we place ourselves in your hands. (*To audience.*) The play begins. (*Exits.*)

(PHILIA *appears at the window of* LYCUS' *house;* HERO *appears on the balcony of* SENEX's *house.* SENEX *enters from his house and calls.*)

Senex. Slaves! (PROTEANS *enter from* SENEX's *house, dressed as slaves; they cringe.*) We are about to start our journey. My robe. (PROTEANS *place his robe on him.*) My wreath. (PROTEANS *place wreath on his head.*)

Domina. (*Appearing in doorway of* SENEX's *house.*) Senex!

Senex. (*Frowns.*) My wife.

Domina. Slaves! Stop cringing and fetch the baggage!

Proteans. (*Exiting into* SENEX's *house.*) Yes, yes, yes.

Domina. Senex, you are master of the house and no help at all. Where is Pseudolus? Where is Hysterium? Summon them! (SENEX *is about to speak,* DOMINA *calls out.*) Pseudolus! Hysterium!

(HYSTERIUM *enters from* SENEX's *house. During the following,* SENEX *drifts toward* LYCUS' *house.*)

Hysterium. Ah, Madam, you called?

Domina. Yes, Hysterium.

Hysterium. And I answered. Ever your humble. (*Kisses the hem of her cape.*)

Domina. Have you prepared my potions?

Hysterium. (*Holds up small bag.*) Yes,

madam. In addition to your usual potions, I have included one for tantrums and one for queasiness.

Domina. Thank you, Hysterium, slave of slaves.

Hysterium. I live to grovel. (*Kisses her hem.* DOMINA *calls to* HERO *on balcony of* SENEX's *house.*)

Domina. Hero, come kiss your mother goodbye.

Hero. Yes, mother, (*Exits into* SENEX's *house.* SLAVES *come out of* SENEX's *house, carrying baggage.*)

Domina. Slaves, take that baggage and go before us, you clumsies!

Proteans. (*As they scurry off.*) Yes, yes, clumsies, yes.

Domina. Senex! Come away from that house of shame!

Senex. (*Approaching her.*) I was just standing there saying, "Shame, shame, shame!"

Domina. Hysterium!

Hysterium. Yes, madam?

Domina. Where is Pseudolus?

Hysterium. Where is he indeed! I have not seen him since he dressed Hero this morning.

Domina. Tell him that while we are gone, he is to watch over Hero. He is to keep him cheerful, well-fed, and far from the opposite sex.

Senex. My dear, the boy has to learn sometime.

Domina. And when that time comes, *you* shall tell him . . .

Senex. Yes, dear.

Domina. . . . what little you know. Now, go and fetch the gift we bring my mother.

Senex. Yes, dear. (*Exits into his house, as* HERO *enters from it.*)

Hero. Good morning, father.

Domina. Ah, Hero. Your father and I are off to visit my mother in the country. What a joy it would be were you to accompany us. But, alas, the sight of anyone in good health fills my mother with rage. (SENEX re-enters carrying a bust of DOMINA.) Ah, there I am. Do you think it will please my mother?

Hysterium. Oh, yes, madam, The crafts-manship is superb.

Domina. And the resemblance?

Hysterium. Frightening..

Domina. The time of farewell is at hand. Hysterium, Slave-in-Chief, here are my husband's final instructions. (SENEX *opens his mouth to speak; she continues.*) In his absence, his entire household is in your spotless care. Your word shall be absolute, your authority unquestioned.

Senex. And furthermore—

Domina. We are on our way!

Senex. (*Mutters.*) We are on our way.

Domina. Farewell, beloved son. Fare-well, thoughtful Hysterium. Senex, come along! And carry my bust with pride. (*Exits. A pause, and then her voice is heard.*) Senex!

Senex. Yes, dear. (*To audience.*) A les-son for you all. Never fall in love during a total eclipse! (*Exits.*)

Hysterium. (*To audience.*) Well, to work, to work! Now that I am com-pletely in charge, I'm going to be a very busy slave. (*Sees* HERO, *who has drifted toward* LYCUS' *house, pulls him away.*) Here! Come away from there. You must never know what goes on in that house.

Hero. But I do know.

Hysterium. You do? (HERO *nods.*) Isn't it amazing? Well, I can't stand here talking. (*Goes to* SENEX's *house, picks something from a column, stamps on it, grimaces, enters house, calling*) Pseudolus!

(HERO *watches him go, then turns to the audience.*)

Hero. (*Sings:*) Now that we're alone,
May I tell you
I've been feeling very strange?
Either something's in the air
Or else a change
Is happening in me.
I think I know the cause,
I hope I know the cause.
From everything I've heard,
There's only one cause it can be . . .

Love, I hear,
Makes you sigh a lot.
Also, love, I hear,
Leaves you weak.

Love, I hear,
Makes you blush
And turns you ashen.
You try to speak with passion.
And squeak . . .
I hear.
Love, they say.
Makes you pine away,
But you pine away
With an idiotic grin.
I pine, I blush,
I squeak, I squawk.
Today I woke
Too weak to walk.
What's love, I hear,
I feel . . . I fear . . .
I'm in.

(*Sighs*)

See what I mean?
Da-da-da-da-da-da-da . . .
(I hum a lot, too.)
I'm dazed, I'm pale,
I'm sick, I'm sore;
I've never felt so well before!
What's love, I hear,
I feel . . . I fear . . .
I know I am . . .

I'm sure . . . I mean . . .
I think . . . I trust . . .
I pray . . . I must
Be in!
Forgive me if I shout . . .
Forgive me if I crow . . .
I've only just found out
And, well . . .
I thought you ought to know.

(PROTEANS *enter dressed as* CITIZENS, *holding* PSEUDOLUS *by the arms. They utter obviously fake chatter.*)

Hero. Pseudolus!

First Citizen. (*Salutes.*) Citizen! This is your slave? He was parading as a citizen.

Pseudolus. Believe me, master, I was not parading. This is parading. (*Demonstrates.*) I was walking. (*He starts to walk off.* CITIZEN *stops him.*)

Second Citizen. Come back here!

Third Citizen. (*To* HERO.) He invited us to game with him, and, in a matter of moments, he had taken all our money.

First Citizen. He was using weighted dice!

Hero. (*To* PSEUDOLUS.) Return the money.

Second Citizen. He took nine minae.

Pseudolus. Nine?! I took seven!

Hero. Give them nine.

Pseudolus. (*Handing coins to* CITIZEN.) One, two, three, four. I am being cheated out of the money I won fairly.

Hero. Pseudolus!

Pseudolus. (*Giving* CITIZENS *coins.*) Seven, eight.

First Citizen. What happened to five and six?

Pseudolus. I'm coming to them. Nine, five, six! (*Hands them three more coins.*)

Second Citizen. Come, fellow citizens! (CITIZENS *exit, chattering.*)

Pseudolus. (*Sheepishly.*) I should be whipped . . . gently. But I only did it for money. I thought if I could raise enough you'd let me buy my freedom from you.

Hero. Oh, Pseudolus, not again!

Pseudolus. It's all I think about. I hate being a slave.

Hero. Better a slave than a slave to love.

Pseudolus. That's easy for you to . . . Love? You? Tell me, master, who is she? Anyone I know?

Hero. Sometimes you can see her through that window. (*Points to* LYCUS' *house.*)

Pseudolus. Through that win— (*Horrified.*) A courtesan in the house of Lycus? Your parents would be outraged if they could hear you.

Hero. I don't care!

Pseudolus. Do you know how many minae a girl like that would cost?

Hero. And worth every drachma! Oh, Pseudolus, I would give anything for her.

Pseudolus. You would? You really love this girl? (HERO *sighs.*) I like the way you said that. Now, you cannot afford to buy this girl, but in spite of that, suppose someone, someone with tremendous cunning and guile, could arrange for her to be yours.

Hero. Yes?

Pseudolus. If that someone could arrange it, what would you give me?

Hero. Everything!

Pseudolus. Everything? What do you own? Twenty minae, a collection of sea shells and me.

Hero. Right.

Pseudolus. You don't have to give me the twenty minae, or the sea shells.

If I get you that girl, just give me me.
Hero. Give you you?
Pseudolus. My freedom.
Hero. Pseudolus! People do not go about freeing slaves.
Pseudolus. Be the first! Start a fashion!
Hero. (*A pause, then:*) Get me that girl!
Pseudolus. And if I can?
Hero. You are free!
Pseudolus. I am what?
Hero. Free!
Pseudolus. (*Sings:*) Free!
Hero. Free!
Pseudolus. (*Sings:*)
Oh, what a word!
Oh, what a word!
(*Speaks:*) Say it again!
Hero. Free!
Pseudolus. (*Sings:*) I've often thought, I've often dreamed
How it would be . . .
And yet I never thought I'd be . . .
(*Speaks:*) Once more.
Hero. Free!
Pseudolus. (*Sings:*) But when you come to think of such things . . .
A man should have the rights that all others . . .
Can you imagine
What it will be like when I am . . .
Can you see me?
Can you see me as a Roman with my head unbowed?
Sing it good and loud . . .
Hero. Free!
Pseudolus. Like a Roman, having rights
And like a Roman, proud!
Can you see me?
Hero. I can see you!
Pseudolus. Can you see me as a voter fighting graft and vice?
Sing it soft and nice . . .
Hero. Free.

Pseudolus. Why, I'll be so conscientious that I may vote twice!
Can you see me?
Can you see me?
When I'm free to be whatever I want to be,
Think what wonders I'll accomplish then!
When the master that I serve is me and just me.

Can you see me being equal with my countrymen?
Can you see me being Pseudolus the Citizen?
Can you see me being—? Give it to me once again!
Hero. Free!
Pseudolus. That's it!
Hero. Free!
Pseudolus. Yes!
Hero. Fr . . .
Pseudolus. (*Claps his hand over* HERO's *mouth.*)
Now, not so fast!
I didn't think . . .
The way I am,
I have a roof,
Three meals a day,
And I don't have to pay a thing.
I'm just a slave and everything's free.
If I were free,
Then nothing would be free,
And if I'm beaten now and then,
What does it matter?
Hero. (*Softly, seductively.*) Free.
Pseudolus. (*Brightening.*)
Can you see me?
Can you see me as a poet writing poetry?
All my verse will be—
Hero. Free!
Pseudolus. A museum will have me pickled for posterity!

Can you see me?

Hero. (*With a grimace.*) I can see you!

Pseudolus. Can you see me as a lover, one of great renown,
Women falling down?

Hero. Free?

Pseudolus. (*Speaks:*) No. (*Then sings:*)
But I'll buy the house of Lycus for my house in town.
Can you see me?
Can't you see me?
Be you anything from king to baker of cakes,
You're a vegetable unless you're free!
It's a little word but, oh, the difference it makes:
It's the necessary essence of democracy,
It's the thing that every slave should have the right to be,
And I soon will have the right to buy a slave for me!
Can you see him?
Well, I'll free him!

When a Pseudolus can move, the universe shakes,
But I'll never move until I'm free!
Such a little word but, oh, the difference it makes:
I'll be Pseudolus the founder of a family,
I'll be Pseudolus the pillar of society,
I'll be Pseudolus the man, if I can only be . . .

Hero. Free!

Pseudolus. Sing it!

Hero. Free!

Pseudolus. Spell it!

Hero. F-r-double—

Pseudolus. No, the long way . . .

Hero. F-R-E-E . . .

Both. FREE!!!

(*Lycus enters from his house.*)

Lycus. What a day! What a day! (*Calls into his house.*) Come out here! PROTEAN, *dressed as* EUNUCH, *enters from house, holding fan.*) What do you think you are doing, Eunuch? I have told you a thousand times not to fan the girls while they're still wet! You'll never learn. You'll be a eunuch all your life! (EUNUCH *exits into house.* LYCUS *turns to audience.*) What a day! I have to go to the Senate this morning. I'm blackmailing one of the Senators. (*Starts off, as* PSEUDOLUS *whispers to* HERO.)

Pseudolus. Quick! Your money bag! (HERO *hands him his money bag.*) Good morning, Lycus. (*Jingles money bag behind* LYCUS' *back.* LYCUS *stops.*)

Lycus. I know that sound, and I love it. (*Turns to* PSEUDOLUS.) Is that money?

Pseudolus. What do you think?

Lycus. How did you come to all this?

Pseudolus. An unexpected legacy. My uncle Simo, the noted Carthaginian elephant breeder, came to an untimely end. He was crushed to death on the last day of the mating season. This morning I bought my freedom.

Lycus. Congratulations!

Pseudolus. With this much left over for one gross indulgence.

Lycus. Good.

Pseudolus. Lycus, I am now in the market for a lifetime companion. Tell me, have you anything lying about in there, anything to satisfy an Olympian appetite?

Lycus. Pseudolus, friend and *citizen*, I have traveled the world in search of beauty, and I can say with modesty that I have the finest assortment in Rome.

Pseudolus. Show me.

(LYCUS *claps his hands.*)

Lycus. Eunuchs! A buyer!

(EUNUCHS *enter from* LYCUS' *house, place stool for* PSEUDOLUS *to sit on.* LYCUS *sings:*)

There is merchandise for every need
At the house of Marcus Lycus.
All the merchandise is guaranteed
At the house of Marcus Lycus.
For a sense of sensuality,
Or an opulence thereof,
Patronize the house of Marcus Lycus,
Merchant of love.

(*Speaks:*) For your most assured approval and your more than possible purchase, here are the fruits of my search. Behold . . . Tintinabula. (TINTINABULA *enters from house, poses.*) Out of the East, with the face of an idol . . . the arms of a willow tree . . . and the pelvis of a camel.

(*She dances.* PSEUDOLUS *looks at* HERO, *who shakes his head "no."*)

Pseudolus. (*To* LYCUS.) Don't you have anyone in there a bit less . . . noisy?

Lycus. I have. May I present Panacea. (PANACEA *enters, poses.*) To make her available to you, I outbid the King of Nubia. Panacea, with a face that holds a thousand promises, and a body that stands behind each promise.

(PANACEA *dances.* HERO *shakes his head "no."* PSEUDOLUS *looks* PANACEA *over, yawns.*)

You are disturbed?

Pseudolus. The proportions. Don't misunderstand me. (*Spreading his hands before her bosom.*) I love the breadth. It's the length. She may be the right length, but is it right for me? (*He stands with her back-to-back.*) Isn't she a bit too short?

Lycus. Definitely not.

Pseudolus. (*Wiggles, then:*) Too tall?

Lycus. No. Like that you look perfect together.

Pseudolus. Yes, but how often will we find ourselves in this position? (*Turns to face her.*) Perhaps if we . . .

Lycus. No need to compromise. Consider the Geminae. (GEMINAE *enter, pose.*) A matched pair. (*They dance.*) Either one a divinely assembled woman, together an infinite number of mathematical possibilities. They are flawless. (HERO *shakes his head "no."*)

Pseudolus. I quite agree. But I am a man of limited means and I don't suppose you'd break up a set.

Lycus. I couldn't. You understand.

Pseudolus. Completely.

Lycus. Fortunately, we still have . . . Vibrata. (VIBRATA *enters, poses.*) Exotic as a desert bloom . . . wondrous as a flamingo . . . lithe as a tigress . . . for the man whose interest is wild life . . .

(VIBRATA *sings, dances.* HERO *shakes his head "no."* PSEUDOLUS *goes to* VIBRATA.)

Pseudolus. Lycus, all that I can see is a sight to behold, but I keep feeling there is something wrong. Perhaps a cleft palate, a hammer toe . . .

Lycus. Wait. I know exactly what you want. May I present . . . Gymnasia. (GYMNASIA *enters, does a bump.* PSEUDOLUS *falls off stool.* HERO *shakes his head "no," but* PSEUDOLUS *is completely captivated.*) Gymnasia, a giant stage on which a thousand dramas can be played.

(PSEUDOLUS *circles her, stops behind her, gestures to* LYCUS.)

Pseudolus. Lycus, could I see you back here a moment? (LYCUS *disappears behind* GYMNASIA. *He and* PSEUDOLUS *gesture.* PSEUDOLUS *steps into the clear.*) Two hundred minae?! For what?!

Lycus. Figure it out for yourself.

Pseudolus. Yes, it is a fair price by the pound. But what disturbs me, frankly, is the upkeep. Perhaps you would have more success selling her to some fraternal organization. A group dedicated to good works. But on the other hand . . . (*Puts his head on her bosom.*)

Hero. Pseudolus!

Pseudolus. Yes, darling?

Hero. (*Pulls him aside.*) Do you want your freedom?

Pseudolus. (*Looks back at* GYMNASIA.) More than ever. (*To* LYCUS.) May I see the next girl?

Lycus. That is the entire lot. Surely there is one among these to satisfy you.

Pseudolus. As yet I have not seen exactly what I had in mind.

Lycus. (*Clap hands.*) Courtesans! Out of the sun and into the house. I shall return in time to lead you in midday prayers.

(COURTESANS *and* EUNUCHS *exit.* PHILIA's *head appears in upper window of* LYCUS' *house.*)

Hero. (*Whispers to* PSEUDOLUS.) Pseudolus, there she is!

Pseudolus. (*To* LYCUS.) Oh, you fox! "That is the entire lot." Did I not just spy a golden head and a pair of sky blue eyes? A body clad in flowing white? (HERO *shakes his head "yes" violently.*)

Lycus. Oh, that one. A recent arrival from Crete. A virgin.

Pseudolus. (*Nudging* HERO.) A virgin.

Hero. (*Mouths speech.*) A virgin!

Pseudolus. (*To* LYCUS.) Well??

Lycus. Only yesterday she was sold.

Hero. Sold! (*Draws his dagger melodramatically.* PSEUDOLUS *wrests it from him.*)

Pseudolus. Behave yourself! (*Begins casually cleaning his nails with dagger.*) She was sold?

Lycus. To the great captain, Miles Gloriosus, who comes this day to claim her. She cost 500 minae.

Pseudolus. (*Amazed.*) Five hundred!

Lycus. A great sum, to be sure. But being a man of conquest, his heart was set on a virgin.

Pseudolus. You say she just arrived from Crete?

Lycus. Yes.

Pseudolus. Mmm. I hope the great captain is kind to her. She deserves a bit of affection before . . . (*Sighs, then to* HERO:) Tragic, is it not? (HERO *moans.*)

Lycus. What is tragic?

Pseudolus. The news from Crete.

Lycus. What news?

Pseudolus. Why should I darken your day? (*Heaves a deep sigh.*) Farewell, Lycus.

Lycus. (*Grabs him.*) What is the news?

Pseudolus. What news?

Lycus. The news from Crete.

Pseudolus. I heard it. Tragic.

Lycus. (*Shakes him.*) Pseudolus!

Pseudolus. You force me to tell you! Crete is ravaged by a great plague.

People are dying by the thousands.

Lycus. But this girl is healthy. She goes smiling through the day.

Pseudolus. She doesn't! I thought you knew. When they start to smile, the end is near.

Lycus. No!

Pseudolus. Yes. I am told it is lovely now in Crete. Everyone lying there, smiling.

Lycus. Is it contagious?

Pseudolus. Did you ever see a plague that wasn't?

Lycus. My other girls!

Pseudolus. You had best get her out of there.

Hero. Yes!

Lycus. And then?

Pseudolus. I could look after her until the captain comes.

Hero. He could!

Lycus. But would *you* not be . . . ?

Pseudolus. I have already had the plague. I would tell you about it but . . . (*Pantomimes disgust.*)

Lycus. I do hope she lives until the captain gets here. (*Exits into his house.*)

Hero. (*Elated.*) Pseudolus, I am to be with her!

Pseudolus. Until the captain arrives. (*He hands back the money bag and dagger.*)

Hero. (*Sadly.*) Yes.

Pseudolus. Wait! (*Thinks a moment.*)

Hero. Yes?

Pseudolus. A brilliant idea!

Hero. Yes?

Pseudolus. That's what we have to find. A brilliant idea.

Hero. You must find one.

(*Lycus speaks into his house, as he backs out of it.*)

Lycus. Come, come, my dear. This way.

Don't touch that pillar. Here is someone I want you to meet. (*Philia enters, carrying a bag.*) Philia, this is Pseudolus. You are to stay with him until the captain comes. It will not be long. (*Aside to Pseudolus.*) Pseudolus! Thank you, Pseudolus. If none in the house were to your liking, there will soon be new arrivals. You shall have first choice, because, Pseudolus, you are a friend. (*Bows.*)

Pseudolus. (*Returning the bow.*) And you, Lycus, are a gentleman and a procurer. (*Lycus exits. Hero and Philia stand staring at each other. Pseudolus looks at them fondly, then turns to audience.*) There they are. Together. And I must keep them that way, together, if I am to be free. What to do? What to do? (*To himself.*) I need help. I'll go to the harbor. There I may find a way out! I am off! The captain! (*Hero and Philia turn to him, alarmed.*) Watch for him. He may arrive this way . . . (*Philia turns from Hero, looks off.*) . . . or he may arrive this way. (*Hero turns, looks off.*) No, no. You watch this way. (*Turns Philia around.*) And you watch that way. (*Turns Hero around. Hero and Philia now face each other.*) Much better. (*Starts to exit, stops, addresses audience.*) Don't worry. Nothing will happen. He's a virgin, too. (*Runs off.*)

Philia. My name is Philia.

Hero. Yes.

Philia. I do not know your name, but you have beautiful legs.

Hero. My name is Hero and . . . uh . . . you have beautiful legs . . . I imagine.

Philia. I would show them to you, but they are sold.

Hero. I know.

Philia. Along with the rest of me. I cost 500 minae. Is that a lot of money?

Hero. Oh, yes.

Philia. More than 300?

Hero. Nearly twice as much.

Philia. Those are the two numbers that mix me up, three and five. I hope that captain doesn't expect me to do a lot of adding.

Hero. You can't add?

Philia. We are taught beauty and grace, and no more. I cannot add, or spell, or anything. I have but one talent. *(Sings:)*
I'm lovely,
All I am is lovely,
Lovely is the one thing I can do.
Winsome,
What I am is winsome,
Radiant as in some dream come true.
Oh,
Isn't it a shame?
I can neither sew
Nor cook nor read nor write my name.
But I'm happy
Merely being lovely,
For it's one thing I can give to you.

Hero. (*Speaks.*) Philia . . .

Philia. Yes?

Hero. Say my name!

Philia. Just say your name?

Hero. Yes.

Philia. Very well. (*A blank look.*) I have forgotten it.

Hero. (*Disappointed.*) It's Hero.

Philia. Forgive me, Hero. I have no memory for names.

Hero. You don't need one. You don't need anything. (*Sings:*)
You're lovely,
Absolutely lovely,
Who'd believe the loveliness of you?
Winsome,

Sweet and warm and winsome,
Radiant as in some dream come true.
Now
Venus would seem tame,
Helen and her thou-
Sand ships would have to die of shame,

Both. And I'm happy,
Happy that you're (I'm) lovely,
For there's one thing loveliness can do:
It's a gift for me to share with you!

(*They kiss.*)

Hero. Do you know? I've never been kissed before.

Philia. That's the very first thing they teach us.

Hero. Philia . . . I love you.

Philia. And I love you.

(*They embrace as* HYSTERIUM *enters from* SENEX's *house, muttering.*)

Hysterium. Pseudolus! Where is that—? (*Sees* HERO *and* PHILIA.) Oh, no! (*Rushes at them.*) No, no, no, no!

Hero. (*Frightened.*) Hysterium—this is Philia.

Hysterium. Never mind who she is, who is she? Where is she from?

Hero. (*Haltingly.*) She is from the house of Lycus.

Hysterium. A courtesan!

Philia. I am a virgin.

Hysterium. (*With a fake smile.*) Of course. Hero, this will never do. Never, never. Bid farewell to this young lady so that she can go about her . . . uh . . . business.

Hero. But Pseudolus said—

Hysterium. Pseudolus! I might have known!

(PSEUDOLUS *runs on.*)

Pseudolus. Hero! Master!

Hysterium. Pseudolus! (PSEUDOLUS reacts, *polishes pillar of house.*) Pseudolus!

Pseudolus. Yes, Hysterium?

Hysterium. Pseudolus!

Pseudolus. Pronounced perfectly! You know, a lot of people say *Pseudolus*, and I hate it. (*Aside to* HERO). Show the girl our garden.

(HERO *and* PHILIA *exit behind* SENEX's *house.*)

Hysterium. How dare you! Arranging an assignation between an innocent boy and a you-know-what! (*He starts after the couple.*)

Pseudolus. (*Stopping him.*) Hysterium, there is something you should know about that you-know-what.

Hysterium. What?

Pseudolus. That girl, about whom you think the worst, is my daughter.

Hysterium. Your what?

Pseudolus. My daughter. You've heard me speak of her.

Hysterium. Never!

Pseudolus. Well, I don't like to talk about her. (*Polishes pillar.*)

Hysterium. That girl is not your daughter.

Pseudolus. My sister?

Hysterium. I shall go tell his parents.

Pseudolus. Wait! Hysterium, the truth. She has been sold to a captain who comes any moment now to claim her.

Hysterium. Oh . . .? I go tell his parents!

Pseudolus. I go with you!

Hysterium. You don't want to be there when I tell them about you!

Pseudolus. No, I want *you* to be there when I tell them about *you!*

Hysterium. Tell them *what* about me? I have nothing to fear. I am a pillar of virtue. I go. (*Starts to leave.*)

Pseudolus. I think it might be of interest to the family that their slave-in-chief, their pillar of virtue, has secreted within the confines of his cubicle Rome's most extensive and diversified collection of erotic pottery.

(HYSTERIUM *freezes in horror.*)

Hysterium. Pseudolus! (*Calls out.*) Hero!

Pseudolus. Tell me, where did you ever get that fruit bowl with the frieze of . . . ? (*Indicates an erotic pose or two.*)

Hysterium. Pseudolus! (*Calls again.*) Hero!

(HERO *and* PHILIA *enter.*)

Hysterium. Hero, as you know, your mother and father placed me in charge of your innocence. However, I have decided to allow you to remain with the girl until the arrival of her captain.

Hero. Oh, Philia! (*Embraces her.*)

Hysterium. Here! Stop doing that! (*Separates them.*) You could hurt each other! (*Exiting into* SENEX's *house.*) Ohhhhh!

Pseudolus. Master, I said we needed a brilliant idea.

Hero. Yes?

Pseudolus. I have been to the harbor, and I have found one. Come along!

Philia. Are we going somewhere?

Pseudolus. *You* are. You have your belongings. (*To* HERO.) Let us fetch yours.

Hero. Where are we to go?

Pseudolus. Away.

Hero. *Where* away?

Pseudolus. *Far* away!

Hero. But my family . . .

Philia. My captain . . .

Pseudolus. There is only room for two of you.

Hero. Where?

Pseudolus. (*Sings:*)
In the Tiber there sits a boat,
Gently dipping its bow,
Trim and tidy and built to float.
Pretty little picture?
Now . . .
Put a boy on the starboard side,
Leaning out at the rail.
Next to him put a blushing bride,
Slim and slender and starry-eyed.
Down below put a tiny bed.
The sun gets pale,
The sea gets red,
And off they sail on the first high tide,
The boat and the bed and the boy
and the bride!

It's a pretty little picture, oh, my!
Pretty little picture, how true!
Pretty little picture which I,
Pseudolittlelus, give to you!

Feel the roll of the playful waves!
See the sails as they swell!
Hear the whips on the galley slaves!
Pretty little picture?
Well . . .
Let it carry your cares away,
Out of sight, out of mind,
Past the buoy and through the bay—
Soon there's nothing but sea and
spray.
Night descends and the moon's
aglow.
Your arms entwined,
You steal below,
And far behind at the edge of the
day,
The bong of the bell of the buoy in
the bay,
And the boat and the boy and the
bride are away!

It's a pretty little picture so share
As the little boat sails to sea.
Take a little trip free as air,
Have a little freedom on me!

Hero and Philia. No worries,
No bothers,
No captains,
No fathers!

Pseudolus. In the ocean an island waits,
Smooth and sandy and pink,
Filled with lemons and nuts and
dates.
Pretty little picture?
Think:
In a cottage of cypress trees,
Sea-shells dotting the door,
Boy and bride live a life of ease,
Doing nothing but what they please.
And every night when the stars
appear,
There's nothing more to see or hear,
There's just the shore
Where the lovers lie,
The sand and the sea and the stars
and the sky,
And the sound of a soft little satisfied
sigh . . .

(Hero *and* Philia *sigh.*)

All. All your petty little problems will
cease,
And your little blessings will flow,
And your little family increase.
Pretty little picture?

Pseudolus. No, no!
Pretty little masterpiece!

All. Pretty little picture!

Pseudolus. (*Speaks*) Come! We go!

Hero. Yes!

Philia. Wait! I cannot go.

Pseudolus. Why can you not?!

Philia. As long as the captain has a
contract I must go with him. That
is the way of a courtesan.

Hero. Oh, Venus, why did you bring us together, only to part us?

Philia. Be brave, Hero.

Hero. For us there will never be happiness.

Philia. We will have to learn to be happy without it.

Pseudolus. (*To audience.*) Have you been listening? Do you believe this? And not a word about me or my freedom. (*Firmly.*) She *must* go with him!

Philia. This waiting out here is torture. Why doesn't he come and take me?

Pseudolus. In good time you will be taken. But not on the street. Inside.

Philia. You will tell me when he comes?

Pseudolus. I shall have him knock. On the door. Three times.

Philia. That's two and one more?

Pseudolus. Correct. Three times. Now, in, in, in.

(PHILIA *exits into* SENEX's *house.*)

Hero. (*Despondently.*) Pseudolus.

Pseudolus. (*Confidently.*) She will go with you.

(HYSTERIUM *enters from* SENEX's *house.*)

Hysterium. Hero, I am off to market. While you are alone with the girl, remember who you are. (HERO *exits into* SENEX's *house.*) I have yet to begin my daily chores.

Pseudolus. Hysterium, before you go. Just one more favor.

Hysterium. What is it?

Pseudolus. May I borrow your book of potions?

Hysterium. Oh, no, no, no! That stays right here . . . (*Pats his back pocket.*) . . . where it belongs. (*Calls off.*) You there, bird seller! What do you have in the way of a plump peahen? (*As*

he exits, PSEUDOLUS *deftly lifts potion book from* HYSTERIUM's *back pocket.*)

Pseudolus. (*Addresses audience.*) His book of potions! And my pass to freedom! What I need is his sleeping potion. With a drop or two of that, the breath stops short, the eyes slam shut, the body hangs limp. I shall mix a few drops in a beaker of wine and give it to the girl to drink. I show Lycus that she has died of the plague and tell Hero to dispose of the body. Then they to the boat, I to the hills, (*Points to audience.*) and you to your homes. (*Looks through pages, then at audience.*) I just remembered something frightening. I cannot read! (*Calls.*) Hero! Come out here. (HERO *enters from* SENEX's *house.*) Call these pages off to me.

Hero. Not now?!

Pseudolus. Yes, now! Read!

Hero. (*Reading as he turns pages.*) "Fever Potion" . . . "Headache Potion" . . . "Passion Potion" . . . "Sleeping Potion" . . .

Pseudolus. That's it! The formula. What do we need? The ingredients?

Hero. "The eye of an eel."

Pseudolus. That we have.

Hero. "The heart of a snail."

Pseudolus. That we have.

Hero. "A cup of mare's sweat."

Pseudolus. Mare's sweat? That we have not.

Hero. Why are you preparing this?

Pseudolus. I intend to give it to the girl. Asleep, she will go with you.

Hero. She will?

Pseudolus. (*Worried.*) Mare's sweat . . .

Hero. Where will you find it?

Pseudolus. Leave that to me. *You* go to the harbor! Give the boatman twenty minae and tell him that you sail with him this day! *I* shall prepare the potion!

Hero. This is exciting!

Pseudolus. Isn't it? Go! (HERO *exits.*) Mare's sweat! Where am I going to find mare's sweat on a balmy day like this? (PSEUDOLUS *exits, as* SENEX *enters with* DOMINA's *bust, calling.*)

Senex. Pseudolus! Pseudolus! . . . He could have taken this to the stone-cutter for me. (*To audience.*) I dropped it, and now the nose has to be re-sharpened. Hysterium will take it for me. (*Goes to his house, kicks door three times. A pause, then* PHILIA *enters from the house, arms outstretched.*)

Philia. Take me! (SENEX *looks around.*) Take me!

Senex. What did you say?

Philia. Take me!

Senex. One moment. (*Puts statute on stoop, starts for* PHILIA, *returns to statue, and turns its face away from* PHILIA.)

Philia. Here on the street if you like! My body is yours. Say it. Say it!

Senex. (*Looks around, then quickly.*) Your body is mine.

Philia. Then take me! (*Throws herself at him.*) Is this not what you want?

Senex. It does cross my mind now and then.

Philia. You must know one thing.

Senex. What is that?

Philia. Though you have my body, you shall never have my heart.

Senex. Well, you can't have everything. (*Looks heavenward.*) A thousand thanks, whichever one of you did this. (*She seizes him. They hold their embrace as* PSEUDOLUS *enters, carrying a vial. Not seeing* SENEX *and* PHILIA, *he addresses the audience.*)

Pseudolus. Would you believe it? There was a mare sweating not two streets from here. (*Holds up vial, sees embrace.* SENEX's *face is hidden from him.* PSEUDOLOUS *turns to audience.*) Gets to look more like his father every day!

Philia. (*Still in* SENEX's *arms.*) Pseudolus, he is here.

Pseudolus. No!

(SENEX *looks from* PHILIA *to* PSEUDOLUS, *then back to* PHILIA.)

Senex. Remember where we stopped. (*Slips out from under her, goes to* PSEUDOLUS.)

Pseudolus. Sir, you're back.

Senex. (*Holding his spine.*) She almost broke it.

Pseudolus. You've returned.

Senex. Yes!

Pseudolus. Unexpectedly!

Senex. Apparently! Who is she?

Philia. I shall await your bidding.

Senex. Yes, dear.

Philia. Ever your servant. (*Bows, exits into* SENEX's *house.*)

Senex. (*Sighs.*) Ever my servant.

Pseudolus. (*Quickly.*) Yes, sir. Your servant. Your new maid. We needed someone to help.

Senex. A new maid. She seems very loyal.

Pseudolus. And very efficient and very courteous and very thoughtful.

Senex. Maids like me. I'm neat. I like maids. *They're* neat. Something no household should be without. (*Sings,* PSEUDOLUS *all the while encouraging him, in song.*)

Everybody ought to have a maid.

Pseudolus. Everybody ought to have a maid.

Senex. Everybody ought to have a working girl,

Everybody ought to have a lurking
  girl
To putter around the house.

Everybody ought to have a maid.
Pseudolus. Everybody ought to have a
maid!
Senex. Everybody ought to have a
  menial,
Consistently congenial
And quieter than a mouse.
Oh! Oh! Wouldn't she be delicious,
Tidying up the dishes,
Neat as a pin?
Oh! Oh! Wouldn't she be delightful,
Sweeping out, sleeping in?
Everybody ought to have a maid!
Pseudolus. Everybody ought to have a
maid!
Senex. Someone whom you hire when
  you're short of help
To offer you the sort of help
You never get from a spouse!
Fluttering up the stairway,
Shuttering up the windows,
Cluttering up the bedroom,
Buttering up the master,
Puttering all around
The house!

(PSEUDOLUS *pantomimes a maid.*)

Oh! Oh! Wouldn't she be delicious,
Tidying up the dishes,
Neat as a pin?
Oh! Oh! Wouldn't she be delightful,
Sweeping out, sleeping in?
Everybody ought to have a maid!
Someone who, when fetching you
  your slipper, will
Be winsome as a whipoorwill
And graceful as a grouse!
Skittering down the hallway,
Flittering through the parlor,
Tittering in the pantry,
Littering up the bedroom,

Puttering all around
The house!

(HYSTERIUM *enters, reacts at the
sight of* SENEX. PSEUDOLUS *whispers
to him.*)

Hysterium. (*Speaks.*) A maid?
Pseudolus. A maid.
Senex. A maid.
All. A maid! (*Sing:*)
  Everybody ought to have a maid.
  Everybody ought to have a serving
    girl,
  A loyal and unswerving girl
  Who's quieter than a mouse.
  Oh! Oh!
  Think of her at the dustbin,
  'Specially when she's just been
  Traipsing about.
  Oh! Oh!
  Wouldn't she be delightful?
Hysterium. Living in . . .
Senex. Giving out . . .
All. Everybody ought to have a maid.
  Daintily collecting bits of paper 'n'
    strings,
  Appealing in her apron strings,
  Beguiling in her blouse!
Hysterium.
  Pattering through the attic,
Senex. Chattering in the cellar,
Pseudolus. Flattering in the bedroom,
All. Puttering all around the house,
  The house,
  The house!

(LYCUS *enters.* HYSTERIUM *whispers
to him.*)

Lycus. (*Speaks.*) A maid?
Hysterium. A maid.
Pseudolus. A maid.
Senex. A maid.
All. (*Sing:*) Everybody ought to have a
  maid,

Someone who's efficient and reliable,
Obedient and pliable
And quieter than a mouse.
Oh! Oh! Wouldn't she be so nimble,
Fiddling with her thimble,
Mending a gown?
Oh! Oh! Wouldn't she be delightful?
Lycus. Cleaning up . . .
Senex. Leaning down . . .
All. Everybody ought to have a maid!
Someone who'll be busy as a bumble-
bee
And, even if you grumble, be
As graceful as a grouse!
Lycus. Wriggling in the anteroom,
Hysterium. Jiggling in the living-room,
Pseudolus. Giggling in the dining-room,
Senex. Wiggling in the other rooms,
All. Puttering all around
The house!
The house!
The house!

(*Lycus exits into his house.*)

Senex. I know how busy both of you
are. Therefore, it is for *me* to instruct
her in the niceties of housework.
(*Starting for his house.*) We shall
start in my room.
Hysterium. Sir!
Pseudolus. Sir, your son is in there!
Senex. Oh! (*Thinks a moment, then:*)
Before my friend and neighbor, Erronius, went abroad in search of his
children stolen in infancy by pirates,
he asked me to look into his house
from time to time. (*Goes to Erronius' house, and takes key from ledge
over door.*) This seems as good a
time as any. (*Opens door.*) I shall
have a chat with the girl in here.
Send her to me.
Pseudolus. Sir.
Senex. (*Growing impatient*). Yes?

Pseudolus. Only my great devotion to
you allows me to speak so frankly.
(*Unseen by* Senex, Pseudolus *sprin-
kles contents of vial on him.*) You
trudged along the road quite some
way, and I fear that the great physical exertion . . . (*Sniffs.*)
Senex. (*Sniffing.*) Is that me?!
Pseudolus. Yes, sir.
Senex. My heavens, I smell like an overheated horse! I shall have to bathe.
Pseudolus. At least!

(Senex *exits into* Erronius' *house.*)

Hysterium. Why did I let her in the
house? I should never have listened
to you!
Pseudolus. Everything is going to be
fine, pussycat. (*Hands him potion
book.*)
Hysterium. Oh, you! You just see that
she gets out of that house.
Pseudolus. (*Picking up statue.*) And
you just see that he *stays* in *that*
house. Keep calm! (*Exits into* Senex's
house.)
Hysterium. Calm? Calm? Mustn't be
excited. Calm. Calm. (*Sings ex-
citedly:*)
I'm calm, I'm calm,
I'm perfectly calm,
I'm utterly under control.
I haven't a worry—
Where others would hurry,
I stroll.
(*He runs frantically around the
stage.*)
I'm calm, I'm cool,
A gibbering fool
Is something I never become!
When thunder is rumbling
And others are crumbling,
I hum.
(*He tries to hum; it becomes a stifled
scream.*)

I must think calm, comforting things:
Butterfly wings,
Emerald rings.
Or a murmuring brook,
Murmuring, murmuring, murmuring
. . .
Look:
(*Steadying his hands, seemingly calm.*)
I'm calm, I'm calm,
I haven't a qualm,
I'm utterly under control.
Let nothing confuse me
Or faze me—
(*Yawns.*)
Excuse me—
I'm calm,
Oh, so calm,
Oh, so . . .

Senex. (*Calls from inside* Erronius' *house.*) Hysterium! (Hysterium *runs into* Senex's *house.*)
(Proteans, *dressed as* Sailors, *enter with bags, drop them, as* Erronius *enters behind them.*)

Erronius. Bring up the baggage. Fetch the rest from the harbor. (Sailors *exit.*) Ah, home at last! After years of searching for my long lost children. (Hysterium *enters from* Senex's *house, carrying a plucked chicken, reacts in horror.*) How good it is to see this street once more. These tired old eyes fill with tears at the sight of the little they see. (*Bumps into* Hysterium.) Pardon me, young woman, I was just . . . that is . . . I mean to say . . . Ah, lovely baby. (*Pats chicken.*) About the age of my children when they were stolen by pirates. (*Going toward his house.*) Well, at least I have the comfort of my lonely house.

(Hysterium *rushes to the door of* Erronius' *house.*)

Hysterium. Sir!

Erronius. And who are you?

Hysterium. Hysterium, sir, servant to Senex.

Erronius. (*To pillar.*) Yes, of course, I should have known you anywhere. (Senex *is heard singing from inside house a bit of* "Everybody Ought to Have a Maid.") What was that?

Hysterium. I didn't hear anything. (Senex *sings a bit more.*) I didn't hear that either.

Erronius. What was that?

Hysterium. What was what?

Erronius. (*Pointing to his house.*) That!

Hysterium. That what?

Erronius. That eerie sound.

Hysterium. Eerie?

Erronius. Eerie, as if haunted.

Hysterium. (*To himself.*) Eerie, as if haunted? (*To* Erronius.) Sir, what I am about to tell you is eerie . . . Your house is . . . haunted.

Erronius. Haunted?

Hysterium. As haunted as the day is long!

(Pseudolus *enters, stirring the potion, listens.*)

Erronius. Impossible! My house haunted, you say? Strange.

Hysterium. But true. Perhaps you ought to stay with relatives . . . distant relatives.

Erronius. Yes! No! Fetch me a soothsayer.

Hysterium. A soothsayer?

Erronius. Yes, I must have him search my house immediately.

(Pseudolus *puts a cloth over his head, runs to* Erronius, *and chants ghoulishly.*)

Pseudolus. You are in need of a soothsayer?

Erronius. How did you know?

Pseudolus. I'd be a fine soothsayer if I didn't!

Erronius. There is a spirit in my . . .

Pseudolus. Silence! I am about to say the sooth! Wait! (*Chants incoherently.*) I see it. I see everything. (HYSTERIUM *steps behind* ERRONIUS, *pantomimes distance.*) You have been abroad.

Erronius. Yes, yes.

Pseudolus. For . . . (*Looks at* HYSTERIUM, *who flashes his ten fingers twice.*) . . . twenty years! (ERRONIUS *nods vigorously.* HYSTERIUM *shades his eyes with one hand.*) You have been searching . . . for . . . (HYSTERIUM *cradles his arms, rocks them.*) A child! (HYSTERIUM *holds up two fingers.*) Two children!

Erronius. Yes, yes!

(HYSTERIUM *flexes his muscles.*)

Pseudolus. A fine, big boy.

Erronius. Yes.

Pseudolus. And . . . (HYSTERIUM *places hand on his hip, pantomimes a girl.*) A strange, little boy. (HYSTERIUM *shakes his head "no."*) A girl! A girl! A boy and a girl!

Erronius. Yes! Can you find them for me?

Pseudolus. Certainly. I can find them for you.

Erronius. (*Takes ring from his finger, gives it to* PSEUDOLUS.) Each wears a ring on which is engraven a gaggle of geese.

Pseudolus. A gaggle of what?

Erronius. A gaggle of geese. Look! (*Points to ring.*) There are only two others like it in the world. And my children wear them.

Pseudolus. How many geese in a gaggle?

Erronius. At least seven.

Pseudolus. Seven? Then before I say the sooth again you must walk seven times around the seven hills of Rome.

Erronius. Seven times?

Hysterium. Slowly.

Erronius. Seven times around the seven hills? (SAILORS *enter with more baggage.*) Take it all back to the harbor! (*Proudly.*) My house is haunted. (SAILORS *exit with baggage.* SENEX *is heard singing again.* PSEUDOLUS *joins in, eerily.*) And the spirit?

Pseudolus. It shall be gone by the time you have done my bidding.

Erronius. Thank you.

Pseudolus. To the hills!

Erronius. To the hills! (*He starts for the footlights,* PSEUDOLUS *and* HYSTERIUM *stop him, head him toward the wings.*)

Hysterium. This is the way, sir!

Erronius. Thank you, young woman! (*Exits.*)

Pseudolus. (*Calls.*) Sir, you forgot your gaggle! (*Puts ring on his own finger.*)

(SENEX *enters from* ERRONIUS' *house.*)

Senex. Hysterium!

Hysterium. Sir!

Senex. Prepare my bath!

Hysterium. Yes, sir! (*Runs into* ERRONIUS' *house.*)

Senex. Ah, Pseudolus, that little maid. Do you know what her first words were to me? She said, "Take me."

Pseudolus. (*Picking up potion bowl.*) And you shall, sir.

Senex. . . . . I'll try.

Pseudolus. (*Exiting into* SENEX's *house.*) Yes, sir.

Senex. (*Starting into* ERRONIUS' *house.*) Remember, Hysterium, Not too hot and not too cold.

(HERO *runs on, calling.*)

Hero. Philia! Philia!

Senex. Son!

Hero. Father! Where's Mother?

Senex. (*Frightened, turns.*) Where?! (*Realizes.*) Oh. I—I have returned without her. Pressing business. (Philia *appears on balcony of* Senex's *house.*) Lovely new maid.

Hero. New maid?

Senex. Pseudolus told me about it.

Hero. Oh.

Senex. (*To* Philia.) Presently, my dear.

(Philia *withdraws into house, waving.* Senex *turns to audience, sings:*)

Why did he look at her that way?

Hero. (*Sings, to audience:*)
Why did he look at her that way?

Both. Must be my imagination . . .

Senex. She's a lovely blooming flower,
He's just a sprout—impossible!

Hero. She's a lovely blooming flower,
He's all worn out—impossible!

Senex. Just a fledgling in the nest . . .

Hero. Just a man who needs a rest . . .

Senex. He's a beamish boy at best . . .

Hero. Poor old fellow . . .

Senex. He's a child and loves a test
He's too young to pass—impassable!

Hero. He has asthma, gout, a wife,
Lumbago and gas—irascible!

Senex. Romping in the nursery . . .

Hero. He looks tired . . .

Senex. (*To* Hero, *warmly.*)
Son, sit on your father's knee.

Hero. (*To* Senex, *warmly.*)
Father, you can lean on me.

Both. (*To audience.*) Him?
Impossible!

Hero. But why did she wave at him that way?

Senex. Why did she wave at him that way?

Both. Could there be an explanation?

Hero. Women often want a father,

She may want mine—it's possible!

Senex. He's a handsome lad of twenty,
I'm thirty-nine—it's possible!

Hero. Older men know so much more . . .

Senex. In a way, I'm forty-four . . .

Hero. Next to him, I'll seem a bore . . .

Senex. All right, fifty!

Hero. Then again, he *is* my father,
I ought to trust—impossible!

Senex. Then again, with love at my age,
Sometimes it's just—impossible!

Hero. With a girl, I'm ill-at-ease . . .

Senex. I don't feel well . . .

Hero. (*To* Senex, *helplessly.*)
Sir, about those birds and bees . . .

Senex. (*To* Hero, *helplessly.*)
Son, a glass of water, please . . .

Both. (*To audience.*)
The situation's fraught,
Fraughter than I thought,
With horrible,
Impossible
Possibilities!

Senex. (*Calling to his house.*) Pseudolus! (*To* Hero.) Son, it grieves me to see a boy your age moping about the house. (Pseudolus *enters, stirring potion.*) Pseudolus, I want you to take Hero to the baths.

Hero. Sir!

Pseudolus. Very good, sir. Allow me to finish a brew master Hero asked me to prepare. (*To* Hero.) Master, I shall meet you in front of the baths of Aqua Salina. You know where it is? Next to the harbor. And I shall have a surprise for you.

Hero. Oh, yes. Yes, of course. Farewell, father. Farewell, Pseudolus. (*Exits.*)

Senex. Well, he to his bath and I to mine.

(Hysterium *enters from* Erronius' *house, wiping hands on tunic.*)

Hysterium. Just the way you like it, sir.

Senex. One thing more, Hysterium.

Hysterium. Yes, sir?

Senex. I shall need a complete change of garb. Let me see . . . my tunic with the tassels!

Hysterium. Sir, it needs taking in.

Senex. Well, take it in and bring it out! (*Exits into* ERRONIUS' *house.*)

(HYSTERIUM *exits into* SENEX'S *house singing a bit of "I'm Calm."* LYCUS *enters from his house.*)

Lycus. Pseudolus! The girl! I want to know the worst. How is she?

Pseudolus. She is very low.

Lycus. Still smiling?

Pseudolus. Laughing! (LYCUS *reacts in horror.*) There is one hope! I have prepared a plague potion. If it is not too late, we may yet save her life.

Lycus. Give it to her!

Pseudolus. Yes!

(PSEUDOLUS *starts for* SENEX'S *house as a* FANFARE *is heard and a* PROTEAN, *dressed as a* SOLDIER, *enters, carrying a spear.*)

Soldier. Ho, there! (*They turn, stare at him with horror.*) I seek the house of Marcus Lycus.

Lycus. (*Stammering superbly.*) Who heeks the souse of Mycus Leecus?

Pseudolus. (*A hand on* LYCUS' *shoulder.*) Hold, sir.

Lycus. But he . . . who . . .

Pseudolus. You're not holding. (*To* SOLDIER, *enunciating grotesquely.*) Who is he who seeks the house of Marcus Lycus?

Soldier. A foot soldier of Captain Miles Gloriosus! (*Executes an elaborate salute.*)

Pseudolus. Smartly done!

Soldier. My captain has dispatched me to inform you that he is but half a league away. Prepare to greet him! (*Salutes, exits. Another* FANFARE *is heard.*)

Pseudolus. Half a league!

Lycus. We have only moments!

Pseudolus. I'll give her the potion!

Lycus. Yes!

Pseudolus. Yes! (*Starts for* SENEX'S *house.*)

Lycus. Wait!

Pseudolus. (*Returns to* LYCUS.) What?

Lycus. Don't leave me!

Pseudolus. Why not?

Lycus. He's coming!

Pseudolus. I know he's coming!

Lycus. (*Takes bowl from him.*) You speak to him. *I'll* give her the potion!

Pseudolus. Wait! You can't give her the potion!

Lycus. Why not?

Pseudolus. You'll catch the plague!

Lycus. (*Hands him bowl quickly.*) Oh, I don't want the plague!

Pseudolus. I've got to give her the potion!

Lycus. Yes!

Pseudolus. Yes! (*Starts for* SENEX'S *house.*)

Lycus. Wait!

Pseudolus. What? (*Returns to* LYCUS.)

Lycus. She is in the house of Senex!

Pseudolus. What will we do? . . . Does he know which house is your house?

Lycus. No!

Pseudolus. (*Points to* SENEX'S *house.*) *This* is your house!

Lycus. Will he believe it?

Pseudolus. Get the girls!

Lycus. Good!

Pseudolus. I'll give her the potion!

Lycus. And I'll get the girls!

Pseudolus. Good!

Lycus. Yes!

Pseudolus. Yes! (*Starts for* SENEX'S *house.*)

Lycus. Wait!

Pseudolus. (*Returns to* LYCUS.) *What is it??!!*

Lycus. I forgot.

Pseudolus. Lycus, we must not lose our heads!

Lycus. Yes! No!

Pseudolus. (*Screams.*) We must remain calm!

(FANFARE *is heard.*)

Lycus. Pseudolus, *you* must speak to the captain! I have no talent for bravery.

Pseudolus. You grant me permission to represent you?

Lycus. Complete!

Pseudolus. All right. Collect the courtesans and bring them out. Then you are to wait in your house.

Lycus. Pseudolus, I am eternally grateful! I am your friend until death!

Pseudolus. Go!

Lycus. Yes!

Pseudolus. Yes! (*Starts for* SENEX'S *house.*)

Lycus. Wait!

Pseudolus. (*Stops, yells.*) No!

(A FANFARE, *and* TWO PROTEANS, *dressed as* SOLDIERS, *enter, come to a smart halt.* LYCUS *ducks into his house.* PSEUDOLUS *puts down potion bowl.*)

Second Soldier. Ho, there!

Third Soldier. We seek the house of Marcus Lycus!

Pseudolus. Who seeks the mouse of Larcus Heekus?

Third Soldier. Foot soldiers of Captain Miles Gloriosus.

Second Soldier. He is but a quarter of a league away and bids you honor this. (*Hands* PSEUDOLUS *parchment.*)

Pseudolus. (*Studies parchment.*) Oh, yes, of course.

Second Soldier. You know what this is?

Pseudolus. Of course I know what this is. This is writing.

Third Soldier. It is your contract with the captain.

Pseudolus. And a pretty piece of work. What is this word here?

Third Soldier. That is "Lycus."

Pseudolus. Oh, yes. Then you realize whom you are speaking to.

Second Soldier. Yes, sir.

Third Soldier. And do you see what it says there? (*Points to another spot.*)

Pseudolus. It says . . . words. And I intend to stand behind those words, or my name is not Marcus Lycus!

(HYSTERIUM *enters from* SENEX'S *house.*)

Hysterium. Pseudolus!

Pseudolus. (*Without missing a beat.*) Or my name is not Pseudolus Marcus Lycus! A moment. I must have a word with my eunuch. (*To* HYSTERIUM.) Come here, eunuch! (*Takes* HYSTERIUM *aside.*)

Hysterium. How dare you call me that?

Pseudolus. You know it's not true, and I know it's not true, so what do we care what they think?

Hysterium. Those soldiers, have they come for the girl? I'll go right in and get her.

Pseudolus. They have not come for the girl. They have come for me.

Hysterium. What?

Pseudolus. Hysterium, I have never told you this, but years ago I deserted from the army.

Hysterium. No!

Pseudolus. Sh! I was very young. I wanted to be an archer. Instead, they made me a slinger. Then, one day, at the height of a battle, I lost my head. I arched when I should have slung. I had to flee.

Hysterium. And now they have found

you. Oh, Pseudolus!

Pseudolus. Sh! They are looking for Pseudolus. I told them I am Lycus.

Hysterium. And Lycus you are! Rely on me!

Pseudolus. I must. (*Picks up potion bowl.*) Hysterium, more bad news!

Hysterium. I hope it's good.

Pseudolus. It's terrible! The girl refuses to go with her captain. That is why I have prepared your sleeping potion. You are to give her a drop or two in a beaker of wine, and upon hearing me say, "Present the bride," carry her out in your arms!

Hysterium. Trust me, Pseu— (*Catches himself, then loudly.*) Trust me, Lycus! (*Takes bowl from* Pseudolus, *speaking for* Soldiers' *benefit.*) I go, Lycus. Farewell, Lycus! (*Exits into* Senex's *house.*)

Pseudolus. (*To* Soldiers.) Bid your captain come! His bride awaits him! (*Soldiers execute fancy salute, run off.* Pseudolus *calls out.*) Lycus! The girls! Quickly!

Lycus. (*Opening his door.*) Yes! (*Calls into house.*) Eunuchs! The girls! Quickly! (*To* Pseudolus.) We shall pose them informally!

Pseudolus. Give the place a friendly look.

(Eunuchs *herd* Courtesans *out of house.*)

Eunuch. Hurry, there! Hurry! Hurry!

Gymnasia. Don't you lower your voice to me!

Lycus. You are to do exactly as Pseudolus bids. He will represent me.

Pseudolus. (*Points to* Senex's *house.*) All you girls over here! Now, you eunuchs . . . (*Indicates manly pose he wants them to assume.* Eunuchs *squeal with delight.*) Lycus, do we really need these eunuchs?

Lycus. (*To* Eunuchs.) Into the house.

Eunuchs. (*Chirping.*) Into the house! Into the house! (Eunuchs *exit into* Lycus' *house.* Pseudolus *proceeds to arrange* Courtesans.)

Pseudolus. (*To* Panacea.) You there. (*To* Tintinabula *and* Vibrata.) You there. (*To* Geminae.) You there. (*To* Gymnasia.) You there . . . Oh, there's so much of you there! (*Leans on her bosom, as* Erronius *enters.*)

Erronius. (*To audience.*) First time around! (All *watch as he crosses the stage, and exits.*)

Pseudolus. (*To* Courtesans.) Now, may I have your attention? You are about to meet a great captain. Remember who you are and what you stand for. Now, will you all please strike . . . vocational attitudes? (Courtesans *strike poses.*) Perfect! I would like a mosaic of this scene. An entire wall made up of—

(Fanfare *is heard.*)

Lycus. The Captain! Pseudolus, again my heartfelt—

Pseudolus. In! In!

(Lycus *exits into his house.* A Second Fanfare *is heard.*)

Miles' Voice. (*Offstage.*) Stand aside, everyone! I take large steps! (*He enters with* Soldiers, *counting off.*)

Soldiers. One, two, one, two . . .

Miles. We not only fought but we won, too!

Soldiers. One, two, one two . . . Left, right, left, right . . .

Miles. There's none of the enemy left, right?

Soldiers. Right! Left! . . . uh . . . Ri— uh—left! (*Utter confusion.*)

Miles. Halt!

Pseudolus. (*Saluting.*) Hail, Miles Gloriosus!

Miles. You are?
Pseudolus. Marcus Lycus, sir. I am dazzled by your presence.
Miles. Everyone is.
Pseudolus. (*Indicating* SENEX's *house.*)
Welcome to my house, great captain.
Your bride awaits you.
Miles. My bride! (*Sings:*)
My bride! My bride!
I've come to claim my bride,
Come tenderly to crush her against
my side!
Let haste be made,
I cannot be delayed!
There are lands to conquer,
Cities to loot,
And peoples to degrade!
Soldiers. Look at those arms!
Look at that chest!
Look at them!
Miles. Not to mention the rest!
Even I am impressed.

My bride! My bride!
Come bring to me my bride!
My lust for her no longer can be
denied!
Convey the news,
I have no time to lose!
There are towns to plunder,
Temples to burn
And women to abuse!
Soldiers. Look at that foot!
Look at that heel!
Mark the magnificent muscles of
steel!
Miles. I am my ideal!
I, Miles Gloriosus,
I, slaughterer of thousands,
I, oppressor of the meek,
Subduer of the weak,
Degrader of the Greek,
Destroyer of the Turk,
Must hurry back to work!
Miles. I, Miles Gloriosus,
Courtesans. Him, Miles Gloriosus,

Soldiers. A man among men!
Miles. I, paragon of virtues,
Courtesans. Him, paragon of virtues,
Soldiers. With sword and with pen!
Miles. I, in war the most admired,
All. Himmm!
Miles. In wit the most inspired,
All. Himmmm!
Miles. In love the most desired,
All. Himmm!
Miles. In dress the best displayed,
I am a parade!
Soldiers. Look at those eyes,
Cunning and keen!
Look at the size of those thighs,
Like a mighty machine!
Pseudolus. Those are the mightiest
thighs that I ever have theen!
I mean . . .
Miles. My bride! My bride!
Inform my lucky bride:
The fabled arms of Miles are open
wide!
Make haste! Make haste!
I have no time to waste!
There are shrines I should be sacking,
Ribs I should be cracking,
Eyes to gouge and booty to divide!
Bring me my bride!
Soldiers. Bring him his bride!
All. Bring him his bride!

(PSEUDOLUS *goes to door of* SENEX's
house.)

Pseudolus. Present the bride! (FAN-
FARE.) Pay homage all! Here, in one
being is Juno, Diana, and Venus.
(ALL *kneel.*) Present the bride!
(FANFARE. PSEUDOLUS bows. HYSTER-
IUM *enters.* PSEUDOLUS *turns to*
MILES.) A short delay, sir! (*Pulls*
HYSTERIUM *aside.*) What happened?
Hysterium. I'll tell you what happened!
Nothing! She won't drink!
Pseudolus. What?

Hysterium. She says on Crete her religion forbids it.

Pseudolus. He had to fall in love with a religious Cretan! *I'll* get her to drink! (*To* MILES.) Captain, forgive the girl. She primps and preens. She wants to be worthy of so great a warrior.

(*Exits into* SENEX's *house with* HYSTERIUM.)

Miles. Understandable I *am* a legend in my own time. (*Laughs.* SOLDIERS *join in.*) Men! Close ranks! (*They do.*) Stand tall! (PSEUDOLUS *enters from* SENEX's *house.*) Lycus! (LYCUS *peeks out of upper window of his house, listens.*) Where is my bride?

Pseudolus. Did she not come through this door?

Miles. No! What are you saying, man?

Pseudolus. The virgin has escaped!

Miles. Oh, no! The beautiful bride I bargained for!

Pseudolus. Vanished!

Miles. This is monstrous!

Pseudolus. It certainly is. But look at it this way. Since I cannot deliver her to you, you do not have to pay me the 500 minae.

Miles. I *paid* you the 500 minae! (PSEUDOLUS *reacts.*) Through my agents. Has the money escaped as well?

Pseudolus. There has been a little mistake. (*Laughs*) I was only joking. Lycus will pay you.

(LYCUS *groans, disappears from window.*)

Miles. What?

Pseudolus. I was helping out a friend.

Allow me, great captain. (*He goes to* LYCUS' *house, pulls* LYCUS *out.*) Come out here! (*To* MILES.) Here is your man! (*To* LYCUS.) Tell him! Tell him who I am!

(HYSTERIUM *enters from* SENEX's *house.*)

Lycus. Everyone knows who you are, Lycus.

Hysterium. Of course. He is Marcus Lycus.

Pseudolus. No! No! *He* is Lycus. *This* is his house!

Lycus. (*To* MILES.) Look within, sir. You will find none here but hooded men. We are a holy order. An ancient brotherhood of lepers. (MILES *backs away.*) Unclean! Unclean! And bless you, Lycus! (*He backs offstage.*)

Miles. What now, Lycus?

Pseudolus. What?

Miles. I shall tell you what! With axe and pike, my soldiers shall raze this house to the ground!

Hysterium. (*Fainting.*) Our beautiful house!

Miles. And you, you shall receive the maximum punishment, death!

(COURTESANS *scream.*)

Pseudolus. Please, sir, please! May I be allowed a word?

Miles. A word?

Pseudolus. One word.

Miles. It had better be a good one.

Pseudolus. Oh, it is, sir!

Miles. What is it?

Pseudolus. (*To audience.*) Intermission!

END OF ACT I

ACT II

The scene is the same as for Act I. This time PROLOGUS is played by SENEX rather than by PSEUDOLUS. As the characters enter, they assume the positions in which we last saw them at the end of ACT I.

Prologus. Welcome again, playgoers. You are about to witness the second half of our play. (*Signals orchestra, which plays under following.*) Permit me to remind you where we were when last you saw us. The virgin . . . (PHILIA *enters.*) . . . was waiting . . . that's what they do best . . . waiting here in the house for her captain to claim her. She has refused to drink the potion on religious grounds. (PHILIA *exits into* SENEX's *house.*) Lycus . . . (LYCUS *enters.*) . . . skulks about the city, searching for Philia. (LYCUS *exits.*) Hero . . . (HERO *enters.*) . . . is at the baths where he sits and soaks. (HERO *exits.*) His mother . . . (DOMINA *enters, crosses stage, exits.*) . . . is on the way to the country to visit *her* mother. A hundred and four years old, and not one organ in working condition. The courtesans . . . (COURTESANS *enter*) . . . Miles Gloriosus and his mighty warriors . . . (MILES, SOLDIERS *enter.*) . . . Hysterium and Pseudolus are here. (HYSTERIUM, PSEUDOLUS *enter.*) And I, Senex, await the maid in my neighbor's house, hopefully about to sow my last oat, if memory serves. Let the play continue! (SENEX *exits into* ERRONIUS' *house.*)

Pseudolus. (*To* MILES.) Sir! I . . .

Miles. (*To* SOLDIERS.) Gag him! (SOLDIER *grabs* PSEUDOLUS *from behind, clamps hand over his mouth.*) And now I rid Rome of a rascal! (*He draws sword and lunges at* PSEUDO-LUS, *who whirls around. The sword jabs* SOLDIER *in the rear.* SOLDIER *releases* PSEUDOLUS, *and jumps away, rubbing sore spot.* MILES *advances on* PSEUDOLUS.*) You . . .

Pseudolus. (*Backing away.*) Sir! (MILES *stalks him.*) The girl must be near at hand. If you kill me you deprive yourself of seeing a face so fair, a heart so pure, a body so undulating . . . (MILES *lowers his sword.* PSEU-DOLUS, *sensing success, presses on.*) She is magnificence personified! If you had been born a woman, you would have been she!

Miles. As magnificent as that?

Pseudolus. Yes, sir. Spare me! I am sure she can be found.

Miles. You are?

Pseudolus. Yes, sir. I shall give you a list of ten or twenty places you might look for her.

Miles. *You* shall look for her!

Pseudolus. Me? With this bad leg? (*He limps horribly.* MILES *grabs him.*)

Miles. With that bad leg!

Pseudolus. Yes, it will do it good. And where may I deliver the girl? I mean, where will you be?

Miles. (*Points to* SENEX's *house.*) Waiting here in your house.

Hysterium. No!

Miles. No?!

Hysterium. I meant "yes," it just came out "no."

Miles. (*To* PSEUDOLUS.) And to assure your return . . . Men! You are to go with him.

Pseudolus. Sir, before I go, a word with my eunuch.

Miles. Be brief.

Pseudolus. Yes, sir. Come here, eunuch. (*Pulls* HYSTERIUM *aside.*) Hysterium, this is what you must do. Hide the girl, up on the roof.

Hysterium. Why?

Pseudolus. Why not? Go.

(HYSTERIUM *exits into* SENEX's *house.*)

Pseudolus. My eunuch is making sure the house is fit to receive so illustrious a visitor.

Miles. I have been put off enough for one day! (*Turns to enter* SENEX's *house, stops, as* ERRONIUS *enters.*)

Erronius. The second time around! (*Exits.*)

Miles. Lycus!

Pseudolus. Yes, sir! (*Calls to* SENEX's *house.*) Ready?

Hysterium. (*From inside house.*) Ready!

Pseudolus. All is ready, sir. There is food and drink within. And the girls will sing and dance for you.

(COURTESANS *exit into* SENEX's *house.*)

Miles. You have but one hour. Men, you are to hound his every step.

(MILES *exits into* SENEX's *house.* PSEUDOLUS *circles stage, followed by* SOLDIERS, *they exit.* SENEX *appears in window of* ERRONIUS' *house.*)

Senex. Hysterium!

(HYSTERIUM *enters from* SENEX's *house.*)

Hysterium. Yes, sir!

Senex. Tell the little maid I am almost ready.

Hysterium. Sir, I must say this to you. Abandon this mad adventure! Think of your wife on the way to the country!

Senex. That, Hysterium, is the country's problem.

Hysterium. Yes, sir.

Senex. Hysterium, one thing more. You know that potion you prepare that so fills one with passion, one can almost perform miracles?

Hysterium. Yes, sir. We have some left over from your last anniversary.

Senex. Bring it to me, now, slave-in-chief. (*Withdraws from window.*)

Hysterium. Slave-in-chief! I wonder how many slaves-in-chief have a master in the tub, a house full of courtesans, and a virgin on the roof!

(*He exits into* SENEX's *house, as* PSEUDOLUS *enters, closely followed by* SOLDIERS. PSEUDOLUS *does several intricate maneuvers which the* SOLDIERS *carefully follow. The maneuvers become more elaborate.* PANACEA *enters from* SENEX's *house, and the* SOLDIERS *follow her off.*)

Pseudolus. (*To audience.*) Just one hour. Pretending she was dead was the perfect plan. If only Philia had taken one sip . . . It still is the perfect plan, if I can only find a body. A body. (*An inspiration.*) Gusto! Gusto, the bodysnatcher! He owes me a favor! (*He runs off, not seeing* DOMINA, *who enters.*)

Domina. (*To audience.*) Since sending my husband back to Rome, I have been haunted by the premonition that he is up to something low. (*Calls.*) Hysterium!

Hysterium. (*Entering from* SENEX's *house with cup.*) Coming master . . . mistress! You're home!

Domina. And parched with thirst, ever-thoughtful Hysterium. (*Reaches for cup, he pulls it away.*)

Hysterium. No! It's a potion!

Domina. What sort of potion?

Hysterium. To make you thirsty. And you're already thirsty, so you don't need it. (*Puts cup near* ERRONIUS' *house.*)

Domina. Thirst is the lesser of my problems. Hysterium, on the best of intuition, I believe my husband is fouling the nest.

Hysterium. No! Never!

Domina. Never? Old friend and confidant, you are talking to a woman who faces facts. (*Sings:*)
For over thirty years,
I've cried myself to sleep,
Assailed by doubts and fears
So great the gods themselves would weep!
The moment I am gone,
I wonder where he'll go.
In all your simple honesty,
You can't begin to know . . .
Ohhhh. . . .
(*Wailing tenderly.*)
I want him,
I need him,
Where is he?
(*Furiously.*)
That dirty old man is here somewhere,
Cavorting with someone young and fair,
Disporting in every shameless whim,
Just wait till I get my hands on him!
(*Tenderly.*)
I'll hold him,
Enfold him,
Where is he?
(*Furiously.*)
That dirty old man, where can he be?

Profaning our vows for all to see,
Complaining how he's misunderstood,
Abusing me (if he only would!)
Oh, love,
Sweet love,
Why hide?
You vermin, you worm, you villain!
Come face,
Embrace
Your bride!
Wherever he is, I know he's still an Angel,
My angel!
Where is he,
That dirty old man divine?
I love him,
I love him,
That lecherous, lewd, lascivious,
Loathsome, lying, lazy,
Dirty old man of mine!

Miles' Voice. (*From inside* SENEX's *house.*) Why?

Domina. Ah, I hear him now!

Miles' Voice. Why must I always be surrounded by fawning admirers?

Domina. (*To* HYSTERIUM.) That is not my husband's voice. Tell me, who is in my house?

Hysterium. I think it's a captain.

Domina. A captain?

Hysterium. Yes . . . he thinks that . . . your house . . . is the . . . I hope you do not object to my offering him your hospitality.

Domina. Object? When, I, myself, am the daughter of a Roman general? Hysterium, I must meet him.

Hysterium. You wouldn't like him. He's very vulgar.

Domina. All soldiers are, in a grand sort of way.

(*MILES appears in doorway.*)

Miles. . . . interminable! (*Shouts at* Hysterium.) Bring more food and drink, eunuch!

Hysterium. (*To* Domina.) You see?

Domina. Captain, I was just coming inside to give you a proper welcome.

(Hysterium *winces.*)

Miles. (*Thinking she is one of* Lycus' *girls.*) You are of this house?

Domina. For years and years. You know, Captain, my father was General Magnus. On the last anniversary of his death, I entertained over two hundred officers.

Miles. Two hundred? By yourself?

Domina. Of course not. Hysterium here was a big help. (Hysterium *smiles proudly, then reacts painfully.*) But now my business takes me to the Forum, but I shall return. And for the length of your stay I shall bend over backwards to please you.

Miles. (*Horrified.*) That will not be necessary! (*Exits into* Senex's *house.*)

Domina. (*To* Hysterium.) I do wish I could chat on with him, but I must find out why my husband was so anxious to return to Rome. Hysterium, when next we meet I shall be in some form of disguise. If you recognize me, not a word. (*Waving to* Miles, *who appears in door of house.*) Until later, Captain. (Miles *moans, exits into house.* Domina *starts off, as* Pseudolus *enters, sees her, starts polishing pillar.*) Ah, Pseudolus, busy as ever.

Pseudolus. Yes, madam. (*She exists.* Pseudolus *rushes to* Hysterium) She's back!

Hysterium. Yes!

Pseudolus. What has happened?

Hysterium. What *hasn't* happened?

Pseudolus. All right, what *hasn't* happened? She hasn't found out anything, has she?

Hysterium. No!

Pseudolus. Good!

Hysterium. But she will, and she'll kill me!

Pseudolus. No, she won't!

Hysterium. No, she won't. I'll kill myself! I can do it painlessly. If she does it, it will hurt. I must do it. I have besmirched the honor of my family. My father will turn in his grave!

Pseudolus. Your father is alive.

Hysterium. This will kill him!

Pseudolus. Are you finished? Now, listen to this. I have really shocking news.

Hysterium. What?

Pseudolus. You know Gusto, the body-snatcher? (Hysterium *nods.*) He died this morning.

Hysterium. No! I saw him only yesterday. When is he to be buried?

Pseudolus. They don't know. Someone snatched the body.

Hysterium. Isn't that a sha—? (*Does a take.*) Why are we crying over a dead body-snatcher?!

Pseudolus. Because he could have helped us. He could have lent us a body. (*Puts his hand on* Hysterium's *shoulder.*)

Hysterium. A body?

Pseudolus. A body (*A gleam comes into his eye, starts running his hand over* Hysterium's *shoulder and chest.*) A body. Hysterium, would you like everything to be the way it was when you woke up this morning?

Hysterium. In a minute!

Pseudolus. That's all it will take. Come! (*Pulls* Hysterium *toward* Lycus' *house.*)

Hysterium. In here?
Pseudolus. In here!
Hysterium. Where did you get the money? (PSEUDOLUS *pulls* HYSTERIUM *into* LYCUS' *house.*)

(SENEX *enters from* ERRONIUS' *house, inhales deeply.*)

Senex. Mmmmmmm. (*To audience.*) Something smells divine, and it's me. I just took the most luxurious bath. The oil, the essences. Oh, spectators, I would love to pass among you so that each and every one might get a good whiff. (*Calls.*) Philia! (*To himself.*) Mustn't shout. I have to save every bit of energy. (*Gently.*) Philia!

(PHILIA *appears on roof of* SENEX's *house.*)

Philia. Yes, master? Master?
Senex. (*Looks around for her, then sees her on roof.*) Ah, my dear. No need to dust up there. Come to me.
Philia. I am yours.
Senex. Yes, my dear. But not on the roof. Join me in this house.
Philia. Yes, sir.

(SENEX *exits into* ERRONIUS' *house. As* PHILIA *disappears from roof,* MILES *appears on balcony of* SENEX's *house.*)

Miles. Oh, where is he? If he does not bring me my bride he shall see me at the height of my wrath. (*He looks down, gets dizzy, emits a tiny scream, and staggers back into house.*)

(PHILIA *enters from* SENEX's *house, as* HERO *runs on.*)

Hero. Philia!
Philia. In time to say farewell.
Hero. Did not Pseudolus give you a beaker of wine?

Philia. My religion forbids the drinking of wine.
Hero. Oh, no!
Philia. Oh, yes.
Hero. Oh, Philia.
Philia. The captain. I must go to him.
Hero. I hate him.
Philia. So do I. And I have a way to make him suffer. (*Sings:*)
Let the captain wed me and woo me,
I shall play my part!
Let him make his mad passion to me,
You will have my heart!
He can have the body he paid for,
Nothing but the body he paid for!
When he has the body he paid for,
Our revenge will start!

When I kiss him,
I'll be kissing you,
So I'll kiss him morning and night,
That'll show him!

When I hold him,
I'll be holding you,
So I'll hold him ten times as tight,
That'll show him, too!

I shall coo and tenderly stroke his hair.
Wish that you were there—
You'd enjoy it!

When it's evening
And we're in our tent for two,
I'll sit on his knee,
Get to know him
Intimately,
That'll show him
How much I really love you!

(PSEUDOLUS *enters from* LYCUS' *house.*)

Hero. Pseudolus!
Pseudolus. What has happened? Why are you not on the . . . ?

Hero. Her captain has come!

Pseudolus. Where is he?

Philia. (*Points to* ERRONIUS' *house.*) In there.

Pseudolus. In there . . . ? (*Realizes she is referring to* SENEX.) No, no, he *was* in there. He had to go to the Senate for an unexpected ovation.

Hero. Really?

Pseudolus. (*Shaking his head "no."*) Of course.

Philia. Does he still want me to wait on the roof?

Pseudolus. Yes.

Miles' Voice. (*From inside* SENEX'S *house.*) Leave me alone!

Pseudolus. No! Wait—uh—in the garden!

Philia. In the garden?

Pseudolus. Yes. Behind that large clump of myrrh!

Philia. You will tell me when he comes?

Pseudolus. Don't we always?

Philia. Oh, Hero, if only you could buy me from the captain.

Pseudolus. If Hero has the captain's contract, you will go with him? (PHILIA *nods "yes."*) It shall be arranged. Into the garden. (HERO *and* PHILIA *exit into garden behind* SENEX'S *house.* PSEUDOLUS *hums "Free" as he pushes bench center stage. He calls:*) Come out here! Come on out!

(HYSTERIUM *enters from* LYCUS' *house in virgin's dress and wig to resemble* PHILIA.)

Hysterium. You didn't tell me I'd have to be a girl!

Pseudolus. A dead girl! The captain will see you, go on his way, and all will be well.

Hysterium. No! It won't do! (*He starts back into* LYCUS' *house.*)

Pseudolus. (*Stopping him.*) Please, Hysterium. We must convince the captain.

Hysterium. That I am a beautiful dead girl?

Pseudolus. Yes.

Hysterium. He'll never believe it.

Pseudolus. He will. You're delicious.

Hysterium. What if he tries to kiss me?

Pseudolus. He won't kiss you.

Hysterium. How can he help it if I'm so delicious?

Pseudolus. Hysterium, please—just lie on the bench.

Hysterium. He'll never believe I'm a girl. Look at me. Just look at me.

Pseudolus. I can't take my eyes off you. (*Sings:*)
You're lovely,
Absolutely lovely,
Who'd believe the loveliness of you?

Hysterium. No! (*He starts away.*)

Pseudolus. Come back! (*Sings:*)
Perfect,
Sweet and warm and winsome,
Radiant as in some dream come true.
Now
Venus will seem tame,
Helen and her thousand ships,
Will have to die of shame!
(HYSTERIUM *is becoming convinced;* PSEUDOLUS *presses his advantage.*)
You're so lovely.
Frighteningly lovely,
That the world will never seem the same!

(*He gently forces* HYSTERIUM *to lie back on the bench, folds his arms. Speaks:*) Now, lie there, close your eyes, and think dead thoughts. Good! (*Starts into* SENEX'S *house, stops, with disgust, as* HYSTERIUM *sits up and sings.*)

Hysterium. I'm lovely,

Absolutely lovely,
Who'd believe the loveliness of me?
Perfect,
Sweet and warm and winsome,
Radiant as in some dream come true.

(PSEUDOLUS *forces him down on bench.*)

Now . . .
(SPEAKS:) Shouldn't I have jewelry?
Pseudolus. Jewelry? (*Thinks a moment, takes* ERRONIUS' *ring from his finger, slips it on* HYSTERIUM.)
Hysterium. Flowers.
Pseudolus. What?
Hysterium. I should have flowers. (PSEUDOLUS *runs to garden for flower, gives it to* HYSTERIUM, *who sings:*)
I'm so lovely,
Pseudolus. (*Sings:*) Literally lovely—
Both. That the world will never seem the same—
Pseudolus. You're so lovely—
Both. That the world will never seem the same!
(PSEUDOLUS *gets him down on the bench once more, covers his face with the veil, and folds his arms.*
Pseudolus. Fold the arms!
Hysterium. (*Sitting up.*) Any coins he puts in my eyes, I keep!

(PSEUDOLUS *pushes* HYSTERIUM *down.*)

First Soldier's Voice. (*Offstage.*) Ho, there! (SOLDIERS *run on in pursuit of* PANACEA, *who ducks into* SENEX's *house. Pseudolus stops* SOLDIERS.)
Pseudolus. I have been looking everywhere for you. Here is your captain's bride. Dead! (SOLDIERS *crowd around* HYSTERIUM.) Give her air! (*They jump back.*) You had best break the sad news to your captain. (SOLDIER *enters* SENEX's *house reluctantly.* PSEUDOLUS *looks at* HYSTERIUM, *then to*

SOLDIERS.) A virgin. A lot of good it did her.

(MILES *enters with* SOLDIER.)

Miles. Oh, grievous day. Men, support me! (SOLDIERS *hold him.*) How? How did she die?
Pseudolus. Well, she just sort of rolled over and . . .
Miles. Spare me! I cannot control my tears. I must cry.
Pseudolus. Go ahead, you'll feel better. Now that you have seen her, sir, I suggest you depart and torture yourself no longer. If you'll give me the contract, I—I shall dispose of the body.
Miles. Ghoul! I will not leave without the comfort of a proper funeral service! (HYSTERIUM *shakes his head* "no." PSEUDOLUS *blocks* MILES' *view.*)
Pseudolus. Sir, do you have time for that? I mean, isn't there a war somewhere you should be—
Miles. Silence! I insist on conducting a funeral.
Pseudolus. Yes, sir.
Miles. We need mourners.
Pseudolus. We have them. (*To* SOLDIERS.) Hold him firmly. (SOLDIERS *hold* MILES. PSEUDOLUS *exits into* SENEX's *house.*)
Miles. The poor girl. To have died so young, without ever having experienced . . . me.

(PSEUDOLUS *re-enters.*)

Pseudolus. Sir, they will be here presently. While we wait, would you like something to eat?
Miles. No, thank you. (*Wails, then blubbers.*) Oh, her bridal bower becomes a burial bier of bitter bereavement.
Pseudolus. Very good. Can you say,

Zero Mostel as Pseudolus, with Jack Gilford (on his back) and Ronald Holgate, at the Alvin Theater, New York, May 1962. (Van Williams)

"Titus, the tailor, told ten tall tales to Titania, the titmouse?"

Miles. Do not try to cheer me. I am inconsolable!

(COURTESANS *enter from* SENEX'S *house, with little black handkerchiefs.*)

Pseudolus. Gather around, handmaidens of sorrow.

Miles. (*Sings:*) Sound the flute,
Blow the horn,
Pluck the lute,
Forward . . . mourn!

(SOLDIERS *and* COURTESANS *wail so effectively that even* HYSTERIUM *is affected.*)

Pseudolus. (*Tragically, over the body.*)
All Crete was at her feet,
All Thrace was in her thrall.
All Sparta loved her sweetness and Gaul . . .
And Spain . . .

Miles. And Greece . . .

Pseudolus. And Egypt . . .

Miles. And Syria . . .

Pseudolus. And Mesopotamia . . .

Mourners. All Crete was at her feet.
All Thrace was in her thrall.
Oh, why should such a blossom fall?

(COURTESANS *pound on bench, frightening* HYSTERIUM, *who falls to the floor. He scrambles back on bench, lies there, his arms unfolded.*)

Miles. Speak the spells,
Chant the charms,
Toll the bells,
Pseudolus. Fold the arms!

(HYSTERIUM *slowly folds his arms.*)

Sir, on behalf of the body, I want to thank you for a lovely funeral. I don't know about you, but I've suffered enough. If you will just give me the contract, I shall take the body and . . .
Miles. (*Singing away:*)
Strew the soil,
Strum the lyre,
Spread the oil,
Build the pyre!
Pseudolus. A pyre? What kind of pyre?
Miles. A pyre of fire!
Pseudolus. Oh, a fire pyre!
Miles. She must be burned!
Pseudolus. Burned? Sir . . .
Miles. I want her ashes!
Pseudolus. Captain, I implore you. It is not for us to destroy such loveliness. The Gods are awaiting her. They would not be happy if we sent up a smoked virgin!
Miles. I cannot afford to offend the Gods.
Pseudolus. Who can?
Miles. (*Sings:*)
All Crete was at her feet,
But I shall weep no more.
I'll find my consolation as before
Among the simple pleasures of war!

Bring me the contract. (SOLDIER *hands him contract.*) I give her to the gods. (*Puts contract on* HYSTERIUM.) Take her then and lay her to rest. And I shall go my melancholy way. Men. (*Starts to go, stops.*) Wait. A farewell kiss.
Pseudolus. Of course (*Kisses* MILES *on the cheek.*)
Miles. Not you! (*Pushes him aside, bends over* HYSTERIUM.)
Pseudolus. Sir! You mustn't!
Miles. Why not?
Pseudolus. It could make you very sick. The truth is, she died of an illness contracted on Crete.
Miles. What illness?
Pseudolus. The plague!

(*There is general pandemonium.* COURTESANS *scream "The plague, the plague!" run about wildly, exiting in all directions.*)

Miles. Silence!
Pseudolus. The plague! The plague! Run for your lives! (*To audience.*) Don't just sit there! Run!

(MILES *grabs* PSEUDOLUS.)

Miles. There is no plague!
Pseudolus. What?
Miles. I have returned this day from Crete, and there is no plague.
Pseudolus. Then what was everyone yelling about?

(LYCUS *enters, hides behind pillar.*)

Miles. This girl is alive!
Hysterium. (*Jumps up.*) And she's going to stay that way! (*Runs off.*)
Miles. Stop! After her, men! (SOLDIERS *run off.*)
Pseudolus. I'll get her! (*Runs off in opposite direction.*)
Miles. Wait! (*Chases* PSEUDOLUS.)
Lycus. Now *all* the courtesans have escaped. Eunuchs! I stand to lose a for-

tune in flesh! (EUNUCH *enters from* LYCUS' *house.*) Find the girls! Bring them back! (EUNUCH *exits, chattering.* LYCUS *exits.* HYSTERIUM *re-enters, hiding face with leafy branch.*)

Hysterium. I've got to get out of these clothes!

(SENEX *enters from* ERRONIUS' *house, spots* HYSTERIUM, *goes to him.*)

Senex. Ah, there you are, my little dove! (*Cooing.*) You don't have to be afraid of me. (*Leads* HYSTERIUM *to bench, seats him on his lap.*) My slave has prepared a little feast. I want you to serve it to me in there. (*Points to* ERRONIUS' *house.*) Do you understand? Go, then.

(*They wave to each other, as* HYSTERIUM *exits into* SENEX'S *house.* SENEX *exits into* ERRONIUS' *house, singing "Everybody Ought to Have a Maid."* HYSTERIUM *pokes his head out of door and ducks back into house as he sees* EUNUCH *enter with* Vibrata. EUNUCH *pushes her into* LYCUS' *house, exits, chattering.* HYSTERIUM *starts out of house once more as* PSEUDOLUS *runs on, kicks him from behind.*)

Hysterium. PSEUDOLUS!

Pseudolus. I ought to give you worse than that! What did you do with the contract?

Hysterium. I lost it.

Pseudolus. You find it or you're going to get one of the great beatings of all time!

Miles' Voice. (*Offstage.*) He dies!

Pseudolus. Look out! (PSEUDOLUS *and* HYSTERIUM *run off in opposite directions.* MILES *runs on.*)

Miles. This way men! I have found her! (*Runs off after* HYSTERIUM, *shouting.*)

(SOLDIER *enters and runs off.* DOMINA *enters, disguised in virgin's dress and veil, removes veil from her face, addresses audience.*)

Domina. If it's a pretty face he wants . . . (PSEUDOLUS *enters behind her, gives her a swift kick. She screams. He exits.* LYCUS *enters, she turns.*) How dare you! (*She slaps* LYCUS.)

Soldier's Voice. (*Offstage.*) Here she is! Men, the virgin!

(SOLDIER *runs on, chases* DOMINA *and* LYCUS *off.* EUNUCH *enters with* PANACEA *and* TINTINABULA, *pushes them into* LYCUS' *house. He exits, chattering.* MILES *enters, as* DOMINA *re-enters.*)

Miles. My virgin!

Domina. Sir, I am not anybody's virgin.

Miles. You made that more than clear when last we met! (*He runs off.* HYSTERIUM *runs on, behind* DOMINA.)

Hysterium. The cause of it all! (*Kicks* DOMINA *in the rear. She screams. He hides behind pillar, as* LYCUS *runs on.*)

Domina. You, again! (*Swings at* LYCUS, *misses, chases him off.* HYSTERIUM *runs to* LYCUS' *house.*)

Hysterium. I have to get out of these clothes!

(SENEX *enters from* ERRONIUS' *house.*)

Senex. No, no, my dear. Wrong house. (*Chases* HYSTERIUM *around his house.*)

Hysterium. (*As he comes around the first time.*) Leave me alone!

Senex. (*Following him on the run.*) Ah, you're beautiful when you're angry!

(HERO *appears on balcony of* SENEX's *house, calls.*)

Hero. Philia! Philia! (*Exits into house.* HYSTERIUM *re-appears from behind* SENEX's *house.*)

Hysterium. Second time around! (*Exits into* SENEX's *house.*)

(PSEUDOLUS *runs on, chased by* SOLDIERS *who come at him from different directions.* PSEUDOLUS *leads them among the pillars, swings doors open, knocks two of them out and into the wings, trips* THIRD SOLDIER *who falls.* PSEUDOLUS *runs to him, takes contract from his belt.* HERO *appears on balcony.*)

Hero. All is lost?

Pseudolus. All is won! The contract!— This is what you must do—

(HERO *exits into house, as* MILES *runs on, sword drawn.* PSEUDOLUS *cowers.*)

Miles. You die! (LYCUS *runs on.*) The leper!

Lycus. Unclean! Unclean!

(MILES, PSEUDOLUS, *and* LYCUS *run off, each in a different direction.* SENEX *appears on the roof of his house, coos.*)

Senex. I know you're up here somewhere, my dear. Philia! Philia!

(*He disappears from roof as* PHILIA *enters from behind* SENEX's *house.*)

Philia. I thought I heard someone call my name. (*Exits into* SENEX's *house.*)

(EUNUCH *enters with one* TWIN, SECOND EUNUCH *enters with other* TWIN; *they bump into each other, scream, recognize each other, then all exit into* LYCUS' *house.* DOMINA *enters, hides behind pillar as* PSEUDOLUS, *disguised as eunuch, enters, chattering leading* GYMNASIA, *exits with her into* LYCUS' *house.*)

Domina. That is where my husband is! (*Knocks on* LYCUS' *door.*) I know what goes on in there!

(PSEUDOLUS *appears in upper window of* LYCUS' *house.*)

Pseudolus. Who doesn't?!

(DOMINA *goes to* SENEX's *house, cautiously looks around. Unseen by her,* HYSTERIUM *enters from same house, looks around, then* PHILIA *also enters from house, looking about. They just miss seeing each other as they go in and out of the swinging doors. Suddenly they see one another, scream, and run behind* SENEX's *house.* PSEUDOLUS *enters from* LYCUS' *house, runs to* SENEX's *house, opens door. As* PHILIA *runs on from behind house, he pushes her through the doorway, As* HYSTERIUM *passes,* PSEUDOLUS *kicks him and* HYSTERIUM *tumbles into* ERRONIUS' *house.* DOMINA *chases after* HYSTERIUM. *She is followed by* SENEX *who catches her at* ERRONIUS' *door, pushes her in, triumphantly.*)

Senex. At last!

(HERO *re-appears on balcony.*)

Pseudolus. Hero! The contract! (*Throws contract to him.*) To the harbor!

Hero. What will happen to you?

Pseudolus. Nothing. I have a potion which will make me appear as if dead.

(HERO *exits into house.* SOLDIER *staggers to his feet.*)

Soldier. You are under arrest!

(PSEUDOLUS *blows at him,* SOLDIER *falls back down.* DOMINA *enters from* ERRONIUS' *house, followed by* SENEX. PSEUDOLUS *ducks into* SENEX's *house.*)

Domina. Dearest Senex, you saw through my disguise!

Senex. Yes, beloved. (*She embraces him. He looks around for* PHILIA.)

Domina. Forgive me for mistrusting you. My darling, it's just that you have been a little distant these last twenty-nine years.

Senex. (*Starts backing off.*) Yes, beloved, yes.

Domina. Where are you going?

Senex. Business. Pressing business. (*He runs off.*)

Domina. (*Following him.*) Senex! Senex! (*Exits.*)

Erronius. (*Entering.*) Third time around! (*Starts toward his house, as* HYSTERIUM *enters from it. Seeing* ERRONIUS, *he darts back in.*) The spirit! (*Sneaks over to side of his house.* HYSTERIUM *peeks out of door, and not seeing* ERRONIUS, *tip-toes out.*) Who are you? (HYSTERIUM *trips and falls.* ERRONIUS *helps him up.*) Let me help you.

Hysterium. Thank you. I am quite all right.

Erronius. (*Seeing ring.*) Wait!

Hysterium. What is it?

Erronius. My dear one! My sweet one! My little one! (*Kisses* HYSTERIUM.)

Hysterium. Why do older men find me so attractive?

Erronius. My daughter!

Hysterium. What?

Erronius. You wear the ring with the gaggle of geese!

Hysterium. I am not your daughter!

(MILES *and* THREE SOLDIERS *run on, spot* HYSTERIUM.)

Miles. There she is!

Erronius. Yes!

Miles. My virgin!

Erronius. Those filthy pirates!

Hysterium. I am not your daughter! I . . . uh . . . I am an Etruscan dancer. (*He dances a few steps as* SENEX *re-enters.*)

Senex. Dancing with impatience, my dear?

Miles. Who is it speaks so boldly to my virgin?

Senex. Your what? She is my maid!

Erronius. She is my daughter!

(*All tug at* HYSTERIUM.)

Hysterium. Please! No fighting! That hurts! Please! (*In the tussle, without knowing it,* HYSTERIUM *loses his wig.*)

Miles. You are not the virgin!

Hysterium. (*Walks into* ERRONIUS' *arms.*) Of course not! I am this old man's baby daughter.

Senex. Hysterium!

Miles. The eunuch!

Erronius. My daughter is a eunuch?

Miles. Seize that man! (*Points to* HYSTERIUM. SOLDIERS *point swords at him.*)

Domina. (*Entering.*) Senex!

Miles. You, again?

Senex. Sir, You are speaking to my wife!

Miles. You are married to that . . . that . . .

Senex. Yes, I am married to that . . . that! And I shall thank you to release my slave and remove yourself from in front of my house!

Miles. Your house? This is the house of Lycus.

Domina. Lycus?

(*All babble at once.*)

Miles. Quiet! I declare this area under martial law!

Pseudolus. (*Entering from* SENEX'S *house and indicating* HYSTERIUM.) Release that man!

Miles. Release that man! (*Recognizes* PSEUDOLUS.) You!

Pseudolus. Sir, this quivering creature is blameless. It is I, and I alone, who have caused you this grief.

Miles. Men, unseize him and seize him! (SOLDIERS *surround* PSEUDOLUS.) And now, death by evisceration!

(PSEUDOLUS *reacts horribly.*)

Hysterium. Oh, Pseudolus!

Pseudolus. Calm, my friend. (*To* MILES.) Sir, I believe a doomed man is allowed a final request?

Miles. Yes.

Pseudolus. Allow me to take my own life.

Miles. Sir, I have seen kings with less courage.

Pseudolus. So have I. Hysterium, the potion. You know the one I mean.

Hysterium. The potion? (*Picks up cup from where he placed it earlier.*)

Pseudolus. Thank you, dear friend. Give the hemlock to Socrates.

Hysterium. (*To* SOLDIERS.) Which one of you is Socrates?

Pseudolus. Give me that! (*Takes cup, raises it.*) I go to sail on uncharted seas. To the harbor, *to the harbor* . . . (PHILIA *and* HERO *sneak out of* SENEX'S *house, exit unseen.*) . . . from which no mariner returns. Farewell. (*Drains potion, dies noisily and elaborately.* MILES *leans over him.*) Kiss me! (*He has taken the passion potion, jumps up.*) Somebody kiss me! Anybody! (*To* HYSTERIUM.) I could kill you . . . you darling!

Miles. Seize him! (SOLDIER *grabs* PSEUDOLUS *from behind.*)

Pseudolus. Thank you! I needed that!

Miles. Stop that! (*Smacks* PSEUDOLUS *in back of head.*)

(LYCUS *enters with* PHILIA. HERO *follows.*)

Lycus. Great Miles Gloriosus! I would not reveal my true identity until I could deliver that which I had promised. Sir, I am Lycus. Philia, go to the man who bought you.

(PHILIA *sighs, goes to* SENEX, DOMINA *reacts.*)

Senex. No, no.

Philia. Aren't you the . . . ?

Senex. Quiet! We're under martial law.

Lycus. There is the captain! Captain, here is your virgin.

Miles. And worth the waiting for. (*To* PSEUDOLUS.) Out of the great joy of the occasion, forgiveness. You are free.

Pseudolus. Free . . . to be a slave. (*Slumps against pillar.*)

Erronius. I cannot understand it. There was the ring. The ring with the gaggle of geese.

Miles. What did you say, old man? (MILES *extends his hand.*)

Erronius. The ring!

Miles. Father!

Erronius. You've grown! (*They embrace.*)

Philia. (*Showing ring on chain about her neck.*) Are these many geese a gaggle?

Erronius. How long have you had this?

Philia. I've had this since, I don't know when I've had this since.

Erronius. My daughter!

Miles. My sister?!

Hysterium. Pseudolus, did you hear that?

Pseudolus. Silence! Stand back, everyone! My dear old man, I take it your daughter is free born?

Erronius. Without a doubt!

Pseudolus. Lycus, as all of us know, the penalty for selling a free-born citizen is to be trampled to death by a water buffalo in heat!

Miles. Seize him!

Lycus. Careful, I'm a bleeder!

Pseudolus. (*To* LYCUS.) Bring out those girls! (*To audience.*) I told you this was to be a comedy! (As LYCUS *brings* COURTESANS *out of his house.*) Hero!

Hero. Mother and father, I wish to marry.

Senex. (*Aside to* HERO.) Son, if you are only as happy as your mother and I . . . my heart will bleed for you.

Pseudolus. (*Sings to audience, indicating* HERO *and* PHILIA.)
Lovers divided
Get coincided.
Something for everyone—

Hero and Philia. A comedy tonight!

Pseudolus. (*Indicating* SENEX *and* DOMINA.)
Father and mother
Get one another.

Domina. Something for everyone—

Senex. A tragedy tonight!

Miles. (*Holding the* GEMINAE.)
I get the twins!
They get the best!

Erronius. I get a family . . .

Hysterium. I get a rest.

Soldiers. (*Holding the other* COURTE-SANS.)
We get a few girls.

Lycus. I'll get some new girls.

Pseudolus. I get the thing I want to be:
Free!

All. Free! Free! Free! Free! Free!

(PSEUDOLUS *exits joyfully.*)

Nothing for kings,
Nothing for crowns,
Something for lovers, liars, and clowns!
What is the moral?
Must be a moral.
Here is the moral, wrong or right:

Pseudolus. (*Re-enters with* GYMNASIA.)
Morals tomorrow!

All. Comedy tonight!

CURTAIN

A marble model of a Roman stage in the Museo Nazionale Romano delle Terme, Rome, showing the *scaenae frons* with its large center door (regia) and two side doors (hospitalia), flanked by arches with rectangular sinkings, probably for the insertion of paintings. (Library and Museum of the Performing Arts, Lincoln Center)

(*Above*) The Salzburg production of *Everyman*. In this scene Jedermann is entertaining his guests at a banquet only a moment before Death seizes him. The façade of the Cathedral is in the background. (*Below*) The Nederlandse Comedie production of *Elckerlyc* in Delft, Holland. Elckerlyc is shown surrounded by relatives and friends in this rather simple, religious version of *Everyman*, performed in front of the Prinsenhof. (Netherlands Information Service—Lemaire en Wennink)

Everyman

~~~~~~

INTRODUCTION: THE MEDIEVAL PLAYWRIGHT

The most significant fact about the medieval playwright is his anonymity; the dedicated men who created the tremendous body of medieval drama, like those who built the great cathedrals, did so, not for personal fame, but for the good of the Church, the salvation of men's souls, and the greater glory of God. Though the names of few English dramatists who wrote prior to the sixteenth century have come down to us, we may be certain that all of them were connected in some way with the Church. From the tenth to the sixteenth century, hundreds of monks, priests, and brothers occupied themselves with the composition and revision of religious plays, from the simple tropes to the technically complex "moralities." These men were not "original" artists; they did not create their own material, but drew upon the stories in the Bible, the legends of the saints, or the dogmas of the Church, which they adapted and dramatized.

For almost a thousand years after the death of Christ, His life story was repeated in the liturgy and in the ritual of all the churches in Christendom. One of the most dramatic stories in the world, it was told in Latin to people who understood no Latin and who knew very little about the Bible, since they could not read. It was the problem of the Church to present to the congregation vivid images to illustrate the story of Christ's birth, passion, and resurrection. The Church began to present spectacles in which action alone revealed the content. Three dramatic essentials—action, costume, and music—were adopted by the Church and the service became more ornate and theatrical. The Easter service and the Christmas service were the most elaborate. By the end of the ninth century, in an elementary form of dramatic dialogue, Latin words were fitted to the special music sung on the high festivals. These brief exchanges of speech, which were introduced into the chanted liturgy, were known as tropes, and the men who wrote them were the forerunners of the playwrights.

By processes of growth and elaboration, the simple dialogue and action of the tropes ultimately resulted in full-length and highly developed dramas. In their first stage, these were called mystery plays and were based mainly on the events set forth in the Old and New Testaments. By the twelfth century practically all of the Bible, from the creation of the World to the Day of Judgment, had been dramatized in well-developed one-act episodes, and the dialogue was no longer written in Latin but in English. The mysteries became enormously popular and attracted great and unruly crowds to the churches.

In response to a demand for greater realism came the miracle plays, a more advanced and more secular form of the drama, which not only dealt with the Scriptures but also presented stories from the lives of the saints. The dramas were embellished with apocryphal and extraneous material, most of which was coarse and farcical; Noah's wife was usually drunk and King Herod ranted and swore.

The great cycle of plays had become so worldly and corrupt by the fourteenth century that it was ordered out of the church, and control over the liturgical drama passed from the hands of the clergy to those of laymen. The plays were taken over by the craft and trade guilds, the most important organizations in the social and economic life of a medieval town, and changed from an indoor cere-monial rite to an outdoor show. Within the church, the plays had been presented at Christmas and Easter, but the cold, wet weather in England at these seasons was unfavorable for outdoor presentations; when they left the church, therefore, the plays were incorporated into the celebration of Corpus Christi Day, a street festival in honor of the Sacrament, in existence since 1316 and occurring yearly late in May or early in June. The miracle plays immediately became the most exciting part of the procession. Although no longer Church-sponsored, the plays were revised, adapted, and elaborated from year to year by ecclesiastical writers especially employed for the purpose. The number of men engaged in this task may be judged by the fact that every important university, cathedral, and market town in England had its own cycle of plays, though only four cycles have come down to us: the York cycle of 48 plays, the Wakefield or Towneley cycle of 32 plays, the Chester cycle of 25 plays, and the Coventry cycle of 42 plays. Usually the cycle was played in one day, from sunrise to sundown, but in some towns the pageants took from three days to a full week. At Chester, they were performed on the Monday, Tuesday, and Wednesday of Whitsun week.

The final development of religious drama was the morality play, which ap-peared about the middle of the fourteenth century. The moralities were more original in invention and more complex in structure than the mystery or miracle plays; their plots were not drawn from Scripture but from well-known allegorical tales, and their characters were personifications of such abstract ideas as Wealth, Lust, and Faith. Virtue and Vice were repeatedly shown struggling for possession of Man's soul. The morality play attempted to furnish answers to the question, "What must I do—what must I believe—to be saved?" In its later development this type of play became dull, narrow, and essentially sectarian, its didacticism relieved only by the scenes of low humor; but the finest example of the morality play is a genuinely profound and moving drama called *Everyman*.

Some scholars believe that *Everyman* is a translation from a Dutch play called *Elckerlyc*, or that both plays have a common source in a Latin work called *Homulus*. It is more likely, however, judging from internal evidence and from the spirit of the piece, that the play is of English origin. It may have been written around 1475 in the reign of Edward IV.

Although we do not know the name of the play's author or a single biographical fact concerning him, it is safe to say that *Everyman* is the work of a priest or theologian. Everyman, for example, puts on the jewel of penance, later wears the robe of contrition, and then takes the seven "blessed sacraments," including "holy and extreme unction." In the final scene of the play, Everyman, holding a small wooden cross, asks his companions to touch it; in this symbolic gesture, the various personages who are the abstract concepts of Everyman's own potentialities —his strength, intellect, five wits, beauty, conscience, and good deeds—signify the full resignation of all the powers of body and soul in the acceptance of death according to God's will. The play is thus a graphic expression of Catholic doctrine relating to sin and contrition, confession, grace, and salvation.

The original source of the story of *Everyman* is the old Buddhist parable of Barlaam and Josaphat in which a man, ordered to appear before his king, applied for help to his three friends; but only one of them, who symbolized his virtue and whom he had always neglected, readily offered to accompany him and plead for him. Further details for the play were borrowed from a Scottish version of Barlaam, in which the virtuous friend was called Good Deeds. This name was particularly useful to the author of *Everyman*, for according to Catholic doctrine, good deeds—consisting chiefly of prayer, fasting, and almsgiving—are necessary to atone for evil and to obtain grace. The writer of *Everyman* also made use of ideas, themes, and actual expressions which had appeared in earlier moralities, *The Pride of Life, The Castle of Perseverance,* and *The Debate of the Body and the Soul,* and in various tales of Chaucer (*Pardoner's* and *Parson's,* for instance) which dealt with religious pilgrimages and repentance. But if this unknown playwright borrowed freely from earlier works, he also made great contributions to later morality plays as well as to the secular drama of the present day.

Everyman has a very simple plot. The strength of the play lies in the skill with which the individual scenes are developed. Although it is an allegory, the story appears to concern itself with an ordinary journey. Death, sent by God, tells Everyman to prepare himself for a long pilgrimage; the language Death uses is poignant and Everyman is struck to the heart with terror. After Death departs, Everyman appeals to his friends (Fellowship), to his close and distant relatives (Kindred and Cousin), and to his worldly possessions (Goods), but they all desert him. Good Deeds alone will accompany him, and she introduces him to her sister, Conscience, who leads him to Confession. Everyman is advised to surround himself with his most intimate friends, Intellect, Strength, Five Wits, and Beauty, and they remain close by until he approaches the very end of his journey; then one by one they leave him until, at the last, he is sustained by Good Deeds alone.

Although the author of *Everyman* depicts life in this world as a spiritual adventure, he makes this abstract concept convincingly concrete by introducing into his play human situations and vivid figures. By creating characters whose reasoning is psychologically sound and whose behavior is recognizably realistic, the author manages to engage the interest and sympathy of his audiences. Everyman, for instance, lonely and terrified in the face of death, is thoroughly understandable and moving; while the figures who surround him and display various human weaknesses, also evoke pathos and pity. Such characters are not arid personifications but possess genuine and fundamental attributes common to all of us.

The theme and structure of the play are superior to the poetry in which it is written, for the style and language are rugged and rather awkward. This irregularity and clumsiness of the outward form is a natural consequence of the conditions under which the morality was composed. It is evident that the playwright did not aim at producing a pleasing pastime, but rather an unwelcome warning; a dismal, but highly necessary, admonition. That *Everyman* was extremely popular, nevertheless, with early English audiences is attested to by the fact that four different editions of the play are extant. John Skot's edition, believed to have been published about 1530, is the basis of the version in modern English printed in this volume.

By 1550 the force of religious drama had been spent. Many men who still had religious connections were making names for themselves by writing secular interludes and chronicle history plays. This was the beginning of the literary drama in England; shortly thereafter, the first tragedies and comedies, composed in imitation of ancient classical works, made their appearance and laid the groundwork for the masterpieces of the Elizabethan age.

PRODUCTION IN THE MIDDLE AGES

The decline of the Roman Empire brought with it the degradation of classical tragedy into pantomime, and of classical comedy into farce. The tragic actor became the *pantomimus* who danced out the story of a play to the accompaniment of music, and the comic actor put on vulgar displays for the delight of ignorant audiences. The Christian church preached vehemently against these coarse and sensuous exhibitions to which the multilingual and degraded population flocked; but more important than the opposition of the Church was the contempt of the barbarians of the later invasions. The Church and the barbarians between them dealt the theater in Rome a death blow from which it never recovered, and public entertainment ended with the fall of the Empire.

Between the sixth and the tenth century, wandering mimes, jugglers, and acrobats, who were looked upon as outcasts and vagabonds, roved from town to town and with their comic antics and tricks provided entertainment for the nobleman in his home and for idle crowds in the public squares, while the ancient theater buildings fell into decay. Buildings specially constructed for the performance of plays were not to make their appearance again until the Renaissance.

Paradoxically, it was the Christian church, the formidable adversary of the drama, that actually brought the theater to life again in the Middle Ages. In seeking a way to impress the lessons of the Scriptures more forcefully on the minds of unlettered people, the Church introduced the tropes into the liturgy. The growth and development of these scenes led, as we have seen, to the creation of the mystery, miracle, and morality plays. In mounting these plays effectively, the Church became as great a producing organization as any that had existed in classical times.

The Theater

By the end of the tenth century, the churches were serving as "theaters" during the Christmas and Easter holidays. For the Easter trope, the altar at first symbolized the tomb in which the body of Christ was laid, but not very long afterwards an actual sepulcher with a lid was built of wood or iron and was set up in the north aisle. If more than one locale was required, as for the Christmas drama, Herod's Court was placed in one aisle and the manger in another. This led to the convention of setting up all the scenes of action at one time before the audience. The platform or stalls where the action took place were called *mansions* or houses and these were arranged in regular places in the church. Heaven was usually in the vicinity of the high altar, and nearby were the mansions of the holy characters; while Hell, which served as the abode of the devils, was located at the opposite side of the church building and the houses of the damned were situated near it. The actors moved from station to station around the interior of the church as they presented their long cycle of plays which was a dramatization of the Bible from Creation to Doomsday.

When the drama left the precincts of the church and became part of the Corpus Christi Day procession, the long cycles were broken up into separate scenes, each of which became the property of one of the trade guilds of the town, the members of the guild being made responsible for its production. Some of the guilds chose to produce scenes which were particularly related to their trades; the shipwrights took over *The Building of the Ark,* the fishers and mariners *Noah and the Flood,* and the butchers *The Crucifixion.*

Since the plays were performed as part of a procession, the stationary stage, or *mansion,* was replaced by the pageant-wagon. This was a scaffold on wheels that could be dragged through the streets, something like our modern "floats," but two stories high; the lower story was curtained off and used as a dressing room, while the upper story, reached by a ladder, served as a stage. When the pageant-wagon stopped at the stations in the town where people had gathered to see the plays, the actors performed not only on the upper story of the wagon but descended to the street and used the open area (called the *platea*) in front of the wagon.

It is quite likely that the earliest Morality plays were presented in cyclic form, that is, in a series of scenes on moving pageant-wagons, but by the late fifteenth century, with the appearance of such full-length works as *The Castle of Perseverance* and *Everyman,* the method of production had changed radically. The full-fledged Morality was not performed by the members of a guild but by a troupe of traveling players at one time and at one place, probably the town square or village green. The plays were advertised in advance and audiences gathered at the appointed place on the day of the performance; this was standard practice for the roving acting companies but its major drawback was that the players had to pass the hat for contributions in order to stay in business. The solution to the problem lay in finding a nobleman who would subsidize the company, or an inn yard which could be rented and filled with people who were willing to pay the price of admission. These conditions of production actually came into use during the first half of the sixteenth century and served for the presentation of interludes and chronicle history plays. The inn yard, as we shall see, was the immediate precursor of the Elizabethan theater.

The Audience

It was not for an "audience" that the earliest medieval drama was written but for a church congregation. Very little mention is made of the first spectators since they probably preserved an attitude of silent and serious devotion as the tropes were being enacted. There are a few facts concerning them, however, of which we are quite certain: They were all members of the same religious faith; they represented, socially, a cross-section of the population from prince to peasant; they probably attended services in increasing numbers as a result of the pleasure they took in the literary and dramatic embellishments of the liturgy; and, finally, with the introduction of a great deal of secular material into the plays, their boisterousness and loss of reverence made their presence in the church undesirable.

The miracle plays, which were performed on pageant-wagons that were trundled through the public streets, attracted much more heterogeneous and unruly audiences. The people got up at about four in the morning on Corpus Christi Day and took their places at the city gate, on the village green, and at the various other stations in the town where the wagons were scheduled to stop. Some sat in convenient windows or on wooden "bleachers" erected for the occasion. People of all faiths, or of no faith, were attracted—nobles, clergy, merchants, craftsmen, peasants, and paupers, all joking and jostling, exchanging obscene remarks with the actors and giving vent to ribald laughter. The coarseness and blasphemy that had been kept under a modicum of restraint within the church went completely out of bounds in the market-place.

The audience which later attended the moralities was more subdued and intent, since the plays contained literary, ideological, and theatrical elements that were rather complex; and if admission fees were charged for these performances, the audience was still more select and restrained than the roving street crowds.

The sixteenth century brought an additional refinement of the audience, but even in the heyday of the Elizabethan drama playgoers were not in the habit of listening with rapt attention unless a particular character or scene captivated them. It was much more common practice for them to gape and to gossip and to stuff themselves with food while the play was going on. It was at this time, in fact, that the "private playhouses" were created for the ladies and gentlemen who were willing to pay extremely high prices in order to escape the "noisy rabble" that haunted the public theaters.

The Actors

The medieval actor was primarily an amateur; it was not until the last days of the fifteenth century that semiprofessional and professional acting troupes came into existence. The first "actors," of course, were the priests and minor canons in the churches who chanted the tropes in Latin. By the end of the tenth century they had received specific directions for the enactment of their parts from Bishop Ethelwold of Winchester, who wrote concerning the proper method of performing the *Quem Quaeritis:*

> While the third lesson is being chanted, four brethren [of the church] shall costume themselves. One of these, dressed in an alb [a white linen robe], shall enter as though to take part in the service, and, stationing himself at the tomb [altar] without attracting attention, shall sit there quietly with a palm-branch in his hand. Then the other three shall approach dressed in copes [long, flowing garments], bearing in their hands censers with burning incense, and walking carefully as those who seek something, approach the tomb. When he who sits there beholds the three approach, he shall begin to sing in a soft, sweet voice, "Whom do you seek?" And when he has sung it to the end, the three shall reply in unison, "Jesus of Nazareth"; and he shall say, "He is not here . . ." And he shows them the place bare save for the linens from Christ's body . . . and they shall hold them up in the face of the clergy, as if to demonstrate that the Lord has risen and is no longer wrapped in them. They shall sing the anthem, "The Lord is Risen from the Tomb," and shall place the linens upon the altar. Then the priest, sharing their joy at the triumph of Christ over death, shall begin the hymn, "We praise Thee, O Lord," and this begun, all the bells chime out together.

Ethelwold became, in effect, one of our first play directors; and here we see him concerned with principles of staging and acting that have persisted to the present day. The Angel is to enter "without attracting attention," which modern directors would term "stealing" into place; the Three Marys are to pretend they are seeking something, which is the imitation of an action; the properties and costumes help to characterize the actors—the voluminous copes, for instance, heighten the illusion that the three priests, acting the Marys, are women; and, most significantly, there are specific directions for the interpretation, or "reading" of the lines, indicating the emotional and tonal qualities desired.

Since medieval drama was as international as the Church that sponsored it, the techniques of production varied only slightly from country to country. In the French mystery play *The Representation of Adam*, dating from the twelfth century, the text embodies explicit directions to the actor. It says:

> Adam shall be trained well to speak at the right moment, so that he may come neither too soon nor too late. Not only he, but all shall be well practiced in speaking calmly, and making gestures appropriate to the things they say; they shall neither add nor omit any syllable of the meter; all shall express themselves in a distinct manner, and say in consecutive order all that is to be said.

And in *Herodes*, an English play of roughly the same period, the actor who was to assume the title role was expressly instructed to "tear a passion to tatters." The directions state:

Then let Herod, having seen the prophecy, kindled with rage, hurl the book to the floor; but let his son, hearing the tumult, advance to calm his father.

When, in the fourteenth century, control over the liturgical drama passed from the Church to the craft guilds, the priests began to withdraw as actors and the members of the guild took over as performers. The great care which the towns took in selecting players for their pageants and in providing beautiful, eye-filling productions was based less on their religious devotion than on their business acumen. The plays attracted great crowds to the towns, where local merchants were eager to receive them, and where high prices were charged for convenient places to view the performances. It was for this reason that the civic authorities involved themselves in the production of the plays; if a town was particularly generous in its treatment of players, people with acting talent would come to it from neighboring towns, from other cycle-towns, and from London. No expense was spared in entertaining the actors. The companies not only paid the actors for their services, but also kept them generously supplied with food and drink. Although the actors were expected to be letter perfect in their parts, a prompter was paid to hold the book and supply the lines when lapses occurred. The actors often rehearsed for weeks before the performance; if their memories failed too often, or they acted carelessly, both they and their companies were fined for the dishonor which they had brought on the town—they by their pageant-masters, and their companies by the town council.

The account-books of the guilds give us some idea of what the actors received for their services. A man who hanged Judas got only fourpence, but he received an additional fourpence for crowing like a cock when Peter denied his Lord; four Saved Souls were paid five shillings and four Damned Souls received an equal amount. A man who played God earned sixpence, while the actors who portrayed Noah and his wife received one shilling and sixpence between them; eleven years later, in 1494, God's salary was raised to tenpence and Noah and Mrs. Noah earned one shilling and eightpence.

The roles that the medieval actors were called upon to portray did not require "characterization" in the modern sense of the word, as the figures in the cycle plays were mainly one-dimensional and fell into one of three well-defined groups. First, there were the serious characters who won the audience's reverence or sympathy: God, Christ, Mary, Abraham and Isaac, the Good Angels, and the Saved Souls. In the second group were the characters who, mainly because of their opposition to Christ, aroused the hatred or scorn of the spectators; these included Judas, Herod, Annas and Caiaphas, and Pilate. The third group consisted of the supporting characters who might be good or evil, serious or comic, depending upon the purpose of the episode in which they appeared; among these were Mrs. Noah, Mak, the Soldiers at Christ's tomb, Lucifer, and a huge assortment of Devils.

The actors in the first group, who strove to evoke awe and respect, were rather restrained in their speech and in their body movements, since they usually expressed the quieter emotions of joy and hope, pity and pain. Those in the second group—the tyrants and the enemies of Christ—used voice, gesture, and grimace with unrestrained violence and passion, which accounts for the indelible impression they made upon the minds of the spectators, and for their enormous popularity. The actors in the third group were mostly comedians who keyed their performances to the taste of the illiterate street crowd; they specialized in knock-about farce seasoned with coarse jests and japes. The expert comic actor had the combined talents of the clown, the dancer, the juggler, and the acrobat, and when he represented a devil or an evil spirit he went to the most extreme lengths in leaping, shouting, and making hideous faces.

With the decline of religious feeling in the fourteenth and fifteenth centuries, people began to lose interest in the long cycle plays, and the guilds no longer found it profitable to support them. But the attraction of the drama still held, and a number of skilled players, aware of the opportunities in a new and uncrowded field, deserted their regular trades and became "strollers." By giving up their memberships in the craft guilds, the players entered the ranks of vagabonds and masterless men, subject to arrest and imprisonment; but that did not deter them from traveling about the country and practicing their art. Morality plays and interludes, which admitted more and more secular and comic elements as time went on, formed the stock in trade of the strolling players.

These companies performed on the village green, in town halls, and in the homes of members of the nobility; the acting troupe usually consisted of only four men and a boy, so that it was often necessary for each of the actors to fill two or three parts in the play. The strollers faced many other difficult conditions. In the first place, they had to work with very poor material; they themselves recognized that their plays were crude, but they did not have the ability to improve them. Then they had to drum up their own audiences; this meant riding around the countryside continually to announce the performances a week in advance of the dates on which they were to be given. Furthermore, since the contributions of the spectators were made on a voluntary basis, the livelihood of the players was extremely precarious. Actors had to resort to tricks and devices of many kinds in order to make audiences part with their money. The appearance of the comic devil, who was always a popular figure, was withheld, for example, until after the collection plate had been passed; and suggestive actions and coarse jokes became standard features of the performance.

Because their financial gains were so small and the manner in which they got them so unconventional, itinerant players found that their reputations were deteriorating rapidly and stringent statutes were being passed against them. These local laws severely hampered the activities of the strolling players. The more talented among them managed to escape from this difficult situation by putting themselves under the protection of important personages, for as "servants" of the great they could no longer be classed as vagabonds. Actors who wore the badges of noble houses could travel about without fear of being molested, and from the fifteenth century on we hear of strolling companies operating under this arrangement. It was not until the sixteenth century, however, when men like the Earl of Leicester and Lord Strange lent their names and their support to companies of players that the greatest troupes of the Elizabethan era developed. Inept and anonymous as he was, the strolling player formed an important link in the chain that led from the old mimes and minstrels to the masters of tragic and comic acting who appeared in the plays of Shakespeare.

Scenery and Lighting

The medieval stage did not lack scenery, but it was usually simple and inclined to be symbolic. The altar of the church originally stood as a symbol for the tomb of Christ; later a simple tomb of wood or iron was built. The various mansions or houses, that were set up inside the church for the dozen or so scenes of action required in the early liturgical plays must have been small and plainly furnished or the aisles could not have accommodated them.

Heaven, in the French mystery play of *Adam*, was to be decorated as follows: "Paradise shall be situated in a rather prominent place, and is to be hung all around with draperies and silk curtains to such a height that the persons who find themselves in Paradise are seen from their shoulders upward. There shall be seen sweet smelling flowers and foliage; there shall be different trees covered with fruit, so that the place may appear very agreeable."

If Heaven was most tasteful and attractive in its décor, Hell was most elaborate and terrifying; for Hell-mouth a great dark hole was necessary into which the capering devils dragged the sinners and from which huge billows of smoke issued forth along with the clash of pots and kettles and shouts of jubilation.

The scenery on the upper level of the pageant-wagon could not have been large or ornate because of the limited space; and yet fountains, arbors, and even clouds were constructed there. Even simultaneous staging was frequently practiced; if two scenes, a forest and a palace, for example, were required for a play, both would be indicated on the pageant-wagon at the same time. At one side of the stage, two trees would represent the forest; at the other side of the stage, a large gilded chair would represent the throne in the palace. The actor, having to make a journey from the forest to the palace, would leave his position near the trees, circle the stage several times, and come to a halt near the chair.

The setting for the Christ child in the manger, which should have been simple, was presented rather lavishly by the mercers of Chester, who decorated their pageant-wagon with yards of velvet, satin, and silk damask in various colors and of silk taffeta of parrot green.

The sets used for the morality plays, which were mounted in open fields or in town squares and which therefore had to be transportable, could not have been any more elaborate than those used on the pageant-wagons. Pageant-wagons, in fact, or two-story scaffolds which resembled them, might very well have served as the settings for *The Castle of Perseverance* and for *Everyman*. The manuscript of the former play merely calls for a castle and close to it a bed for Mankind; *Everyman*, too, could be adequately performed on a two-story scaffold with an open playing space around it. The open space, or *platea*, was an unlocalized stage, which means that it might represent any place. It might be neutral territory, or it might represent a very definite locality made clear to the audience by the words and actions of the characters. This convention of a clearly defined house with an unlocalized stage in front of it was carried over into the Elizabethan theater.

From all accounts, there was a notable absence of realism in the scenery, nor could there have been many realistic lighting effects, as the plays were presented outdoors in ordinary daylight. This made it necessary for the writers of the medieval period, as it did for the Elizabethans much later, to establish time and place by putting such information into the speeches of the actors. In the Towneley *Jacob*, the old patriarch announces:

> The sun is down, what is best?
> Here purpose I all night to rest;
> Under my head this stone shall lie;
> A night's rest take will I.

Special lighting effects, such as burning candles and flaming torches, as well as the more elaborate spectacle of houses or altars being consumed by fire, were much in use.

Costumes and Make-up

If the medieval actor received rather scant help from the scenery, he relied very heavily upon costumes, make-up, and properties to strengthen his characterization. But since the medieval man knew little and cared less about historical accuracy, theatrical costumes might be realistic, symbolic, or fantastic, with all three styles frequently used in a single play.

The priests who took part in the presentation of the tropes, even when representing secular figures, wore lavish church vestments known as albs and copes, and carried palm branches and censers in their hands. The manuscript of the play of *Adam* directs that "the Savior shall appear, robed in a dalmatica [an elaborate ecclesiastical garment]; Adam and Eve place themselves in front of him, Adam dressed in a red tunic, Eve in a white garment and white silk veil."

While the liturgical plays were put on under its sponsorship, the Church provided all costumes and properties; but after the plays were taken over by the trade guilds, the costumes and properties were generally made by guild members. Ecclesiastical gowns and utensils needed for certain scenes might be borrowed, rented, or bought from the Church. Since the aim of each pageant-master was to be ostentatious rather than correct, the productions, on the whole, were rich, gaudy, splendid, and anachronistic.

God was usually represented only by a voice, but when He did appear on stage it was with a gilded face and in a costume of white leather, possibly also gilded; one property list calls for "five sheep-skins for God's coat." Christ, too, was clothed in white leather to symbolize nakedness and purity. Adam and Eve, the only other characters one might expect to see unclothed, apparently wore costumes of some sort. In the property list of the Norwich grocers' *Creation of Eve*, we find "a red rib, a tail for the Serpent, two coats and a pair of dyed stockings for Eve, a coat and dyed stockings for Adam, and two wigs for Adam and Eve."

The Saints and Prophets were generally dressed in church vestments—dalmatics and stoles. Some were further individualized by special costumes and properties: John the Baptist wore a shaggy cloak, had long hair and a beard, and carried a palm-branch; Moses held the Tables of the Law; and Balaam plied his spurs to the ass (made of wood or canvas) upon which he rode.

The "villains" were dressed with equal care, their costumes very often being more intricate and more interesting than those of the holier characters. Herod was an extremely ostentatious figure, who frequently wore armor and a sword. Judas traditionally appeared in a red wig and a red beard. Lucifer as the "angel bright" was dressed in white and gold, but after his fall he became a "devil full dark" and appeared in black. Similarly, the Good Angels and the Saved Souls wore white, while their evil counterparts wore black.

Symbolic and fantastic costumes persisted down to the sixteenth century and were much in evidence in the morality plays. In *The Castle of Perseverance*, the four daughters of God wore cloaks whose colors had symbolic significance: Mercy appeared in white, Righteousness in red, Truth in green, and Peace in black.

The costumes of the devils, particularly of the Vice, or comic devil, were extravagantly fantastic and specially designed, with grotesque animal heads and bodies, to frighten and impress the spectators. A stage property particularly characteristic of the devil, and one of which he made frequent use, was gunpowder—possibly because it suggested fire and brimstone. An extremely interesting description of a performance put on by devils states: "These devils were all clad in skins of wolves, calves, and rams, surmounted with sheep-heads, bullhorns, and cockscombs, with girdles of thick skins, from which hung cows' or mules' bells with horrible noise. Some carried in their hands black rods full of squibs [firecrackers]; others long flaming spars, on which at each turn they threw handfuls of powdered resinous pitch from which issued terrible flame and smoke."

The figure of Death in *Everyman* was made up to look like a skeleton and carried a scythe, or a six-foot length of board to symbolize a coffin.

Such startling and spectacular effects help to account for the popularity of the medieval theater.

Music and Dance

The medieval drama grew out of, and was always closely associated with, music. The chanted liturgy gave birth to the trope and the trope itself was chanted. As the mystery and miracle plays developed, the singing of the church choir supplied background accompaniment to the dramatic action.

There was a general hostility toward the practical use of musical instruments in the medieval Church, perhaps because they had been used by minstrels for many centuries to accompany romantic and bawdy songs; but once the drama left its religious confines, it drew many minstrels and musicians into its own orbit.

The trade guilds hired expert instrumentalists as well as the best available actors to enliven their productions. The musicians supplied background music for the plays; their tones were soft and sweet for certain dramatic moments, loud and furious for others. Music was even introduced on occasions which we would consider most inappropriate for it; for the scene depicting Christ disputing with the doctors in the temple, for example, the Chester smiths were advised to "get minstrels with pipes, tabors, and flutes" to accompany the action.

In addition to instrumental music, there was a great deal of singing, both accompanied and unaccompanied, in the cycle plays. Many of them end with the characters or with a chorus of angels intoning the *Te Deum*. In the Coventry play, *The Magi, Herod, and the Slaughter of the Innocents*, three songs are sung; one of them is a touching lullaby addressed by a chorus of women to their infants in arms.

Music played an even more important part in the productions of the strolling players. To begin with, it was necessary for the strollers to send banner-bearers ahead of the company to announce the plays, present their authority for performing them, and ask that the audience gather on time and create no disturbance. These "advance men" undoubtedly entered the various towns sounding their pipes and drums in order to attract crowds to whom they could make their announcements. Then songs, dances, and incidental music were introduced into the performances not only to heighten the theatrical effectiveness of the dramatic action but for the sheer entertainment of the pleasure-seeking audiences.

The musical element certainly became more pronounced as the plays turned from religious to secular subjects. The musical instruments most commonly used to accompany the speech, the songs, and the dances in medieval drama were lutes, psalteries, viols, trumpets, horns, flutes, pipes, drums, and bells. Music became so integral a part of theatrical production that when the first regular theater was built in 1576 a Music Room was provided for the men who supplied the musical accompaniment for the Elizabethan drama.

THE PRODUCTION RECORD

Everyman was originally produced during the second half of the fifteenth century and was performed with fair regularity for about seventy-five years by semiprofessional and professional acting companies. Although the play was known in Holland as well as in England, no production records regarding it survive from that period in either country.

After a lapse of about four hundred years, William Poel, the founder of the Elizabethan Stage Society, mounted the first modern production of the old morality play on July 7, 1901, in the Great Hall of the Charterhouse in London. Poel directed the play, designed the set and costumes, and, in the role of Death, gave a remarkable and grotesque study of the character; in later productions he took the part of God. The play was acted in strict accordance with the text; there were no cuts, alterations, or transpositions. Poel always insisted upon the rapid and clear speaking of the verse with varied emphasis. The scenery represented the interior of a medieval chapel, but the playing area remained bare. The costumes were copied from those worn by the figures in early-fifteenth-century

Flemish tapestries, which suggests that Poel was among those who believed that the play was originally Dutch.

After its premiere, the play was repeated on the 13th and the 20th of July, 1901, in the Master's Court of the Charterhouse, in outdoor performances. For the next fifteen years, Poel mounted innumerable productions of the play in theaters, churches, college quadrangles, and public halls, indoors and out, in various sections of London. Many actors who were later to become famous appeared in these early productions; among them were Edith Wynne-Matthison, Charles Rann Kennedy, Lewis Casson, Robert Atkins, and Russell Thorndike. Early in the play's career, Philip Ben Greet, became associated with Poel as co-producer, director, and actor, and it was Ben Greet who brought *Everyman* to America.

In 1911 Max Reinhardt, the great German director, having seen Poel's production of the play, decided to mount his own version of *Everyman*. The script was revised and modernized by the poet and playwright Hugo von Hofmannsthal, and an original musical score was composed for the production by Einar Nilson. The premiere of *Jedermann*, as the play was called in German, took place on December 1 at the Zirkus Schumann in Berlin. Hofmannsthal removed from the old morality play a great deal of the religious ritual and dogma that emphasized Everyman's approaching death, and highlighted instead the protagonist's insatiable lust for life. An elaborate and spectacular banquet scene—involving singing, dancing, feasting, and lovemaking—became the central feature of the German production. The play was done in arena style in a huge old circus building but Reinhardt had no trouble filling the house. Except during World War II, *Jedermann* has been performed regularly each year in the Salzburg Cathedral square, where it may still be seen during the summer season.

The medieval pageant-wagon. The engraving was based on contemporary descriptions. The wagons were wheeled into town squares for the performances, and the audience crowded around them.

ACTING THE PART OF JEDERMANN
An Interview with Will Quadflieg

Will Quadflieg, one of the stars of the German theater, a handsome and vital man, has been playing the title role of Jedermann since 1951. When Quadflieg took over the part, he realized that he was carrying on an important tradition at the Salzburg Festival; Alexander Moissi, who created the role for Reinhardt, had achieved world-wide fame as Everyman, and, after the Second World War, Attila Hörbiger also won acclaim for his performance.

In 1951 Quadflieg was thirty-six years old and a matinee idol; he confesses today that he suffered then from the same weaknesses of character that beset Everyman—an extravagant love of life, and an excessive earthiness, materialism, and superficiality. For that first season, Quadflieg went through five weeks of intensive rehearsal under the direction of Ernst Lothar, but lacking a perspective on the character he was portraying, his performances left a great deal to be desired.

Now that he is ten years older, has suffered many profound and enlightening experiences, has an entirely different outlook on life, has studied the character of Everyman more seriously, and has enacted it more than fifty times, he feels that he has made the role his own. He now comes to Salzburg for only the last week of rehearsals, but the continuing development of his own personality has enabled him to enrich his performance to a greater degree every summer.

"Time passes mercilessly," says Quadflieg, "and it becomes a conscious and poignant experience when the members of the company greet each other each year. Many a colleague who had been playing with us for years has passed away, and now another dresses in his costume and speaks his words. We ourselves, those who go on playing, have changed and developed. It rarely happens in the life of an actor that every year he is able to shape the same role anew with unbroken continuity, and let his own inner and outer maturation flow into the formation of the character. The main point, however, is to find a new approach each time the part is played. My basic concept is that Everyman has been completely seduced by the good things of the world—food, women, clothes, and all sensual pleasures—and is too unmindful of the life of the spirit. That is the impression I try to create as forcefully as I can. Obviously, this idea never occurred to me when I myself resembled Everyman, but as I've grown older and more mature, I've also become more objective and am now able, paradoxically, to portray Everyman's weaknesses not only with greater understanding but with greater abandon and verisimilitude. There is a little chapel not far from the cathedral square where the figure of Christ on the Cross writhes in intense suffering; I go there often to study it because this religious work seems to me to have the same meaning as the play; at any rate, both point the way to Man's redemption."

From a technical point of view, says Quadflieg, performing on an outdoor stage presents special difficulties for the actor. He is not assisted by lighting, scenery, or any of the other productional advantages of an indoor theater. The actor never feels so alone and so completely thrown upon his own resources as when he plays out-of-doors. "You are the loneliest man in the world," says Quadflieg, "because all of your power and skill must come from within."

The first problem is that of controlling the audience's concentration and attention; getting close to the audience is most difficult when the sun is shining and the wind is blowing. The actor's only solution is to develop his powers of projection. Then there is the problem of the language barrier; Jedermann speaks German while at least half the audience has no knowledge of the language. To reach people who do not understand what is being said, the actor must be in command of a rich "vocabulary" of gesture, miming, facial expression, and vocal variety. "The object," Quadflieg believes, "is to find the religious ecstasy in the role, sometimes attained only for seconds, but if it can be found the audience can be reached. In this connection, 'breath' and 'spirit' are very closely related; if the actor has great reserves of breath an impression of 'breadth' of spirit is communicated to the audience. But the task of the actor is more difficult today than it was when *Jedermann* was first performed, because the world is certainly 'colder' and more lacking in faith. It cannot be denied that when Alexander Moissi spoke the Lord's Prayer for the first time the emotional and spiritual conditions were essentially different from those of the present. Now it almost verges on the blasphemous to utter the Lord's Prayer in the presence of a crowd of people that has flocked together from every corner of the globe to 'take the show in' with their cameras instead of with their hearts, so that it is absolutely incumbent upon the actor to make the audience believe that the prayer issues from the distress, the anxiety, the sweat, and the tears of a lost soul. The basic facts and truths of life remain the same, but searching, erring man, enslaved by matter, is, today, more than ever, in need of insight, of self-realization, and of mercy."

Quadflieg is of the opinion that in playing Everyman he is acting in the great tradition not only of those who went before him in this particular role but of all the actors of the Greek and medieval theaters who performed out-of-doors before large groups of people in plays of religious significance. That is the "great world theater." In such a theater modern techniques of acting are useless. The object is to combine the ancient form of acting with the modern world of nerves; instead of psychological introspection, the actor must work for physical projection —instead of cultivating his sensitivity, he must develop his throat, chest, and belly, his physiological and psychic force and power. Although *Jedermann* is written in rhymed couplets, Quadflieg acts against the lines with rich humor and forceful realism, "because the main job is to seize the audience and take it with you at every moment."

Quadflieg defines acting as "a controlled trance"—a balance between the intellect and the emotions; it is reality governed by form and style. But the word "trance" is misleading if it suggests effortlessness, for the role of Everyman is so taxing that Quadflieg did not want to play it in 1959; he wanted a rest from it for a year, but he finally gave in to the director's entreaties. Here again there is a challenge for the actor, for no matter how tired or drained he feels, his performance must always be fresh and alive even if he is acting "with his blood." "I agreed to do it again," says Quadflieg, "because the Cathedral rises behind and above us like a protecting shield, and the old, grand architecture of the cathedral square—strong with its timeless and incomparable form—surrounds, sustains, and succors us."

THE FIGURE OF DEATH
An Interview with Ernst Deutsch

Ernst Deutsch, an actor on the German-speaking stage for over thirty-five years, who appeared in many of Reinhardt's outstanding productions, has been performing the role of Death in the Salzburg *Jedermann* for more than a decade. Although the role is not a long one, the actor has worked continually on the intricacies of its interpretation and as a result is able to create a powerful and terrifying impression. One of the gestures that he is called upon to make is, Deutsch believes, the most significant in the entire play. That gesture is made at the moment when Death stands face to face with Everyman who is carousing at a banquet and is oblivious of the fact that his last hour is at hand. Everyman speaks scornfully to Death. In reply, Death merely lifts his hand and places it over the heart of Everyman who collapses with an expression of pain and astonishment on his face. It is this gesture, as Deutsch sees it, that contains the quintessence not only of his characterization but also of the central theme of the play.

The part of Death has been called metaphorical and other-worldly and the actor is made up, therefore, in nonrealistic garb. His costume, like the one that William Poel designed for this character, is based on the medieval practice of representing Death as a skeleton. Deutsch's head is completely hidden by a mask that was actually molded from his own features and then painted to show hollow eyes and cheeks and a skull as bald as bone. The actor's body is covered by a tight-fitting black cotton tricot leotard on which are painted the white bones of a skeleton. Over the costume, Deutsch wears a full black cape with a tall, standing collar. Death envelops himself in the cape when he speaks to Everyman.

Death appears in only four scenes in the play. He is seen for the first time when the Lord summons him and orders him to go as a messenger in search of Everyman. He seems, on this occasion, to rise up out of the earth, as he climbs the stairs behind the platform stage. After the Lord has dismissed him, Death returns the way he came. The "ascending" and "descending" of this figure symbolize his connection with the underworld.

Death's second appearance occurs during the banquet scene. Everyman leaves his seat and strolls off with the Courtesan; Death silently enters and takes Everyman's place at the table. None of the guests is aware of Death's presence; suddenly Everyman turns around, sees Death, and sinks down in a faint. Then Death disappears without having uttered a word. Hofmannsthal obviously borrowed this scene from Shakespeare's *Macbeth,* with Death and Everyman in the roles of Banquo's ghost and the King.

Everyman is sitting at the table, reveling with his companions, when Death enters for the third time. The black-robed figure rises directly behind the chair of Everyman and seems to tower above him (the actor has actually mounted an extra little platform that is invisible to the audience). Everyman asks, "And who's there behind me?" Death replies, "I was sent to thee . . . ," whereupon Everyman begins to laugh in ridicule at the unbidden guest. Death slowly raises his arm to its full length, reaches over Everyman's shoulder, and places his hand upon Everyman's heart. Everyman sinks down but does not die; then a conversation follows between Everyman and Death. Death advises the stricken man to use well the short time remaining to him and to be a good Christian, and then he departs.

Later in the play, at the very moment before Everyman rejects Mammon (his wealth), Death appears for the last time, looks deeply at Everyman, raises his arm in a beckoning gesture—as if to announce that it is time for Everyman to answer the Lord's summons—and then leaves without speaking a word.

From the point of view of the number of lines assigned him, Death has a negligible part in the play; and yet each appearance of this character is so fraught with meaning, and the moment at which his cold hand falls upon Everyman's heart is a symbol of such universal significance, that a chill grips the heart of every spectator and the actor becomes aware of the great importance of his role.

〰 *Everyman*

PUT INTO MODERN ENGLISH BY RANDOLPH GOODMAN

CHARACTERS

GOD (Adonai)

MESSENGER	CONSCIENCE
DEATH	CONFESSION
EVERYMAN	BEAUTY
FELLOWSHIP	STRENGTH
KINDRED	INTELLECT
COUSIN	FIVE SENSES
GOODS	ANGEL
GOOD DEEDS	DOCTOR OF THEOLOGY

Here begins a tale of how the High Father of heaven sends Death to summon every creature to come and give an account of his life in this world; and it is in the manner of a moral play.

(*Enter* MESSENGER *as Prologue.*)

Messenger. I hope that you in the audience
Will watch this drama with reverence;
It is called *The Summoning of Everyman,*
And in the form of a moral play
Tells of the few days we are given to spend,   5
How we live our lives, and how they end.
This matter is awesome truly,
But the purpose of it is holy
And sweet to bear away.
The story says: Man, in the beginning,   10
Take heed, and give deep thought to the ending,
Be you ever so merry today!
In the beginning you think sin very sweet;
But in the end it causes the soul to weep,
When the body lies in clay.   15
Here you will see how Fellowship and Jollity,
Strength, Pleasure, and Beauty,
Will fade from you like the flower in May.
And you will see how our heaven's King
Calls Everyman to a general reckoning.   20
Now listen, and hear what he has to say. (*Exit* MESSENGER.)

(GOD *speaks.*)

God. I perceive, here in my majesty,
How ungrateful to me is all mankind,
Living without dread in worldly prosperity;
Without spiritual insight, the people are so blind   25
And drowned in sin, they know me not for their God;
Only worldly riches is on their mind,
They fear not my righteousness, my sharp rod.
My law that I taught, when I died for them,
They clean forget, and the shedding of my blood.   30
I was hanged between two, no one can deny;
To bring life to them I consented to die;
I healed their feet; my head was torn with thorns.
I could do no more than I did, truly;
And now I see the people all forsake me.   35
They commit the seven deadly sins damnable,
So that pride, avarice, wrath, and lechery
Are now in the world made so commendable,
That men cannot hope to live in the angels' company.
Every man seeks thus after his own pleasure,   40
And yet his life is by no means secure.
I see the more that I forbear
The worse they are from year to year.
Everything alive degenerates;
Therefore I will make great haste
To have a reckoning of every man's person;   46
For, if I leave the people thus alone
In their lives and wicked tempers,
Surely they will become much worse than beasts.
For now they eat each other up with envy,   50
Not one so much as thinks of charity.
I had hoped that every man

Would dwell forever in my glory,
And I decreed that all be saved;
But now I see, like outcast traitors,
all depraved,   55
They neither thank me for the joy I
meant for them,
Nor even for the life I have lent to
them.
I offered the people abundant mercy,
But there are few who pray for it
earnestly.
They are so encumbered with
worldly riches   60
That instead of mercy I must do jus-
tice
On every man living without fear.
Where are you, Death, you mighty
messenger?

(*Enter* DEATH.)

Death. Almighty God, I am here at
hand
To submit to your will and obey your
command.   65
God. Go now to Everyman,
And tell him, in my name,
Of a pilgrimage he must undertake,
Which he in no way may escape;
And that he must bring with him a
strict reckoning   70
Without delay or tarrying.
Death. My Lord, in the world I will run
everywhere,
And sternly search out both rich and
poor;

(GOD *withdraws.*)

I will attack every man who lives like
a beast,
Against God's laws, with no fear in
his heart.   75
He who loves riches I will strike with
my dart,
To blind his sight, and bar him from
heaven.
Unless Alms is his good friend,

He shall dwell in hell till the world
shall end.   79

(*Enter* EVERYMAN.)

Look, there I see Everyman walking;
He gives little thought to my coming.
His mind is on fleshly lusts and on
treasure,
Which shall make him endure pain
without measure,
Before the Lord, heaven's King.
Everyman, stand still! Where are you
going   85
So blithely? Have you forgotten your
Maker?
Everyman. Why do you ask?
Do you really want to know?
Death. Yes, I do. Listen to me:
I have been sent to you hastily   90
By God in his majesty.
Everyman. What, sent to me?
Death. Yes, certainly.
Though you have forgotten him
here,
He thinks of you in the heavenly
sphere,   95
As, before we part, you shall know.
Everyman. What does God desire me to
do?
Death. That will not take me long to
say:
He wants to have a reckoning
Without any longer delay.   100
Everyman. To give such a reckoning, I
need more than a day;
For this grave matter fills my heart
with dismay.
Death. You must take on yourself a
long journey;
And bring your book of account with
you,
And make very sure your reckoning
is true,   105
For to come back there is no way.
Then you shall answer to God, and
show

Your many bad deeds, and the few
   that are good,
How you have spent your life, and
   used every sharp device,
Before the great Lord of Paradise.
Now let us set about making that
   journey,   111
And, I want you to know, you shall
   have no attorney.
Everyman. I am not ready to give such
   a reckoning.
   I do not know you. Whose messenger
   are you?
Death. I am Death, who fears no man,
   Defeats every man, and spares no
     man;   116
   For it is God's commandment
   That all should be obedient to me.
Everyman. Oh, Death, you come when
   I have you least in mind!
   Yet it lies in your power to save me;
   I will give you a share of my goods,
     if you will be kind;   121
   Yes, a thousand pounds you shall
     have,
   If you put off this matter till another
     day.
Death. Everyman, I cannot do it; there
   is no way.
   I do not care for gold, silver, or
     riches,   125
   Nor for popes, emperors, kings,
     dukes, nor princes;
   For, if I would accept great gifts,
   I could own the whole world;
   But my custom is just the contrary.
   I grant you no delay. Come along,
     and do not tarry.   130
Everyman. Alas, shall I have no longer
   stay?
   I see very well Death gives no warn-
     ing!
   Just to think of you makes my heart
     sick,
   For my record-book is so unpre-
     pared.

Everyman and Death depicted in a woodcut, the frontispiece to John Skot's edition
of the play (*c.* 1530).

   If I could have just twelve more
     years,   135
   My book of accounts I would make
     so clear
   That my life's record I could show
     without fear.
   Therefore, Death, I beg you, for
     God's mercy,
   Spare me till I find myself some rem-
     edy.
Death. It is useless now to cry, weep,
   and pray;   140
   No, set off quickly on your journey,
   And test your friends if you can;
   For well you know time waits for no
     man,
   And in this world each living crea-
     ture
   For Adam's sin must die in the
     course of nature.   145
Everyman. Death, if I go before heav-
   en's King
   And truly make my reckoning,
   Tell me, for charity's sake,

Shall I ever again come back?

Death. No, Everyman, once you are there,   150
You may never again come here.
That is true. Trust me.

Everyman. Oh, gracious God, on your high throne in heaven,
Have mercy on me in this time of need!
Shall I have no earthly company of my acquaintance   155
To go with me, and take the lead?

Death. Yes, if there are any so foolhardy
As to go with you and keep you company.
Quick, get you gone to God's magnificence,
And give your reckoning in his presence.   160
Do you think that your life was given to you,
And your worldly goods were gifts also?

Everyman. I had thought so, truly.

Death. No, no; they were only lent to you;
For as soon as you are gone,   165
Another shall have them a while, and then move on,
Just as you have done.
Everyman, you are mad! You have your five senses,
And here on earth will not cleanse your life;
And then I come, suddenly.   170

Everyman. Oh, wretched coward, where shall I flee,
That I may escape this endless sorrow?
Oh, gentle Death, spare me till tomorrow,
That I may alter my ways
With deep meditation.   175

Death. No, I will not consent to that;

I will reprieve no man;
But I shall suddenly strike to the heart
With no meditation at all.
And now I will take myself out of your sight;   180
See that you make yourself ready at once,
For you may well say that this is the day
That no man living can keep away.

(*Exit* DEATH.)

Everyman. Alas, I must sigh! Alas, I must weep!
There is no one who will accompany me   185
To help or guard me on my journey;
A worthy account-book I failed to keep.
Now how shall I escape punishment and scorn?
I wish to God I had never been born!
To my soul it would have been a great gain;   190
For now I fear I shall suffer great pain.
The time passes. Oh, help me, Lord, who made everything!
For though I mourn, it accomplishes nothing.
The day passes, and is almost gone;
I do not know what is to be done.
To whom shall I complain of this painful trip?   196
What if I speak of it to Fellowship,
And tell him of this unlooked for event?
My trust in him will not be misplaced;
We have in this world for many a day   200
Been the best of friends in sport and play.
I see him coming, certainly.

I am sure he will bear me company;
I will speak to him and ease my sorrow.

(FELLOWSHIP *enters.*)

We meet just in time, Fellowship.
Good morrow!   205
Fellowship. Good morning, Everyman.
A hearty good day!
Friend, why do you stare in such a
pitiful way?
If anything is wrong, you must tell
me,
And I will find a remedy.
Everyman. Yes, good Fellowship, yes;
I am in great jeopardy.   211
Fellowship. Tell me what is on your
mind, dear friend;
I will not desert you until my life's
end,
If you are looking for good company.
Everyman. That was well spoken, and
lovingly.   215
Fellowship. But I must know the cause
of your unhappiness;
It grieves me to see you in any distress.
If you have been wronged, you shall
be revenged,
Though I am slain for you, and my
blood is shed,
And I know beforehand that I shall
be dead.   220
Everyman. Really, Fellowship! Many
thanks.
Fellowship. Oh, there is nothing to
thank me for.
Tell me your trouble, and say no
more.
Everyman. If I should open my heart to
you,
And you were to make light of the
matter,   225
And lend no comfort when you have
heard me through,

Then I should be ten times sadder.
Fellowship. Sir, what I say I will do indeed.
Everyman. Then you are surely a friend
in need:
I have always found you true before.
Fellowship. And so you shall for ever
more;   231
For if, in faith, you go to hell,
I will not forsake you on the way!
Everyman. You speak like a good
friend; I believe you well.
I shall repay you, if I can.   235
Fellowship. I ask no repayment, Everyman!
For he who says, and does not do,
Is not a worthy man, or true;
So tell me what you have on your
mind,   239
As to a friend most loving and kind.
Everyman. I shall tell you how it is:
I am commanded to go on a journey,
A long, hard, and dangerous way,
And give a strict account without
delay,
Before the high judge, Adonai.   245
Therefore, I beg you, keep me company,
As you have promised, on this journey.
Fellowship. That is trouble indeed. And
promise is duty;
But if I should take such a voyage
upon me,
I know very well, it should be to my
pain;   250
And it certainly makes me afraid.
But let us talk of it here as well as
we can,
For your words would frighten a
fearless man.
Everyman. Why, if I had need of you,
you said,
You would never forsake me, alive or
dead,   255

Though I went to hell, truly.

Fellowship. So I said, certainly,

But I was speaking in jest, not seriously;

And besides, if we took such a journey,

When should we come back again?

Everyman. Never again. Not till Judgment Day.   261

Fellowship. Believe me, then I will never go there!

Who has brought you this message?

Everyman. It was Death, who was with me here.

Fellowship. Then, by God, who redeemed us all,   265

If Death was the messenger,

I will not go on that loathsome journey

For any man alive today—

Not for the father that begot me!

Everyman. You promised otherwise, by God.   270

Fellowship. I know very well I did, that's true;

But if you wanted to eat, drink, and be merry,

Or visit carefree women for company,

I would not desert you from dark to dawn,   274

And there you may trust me, truly!

Everyman. Yes, for that you would be ready;

And would sooner apply your mind

To merriment, pleasure, and play,

Than to keep me company on my long journey.

Fellowship. Now, believe me, I will not go that way.   280

But for a murder, if there is someone to kill,

In that I will help you with a good will.

Everyman. Oh, that is a stupid remark indeed!

Good fellow, help me in my adversity;

We have long been friends, and now I am in need;   285

And so, gentle Fellowship, consider me.

Fellowship. Whether we have been friends or no,

By Saint John, I will not go with you.

Everyman. But, I beg you, take the trouble, and do so much for me

As to walk with me a way, as an act of charity,   290

And comfort me till I reach the edge of town.

Fellowship. No, even if you give me a new gown,

Not a foot with you will I go;

But, if you had stayed, I would not have left you so.

Now, God speed you on your journey, man,   295

For I will leave you as fast as I can.

Everyman. Where are you going, Fellowship? What am I to do?

Fellowship. Well, by my faith, to God I commend you.

Everyman. Farewell, good Fellowship! For you my heart is sore;

Goodbye for ever! I shall see you no more!   300

Fellowship. Farewell, Everyman! The end comes without warning;

For your sake I will remember that parting is mourning.

(*Exit* FELLOWSHIP.)

Everyman. Alas! shall we thus part company indeed—

Oh, help, Blessed Lady!—without any more concern?

If Fellowship has forsaken me in my great need,   305

Where in this world for help shall I turn?

Fellowship used to make merry with
    me,
And now he feels no sorrow for me.
It is said, "In prosperity a man may
    find friends,   309
But in adversity the friendship ends."
Now for help to whom shall I flee,
Since Fellowship has forsaken me?
To my kinsmen I will appeal,
And beg them to help me in my or-
    deal;
I think they will come to the aid of a
    man,   315
For kinsmen will always do what
    they can.
I will go test, for there I see them,
Whether they are now true friends
    and kinsmen.

(*Enter* KINDRED *and* COUSIN.)

Kindred. Here we are now, at your
    urgent call.
I beg you, Cousin, tell us all,   320
Whatever is wrong, and do not spare
    us.
Cousin. Yes, Everyman, and make clear
    to us
If you have a mind to go anywhere,
For we will live and die together.
Kindred. In wealth and woe we will
    stand by you, truly;   325
And to his kin a man may speak
    freely.
Everyman. Thank you, my friends and
    kinsmen kind.
Now I shall tell you the grief on my
    mind.
I was commanded by a messenger,
Who is a high King's chief officer,   330
To make a pilgrimage and face great
    pain,
And I know I shall never come back
    again;
I must also give a strict reckoning,
For I have a great enemy who is
    beckoning   334

Me to evil and seeks my surrender.
Kindred. What account is that which
    you must render?
I would like to know.
Everyman. I must tell of all my works:
How I have lived, and spent my
    days:
And all the bad deeds I have done 340
In my time, since life was lent me;
And all the virtues I have managed
    to shun.
Therefore, I beg you, go there with
    me,
To help clear my account, for holy
    charity.
Cousin. What, to go there? Is that what
    you called us for?   345
No, Everyman, I had rather fast on
    bread and water
For the next five years or more.
Everyman. Alas, that ever I was born!
For now, if you desert me,
I shall never be happy.   350
Kindred. Oh, what a clown you are,
    Everyman!
Be brave. There is no need to moan.
But of one thing I warn you, by Saint
    Anne,
As far as I am concerned, you shall
    go alone.
Everyman. Dear Cousin, tell me, will
    you not go?   355
Cousin. No, by our Lady! I have a
    cramp in my toe.
Trust not to me, for as God is my
    judge,
When you need me most, I will not
    budge.
Kindred. It is no use to try to persuade
    us.
If you take my maid, I will not make
    a fuss;   360
She loves to go to feasts, to make
    merry,
To dance, to go out, and to gad
    about.

I will give her leave to help you on
that journey,
If you and she can agree.
Everyman. Now tell me what you really
have in mind.   365
Will you go with me, or remain be-
hind?
Kindred. Remain behind? Yes, that I
will do, I say!
Therefore farewell till another day.

(*Exit* Kindred.)

Everyman. How can I be merry or
glad?
For men make fine promises, and
boast,   370
And yet desert me when I need them
most.
I am deceived, and that makes me
sad.
Cousin. Cousin Everyman, farewell for
now,
I certainly will not go with you;
My own account is in a very bad
way;   375
I have to improve it, and so I must
stay.
So God help you, and now I must go.

(*Exit* Cousin.)

Everyman. Oh, dear Lord, has it all
come to this?
Fine words make fools glad. That is
true.
They promise easily, but they will
not do.   380
My kinsmen promised me faithfully
To remain with me steadfastly,
But very fast they ran away;
And Fellowship promised in the
same way.
What friend is it best for me to seek
out?   385
I am wasting my time here hanging
about.

Now something comes to my mind,
which is:
All my life I have loved riches.
If only my Goods might help me
now,
He would make my heart very light,
I vow.   390
I will speak to him of my distress.
Where are you, my Goods and
riches?

(Goods *speaks from a corner.*)

Goods. Who calls me? Everyman?
What? Are you in a hurry?
I lie here in a corner, bound down
and piled high,
Locked in chests and in sacks,   395
In bags and in packs. As you can see,
I cannot move; under such stacks I
lie.
What do you want? Tell me quickly.
Everyman. Come to me, Goods, as fast
as you can,
For I must have your advice.   400
Goods. Sir, if in this world you have
sorrow or adversity,
I can help you with a remedy
quickly.
Everyman. It is another distress that
troubles me;
It is not of this world, I must tell you
so.
I am sent for, another way to go, 405
To give a strict account in general
Before the highest deity of all.
All my life you have given pleasure
to me,
And so I beg you to go with me,
And, perhaps, help clean and purify
410
My record before God Almighty;
For it is always said and sung,
That money makes everything right
that is wrong.

Goods. No, Everyman, I sing another song.

I follow no man on such voyages;   415
For, if I went with you,
My being there would make it much worse for you;
Because you have kept me, and nothing else, in your thought,
I have caused your account to amount to nought.   419
So your record is faulty from A to Z,
And that is because of your love of me.

Everyman. That would make me lament,
On the fearful day of judgment.
Get up, let us go there together.

Goods. No, not so! I am too tender, I would not survive;   425
Not one foot will I follow any man alive.

Everyman. Alas, I have loved you and had great pleasure
All the days of my life in goods and treasure.

Goods. And for that you will be damned;
I am not lying!
My love is contrary to the love everlasting;   430
But if you had loved me moderately,
And had given to the poor a part of me,
You would not be in such despair,
Nor in this great sorrow and care.

Everyman. Oh, I was deceived before I was aware!   435
And I blame it all on misspending my time.

Goods. What, do you think that I am yours?

Everyman. Yes, so I thought.

Goods. No, Everyman, I say no.
Just for a time you had the loan of me,   440
And lived for a while in prosperity.
It is my nature to cause men to sin;

If I save one, a thousand I ruin.
Do you think that I will follow you
From this world? No, that is not true.

Everyman. I had thought otherwise.

Goods. So you see, Goods is the thief of your soul;   447
For when you are dead, I repeat the play—
And deceive another in the same way
As I have done you, and all to his soul's decay.   450

Everyman. Oh, false Goods, cursed may you be,
You traitor to God, you have deceived me
And caught me in your snare!

Goods. Well, you brought yourself despair,
And I am glad;   455
It makes me laugh, I cannot be sad.

Everyman. Oh, Goods, for so long you have had my heartfelt love;
I gave you what I owed to the Lord above.
But will you not go with me indeed?
The truth I beg you to say.   460

Goods. No, so help me God!
I say farewell, farewell, good day.

(*Exit* Goods.)

Everyman. Oh, to whom shall I make my plea
To go with me on this sad journey?
First Fellowship said that he would go;   465
His words were very pleasant and sweet,
But shortly afterwards he said no.
Then I spoke to my kinsmen, in deep despair,
They also gave me words that were fair.
They lacked for no fair words to spend,   470
But all deserted me in the end.

Then I went to my Goods, that I
　loved best,
In hope to have comfort, but there I
　had least.
For my Goods seemed very happy to
　tell　　　　　　　　　　　　474
How many men he had sent to hell.
It made me feel so low and ashamed,
I know I really deserve to be
　blamed;
I am filled with loathing and self-
　hate.
To whom shall I turn for advice so
　late?
I think that I shall never succeed　480
Until I seek out my one Good Deed.
But, alas, she is so weak
That she can neither walk nor speak;
And yet I will gamble on her now.
My Good Deeds, where are you?　485

(GOOD DEEDS *speaks from the
ground.*)

Good Deeds. Here I lie, cold, on the
　ground.
Your sins have me so bound down
That I cannot stir.
Everyman. Oh, Good Deeds, I live in
　fear!
I beg you to advise me here;　　490
Your help now would be most wel-
　come.
Good Deeds. Everyman, I understand
That you have been summoned to
　give an account
Before the high judge, the heavenly
　King;
If you do as I say, I will go with you
　on that journey.　　　　　　495
Everyman. That is why I come to you
　to make my plea;
I hope that you will go with me.
Good Deeds. I would gladly go, but I
　cannot stand, believe me.

Everyman. Why, has something hap-
　pened to you?
Good Deeds. Yes, indeed, and I must
　thank you;　　　　　　　　500
If you had paid more attention to
　me,
Your book of accounts would be
　ready, you see.

(GOOD DEEDS *shows him the Book.*)

Look, the book of your works and
　your deeds
Lies under your feet,
To your soul's heaviness.　　　505
Everyman. Oh, dear Lord, help me!
There is not one letter here that I
　can see.
Good Deeds. Your account is black in
　this time of distress.
Everyman. Good Deeds, I beg you to
　help me in my need,
Or else I am for ever damned, in-
　deed;　　　　　　　　　　510
Show me how to make my reckoning
Before the Redeemer of everything,
Who is, and was, and ever shall be
　King.
Good Deeds. Everyman, I am sorry for
　your fall,
And would gladly help you if I
　could, at all.　　　　　　　515
Everyman. Good Deeds, I beg you to
　give me your advice.
Good Deeds. That I shall gladly do;
Though at the moment I cannot
　walk,
I have a sister who will go with you.
She is called Conscience, and will
　stay with you,　　　　　　520
And help you to make that dreadful
　reckoning.

(*Enter* CONSCIENCE.)

Conscience. Everyman, I will go with
　you, and be your guide;

In your great need, I will walk by
   your side.
Everyman. I am in good condition now
   in every thing,
   And am wholly content with this
   good thing,   525
Thanks to God my Creator.
Good Deeds. And after she has brought
   you there,
   Where you shall be healed of your
   pain,
   Then go with your reckoning and
   Good Deeds together,
   And be joyful at heart again   530
Before the blessed Trinity.
Everyman. Oh, Good Deeds, you give
   me
   Great contentment, certainly,
   With your sweet words.
Conscience. Now let us go together lov-
   ingly   535
   To that cleansing river, Confession.
Everyman. Oh, I weep for joy; I wish
   we were there!
   But, I beg you to tell me, if you will,
   Where Confession, that holy man,
   dwells.   539
Conscience. In the house of salvation;
   We shall find him in that place,
   That shall comfort us, by God's
   grace.

   (CONSCIENCE *takes* EVERYMAN *to*
   CONFESSION.)

   Here is Confession. Kneel down and
   ask mercy,
   For he is highly esteemed by God Almighty.
Everyman. (*Kneeling*) Oh, glorious
   fountain, that purifies all uncleanli-
   ness,   545
   Wash the dark spots of vice from me,
   So that no sin may be seen in me.
   I come with Conscience for my redemption,

And offer sincere and complete re-
   pentance;
For I am commanded a pilgrimage to
   take,   550
And a strict account before God to
   make.
Oh, hear me, Confession, guide to
   salvation.
Help my Good Deeds; oh, answer
   my plea.
Confession. I well know your sorrow,
   Everyman,
And because with Conscience you
   come to me,   555
I will comfort you as well as I can,
And a precious jewel you will get
   from me,
Called penance, the enemy of adver-
   sity;
You shall chastise your body with it,
And with self-denial, and devotion to
   God's service.   560
Here you shall receive that scourge
   from me,

(*Gives* EVERYMAN *a whip.*)

Which is harsh punishment that you
   must endure
To remember your Savior was
   scourged for you
With sharp whips, and suffered it patiently;
So must you, before you end your
   painful pilgrimage.   565
Conscience, look after him on this
   voyage,
And by that time Good Deeds will
   be with you.
But in any case you may be sure of
   mercy,
For your time draws quickly to an
   end. If you want to be
Saved, seek God's help, and He will
   grant it, truly.   570

When man beats himself with the
whip of remorse,
The oil of forgiveness shall heal him,
of course.

(*Exit* CONFESSION; EVERYMAN *rises.*)

Everyman. Thanks be to God for his
gracious work!
It is time now for my penance to
begin;
God's grace has rejoiced and light-
ened my heart,   575
Though the knots of the whip hurt,
and burn within.
Conscience. Be sure you do your penance, Everyman,
In spite of the pain it causes you;
And Conscience will gladly give you
advice
How to make your account without
blemish or vice.   580

(EVERYMAN *kneels.*)

Everyman. Oh eternal God, oh heavenly
being,
Oh way of righteousness, oh goodly
vision,
Who came to earth through a virgin,
pure,
And sought to bring every man the
redemption
Which Adam forfeited by his disobe-
dience.   585
Oh blessed Godhead, elect and high
divinity,
Forgive my grievous offenses;
I plead for mercy in your presence.
Oh spiritual treasure, ransomer and
redeemer,   589
The hope and guide of all the world,
Mirror of joy, and founder of mercy,
By which heaven and earth are illu-
minated,
Hear my clamorous lament, though it
comes late.

Receive my prayers, in your benefi-
cence;
Though I have committed abomina-
ble sins,   595
Let my name be written on the table
of penance.
Oh, Mary, pray to the Maker of every-
thing,
To help me at my ending;
And save me from the power of my
enemy,
For Death now attacks me strongly.
Oh, Lady, through the mediation of
your prayer,   601
In your Son's glory let me share,
Since by means of his passion he
made men whole,
I pray you, help me to save my soul.

(EVERYMAN *rises.*)

Conscience, give me the scourge of
penance;   605
With it my flesh shall be redeemed.
I will now begin, if God give me
grace.
Conscience. Everyman, God gives you
time and opportunity!
So I entrust you to the hands of our
Savior;
Now you may make your reckoning
sure.   610
Everyman. In the name of the Holy
Trinity,
I shall harshly punish my body.

(EVERYMAN *scourges himself.*)

Take this, body, for the sin of the
flesh!
Because you delighted in fine clothes
and sweet scent,
And led me into the path of damnation,   615
You must suffer these strokes as punishment.

This penance is the clear water of
glory

That will quench the sharp flames of
purgatory.

(GOOD DEEDS *rises from the ground.*)

Good Deeds. I thank God, now I can
walk and go,

And I am cured of my sickness and
woe.   620

Therefore with Everyman I will go
everywhere;

His good works I will help him to
declare.

Conscience. Now, Everyman, be merry
and glad!

Your Good Deeds stand by you, you
must not be sad.

Now your Good Deeds, whole and
sound,   625

Can stand upright upon the ground.

Everyman. My heart is light, and shall
be evermore.

Now I will do greater penance than
before.

Good Deeds. Everyman, pilgrim, my
special friend,   629

May you be blessed to the very end.

Eternal glory is prepared for you.

You have made me well and happy,
too,

So I will stand by you in every trial.

Everyman. Welcome, Good Deeds; just
to hear your voice

Makes me weep for the sweetness of
love.   635

Conscience. Be sad no more, but forever rejoice;

God sees your life from his throne
above.

Put on this garment for your own
good,

It is wet with your tears;

You will want it when you stand before God,   640

When you have come to your journey's end.

Everyman. Gentle, Conscience, what do
you call it?

Conscience. It is the garment of sorrow;

It will deliver you from pain;

It is called contrition,   645

And begets forgiveness;

It is most pleasing to God.

Good Deeds. Everyman, will you wear
it for your salvation?

(EVERYMAN *puts on the robe of contrition.*)

Everyman. A blessing on Jesus, Mary's
Son,

For now I have put on contrition. 650

So let us go on without tarrying;

Good Deeds, have I cleared my reckoning?

Good Deeds. Yes, indeed, I have it
here.

Everyman. Then I trust I need not fear.

Now, friends, let us not separate. 655

Conscience. No, Everyman, we will not
do that.

Good Deeds. But you must take with
you

Three persons of great power.

Everyman. Who should they be?

Good Deeds. They are called Intellect
and Strength   660

And Beauty, who must not remain
behind.

Conscience. You must also keep in mind

Your Five Senses, as your counselors.

Good Deeds. You must have them ready
at all hours.

Everyman. How shall I get them to appear?   665

Conscience. You must call them all together;

They will hear you at once and consent.

Everyman. My friends, come here and be present,
Intellect, Strength, my Five Senses, and Beauty.

(*Enter* BEAUTY, STRENGTH, INTELLECT, *and* FIVE SENSES.)

Beauty. Here, at your call, we come to you.   670
What is it you want us to do?
Good Deeds. To go with Everyman, if you will,
And help him on his pilgrimage.
Will you go with him or not on that voyage?
Strength. We will all take him there,
And will help and comfort him, believe me.   676
Intellect. And all of us will go together.
Everyman. Almighty God, praised may you be!
I thank you for letting me bring
My Strength, Intellect, Beauty, and Five Senses here.
Now I lack nothing;   680
And my Good Deeds and Conscience clear
Are all together at my command here.
I need nothing more for God's business.
Strength. And I, Strength, will stand by in your distress,
Though you find yourself on a battleground.   685
Five Senses. We will follow you all around,
And never desert you in joy or sorrow.
Beauty. Nor will I, until death's hour,
No matter what may come of it.
Intellect. Everyman, take thought first of all;   690
Go, after reflecting well and deliberating.

We want you to leave with the confident feeling
That all shall be well.
Everyman. Listen, my friends, to what I have to tell:
I beg God to reward you in his heavenly sphere.   695
Now I want you all to hear,
While all of you are present,
How I make my will and testament:
Half my goods I will freely give away
To charity, for a worthy cause;   700
And the other half shall still remain
In bequest, to be returned where it ought to be.
I do this in spite of the fiend of hell,
To be free of his power to harm me
From this day and forever after.   705
Conscience. Everyman, listen to what I say:
Go and seek out a priest today
And receive from him, as soon as you can,
The holy sacraments, and then
See that you quickly come back again.   710
We will all wait for you here.
Five Senses. Yes, Everyman, hurry and prepare yourself.
There is no emperor, king, duke, nor baron,
Who has as much of God's authority
As the humblest priest you may go to see;   715
For he bears the keys of the blessed sacraments,
Benign and pure, and is in charge
Of man's redemption, which is always sure.
God gave us this medicine for the soul,
Knowing in his heart it would make us whole,   720
Here in this brief and painful life.

The blessed sacraments are seven:

Baptism, confirmation, ordination to the priesthood,

The sacrament of God's flesh and blood,

Marriage, extreme unction, and penance. 725

These seven are good to keep in remembrance;

They are full of grace and of high divinity.

Everyman. I will gladly receive that Holy Body

And meekly to my spiritual father I will go.

Five Senses. Everyman, that is the best thing you can do. 730

God will grant salvation to you,

For the priests excel in everything;

They explain Holy Scripture when they teach,

Turn man from sin, and put heaven within his reach; 734

God has given more power to them

Than to any angel that is in heaven.

With five words, it is understood,

He turns God's body into flesh and blood

When he holds wine and wafer in his hands.

The priest binds and unbinds all bonds, 740

Both on earth and in heaven.

He administers the sacraments seven.

We kiss his feet, since he is worthy of it,

For he is the surgeon who cures deadly sin; 744

We can find no remedy under God,

Except from the priesthood.

Everyman, God gave priests that dignity,

And set them here among us in his place,

So they rank above angels in degree.

(*Exit* EVERYMAN *to receive the last rites.*)

Conscience. If priests are good, they have such rank, surely. 750

When Jesus hung on the cross in great pain,

Out of his blessed heart he gave us

Those same sacraments to save us;

Yes, the Lord gave, he did not sell them to us.

Therefore Saint Peter the Apostle proclaims 755

That the Lord's curse sharply stings

Those who buy or sell their Savior,

Or give or take money for spiritual things.

Sinful priests set a bad example for sinners;

Their children sit by other men's fires, I have heard; 760

And some seek wanton women's company

In unclean lives of lust and lechery:

Their sins have made them blind.

Five Senses. I trust to God no such may we find. 765

Therefore let us honor the priesthood,

And follow their doctrine for our soul's good.

They are our shepherds, we are their sheep;

From error they lead us, and in safety keep.

Peace, Everyman is coming in sight;

He has truly performed every rite. 770

Good Deeds. I think it is he, indeed.

(*Re-enter* EVERYMAN.)

Everyman. Now may the Lord bless you all.

I have received the sacraments for my redemption,

And even my extreme unction:

May all those be blessed who counseled me to take it! 775

And now, friends, let us go without
    delay;
I thank God that you have stood by
    me so long.
Now each of you put your hand on
    this cross,
And quickly follow me.
I will lead you to where I would like
    to be;
God be our guide! 780
Strength. Everyman, we will not part
    from you,
Until your long voyage is through.
Intellect. I, Intellect, will also be your
    guard.
Conscience. Although this pilgrimage is
    very hard,
I will never leave your side. 785
Strength. Everyman, I will do as much
    for you
As ever I did for Judas Maccabeus.

(EVERYMAN *approaches the grave.*)

Everyman. Alas, I am so faint I cannot
    stand;
My legs are beginning to fold.
Friends, let us not return again to
    this land, 790
Not for all the world's gold;
For into this cave I must creep,
And turn to earth, and there to sleep.
Beauty. What, into this grave? Alas!
Everyman. Yes, and you shall decay
    there, utterly. 795
Beauty. You mean, I should wither
    here?
Everyman. Yes, by my faith, and never
    again appear.
We shall live in this world no more,
But in heaven before the highest
    Lord.
Beauty. Then I cancel my promise.
    Adieu, by Saint John! 800
I bow to you now, and I shall be
    gone.

Everyman. But, Beauty, where are you
    going?
Beauty. Quiet! I am deaf. I will not look
    back,
Not if you gave me all the gold in
    your sack.

(*Exit* BEAUTY.)

Everyman. Alas, in whom can I put my
    trust? 805
Beauty is leaving me very fast;
She promised to stay with me to the
    last.
Strength. Everyman, I will also desert
    and deny you.
Your game in no way pleases me.
Everyman. Why, then, you will all de-
    sert me! 810
Sweet Strength, remain a little while!
Strength. No, sir, by the cross of grace!
I will hurry away from you,
Though you weep till your heart
    breaks in two.
Everyman. You said you would always
    see me through. 815
Strength. Yes, but I have gone far
    enough with you.
You are old enough, it seems to me,
Your own pilgrimage to oversee.
I am sorry that I came here with you.
Everyman. Strength, I am to blame for
    displeasing you; 820
Still a vow is a debt, you are well
    aware.
Strength. In faith, I do not care.
You are just a fool to complain;
You spend your speech and waste
    your brain. 824
Go, thrust yourself into the ground.

(*Exit* STRENGTH.)

Everyman. I expected to find him more
    trustworthy;
But he who trusts in his Strength

Will be decieved by him at length.
Both Strength and Beauty have for-
saken me;
Though they made their fine vows so
lovingly.   830
Intellect. Everyman, after Strength, I
will be gone;
As for me, I will leave you alone.
Everyman. Why, Intellect, will you de-
sert me, too?
Intellect. Yes, in truth, I will part from
you,
For when Strength leaves life and
limb,   835
I always follow after him.
Everyman. But, I beg you, for the love
of the Trinity,
Look into my grave just once with
pity.
Intellect. No, so near I will not come;
Farewell, every one!   840

(*Exit* INTELLECT.)

Everyman. Oh, all things fail me, save
God, I detect—
Beauty, Strength, and Intellect;
For when Death blows his blast,
They all run from me very fast.
Five Senses. Everyman, I will do as the
others do,   845
Forsake you now, and take my leave
of you.
Everyman. Alas, then I must weep and
wail,
For I took you for my best friend.
Five Senses. I cannot help you in your
travail;
So farewell, this is the end.   850

(*Exit* FIVE SENSES.)

Everyman. Oh Lord, help me! All have
forsaken me.
Good Deeds. No, Everyman, I will
stand by you.

I will not forsake you, indeed;
You shall find me a true friend in
your need.   853
Everyman. Many thanks, Good Deeds!
Now I know who my true friend is.
They have forsaken me, every one,
Though I loved them better than my
Good Deeds alone.
Conscience, will you forsake me too?
Conscience. Yes, Everyman, when you
go to your Death;
But not yet, no matter the danger. 860
Everyman. I thank you, Conscience,
with all my heart.
Conscience. No, I will not yet from
here depart
Till I see what shall become of you.
Everyman. I think, alas, that now I
must be gone
To pay my debts and make my reck-
oning,   865
For my time, I see, is quickly pass-
ing.
Take this example, all you who hear
and see
How those I loved best were quick to
forsake me,
Except my Good Deeds who stands
by me truly.
Good Deeds. All earthly things are but
vanity.   870
Beauty, Strength, and Intellect desert
all men,
As do false speaking friends and
kinsmen—
All leave you, but I, your own Good
Deeds.
Everyman. Have mercy on me, God Al-
mighty;
And stand by me, holy Mother and
Maid.   875
Good Deeds. I will speak for you; do
not be afraid.
Everyman. God have mercy; let me not
cry in vain.

Good Deeds. Hasten our dying and diminish our pain;
Let us go and never come again.

Everyman. Into your hands, Lord, I commend my soul.   880
Receive it, Lord, that it may not be lost.
As you redeemed me, so defend me
From the foul fiend whom I fear most,
That I may appear with that blessed host
That shall be saved on Judgment Day.   885
Into your hands, Lord without limit
And everlasting, *I commend my spirit.*

(EVERYMAN *and* GOOD DEEDS *descend into the grave.*)

Conscience. Now he has suffered what all of us shall endure;
But Good Deeds shall make all of us secure.
Now he has reached the ending;   890
It seems to me I hear angels singing,
And making great joy and melody
Where Everyman's soul shall live for eternity.

(*Exit* CONSCIENCE; *an* ANGEL *appears.*)

Angel. Come, excellent chosen spouse, to the Lord!
Hereabove you shall go   895
Because of your uncommon virtue.
Now the soul from the body will disappear,
And your reckoning is crystal clear.
Arise now into the heavenly sphere,

(*To the audience.*)

And all of you shall go that way,   900
Who live pure lives before Judgment Day.

(*Enter a* DOCTOR OF THEOLOGY *as Epilogue.*)

Doctor. This moral men should keep in mind.
You listeners, take heed, both old and young,
And avoid Pride, for he deceives you in the end;
And remember Beauty, Five Senses, Strength, and Intellect,   905
All forsake every man at last,
While his good deeds forever stand fast.
But beware, for if they are few,
Before God, they will be of no help at all;
There will be no excuse then for any man.   910
Alas, what shall he do then?
For, after death, no man can make amends,
For then all mercy and all pity ends.
If his account, when he comes, is dark and dire,
God will say: "*Depart, you accursed, into everlasting fire.*"   915
But he whose account is whole and sound,
High in heaven shall he be crowned;
May God bring us all into that place,
That we may live, body and soul, in grace.
And may the Trinity help us then! 920
And, for Saint Charity, let us say Amen.

Thus ends this moral play of EVERYMAN.

Macbeth

WILLIAM SHAKESPEARE

INTRODUCTION

William Shakespeare, son of John Shakespeare and Mary Arden, was born on or about April 23, 1564, in Stratford-on-Avon, England. We first hear of his connection with the London theater in 1592 and by 1594 he had become a member of the Lord Chamberlain's Company and shared in the profits as actor and playwright.

It was with this company that he was affiliated for the rest of his life; and for its notable members, headed by Richard Burbage, the finest actor of his day, he wrote at least two plays a year for twenty consecutive years. The actors became the close personal friends of the playwright, and after his death his plays were collected and published in the First Folio (1623) by two of them—Heminges and Condell. The company performed at The Theatre and The Curtain until its new house, The Globe, was opened in 1599. In addition to The Globe, which was situated in the new theater district on the Bankside south of the Thames, the company also bought and refurbished an indoor theater called Blackfriars which was used mainly in the winter. In 1603, ten days after he came to the throne, James I issued an order placing the Chamberlain's Men under his own patronage and bestowing upon them the new title "The King's Men" by which name they were known thereafter. The company was the most successful in London and brought those who shared in its profits great wealth.

In 1611, at the age of forty-seven, Shakespeare retired to Stratford a wealthy man. On April 23, 1616, he died, and was buried in the village church in which he had been baptized. He was survived by his wife and by two daughters, both of whom were married; his son, Hamnet had died in 1596.

It is customary to divide Shakespeare's career as a playwright into four periods. These were once regarded as reflecting his own emotional and intellectual history, but a wider study of the Elizabethan drama has made it clear that changes in the technique, type, and tone of his plays were the results of external conditions rather than inner forces. The first period, extending from 1590 to 1596, is that during which he experimented with a number of kinds of comedy: classical, euphuistic, and romantic. The second period, running from 1596 to 1601, is that of the great history plays. The third period, from 1601 to 1608, is that of the great tragedies and the "bitter" comedies. The final period, 1608 to 1611, is that of the romances; but as late as 1613, after he had apparently retired, he collaborated with John Fletcher in *Henry VIII* and probably in *The Two Noble Kinsmen.*

The uniqueness of Shakespeare's genius is universally admitted; it is so overwhelming, in fact, that some believe that he could not have been the author of the plays ascribed to him in view of his conventional background and uneventful existence. A careful analysis of the plays indicates, however, that his very conventionality is the basis for his continuing appeal. His moral values are the generally accepted ones; his view of life is never sordid; his treatment of women, children, the aged, and unfortunate is sympathetic, and his characteristic viewpoint is distinctly idealistic.

Macbeth was the last of the four great tragedies to be written by Shakespeare when his creative powers were at their height. The play had been preceded by *Hamlet, Othello,* and *King Lear. Macbeth* can be dated with some degree of assurance in 1606. The subject of the play may have been suggested to Shakespeare by an entertainment presented to King James at Oxford in August, 1605, in which three youths dressed as sibyls recited some Latin verses containing the old prophecy that Banquo's descendants should be kings. Since James claimed descent from Banquo, the performance naturally pleased him, though he usually had very little patience with plays of any sort. He did not share Elizabeth's interest in the theater. It is believed that, called upon to provide a play for the entertainment of James and his brother-in-law, King Christian of Denmark, who was visiting England in 1606, Shakespeare was careful to choose a subject that he knew was of interest to the king and made sure, furthermore, not to write at great length. *Macbeth* is the shortest of all Shakespeare's plays except for the *Comedy of Errors;* the text, which we know only from the First Folio, shows many corruptions as if it had been hastily written or carelessly cut.

The source of the material for *Macbeth* was Holinshed's *Chronicles of England, Scotland, and Ireland,* from which Shakespeare had drawn the subjects for his English history plays. From Holinshed came the salient facts about Macbeth and Banquo, the witches on the heath, their prophecies, and the various incidents that follow from them in the play. But according to this account, Macbeth managed to kill King Duncan during a battle, an incident which Shakespeare rejected probably because of its commonplaceness. In another tale in Holinshed, he read of King Duff, who was murdered in his sleep in the castle of Donwald by a subject ambitious for the crown, acting on his wife's instigation. Shakespeare did not hesitate to depart from historical accuracy by combining these two unrelated stories; by so doing he heightened the interest, the dramatic value, and the impact of his play. All of the action in the scenes involving the witches was original with Shakespeare, as was the dinner scene in which Banquo's ghost returned to confront his murderer. The playwright knew that witches, prophecies, and ghosts would please the king, who was a confirmed believer in the supernatural, and therefore, in the final Witch Scene (IV, 1) he went so far as to introduce Banquo's descendants in a parade of apparitions, with the last spirit carrying "twofold balls and treble scepters," the insignia of King James. But these were merely theatrical trappings, for the story that really interested Shakespeare concerned a man whose unbridled ambitions led him into evil from which, despite his agonies of remorse, he could not escape.

The plot-line of *Macbeth* is extremely simple—the simplest of all the tragedies —for the central figure supplies the main driving power of the action which is straightforward and unswerving from beginning to end. Macbeth and Banquo, two Scottish generals who are on their way home after a victorious battle, cross a deserted heath and there meet three old hags who prophesy that Macbeth shall be the Thane of Cawdor and later on shall be king, while Banquo shall be the father of kings though not one himself. Shortly thereafter a messenger arrives and addresses Macbeth as the Thane of Cawdor, a title just granted him by the king as a reward for his services. The witches' prophecy already seems to be coming true; to hasten its fulfillment, Lady Macbeth urges her husband to murder the king who has come on a visit to their castle. With the assistance of his wife, Macbeth kills Duncan, whose sons flee the country in terror, making it appear as if they had been implicated in the crime. Macbeth is crowned king of Scotland, but he is troubled in his conscience, and also disturbed by the prediction that Banquo's children are to inherit the throne. Fearing that Banquo will take matters into his own hands just as he himself had done, Macbeth arranges for the murder of Banquo and his only son, Fleance. Banquo is killed but Fleance escapes. Macbeth gives a great dinner for the members of the court and is about to take his seat at table when he sees the ghost of Banquo; it is visible to Macbeth alone but his frenzied and incriminating remarks break up the feast. Macbeth then goes to consult the witches about the future and is assured that Banquo's descendants will reign; he is also told to beware Macduff. After his interview with the witches he is greeted with the news that Macduff has fled to England, whereupon he orders the murder of Lady Macduff and her children. Macbeth starts a reign of terror and persecution. Lady Macbeth, who before the murder of Duncan appeared to be stronger than her husband, is now completely overcome by remorse and guilt and, with unsettled mind, dies, probably by her own hand. Macduff leads an army against Macbeth's castle at Dunsinane, the soldiers covering their advance with branches cut from the trees of Birnam wood. Macbeth's nerves are shaken, for the sight recalls two other predictions made by the witches: that he would not be vanquished until Birnam wood came to Dunsinane and that he would not yield to a man born of woman. The castle is attacked and during a hand-to-hand conflict with Macduff, Macbeth learns that his opponent was taken prematurely from his mother's womb. Macbeth realizes that he is doomed, but with great natural courage goes on fighting until he falls.

The play has no subplots and no unnecessary characters; it resembles a Greek tragedy in its stark beauty and its terrifying atmosphere. There are even more specific resemblances: the witches, like the Delphic oracle, announce the hero's fate, but he is powerless to avoid it; the supernatural plays an important part in the lives of the characters; and like Medea, Lady Macbeth, a passionate and faithful wife, does not hesitate to commit crimes for her husband's benefit.

Shakespeare's characterization of Macbeth and Lady Macbeth is superb. As husband and wife these two are well matched, since both are moved by the same passion of ambition; both are haughty and authoritarian; and both, in their egotism, show arrogance toward their inferiors. But they differ from each other in one important respect: Macbeth has a powerful imagination which almost prevents him from killing Duncan, for he seems conscious of what is to follow, and his deep remorse comes as a natural aftermath. Lady Macbeth, on the other hand, suppresses her imagination along with her femininity and sensitivity, and it is not until she sees the shocked faces of the guests at the banquet as her husband betrays himself that the enormity of their crime comes home to her. She faints at the knowledge and from that point on her personality disintegrates rapidly. When we see her for the last time in the sleep-walking scene, we realize how important she has been to the play. The second half of the play is certainly less interesting than the first because of Lady Macbeth's almost total absence from the scene.

The language of the play is unusual for its speed and economy; the condensation of ideas produces many oracular statements and the dialogue bristles with dramatic irony. As he approaches the estate of Macbeth, Duncan remarks, "This castle hath a pleasant seat," but it is there that he meets his death; in urging her husband to kill the king, Lady Macbeth says,

> A little water clears us of this deed:
> How easy is it then,

light words that have a terrible echo in the sleep-walking scene. In 1606, Shakespeare was still experimenting with blank verse so that the meter of the poetry in *Macbeth* looks forward to the freedom he allowed himself in his later plays. The thoughts rush on from line to line—they are not end-stopped—and build in each speech to a climactic effect.

There are two predominant images in the play, darkness and blood. All the scenes but three occur either in the blackness of night or in some dark place. The witches on the heath or in their cave, the murder scenes, the banquet scene, and the sleep-walking scene all take place in thick or subdued light. Three times only during the play does the sun shine: once, at the beginning, most ironically, when Duncan draws near Macbeth's castle of death at Inverness; then in the England scene; and again, at the very end, when Macduff invades Macbeth's castle at Dunsinane and symbolically restores the light to Scotland.

The images involving blood begin at the very opening of the play with the appearance of the bleeding sergeant who, reporting Macbeth's valor in battle, says that his sword "smoked with bloody execution"; then follow the "bloody dagger" that tempts Macbeth to murder, the hands deeply stained in Duncan's blood, the "blood-bolter'd" face of Banquo's ghost, Macbeth's remark that he has waded so deeply in blood that to go back would be no better than to go on, Lady Macbeth's attempt to wash the smell of blood from her hands, the image of Scotland bleeding to death from the wounds inflicted by Macbeth, and, at the close of the play, Macbeth likened by Macduff to a bloody villain and a butcher. And, yet, the final impression left by the play, though harrowing, is not revolting, because of Shakespeare's supreme ability to create characters so human that we are forced to suspend judgment upon actions which arouse deep feelings of pity and terror.

The theme of *Macbeth* might very well be expressed in the words with which Euripides concluded *Medea*: "Those things we count on do not come to pass, while the things we do not dream of are bound to happen." Shakespeare makes it abundantly clear that no man is able to arrange his future or to control his fate; and certainly not the man who meddles with evil and thus willfully exposes himself to the hazards of retaliation and chance. Banquo committed no active wrong, and yet in a sense he had to pay for condoning evil, for he stood silently by, suppressing his knowledge of the witches' predictions while Macbeth took advantage of them and pursued his career of crime. That does not mean that Shakespeare subscribed to the idea of "poetic justice"—punishment for the bad, rewards for the good; Duncan did not deserve to be murdered, nor did Lady Macduff and her children, but that is the unaccountable way in which things happen in this uncertain world. Shakespeare does not deny the existence of free will—Macbeth acts with full consciousness of what he is doing, as does Macduff when he goes off to England for aid—but the results are always in doubt.

About one thing Shakespeare leaves no doubt: Macbeth was a man full of "the milk of human kindness," frank, sociable, and generous, who was tempted to a life of crime by excellent opportunities, the instigations of his wife, and prophetic warnings, and thoughtlessly cast away his loyalty and his virtue. The tragedy lies in the fact that Macbeth "had to pay with his life, for the murder of his principles." And here we have a clue to the profound significance of the witches, who, while they clearly echo emotional drives and deep, unconscious self-knowledge, relate at the same time to the blind, inchoate forces of evil that are at large in the world. Men are thereby seduced, both from within and without, not only to destroy others but to waste their own most precious endowments. Such subtleties, with which the play is rich, help to account for its lasting power and importance.

PRODUCTION IN THE ELIZABETHAN THEATER

The Theater

Before there were any theaters in London, the acting companies gave public performances in the courtyards of such inns as The Bell, The Crosskeys, The Bull, and The Bel Savage. These yards were rectangular or square, surrounded on four sides by the inn but open to the sky. A platform stage was erected at one end of the yard, and the audience entered from the street through an archway at which a money-gatherer was stationed. Galleries, or balconies, ran around the interior of the court, overlooking the yard, and provided excellent locations from which the guests of the inn could watch the plays; these spectators, too, rewarded the players. But the innyards presented certain disadvantages, since the actors were at the mercy of the landlords who demanded a large share of their profits and imposed restrictive rules and regulations upon them, as did the civic authorities who looked upon players as a public menace.

The Globe Theater, London, where *Macbeth* had its première. *(Above)* A contemporary engraving of the exterior. (British Information Service) *(Left)* A model of the interior, at Hofstra College, Hempstead, New York, as reconstructed by John Cranford Adams and Irwin Smith. Notice the absence of seats in the pit. (W. Kilmer—J. C. Adams)

In 1574, Queen Elizabeth, who defended the acted drama against the attacks of the city government, granted a special license to James Burbage and four fellows of the company of the Earl of Leicester to exhibit all kinds of stage plays during the Queen's pleasure in any part of England, "as well for the recreation of her loving subjects as for her own solace and enjoyment." The very next year, however, the mayor and corporation of London formally expelled all players from the city.

Actors had always been at the mercy of the city officials and of the Puritans who complained that public performances attracted great crowds of unruly people, were the breeding-place of infections and plagues, provided a hangout for pickpockets, prostitutes, and other low characters, caused people to waste money on entertainment that should have been spent on more substantial commodities, and, worst of all, were "the sink of all sin" and the enemy "to virtue and religion." None of this was literally true, but in order to escape from these restrictions and reproaches, James Burbage conceived the idea and drew up plans for a building to be devoted solely to the presentation of plays. This theater, the first of its kind in England, would be his own, and so he would be unhampered by the landlords of the inns; and if he selected its site carefully, the City Fathers would have no power over him. He had four locations to choose from; these were the so-called "liberties," the lands taken over from the Catholic church and still held by the Crown free of all city control. He decided to build his playhouse in the Liberty of Holywell, on the edge of Finsbury Fields, a public playground in the north of London to which crowds of people went in a holiday mood seeking pleasure and recreation.

The Theatre, as the playhouse was called, began to go up in April, 1576, and showed clearly that it embodied the best features of the bull- and the bear-baiting rings as well as those of the innyards. Like the bull-ring, it was circular in shape to accommodate large numbers of people and provide excellent sight-lines; like the innyards it had a platform stage and balconies around the interior. In 1577 another playhouse, The Curtain, was built close by The Theatre, and this, too, came under the control of Burbage. Their design served, with improvements, as the model for all the theaters of the period.

When James Burbage died in 1597, his property was left to his sons, Cuthbert and Richard, who two years later formed a company with the actors in the troupe, including William Shakespeare, John Heminges, Augustine Phillips, Thomas Pope, and Will Kempe, for the erection of a new house to replace The Theatre. The old building was torn down and the timber was transported to the south bank of the Thames, which had become the new theater district; there, with the assistance of Peter Street, an expert carpenter and builder, the Burbages built the celebrated Globe Theater.

There have been some rather detailed conjectures about the physical structure of the Globe, but few actual records survive. The house, it is said, was octagonal in shape and open to the sky; it was three stories high and accommodated over two thousand people. The building had two entrances—one in front for the audience; one in the rear for the actors, musicians, and the personnel of the theater. Inside the building, a rectangular platform stage—about 40 feet wide, 25 feet deep, and 6 feet high—projected into the middle of the yard. There were no seats on the ground floor; the audience, called "groundlings," stood in front of and on both sides of the stage. Around and above the yard ran three galleries approached by interior stairs and divided into "rooms" or boxes where the better class of spectators sat on stools. Over a large part of the platform stage there extended a wooden roof, called "the heavens" or "the shadow," which was supported by two pillars that rested on the stage; the roof served partly to protect the actors from bad weather, but primarily to contain the machinery needed to let down such stage properties as thrones or to "fly" actors impersonating fairies or gods. At the rear of the stage there was a deep recess, or alcove, called an "inner stage," that was curtained off and also served as a playing area, mainly for interior scenes. On the right and left at the rear of the platform, there were doors leading into the tiring-house, where the dressing rooms were situated; these doors were used for entrances and exits by the players. In the floors of the platform and of the inner stage there were trapdoors through which actors or properties such as the Witches' cauldron in *Macbeth*, could be made suddenly to appear or disappear. On each of the three stories there was a recess above the inner stage; the recess on the second floor, like the one below it, was curtained off and served as an acting area—for balcony or battlements; the alcove on the third floor was called the Music Room as it was used by the men who supplied the musical accompaniment to the play. Above the "heavens" were little huts and a tower; the huts were used by the sound-effects men and possibly for the storage of costumes and properties; from the tower a flag was unfurled on the days that performances were given in the theater, and in the tower there was a great bell; also from the tower a trumpeter blew three blasts on his horn to announce the beginning of the play. Over the front door of the theater swung a wooden sign showing Hercules carrying the globe on his back, and under him appeared the legend, *Totus mundus agit histrionem* (All the world's a stage).

Admission to the theater was a penny; this entitled the person to stand in the yard. To sit or stand in the galleries, the spectator was required to pay an extra penny or two depending upon the location.

The first Globe playhouse had a thatched roof which proved the theater's undoing. In 1613, at the premiere performance of *Henry VIII*, by Shakespeare and Fletcher, a cannon was fired from one of the huts to signal the entrance of the king at a dramatic moment in the play; some of the sparks or wadding from the cannon lighted on the thatch and in less than an hour the theater was burned to the ground, luckily with no fatalities. One stanza of a popular ballad of the day reports:

> Out run the knights, out run the lords,
> And there was great ado;
> Some lost their hats, and some their swords;
> Then out run Burbage, too.

The following year the New Globe was erected on the old site; it was more beautiful and lavish than the former house, and this time it was roofed with tiles.

Scenery, Lighting, Properties

There was a certain amount of built and painted scenery, flat and three-dimensional pieces, on the Elizabethan stage, as we learn from the *Diary* of Philip Henslowe, one of the important theater-owners of the period; but the scenery was used as it had been in the medieval period, rather than it is in modern times. The modern theater has what is known as a "picture-frame" stage, which is entirely concealed by a front curtain. When the curtain is drawn up, it is as if the wall of a room has been removed, allowing us an intimate view of the goings on inside. The scenery in the modern theater usually represents a definite place at a definite time, a scene-change being a major operation accomplished behind a lowered curtain. The Elizabethan theater, like the medieval, had no front curtain, and the platform stage was unlocalized; that is, it was neutral ground that might represent a public square, a forest, a street, or a seacoast, in rapid succession. This feat was performed by a stagehand who, in full view of the audience, carried on and off such simple set-pieces and properties as a rock, a tree, or a gate. In addition to these significant and movable items, the lines of the play would indicate the locale and the time of day or night at the opening of each scene; it was up to the audience to exercise its imagination and supply the missing details in the décor. On this type of stage, different times and places could succeed each other as rapidly as stagehands and actors came and went.

The inner stage and the chamber above it were curtained off, as has been said, so that it was possible for these areas to be furnished to represent definite places —a bedroom, a prison, or a throne-room. Painted canvas or tapestries were hung in the alcoves to help suggest locale; if a tragedy was being performed, the draperies were black. Very often the inner stage and the platform were combined into a single set; the curtain would open and disclose, for instance, that the inner stage was a throne-room—king and queen would be seated on two large gilded chairs and courtiers stood about. As the scene progressed, the actors would move out of the alcove on to the platform, thus making that area part of the throne-room; in similar manner various other acting areas could be used in combination, thus giving the Elizabethan stage enormous flexibility, variety, and interest.

The Elizabethan play took two and one half to three hours to perform and was presented in the afternoon from three to six in the summer and from two to five in the winter. In this open-air theater, general illumination was provided by natural daylight; the platform always had enough light upon it, and even the alcoves, under the "heavens," were amply lit. But many scenes were supposed to take place at night or in the darkness of caves and cells, and this provided the opportunity for the use of torches, cressets, candles, and lanterns. *Macbeth,* which was called in its entirety "a thing of night," has scene after scene in which special lighting is obligatory: cressets affixed to walls to cast flickering lights on bloody daggers or bloody hands; sad, fluttering candles for the sleep-walking scene; and lurid, miasmic flames for the cauldron of the witches. The fact that all of these things were going on in broad daylight did not disturb the Elizabethan spectator; it was one of the conventions of his theater which he accepted.

The properties in use on the Elizabethan stage served an impressionistic or a symbolic rather than a realistic purpose. Large gilded chairs would signify a throne-room; a fourposter, a bedroom; and a rough-hewn table and some stools, a tavern. The locales changed so quickly that it would have been impossible to "dress a set" in minute detail. There were innumerable hand properties—daggers and swords, fans, handkerchiefs, goblets, musical instruments, and, in the Senecan melodramas, such as *Titus Andronicus*, several heads and hands—but all of these were carried on and off by the actors.

The arras, an imitation tapestry, or "painted cloth," was one type of hanging, but there were various kinds of curtains, all easily removable; and the floors of all the acting areas were covered with rushes, a kind of dried grass, in lieu of carpeting. The rushes were swept out after each performance, and the stage was freshly strewn for the next. Occasionally we hear of matting or rugs being used.

The Actors

Three classes of persons were connected with the theaters: sharers, hirelings, and servants. The "sharers" were the most important actors, who actually made up the "company," and who divided among themselves the money taken in each day at the door; according to their importance, some received whole shares, others half-shares. The "hirelings" were actors of lower rank who did not share in the large profits of the theater but were engaged by the company at a fixed and rather small salary. Many of these were young people who were regarded as apprentices and as possible future sharers, depending upon their development. Musicians were also engaged on a salary basis. The "servants" were employed by the company as prompters, stagehands, property-keepers, money-gatherers, and caretakers of the building.

The actors in the Elizabethan theater were all male; women were not permitted to appear upon the stage. The parts of young women were played by boys, those of old women or of hags, like the witches in *Macbeth*, were played by men. In the days before the theaters were built, a traveling company of players would consist of four or five men and one or two boys; the plays they performed often contained as many as twenty or thirty characters, so that each actor was required to play several parts. This practice of doubling actually remained in force and developed into a high art in Shakespeare's company, which at its peak employed only twelve men and six boys. Yet the cast of *Macbeth* lists twenty-eight characters and requires, in addition, Apparitions, Lords, Gentlemen, Officers, Soldiers, Murderers, Attendants, and Messengers. An analysis of the play will show that only Macbeth and Lady Macbeth remain throughout the action, while the other characters make brief appearances; Malcolm and Macduff, for example, have important scenes at the beginning and the end of the play, but would be free to double at other times.

Each actor in Shakespeare's company, particularly the stars or sharers, had his

(*Above*) Macbeth and Banquo meeting the "fairies or nymphs" on the heath. From a woodcut illustrating Holinshed's *Chronicles* (1587), the source of Shakespeare's play. (*Below*) In a nineteenth-century production, Mrs. Pritchard, Garrick's leading lady, carries the candle in the sleep-walking scene. Mrs. Siddons put the candle down. (Yale Theater Collection) (*Right*) An eighteenth-century production, in an engraving from Nicholas Rowe's 1709 edition of Shakespeare. Garrick, like the actor here, wore small-clothes. (Columbia University Library)

specialty. Richard Burbage was the leading man; he created the roles of Richard III, Romeo, Hamlet, Othello, Macbeth, and King Lear; Will Kempe, a low comedian, played such parts as Dogberry in *Much Ado about Nothing* and Bottom in *A Midsummer Night's Dream;* his place in the company was later taken by a more subtle and refined comedian, Robert Armin, who acted the First Grave-digger in *Hamlet* and the Fool in *King Lear;* John Heminges specialized in old men: Polonius in *Hamlet* and Brabantio in *Othello;* while Augustine Phillips and Thomas Pope may have played the fickle lovers or the bragging soldiers.

The actors were trained, as in other Elizabethan professions, under an apprenticeship system. A boy would start at the age of ten and be required to pay a sum of money to the master for whom he would work for seven years without receiving a salary; in return he would be given board and lodging and taught his trade thoroughly. The experienced actor would teach the boy in his care to play women's parts and also the type of part in which the older actor specialized so that his apprentice might become his successor. It is believed that the boys were hired in pairs: two who were about ten years of age, two about twelve to fourteen, and two between fifteen and eighteen. The eldest would serve as leading ladies as long as their voices and bodily development allowed, then they would graduate into adult roles, at which point a new pair of ten-year-olds would be taken on. An effort would be made to select a serious, blond, blue-eyed boy along with a boy who was small and dark for comedy; these types are paired in many of Shakespeare's plays. Some of these boys, such as Nathaniel Field and Richard Robinson, went on to become celebrated actors and writers and sharers in the company. Sir Laurence Olivier, in modern times, began his acting career at fifteen by playing Katharine in *The Taming of the Shrew* at Stratford-on-Avon.

In acting the women's parts, the boys played with great simplicity, directness, and restraint; Shakespeare, in fact, underemphasized sex in these roles. In many of the comedies, furthermore, the heroines disguised themselves as boys.

It is more difficult to attempt to describe the acting style of the adults. It could not have been as naturalistic as that of our own day, principally because the dialogue was written in verse. It must to some extent have been stylized and declamatory, although we know from Hamlet's advice to the Players that Shakespeare deplored ranting and bombast and broad, empty gestures. We deduce from Hamlet's speech the following set of rules for the actor: The speeches were to be spoken rapidly but intelligibly; the body movements and gestures were to be natural; the energy and emotions were to be under control at all times; the actor was to identify himself closely not only with the character he was playing but also with the customs and conventions of his day; and, finally, the actor was not to play down to his audience and be satisfied with cheap effects, but was to strive for the approval of the serious and discerning playgoer, rare as he might be.

Costumes

All Elizabethan plays were done, so to speak, in modern dress; that is, the costumes of the actors were the last word in contemporary fashion. The women wore the wide-spreading farthingale made of satin, velvet, taffeta, cloth of gold, silver, or copper, and the ruff of stiff lawn. The person was ornamented with gold and silver jewelry, precious stones, and strings of pearls. The men wore doublet and hose made of rich and contrasting materials, trimmed with lace of gold, silver, or thread; the jacket and cloak were made of silk or velvet; the ruffs, of stiff lawn; the shoes of fine, soft leather; and the outer robes were heavily furred. The actors, like the fops and ladies of the period, were also interested in the high styles of foreign countries and so appeared in German trunks, French hose, Spanish hats, and Italian cloaks confusingly mixed. The satirists of the day ridiculed these fashions, and clowns appeared on the stage in exaggerated parodies of them. In *The Merchant of Venice* (I, 2), Portia remarks of a young English nobleman: "How oddly he is suited! I think he bought his doublet in Italy, his round hose in France, his bonnet in Germany. . . ."

The colors too were dazzling and symbolic. One gown was white, gold, silver, red, and green; another was black, purple, crimson, and white; and there were dresses of such delicate tints as coral pink, silver, and gray. These, among many others, were the colors of the nobility and the courtiers, while servants were limited to dark blue or mustard-colored garments. Green sleeves, which became celebrated in song, were the mark of the courtesan.

In addition to their secular garments, the actors wore elaborate robes of state, impressive ecclesiastical vestments, and the various military and civic uniforms of the day.

Elizabethan stage costumes were undoubtedly magnificent and costly; they represented, in fact, the most expensive item in the production budget. One producer paid a dramatist 8 pounds for a play, then spent 20 pounds on a gown for the leading lady; another garment cost more than the theater took in in a week. But there was obviously a need for this spectacular display to offset the paucity of scenery and to satisfy the demand of the audience for eye-filling splendor and pageantry.

It did not in the least disturb the playgoer that Timon of Athens, Julius Caesar of Rome, and Cleopatra of Egypt all wore Elizabethan costumes. Nor did he appear to be bothered by the fact that ancient and contemporary costumes were worn side by side, a man in medieval armor talking to one in a fashionable doublet, with the occasional intermixture of such foreign items as a Moor's robe, a Turkish turban, or Shylock's "Jewish gaberdine." No attempt was made to achieve complete historical accuracy of costume until the nineteenth century.

A number of fantastic costumes were in use for fairies, devils, and clowns, but these were patterned mainly on traditional representations which had come down from the medieval mystery and miracle plays. The devils wore tails, cloven hoofs, and horns; the clowns were dressed like country yokels or wore the red and yellow motley of the fool; ghosts usually wore sheets, though that of Hamlet's father appeared in full armor; the witches in *Macbeth* wore ugly masks and fright wigs.

The costumes were acquired in various ways and might belong to the company jointly or to the individual actors. Some new garments were bought but these were so expensive as to be almost prohibitive; an effort was therefore made to get hold of secondhand clothing. Many courtiers, either because they were in need or because they did not wish to be seen too frequently in the same outfits, sold their finery to the players. Upon the deaths of some noblemen their expensive clothes were willed to servants or to poor relatives who sold them in turn to the actors. After the death of Mary of Scotland her wardrobe was turned over to Queen Elizabeth who presented these beautiful gowns to actors in lieu of a fee. If a theatrical company failed, its costumes were sold to active competitors. Some theater owners rented their costumes to other companies; and each company had at least one or two tailors in regular employ who busily altered or renovated the costumes on hand.

We may gain some notion of the magnitude of the problem faced in costuming the players when we realize that successful companies produced as many as forty plays in a season.

Music and Dance

The Elizabethan age was a highly musical one; instrumental and vocal music in solo or concert enlivened all public and private occasions. The Elizabethan play was accompanied almost throughout by music that either served an integral dramatic purpose or was merely incidental to the action.

There were four basic types of music used in the plays: military and ceremonial music, songs sung either with or without instrumental accompaniment, incidental instrumental music played as an accompaniment to dancing, action, or speech, and unmotivated background music used to create a special mood or atmosphere. In addition, many sound effects were employed to heighten the aural appeal of the plays by arousing tensions and simulating reality. In A Midsummer Night's Dream, the musicians may actually have appeared on the stage, but usually the music emanated from the Music Room on the second gallery above the stage.

The military and ceremonial music was used most frequently in the chronicle history plays, but was also employed in the tragedies. Such directions in the text as "alarums and excursions" called for the blast of trumpets, clash of cymbals, and roll of drums. Charges and retreats required trumpets, as did fanfares or flourishes which announced the entry of royal or noble persons. The hautboy, forerunner of the oboe, was another instrument much used in military scenes.

Many songs found their way into the plays. Shakespeare composed a number of original ones; others were popular songs of the day, or old traditional airs. The clown Feste, in Twelfth Night, sings an ancient ballad "Come Away, Death" accompanied by instrumentalists who are on stage. But the old drinking song, "And let me the canikin clink, clink," sung in the tavern scene in Othello, was unaccompanied except by the banging of tankards.

From the Music Room came the background, or "still," music, as it was called, which helped to intensify the terrifying atmosphere and eerie mood of the Apparition and Witch scenes in Macbeth. A thunderclap is heard as each Apparition appears and his passage across the stage must have been accompanied by strange unearthly sounds; the dance of the witches, too, which was frenzied and frightening, must have been done to music.

Sound effects were closely related to musical effects and were frequently called for in the plays. Thunder, the clashing of metal and clanking of chains, cannon shots and fireworks, the tolling of bells, and winding of hunting horns are only a few of the sounds which the Elizabethan stagehands had to produce.

Dancing, like music, was immensely popular in the social life of the time and played an equally important part in many of the plays. The most popular court dances were the allemande, the courante, the galliard, the lavolta, and the pavan; while the most celebrated country dances were Sellenger's Round and the Hay. Each dance had its own traditional music. Many of the comedies ended with the gayer of these dances, while the more stately dances helped to advance the plots of the serious plays. Shakespeare made use of dances in this dual way—to entertain the audience at his comedies and to heighten the dramatic action in his tragedies. It is at a great formal dance, to which he has come in order to see Rosaline, that Romeo first meets Juliet. And just before the King appears at Cardinal Wolsey's supper-dance, in *Henry VIII*, there is the stage direction, "Drum and trumpet; chambers discharged." As we have noted, at this play's premiere the firing of the cannon caused the Globe Theatre to burn to the ground, but the audience was so enthralled by the music, dancing, and sound effects going on at the moment, that they barely escaped with their lives.

The Audience

The Elizabethan theater was the most democratic institution in an undemocratic age. The audience was socially, economically, and educationally heterogeneous; every class was represented, from cutpurse to courtier.

Many Londoners were indifferent to the theater; others were openly hostile for religious reasons; but those who went attended more or less regularly once a week. It is believed that about 15,000 a week went in 1595, when two companies were operating; 18,000 went in 1601, when four companies were operating; and 21,000 went in 1605, when five companies were operating. By occupation, the largest single group in the audience, about 71 percent, consisted of shopkeepers and craftsmen; the second largest group, about 22 percent, was made up of porters, servants, laborers, with a sprinkling of such miscellaneous characters as prostitutes and pickpockets; the remaining 7 percent was accounted for by members of the nobility, professional men, and the gentry. Men, women, and children attended.

The Elizabethan playhouse accommodated from 2,000 to 2,500 people, but usually played to only half of capacity. On holidays, however, or on days when a special old favorite or a new play was being presented, the house would be jammed; then about one-third of the audience would stand in the yard, while the rest sat or stood in the galleries.

The penny paid as general admission had the buying power equivalent to the price of a movie today, so that the extra pennies charged for the better locations made those seats rather expensive. Only one other place in the theater commanded a higher price: sixpence was charged for a stool on the stage. Young gallants—wealthy playboys—who put on their finest clothes and went to the theater not to see the play but to be seen themselves would occupy these prominent places. The custom of sitting on the stage persisted until the eighteenth century when David Garrick abolished it.

All of the members of the audience put on their best clothes when they went to the theater, but the gallants outdid everyone except perhaps the members of the nobility. The audience was generally relaxed and in a gay mood; people smoked, ate oranges, and nuts during the performance. They cracked the nuts between their teeth and sometimes annoyed the actors and other members of the audience with the sound.

Although the enemies of the theater claimed that audiences were unruly and given to fighting and rioting, unbiased observers of the time speak only of the excellent behavior and rapt attention of the spectators, who laughed, applauded, and wept when their emotions were stirred, hissed or booed when they were displeased, but most of the time listened in interested silence.

The general mingling in the theater of people from all walks of life was a major cause of complaint on the part of public officials and Puritans, who were bent upon maintaining class distinctions and social barriers; but it gave the playwright the unique opportunity of appealing to individuals not as members of a class but as human beings with wide and varied backgrounds and tastes, and in so doing to write great plays of universal significance. This was the Elizabethan audience's contribution to the plays of Shakespeare.

THE PRODUCTION RECORD

Macbeth was especially written to entertain King James I and his guest, King Christian IV of Denmark, at Hampton Court on August 7, 1606. (See *The Royal Play of Macbeth* by Henry N. Paul, Macmillan, N.Y., 1950.) The play was acted at court by Richard Burbage and the King's Men and, a month or so later, was given its first public performance at the Globe Theatre. It was immediately successful and often repeated. At some time between 1610 and 1612, it is believed, the figure of Hecate and three additional witches, who sang and danced, were introduced into the play from Thomas Middleton's work *The Witch*. Since this was in line with the audience's growing taste for spectacle, the play was presented in this manner until the Puritans closed the theaters in 1642.

With the restoration of the drama, Sir William Davenant, who claimed to be Shakespeare's godson, was given authority by the king "to reform and make fit" for the audiences of 1660 the plays of the earlier period. Davenant lost no time in "improving" *Macbeth* by turning it into something like an opera. His version of the play was described as follows: "The Tragedy of Macbeth, alter'd by Sir William Davenant; being drest in all its Finery, as new Cloaths, new Scenes, Machines, as flyings for the Witches; with all the Singing and Dancing in it: The first compos'd by Mr. Lock, the other by Mr. Channell and Mr. Joseph Priest; it being all Excellently perform'd, being in the Nature of an Opera, it Recompenc'd double the Expense; it proves still a lasting play."

In January, 1744, David Garrick announced that he would produce *Macbeth* "as written by Shakespeare." James Quin, a rival actor, was surprised and shocked; he asked, "What does he mean? Don't I play *Macbeth* as written by Shakespeare?" Garrick removed all of Davenant's ineptly written scenes involving Lady Macduff and her morals, but in his zeal he went so far as to cut Shakespeare's scene of the murder of her children. The drunken porter was also cut out; but the witches with their singing, dancing, and cavorting, were retained, and many additional apparitions were introduced. For Macbeth's death scene, Garrick wrote a speech in which he mentioned "with dying breath, his guilt, delusion, the witches, and those horrid visions of future punishment, which must ever appall and torture the last moments of such accumulated crimes." Garrick was concerned, too, with the costumes in his plays; he mentions the red coats of Macbeth and Banquo, and says that Macbeth's night gown [dressing gown] "ought to be a Red Damask, and not the frippery flower'd one of a Foppington." In accordance with the

Charles Kean's 1853 production was noted for historical accuracy of costumes and scenery. The Ghost of Banquo appeared inside the column at left. (Victoria and Albert Museum, Enthoven Collection)

Two twentieth-century productions of *Macbeth*. (*Above*) The Negro theater unit of the WPA Federal Theater Project performed the play in New York City in 1936. The witches' scenes were conceived as voodoo rituals. Note the reclining skeleton on the backdrop. (Culver Service) (*Opposite*) At the National Theater in Munich in 1967, Verdi's opera *Macbeth* was transplanted to the age of technology. One interior set was a stylized entryway within the fortress. (German Information Service)

fashion of the time, all the actors wore wigs, so we are not surprised to learn that Banquo's ghost also appeared in a tie-wig.

Garrick wrote the following remarks as to the manner in which the actor playing Macbeth should behave after the murder of Duncan:

He should at that time, be a moving statue, or indeed a petrified man; his eyes must speak, and his tongue be metaphorically silent; his ears must be sensible of imaginary noises, and deaf to the present and audible voice of his wife; his attitude must be quick and permanent; his voice articulately trembling, and confusedly intelligible; the murderer should be seen in every limb, and yet every member, at that instant, should seem separated from his body, and his body from his soul. This is the picture of a complete regicide . . . I hope I shall not be thought minutely circumstantial, if I should advise a real genius to wear cork heels to his shoes, as in this scene he should seem to tread on air, and I promise him he will soon discover the great benefit of this (however seemingly trifling) piece of advice.

The next great innovation in the play was in the acting of Mrs. Sarah Siddons, who first performed the role in 1785 and continued in it for a quarter of a century. Mrs. Siddons depicted Lady Macbeth as an iron woman. From her first

scene she showed the decisiveness of the whole character and the daring steadiness of her mind, which could be disturbed by no scruple, intimidated by no danger. When she came on with the letter from Macbeth, in her first entrance, her face, her form, and her deportment gave the impression that she was possessed by a demon. She read the whole letter with the greatest skill and novelty and after an instant of reflection, exclaimed,

> Glamis thou art, and Cawdor—and shalt be
> What thou art promised.

The amazing burst of energy upon the words "shalt be" perfectly electrified the house. In the performance of the sleep-walking scene, Mrs. Siddons differed essentially from every other actress. "The actresses previous to herself," the account continues, "rather glided than walked, and every other action had a feebler character than is exhibited by one awake. Their figure, too, was kept perpendicularly erect, and the eye, though open, studiously avoided motion. . . . Mrs. Siddons seemed to conceive the fancy as having equal power over the whole frame, and all her actions had the wakeful vigor; she laded the water from the imaginary ewer over her hands—bent her body to listen to the sounds presented by her fancy, and hurried to resume the taper where she had left it, that she might with all speed drag her pallid husband to their chamber."

Every important English actor of the nineteenth century—John Kemble, Edmund Kean, Charles Kemble, Charles Macready—appeared in an elaborately mounted production of *Macbeth*, but it never occurred to these men to act the play as it had originally been written. That honor belongs to Samuel Phelps, who in 1847 produced the play from the text of the First Folio. It had not been done in this manner for about two hundred years. Phelps's actors wore "primitive mantles, with their heavy bars and ponderous folds," harmonizing well "with our notions of the early, almost traditional period of the play." Sir Laurence Olivier's production at Stratford-on-Avon in 1955 was conceived in similar fashion.

It was not until the present century that any serious or concerted effort was made to present Shakespeare's plays exactly as they were written, in conditions approximating to those of their original performance, that is, on a platform stage without scenery. Credit for initiating the return to this mode of production must go to William Poel, who in 1895 founded the Elizabethan Stage Society, and under its auspices put on many of Shakespeare's plays as he conceived that they had been done at the Globe. Poel insisted upon the rapid and clear speaking of the verse, with varied emphasis, and introduced startling stage business so as not to permit the attention of the audience to flag for an instant. He produced *Macbeth* in 1909, with Hubert Carter in the title role and Lillah McCarthy as Lady Macbeth; the Three Witches were played by the Irish actors William, Frank, and Brigit Fay, whose heavy brogues lent a strange, foreign quality to the proceedings. During the banquet scene, the ghost of Duncan as well as the ghost of Banquo appeared, and Poel showed that there was some warrant for this in the text.

Poel's work met with the opposition of the old-line producers, the objections of the critics, and the indifference of the public; but he left his mark unmistakably upon the more sensitive, intelligent, and enterprising members of his profession. Those who felt his influence and enlarged upon his ideas include Ben Greet, Gordon Craig, Max Reinhardt, Granville-Barker, Tyrone Guthrie, E. Martin Browne, Peter Brook, John Gielgud, and Laurence Olivier.

During 1948 and 1950, Margaret Webster's Travelling Shakespeare Company took two plays—*Hamlet* and *Macbeth*—to high schools, colleges, and universities in various parts of the United States. The problem of the designer was to create scenery that would take up little space and could be packed with speed. Wolfgang Roth solved the problem by using telescoped booms, hanging the front curtain on a wire, the other curtains on aluminum pipes, and painted scenery that rolled up like blinds. Rearranged in different ways the curtains and simple platforms served for both plays. All of the scenery and props were carried in a single truck, while the acting company traveled in a bus.

The most expert and exciting production of *Macbeth* to be presented in English in recent years was that done by Laurence Olivier and Vivien Leigh at the Shakespeare Memorial Theatre, Stratford-on-Avon, in the summer of 1955. The

The 1955 Stratford-on-Avon production. (*Left*) Sketch by Roger Furse of Laurence Olivier in the "nightshirt" costume for the porter's scene. (*Right*) Vivien Leigh and Olivier. (Angus McBean)

play was directed by Glen Byam Shaw, a Poel disciple, and designed by Roger Furse in colorful and primitive style. Olivier's performance, amply supported by voice and physique, created an overwhelming image of naked force and emphasized, at the same time, the perverse use to which this enormous force was being put. Olivier prepared a motion picture version of the play, but lack of financial backing held up its production.

Macbeth has been filmed several times, by amateurs as well as by professionals; two interesting screen versions were those produced by Reliance and by Republic Pictures. The earlier film was done in 1916 with Sir Herbert Tree and Constance Collier in the title roles; the 1948 version featured Orson Welles, his speech thick with Scottish burrs, and a musical score by Jacques Ibert. A Japanese screen adaptation of *Macbeth, The Throne of Blood* (*Kumonosu-Jo*), was produced by the Toho Company in 1957; the story was set in sixteenth-century Japan when the war lords battled each other for supremacy. The role of Lord Washizu (Macbeth) was played by Toshiro Mifune, and Isuzu Yamada enacted the part of Lady Washizu. Akira Kurosawa, Japan's most gifted director, was in charge of the production; although it lacked the greatness of the play, the film had scenes of unusual power; two in particular—the forest moving toward the castle and Washizu meeting his death—have seldom been matched on the screen for beauty or terror. Several television versions of the play have also been done.

LILLAH McCARTHY AS LADY MACBETH

[From June 22 to 26, 1909, Lillah McCarthy and Evelyn Weeden alternated in the role of Lady Macbeth in William Poel's production of the play at the Fulham Grand Theatre, London. Miss McCarthy made a detailed record of Poel's method of work of which the following is an excerpt:]

Make-up. Hair, bright red. Face, pink flush. Eyelids painted light green. Flecks of gold under the eyes. Eyebrows, same color as hair. Mouth very clear, carmine. Neck, white and pale blue. Hands likewise.

The hair or wig was specially handled: the forehead was built up high and broad; the hair was dressed well back from the ears, and swept into towering form from the forehead in front and the neck in back.

Carriage Style. The head was held high, the shoulders up, the spine straight, the legs and feet together. In the movements, there was to be a slight swing from side to side, not up and down.

Costumes. The characters had to wear the correct Elizabethan dress which Poel had copied from models in the art galleries. The wardrobe which he had collected was large and very beautiful as was his collection of stage jewellery.

Rehearsals. William Poel was insistent on the strictest observance of the precise details of rhythm, diction, voice, gesture, carriage, and make-up. He was ruthless in rehearsal. He rehearsed each of us one at a time. We were made to repeat after him our lines until we had got the rhythm and then the right expression of the passion or the tenderness or other essential of the part which the character demanded. While one of us was being rehearsed, the others sat at the back of the room in order to learn how to act.

Poel insisted on the *youth* of Shakespeare's leading characters. They were young boys and girls. Even the "old" parts were by no means aged; Lady Macbeth was thirty-five or so. Youth was exuberant in Shakespeare and old age was only a dim background.

Poel's rehearsing of *Macbeth* was the most tremendous dramatic experience I have ever known. Macbeth, a visionary: no mere murderous plotter. The vision of the deed obsessed him before he perpetrated it and pursued him after the deed was done with fear and apprehension and always his voice echoes chorus-like, haunting and terrible, the voice of a lost soul, itself agonised by the sense of its loss. Lady Macbeth—the realist, devilishly practical. No imagination for her but greed: the greed to govern, too great a greed, so great that it destroys her grasping mind, destroys his also, leaving only the mad and despairing vision of "tomorrow and tomorrow. . . ."

The discipline of William Poel's rehearsals sometimes wore me down. But I emerged from it knowing something. Poel scorned convention and tradition. He gave a brilliant example of his contempt for custom and of his genius when, in the "sleep-walking" scene, he made me, Lady Macbeth, as the scene opens sit at my dressing-table and begin to take off my rings and loosen my hair. The actress, who must presently reach such a dreadful climax of despair, can only rise to it if she begins on the lowest note in the scale of emotions. The tension of apprehension which the silence evokes will, moreover, have pity blended with it; pity for the poor distraught woman doing with hesitating fingers these trivial things of her daily life.

SOME REMARKS ON *Macbeth*
An Interview with Laurence Olivier

Sybil Thorndike once told Olivier, "You must be married to play *Macbeth*." This is not the portrait of a single man; it is not the fissure in the statue, and the statue crumbling. It is a dramatization of the kinship of two bed-fellows, and the actor must be conscious of the other person, his mate, on the stage.

The man in this case has imagination; the woman has none. It is the ability to foresee and to foreknow that at one and the same time provides the bait, and tortures the conscience. The two—husband and wife—pass each other; they do not meet. But as they move closer and then apart, the varying distances of their feeling and understanding are clearly shown. The journey of the plot, therefore, is forever fluctuating; it moves and ceases, flares and fails as does the relationship between Macbeth and Lady Macbeth.

The great moment, early in the play, is the meeting with the Witches. Macbeth's first line, "So foul and fair a day I have not seen," not only echoes the incantation of the Weird Sisters ("Fair is foul, and foul is fair") but is an excellent foreshadowing of the contrasts and conflicts, the tangled emotions that weave their way through the play. In the brilliant scene (I, 7) in which Macbeth is contemplating Duncan's murder, he tries to think "fairly" of his duty to his kinsmen and king but admits that he is "foully" driven to commit the crime by his vaulting ambition. It is a key moment, in which the absolute duplicity of his nature is revealed. Lady Macbeth is completely aware of it and is merely waiting for him to make a slip of the tongue to show that he will comply with her wishes and commit the murder. He gives himself away at last when he utters the lines:

> Bring forth men-children only;
> For thy undaunted mettle should compose
> Nothing but males.

The double pun of "mettle" for metal and "males" for coats of mail springs directly from his overheated imagination which already foresees the battles that are to ensue, and it is only later that he announces, "I am settled. . . ." Lady Macbeth, however, knows that he will do it long before he agrees to; she has known it all along.

The important thing to remember about this ill-starred couple is that they are human beings and not monsters. Lady Macbeth feels that she has a genuine right to the throne because her ancestors occupied it until Duncan's forebears treacherously usurped it; Macbeth, too, has a claim not only because he is first cousin to the king but because he has rendered meritorious service to his country on the field of battle. They have talked these things over at night, as husbands and wives do, and convinced themselves that there is ample justification for the murder. But Lady Macbeth cautions her husband about his guilty look:

> Your face, my thane, is as a book, where men
> May read strange matters.

She urges him to leave "matters" to her:

> . . . you shall put
> This night's great business into my dispatch,
> Which shall to all our nights and days to come
> Give solely sovereign sway, and masterdom.

When the moment comes to do the deed, however, she boggles at it and returns with the excuse:

> Had he [the king] not resembled
> My father as he slept, I had done't.

That is the beginning of the journey through hell for Macbeth and Lady Macbeth; deeper and deeper they wade in a pool of blood, and she goes down before he does.

From the very first moment that he contemplates the murder of the king, Macbeth's piercing imagination makes it clear that he is bound to fail; he is aware

> that we but teach
> Bloody instructions, which being taught, return
> To plague the inventor.

And when failure finally stares him in the face he is forced to capitulate, but not before he cries:

> be these juggling fiends no more believ'd,
> That palter with us in a double sense,
> That keep the word of promise to our ear,
> And break it to our hope.

This is the sort of rationalization that self-deception provides for one.

"Macbeth is the sort of man who makes you feel a little uncomfortable," says Olivier. "I tried to simulate a certain edgier, more resolute voice than I've really got, and to convey an impression of more power than the man sitting before you really suggests." Olivier first played Macbeth, unsuccessfully, at the Old Vic in 1937 but the intervening years have brought him many rich experiences both as a man and as an actor; he says: "You can't possibly play Macbeth without drawing on every single thing you have. You've got to give it everything you've ever done —Hamlet, Richard III, Malvolio, Henry V. There's no hope if you're not repeating yourself, and not making use of what you've learned."

SCENERY AND COSTUMES FOR OLIVIER'S *Macbeth*
An Interview with Roger Furse

Roger Furse, who had played an important part in the design of all of Laurence Olivier's Shakespearean films, was asked to create the scenery and costumes for the Olivier production of *Macbeth* at Stratford-on-Avon. Furse had about six months in which to think his ideas through and work them out in detail, and during that time the basic concept for the production was thoroughly discussed with Glen Byam Shaw, who directed the play, and with Olivier himself. It was decided that the production was to give the impression of power, speed, and fury, and that the heightened tempo of the action would demand quick changes of scenery which could best be accomplished by the use of flat drops and painted effects. It was also felt that the décor should have a barbaric simplicity which Furse conceived of in terms of rough-hewn stone and "pointed" arches which would be unusually fierce and primitive.

Although *Macbeth* was his favorite among the Shakespearean tragedies, Furse had never done the play before and was casting about in his mind for some way to give it a "sharp" look. He had designed the sets for Olivier's film version of *Hamlet* and remembered that during the scene between Hamlet and Polonius, when the young man addressed the older one in a very cutting manner, he had wanted the scenery to have an equally sharp and knifelike effect; so, as Hamlet quits the scene, we see behind him a series of pointed arches which are meant to reinforce the emotional quality of the moment. The idea of pointed arches originally came to Furse in the form of images of the wooden arches used in archaic Norwegian architecture. He had been thinking of the north, its relationship to the Hamlet story, saw the jutting edges of the timber structures in his mind's eye, adapted them for the stone castle at Elsinore, and then for the castle at Dunsinane, even incorporating them into such a detail as the tall pointed backs of the thrones occupied by Macbeth and his queen.

The walls, steps, battlements, and other architectural features, were made of flats, cloth, and board, as already mentioned, painted to simulate the texture of stone. The interior of Macbeth's castle at Inverness was interesting in that it was shown as a two-story structure, with the bedrooms on the upper level and the public rooms on stage level; a flight of stone steps on one side of the stage led up to the door of Duncan's chamber which was visible to the audience, and another flight of steps on the other side of the stage led to the chamber of the Macbeths. This arrangement made it possible for the audience to see Macbeth and Lady Macbeth enter and leave the room of their victim, and also to observe with heightened interest the horrified expressions on the faces of the men who discover the deed. The mechanically operated elevator-platform with which the stage at Stratford is equipped served in this scene as the upper story of the castle; in other scenes it represented the battlements at Inverness and Dunsinane, and supported the Weird Sisters in midair in their first appearance.

The outdoor scenes were distinguished by their contrasting moods. The scene on the heath, at the opening of the play, was backed by a cyclorama; in front of this were some ground rows of mountains and rocks; the elevator-platform was slightly raised, and from it steps led down toward the footlights; on the steps were some stylized stones. The scene was painted and lighted to suggest cloudiness and storm and to establish a threatening and foreboding mood. The scene in England, which represents a clearing in the woods, was done, on the other hand, in delicate greens and blues and, according to Furse, seemed out of keeping with the rest of the production because it comes without preparation and is basically pathetic and sentimental, in contrast to the coldness and brutality of the rest of the play. The back cloth was painted to depict a blue sky and soft, green hills, and in front of this was a thick grove of trees (cut-outs), which were made to look "chunky" and stylized; downstage, there was a section of broken wall on which the actors could sit. The England scene would have been entirely out of place, Furse feels, if the director had not conceived of a brilliant device to tie the scene in which Lady Macduff and her children are murdered to the scene that follows in England in which Macduff learns of the destruction of his family; as the assassin's dagger was driven home, Lady Macduff emitted an ear-piercing scream that did not die out as the murder scene ended but carried over into the opening of the England scene, thus bridging the two.

For the sleep-walking scene, there were three alleys of arches made up of four cut cloths and a backing; the openings cut in the cloths that hung toward the front of the stage were larger than the openings in the cloths at the rear, which produced an effect of perspective in depth; the stage was dimly lighted, but shafts of brighter light fell through the arches, increased the sense of distance, and gave an eerie quality to the scene; the arches at the front were red and shaded down to black at the back; they were not regular or symmetrical but seemed to be edged with blocks of rough-hewn stone upon which the light fell. In this production, Lady Macbeth did not descend from her chamber but, at the opening of the scene, advanced toward the audience from the farthest point upstage, and moved slowly through the series of arches and through the shafts of light, in and out of the shadows, going back at the end of the scene the way she had come.

The final scenes of the play, representing the battlements of Dunsinane, were conceived as a series of levels and steps, and the lighting suggested the reddish hues of blood.

The color scheme for the entire production was humorously known as "Furse's old dried blood"; it was composed mainly of reds and browns, rust-color, black, and green. A year or so after he had done this production, Furse was traveling with Olivier through the highlands of Scotland in search of "locations" for the then contemplated film version of Macbeth; it was midwinter and Furse was struck by the colors of the rocks, the dead bracken, dead heather, the lichens and iodine in the streams, which painted the Scottish landscape in the exact shades of red, brown, rust, green, and black that he had used for his stage sets.

Glen Byam Shaw's conception for the treatment of the Weird Sisters was highly original. He decided to present the witches, when they first appear, as if they were flying about in the murky air above the heath. To achieve this effect, the elevator-platform was raised to a great height and the witches were grouped on it, behind a gauze curtain. They made their second appearance on the heath on stage level, again in murky light; the third time they appeared, they were in a deep cave into which Macbeth had to descend in order to consult with them. These witches clearly exerted their supernatural powers in the air, on the earth, and in the dark subterranean regions. The witches' cauldron was placed over a trap-door in the stage and the apparitions came up from below and emerged from the mouth of the cauldron; the voices of the apparitions corresponded to those of Duncan, Banquo, and others with whom they stood in symbolic relationship; other symbols, too, forecasting action to come, emerged from the cauldron, such as the bough of a tree presaging Birnam Wood, and the head of Macbeth on a spear.

Since modern playgoers are cynical concerning the idea of ghosts, Roger Furse is of the opinion that stage apparitions ought to be made to seem as "real" as possible if the intention is to frighten the audience. It was for this reason that he first thought of presenting one of the witches as a ravishingly beautiful girl and rendered her that way in his sketches, but she so closely resembled a Charles Addams creation that he had to discard the idea for fear of causing laughter. In his television production of *Macbeth* in November, 1960, George Schaefer used this very interpretation and was praised for his conception of the apprentice witch.

The treatment of the Weird Sisters met with mixed reactions among the critics but their comments concerning the scenery were generally complimentary; one reviewer called the castle settings "monolithic" and said that the landscapes were "posterlike"; another remarked that the sets were "night-blue and darkly red (the hue of congealed blood)"; a third said, "Furse's settings hold the note of doom, although his Dunsinane battlements remind me of an earthquake-tilted church-yard"; and a fourth noted that the settings gave "the impression of rude and massive halls and storm-wracked wastes in which the gloomy and lurid story unfolded itself with perfect propriety." Two moments, involving the scenery, were thought to be particularly effective. Toward the beginning of the play, Lady Macbeth appeared against the blue, midnight sky up among the arches of Inverness Castle and the stage was filled with poignancy and beauty; and in the final duel, Macduff followed the retreating Macbeth up a winding flight of steps at Dunsinane. There was a last cut-and-thrust with the daggers, and they disappeared. At the next moment, against a sky suddenly clear and serene, Malcolm invited his Earls to see him crowned at Scone, and the beauty of this scene was not marred by the showing of "the usurper's cursed head."

In dressing the actors, it was Roger Furse's idea to design very simple clothes rather than "costumes," nor did he want to emphasize their "Scottishness" but attempted only to hint at it.

"I had no intention," said Furse, "of getting the actors up in vests of shaggy fur, boots in the same style, and double horns on their heads in primitive Scottish fashion. I chose, as a suitable and attractive period, the early Middle Ages—the

tenth and eleventh centuries—and studied the scenes depicted in the Winchester
Bible in order to adapt the style of clothing shown in the illuminations."

As Macbeth, Laurence Olivier was dressed mainly in browns, reds, and black;
for the banquet scene, he wore a scarlet cloak over a dark green tunic, and a
heavy, ornate crown. Although Macbeth's clothes—tunics, hose, leggings, and
cloaks—resembled those of the other men in style, they were much richer in color
and fabric, more highly decorated, and more striking. He also wore heavy golden
rings and a massive brooch that held his cloak at the right shoulder. Olivier's
make-up was very simple; his hair was soft and wavy and covered his ears, giving
his head a slight fullness, but the hair did not reach below the neckline at the
back; he had a mustache and a thin beard that outlined his jaw.

As played by Vivien Leigh, Lady Macbeth's glowing beauty helped to explain
the influence she exercised over her husband. In her first appearance, the actress
wore a gown of dull, mossy green. After the coronation, she was attired in a
gown of peacock blue-green that was shiny and seductive; from the waist and
shoulders fell panels of cloth decorated with gold; the skirt had a very long train
and was embroidered along the edges. Her robes of state included a voluminous
red cloak that had gold brooches at each shoulder from which wide gleaming
streamers fell to her waist. She wore a red wig, a large crown, and long pendant
earrings. Heavy costume jewelry consisting of square or rectangular brooches,
bracelets, and rings completed the outfit. For the sleepwalking scene, she appeared in pale night-clothes which were not white but seemed to be so in
contrast to the gunmetal dressing-gown that was thrown over her shoulders; the
dressing-gown was carefully draped for each performance so that it was crooked
and awry and gave her a weird and smoky look. It is interesting to note that
during the intensive study that she did in preparation for the part, Vivien Leigh
learned that Lady Macbeth's first name was Gruach, or Grace; although Miss
Leigh could work no grace into Lady Macbeth's spirit, she was the epitome of
grace in all her movements.

Civilian clothes for the men consisted of long-sleeved tunics, skirts, hose, and
cross-gartered leggings; a long piece of material was worn over one shoulder like
a plaid, and a leather pouch on a belt hung in front, from the waist, to suggest a
sporran. The fighting men wore leather armor, hard helmets of papier-mâché to
represent leather, and soft leather boots, some of which had rough skin on the
outside. Several of the soldiers had belts over one shoulder as well as around the
waist, and above this was the plaid, held in place by a large brooch at the left
shoulder. No mail or metal armor was used.

After the murder of Duncan, the men awakened from their sleep appeared in
long hose made of tightly fitting soft wool, some with plaids slung over their bare
shoulders, others in unbelted tunics which gave them a "nightshirty" look. The
Messenger who came to warn Lady Macduff was conceived of, for this production, as a shepherd who carried a crook and wore a fleece coat and leggings of
a dirty off-white. The Porter, too, was dirty and patchy, his clothes covered with
wine and egg stains; he wore a belt to which keys were attached and entered
carrying his boots, which he put on during the scene.

The men's make-up did not have a smooth and finished look but was intended to be a bit sweaty; many of the men were sparsely bearded. The fabrics for all the costumes were treated in various ways: The cloth was lightly painted to give a tartan effect; the edges of the skirts were decorated; the leather, papier-mâché, and other materials were sprayed with paint, roughed, bruised, tinted, or toned to suggest the contours of the body. The women's gowns, in particular, were designed to accentuate the physique. They were low-waisted and tight-fitting, and made of soft, clinging materials. In order to achieve a high-bosomed effect, shadows were painted on the gown under the breasts. In several instances, Furse painted the anatomy on the costumes of both men and women; shadows and highlights indicated breasts, ribs, navels, and crotches. The purpose was to emphasize the fact that the clothing was not merely hanging on the body but actually fitted the form.

Roger Furse began work on the production of *Macbeth* with a series of mental images of the sets and costumes that he wanted to use; he made rough sketches of these and took them to the director for approval. Then he drew his ground plans; these are especially complex for productions at Stratford because the use of the elevator-platform is involved and because plays are presented there in repertory, which means that the scenery for several plays must be taken into consideration, in order to avoid hanging and storing conflicts. Some of the scenery may be left in the flies, but most of it has to be taken down to make way for the other productions.

From the ground plans, Furse makes a rough model of the set in order to get the proportions of the elements before proceeding with exact measurements; the main items of scenery are done first so that he will have enough time to work out the snags, and also because building and painting take longer than other jobs. Furse thinks out a palette of colors in his mind and then works out the colors of the costumes as they will be seen against the colors of the scenery; since the costumes must stand out from the scenery, subtleties in harmony and contrast have to be devised.

The job of designing the sets and costumes for *Macbeth* took half a year of intensive work; Furse was occupied the entire time conceiving, executing, and supervising the job from beginning to end. He was not permitted, however, to assume the entire responsibility for the lighting of the production but had to work in consultation with the lighting designer of the Stratford Memorial Theatre.

"A designer has to make financial sacrifices to work at Stratford," says Mr. Furse, "but it is a rewarding experience in other ways. The films certainly pay much better and plans for the filming of *Macbeth* have proceeded to an advanced stage. With Olivier, I worked out the picture scene by scene, even down to the timing of each scene. Every set was planned to fit the locations we selected in Scotland where the film is to be made; the scale and mood of the country are exactly right for the screen. But Scotland is becoming "civilized" so fast—so many telephone poles and TV aerials are going up all over the place—that unless we shoot the film soon the locations we've selected will be useless."

The Tragedy of Macbeth

DRAMATIS PERSONÆ.

DUNCAN, King of Scotland.

MALCOLM,
DONALBAIN, } his sons.

MACBETH,
BANQUO, } Generals of the Scottish Army.

MACDUFF,
LENNOX,
ROSS,
MENTEITH, } Noblemen of Scotland.
ANGUS,
CAITHNESS,

FLEANCE, Son to Banquo.

SIWARD, Earl of Northumberland, General of the English forces.

YOUNG SIWARD, his son.

SEYTON, an Officer attending on Macbeth.

Boy, son to Macduff.

A Sergeant.

A Porter.

An Old Man.

An English Doctor.

A Scottish Doctor.

LADY MACBETH.

LADY MACDUFF.

A Gentlewoman, attending on Lady Macbeth.

Three Witches.

HECATE.

The Ghost of Banquo.

Apparitions.

Lords, Gentlemen, Officers, Soldiers, Murderers, Messengers, Attendants.

SCENE.—SCOTLAND; ENGLAND.

ACT I. SCENE I.
SCOTLAND. AN OPEN PLACE.

(*Thunder and lightning. Enter three* WITCHES.)

1. Witch. When shall we three meet again
In thunder, lightning, or in rain?
2. Witch. When the hurlyburly's done,
When the battle's lost and won.

3. Witch. That will be ere the set of sun.　　　　　　　　　　5
1. Witch. Where the place?　　　　.
2. Witch.　　　　　Upon the heath.
3. Witch. There to meet with Macbeth.
1. Witch. I come, Graymalkin!
2. Witch. Paddock calls.
3. Witch.　　　　　Anon!
All. Fair is foul, and foul is fair.　　10
　Hover through the fog and filthy air.
　(*Exeunt.*)

Scene ii. A camp near Forres.

(*Alarum within. Enter* King Duncan, Malcolm, Donalbain, Lennox, *with* Attendants, *meeting a bleeding* Sergeant.)

King. What bloody man is that? He can report,
　As seemeth by his plight, of the revolt
　The newest state.[1]
Mal.　　　　　This is the sergeant
　Who like a good and hardy soldier fought
　'Gainst my captivity. Hail, brave friend!　　　　　　5
　Say to the King the knowledge of the broil [2]
　As thou didst leave it.
Serg.　　　　　Doubtful it stood,
　As two spent swimmers that do cling together
　And choke their art. The merciless Macdonwald
　(Worthy to be a rebel, for to that　10
　The multiplying villanies of nature
　Do swarm upon him) from the Western Isles
　Of kerns and gallowglasses[3] is supplied;

1. Latest news.
2. Battle.
3. Irish soldiers.
4. Doomed.
5. Favorite.

And Fortune, on his damned [4] quarrel smiling,
　Show'd like a rebel's whore. But all's too weak;　　　　　15
　For brave Macbeth (well he deserves that name),
　Disdaining Fortune, with his brandish'd steel,
　Which smok'd with bloody execution
　(Like valor's minion[5]), carv'd out his passage
　Till he fac'd the slave;　　　20
　Which[6] ne'er shook hands nor bade farewell to him
　Till he unseam'd him from the nave[7] to th' chaps[8]
　And fix'd his head upon our battlements.
King. O valiant cousin! worthy gentleman!
Serg. As whence the sun 'gins his reflection　　　　　25
　Shipwracking storms and direful thunders break,
　So from that spring whence comfort seem'd to come
　Discomfort swells. Mark, King of Scotland, mark.
　No sooner justice had, with valor arm'd,
　Compell'd these skipping kerns to trust their heels　　　30
　But the Norweyan lord, surveying vantage,
　With furbish'd arms and new supplies of men,
　Began a fresh assault.[9]
King.　　　　　Dismay'd not this
　Our captains, Macbeth and Banquo?
Serg.　　　　　Yes,

6. Macbeth.
7. Navel.
8. Jaws.
9. After the defeat of Macdonwald's men, the Norwegians attacked.

As sparrows eagles, or the hare the
lion.[10]   35
If I say sooth, I must report they
were
As cannons overcharg'd with double
cracks, so they
Doubly redoubled strokes upon the
foe.
Except[11] they meant to bathe in
reeking wounds,
Or memorize[12] another Golgotha,   40
I cannot tell—
But I am faint; my gashes cry for
help.
King. So well thy words become thee
as thy wounds;
They smack of honor both. Go get
him surgeons.

(*Exit* SERGEANT, *attended.*)
(*Enter* ROSS.)

Who comes here?
Mal.   The worthy Thane of Ross.   45
Len. What a haste looks through his
eyes! So should he look
That seems to speak things strange.
Ross.   God save the King!
King. Whence cam'st thou, worthy
thane?
Ross.   From Fife, great King,
Where the Norweyan banners flout
the sky
And fan our people cold. Norway
himself,[13]   50
With terrible numbers,
Assisted by that most disloyal traitor
The Thane of Cawdor, began a
dismal conflict,
Till that Bellona's bridegroom, lapp'd
in proof,[14]

Confronted him with self-compari-
sons,[15]   55
Point against point, rebellious arm
'gainst arm,
Curbing his lavish spirit; and to con-
clude,
The victory fell on us.
King.   Great happiness!
Ross.   That now
Sweno, the Norways' king, craves
composition;[16]
Nor would we deign him burial of
his men   60
Till he disbursed, at Saint Colme's
Inch,[17]
Ten thousand dollars to our general
use.
King. No more that Thane of Cawdor
shall deceive
Our bosom interest. Go pronounce
his present death
And with his former title greet Mac-
beth.   65
Ross. I'll see it done.
Dun. What he hath lost noble Macbeth
hath won.

(*Exeunt.*)

SCENE III. A BLASTED HEATH.

(*Thunder. Enter the three* WITCHES.)
1. Witch. Where hast thou been, sister?
2. Witch. Killing swine.
3. Witch. Sister, where thou?
1. Witch. A sailor's wife had chestnuts
in her lap
And munch'd and munch'd and
munch'd. 'Give me,' quoth I.   5
'Aroint[1] thee, witch!' the rump-fed
ronyon[2] cries.

---

10. As sparrows dismay eagles, etc.
11. Whether.
12. Make memorable.
13. The King of Norway.
14. Macbeth in armor.

15. Matched him stroke for stroke.
16. A peace treaty.
17. Island in the Firth of Forth.
1. Begone.
2. Mangy woman.

Her husband's to Aleppo gone, mas-
ter o' th' Tiger;³
But in a sieve I'll thither sail
And, like a rat without a tail,
I'll do, I'll do, and I'll do.   10
2. *Witch.* I'll give thee a wind.
1. *Witch.* Th' art kind.
3. *Witch.* And I another.
1. *Witch.* I myself have all the other,
And the very ports they blow,   15
All the quarters that they know
I' th' shipman's card.
I will drain him dry as hay.
Sleep shall neither night nor day
Hang upon his penthouse lid.   20
He shall live a man forbid.
Weary sev'nights, nine times nine,
Shall he dwindle, peak, and pine.
Though his bark cannot be lost,
Yet it shall be tempest-tost.   25
Look what I have.
2. *Witch.* Show me! show me!
1. *Witch.* Here I have a pilot's thumb,
Wrack'd as homeward he did come.

(*Drum within.*)

3. *Witch.* A drum, a drum!   30
Macbeth doth come.
All. The Weird Sisters,⁴ hand in hand,
Posters of ⁵ the sea and land,
Thus do go about, about,   34
Thrice to thine, and thrice to mine,
And thrice again, to make up nine.
Peace! The charm's wound up.

(*Enter* MACBETH *and* BANQUO.)

Macb. So foul and fair a day I have not
seen.
Ban. How far is't call'd to Forres? What
are these,
So wither'd, and so wild in their attire,   40

That look not like th' inhabitants o'
th' earth,
And yet are on't? Live you? or are
you aught
That man may question? You seem to
understand me,
By each at once her choppy⁶ finger
laying
Upon her skinny lips. You should be
women,   45
And yet your beards forbid me to
interpret
That you are so.
Macb. Speak, if you can. What are you?
1. *Witch.* All hail, Macbeth! Hail to
thee, Thane of Glamis!
2. *Witch.* All hail, Macbeth! Hail to
thee, Thane of Cawdor!
3. *Witch.* All hail, Macbeth, that shalt
be King hereafter!   50
Ban. Good sir, why do you start and
seem to fear
Things that do sound so fair? I' th'
name of truth,
Are ye fantastical, or that indeed
Which outwardly ye show? My noble
partner
You greet with present grace and
great prediction   55
Of noble having and of royal hope,
That he seems rapt withal.⁷ To me
you speak not.
If you can look into the seeds of time
And say which grain will grow and
which will not,
Speak then to me, who neither beg
nor fear   60
Your favors nor your hate.
1. *Witch.* Hail!
2. *Witch.* Hail!
3. *Witch.* Hail!

3. Name of a ship.
4. Goddesses of Destiny.
5. Swift travelers over.

6. Chapped.
7. Carried away by it.

1. Witch. Lesser than Macbeth, and
   greater.   65
2. Witch. Not so happy, yet much happier.
3. Witch. Thou shalt get[8] kings, though
   thou be none.
   So all hail, Macbeth and Banquo!
1. Witch. Banquo and Macbeth, all
   hail!
Macb. Stay, you imperfect[9] speakers,
   tell me more!   70
   By Sinel's[10] death I know I am Thane
   of Glamis;
   But how of Cawdor? The Thane of
   Cawdor lives,
   A prosperous gentleman; and to be
   King
   Stands not within the prospect of be-
   lief,
   No more than to be Cawdor. Say
   from whence   75
   You owe this strange intelligence, or
   why
   Upon this blasted heath you stop our
   way
   With such prophetic greeting. Speak,
   I charge you.

   (*Witches vanish.*)

Ban. The earth hath bubbles, as the
   water has,
   And these are of them. Whither are
   they vanish'd?   80
Macb. Into the air, and what seem'd
   corporal melted
   As breath into the wind. Would they
   had stay'd!
Ban. Were such things here as we do
   speak about?
   Or have we eaten on the insane root[11]
   That takes the reason prisoner?   85

Macb. Your children shall be kings.
Ban.   You shall be King.
Macb. And Thane of Cawdor too. Went
   it not so?
Ban. To th' selfsame tune and words.
   Who's here?

   (*Enter* Ross *and* ANGUS.)

Ross. The King hath happily receiv'd,
   Macbeth,
   The news of thy success; and when
   he reads   90
   Thy personal venture in the rebels'
   fight,
   His wonders and his praises do con-
   tend
   Which should be thine or his. Silenc'd
   with that,
   In viewing o'er the rest o' th' self-
   same day,
   He finds thee in the stout Norweyan
   ranks,   95
   Nothing afeard of what thyself didst
   make,
   Strange images[12] of death. As thick
   as hail
   Came post with post,[13] and every one
   did bear
   Thy praises in his kingdom's great
   defense
   And pour'd them down before him.
Ang.   We are sent   100
   To give thee from our royal master
   thanks;
   Only to herald [14] thee into his sight,
   Not pay thee.
Ross. And for an earnest[15] of a greater
   honor,
   He bade me, from him, call thee
   Thane of Cawdor;   105

8. Beget.
9. Puzzling.
10. Macbeth's father.
11. A root supposed to cause insanity.

12. Horrible forms.
13. Messenger after messenger.
14. Conduct.
15. Pledge.

In which addition,[16] hail, most worthy
    Thane!
    For it is thine.
Ban.   What, can the devil speak true?
Macb. The Thane of Cawdor lives. Why
    do you dress me
    In borrowed robes?
Ang.   Who was the Thane lives yet,
    But under heavy judgment[17] bears
    that life   110
    Which he deserves to lose. Whether
    he was combin'd
    With those of Norway, or did line[18]
    the rebel
    With hidden help and vantage, or
    that with both[19]
    He labor'd in his country's wrack, I
    know not;
    But treasons capital, confess'd and
    prov'd,   115
    Have overthrown him.
Macb. (*aside*) Glamis, and Thane of
    Cawdor!
    The greatest is behind.[20]—(*To* Ross
    and Angus) Thanks for your pains.
    (*Aside to* Banquo) Do you not hope
    your children shall be kings,
    When those that gave the Thane of
    Cawdor to me
    Promis'd no less to them?
Ban. (*aside to* Macbeth) That, trusted
    home,[21]   120
    Might yet enkindle you unto the
    crown,
    Besides the Thane of Cawdor. But 'tis
    strange!
    And oftentimes, to win us to our
    harm,
    The instruments of darkness tell us
    truths,   124

Win us with honest trifles, to be-
    tray 's
    In deepest consequence.—
    Cousins, a word, I pray you.
Macb.   (*aside*) Two truths are told,
    As happy prologues to the swelling[22]
    act
    Of the imperial theme.—I thank you,
    gentlemen.—   129
    (*Aside*) This supernatural soliciting[23]
    Cannot be ill; cannot be good. If ill,
    Why hath it given me earnest of suc-
    cess,
    Commencing in a truth? I am Thane
    of Cawdor.
    If good, why do I yield to that sug-
    gestion
    Whose horrid image doth unfix my
    hair   135
    And make my seated [24] heart knock
    at my ribs
    Against the use of nature? Present
    fears
    Are less than horrible imaginings.
    My thought, whose murder yet is but
    fantastical,
    Shakes so my single state of man that
    function   140
    Is smother'd in surmise and nothing
    is
    But what is not.
Ban.   Look how our partner's rapt.
Macb. (*aside*) If chance will have me
    King, why, chance may crown me,
    Without my stir.[25]
Ban.   New honors come upon him,
    Like our strange[26] garments, cleave
    not to their mold [27]   145
    But with the aid of use.
Macb. (*aside*) Come what come may,

---

16. Title.
17. Sentence.
18. Aid.
19. Macdonwald and the King of Norway.
20. Still to come.
21. If you believe it.

22. Magnificent.
23. Prediction.
24. Firm.
25. Stirring.
26. New.
27. Do not fit.

Time and the hour runs through the
roughest day.

Ban. Worthy Macbeth, we stay upon
your leisure.

Macb. Give me your favor.[28] My dull
brain was wrought
With things forgotten. Kind gentle-
men, your pains   150
Are regist'red where every day I turn
The leaf to read them.[29] Let us to-
ward the King.
(*Aside to* Banquo) Think upon what
hath chanc'd; and, at more time,
The interim having weigh'd it,[30] let
us speak
Our free hearts each to other.

Ban. (*aside to* Macbeth) Very gladly.

Macb. (*aside to* Banquo) Till then,
enough.—Come, friends.   156

(*Exeunt.*)

Scene iv. Forres. The palace.

(*Flourish. Enter* King Duncan, Lennox, Malcolm, Donalbain, *and* Attendants.)

King. Is execution done on Cawdor?
Are not
Those in commission yet return'd?

Mal.   My liege,
They are not yet come back. But I
have spoke
With one that saw him die; who did
report
That very frankly he confess'd his
treasons,   5
Implor'd your Highness' pardon, and
set forth
A deep repentance. Nothing in his
life
Became him like the leaving it. He
died

As one that had been studied [1] in his
death
To throw away the dearest thing he
ow'd   10
As 'twere a careless trifle.

King.   There's no art
To find the mind's construction[2] in
the face.
He was a gentleman on whom I built
An absolute trust.

(*Enter* Macbeth, Banquo, *and* Angus.)

                    O worthiest cousin,
The sin of my ingratitude even now
Was heavy on me! Thou art so far
before   16
That swiftest wing of recompense is
slow
To overtake thee. Would thou hadst
less deserv'd,
That the proportion both of thanks
and payment
Might have been mine! Only I have
left to say,   20
More is thy due than more than all
can pay.

Macb. The service and the loyalty I
owe,
In doing it pays itself. Your Highness' part
Is to receive our duties; and our
duties
Are to your throne and state children
and servants,   25
Which do but what they should by
doing everything
Safe toward your love and honor.

King.   Welcome hither.
I have begun to plant thee and will
labor

---

28. Pardon.
29. In my memory.
30. Having considered it meanwhile.

1. As if he had studied the art of dying.
2. Intention.

To make thee full of growing. Noble
   Banquo,
That hast no less deserv'd, nor must
   be known   30
No less to have done so, let me infold
   thee
And hold thee to my heart.
Ban.   There if I grow,
   The harvest is your own.
King.   My plenteous joys,
   Wanton in fulness, seek to hide them-
      selves
   In drops of sorrow. Sons, kinsmen,
      thanes,   35
And you whose places are the near-
   est, know
We will establish our estate upon
Our eldest, Malcolm, whom we name
   hereafter
The Prince of Cumberland; which
   honor must   39
Not unaccompanied invest him only,
But signs of nobleness, like stars, shall
   shine
On all deservers. From hence to In-
   verness,
And bind us further to you.
Macb. The rest is labor, which is not
   us'd for you!
I'll be myself the harbinger,[3] and
   make joyful   45
The hearing of my wife with your
   approach;
So, humbly take my leave.
King.   My worthy Cawdor!
Macb. (*aside*) The Prince of Cumber-
   land! That is a step
On which I must fall down, or else
   o'erleap,
For in my way it lies. Stars, hide your
   fires!   50
Let not light see my black and deep
   desires.

The eye wink at the hand;[4] yet let
   that be,
Which the eye fears, when it is done,
   to see.

(*Exit.*)

King. True, worthy Banquo: he is full
   so valiant,[5]   54
And in his commendations I am fed;
It is a banquet to me. Let's after him,
Whose care is gone before to bid us
   welcome.
It is a peerless kinsman.

(*Flourish. Exeunt.*)

SCENE V. INVERNESS. MACBETH'S CASTLE.

(*Enter* MACBETH'S WIFE, *alone, with
a letter.*)

Lady. (*reads*) 'They met me in the
   day of success; and I have learn'd
   by the perfect'st report they have
   more in them than mortal knowledge. When I burn'd in desire to
   question them further, they made
   themselves air, into which they
   vanish'd. Whiles I stood rapt in
   the wonder of it, came missives
   from the King, who all-hail'd me
   Thane of Cawdor, by which title,
   before, these Weird Sisters saluted
   me, and referr'd me to the coming
   on of time with "Hail, King that
   shalt be!" This have I thought good
   to deliver thee, my dearest partner
   of greatness, that thou mightst not
   lose the dues of rejoicing by being
   ignorant of what greatness is
   promis'd thee. Lay it to thy heart,
   and farewell.'   21

Glamis thou art, and Cawdor, and
   shalt be—

---

3. Messenger.
4. Let the eye not see what the hand does.

5. As valiant as you say he is.

What thou art promis'd. Yet do I fear thy nature.
It is too full o' th' milk of human kindness
To catch the nearest way. Thou wouldst be great;   25
Art not without ambition, but without
The illness[1] should attend it. What thou wouldst highly,
That wouldst thou holily; wouldst not play false,
And yet wouldst wrongly win. Thou'ldst have, great Glamis,
That which cries 'Thus thou must do,' if thou have it;   30
And that which rather thou dost fear to do
Than wishest should be undone. Hie thee hither,
That I may pour my spirits in thine ear
And chastise with the valor of my tongue
All that impedes thee from the golden round [2]   35
Which fate and metaphysical [3] aid doth seem
To have thee crown'd withal.

(*Enter* MESSENGER.)
                    What is your tidings?
Mess.   The King comes here to-night.
Lady.   Thou'rt mad to say it!
Is not thy master with him? who, were't so,   39
Would have inform'd for preparation.
Mess. So please you, it is true. Our Thane is coming.
One of my fellows had the speed of him,[4]

Who, almost dead for breath, had scarcely more
Than would make up his message.
Lady.   Give him tending;
He brings great news.
(*Exit* MESSENGER.)
                    The raven himself is hoarse
That croaks the fatal entrance of Duncan   46
Under my battlements. Come, you spirits
That tend on mortal thoughts, unsex me here,
And fill me, from the crown to the toe, top-full
Of direst cruelty! Make thick my blood;   50
Stop up th' access and passage to remorse,
That no compunctious visitings of nature[5]
Shake my fell purpose nor keep peace between
Th' effect and it! Come to my woman's breasts
And take my milk for gall, you murd'ring ministers,   55
Wherever in your sightless[6] substances
You wait on nature's mischief! [7] Come, thick night,
And pall [8] thee in the dunnest[9] smoke of hell,
That my keen knife see not the wound it makes,
Nor heaven peep through the blanket of the dark   60
To cry 'Hold, hold!'

(*Enter* MACBETH.)
                    Great Glamis! worthy Cawdor!

1. Evil nature.
2. The crown.
3. Supernatural.
4. Outran him.
5. Instinctive feelings of pity.
6. Invisible.
7. Serve evil.
8. Wrap.
9. Blackest.

MACBETH 195

Greater than both, by the all-hail
hereafter!
Thy letters have transported me be-
yond
This ignorant present, and I feel
now   64
The future in the instant.¹⁰
Macb.   My dearest love,
Duncan comes here to-night.
Lady.   And when goes hence?
Macb. To-morrow, as he purposes.
Lady.   O, never
Shall sun that morrow see!
Your face, my Thane, is as a book
where men
May read strange matters. To be-
guile the time,¹¹   70
Look like the time;¹² bear welcome
in your eye,
Your hand, your tongue; look like the
innocent flower,
But be the serpent under't. He that's
coming
Must be provided for; and you shall
put
This night's great business into my
dispatch,   75
Which shall to all our nights and
days to come
Give solely sovereign sway and mas-
terdom.
Macb. We will speak further.
Lady.   Only look up clear.
To alter favor ever is to fear.¹³
Leave all the rest to me.   80

(*Exeunt.*)

SCENE VI. INVERNESS. BEFORE MACBETH'S
CASTLE.

(*Hautboys and torches. Enter* KING
DUNCAN, MALCOLM, DONALBAIN,

BANQUO, LENNOX, MACDUFF, ROSS,
ANGUS, *and* ATTENDANTS.)
King. This castle hath a pleasant seat.
The air
Nimbly and sweetly recommends it-
self
Unto our gentle senses.
Ban.   This guest of summer,
The temple-haunting martlet,¹ does
approve
By his lov'd mansionry² that the
heaven's breath   5
Smells wooingly here. No jutty,
frieze,
Buttress, nor coign of vantage, but
this bird
Hath made his pendent bed and pro-
creant cradle.
Where they most breed and haunt,
I have observ'd
The air is delicate.

(*Enter* LADY MACBETH.)

King. See, see, our honor'd hostess! 10
The love that follows us sometime is
our trouble,
Which still we thank as love. Herein
I teach you
How you shall bid God 'ild³ us for
your pains
And thank us for your trouble.
Lady.   All our service
In every point twice done, and then
done double,   15
Were poor and single business to
contend
Against those honors deep and broad
wherewith
Your Majesty loads our house. For
those of old,⁴

10. You seem already to be king.
11. To deceive the world.
12. Wear an appropriate expression.
13. To change your facial expression is to
betray yourself.

1. A small bird.
2. Demonstrates by choosing this place for
his nest.
3. Reward.
4. Past honors.

And the late[5] dignities heap'd up to them,   19
We rest your hermits,[6]

King. Where's the Thane of Cawdor?
We cours'd him at the heels and had a purpose
To be his purveyor;[7] but he rides well.
And his great love, sharp as his spur, hath holp[8] him
To his home before us. Fair and noble hostess,
We are your guest to-night.

Lady.   Your servants ever 25
Have theirs, themselves, and what is theirs, in compt,
To make their audit at your Highness' pleasure,
Still to return your own.[9]

King.   Give me your hand;
Conduct me to mine host. We love him highly
And shall continue our graces towards him.   30
By your leave, hostess.

(*Exeunt.*)

SCENE VII. INVERNESS. MACBETH'S CASTLE.

(*Hautboys. Torches. Enter a* SEWER,[1] *and divers* SERVANTS *with dishes and service, and cross the stage. Then enter* MACBETH.)

Macb. If it were done when 'tis done, then 'twere well
It were done quickly. If th' assassination
Could trammel up the consequence,[2] and catch,

With his surcease,[3] success; that but this blow
Might be the be-all and the end-all here,   5
But here, upon this bank and shoal of time,
We'ld jump[4] the life to come. But in these cases
We still have judgment here, that we but teach
Bloody instructions, which, being taught, return
To plague th' inventor. This even-handed justice   10
Commends th' ingredients of our poison'd chalice
To our own lips. He's here in double trust:
First, as I am his kinsman and his subject—
Strong both against the deed; then, as his host,
Who should against his murderer shut the door,   15
Not bear the knife myself. Besides, this Duncan
Hath borne his faculties so meek, hath been
So clear in his great office, that his virtues
Will plead like angels, trumpet-tongu'd, against
The deep damnation of his taking-off;   20
And pity, like a naked new-born babe,
Striding the blast, or heaven's cheru-bin, hors'd
Upon the sightless couriers of the air,

5. Recent.
6. Worshipers.
7. Forerunner.
8. Helped.
9. We owe you our duty, and we are ready to pay it.

1. Butler.
2. Put an end to the matter.
3. Duncan's death.
4. Risk.

Shall blow the horrid deed in every
eye,
That tears shall drown the wind. I
have no spur   25
To prick the sides of my intent, but
only
Vaulting ambition, which o'erleaps
itself
And falls on th' other side.

(*Enter* LADY MACBETH.)
                    How now? What news?
Lady. He has almost supp'd. Why have
you left the chamber?
Macb. Hath he ask'd for me?
Lady.   Know you not he has?   30
Macb. We will proceed no further in
this business.
He hath honor'd me of late, and I
have bought
Golden opinions from all sorts of
people,
Which would be worn now in their
newest gloss,
Not cast aside so soon.
Lady.   Was the hope drunk   35
Wherein you dress'd yourself? Hath
it slept since?
And wakes it now to look so green
and pale
At what it did so freely? From this
time
Such I account thy love. Art thou
afeard
To be the same in thine own act and
valor   40
As thou art in desire? Wouldst thou
have that
Which thou esteem'st the ornament
of life,
And live a coward in thine own
esteem,
Letting 'I dare not' wait upon 'I
would,'

Like the poor cat i' th' adage? [5]
Macb.   Prithee peace!   45
I dare do all that may become a man.
Who dares do more is none.
Lady.   What beast was't then
That made you break this enterprise
to me?
When you durst do it, then you were
a man;
And to be more than what you were,
you would   50
Be so much more the man. Nor time
nor place
Did then adhere,[6] and yet you would
make both.
They have made themselves, and
that their fitness now
Does unmake you. I have given suck,
and I know
How tender 'tis to love the babe that
milks me.   55
I would, while it was smiling in my
face,
Have pluck'd my nipple from his
boneless gums
And dash'd the brains out, had I so
sworn as you
Have done to this.
Macb.   If we should fail?
Lady.   We fail?
But screw your courage to the stick-
ing place,   60
And we'll not fail. When Duncan is
asleep
(Whereto the rather shall his day's
hard journey
Soundly invite him), his two cham-
berlains
Will I with wine and wassail [7] so con-
vince
That memory, the warder of the
brain,   65
Shall be a fume, and the receipt of
reason

5. The cat wanted to eat fish but didn't want
to wet her feet.
6. Were then suitable.
7. Punch.

A limbeck[8] only. When in swinish
sleep
Their drenched natures lie as in a
death,
What cannot you and I perform upon
Th' unguarded Duncan? what not
put upon   70
His spongy[9] officers, who shall bear
the guilt
Of our great quell?[10]

Macb. Bring forth men-children only;
For thy undaunted mettle should
compose
Nothing but males. Will it not be
receiv'd,
When we have mark'd with blood
those sleepy two   75
Of his own chamber and us'd their
very daggers,
That they have done't?

Lady.   Who dares receive it other,
As we shall make our griefs and
clamor roar
Upon his death?

Macb.   I am settled and bend up
Each corporal agent[11] to this terrible
feat,   80
Away, and mock the time[12] with fair-
est show;
False face must hide what the false
heart doth know.

(*Exeunt.*)

ACT II. SCENE I. INVERNESS.
COURT OF MACBETH'S CASTLE.

(*Enter* BANQUO, *and* FLEANCE *with
a torch before him.*)

Ban. How goes the night, boy?
Fle. The moon is down; I have not
heard the clock.
Ban. And she goes down at twelve.

Fle.   I take't, 'tis later, sir.
Ban. Hold, take my sword. There's
husbandry in heaven;
Their candles are all out. Take thee
that too.   5
A heavy summons lies like lead upon
me,
And yet I would not sleep. Merciful
powers,
Restrain in me the cursed thoughts
that nature
Gives way to in repose!

(*Enter* MACBETH, *and a* SERVANT
with a torch.)

Give me my sword.
Who's there?   10
Macb. A friend.
Ban. What, sir, not yet at rest? The
King's abed.
He hath been in unusual pleasure
and
Sent forth great largess to your of-
fices.
This diamond he greets your wife
withal   15
By the name of most kind hostess,
and shut up
In measureless content.

Macb.   Being unprepar'd,
Our will became the servant to de-
fect,[1]
Which else should free have wrought.

Ban.   All's well.
I dreamt last night of the three Weird
Sisters.   20
To you they have show'd some truth.

Macb.   I think not of them.
Yet when we can entreat an hour to
serve,
We would spend it in some words
upon that business,

---

8. A still.
9. Drunken.
10. Murder.

11. Bodily faculty.
12. Deceive everyone.
1. We did not entertain the king properly.

If you would grant the time.

Ban.   At your kind'st leisure.

Macb. If you shall cleave to my con-
    sent, when 'tis,[2]   25
It shall make honor for you.

Ban.   So I lose none
    In seeking to augment it but still
        keep
My bosom franchis'd [3] and allegiance
        clear,
I shall be counsell'd.

Macb.   Good repose the while!

Ban. Thanks, sir. The like to you!   30

(*Exeunt* BANQUO *and* FLEANCE.)

Macb. Go bid thy mistress, when my
    drink is ready,
She strike upon the bell. Get thee to
        bed.

(*Exit* SERVANT.)

Is this a dagger which I see before
        me,
The handle toward my hand? Come,
    let me clutch thee!
I have thee not, and yet I see thee
        still.   35
Art thou not, fatal vision, sensible
To feeling as to sight? or art thou but
A dagger of the mind, a false cre-
        ation,
Proceeding from the heat-oppressed
        brain?
I see thee yet, in form as palpable   40
As this which now I draw.
Thou marshall'st me the way that I
        was going,
And such an instrument I was to use.
Mine eyes are made the fools o' th'
        other senses,
Or else worth all the rest. I see thee
        still;   45

And on thy blade and dudgeon[4]
    gouts[5] of blood,
Which was not so before. There's
    no such thing.
It is the bloody business which in-
    forms
Thus to mine eyes. Now o'er the one
    half-world
Nature seems dead, and wicked
    dreams abuse
The curtain'd sleep. Now witchcraft
    celebrates
Pale Hecate's offerings; and wither'd
    murder,
Alarum'd by his sentinel, the wolf,
Whose howl's his watch, thus with
    his stealthy pace,
With Tarquin's ravishing strides,
    towards his design   55
Moves like a ghost. Thou sure and
    firm-set earth,
Hear not my steps which way they
    walk, for fear
Thy very stones prate of my where-
    about
And take the present horror from the
    time,
Which now suits with it. Whiles I
    threat, he lives;   60
Words to the heat of deeds too cold
    breath gives.

(*A bell rings.*)

I go, and it is done. The bell invites
    me.
Hear it not, Duncan, for it is a knell
That summons thee to heaven, or to
    hell.

(*Exit.*)

SCENE II. INVERNESS. MACBETH'S CASTLE.

(*Enter* LADY MACBETH.)

2. If you will side with me when the time
    comes.
3. Free from guilt.

4. Hilt.
5. Big drops.

Lady. That which hath made them
drunk hath made me bold;

What hath quench'd them hath given
me fire. Hark! Peace!

It was the owl that shriek'd, the fatal
bellman

Which gives the stern'st good-night.
He is about it.

The doors are open, and the surfeited
grooms   5

Do mock their charge with snores. I
have drugg'd their possets,[1]

That death and nature do contend
about them

Whether they live or die.

Macb. (*Within.*) Who's there? What,
ho?

Lady. Alack, I am afraid they have
awak'd,   10

And 'tis not done! Th' attempt, and
not the deed,

Confounds us. Hark! I laid their daggers ready;

He could not miss 'em. Had he not
resembled

My father as he slept, I had done't.

(*Enter* MACBETH.)

                              My husband!

Macb. I have done the deed. Didst
thou not hear a noise?   15

Lady. I heard the owl scream and the
crickets cry.

Did you not speak?

Macb.   When?

Lady.   Now.

Macb.   As I descended?

Lady. Ay.

Macb. Hark!

Who lies i' th' second chamber?

Lady.   Donalbain.   20

Macb. This is a sorry sight.

(*Looks on his hands.*)

Lady. A foolish thought, to say a sorry
sight.

Macb. There's one did laugh in's sleep,
and one cried 'Murder!'

That they did wake each other. I
stood and heard them.

But they did say their prayers and
address'd them   25

Again to sleep.

Lady. There are two lodg'd together.

Macb. One cried 'God bless us!' and
'Amen!' the other,

As[2] they had seen me with these
hangman's hands.

List'ning their fear, I could not say
'Amen!'

When they did say 'God bless us!'

Lady. Consider it not so deeply.   30

Macb. But wherefore could not I pronounce 'Amen'?

I had most need of blessing, and
'Amen'

Stuck in my throat.

Lady. These deeds must not be thought
After these ways. So, it will make us
mad.

Macb. Methought I heard a voice cry
'Sleep no more!   35

Macbeth does murder sleep'—the innocent sleep,

Sleep that knits up the ravell'd sleave
of care,

The death of each day's life, sore
labor's bath,

Balm of hurt minds, great nature's
second course,

Chief nourisher in life's feast.

Lady.   What do you mean?   40

Macb. Still it cried 'Sleep no more!' to
all the house;

'Glamis hath murder'd sleep, and
therefore Cawdor

1. A milk punch.   2. As if.

Shall sleep no more! Macbeth shall
sleep no more!'
Lady. Who was it that thus cried?
Why, worthy Thane,
You do unbend your noble strength
to think   45
So brainsickly of things. Go get some
water
And wash this filthy witness from
your hand.
Why did you bring these daggers
from the place?
They must lie there. Go carry them
and smear
The sleepy grooms with blood.
Macb.   I'll go no more. 50
I am afraid to think what I have
done;
Look on't again I dare not.
Lady.   Infirm of purpose!
Give me the daggers. The sleeping
and the dead
Are but as pictures. 'Tis the eye of
childhood
That fears a painted devil. If he do
bleed,   55
I'll gild the faces of the grooms
withal,
For it must seem their guilt.

(*Exit. Knocking within.*)

Macb.   Whence is that knocking?
How is't with me when every noise
appals me?
What hands are here? Ha! they pluck
out mine eyes!
Will all great Neptune's ocean wash
this blood   60
Clean from my hand? No. This my
hand will rather
The multitudinous seas incarnadine,
Making the green one³ red.

(*Enter* LADY MACBETH.)

3. All.
4. Your self-control has deserted you.

Lady. My hands are of your color, but
I shame
To wear a heart so white. (*Knock.*)
I hear a knocking   65
At the south entry. Retire we to our
chamber.
A little water clears us of this deed.
How easy is it then! Your constancy
Hath left you unattended.⁴ (*Knock.*)
Hark! more knocking.
Get on your nightgown, lest occasion
call us   70
And show us to be watchers. Be not
lost
So poorly in your thoughts.
Macb. To know my deed, 'twere best
not know myself.

(*Knock.*)

Wake Duncan with thy knocking! I
would thou couldst!

(*Exeunt.*)

SCENE III. INVERNESS. MACBETH'S
CASTLE.

(*Enter a* PORTER. *Knocking within.*)

Porter. Here's a knocking indeed! If a
man were porter of hell gate, he
should have old turning the key.
(*Knock.*) Knock, knock, knock!
Who's there, i' th' name of Belze-
bub? Here's a farmer that hang'd
himself on th' expectation of plenty.
Come in time! Have napkins enow¹
about you; here you'll sweat for't.
(*Knock.*) Knock, knock! Who's
there, in th' other devil's name?
Faith, here's an equivocator,² that
could swear in both the scales
against either scale; who committed treason enough for God's sake,
yet could not equivocate to heaven.

1. Handkerchiefs enough.
2. Liar.

O, come in, equivocator! (*Knock.*)
Knock, knock, knock! Who's there?
Faith, here's an English tailor come
hither for stealing out of a French
hose. Come in, tailor. Here you
may roast your goose. (*Knock.*)
Knock, knock! Never at quiet!
What are you? But this place is
too cold for hell. I'll devil-porter
it no further. I had thought to have
let in some of all professions that
go the primrose way to th' everlasting bonfire. (*Knock.*) Anon,
anon! (*Opens the gate.*) I pray
you remember the porter.   31

(*Enter* MACDUFF *and* LENNOX.)

Macd. Was it so late, friend, ere you
   went to bed,
That you do lie so late?
Port. Faith, sir, we were carousing till
   the second cock; and drink, sir, is a
   great provoker of three things.   36
Macd. What three things does drink
   especially provoke?
Port. Marry, sir, nose-painting, sleep,
   and urine. Lechery, sir, it provokes,
   and unprovokes: it provokes the
   desire, but it takes away the performance. Therefore much drink
   may be said to be an equivocator
   with lechery: it makes him, and it
   mars him; it sets him on, and it
   takes him off; it persuades him,
   and disheartens him; makes him
   stand to, and not stand to; in conclusion, equivocates him in a sleep,
   and, giving him the lie, leaves
   him.   51
Macd. I believe drink gave thee the lie
   last night.
Port. That it did, sir, i' the very throat
   on me; but I requited him for his
   lie; and, I think, being too strong

for him, though he took up my
legs sometime, yet I made a shift
to cast him.   58
Macd. Is thy master stirring?

(*Enter* MACBETH.)

Our knocking has awak'd him; here
he comes.
Len. Good morrow, noble sir.
Macb.   Good morrow, both.
Macd. Is the King stirring, worthy
   Thane?
Macb.   Not yet.   62
Macd. He did command me to call
   timely on him;
I have almost slipp'd the hour.
Macb.   I'll bring you to him.
Macd. I know this is a joyful trouble to
   you;   65
But yet 'tis one.
Macb. The labor we delight in physics[3]
   pain.
This is the door.
Macd.   I'll make so bold to call,
For 'tis my limited service.[4]

(*Exit.*)

Len. Goes the King hence to-day?
Macb.   He does; he did appoint so.
Len. The night has been unruly. Where
   we lay,   71
Our chimneys were blown down;
   and, as they say,
Lamentings heard i' th' air, strange
   screams of death,
And prophesying, with accents ter-
   rible,
Of dire combustion[5] and confus'd
   events   75
New hatch'd to th' woeful time. The
   obscure bird [6]
Clamor'd the livelong night. Some say
   the earth
Was feverous and did shake.

3. Cures.
4. Assigned duty.
5. Social upheaval.
6. The owl.

Macb.   'Twas a rough night.
Len. My young remembrance cannot
    parallel
    A fellow to it.   80

(*Enter* MACDUFF.)

Macd. O horror, horror, horror! Tongue
    nor heart
    Cannot conceive nor name thee!
Macb. and Len. What's the matter?
Macd. Confusion now hath made his
    masterpiece!
    Most sacrilegious murder hath broke
        ope   85
    The Lord's anointed temple and stole
        thence
    The life o' th' building!
Macb.   What is't you say? the life?
Len. Mean you his Majesty?
Macd. Approach the chamber, and de-
    stroy your sight
    With a new Gorgon. Do not bid me
        speak.   90
    See, and then speak yourselves.

(*Exeunt* MACBETH *and* LENNOX.)
                        Awake, awake!
    Ring the alarum bell. Murder and
        treason!
    Banquo and Donalbain! Malcolm!
        awake!
    Shake off this downy sleep, death's
        counterfeit,
    And look on death itself! Up, up, and
        see   95
    The great doom's image! Malcolm!
        Banquo!
    As from your graves rise up and walk
        like sprites
    To countenance this horror! Ring the
        bell!

(*Bell rings.*)
(*Enter* LADY MACBETH.)

Lady. What's the business,
    That such a hideous trumpet calls to
        parley   100

    The sleepers of the house? Speak,
        speak!
Macd.   O gentle lady,
    'Tis not for you to hear what I can
        speak!
    The repetition in a woman's ear
    Would murder as it fell.

(*Enter* BANQUO.)
                        O Banquo, Banquo,
    Our royal master's murder'd!
Lady.   Woe, alas! 105
    What, in our house?
Ban.   Too cruel anywhere.
    Dear Duff, I prithee contradict thy-
        self
    And say it is not so.

(*Enter* MACBETH, LENNOX, *and*
Ross.)

Macb. Had I but died an hour before
    this chance,
    I had liv'd a blessed time; for from
        this instant   110
    There's nothing serious in mortality;
    All is but toys; renown and grace is
        dead;
    The wine of life is drawn, and the
        mere lees
    Is left this vault to brag of.   114

(*Enter* MALCOLM *and* DONALBAIN.)

Don. What is amiss?
Macb.   You are, and do not know't.
    The spring, the head, the fountain of
        your blood
    Is stopp'd, the very source of it is
        stopp'd.
Macd. Your royal father's murder'd.
Mal.   O, by whom?
Len. Those of his chamber, as it seem'd,
        had done't.
    Their hands and faces were all badg'd
        with blood;   120
    So were their daggers, which unwip'd
        we found
    Upon their pillows.

They star'd and were distracted. No man's life
Was to be trusted with them.

Macb. O, yet I do repent me of my fury   125
That I did kill them.

Macd.   Wherefore did you so?

Macb. Who can be wise, amazed, temperate, and furious,
Loyal and neutral, in a moment? No man.
The expedition of my violent love
Outrun the pauser, reason. Here lay Duncan,   130
His silver skin laced with his golden blood,
And his gash'd stabs look'd like a breach in nature
For ruin's wasteful entrance; there, the murderers,
Steep'd in the colors of their trade, their daggers
Unmannerly breech'd⁷ with gore. Who could refrain   135
That had a heart to love and in that heart
Courage to make 's love known?

Lady.   Help me hence, ho!

Macd. Look to the lady.

Mal. (*Aside to* DONALBAIN.) Why do we hold our tongues,
That most may claim this argument for ours?   140

Don. (*Aside to* MALCOLM.) What should be spoken here, where our fate,
Hid in an auger hole, may rush and seize us?
Let's away.
Our tears are not yet brew'd.

Mal. (*Aside to* DONALBAIN.) Nor our strong sorrow   145
Upon the foot of motion.

Ban.   Look to the lady.

(LADY MACBETH *is carried out.*)
And when we have our naked frailties hid,
That suffer in exposure, let us meet
And question this most bloody piece of work,
To know it further. Fears and scruples shake us.   150
In the great hand of God I stand, and thence
Against the undivulg'd pretense I fight
Of treasonous malice.

Macd.   And so do I.

All.   So all.

Macb. Let's briefly put on manly readiness
And meet i' th' hall together.

All.   Well contented.   155

(*Exeunt all but* MALCOLM *and* DONALBAIN.)

Mal. What will you do? Let's not consort with them.
To show an unfelt sorrow is an office
Which the false man does easy. I'll to England.

Don. To Ireland I. Our separated fortune
Shall keep us both the safer. Where we are,   160
There's daggers in men's smiles; the near in blood,⁸
The nearer bloody.⁹

Mal. This murderous shaft that's shot
Hath not yet lighted, and our safest way
Is to avoid the aim. Therefore to horse!
And let us not be dainty of leavetaking   165

7. Rudely covered.
8. The more closely related to the King—.
9. The more danger.

But shift[10] away. There's warrant in that theft
Which steals itself when there's no mercy left.

(*Exeunt.*)

SCENE IV. INVERNESS. OUTSIDE MACBETH'S CASTLE.

(*Enter* ROSS *with an* OLD MAN.)

Old Man. Threescore and ten I can remember well;
Within the volume of which time I have seen
Hours dreadful and things strange; but this sore night
Hath trifled former knowings.
Ross. Ah, good father,
Thou seest the heavens, as troubled with man's act,   5
Threaten his bloody stage.[1] By th' clock 'tis day,
And yet dark night strangles the traveling lamp.
Is't night's predominance, or the day's shame,
That darkness does the face of earth entomb
When living light should kiss it?
Old Man.   'Tis unnatural,   10
Even like the deed that's done. On Tuesday last
A falcon, tow'ring in her pride of place,
Was by a mousing owl hawk'd at and kill'd.
Ross. And Duncan's horses (a thing most strange and certain),
Beauteous and swift, the minions of their race,   15
Turn'd wild in nature, broke their stalls, flung out,
Contending 'gainst obedience, as they would make
War with mankind.
Old Man. 'Tis said they eat each other.
Ross. They did so, to th' amazement of mine eyes
That look'd upon't.

(*Enter* MACDUFF.)

Here comes the good Macduff.
How goes the world, sir, now?   21
Macd.   Why, see you not?
Ross. Is't known who did this more than bloody deed?
Macd. Those that Macbeth hath slain.
Ross.   Alas, the day!
What good could they pretend?
Macd.   They were suborn'd.[2]
Malcolm and Donalbain, the King's two sons,   25
Are stol'n away and fled, which puts upon them
Suspicion of the deed.
Ross.   'Gainst nature still!
Thriftless ambition, that wilt ravin up[3]
Thine own live's means! Then 'tis most like
The sovereignty will fall upon Macbeth.   30
Macd. He is already named, and gone to Scone
To be invested.
Ross.   Where is Duncan's body?
Macd. Carried to Colmekill,
The sacred storehouse of his predecessors
And guardian of their bones.
Ross.   Will you to Scone?   35
Macd. No, cousin, I'll to Fife.
Ross.   Well, I will thither.
Macd. Well, may you see things well done there. Adieu!
Lest our old robes sit easier than our new!
Ross. Farewell, father.

10. Steal.
1. The earth.

2. Bribed.
3. Devour.

Old Man. God's benison go with you,
and with those   40
That would make good of bad, and
friends of foes!

(*Exeunt omnes.*)

ACT III. SCENE I. FORRES. THE PALACE.

(*Enter* BANQUO.)

Ban. Thou hast it now—King, Cawdor,
Glamis, all,
As the weird women promis'd; and
I fear
Thou play'dst most foully for't. Yet it
was said
It should not stand in thy posterity,
But that myself should be the root
and father   5
Of many kings. If there come truth
from them
(As upon thee, Macbeth, their
speeches shine),
Why, by the verities on thee made
good,
May they not be my oracles as well
And set me up in hope? But, hush, no
more!   10

(*Sennet*[1] *sounded. Enter* MACBETH,
as King; LADY MACBETH, *as Queen;*
LENNOX, ROSS, LORDS, *and* ATTEND-
ANTS.)

Macb. Here's our chief guest.
Lady.   If he had been forgotten,
It had been as a gap in our great
feast,
And all-thing unbecoming.
Macb. To-night we hold a solemn sup-
per, sir,
And I'll request your presence.
Ban.   Let your Highness   15
Command upon me, to the which my
duties
Are with a most indissoluble tie
For ever knit.

1. Trumpet call.

Macb.   Ride you this afternoon?
Ban. Ay, my good lord.   20
Macb. We should have else desir'd
your good advice
(Which still hath been both grave
and prosperous)
In this day's council; but we'll take
to-morrow.
Is't far you ride?
Ban. As far, my lord, as will fill up the
time   25
'Twixt this and supper. Go not my
horse the better,
I must become a borrower of the
night
For a dark hour or twain.
Macb.   Fail not our feast.
Ban. My lord, I will not.
Macb. We hear our bloody cousins are
bestow'd   30
In England and in Ireland, not con-
fessing
Their cruel parricide, filling their
hearers
With strange invention. But of that
to-morrow,
When therewithal we shall have
cause of state
Craving[2] us jointly. Hie you to horse.
Adieu,   35
Till you return at night. Goes Fleance
with you?
Ban. Ay, my good lord. Our time does
call upon 's.
Macb. I wish your horses swift and sure
of foot,
And so I do commend you to their
backs.
Farewell.   40

(*Exit* BANQUO.)

Let every man be master of his time
Till seven at night. To make society
The sweeter welcome, we will keep
ourself

2. Concerning.

Till supper time alone. While then,
  God be with you!

(*Exeunt all but* MACBETH *and a*
SERVANT.)

Sirrah, a word with you. Attend those
  men   45

Our pleasure?

Serv. They are, my lord, without the
  palace gate.

Macb. Bring them before us.

(*Exit* SERVANT.)

              To be thus[3] is nothing,

But to be safely thus. Our fears in
  Banquo

Stick deep; and in his royalty of
  nature   50

Reigns that which would be fear'd.
  'Tis much he dares,

And to that dauntless temper of his
  mind

He hath a wisdom that doth guide
  his valor

To act in safety. There is none but he

Whose being I do fear; and under
  him   55

My Genius is rebuk'd, as it is said

Mark Antony's was by Cæsar. He
  chid the sisters

When first they put the name of King
  upon me,

And bade them speak to him. Then,
  prophet-like,

They hail'd him father to a line of
  kings.   60

Upon my head they placed a fruitless
  crown

And put a barren sceptre in my gripe,

Thence to be wrench'd with an un-
  lineal hand,

No son of mine succeeding. If't be so,

For Banquo's issue have I filed my
  mind;   65

For them the gracious Duncan have
  I murder'd;

Put rancors in the vessel of my peace

Only for them, and mine eternal
  jewel [4]

Given to the common enemy of man[5]

To make them kings, the seed of
  Banquo kings!   70

Rather than so, come, Fate, into the
  list,

And champion me to th' utterance!
  Who's there?

(*Enter* SERVANT *and two* MURDER-
ERS.)

Now go to the door and stay there
  till we call.

(*Exit* SERVANT.)

Was it not yesterday we spoke together?

Murderers. It was, so please your Highness.

Macb.   Well then, now   75

Have you consider'd of my speeches?
  Know

That it was he, in the times past,
  which held you

So under fortune, which you thought
  had been

Our innocent self. This I made good
  to you

In our last conference, pass'd in pro-
  bation with you   80

How you were borne in hand, how
  cross'd; the instruments;

Who wrought with them; and all
  things else that might

To half a soul [6] and to a notion[7]
  craz'd

Say 'Thus did Banquo.'

1. Mur.   You made it known to us

Macb. I did so; and went further, which
  is now   85

---

3. King.
4. Immortal soul.
5. The devil.

6. A half-wit.
7. Mind.

Our point of second meeting. Do you find
Your patience so predominant in your nature
That you can let this go? Are you so gospell'd
To pray for this good man and for his issue,
Whose heavy hand hath bow'd you to the grave   90
And beggar'd yours for ever?
1. Mur.   We are men, my liege.
Macb. Ay, in the catalogue ye go for men,
As hounds and greyhounds, mongrels, spaniels, curs,
Shoughs, water-rugs, and demi-wolves are clept
All by the name of dogs. The valued file   95
Distinguishes the swift, the slow, the subtle,
The housekeeper, the hunter, every one
According to the gift which bounte-ous' nature
Hath in him closed; whereby he does receive   99
Particular addition, from the bill
That writes them all alike; and so of men.
Now, if you have a station in the file,
Not i' th' worst rank of manhood, say't;
And I will put that business in your bosoms
Whose execution takes your enemy off,   105
Grapples you to the heart and love of us,
Who wear our health but sickly in his life,
Which in his death were perfect.
2. Mur.   I am one, my liege,
Whom the vile blows and buffets of the world
Have so incensed that I am reckless what   110
I do to spite the world.
1. Mur.   And I another,
So weary with disasters, tugg'd with fortune,
That I would set my life on any chance,
To mend it or be rid on't.
Macb.   Both of you
Know Banquo was your enemy.
Murderers.   True, my lord.   115
Macb. So is he mine; and in such bloody distance
That every minute of his being thrusts
Against my near'st of life; and though I could
With barefaced power sweep him from my sight
And bid my will avouch it, yet I must not,   120
For certain friends that are both his and mine,
Whose loves I may not drop, but wail his fall
Who I myself struck down. And thence it is
That I to your assistance do make love,
Masking the business from the com-mon eye   125
For sundry weighty reasons.
2. Mur.   We shall, my lord,
Perform what you command us.
1. Mur.   Though our lives—
Macb. Your spirits shine through you.
Within this hour at most
I will advise you where to plant your-selves,
Acquaint you with the perfect spy o' th' time,   130

The moment on't; for't must be done
  to-night,
And something from the palace; al-
  ways thought
That I require a clearness;[8] and with
  him,
To leave no rubs nor botches in the
  work,
Fleance his son, that keeps him com-
  pany,   135
Whose absence is no less material to
  me
Than is his father's, must embrace
  the fate
Of that dark hour. Resolve yourselves
  apart;[9]
I'll come to you anon.
Murderers.   We are resolv'd, my lord.
Macb. I'll call upon you straight. Abide
  within.   140

(*Exeunt* Murderers.)

It is concluded. Banquo, thy soul's
  flight,
If it find heaven, must find it out tonight.

(*Exit.*)

Scene ii. Forres. The palace.

(*Enter* Lady Macbeth *and a* Servant.)

Lady. Is Banquo gone from court?
Serv. Ay, madam, but returns again to-
  night.
Lady. Say to the King I would attend
  his leisure
For a few words.
Serv.   Madam, I will.

(*Exit.*)

Lady.   Naught's had, all's spent,
  Where our desire is got without content.   5

'Tis safer to be that which we destroy
Than by destruction dwell in doubtful joy.

(*Enter* Macbeth.)

How now, my lord? Why do you
  keep alone,
Of sorriest fancies your companions
  making,
Using those thoughts which should
  indeed have died   10
With them they think on? Things
  without all remedy
Should be without regard. What's
  done is done.
Macb. We have scotch'd the snake, not
  kill'd it.
She'll close, and be herself, whilst our
  poor malice
Remains in danger of her former
  tooth.   15
But let the frame of things disjoint,[1]
  both the worlds suffer,
Ere we will eat our meal in fear and
  sleep
In the affliction of these terrible
  dreams
That shake us nightly. Better be with
  the dead,
Whom we, to gain our peace, have
  sent to peace,   20
Than on the torture of the mind to
  lie
In restless ecstasy. Duncan is in his
  grave;
After life's fitful fever he sleeps well.
Treason has done his worst. Nor steel
  nor poison,
Malice domestic, foreign levy, noth-
  ing,   25
Can touch him further.
Lady.   Come on.
Gentle my lord, sleek o'er your rug-
  ged looks;

8. I must not be suspected.
9. Decide for yourselves.

1. The universe collapse.

Be bright and jovial among your guests to-night.

Macb. So shall I, love; and so, I pray, be you.

Let your remembrance apply to Banquo;   30

Present him eminence both with eye and tongue—

Unsafe the while, that we

Must lave our honors in these flattering streams

And make our faces vizards to our hearts,

Disguising what they are.

Lady.   You must leave this. 35

Macb. O, full of scorpions is my mind, dear wife!

Thou know'st that Banquo, and his Fleance, lives.

Lady. But in them Nature's copy's not eterne.

Macb. There's comfort yet! They are assailable.

Then be thou jocund. Ere the bat hath flown   40

His cloister'd flight, ere to black Hecate's summons

The shard-borne beetle with his drowsy hums

Hath rung night's yawning peal, there shall be done

A deed of dreadful note.

Lady.   What's to be done?

Macb. Be innocent of the knowledge, dearest chuck,   45

Till thou applaud the deed. Come, seeling² night,

Scarf up the tender eye of pitiful day,

And with thy bloody and invisible hand

Cancel and tear to pieces that great bond ³

Which keeps me pale! Light thickens, and the crow   50

Makes wing to th' rooky wood.

Good things of day begin to droop and drowse,

Whiles night's black agents to their preys do rouse.

Thou marvel'st at my words; but hold thee still:

Things bad begun make strong themselves by ill.   55

So prithee go with me.

(*Exeunt.*)

SCENE III. FORRES. A PARK NEAR THE PALACE.

(*Enter three* MURDERERS)

1. Mur. But who did bid thee join with us?

3. Mur.   Macbeth.

2. Mur. He needs not our mistrust, since he delivers

Our offices, and what we have to do,

To the direction just.

1. Mur.   Then stand with us.

The west yet glimmers with some streaks of day.   5

Now spurs the lated traveller apace

To gain the timely inn, and near approaches

The subject of our watch.

3. Mur.   Hark! I hear horses.

Ban. (*Within.*) Give us a light there, ho!

2. Mur.   Then 'tis he! The rest

That are within the note of expectation¹   10

Already are i' th' court.

1. Mur.   His horses go about.

3. Mur. Almost a mile; but he does usually,

So all men do, from hence to th' palace gate

2. Blinding.
3. Banquo's life.

1. The invited guests.

Make it their walk.

(*Enter* Banquo, *and* Fleance *with a torch.*)

2. Mur.   A light, a light!
3. Mur.   'Tis he.
1. Mur. Stand to't.   15
Ban. It will be rain to-night.
1. Mur.   Let it come down!

(*They fall upon* Banquo.)

Ban. O, treachery! Fly, good Fleance, fly, fly, fly!
Thou mayst revenge. O slave!

(*Dies.* Fleance *escapes.*)

3. Mur. Who did strike out the light?
1. Mur.   Was't not the way?
3. Mur. There's but one down; the son is fled.
2. Mur.   We have lost   20
Best half of our affair.
1. Mur. Well, let's away, and say how much is done.

(*Exeunt.*)

SCENE IV. FORRES. HALL IN THE PALACE.

(*Banquet prepared. Enter* MACBETH, LADY MACBETH, ROSS, LENNOX, LORDS, *and* ATTENDANTS.)

Macb. You know your own degrees, sit down. At first
And last the hearty welcome.
Lords.   Thanks to your Majesty.
Macb. Ourself will mingle with society
And play the humble host.
Our hostess keeps her state, but in best time   5
We will require her welcome.
Lady. Pronounce it for me, sir, to all our friends,
For my heart speaks they are welcome.

(FIRST MURDERER *appears at the door.*)

1. Respond to.

Macb. See, they encounter[1] thee with their hearts' thanks.
Both sides are even. Here I'll sit i' th' midst.   10
Be large in mirth; anon we'll drink a measure
The table round. (*Goes to the door.*)
There's blood upon thy face.
Mur. 'Tis Banquo's then.
Macb. 'Tis better thee without than he within.
Is he dispatch'd?   15
Mur. My lord, his throat is cut. That I did for him.
Macb. Thou art the best o' th' cut-throats! Yet he's good
That did the like for Fleance. If thou didst it,
Thou art the nonpareil.
Mur.   Most royal sir,
Fleance is scap'd.   20
Macb. (*Aside.*) Then comes my fit again. I had else been perfect;
Whole as the marble, founded as the rock,
As broad and general as the casing air.
But now I am cabin'd, cribb'd, confin'd, bound in
To saucy doubts and fears.—But Banquo's safe?   25
Mur. Ay, my good lord. Safe in a ditch he bides,
With twenty trenched gashes on his head,
The least a death to nature.
Macb.   Thanks for that!
There the grown serpent lies; the worm that's fled
Hath nature that in time will venom breed,   30
No teeth for th' present. Get thee gone. To-morrow
We'll hear ourselves[2] again.

2. Confer with each other.

(*Exit* MURDERER.)

Lady.   My royal lord,
You do not give the cheer. The feast is sold
That is not often vouch'd, while 'tis a-making,
'Tis given with welcome. To feed were best at home.   35
From thence, the sauce to meat is ceremony;
Meeting were bare without it.

(*Enter the* GHOST OF BANQUO, *and sits in* MACBETH'S *place.*)

Macb.   Sweet remembrancer!
Now good digestion wait on appetite,
And health on both!

Len.   May't please your Highness sit.

Macb. Here had we now our country's honor, roof'd,   40
Were the graced person of our Banquo present;
Who may I rather challenge for unkindness
Than pity for mischance!

Ross.   His absence, sir,
Lays blame upon his promise. Please't your Highness
To grace us with your royal company.   45

Macb. The table's full.

Len.   Here is a place reserved, sir.

Macb. Where?

Len. Here, my good lord. What is't that moves your Highness?

Macb. Which of you have done this?

Lords.   What, my good lord?

Macb. Thou canst not say I did it.
Never shake   50
Thy gory locks at me.

Ross. Gentlemen, rise. His Highness is not well.

Lady. Sit, worthy friends. My lord is often thus,

And hath been from his youth. Pray you keep seat.   54
The fit is momentary; upon a thought
He will again be well. If much you note him,
You shall offend him and extend his passion.
Feed, and regard him not.—Are you a man?

Macb. Ay, and a bold one, that dare look on that
Which might appal the devil.

Lady.   O proper stuff! 60
This is the very painting of your fear.
This is the air-drawn dagger which you said
Led you to Duncan. O, these flaws and starts
(Impostors to true fear) would well become   64
A woman's story at a winter's fire,
Authorized by her grandam. Shame itself!
Why do you make such faces? When all's done,
You look but on a stool.

Macb. Prithee see there! behold! look! lo! How say you?
Why, what care I? If thou canst nod, speak too.   70
If charnel houses and our graves must send
Those that we bury back, our monuments
Shall be the maws of kites.

(GHOST *vanishes.*)

Lady. What, quite unmann'd in folly?

Macb. If I stand here, I saw him.

Lady.   Fie, for shame!

Macb. Blood hath been shed ere now, i' th' olden time,   75
Ere humane statute purg'd the gentle weal;

Ay, and since too, murders have been perform'd
Too terrible for the ear. The time has been
That, when the brains were out, the man would die,
And there an end! But now they rise again,   80
With twenty mortal murders on their crowns,
And push us from our stools. This is more strange
Than such a murder is.

Lady.   My worthy lord,
Your noble friends do lack you.

Macb.   I do forget.
Do not muse at me, my most worthy friends.   85
I have a strange infirmity, which is nothing
To those that know me. Come, love and health to all!
Then I'll sit down. Give me some wine, fill full.
I drink to th' general joy o' th' whole table,
And to our dear friend Banquo, whom we miss.   90
Would he were here! To all, and him, we thirst,
And all to all.

Lords.   Our duties, and the pledge.

(*Re-enter* GHOST.)

Macb. Avaunt, and quit my sight! Let the earth hide thee!
Thy bones are marrowless, thy blood is cold;
Thou hast no speculation in those eyes   95
Which thou dost glare with!

Lady.   Think of this, good peers,
But as a thing of custom. 'Tis no other.

Only it spoils the pleasure of the time.

Macb. What man dare, I dare.
Approach thou like the rugged Russian bear,   100
The arm'd rhinoceros, or th' Hyrcan tiger;
Take any shape but that, and my firm nerves
Shall never tremble. Or be alive again
And dare me to the desert with thy sword.
If trembling I inhabit then, protest me   105
The baby of a girl.[3] Hence, horrible shadow!
Unreal mock'ry, hence!

(GHOST *vanishes.*)

                    Why, so! Being gone,
I am a man again. Pray you sit still.

Lady. You have displaced the mirth broke the good meeting
With most admired disorder.

Macb.   Can such things be,   110
And overcome us like a summer's cloud
Without our special wonder? You make me strange
Even to the disposition that I owe,[4]
When now I think you can behold such sights
And keep the natural ruby of your cheeks   115
When mine is blanch'd with fear.

Ross.   What sights, my lord?

Lady. I pray you speak not. He grows worse and worse;
Question enrages him. At once, good night.
Stand not upon the order of your going,
But go at once.

3. A weakling.

4. Own.

Len.   Good night, and better health
Attend his Majesty!   121
Lady.   A kind good night to all!

(*Exeunt all but* MACBETH *and* LADY
MACBETH.)

Macb. It will have blood, they say;
    blood will have blood.
Stones have been known to move
    and trees to speak;
Augurs and understood relations
    have
By maggot-pies and choughs and
    rooks brought forth   125
The secret'st man of blood.⁵ What is
    the night?⁶
Lady. Almost at odds with morning,
    which is which.
Macb. How say'st thou that Macduff
    denies his person
At our great bidding?
Lady.   Did you send to him, sir?
Macb. I hear it by the way; but I will
    send.   130
There's not a one of them but in his
    house
I keep a servant fee'd.⁷ I will to-mor-
    row
(And betimes I will) unto the Weird
    Sisters.
More shall they speak; for now I am
    bent to know
By the worst means the worst. For
    mine own good   135
All causes shall give way. I am in
    blood
Stepp'd in so far that, should I wade
    no more,
Returning were as tedious as go o'er.
Strange things I have in head, that
    will to hand,
Which must be acted ere they may
    be scann'd.   140

Lady. You lack the season⁸ of all na-
    tures, sleep.
Macb. Come, we'll to sleep. My strange
    and self-abuse⁹
Is the initiate fear that wants hard
    use.
We are yet but young in deed.¹⁰

(*Exeunt.*)

SCENE V. A HEATH.

(*Thunder. Enter the three* WITCHES,
    meeting HECATE.)

1. Witch. Why, how now, Hecate? You
    look angerly.
Hec. Have I not reason, beldams as you
    are,
Saucy and overbold? How did you
    dare
To trade and traffic with Macbeth
In riddles and affairs of death;   5
And I, the mistress of your charms,
The close contriver of all harms,
Was never call'd to bear my part
Or show the glory of our art?
And, which is worse, all you have
    done   10
Hath been but for a wayward son,
Spiteful and wrathful, who, as others
    do,
Loves for his own ends, not for you.
But make amends now. Get you gone
And at the pit of Acheron   15
Meet me i' th' morning. Thither he
Will come to know his destiny.
Your vessels and your spells provide,
Your charms and everything beside.
I am for th' air. This night I'll spend
Unto a dismal and a fatal end.   21
Great business must be wrought ere
    noon.
Upon the corner of the moon

5. The least suspected murderer.
6. What time is it?
7. A paid spy.

8. Preservative.
9. Self-deception (seeing ghosts).
10. Novices in crime.

There hangs a vaporous drop pro-
  found.   24
I'll catch it ere it come to ground;
And that, distill'd by magic sleights,
Shall raise such artificial sprites
As by the strength of their illusion
Shall draw him on to his confusion.
He shall spurn fate, scorn death, and
  bear   30
His hopes 'bove wisdom, grace, and
  fear;
And you all know security
Is mortals' chiefest enemy.

(*Music and a song within.* 'Come
away, come away,' &c.)

Hark! I am call'd. My little spirit,
  see,
Sits in a foggy cloud and stays for
  me.   35

(*Exit.*)

1. Witch. Come, let's make haste. She'll
  soon be back again.

(*Exeunt.*)

SCENE VI. FORRES. THE PALACE.

(*Enter* LENNOX *and another* LORD.)

Len. My former speeches have but hit
  your thoughts,
Which can interpret farther. Only I
  say
Things have been strangely borne.
  The gracious Duncan
Was pitied of Macbeth. Marry, he
  was dead!
And the right valiant Banquo walk'd
  too late;   5
Whom, you may say (if't please you)
  Fleance kill'd,
For Fleance fled. Men must not walk
  too late.
Who cannot want the thought how
  monstrous
It was for Malcolm and for Donalbain

To kill their gracious father? Damned
  fact!   10
How it did grieve Macbeth! Did he
  not straight,
In pious rage, the two delinquents
  tear,
That were the slaves of drink and
  thralls of sleep?
Was not that nobly done? Ay, and
  wisely too!
For 'twould have anger'd any heart
  alive   15
To hear the men deny't. So that I say
He has borne all things well; and I
  do think
That, had he Duncan's sons under
  his key
(As, an't please heaven, he shall not),
  they should find
What 'twere to kill a father. So should
  Fleance.   20
But peace! for from broad words,
  and 'cause he fail'd
His presence at the tyrant's feasts, I
  hear
Macduff lives in disgrace. Sir, can
  you tell
Where he bestows himself?

Lord.   The son of Duncan,
From whom this tyrant holds the due
  of birth,   25
Lives in the English court, and is
  received
Of the most pious Edward with such
  grace
That the malevolence of fortune
  nothing
Takes from his high respect. Thither
  Macduff
Is gone to pray the holy King upon
  his aid   30
To wake Northumberland and war-
  like Siward;
That by the help of these (with Him
  above

To ratify the work) we may again
Give to our tables meat, sleep to our
   nights,
Free from our feasts and banquets
   bloody knives,   35
Do faithful homage and receive free
   honors—
All which we pine for now. And this
   report
Hath so exasperate the King that he
Prepares for some attempt of war.
Len.   Sent he to Macduff?
Lord. He did; and with an absolute
   'Sir, not I!'   40
The cloudy messenger turns me his
   back
And hums, as who should say, 'You'll
   rue the time
That clogs me with this answer.'
Len.   And that well might
Advise him to a caution t' hold what
   distance
His wisdom can provide. Some holy
   angel   45
Fly to the court of England and un-
   fold
His message ere he come, that a swift
   blessing
May soon return to this our suffering
   country
Under a hand accursed!
Lord.   I'll send my prayers with him.

   (*Exeunt.*)

ACT IV. SCENE I. A CAVERN. IN THE MID-
   DLE, A CAULDRON BOILING.

   (*Thunder. Enter the three* WITCHES.)
1. Witch. Thrice the brinded cat hath
   mew'd.
2. Witch. Thrice and once the hedge-
   pig whin'd.
3. Witch. Harpier cries: 'tis time, 'tis
   time.

1. Witch. Round about the cauldron
   go;
In the poison'd entrails throw.   5
Toad, that under cold stone
Days and nights has thirty-one
Swelt'red venom sleeping got,
Boil thou first i' th' charmed pot.
All. Double, double, toil and trouble;
Fire burn, and cauldron bubble.   11
2. Witch. Fillet of a fenny snake,
In the cauldron boil and bake;
Eye of newt, and toe of frog,
Wool of bat, and tongue of dog,   15
Adder's fork, and blindworm's sting,
Lizard's leg, and howlet's wing;
For a charm of powerful trouble
Like a hell-broth boil and bubble.
All. Double, double, toil and trouble;
Fire burn, and cauldron bubble.   21
3. Witch. Scale of dragon, tooth of
   wolf,
Witch's mummy, maw and gulf
Of the ravin'd salt-sea shark,
Root of hemlock, digg'd i' th' dark;
Liver of blaspheming Jew,   26
Gall of goat, and slips of yew
Sliver'd in the moon's eclipse;
Nose of Turk and Tartar's lips;
Finger of birth-strangled babe   30
Ditch-deliver'd by a drab:
Make the gruel thick and slab.
Add thereto a tiger's chaudron
For th' ingredients of our cauldron.
All. Double, double, toil and trouble;
Fire burn, and cauldron bubble.   36
2. Witch. Cool it with a baboon's blood,
Then the charm is firm and good.

   (*Enter* HECATE.)
Hec. O, well done! I commend your
   pains,
And every one shall share i' th' gains.
And now about the cauldron sing   41
Like elves and fairies in a ring,
Enchanting all that you put in.

(*Music and a song,* 'Black spirits,'
&c. *Exit* HECATE.)

2. Witch. By the pricking of my thumbs,
Something wicked this way comes.
Open locks, 46
Whoever knocks!

(*Enter* MACBETH.)

Macb. How now, you secret, black, and
midnight hags?
What is't you do?
All. A deed without a name.
Macb. I conjure you by that which you
profess 50
(Howe'er you come to know it),
answer me.
Though you untie the winds and let
them fight
Against the churches; though the
yesty¹ waves
Confound and swallow navigation
up;
Though bladed corn be lodged and
trees blown down; 55
Though castles topple on their
warders' heads;
Though palaces and pyramids do
slope
Their heads to their foundations;
though the treasure
Of nature's germens² tumble all together,
Even till destruction sicken—answer
me 60
To what I ask you.
1. Witch. Speak.
2. Witch. Demand.
3. Witch. We'll answer.
1. Witch. Say, if th' hadst rather hear
it from our mouths
Or from our masters.
Macb. Call 'em! Let me see 'em.
1. Witch. Pour in sow's blood, that
hath eaten

1. Foaming.

Her nine farrow; grease that's
sweaten 65
From the murderer's gibbet throw
Into the flame.
All. Come, high or low;
Thyself and office deftly show!

(*Thunder.* FIRST APPARITION, *an
Armed Head.*)

Macb. Tell me, thou unknown power—
1. Witch. He knows thy thought.
Hear his speech, but say thou
naught. 70
1. Appar. Macbeth! Macbeth! Macbeth!
Beware Macduff;
Beware the Thane of Fife. Dismiss
me. Enough.

(*He descends.*)

Macb. Whate'er thou art, for thy good
caution thanks!
Thou hast harp'd my fear aright. But
one word more—
1. Witch. He will not be commanded.
Here's another, 75
More potent than the first.

(*Thunder.* SECOND APPARITION, *a
Bloody Child.*)

2. Appar. Macbeth! Macbeth! Macbeth!
Macb. Had I three ears, I'ld hear thee.
2. Appar. Be bloody, bold, and resolute;
laugh to scorn
The power of man, for none of
woman born 80
Shall harm Macbeth.

(*Descends.*)

Macb. Then live, Macduff. What need
I fear of thee?
But yet I'll make assurance double
sure
And take a bond of fate. Thou shalt
not live!
That I may tell pale-hearted fear it
lies 85

2. Seeds of all living matter.

And sleep in spite of thunder.

(*Thunder.* THIRD APPARITION, *a Child
Crowned, with a tree in his hand.*)

What is this

That rises like the issue of a king
And wears upon his baby-brow the
round
And top of sovereignty?

All.   Listen, but speak not to't.

3. Appar. Be lion-mettled, proud, and
take no care   90
Who chafes, who frets, or where con-
spirers are.
Macbeth shall never vanquish'd be
until
Great Birnam Wood to high Dunsinane Hill
Shall come against him.

(*Descends.*)

Macb.   That will never be.
Who can impress³ the forest, bid the
tree   95
Unfix his earth-bound root? Sweet
bodements,⁴ good!
Rebellion's head rise never till the
Wood
Of Birnam rise, and our high placed
Macbeth
Shall live the lease of nature, pay his
breath
To time and mortal custom. Yet my
heart   100
Throbs to know one thing. Tell me,
if your art
Can tell so much—shall Banquo's
issue ever
Reign in this kingdom?

All.   Seek to know no more.

Macb. I will be satisfied. Deny me this,
And an eternal curse fall on you! Let
me know.   105
Why sinks that cauldron? and what
noise is this?

(*Hautboys.*)

1. Witch. Show!

2. Witch. Show!

3. Witch. Show!

All. Show his eyes, and grieve his
heart!   110
Come like shadows, so depart!

(*A show of eight Kings, the last with
a glass⁵ in his hand; and* BANQUO's
GHOST *following.*)

Macb. Thou art too like the spirit of
Banquo. Down!
Thy crown does sear mine eyeballs.
And thy hair,
Thou other gold-bound brow, is like
the first.
A third is like the former. Filthy
hags!   115
Why do you show me this? A fourth?
Start, eyes!
What, will the line stretch out to th'
crack of doom?
Another yet? A seventh? I'll see no
more.
And yet the eighth appears, who
bears a glass
Which shows me many more; and
some I see   120
That twofold balls and treble sceptres
carry.
Horrible sight! Now I see 'tis true;
For the blood-bolter'd Banquo smiles
upon me
And points at them for his. (*Ap-
paritions vanish.*) What? Is this
so?   124

1. Witch. Ay, sir, all this is so. But why
Stands Macbeth thus amazedly?
Come, sisters, cheer we up his sprites
And show the best of our delights.
I'll charm the air to give a sound
While you perform your antic round,
That this great king may kindly say

---

3. Draft into the army.
4. Prophecies.

5. Mirror.

Our duties did his welcome pay. 132

(*Music. The* WITCHES *dance, and
vanish.*)

Macb. Where are they? Gone? Let this
pernicious hour
Stand aye accursed in the calendar!
Come in, without there!

(*Enter* LENNOX.)

Len.   What's your Grace's will? 135
Macb. Saw you the Weird Sisters?
Len.   No, my lord.
Macb. Came they not by you?
Len.   No indeed, my lord.
Macb. Infected be the air whereon they
ride,
And damn'd all those that trust them!
I did hear
The galloping of horse. Who was't
came by? 140
Len. 'Tis two or three, my lord, that
bring you word
Macduff is fled to England.
Macb.   Fled to England?
Len. Ay, my good lord.
Macb. (*Aside.*) Time, thou anticipat'st[6]
my dread exploits. 144
The flighty purpose never is o'ertook
Unless the deed go with it. From this
moment
The very firstlings of my heart shall
be
The firstlings of my hand. And even
now,
To crown my thoughts with acts, be
it thought and done! 149
The castle of Macduff I will surprise,
Seize upon Fife, give to the edge o'
th' sword
His wife, his babes, and all unfortu-
nate souls
That trace him in his line. No boast-
ing like a fool!

This deed I'll do before this purpose
cool.
But no more sights!—Where are these
gentlemen? 155
Come, bring me where they are.

(*Exeunt.*)

SCENE II. FIFE. MACDUFF'S CASTLE.

(*Enter* MACDUFF'S WIFE, *her* SON,
and ROSS.)

Wife. What had he done to make him
fly the land?
Ross. You must have patience, madam.
Wife.   He had none.
His flight was madness. When our
actions do not,
Our fears do make us traitors.
Ross.   You know not
Whether it was his wisdom or his
fear. 5
Wife. Wisdom? To leave his wife, to
leave his babes,
His mansion, and his titles, in a place
From whence himself does fly? He
loves us not,
He wants the natural touch. For the
poor wren,
(The most diminutive of birds) will
fight, 10
Her young ones in her nest, against
the owl.
All is the fear, and nothing is the
love,
As little is the wisdom, where the
flight
So runs against all reason.
Ross.   My dearest coz,
I pray you school yourself. But for
your husband, 15
He is noble, wise, judicious, and best
knows
The fits o' th' season.[1] I dare not

6. Forestall.

1. Crises of the time.

speak much further;
But cruel are the times, when we are
     traitors
And do not know ourselves; when we
     hold rumor
From what we fear, yet know not
     what we fear,   20
But float upon a wild and violent sea
Each way and none. I take my leave
     of you.
Shall not be long but I'll be here
     again.
Things at the worst will cease, or else
     climb upward
To what they were before.—My
     pretty cousin,   25
Blessing upon you!
Wife. Father'd he is, and yet he's fa-
     therless.
Ross. I am so much a fool, should I stay
     longer,
     It would be my disgrace and your
     discomfort.
     I take my leave at once.

     (*Exit.*)

Wife.   Sirrah, your father's dead;   30
     And what will you do now? How will
     you live?
Son. As birds do, mother.
Wife.   What, with worms and flies?
Son. With what I get, I mean; and so
     do they.
Wife. Poor bird! thou'dst never fear the
     net nor lime,
     The pitfall nor the gin.   35
Son. Why should I, mother? Poor birds
     they are not set for.
     My father is not dead, for all your
     saying.
Wife. Yes, he is dead. How wilt thou
     do for a father?
Son. Nay, how will you do for a hus-
     band?

Wife. Why, I can buy me twenty at
     any market.   40
Son. Then you'll buy 'em to sell again.
Wife. Thou speak'st with all thy wit;
     and yet, i' faith,
     With wit enough for thee.
Son. Was my father a traitor, mother?
Wife. Ay, that he was!   45
Son. What is a traitor?
Wife. Why, one that swears, and lies.
Son. And be all traitors that do so?
Wife. Every one that does so is a traitor
     and must be hanged.   50
Son. And must they all be hanged that
     swear and lie?
Wife. Every one.
Son. Who must hang them?
Wife. Why, the honest men.   55
Son. Then the liars and swearers are
     fools; for there are liars and swear-
     ers enow to beat the honest men
     and hang up them.
Wife. Now God help thee, poor mon-
     key!   60
     But how wilt thou do for a father?
Son. If he were dead, you'ld weep for
     him. If you would not, it were a
     good sign that I should quickly
     have a new father.   65
Wife. Poor prattler, how thou talk'st!

     (*Enter a* MESSENGER.)

Mess. Bless you, fair dame! I am not to
     you known,
     Though in your state of honor I am
     perfect.
     I doubt some danger does approach
     you nearly.
     If you will take a homely² man's ad-
     vice,   70
     Be not found here. Hence with your
     little ones!
     To fright you thus methinks I am too
     savage;

2. Humble.

To do worse to you were fell cruelty,
Which is too nigh your person.
    Heaven preserve you!   74
I dare abide no longer.

(*Exit.*)

Wife.   Whither should I fly?
I have done no harm. But I remember now
I am in this earthly world, where to do harm
Is often laudable, to do good sometime
Accounted dangerous folly. Why then, alas,   79
Do I put up that womanly defense
To say I have done no harm?—What are these faces?

(*Enter* MURDERERS.)

Mur. Where is your husband?
Wife. I hope, in no place so unsanctified   83
Where such as thou mayst find him.
Mur.   He's a traitor.
Son. Thou liest, thou shag-hair'd villain!
Mur.   What, you egg!

(*Stabs him.*)

Young fry of treachery!
Son.   He has kill'd me, mother.
Run away, I pray you!   87

(*Dies.*)
(*Exit* LADY MACDUFF, *crying 'Murder!' and pursued by the* MURDERERS.)

<h3 style="text-align:center">SCENE III. ENGLAND.</h3>
<h4 style="text-align:center">BEFORE KING EDWARD'S PALACE.</h4>

(*Enter* MALCOLM *and* MACDUFF.)

Mal. Let us seek out some desolate shade, and there
Weep our sad bosoms empty.
Macd.   Let us rather

Hold fast the mortal sword and, like good men,
Bestride our downfall'n birthdom. Each new morn
New widows howl, new orphans cry, new sorrows   5
Strike heaven on the face, that it resounds
As if it felt with Scotland and yell'd out
Like syllable of dolor.
Mal.   What I believe, I'll wail;
What know, believe; and what I can redress,
As I shall find the time to friend, I will.   10
What you have spoke, it may be so perchance.
This tyrant, whose sole name blisters our tongues,
Was once thought honest; you have loved him well;
He hath not touched you yet. I am young; but something
You may deserve of him through me,[1] and wisdom   15
To offer up a weak, poor, innocent lamb
T' appease an angry god.
Macd. I am not treacherous.
Mal.   But Macbeth is.
A good and virtuous nature may recoil
In an imperial charge. But I shall crave your pardon.   20
That which you are, my thoughts cannot transpose.
Angels are bright still, though the brightest fell.
Though all things foul would wear the brows of grace,
Yet grace must still look so.
Macd.   I have lost my hopes.

---

1. You may gain something by betraying me.

Mal. Perchance even there where I did
  find my doubts.   25
  Why in that rawness left you wife
  and child,
  Those precious motives, those strong
  knots of love,
  Without leave-taking? I pray you,
  Let not my jealousies be your dis-
  honors,
  But mine own safeties. You may be
  rightly just,   30
  Whatever I shall think.

Macd.   Bleed, bleed, poor country!
  Great tyranny, lay thou thy basis
  sure,
  For goodness dare not check thee!
  Wear thou thy wrongs;
  The title is affeer'd! Fare thee well,
  lord.
  I would not be the villain that thou
  think'st   35
  For the whole space that's in the
  tyrant's grasp
  And the rich East to boot.

Mal.   Be not offended.
  I speak not as in absolute fear of you.
  I think our country sinks beneath the
  yoke,
  It weeps, it bleeds, and each new
  day a gash   40
  Is added to her wounds. I think
  withal
  There would be hands uplifted in my
  right;
  And here from gracious England
  have I offer
  Of goodly thousands. But, for all this,
  When I shall tread upon the tyrant's
  head   45
  Or wear it on my sword, yet my poor
  country
  Shall have more vices than it had
  before,
  More suffer and more sundry ways
  than ever,

  By him that shall succeed.

Macd.   What should he be?

Mal. It is myself I mean; in whom I
  know   50
  All the particulars of vice so grafted
  That, when they shall be open'd,
  black Macbeth
  Will seem as pure as snow, and the
  poor state
  Esteem him as a lamb, being com-
  par'd
  With my confineless harms.

Macd.   Not in the legions 55
  Of horrid hell can come a devil more
  damn'd
  In evils to top Macbeth.

Mal.   I grant him bloody,
  Luxurious, avaricious, false, deceit-
  ful,
  Sudden, malicious, smacking of ev-
  ery sin
  That has a name. But there's no bot-
  tom, none,   60
  In my voluptuousness. Your wives,
  your daughters,
  Your matrons, and your maids could
  not fill up
  The cistern of my lust; and my desire
  All continent impediments would
  o'erbear
  That did oppose my will. Better
  Macbeth   65
  Than such an one to reign.

Macd.   Boundless intemperance
  In nature is a tyranny. It hath been
  Th' untimely emptying of the happy
  throne
  And fall of many kings. But fear not
  yet
  To take upon you what is yours. You
  may   70
  Convey your pleasures in a spacious
  plenty,
  And yet seem cold—the time you may
  so hoodwink.

We have willing dames enough.
There cannot be
That vulture in you to devour so
many
As will to greatness dedicate them-
selves,   75
Finding it so inclin'd.
Mal.   With this there grows
In my most ill-composed affection
such
A stanchless avarice that, were I
King,
I should cut off the nobles for their
lands,
Desire his jewels, and this other's
house,   80
And my more-having would be as a
sauce
To make me hunger more, that I
should forge
Quarrels unjust against the good and
loyal,
Destroying them for wealth.
Macd.   This avarice
Sticks deeper, grows with more per-
nicious root   85
Than summer-seeming lust; and it
hath been
The sword of our slain kings. Yet do
not fear.
Scotland hath foisons[2] to fill up your
will [3]
Of your mere own. All these are
portable,
With other graces weigh'd.   90
Mal. But I have none. The king-becom-
ing graces,
As justice, verity, temperance, stable-
ness,
Bounty, perseverance, mercy, lowli-
ness,
Devotion, patience, courage, forti-
tude,   ·   94
I have no relish of them, but abound

In the division of each several
crime,
Acting it many ways. Nay, had I
power, I should
Pour the sweet milk of concord into
hell,
Uproar the universal peace, confound
All unity on earth.
Macd.   O Scotland, Scotland! 100
Mal. If such a one be fit to govern,
speak.
I am as I have spoken.
Macd.   Fit to govern?
No, not to live. O nation miserable,
With an untitled tyrant bloody-
scepter'd,
When shalt thou see thy wholesome
days again,   105
Since that the truest issue of thy
throne
By his own interdiction stands ac-
curs'd
And does blaspheme his breed? Thy
royal father
Was a most sainted king; the queen
that bore thee,
Oftener upon her knees than on her
feet,   110
Died every day she lived. Fare thee
well!
These evils thou repeat'st upon thy-
self
Have banish'd me from Scotland. O
my breast,
Thy hope ends here!
Mal.   Macduff, this noble passion,
Child of integrity, hath from my
soul   115
Wiped the black scruples, reconciled
my thoughts
To thy good truth and honor. Devil-
ish Macbeth
By many of these trains hath sought
to win me

2. Plenty.

3. Greed.

Into his power; and modest wisdom
plucks me
From over-credulous haste; but God
above   120
Deal between thee and me! for even
now
I put myself to thy direction and
Unspeak mine own detraction, here
abjure
The taints and blames I laid upon
myself   124
For strangers to my nature. I am yet
Unknown to woman, never was for-
sworn,
Scarcely have coveted what was mine
own,
At no time broke my faith, would
not betray
The devil to his fellow, and delight
No less in truth than life. My first
false speaking   130
Was this upon myself. What I am
truly,
Is thine and my poor country's to
command;
Whither indeed, before thy here-
approach,
Old Siward with ten thousand war-
like men   134
Already at a point was setting forth.
Now we'll together; and the chance
of goodness
Be like our warranted quarrel! Why
are you silent?
Macd. Such welcome and unwelcome
things at once
'Tis hard to reconcile.

(*Enter a* DOCTOR.)

Mal. Well, more anon. Comes the King
forth, I pray you?   140
Doct. Ay, sir. There are a crew of
wretched souls

That stay his cure. Their malady con-
vinces[4]
The great assay of art;[5] but at his
touch,
Such sanctity hath heaven given his
hand,
They presently amend.
Mal.   I thank you, doctor.   145

(*Exit* DOCTOR.)

Macd. What's the disease he means?
Mal.   'Tis call'd the evil:
A most miraculous work in this good
king,
Which often since my here-remain in
England
I have seen him do. How he solicits
heaven
Himself best knows; but strangely-
visited people,   150
All swol'n and ulcerous, pitiful to the
eye,
The mere despair of surgery, he
cures,
Hanging a golden stamp about their
necks,
Put on with holy prayers; and 'tis
spoken,   154
To the succeeding royalty he leaves
The healing benediction. With this
strange virtue,[6]
He hath a heavenly gift of prophecy,
And sundry blessings hang about his
throne
That speak him full of grace.

(*Enter* ROSS.)

Macd.   See who comes here.
Mal. My countryman; but yet I know
him not.   160
Macd. My ever gentle cousin, welcome
hither.
Mal. I know him now. Good God betimes remove

4. Baffles.
5. The greatest efforts of medicine.
6. Power.

The means[7] that makes us strangers!
Ross. Sir, amen.
Macd. Stands Scotland where it did?
Ross. Alas, poor country,
Almost afraid to know itself! It can-
not 165
Be call'd our mother, but our grave; where nothing,[8]
But who knows nothing, is once seen to smile;
Where sighs and groans, and shrieks that rent the air,
Are made, not mark'd; where violent sorrow seems
A modern ecstasy.[9] The dead man's knell 170
Is there scarce ask'd for who; and good men's lives
Expire before the flowers in their caps,
Dying or ere they sicken.
Macd. O, relation
Too nice,[10] and yet too true!
Mal. What's the newest grief?
Ross. That of an hour's age doth hiss the speaker; 175
Each minute teems a new one.
Macd. How does my wife?
Ross. Why, well.
Macd. And all my children?
Ross. Well too.
Macd. The tyrant has not batter'd at their peace?
Ross. No; they were well at peace when I did leave 'em.
Macd. Be not a niggard of your speech.
How goes't? 180
Ross. When I came hither to transport the tidings
Which I have heavily borne, there ran a rumor

Of many worthy fellows that were out;
Which was to my belief witness'd the rather
For that I saw the tyrant's power[11] afoot. 185
Now is the time of help. Your eye[12] in Scotland
Would create soldiers, make our women fight
To doff their dire distresses.
Mal. Be't their comfort
We are coming thither. Gracious England hath
Lent us good Siward and ten thou-sand men. 190
An older and a better soldier none
That Christendom gives out.
Ross. Would I could answer
This comfort with the like! But I have words
That would be howl'd out in the desert air,
Where hearing should not latch[13] them.
Macd. What concern they? 195
The general cause? or is it a fee-grief[14]
Due to some single breast?
Ross. No mind that's honest
But in it shares some woe, though the main part
Pertains to you alone.
Macd. If it be mine,
Keep it not from me, quickly let me have it. 200
Ross. Let not your ears despise my tongue for ever,
Which shall possess them with the heaviest sound
That ever yet they heard.

7. Macbeth.
8. No one.
9. An everyday emotion.
10. Narrative too exact.
11. Army.
12. Presence.
13. Catch.
14. Private grief.

Macd.   Humh! I guess at it.
Ross. Your castle is surprised; your wife and babes
Savagely slaughter'd. To relate the manner,   205
Were, on the quarry of these murder'd deer,
To add the death of you.
Mal.   Merciful heaven!
What, man! Ne'er pull your hat upon your brows.
Give sorrow words. The grief that does not speak
Whispers the o'erfraught heart and bids it break.   210
Macd. My children too?
Ross.   Wife, children, servants, all
That could be found.
Macd.   And I must be from thence?
My wife kill'd too?
Ross.   I have said.
Mal.   Be comforted.
Let's make us medicines of our great revenge
To cure this deadly grief.   215
Macd. He has no children. All my pretty ones?
Did you say all? O hell-kite! All?
What, all my pretty chickens and their dam
At one fell swoop?
Mal. Dispute it like a man.
Macd.   I shall do so;   220
But I must also feel it as a man.
I cannot but remember such things were
That were most precious to me. Did heaven look on
And would not take their part? Sinful Macduff,
They were all struck for thee! Naught that I am,   225
Not for their own demerits, but for mine,

Fell slaughter on their souls. Heaven rest them now!
Mal. Be this the whetstone of your sword. Let grief
Convert to anger; blunt not the heart, enrage it.
Macd. O, I could play the woman with mine eyes   230
And braggart with my tongue! But, gentle heavens,
Cut short all intermission. Front to front
Bring thou this fiend of Scotland and myself.
Within my sword's length set him. If he scape,
Heaven forgive him too!
Mal.   This tune goes manly.   235
Come, go we to the King. Our power is ready;
Our lack is nothing but our leave. Macbeth
Is ripe for shaking, and the powers above
Put on their instruments.[15] Receive what cheer you may.
The night is long that never finds the day.   240

(*Exeunt.*)

ACT v. SCENE I.
DUNSINANE. MACBETH'S CASTLE.

(*Enter a* DOCTOR OF PHYSIC *and a* WAITING-GENTLEWOMAN.)

Doct. I have two nights watched with you, but can perceive no truth in your report. When was it she last walked?   4
Gent. Since his Majesty went into the field I have seen her rise from her bed, throw her nightgown upon her, unlock her closet, take forth paper, fold it, write upon't, read it,

15. Urge us on.

afterwards seal it, and again return to bed; yet all this while in a most fast sleep. 12

Doct. A great perturbation in nature, to receive at once the benefit of sleep and do the effects of watching! In this slumb'ry agitation, besides her walking and other actual performances, what, at any time, have you heard her say? 19

Gent. That, sir, which I will not report after her.

Doct. You may to me, and 'tis most meet you should.

Gent. Neither to you nor any one, having no witness to confirm my speech. 26

(*Enter* LADY MACBETH, *with a taper.*)

Lo you, here she comes! This is her very guise, and, upon my life, fast asleep! Observe her; stand close.

Doct. How come she by that light? 30

Gent. Why, it stood by her. She has light by her continually. 'Tis her command.

Doct. You see her eyes are open.

Gent. Ay; but their sense is shut. 35

Doct. What is it she does now? Look how she rubs her hands.

Gent. It is an accustomed action with her, to seem thus washing her hands. I have known her continue in this a quarter of an hour. 41

Lady. Yet here's a spot.

Doct. Hark, she speaks! I will set down what comes from her, to satisfy my remembrance the more strongly. 45

Lady. Out, damned spot! out, I say! One; two. Why then 'tis time to do 't. Hell is murky. Fie, my lord, fie! a soldier, and afeard? What need we fear who knows it, when none can call our power to ac-

count? Yet who would have thought the old man to have had so much blood in him? 54

Doct. Do you mark that?

Lady. The Thane of Fife had a wife. Where is she now? What, will these hands ne'er be clean? No more o' that, my lord, no more o' that! You mar all with this starting. 61

Doct. Go to, go to! You have known what you should not.

Gent. She has spoke what she should not, I am sure of that. Heaven knows what she has known. 66

Lady. Here's the smell of the blood still. All the perfumes of Arabia will not sweeten this little hand. Oh, oh, oh! 70

Doct. What a sigh is there! The heart is sorely charged.

Gent. I would not have such a heart in my bosom for the dignity of the whole body. 75

Doct. Well, well, well.

Gent. Pray God it be, sir.

Doct. This disease is beyond my practice. Yet I have known those which have walked in their sleep who have died holily in their beds. 81

Lady. Wash your hands, put on your nightgown, look not so pale! I tell you yet again, Banquo's buried. He cannot come out on 's grave.

Doct. Even so? 86

Lady. To bed, to bed! There's knocking at the gate. Come, come, come, come, give me your hand! What's done cannot be undone. To bed, to bed, to bed! 91

(*Exit.*)

Doct. Will she go now to bed?

Gent. Directly.

Doct. Foul whisperings are abroad. Un-
　natural deeds　95
　Do breed unnatural troubles. In-
　fected minds
　To their deaf pillows will discharge
　their secrets.
　More needs she the divine than the
　physician.
　God, God forgive us all! Look after
　her;
　Remove from her the means of all
　annoyance,　100
　And still keep eyes upon her. So
　good night.
　My mind she has mated,[1] and
　amazed my sight.
　I think, but dare not speak.
Gent.　Good night, good doctor.

(*Exeunt.*)

SCENE II.
THE COUNTRY NEAR DUNSINANE.

(*Drum and Colors. Enter* MENTEITH,
CAITHNESS, ANGUS, LENNOX, SOL-
DIERS.)

Ment. The English power is near, led
　on by Malcolm,
　His uncle Siward, and the good Mac-
　duff.
　Revenges burn in them; for their
　dear causes
　Would to the bleeding and the grim
　alarm
　Excite the mortified man.
Ang.　Near Birnam Wood　5
　Shall we well meet them; that way
　are they coming.
Caith. Who knows if Donalbain be
　with his brother?
Len. For certain, sir, he is not. I have a
　file

1. Dazed.

Of all the gentry. There is Siward's
　son
And many unrough[1] youths that even
　now　10
Protest their first of manhood.
Ment.　What does the tyrant?
Caith. Great Dunsinane he strongly
　fortifies.
　Some say he's mad; others, that
　lesser hate him,
　Do call it valiant fury; but for cer-
　tain
　He cannot buckle his distemper'd
　cause　15
　Within the belt of rule.
Ang.　Now does he feel
　His secret murders sticking on his
　hands.
　Now minutely revolts upbraid his
　faith-breach.
　Those he commands move only in
　command,
　Nothing in love. Now does he feel
　his title　20
　Hang loose about him, like a giant's
　robe
　Upon a dwarfish thief.
Ment.　Who then shall blame
　His pester'd senses to recoil and
　start,
　When all that is within him does
　condemn
　Itself for being there?
Caith.　Well, march we on　25
　To give obedience where 'tis truly
　owed.
　Meet we the medicine[2] of the sickly
　weal;[3]
　And with him pour we in our coun-
　try's purge
　Each drop of us.

1. Beardless.
2. Malcolm.
3. Realm.

Len. Or so much as it needs
To dew the sovereign flower and
 drown the weeds. 30
Make we our march towards Birnam.

(*Exeunt, marching.*)

SCENE III.

DUNSINANE. A ROOM IN THE CASTLE.

(*Enter* MACBETH, DOCTOR, *and* AT-
TENDANTS.)

Macb. Bring me no more reports. Let
 them[1] fly all!
Till Birnam Wood remove to Dun-
 sinane,
I cannot taint with fear. What's the
 boy Malcolm?
Was he not born of woman? The
 spirits that know
All mortal consequences have pro-
 nounced me thus: 5
'Fear not, Macbeth. No man that's
 born of woman
Shall e'er have power upon thee.'
 Then fly, false thanes,
And mingle with the English epi-
 cures.
The mind I sway by and the heart I
 bear
Shall never sag with doubt nor shake
 with fear. 10

(*Enter* SERVANT.)

The devil damn thee black, thou
 cream-faced loon!
Where got'st thou that goose look?
Serv. There is ten thousand—
Macb. Geese, villain?
Serv. Soldiers, sir.
Macb. Go prick thy face and over-red[2]
 thy fear,
 Thou lily-liver'd boy. What soldiers,
 patch?[3] 15

1. His nobles.
2. Make bloody.
3. Fool.

Death of thy soul! Those linen cheeks
 of thine
Are counsellors to fear. What sol-
 diers, whey-face?
Serv. The English force, so please you.
Macb. Take thy face hence.

(*Exit* SERVANT.)

 Seyton!—I am sick at heart,
When I behold—Seyton, I say!—This
 push 20
Will cheer me ever, or disseat me
 now.
I have lived long enough. My way of
 life
Is fallen into the sere, the yellow
 leaf;
And that which should accompany
 old age,
As honor, love, obedience, troops of
 friends, 25
I must not look to have; but, in their
 stead,
Curses not loud but deep, mouth-
 honor, breath,
Which the poor heart would fain
 deny, and dare not.
Seyton!

(*Enter* SEYTON.)

Sey. What's your gracious pleasure?
Macb. What news more? 30
Sey. All is confirmed, my lord, which
 was reported.
Macb. I'll fight, till from my bones my
 flesh be hacked.
 Give me my armor.
Sey. 'Tis not needed yet.
Macb. I'll put it on.
Send out moe horses,[4] skirr[5] the coun-
 try round; 35
 Hang those that talk of fear. Give me
 mine armor.

4. More horsemen.
5. Scurry.

How does your patient, doctor?

Doct. Not so sick, my lord,
As she is troubled with thick-coming fancies
That keep her from her rest.

Macb. Cure her of that!
Canst thou not minister to a mind diseased, 40
Pluck from the memory a rooted sorrow,
Raze out the written troubles of the brain,
And with some sweet oblivious antidote
Cleanse the stuff'd bosom of that perilous stuff
Which weighs upon the heart?

Doct. Therein the patient 45
Must minister to himself.

Macb. Throw physic to the dogs, I'll none of it!—
Come, put mine armor on. Give me my staff.—
Seyton, send out.—Doctor, the thanes fly from me.—
Come, sir, dispatch.—If thou couldst, doctor, cast 50
The water of my land, find her disease,
And purge it to a sound and pristine health,
I would applaud thee to the very echo,
That should applaud again.—Pull't off, I say.[6]—
What rhubarb, senna, or what purgative drug, 55
Would scour these English hence? Hear'st thou of them?

Doct. Ay, my good lord. Your royal preparation
Makes us hear something.

Macb. Bring it after me! [7]

6. A piece of the armor.
7. The piece of armor.

I will not be afraid of death and bane
Till Birnam Forest come to Dunsinane. 60

(*Exeunt all but the* DOCTOR.)

Doct. Were I from Dunsinane away and clear,
Profit again should hardly draw me here.

(*Exit.*)

SCENE IV.
COUNTRY NEAR BIRNAM WOOD.

(*Drum and colors. Enter* MALCOLM, SIWARD, MACDUFF, SIWARD'S SON, MENTEITH, CAITHNESS, ANGUS, LENNOX, ROSS, *and* SOLDIERS, *marching.*)

Mal. Cousins, I hope the days are near at hand
That chambers will be safe.

Ment. We doubt it nothing.

Siw. What wood is this before us?

Ment. The Wood of Birnam.

Mal. Let every soldier hew him down a bough
And bear't before him. Thereby shall we shadow 5
The numbers of our host and make discovery
Err in report of us.

Soldiers. It shall be done.

Siw. We learn no other but the confident tyrant
Keeps still in Dunsinane and will endure
Our setting down before't.

Mal. 'Tis his main hope; 10
For where there is advantage to be given,
Both more and less[1] have given him the revolt;

1. Men of both high and low rank.

And none serve with him but constrained things,
Whose hearts are absent too.
Macd. Let our just censures
Attend the true event, and put we on
Industrious soldiership.
Siw. The time approaches 16
That will with due decision make us know
What we shall say we have, and what we owe.
Thoughts speculative their unsure hopes relate,
But certain issue strokes must arbitrate; 20
Towards which advance the war.

(*Exeunt, marching.*)

SCENE V.
DUNSINANE. WITHIN THE CASTLE.

(*Enter* MACBETH, SEYTON, *and* SOLDIERS, *with drum and colors.*)
Macb. Hang out our banners on the outward walls.
The cry is still, 'They come!' Our castle's strength
Will laugh a siege to scorn. Here let them lie
Till famine and the ague eat them up.
Were they not forced with those that should be ours, 5
We might have met them dareful, beard to beard,
And beat them backward home.

(*A cry within of women.*)
What is that noise?
Sey. It is the cry of women, my good lord.
(*Exit.*)
Macb. I have almost forgot the taste of fears.

The time has been, my senses would have cool'd 10
To hear a night-shriek, and my fell of hair
Would at a dismal treatise rouse and stir
As life were in't. I have supp'd full with horrors.
Direness, familiar to my slaughterous thoughts,
Cannot once start me.

(*Enter* SEYTON.)
Wherefore was that cry? 15
Sey. The Queen, my lord, is dead.
Macb. She should have died hereafter;
There would have been a time for such a word.[1]
To-morrow, and to-morrow, and to-morrow
Creeps in this petty pace from day to day 20
To the last syllable of recorded time;
And all our yesterdays have lighted fools
The way to dusty death. Out, out, brief candle!
Life's but a walking shadow, a poor player,
That struts and frets his hour upon the stage 25
And then is heard no more. It is a tale
Told by an idiot, full of sound and fury,
Signifying nothing.

(*Enter a* MESSENGER.)
Thou com'st to use they tongue. Thy story quickly!
Mess. Gracious my lord, 30
I should report that which I say I saw,
But know not how to do't.

1. Death.

Macb.   Well, say, sir!

Mess. As I did stand my watch upon the hill,

I look'd toward Birnam, and anon methought

The wood began to move.

Macb.   Liar and slave! 35

Mess. Let me endure your wrath if 't be not so.

Within this three mile may you see it coming;

I say, a moving grove.

Macb.   If thou speak'st false,

Upon the next tree shalt thou hang alive,

Till famine cling thee. If thy speech be sooth,   40

I care not if thou dost for me as much.

I pull in resolution, and begin

To doubt th' equivocation of the fiend,

That lies like truth. 'Fear not, till Birnam Wood

Do come to Dunsinane!' and now a wood   45

Comes toward Dunsinane. Arm, arm, and out!

If this which he avouches does appear,

There is nor flying hence nor tarrying here.

I 'gin to be aweary of the sun,

And wish th' estate o' th' world were now undone.   50

Ring the alarum bell! Blow wind, come wrack,[2]

At least we'll die with harness[3] on our back!

(*Exeunt.*)

SCENE VI.
DUNSINANE. BEFORE THE CASTLE.

(*Drum and colors. Enter* MALCOLM,

SIWARD, MACDUFF, *and their* ARMY, *with boughs.*)

Mal. Now near enough. Your leavy screens throw down

And show like those you are. You, worthy uncle,

Shall with my cousin, your right noble son,

Lead our first battle. Worthy Macduff and we

Shall take upon 's what else remains to do,   5

According to our order.

Siw.   Fare you well.

Do we but find the tyrant's power to-night,

Let us be beaten if we cannot fight.

Macd. Make all our trumpets speak, give them all breath,

Those clamorous harbingers of blood and death.   10

(*Exeunt. Alarums continued.*)

SCENE VII. ANOTHER PART OF THE FIELD.

(*Enter* MACBETH.)

Macb. They have tied me to a stake. I cannot fly,

But bear-like I must fight the course. What's he

That was not born of woman? Such a one

Am I to fear, or none.

(*Enter* YOUNG SIWARD.)

Y. Siw. What is thy name?

Macb.   Thou'lt be afraid to hear it. 5

Y. Siw. No; though thou call'st thyself a hotter name

Than any is in hell.

Macb.   My name's Macbeth.

Y. Siw. The devil himself could not pronounce a title

2. Ruin.

3. Armor.

More hateful to mine ear.

Macb.   No, nor more fearful.

Y. Siw. Thou liest, abhorred tyrant!
With my sword   10
I'll prove the lie thou speak'st.

(*Fight, and* YOUNG SIWARD *slain.*)

Macb.   Thou wast born of woman.
But swords I smile at, weapons laugh
     to scorn,
Brandish'd by man that's of a woman
     born.

(*Exit.*)
(*Alarums. Enter* MACDUFF.)

Macd. That way the noise is. Tyrant,
     show thy face!
If thou be'st slain and with no stroke
     of mine,   15
My wife and children's ghosts will
     haunt me still.
I cannot strike at wretched kerns,
     whose arms
Are hired to bear their staves. Either
     thou, Macbeth,
Or else my sword with an unbat-
     tered edge
I sheathe again undeeded. There
     thou shouldst be.   20
By this great clatter one of greatest
     note
Seems bruited.[1] Let me find him,
     Fortune!
And more I beg not.

(*Exit. Alarums.*)
(*Enter* MALCOLM *and* SIWARD.)

Siw. This way, my lord. The castle's
     gently render'd:[2]
The tyrant's people on both sides do
     fight;   25
The noble thanes do bravely in the
     war;
The day almost itself professes
     yours,

And little is to do.

Mal.   We have met with foes
That strike beside us.

Siw.   Enter, sir, the castle.

(*Exeunt. Alarum.*)

SCENE VIII. ANOTHER PART OF THE FIELD.

(*Enter* MACBETH.)

Macb. Why should I play the Roman
     fool and die
On mine own sword? Whiles I see
     lives, the gashes
Do better upon them.

(*Enter* MACDUFF.)

Macd.   Turn, hellhound, turn!

Macb. Of all men else I have avoided
     thee.
But get thee back! My soul is too
     much charged   5
With blood of thine already.

Macd.   I have no words;
My voice is in my sword, thou
     bloodier villain
Than terms can give thee out!

(*Fight. Alarum.*)

Macb.   Thou losest labor.
As easy mayst thou the intrenchant
     air
With thy keen sword impress as make
     me bleed.   10
Let fall thy blade on vulnerable
     crests.
I bear a charmed life, which must
     not yield
To one of woman born.

Macd.   Despair thy charm!
And let the angel whom thou still
     hast served
Tell thee, Macduff was from his
     mother's womb   15
Untimely ripp'd.

---

1. Announced.

2. Tamely surrendered.

Macb. Accursed be that tongue that tells me so,
For it hath cow'd my better part of man!
And be these juggling fiends no more believed,
That palter[1] with us in a double sense, 20
That keep the word of promise to our ear
And break it to our hope! I'll not fight with thee!

Macd. Then yield thee, coward,
And live to be the show and gaze o' th' time!
We'll have thee, as our rarer monsters are, 25
Painted upon a pole, and underwrit
'Here may you see the tyrant.'

Macb. I will not yield,
To kiss the ground before young Malcolm's feet
And to be baited with the rabble's curse.
Though Birnam Wood be come to Dunsinane, 30
And thou opposed, being of no woman born,
Yet I will try the last. Before my body
I throw my warlike shield. Lay on, Macduff,
And damn'd be him that first cries 'Hold, enough!'

(*Exeunt fighting. Alarums.*)

(*Retreat and flourish. Enter, with drum and colors,* MALCOLM SIWARD, ROSS, THANES, *and* SOLDIERS.)

Mal. I would the friends we miss were safe arrived. 35

Siw. Some must go off; and yet, by these I see,
So great a day as this is cheaply bought.

Mal. Macduff is missing, and your noble son.

Ross. Your son, my lord, has paid a soldier's debt. 39
He only lived but till he was a man,
The which no sooner had his prowess confirm'd
In the unshrinking station where he fought
But like a man he died.

Siw. Then he is dead?

Ross. Ay, and brought off the field. Your cause of sorrow
Must not be measured by his worth, for then 45
It hath no end.

Siw. Had he his hurts before?

Ross. Ay, on the front.

Siw. Why then, God's soldier be he!
Had I as many sons as I have hairs,
I would not wish them to a fairer death.
And so his knell is knoll'd.[2]

Mal. He's worth more sorrow, 50
And that I'll spend for him.

Siw. He's worth no more.
They say he parted well and paid his score,
And so, God be with him! Here comes newer comfort.

(*Enter* MACDUFF, *with* MACBETH'S *head.*)

Macd. Hail, King! for so thou art. Behold where stands
Th' usurper's cursed head. The time is free. 55
I see thee compass'd with thy kingdom's pearl,[3]
That speak my salutation in their minds;
Whose voices I desire aloud with mine—

1. Play false.
2. Tolled.
3. Surrounded by your chief supporters.

Hail, King of Scotland!

All.   Hail, King of Scotland!

(*Flourish.*)

Mal. We shall not spend a large expense of time   60

Before we reckon with your several
loves[4]

And make us even with you. My
thanes and kinsmen,

Henceforth be earls, the first that
ever Scotland

In such an honor named. What's
more to do

Which would be planted newly with
the time—   65

As calling home our exiled friends
abroad

4. Reward your loyalty.

That fled the snares of watchful tyranny,

Producing forth the cruel ministers

Of this dead butcher and his fiend-
like queen,

Who, as 'tis thought, by self and
violent hands   70

Took off her life—this, and what
needful else

That calls upon us, by the grace of
Grace

We will perform in measure, time,
and place.

So thanks to all at once and to each
one,

Whom we invite to see us crown'd at
Scone.   75

(*Flourish. Exeunt omnes.*)

The Misanthrope

MOLIÈRE

INTRODUCTION

Jean-Baptiste Poquelin, better-known as Molière, was born in Paris on January 15, 1622. His father, Jean Poquelin, was an upholsterer and interior decorator, and his mother, Marie Cressé, was the daughter of an upholsterer; both sides of the family were well-to-do. In 1632 Marie died, leaving four children; Jean soon remarried but became a widower again in 1636. This may explain why mothers almost never appear as characters in Molière's plays, for from the age of fourteen he was under the mental and moral influence of his father and grandparents. Jean-Baptiste was educated at the College de Clermont, the best school in Paris, where he distinguished himself both in classics and in philosophy; he completed his education by going to Orleans for a course in law.

His introduction to the theater, and probably his deep love for it, had started long before his school days, however, for his father's shop was situated not very far from two important theatrical sites, the Pont-Neuf and the Rue Mauconseil. At the Pont-Neuf some quack doctors had set up in the street large platform stages upon which comedians acted out plays and farces for the sole purpose of selling patent medicines to the crowds that gathered to watch the free shows. The boy was deeply impressed by the antics of l'Orviétan and Bary, the great comic medicine-men, and stored their tricks and jokes away in his memory for future use. At the corner of the Rue Mauconseil and the Rue Française, even nearer to his father's shop than the Pont-Neuf, stood the Hôtel de Bourgogne, the outstanding theater of the day, where the King's Players put on romantic tragedies and broad farces. The boy was often taken to this theater by his grandfather, Louis de Cressé, who was an ardent playgoer; the tragedies he saw there were second-rate, but the actors of the farces were brilliant and inventive. These actors represented stock characters—The Stingy Father, The Ignorant Doctor, The Bragging Soldier—and performed in the great Italian tradition of improvised comedy, *commedia dell'arte*, making up their lines as they went along; from them, and from the many Italian troupes that later visited Paris, Molière borrowed plot ideas, situations, and actual jests for his own plays.

In 1643, when he was twenty-one, Jean-Baptiste had reached a decision to devote his life to the theater, and for the next thirty years he remained faithful to his profession. He gave up his right to become his father's successor as upholsterer to the King, took possession of a small part of the money that his mother had left him upon her death in 1632, and cast in his lot with the Béjart family.

Jean-Baptiste had fallen in love with Madeleine Béjart, a beautiful, fiery, and gifted girl of twenty-seven who had been an actress for several years, and who, with her brother Joseph and sister Genevieve, now wished to form her own acting company. Madeleine got together about a dozen talented young men and women from well-to-do families and established a dramatic troupe to which she gave the high-sounding name of *L'Illustre Théâtre* (The Illustrious Theater). Jean-Baptiste Poquelin was a member of the original company, which was organized on June 30, 1643; it was shortly after this that he took the surname of Molière, probably to spare his father embarrassment, since actors had no social standing and had even been excommunicated by the church. Though passionately interested in the theater, the members of this newly formed company were unskilled novices for the most part, so that it is no surprise to learn that in the next two years they appeared in three different theaters in various parts of Paris and failed in all of them. These "theaters" were actually indoor tennis courts which had been converted into playhouses by the simple expedient of erecting a platform at one end of the long, narrow room; the audience stood in front of the stage, or sat in the spectators' balcony that ran around three walls and overlooked the playing area. Twice during these early, trying days Molière was arrested for debt and imprisoned, but he was released each time on the bond of a friend. Several of the less hardy members dropped out of the company but the seven who remained, including Molière and the Béjarts, decided to quit Paris and try their luck in the provinces. In 1646 they left the capital and went on a tour of the country that lasted for twelve years.

It was during this period that Molière began to write plays for the company. By the spring of 1658, the playwright's friends were urging him to try his luck once more in Paris. Molière made several trips to the capital, where he managed to get introductions to Cardinal Mazarin and to the King's brother, Philippe, who was known by the title of Monsieur, and who was said to be interested in supporting a dramatic company which would bear his name. The *Illustre Théâtre* left Lyons, acted before Monsieur, and pleased him; then the players were invited to perform for the Court. That was the dream they had had for twelve years while serving their apprenticeship in the provinces.

On the evening of October 24, 1658, Molière acted for the first time before Louis XIV and his courtiers in the Guard Room of the old Louvre Palace on a platform erected at the King's command; the program consisted of Corneille's tragedy *Nicomède*, followed by Molière's farce *The Love-Sick Doctor*, and the whole was brought to a close by a clever speech which Molière addressed to the Court. The evening was a triumph; the King immediately decreed that the company was to be known as the Troupe de Monsieur, and that it was to perform at the Hôtel du Petit Bourbon.

The three most important theaters in Paris at the time were the Hôtel de Bourgogne, the Théâtre du Marais, and the Hôtel du Petit Bourbon, all of which had been developed under the influence of Cardinal Richelieu, who had been intensely interested in every aspect of the theater; he had urged poets to write for the stage, offered pensions to outstanding playwrights and actors, given private performances of new plays in his own home, and in 1641 included in his new palace a magnificent playhouse, later to be known as the Théâtre du Palais Royal. The Petit Bourbon was occupied on Sundays, Tuesdays, and Fridays by an Italian company headed by the celebrated Tiberio Fiorelli whose stage name was Scaramouche; it was in this theater that Molière was granted permission by the King to perform on Mondays, Wednesdays, Thursdays, and Saturdays. The two companies got along admirably and parted friends in July of 1659 when the Italians returned to their own country and left Molière in sole possession of the house.

In November, 1659, Molière opened the season at the Petit Bourbon with an augmented acting company which included the accomplished comic Du Croisy and his wife; the celebrated white-face clown known as Jodolet; and a young actor called La Grange, who became a devoted follower of Molière and the record-keeper for the company. It is from his records that we have learned of the company's casting, performances, payments, and receipts. The first play to be presented at the Petit Bourbon was *Les Précieuses Ridicules* (*The Pretentious Young Ladies*), a comedy in one act which boldly satirized Madame de Rambouillet and her coterie who had set themselves up as the final arbiters of taste and culture in Paris. This was Molière's first attempt at social criticism and proved to be sensationally successful. The King was so pleased that he gave Molière a large gift in cash; but among those whom he had held up to ridicule the playwright made many enemies, and the shrinking receipts of the rival theaters added many more.

In retaliation, these powerful enemies first managed to have Molière's play suspended for fourteen days, then in an effort to drive their adversary out of the city, brought about the complete closing of the Petit Bourbon. Through the good graces of the King, the Théâtre du Palais Royal was turned over to Molière for his own use and was occupied by him for the rest of his life. During the thirteen and a half years that remained to him—a period only slightly longer than that of his twelve-year apprenticeship—Molière worked feverishly, writing, directing, and acting in the thirty-odd plays which have established a reputation that has lasted for three hundred years.

Between 1660 and 1665 French classical comedy assumed a definite form, mainly at the hands of Molière: the masks of the Italians disappeared, characters and situations began to resemble those of contemporary Paris, and plot was developed through the interaction of character rather than through the conduct of intrigues. In *The School for Husbands*, a three-act play in verse, Molière deals with the problems faced by a forty-year-old man who is jealously trying to guard his twenty-year-old wife from the attentions of a younger man. Molière was probably anticipating his own feelings of jealousy, for the play was performed on June 24, 1661, and about eight months later, on February 20, 1662, having just reached the age of forty, the playwright married Armande Béjart, the youngest sister of Madeleine, a beautiful girl of twenty. Armande was a gifted actress, who had been trained for the stage by her sister and by Molière. After her marriage to the dramatist, she took the leading feminine part in each of his plays. For Armande, Molière always wrote parts in which caustic sayings, sharp wit, and a certain amount of coquetry are to be found; the first role of this type is Eliza in *The School for Wives Criticized* and the perfect and final development is Célimène in *The Misanthrope*. Armande bore Molière three children, two of whom died in infancy; the marriage was not a happy one and for several years husband and wife lived apart from each other.

The King recognized Molière's superlative talents and on August 14, 1665, increased the poet's pension and accorded to his acting company the coveted title of "Troupe of the King." In September of the same year, *L'Amour Médecin*, a ballet-play, was written, rehearsed, and acted within a period of five days; it was performed first at Versailles, afterwards in Paris. Molière was obviously working too hard; in December he suffered a serious illness and the Palais Royal had to be closed. It was the beginning of his long struggle against what appears to have been tuberculosis, but he did not let it interfere either with his writing or his acting and, in the last seven years of his life, he produced what are generally considered to be his greatest plays, among them *The Misanthrope, The Doctor in Spite of Himself, George Dandin, Tartuffe* (written in 1664), *The Would-Be Gentleman, The Learned Ladies,* and *The Imaginary Invalid.*

On February 25, 1669, Molière's father died, still unreconciled to the fact that his son had chosen to be a dramatist and actor instead of an upholsterer. Not long afterwards, his friends arranged a reconciliation between Molière and Armande, but it was not a happy state of affairs, for Molière knew that his days were numbered. On February 17, 1672, Madeleine Béjart, his oldest and closest friend, died; in August of the same year, Molière lost his young son; and then began his struggle against the intrigues of the composer, Jean Baptiste Lully, who was in charge of music at the court of Louis XIV. The playwright soon realized that he was out of favor with the King; this rejection coupled with his sorrow over the recent deaths of Madeleine Béjart and of his son and his failing health caused Molière to lose heart.

And yet his newest play, his last, which leveled a blast of ridicule against the medical profession, was one of the cleverest and most vigorous of his comedies. In *The Imaginary Invalid,* Molière himself, physically exhausted and wracked with coughing, played the part of the hypochondriac, Argan. On February 17, 1673, the day of the fourth performance of the play and the very day on which Madeleine had died the year before, Molière was so ill that his wife and his protégé, Michel Baron, begged him not to go to the theater, but he would not take their advice. He said, "There are fifty poor workers who have only their daily wage to live on. What will become of them if the performance does not take place?" During the performance he suffered a hemorrhage but played the piece out to the end. That night, in his house in the Rue Richelieu, he died. The local priests would not listen to the confession of an actor, nor would they permit him to be buried in holy ground; it was only after Armande Béjart enlisted the aid of the King that Molière was buried, four nights later, in the Cemetery Saint-Joseph near the Rue Montmartre. The body of the man who had brought laughter and light to the world was borne to its grave under the cover of darkness.

Three months after the death of Molière, in May, 1673, his company gave up the Palais Royal and bought the Théâtre Guénégaud, whereupon the King ordered Molière's players to merge with the company of the Théâtre du Marais. One of the comedians of the Marais, Guérin d'Estriché, married Armande Béjart in 1677. The two outstanding companies in Paris at this time were the Molière-Marais troupe at the Guénégaud and the company at the Hôtel de Bourgogne, but in 1680 the King decided that these companies should join to form one and, in an order countersigned by Colbert, created the Théâtre-Français, which became the national theater of France. Since Molière's plays made up a considerable part of the repertory, and the troupe at the Théâtre-Français had descended in a straight line from the troupe of Molière, this actor-dramatist is considered one of the founders of the great French theatrical institution, the Comédie-Française, which is sometimes known as the House of Molière.

Molière's comedy has remained for the French the most beloved of all their works, not only because it combines gaiety with extreme restraint in the expression of profound feelings, but also because of its social outlook. An individual's eccentricity in conflict with accepted norms provides the basis for most social comedy, and Molière is the undisputed master of this type; no dramatist has ever displayed a keener social consciousness, a sharper wit, more astute common sense, or more Olympian detachment in depicting the foibles of civilized man than he.

Social comedy differs from romantic comedy in that the latter type puts a heavy emphasis upon story and plot, while the former is concerned with the delineation of character and with social criticism. Sentiment is almost entirely lacking in social comedy; there is hardly a word of genuine tenderness between parents and children, or between brothers and sisters, in all of Molière. Even the tenderness of his lovers is always close to laughter. The most sacred relationships and the most serious situations are made to seem absurd, for the writer of social comedy is a reformer at heart who attacks the follies of society by laughing at them. It is a very difficult art, which explains why even a genius of Molière's stature required a lifetime to perfect it. Because his plays recreate the world he lived in—with its social climbers, doctors, lawyers, prudes, peasants, servants, lecherous old men, and amorous young women, all done so naturally, so spontaneously, so ridiculously, and so like our own world—Molière's work has enduring appeal.

Although *The Misanthrope* has universal significance, it is, at the same time, a perfect example of a neoclassical comedy. The French critics of the seventeenth century, having studied the dramatic precepts of Aristotle and Horace, without, however, having fully understood them, insisted that the playwrights of their own day observe the "laws" of the ancients or suffer the critical consequences. The three unbreakable rules, the critics believed, were the three unities: the unity of action, which meant that a good plot could not have more than one main action and that all minor actions had to be related to it; the unity of time, which meant that an action represented on the stage should consume the same amount of time that it would in real life, and that in no case should it exceed one natural day; and the unity of place, which meant that the physical action of the play should be limited to one place with no change of scene whatsoever. To these "classical" rules, the neoclassical critics added several of their own: A complete play, whether tragedy or comedy, was to consist of five acts in alexandrine verse; only four or five persons of elevated station or character were to be shown; and no incident, violent or otherwise, was to occur on the stage but had to be reported. As the "action" seen by the audience consisted entirely of personages engaged in conversation, the characters were to be evaluated by their quickness of wit and soundness of judgment, while the verse was meant to lift the whole play above the plane of reality. It was expected, in addition, that the characters would be drawn true to human nature so that the audience would recognize its own experiences in the passions and decisions depicted; and, finally, that the dialogue and actions would be appropriate for each character according to his age, sex, and condition with strict adherence to the propriety and decorum suited to people of the upper classes.

The three great dramatists of the period, Corneille, Molière, and Racine, wore the straitjacket of these rules with varying degrees of comfort. Racine, though very unhappy with them, seemed least hampered by the limitations imposed upon him; Corneille departed from the rules when it suited his purpose, as in the case of the *Cid*, but by so doing he started a literary war that lasted for years; while Molière pretended to pay no attention whatsoever to the dictates of the critics, maintaining that he listened only to the public and wrote purely to provide pleasure.

A close examination of *The Misanthrope*, however, clearly shows that in form and content the play is a model of neoclassical correctness. It has a single main action—the play opens with Alceste's determination to learn whether Célimène will marry him, and ends when he gets his answer; the dramatic events consume only a few hours in a single day; and the entire action takes place in the second floor drawing-room of Célimène's house in Paris. The play, moreover, is in five acts and was written in alexandrine verse, a line containing six iambic feet (Wilbur's translation, however, has only five iambic feet to the line); there are just six important characters in the play, and all are members of the upper class; no physical action occurs upon the stage, although a duel, a lawsuit, and several other dramatic incidents are discussed; the language is polished and witty; the psychological motivations are realistic and believable; the dialogue is appropriate to each character; and the utmost decorum is observed even when the antagonists are verbally slashing each other to ribbons. The play's content, like its form, appealed to the tastes of the age in the picture it presented of conventional society and the emphasis it placed upon the exercise of reason, although reason here is shown to be a destructive rather than a constructive force.

The sources of *The Misanthrope* are complicated. In about 1661, Molière wrote a tragedy called *Don Garcia of Navarre, or The Jealous Prince;* the play was a failure. Molière decided to follow it with a comedy on the same theme; the leading characters in the two plays bore a strong resemblance to each other and compromising letters served in both to heighten the intrigue. Because of the similarity of the material, Molière was able to borrow more than one hundred and fifty lines from the unsuccessful tragedy and to work them, without much difficulty, into his new comedy. Some of the characters, such as the fops, are modeled on those in other plays by Molière, particularly the *Impromptu de Versailles;* and a number of minor details were taken from the works of earlier writers.

The major portion of the material, however, was based on Molière's own experience and feelings. For more than two years the playwright had been struggling to have his prohibited works, *Tartuffe* and *Don Juan,* produced in Paris, but at every turn he was thwarted by members of the Court and the Church, by rival poets, and by adherents to the religious sect called the *devots;* he sharply attacks many of these people in *The Misanthrope.* At the same time, the dramatist was having marital difficulties which were soon to force him into an open break with his wife. Molière was inordinately jealous of Armande Béjart, who was young, beautiful, light-hearted, and inclined, perhaps in all innocence, to be a flirt. This husband-wife conflict is clearly reflected in the relationship between Alceste and Célimène.

Molière does not deal in this play with the social order in general but only with Parisian high society, and not even with every phase of that particular class; he says very little, for instance, about religious, political, or economic conditions, or about family relations, and yet he presents a broad canvas upon which are depicted the many lively interests of this social group: its relation to the Court, its amusements, its preoccupation with conversation, law suits, dueling, gossip, portraiture, costume, poetry, and love-making. Add to this the character types ridiculed by Célimène—the nonstop talker, the man who makes a mystery of everything, the bore who mixes only with the nobility, the woman whose visits never end, the critic who likes nothing and works too hard at being clever—and the sum total is a complete exposé of the superficiality and falsity of society.

The plot of *The Misanthrope* is simplicity itself, as it is largely concerned with Alceste's love for Célimène and the reasons for his decision not to marry her. Closely related to this central line are the scenes involving Eliante's and Arsinoé's love for Alceste, the quarrel with Oronte, and the law-suit. Perhaps more attention than was absolutely necessary for the structure of the play was devoted to the scenes between Acaste and Clitandre and between Célimène and Arsinoé, but the dramatic action concludes with the end of the love affair. There are those who maintain that the play is plotless, that it is merely an extended conversation piece, but this is not true. Molière actually displays remarkable skill as a dramatist in the handling of his materials, since the interest is held and heightened by the clever arrangement of events. The three most striking scenes: the sonnet, the verbal portraits, and the women's duel, are distributed among the first three acts, while the fourth act is devoted to the conflict between Alceste and Célimène, and the fifth to the cutting of the knot. All of these situations are so adroitly arranged that there is a definite sense of conflict and climax despite the meagerness of the story. The plot is really incidental, since its function is simply to reveal characters in exemplary situations. Ringing with stage effect, the characters in this play have a social context but no personal history; we are told very little of their past or of their future; they appear, exhibit themselves, and are gone; what is most important are the human traits they reveal in the few moments that they stand before us, their lives arrested and illuminated at a point in time.

Alceste has cast himself in the role of the autocrat and the martyr; he complains of the manners of his contemporaries, their affectations of speech, dress, and behavior; he complains about inferior works of art, about legal procedures, and about the insincerity and infidelity of people in love. He carries his superior notions and ideals to such ridiculous lengths that he succeeds only in defeating himself. Alceste is comic in his lack of a sense of proportion, in the violence of his indignation over small matters, and in the fact that he seems himself to be devoid of a sense of humor; yet, at the same time, his uncompromising honesty wins our admiration, and the intensity of his passion, our sympathy. He has dreamed of an ideal world and follows his aim without regard for his own fortunes or for the feelings of his fellows. He is not a buffoon but neither is he a faultless hero; it is the reality of his character and of his hopes that makes it possible for him to continue to live and to appeal.

Célimène is one of Molière's most brilliant creations; she is beautiful, clever, witty, and cold. She is a widow so that she may entertain freely, but her flirtations lead her into difficulties and make true love impossible for her. She has perfect manners and great tact but is not much troubled by feelings of conscience; she is callous in the manner in which she ridicules her acquaintances, dominates Alceste, and destroys the pretensions of Arsinoé. She has allowed herself to be seduced by society, and consequently she is self-destructive.

Philinte, Alceste's friend, is the intelligent man who is well-adjusted to society. He is not blind to its affectations and faults, but he has learned how to live with them. If he must praise a poor poem, he does so; he knows how to flatter and equivocate, but he retains his personal standards.

Eliante, the most attractive character in the play, is honest and charming. In the expression of her beliefs and in her relationships with others, she is sweet, simple, and sincere. Like Philinte she is warm and direct and knows the meaning of love; these two appear to be the ideal couple.

Arsinoé is a prudish woman who pretends to be high-minded and pure but is actually wicked and hypocritical. After she is defeated by Célimène and rebuffed by Alceste, she displays her stupidity and viciousness by trying to make trouble between them although she can gain nothing by it.

The men in Célimène's entourage—Oronte, Acaste, and Clitandre—are the butts for Alceste's satirical shafts, and at the same time provide a perfect background for his somber figure. The would-be poet and the elegant gallants, who represent the glittering but empty social world of Louis XIV are introduced primarily for the purpose of showing up their mediocrity.

The appeal of *The Misanthrope* lies not only in the skillful arrangement of its incidents, and the richness of its characterization, but in the unusual quality of its verse. In an age of preciosity, when elegant, high-flown, and artificial language was considered the mark of the literary man, Molière's dialogue was notable for its clarity, directness, and force as well as for its heightened realism, its cleverness, and its beauty. Unlike Shakespeare, who was born and bred in the country and whose plays reflect his close observation and love of nature, Molière was by birth and upbringing a city boy, a Parisian, to whom the daffodil, the violet, and the primrose meant nothing. It is safe to say that during the twelve years that he spent wandering through the countryside of France, the only aspect of nature that Molière was aware of was Man. One can almost count on one's fingers the passages in his plays in which he uses nature for the purpose of simile or metaphor, and where he does there is no evidence of direct observation or of deep feeling. Yet his flexible and sonorous verses are alive with vivid images and with subtle, symbolic touches which we find only in the greatest poetry. There is the profound symbolism, for instance, of the veil or the mask to suggest the difference between appearance and reality. Early in the play Philinte informs Alceste that it is not only uncouth but absurd always to speak the naked truth; he says:

> It's often best to veil one's true emotions.
> Wouldn't the social fabric come undone
> If we were wholly frank with everyone?

Later in the play, during the great verbal duel between Célimène and Arsinoé, when these ladies are bent upon unmasking each other, one says:

> if you were more *overtly* good,
> You wouldn't be so much misunderstood; . . .

to which the other replies:

> "What good," they said, "are all these outward shows,
> When everything belies her pious pose?"

Alceste reaches the conclusion that in order to be free to have an honest heart, without masks or veils, one must leave society and live apart from other people.

If *The Misanthrope* has a *theme*, it is extremely difficult to determine exactly what it is. The play has been criticized, by Rousseau among others, on the grounds that Molière has shown the world to be too wicked and that he has permitted the idealist to be defeated while the connivers succeed; actually the reverse is true. Granted that Molière took a dark view of human nature and saw hypocrisy and infidelity on all sides, he was merciless in his castigation of these vices, while he depicted the idealist as a sympathetic figure who has gone woefully astray. We might perhaps come closest to the play's central meaning if we look upon Alceste and Philinte as two aspects of the same character; for we all desire to be individualists and intransigents, like Alceste, while at the same time we are compelled by society to be time-servers and conformists, like Philinte.

Molière always affirmed that "the business of comedy is to represent in a general way all the defects of men, and particularly those of our own age." In

The Misanthrope he produced a play that is not only a perfect example of what he had in mind, but one that has served as a model for countless imitators, none of whom achieved either his deftness or his vitality. The comedy of social criticism, which, to use the playwright's own words, portrays "the manners of the time without aiming at individuals," found its greatest exponent in Molière.

PRODUCTION IN THE NEOCLASSICAL THEATER

The Theater

The social and religious conditions which had created mass audiences for Greek, Roman, and medieval drama had also made outdoor performances feasible, but during the Renaissance both society and the drama became more secular and more commercial and there was a corresponding reduction in the size of the audience and an alteration in the caliber of the people who composed it. The professional neoclassical theater relied for its support mainly upon the king, the members of the nobility, and the upper middle class, and for these people plays were performed indoors.

The earliest indoor theaters were not built specially for dramatic productions but had originally been intended for social gatherings or spectator sports; they had actually been ballrooms or indoor tennis courts which were converted into theaters by the expedient of building a platform at one end of the long, rectangular room. Since the space itself was the wrong shape and the people who renovated it had no principles to guide them (were not aware of the fact, for instance, that the floor of a theater should not be flat but that the seats should rise in tiers), the playhouses of the sixteenth and seventeenth centuries in France were anything but ideal for either playgoers or performers.

An association called the Brotherhood of the Passion ('*Confrérie de la Passion*) made up of artisans and tradesmen whose main avocation had been the performance of mystery plays, had a monopoly on dramatic activity in Paris. They had been in existence since the Middle Ages and had presented plays on outdoor platform stages, but in 1548, when public performances of mysteries were forbidden, the members of the Brotherhood took over the town house of the Dukes of Burgundy and turned the grand ballroom into a theater, the Hôtel de Bourgogne. This was the only theater in Paris until a second troupe established itself in 1634, at an indoor tennis court called the *Jeu de paume du Marais*. Indoor tennis had been a very popular sport but interest in it faded; hence the availability of the deserted courts for use as theaters. It was probably the phenomenal success of the companies at the Bourgogne and the Marais that encouraged the Béjart group to attempt to found a third theater in Paris in 1643.

All of the important Parisian theaters of the seventeenth century had the same physical layout as that of the Hôtel de Bourgogne: The auditorium was a long, narrow room at one end of which there was a narrow, shallow stage; the orchestra floor in front of the stage, called the *parterre* or pit, had no seats but accommodated standees only. For the better class of patrons, there were boxes in the two galleries that ran round the sides of the room, and, beneath the galleries, against the walls, were loges or grandstands built up from the floor. The *"loges de face,"* which faced the stage directly from the rear wall of the theater, were the only ones which provided a suitable view of the stage, but were farthest from it. The other seats faced into the house so that the wealthier patrons had a better view of the crowd in the pit than of the action on the stage. Both auditorium and stage were lighted by candles, and the stage had no curtains.

The two theaters in Paris occupied by Molière and his company after 1658 were the Petit Bourbon and the Palais Royal; both were closely connected with the Court, yet, except for the magnificence of the décor, there was very little structural difference between these houses and the others in the city. The Petit Bourbon was a room about 210 feet long by 64 feet wide, with a deep apse at one end where the uncurtained stage was located; there were two galleries, the higher one set back, and the usual loges around the side walls. Forced out of the Petit Bourbon in 1660, Molière was granted the use of the Palais Royal, the theater which had been built for Cardinal Richelieu in 1637. Although the new house was smaller than the old, it was more richly decorated and was furnished with more complete facilities than any other professional theater then existing in Paris. The auditorium was a lofty, rectangular hall, about 70 feet long and 60 wide, with about two dozen chandeliers to provide illumination. The stage stood at one end of the hall behind an ornamented proscenium frame, the first to appear in any French theater, but still there was no curtain. The stage floor had trap doors in it, and machines were concealed behind the proscenium arch; these were used for spectacles in which objects, like chariots and clouds, or people were made to ascend, descend, or fly. Three galleries, divided into compartments, ran along each side of the house; the lowest gallery had rows of gold-decorated boxes for the highest members of society. The loges, which Molière had brought with him from his former theater, were erected at the rear of the hall.

Great advances were made in the structure of the indoor theater in France during the eighteenth century but that was an age of actors; there were no writers then to compare with Corneille, Racine, or Molière whose masterpieces were performed in their own day under rather crude and primitive conditions in makeshift playhouses.

Brief mention should be made of the outdoor theater at Versailles where ballets and interludes were produced for the entertainment of the King and his Court; the stage was set in the midst of the formal gardens with a natural setting for the background, the acting area was carefully delimited, and the seats of the spectators were arranged in a semicircle facing the stage. Courtly outdoor theaters of this type—and there were several of them—were more traditional in construction and more comfortable than the professional theaters in Paris.

Scenery, Lighting, Properties

The scenery used in the French theaters during the sixteenth and seventeenth centuries was an adaptation of the type in vogue on the medieval platform stage. The mystery plays of the Middle Ages, as has been noted, were performed on a long platform on which stood four or five little buildings, called mansions, representing the various locales to be used during the play. This type of scenery was known as "simultaneous setting" and actually gave the spectators a rough synopsis of the plot; the audience saw immediately that at some time during the play there would be a temple scene, a palace scene, and so on. When an actor emerged from the temple, the audience understood that the stage on which he strode represented the temple grounds; if another actor came out of the palace, then the stage represented the street on which the palace was situated. This was called an "unlocalized stage"; it did not represent a definite locale throughout the play, but varied from scene to scene, taking its character from the buildings around it, and from the entrances and exits of the players whose lines helped to establish their whereabouts.

The Hôtel de Bourgogne, with its tiny stage, did not have room enough for the building of mansions, but such clever designers as Laurent Mahelot and Michel Laurent solved that problem by covering the rear wall of the stage with a painted backcloth on which were depicted, side by side, the various locales required. As the plays became more and more romantic, in addition to temples and palaces, they called for woods, seacoasts, grottoes, and arbors, all of which were duly painted on the back curtain. With the aid of the backcloth, the different compartments could represent any of the settings required for tragedy, comedy, tragicomedy, and pastoral. The most important characteristic of these decorations is that they symbolize rather than represent place, and thus have something in common with Elizabethan staging. The actor, having taken a position either in or in front of a given item of décor, moved downstage, and, by convention, the whole stage would become that place. The audience accepted this convention, but as the plays became more complicated and the compartments multiplied, the result was confusing; the audience was often perplexed as to where the action was taking place. Although this type of staging made excessive demands upon the spectators, the simultaneous setting and the unlocalized stage remained in use well into the seventeenth century and returned to play a prominent part in German expressionism in the early years of our own century. But a great curb was put upon the unlocalized stage by the introduction of neoclassical rules.

When the critics began to insist upon the observance of the unities of action, time, and place, the dramatists were constrained to write plays which called for only a single setting, such as a room in a house, a corner of a garden, or a street. The room would be furnished with no more than a single armchair or table; there might be a bench in the garden; while the street scene would need no properties at all. Many of the plays of Racine and Molière can be acted satisfactorily on a bare stage. *The Misanthrope,* for instance, takes place entirely in one room in Célimène's house, and the essential properties consist of a single chair and three or four letters which are read on stage.

As no front curtain was used in the neoclassical theater, the actors left the stage after each scene. They could not be "discovered" in their places at the opening of a scene, nor could they form a tableau at the end. It was not until the eighteenth century, when designers learned how to construct shiftable scenery and how to use a front curtain, that various locales could be shown in succession and scenes could begin or end with a surprise.

The seventeenth-century theater was lighted by hundreds of candles in chandeliers both in the auditorium and on the stage, but the playhouses were dim nevertheless. There was only general illumination on the stage since the lights could not be controlled easily; they could not be focused on particular areas, spotlighted, dimmed or brightened at will. It was considered a great innovation in stage lighting when at a tragic moment in one production many candles were snuffed out suddenly to produce an eerie effect.

Unlike the tragedies and the high comedies which were considered works of neoclassical art, the comedy-ballets, interludes, and pastorals, which were presented at Court and later at the Palais Royal for the entertainment of the King, made use of an enormous amount of built and movable scenery and many complex properties. Under the direction of an Italian designer, Gaspare Vigarani, a special theater called the *Salle des Machines* was erected with a stage 32 feet wide at the proscenium opening and a depth of about 132 feet. There remarkable effects were obtained, the immense size of the stage permitting the building of temples and houses surrounded by bushes, trees, and mountains; and in the sky there were floating clouds on which sat many gods and goddesses. A movable platform, 40 feet wide by 60 feet long, could raise 60 persons into the air, as well as such properties as great horse-drawn chariots. To light this stage brightly, thousands of candles and oil-lamps were required, many of them concealed behind columns and in the side-wings which had now come into use. To achieve atmospheric effects, lamps were fixed behind bottles filled with colored liquid and metal bowls were placed behind the lights to act as reflectors, thus faint rays of red, blue, or green would be cast upon the stage. The excessive heat and the unpleasant odor of the wax candles and the oil, not to mention the great fire hazard, were part of the early efforts to develop an art of stage lighting.

The theaters of the eighteenth and nineteenth centuries whose stages were cluttered with built and painted scenery carried on the efforts of the *Salle des Machines;* while the realistic theater of our own day, with its "one-set show," has more in common with the neoclassical stage which represented a single room with four doors.

The Actors

The three acting companies which dominated the French theater during the seventeenth century, those of the Hôtel de Bourgogne, the Marais, and the Palais Royal, were all organized along similar lines. Although all were subsidized by the King, they were not united as a single professional group. Each company was independent and self-regulated; each elected its own officers, selected its plays, hired its actors, and had full control over its productions. The company usually bought its plays for a flat fee and owned the works outright; sometimes the dramatist was paid each time his play was performed, but he was not given a regular share in the receipts unless he also happened to be an actor in the troupe. It was customary for the members of the company to settle their financial business each day at the end of the performance. After the audience had departed, the actors took off their makeup, put their costumes away, and gathered in the theater. They counted the money that had been taken in at the box-office, subtracted the amount needed for the running expenses of the theater (heating, lighting, cleaning, and so on), and divided the remainder among the actors according to their status in the company. As in the Elizabethan theater, some actors received full shares, others half or quarter shares; a certain number of employees were on a straight salary basis. When an actor was obliged to retire, he was paid a small pension for the rest of his life by the performer who took his place in the company.

Although successful actors earned a great deal of money, their personal expenses were very high. The largest item in their budgets was the maintenance of their wardrobes. They had to provide their own stage costumes, which were extremely lavish and costly, and in addition were obliged to own very elegant personal clothing because of the society in which they moved. The actors were often summoned to give performances at the palaces in Paris and at Versailles, for which they received extra payment and free food and lodging, but they mingled with members of the nobility and had to look their best.

Each of the three troupes had its own acting style and its own stars. The Italian companies which were so popular throughout this period performed at the Hôtel de Bourgogne and preserved the techniques of the *commedia dell'arte*. Their style of acting was broad and impromptu; much of the dialogue was made up on the spot, although the actors had worked out a synopsis of the plot in advance. Broad comedy, farce, and satire were the strong points of these players; many of their jests were obscene and the performances of the women were in questionable taste.

Another style of play, exemplified by the tragicomedies of Alexandre Hardy, was acted by a native company at the Hôtel de Bourgogne. In their troupe there were three performers who were as skillful in serious plays as they were in comedy; known as Lafleur, Flechelles, and Belleville when they undertook serious roles, they achieved greater fame under the comic names of Gros-Guillaume (Fat William), Gaultier-Garguille (Walter Drainpipe), and Turlupin (Atrocious Punster). As comedians, each had an identifying costume and type of makeup: Gros-Guillaume was enormously fat and wore a costume that emphasized the bulge of his stomach; he covered his face with a thick coating of flour and pretended to be bored with love. Gaultier-Garguille dressed in black, had long stringy gray hair, and wore spectacles that had no lenses; he drew laughs with his bitterness, his carping, and his mimicry. Turlupin had a shock of red hair and wore a loose flowing costume of striped material that looked like the suit of a medieval clown; he played the part of a tricky servant who did not hesitate to pick pockets as a sideline.

The great tragic actors—Montdory, Montfleury, Bellerose, and Floridor—appeared both at the Marais and at the Hôtel de Bourgogne. It was the Marais company that first presented the plays of Corneille and Racine and it was there that the "tragic style" of acting was initiated; it was later taken up and developed by the actors at the Hôtel de Bourgogne. Montdory, the earliest of the great tragic actors in France, was a powerful and vigorous performer with a stentorian voice. In 1636, while appearing in the role of Herod, a character noted for his ranting, his vocal and physical exertions brought on an apoplectic fit that paralyzed his tongue and ended his career. His successors were Bellerose and Montfleury; Bellerose was extremely vain and strutted rather than walked on stage, while Montfleury was a mountain of a man about whom it was said, "He is so fat that it takes several days to give him a sound beating." During his performances, Montfleury wore an iron corset. In addition to their other faults, these two performers developed a tragic style of acting that was unnatural and affected; they chanted their lines as if they were singing and stressed the rhymes of the verse to produce a shrill and bombastic effect. They were unmercifully ridiculed by Molière, but persisted in performing in their declamatory style and established it as a tradition that lasted down to the nineteenth century, mainly because it won the approval of audiences. Floridor, another tragic actor at the Hôtel de Bourgogne, was a brilliant performer with a natural style and had the distinction of being the only member of the company about whom Molière never made a disparaging remark. The comedians at the Bourgogne and the Marais—Raymond Poisson, who created the famous character of Crispin, and Jodolet, the white-faced clown who later joined Molière's company—were original, accomplished, and popular performers.

Molière's company which was housed at the Palais Royal, consisted of the most talented, best trained, and most successful actors in Paris. First among them was Molière himself; he played a great variety of parts, from the buffoon Sganarelle to the almost tragic Alceste. Three other extremely versatile men—Brécourt, La Grange, and Du Croisy—also acted leading roles in a broad range of types; while the smaller character parts were taken by La Thorillière and by Louis Béjart. La Thorillière was a tall, well-built man who played both kings and peasants. Béjart acted old women as well as old men because the actresses of the day refused to play elderly parts. In Le Bourgeois Gentilhomme, the actor Hubert played both the Music Master and Madame Jourdain. Young Michel Baron, Molière's protégé, was a very valuable member of the company who carried on his teacher's style and techniques and became the greatest naturalistic actor in France during the half century after Molière's death.

The women in the troupe were equally adept and portrayed a wide variety of types, for some of which they became famous. Madeleine Béjart usually acted the clever, quick-thinking maid; Armande played cold, sophisticated heroines, such as Célimène in The Misanthrope; Madame Du Parc and Madame Debrie specialized in prudes, coquettes, and ingenues.

Molière was of medium height, attractive, slender, agile and graceful; as an actor he always strove for realistic effects in his own performances, and insisted that the other members of his company perform in the same style. In his one-act play, The Impromptu of Versailles, he severely criticized the company at the Hôtel de Bourgogne for their unrealistic and affected methods and manners. He imitated and satirized each one in turn but leveled his heaviest fire against

Montfleury to whom he alludes as "a king who is very fat, and as big as four men. A king, by Jove, well stuffed out. A king of vast circumference, who could fill a throne handsomely." He objects to the way in which Montfleury delivers his lines, saying that he declaims them in a manner that will make the public applaud him, for when he is supposed to be talking in private with a captain of his guards he uses a demoniacal tone merely for the effect it will produce upon the audience. After imitating one of the leading actresses at the Bourgogne, Molière remarks ironically, "See how natural and impassioned this is. Admire the smiling face she maintains in the deepest affliction."

The advice Molière offers to his own players provides us with an excellent clue to his theories of acting. In *The Impromptu of Versailles,* the playwright-director is surrounded by the members of his company and is about to give each one instructions in his part, when Madame Du Parc complains, "I shall act wretchedly. I do not know why you have given me this ceremonious part. . . . There is no one in the world less ceremonious than I." Molière replies:

"True; and that is how you prove yourself to be an excellent actress, by portraying well a character which is opposite to your own. Try then, all of you, to catch the spirit of your parts aright, and to imagine that you are what you represent."

It is quite clear that within the limitations of the dramatic conventions of the theater for which he wrote, such as the strict verse form of the play and the observation of the rules of decorum, Molière was attempting to create a strong impression of reality.

Costumes

French actors of the seventeenth century, like English actors of the same period, appeared on the stage in contemporary dress; no attempt was made to achieve historical accuracy. If the characters were supposed to represent members of the upper classes they wore clothing that was the last word in current fashion; if they represented characters of a lower social order, they wore the dress of the man in the street.

By 1620 the stiff old styles of farthingales and bombasted and padded limbs, stiff ruffles, and tight waists had given way to a new fashion that called for softly curling tresses, full loose skirts, and dainty ribbons and laces. Men's fashions followed closely upon those of women's, and both revealed the endless possibilities of folds and draperies. About 140 yards of silk ribbon were used in a man's costume for loops, flaps, and rosettes, which were arranged all around the waist and the hems of the coats and breeches, on the shoulders, elbows, garters, sword-belt, hat, and shoes, and even in the hair.

After 1660 a new masculine costume gave the figure a firm outline and a slender and distinguished look. It was a tightfitting coat that reached to the knees, worn over a long vest and narrow knee-breeches. The only lace used was as a cravat and as cuffs, while the ribbons were completely eliminated except for a single bow on the right shoulder (even so sober a person as Alceste is identified as "the man with green ribbons"); but the velvet and gold and silver brocades of which the clothing was made were further embellished with silver and gold embroidery. The favorite jewel was the diamond, which was even used for buttons. Men wore silk stockings and high-heeled shoes; their hats were three-cornered with a low crown, and were often not worn on the head but carried under the arm. Women's fashions resembled men's in attempting to make the figure look slimmer and more dignified; women wore tight-waisted gowns, cut low at the neck, with three-quarter sleeves and trains of varying lengths. The materials were rich and ornate; even the high-heeled shoes were made of embroidered silk.

Men began to wear wigs which were curled or waved, the thick hair reaching below the shoulders. At first the wigs were golden-hued; later they were brown or black. Before the women took to wearing wigs, their heads were adorned with a tall cap, called a *fontange*, made of silk ribbons, starched lace and linen, in which they piled their own hair and created an effect similar to that of the wigs of the men. The fashions of this period had all the splendor and dignity for which the court of Louis XIV was noted, and it was from this time that Paris became known as the fashion center of the world.

In addition to their contemporary clothes, as described above, the actors wore two special costumes called *à la Romaine* and *à la Turque*. For the tragedies in which the action took place in Greece or Rome the actors donned a costume that was more or less modeled on genuine Roman style. It consisted of breastplates, a short skirt, a cloak, a plumed helmet, and high cross-gartered boots. Such a costume was extremely expensive as it was made of very fine materials, including real gold and silver. The Turkish costume consisted of long gowns of rich materials with which were worn silk and brocaded robes, a huge feathered turban, and boots of soft leather; this costume signified that the wearer was of Middle Eastern or of Oriental origin. A third type of stage costume was the fantastic or comic get-up worn by affected or simple-minded people, by yokels and clowns. These were often intended as a form of satire.

Since each costume might cost as much as one or two hundred dollars, the actor who was obliged to appear in thirty-five or forty plays during a season might have a wardrobe that represented an investment of about five thousand dollars, even though some of the clothing was bought secondhand, was obtained as gifts from members of the nobility, or was remodeled from season to season. The posthumous inventory of Molière's costumes showed that as Alceste the actor-playwright had worn "breeches and jacket of a gold-colored and gray striped brocade, lined with tabby, ornamented with green ribbons; the waistcoat of gold brocade, silk stockings and garters."

Although the neoclassical stage was virtually bare of scenery and properties, the actors' costumes were sumptuous, colorful, and eye-filling.

Music and Dance

Music and dance were important elements in French drama from its very beginning. The medieval mystery plays featured solo and choral singing, and the later morality plays concluded with gay folk dances. Such practices continued and developed with the complete approval of the public as well as of the Court.

Louis XIII was so fond of the ballet that the late sixteenth century came to be known as "the age of dancing." He subsidized composers, musicians, and dancers and made sure that these artists were employed to provide entertainment for him. Louis XIV surpassed his father in his love of music and the dance and increased both the subsidies and the opportunities for creative and interpretive artists. The King took part himself in many ballets, and his love of music was so great that he gave his chief composer, Jean Baptiste Lully, unheard-of powers and privileges.

Songs and dances which had nothing at all to do with the story were introduced into many of the comedies of the day; and music was played before, during, and after the performances of tragedies. The King was entertained by the *ballet de cour*, a form of production very much like an extravagant vaudeville show or revue, composed of dances, tableaux, songs, music, and poetry which had no relation to one another.

In 1661 Molière was asked to prepare a work which was to be put on as part of a great festival for the amusement of the King. In collaboration with Lully, Molière wrote his first comedy-ballet, *Les Fâcheux (The Bores)*; this was an enormous innovation in that the songs and dances were integrated with the comedy, and the music not only helped to depict the characters but defined the situations and heightened the mood. In fusing all of these elements, Molière created a form that was to give rise to both comic opera and grand opera in France. Lully learned a great deal about musical drama by working with Molière and the collaboration between the two lasted for ten years, during which time the comedy-ballets created by them became more complex and more brilliant both dramatically and musically.

Each Parisian theater had a group of musicians attached to it, and the actors in the company were proficient vocalists, instrumentalists, and dancers. At the Petit Bourbon and the Palais Royal, the musicians occupied a box adjacent to the stage; while at Versailles an augmented orchestra sat in a pit directly in front of the stage as the musicians do in the modern theater.

The music of the seventeenth century was written mainly for strings. Lully, for instance, was a master of the guitar, the violin, and the clavecin, an early form of the harpsichord; it is significant that his famous orchestra was called "the twenty-four violins of the King," although the group also included such wind instruments as flutes, oboes, and horns.

In the dances of the period, a stock succession of movements was developed until a set rhythmic pattern was established for each; these were the sober allemande, the brisk courante, the slow and stately sarabande, and the lively gigue (jig). The composers of the day also refined and elaborated a number of peasant dances of the French provinces; among them were the *bourrée* (from the Auvergne), the *gavotte* (from the Dauphiné), the *rigaudon* (from Provence), and most important of all, the *minuet* (from Poitou); in addition, certain dances of foreign origin, such as the *anglaise* and the *polonaise*, were introduced at Court and found their way into the plays of the period.

Music and dance were so important in the theater of the seventeenth century

that songs and dances were put on between the acts of even such plays as *Tartuffe*
and *The Misanthrope*. In the latter play, it should be noted, Alceste speaks of
preferring an old song to the tunes written in his day, and at that point in the
play, it is believed, Molière sang *The Old Song of King Henry*. In the preface to
La Grange's *Register*, it is noted that Michel Baron, who took over the role after
Molière's death, had a great success singing the song of *The Misanthrope*, evidently following the example of the author and creator of the character, but the
exact song that was sung is unknown.

The Audience

French playgoers, not very numerous during the seventeenth century, consisted of two separate and widely differing groups. The King and the members
of the Court circle, together with specially invited guests, comprised the first
group. Louis was pleasure-loving and self-indulgent and proved to be an excellent
patron of the drama. Acting companies were called upon frequently and were
rewarded handsomely when they produced their plays at Versailles or at the
various palaces in Paris. Although the royal audiences were highly sophisticated,
their tastes ran generally to great musical spectacles and romantic tragedies.

The second group, and the more substantial audience, was made up of the
general public which frequented the three theaters in Paris on the regular playing
days—Sundays, Tuesdays, and Fridays. A full house at the Palais Royal meant
about 1,000 people, but the theater was seldom filled to capacity. Posters were
put up around town—red for the Hôtel de Bourgogne, green for Molière's theater
—and street criers announced the performances, which were scheduled to begin
at 2 P.M., but usually got started a half-hour to a full hour late.

Members of the upper classes, wealthy merchants, professional men, artisans,
clerks, soldiers, lackeys, playboys, and prostitutes made up the public audiences.
Each occupied the section of the theater suited to his social level or financial
condition; members of the upper classes filled the two lower rows of gold-
decorated boxes, while people of smaller means went to the upper galleries. The
loges at the rear of the parterre were occupied by the well-to-do merchants. The
parterre itself, which was the standing-room directly in front of the stage, was
filled with the clerks, lackeys, soldiers, and members of the lower orders. Some
thirty or forty spectators—mostly young aristocrats who wished to show off—
were allowed to sit on the stage; this practice began when an overflow audience
filled the theater to see Corneille's *Le Cid,* and continued until the eighteenth
century when Voltaire refused to permit spectators to sit on the stage.

The price scale at the Palais Royal was high in comparison with the cost of
admission to the theaters in London and other European cities at that time. A
chair in the lower boxes or on the stage was three dollars; a seat in the loges was
two dollars; the first gallery was one dollar; the second gallery, seventy-five cents;
and the parterre was about fifty cents. Prices were always doubled, or multiplied
even more, for the premiere of a new play, the revival of a popular old one, or
a play that had costly scenery and "machines."

The audience was generally well-behaved, the most unruly groups being the playboys on the stage and the standees. The former often made rude or foolish remarks which annoyed the actors and the other members of the audience, while the standees occasionally became quarrelsome and abusive. This was particularly true when drunken soldiers or the lackeys of great lords thought they had the right to enter the theater without paying; on several occasions they quarreled with and injured the ticket-taker, threatened the actors with bodily harm, broke up the theater, and drove the audience out. But disturbances were rather rare; the audience, which was in a mood for pleasure, usually listened politely to the music played before the performance began as well as during the entr'actes, and bought candy, fruit, and soft drinks from the orange girls who sold these wares.

The general public, with its heterogeneous tastes, provided the greatest stimulus to the playwrights of the day; this was especially true of the crowd in the parterre, which, for all its crudeness, represented the most independent and democratic element in the theater, was most outspoken in its reactions and most appreciative of Molière, when some of his greatest contemporaries were blind to his merits.

THE PRODUCTION RECORD

The first act of *The Misanthrope* was read in public as early as July, 1664, according to Boileau, the poet, critic, and friend of Molière. The play was probably completed by the end of 1665, but the illness and death of Anne of Austria, mother of Louis XIV, caused the closing of the theaters during January and February, 1666, then Easter intervened, and finally the play was launched on June 4, 1666. The play met with only moderate success at its premiere because of the seriousness of the theme and because of the season of the year: then as now the general public preferred light entertainment and new plays were put on in the winter rather than the summer.

Molière himself played Alceste and his wife played Célimène; so much is known for certain. The rest of the casting is conjectural: Eliante and Arsinoé were acted by Du Parc and Debrie, but it is not known which played which; it is believed that La Grange acted Philinte; Du Croisy, Oronte; Hubert, Acaste; and La Thorillière, Clitandre.

We know that Alceste is the most autobiographical of Molière's characters, but we also know that in this play the dramatist was laughing at himself—at his seriousness, his idealism, and his jealousy. Alceste was meant to be lovable and yet ridiculous, and Molière played him for laughs. Later interpreters of the role, as we shall see, attempted to portray Alceste as a tragic figure.

Armande's interpretation of Célimène created as much of a sensation as did her husband's performance, for the actress was considered the perfect embodiment of the role. Scandalmongers immediately decided that the character was drawn from life. A contemporary wrote: "Armande could not brook contradiction, and pretended that a lover ought to be as submissive as a slave." This view might very easily have grown up as a result of her portrayal of Célimène who is all coquetry, egoism, and wit; the truth of the matter is that we know very little

Molière's theaters. *(Above)* The Petit Bourbon, assigned to Molière by Louis XIV. Note the loges and galleries around the sides, the apselike stage, and the absence of proscenium and curtain. *(Right)* Ousted from the Petit Bourbon by the intrigue of his enemies. Molière was granted the use of the Palais Royal, the theater built for Richelieu with proscenium, no curtain, elaborate backstage machinery. (Bibliothèque Nationale)

about Armande's real character but there is no doubt about her great acting ability.

Molière kept *The Misanthrope* in his repertory and performed it for the last time on November 8, 1672, three months before his death.

Between 1680 and 1959, according to the records of the Comédie-Française, *The Misanthrope* was performed about 1,500 times; it ranks fourth in the frequency of production of Molière's plays.

After the death of Molière the role of Alceste was assumed by the dramatist's protégé, Michel Baron, a vigorous man, with a sonorous, exact, and flexible voice; his diction was excellent and varied; he disliked declamation so much that he broke up the alexandrines with pauses and runs, avoided the rhymes, and achieved great subtlety and interest. All of these techniques he had learned from Molière. In 1691, at the height of his fame, Baron left the stage and during his absence the part of Alceste was played by Dancourt. Thirty years later, Baron returned to the Comédie-Française, and on June 1, 1720 he again played Alceste, his favorite role. A playgoer who saw him in the part during this period wrote: "He

not only put a great deal of nobility and dignity into the role but added a delicate polish and a fund of humanity which made one love *The Misanthrope*. He permitted himself a few brusque moments and some humor but always ennobled them by his tone and by his spirit. Nothing crude, nothing gross was uttered by him. Baron was right in his judgment that it was necessary for the actor to adopt a sophisticated tone. By these sensitive means he sweetened the role instead of pushing it too far and exaggerating it. . . . He never declaimed, he spoke. He acted with great sentiment the scene in the fourth act with Célimène; even in his rages he always kept control and showed the deference which one owes to women even when they don't deserve it. Unlike actors of the present [1776], he never made of the misanthrope a grumbler or a boor."

An outstanding actor during the second half of the nineteenth century was Edmond Geffroy, who performed in a passionate and romantic style. He was one of the first actors to portray Alceste as a serious character. He was interested in the psychology of the man, his personal traits and his morals, as well as in his clothing and his external manners. He gave a powerful and moving rendition of the part that led many later actors, down to modern times, to play it in the same way, although such an interpretation was not intended by Molière. Geffroy tended to emphasize the dark and terrible side of a character, for his acting was severe and rather sad, though he was capable of great energetic movements, with his head thrust forward and his eyes half-closed. Geffroy had a very strong historical sense and tried to achieve accuracy and authenticity in his costumes, but that was the period during which many theater people first attempted to reproduce the past with correctness of detail.

The Misanthrope has received a number of productions in the United States, but these were more often in French than in English. It was done for the first time in English by the British-born actor-manager Richard Mansfield, who was also the first to produce Bernard Shaw in America; Mansfield's version of The Misanthrope became part of the actor's repertory and was performed for the last time at the Grand Opera House, Chicago, in May, 1906. The critic for the Chicago Record, May 10, 1906, wrote:

> Mr. Mansfield's revival of The Misanthrope is marked by brilliance of investiture, and his embodiment of Alceste is vibrant with pain. Nervous unrest is curiously blended with spiritual fortitude, the utterance of blistering scorn and the gaze of a commanding eye are frequently shadowed by the proofs of inward doubt and self-pity. He moves in his black habiliments against the silver and white background of Célimène's drawing-room, and he is ever the center of a throng of gaily dressed men and women of the period of Louis XIV. The curls of a full dark wig fall about his anxious countenance. His lips are closely compressed even when he speaks, his nostrils usually dilated, as if ever on the scent of villainy and deceit, his eyes heavy with scorn and grief, his movements swift, decisive and so frequent as to betray the nervous and spiritual stress that drives the man ever onward in the search of ideals and of a peace of mind that as constantly elude him. He speaks rapidly, abruptly, and usually in sharp staccato and makes frequent gestures of protest with upraised hands of startling pallor, and when he does this wide lace cuffs fall back upon his black sleeves. The look of pain and uncertainty is seldom absent from his face. He smiles, but it is always the smile of bitterness. . . .
>
> As a study in deep anguish, none the less unbearable because largely imagined, Mr. Mansfield's Alceste is a remarkable achievement, preserving the tone of saturnine humor subtly displayed and, most essential of all, echoing the tribute Alceste won from his easy-going world—"There is something noble and heroic about him." His Alceste rings with the voice of challenge and is rigid with the attitude of defiance. Withal there are tears in the weary, doubting eyes of the soul that was misunderstood yet understood so much.

On November 12, 1956, the play opened at a tiny off-Broadway house called Theatre East and was presented in English in Richard Wilbur's translation, which had first been used at the Poets' Theatre, Cambridge, Massachusetts, on October 25, 1955.

While the American production was being acted at Theatre East, with its 125 seats, the Madeleine Renaud–Jean-Louis Barrault Company—brought to America by the impresario S. Hurok—opened at the Winter Garden, whose huge proportions more closely resemble those of Molière's Théâtre du Palais Royal, and there

(*Left*) La Thorillière as Philinte and Molière (seated) as Alceste, both in contemporary costumes, as shown in an engraving from the 1684 Amsterdam edition of the play. Note the sparseness of furnishings. (Hachette) (*Above*) A modern-dress version with Célimène (Madeleine Delavaivre) flanked by Acaste (Jacques Ciron) and Clitandre (Etienne Aubray). (French Embassy Information Service)

from February 7 to February 9, 1957, the visiting stars, under the direction of M. Barrault, presented the play in French. The identical production had originally been mounted in Paris on November 6, 1954; the sets were by Pierre Delbée, the costumes by Marcel Escoffier; and Barrault's company was the acme of elegance and zest. The American critics were charmed. Bert McCord of the New York *Herald Tribune*, took occasion to point out the great contrast between the studied acting of the seventeenth century and the naturalistic style of our own day:

> From his company as a whole, M. Barrault has extracted a classical, highly stylized performance calculated to unnerve the more dedicated disciples of the Actors' Studio. The actors flounce, sweep or stalk majestically on stage; they prance and swirl; the act of sitting down is a ceremony to be accomplished with the most flamboyant gestures and waving of plumed hats; they bow low in obeisant humility or rise archly to their full height when insulted. It's all delicious fun.

M. Barrault obviously caught both the spirit and the style of this timeless masterpiece.

The Barrault production, with Madeleine Renaud (seated) as Célimène. Barrault stands in the background. (French Embassy Information Service)

REPERTORY AND *The Misanthrope*
An Interview with Jean-Louis Barrault

Jean-Louis Barrault began his career as an actor in 1931 and served his apprenticeship under the great Charles Dullin; then he studied mime with Etienne Decroux. In 1937 he still considered himself a very imperfect actor; he was full of theories about acting but felt that he needed very much more actual experience. "It was then that I decided to accept every part offered me without reflection," says Barrault, "and so the following season I leapt at the opportunity given me by Alice Cocéa to play the Misanthrope opposite her. For three months I floundered among Alceste's nine hundred lines, which earned me an excommunication from Decroux and a sharp rebuke from Louis Jouvet. But this kind of cold shower knocked off my corners and my star guided me well."

In 1940 Barrault joined the Comédie Française; but six years later, with a change in the administration, those players who wished to leave the state-owned theater were allowed to do so. On September 1, 1946, the actor, with his wife, Madeleine Renaud, and several other colleagues—among them Pierre Bertin, Marie-Helene Dasté, Simone Valere, and Jean-Pierre Granval—set out on a new career. The Madeleine Renaud-Jean-Louis Barrault Company was formed, and established itself at the Marigny Theatre, its headquarters until 1956. The Company toured in many countries and continued to grow and develop; its home is now the state-owned Odeon Theatre. It has a troupe of forty-five actors and a repertory of more than forty plays.

"A company can only be alive if it has a repertory," says Barrault, "and a company can only build up a repertory if it keeps on producing plays one after another and not depending only on those that they have already done well. In order to proceed with these constant changes the company must be able to play, as it were, a number of works at the same time; it must practice a regular, alternating rhythm. With the exception of the Théâtre du Vieux Colombier, that our master Jacques Copeau founded in 1913 and that endured till 1920, there was no example of a private company capable of maintaining this alternating rhythm for more than a short while. To do so was the privilege of the state theaters; the principle was upheld only by virtue of the state subsidy.

"For almost fourteen years we have succeeded in maintaining our rhythm," says Barrault. "The public has become used to it, and we have enjoyed its many advantages. For it is precisely these alternations that have given our work its vitality. If he knows that he will go from a small part today to a big part tomorrow, an actor of high quality is willing to play the small parts, which means that they will be well acted. Playing a number of parts, often entirely different, in a short space of time, the actor grows supple, improves. He does not stiffen, become rusty with routine. And in this jostling of one role against another, the actor's personal, artistic talents become plain; hence it becomes easier to give him the role to which he is best suited. And as they say: 'A play well cast is a play half staged.'

"The constant changes require, no doubt, a large technical staff. This may be costly, but helps to maintain a good team. The scene-shifter, the electrician, the carpenter, all the many tradesmen who collaborate in this fine communal enterprise, are able 'to keep their hands in'; each man's ability is tested and he is made more competent by his varying duties.

"The certainty of seeing a new production at regular intervals has given us a public that is also regular, that follows and supports what we do and enables us to survive in freedom, not at the mercy of the 'passing crowd' that cares only for success. For there is a right that must at times be claimed if you want to chance a bold stroke and contribute your share to the true artistic life of the theater, and that is the 'right to be wrong.' The system of alternation allows us to make mistakes, and our faithful public, ever curious and interested, forgives them. There are numbers of plays that we would never have dared to put on if it were not for the saving grace of alternation.

"We are able, by the same means, to undertake research and, while remaining in constant touch with the classics, to serve the interests of living creative authors.

A study of the classics nourishes the mind and helps it to progress. We are going back to the sources; in our search for the *right tone* we rediscover style; we become fully aware of the intensity, the economy, and the harmony which flow from the exceptional union of good taste and genius. As against this drawing of strength from the classics, we allow ourselves excursions into more or less unknown regions of dramatic art; we are able, as I said, to undertake research. Most writers are ignorant of the full resources of the stage and what can be made of the potentialities of actors. It might be pointed out that the greatest dramatic writers, Shakespeare and Molière, were actors. Our investigations are pursued therefore in a 'clinical' spirit, in the hope that we may, with luck, shed some light on the paths of authorship and, with our special experience, assist young writers in the act of creation. The essential task that we have set before us is to serve present-day authors. We try to be as widely eclectic as possible, however, in our choice of works old and new. In one of our world tours, for example, we presented five plays from various periods: two from the seventeenth century, Lope de Vega's *The Gardener's Dog* and Molière's *Misanthrope;* one from the nineteenth century, Feydeau's *Keep an Eye on Amélie;* and two from the twentieth century, Giraudoux' *Intermezzo* and Claudel's *Christopher Columbus.*

"In our training and practice, although the study of pure diction and the use of words concerns us particularly, we give special attention also to the study of gesture—the most interesting, useful, and deeply poetic performance of pantomime. In fact, we believe that we are developing our art in all its branches in a workmanlike manner, a true spirit of craftsmanship. As for theory, we are inclined to distrust all ready-made ideas and formulas. The stage, like life, is complex and varied; all formulas are good provided they spring from an authentic sensation and, beyond the stirrings of the brain and the senses, reach the heart. That is the reason why, when we give a performance, we are truly rewarded if we feel that our work appeals not only to our own countrymen but reaches a plane of universal humanity; for the theater, like all the arts, is essentially a means of communication, a link between man and man. But drawing its lifeblood from a love of mankind, the theater above all is the art of human communion.

"Molière demonstrates this magnificently in his play *The Misanthrope,* in which we see the human side of the dramatist, urging his idealism upon society, although he is finally forced to withdraw in defeat.

"In studying the play for production, I realized that the characters were all of the high social status which would have permitted them to frequent the Court, and I imagined that the play was being given before the King at the Tuileries or at the palace at St. Germain in one of the great rooms. If the play had been presented at Versailles, it would have been done in the gardens out of doors since the palace was still under construction in 1666. I found it very difficult to make up my mind as to where to set the action, in Célimène's *salon* or in a room in the palace. So I asked Pierre Delbée to design two sets—one an elegant upper-class interior, and the other the interior of a magnificent room in a palace; both were built and used during rehearsals and, finally, with the help of the actors, I decided to use the royal apartment. Throughout the production I was trying to remove the middle-class side of the play and to emphasize the regal side and the set helped my conception; if I had been doing *Tartuffe* or *L'Avare,* I would have used the set I rejected in this instance.

"In playing Alceste, I tried for the characteristics of naïveté, credulity, and optimism. I firmly believe that Alceste is an optimistic person because he is sure that he will succeed in changing mankind and, in the beginning of the play, he is also quite certain that he will be able to change Célimène. He fails in both areas, of course, but his naïveté touches the spectator; Alceste must be charming and seductive. If he is played with too much anger and venom, women would not be attracted to him—as they are; but if he is childlike, petulant, and unreasoning women will be irresistibly drawn to him. Philinte is a pessimist because he does not really believe in men; he knows that they are all bears, monkeys, and wolves. Alceste, on the other hand, foolish as the idea may be, actually believes in the perfectibility of man. He reacts with hatred because of his unrequited love; he is, in short, a frustrated idealist.

"Alceste, in my opinion, was not naturally misanthropic, but became a misanthrope through a series of disappointments. He hopes that men will see his point of view but when they take an opposite course he considers them perverse and flies off the handle. Proof of his sensibility is the fact that Alceste boils over suddenly and loses complete control of his temper. Célimène is the perfect foil for him because she is so cool and self-contained. She is very clever, very intelligent, and reacts almost unconsciously; she operates with feminine intuition, but there is a strong strain of irresponsibility in her.

"I think of Alceste, too, as a Chaplinesque character who wrings both laughter and tears from the audience by creating a feeling of pathos. Because of the ambiguity of the emotions aroused, this was the first play by Molière at which the public smiled quietly instead of laughing uproariously, which is one of the reasons why the play was not an immediate success. The public had come to look upon Molière as a *farceur,* but this play was not 'standard' Molière; the audience was therefore confused and disconcerted. In order to correct the impression and to reinstate himself, so to speak, Molière followed *The Misanthrope* immediately with *The Doctor in Spite of Himself,* a broad and brilliant farce in his more usual vein; and the audience felt that the balance had been restored.

"Molière, like Chaplin, must always make the audience laugh, even in the saddest situations. In *The Misanthrope,* therefore, I played everything very broadly —exaggerated grimaces, broad gestures, and so on; even when Alceste was being most naïve and sincere, I tried to make him look ridiculous. My training in pantomime, I believe, helped me tremendously to achieve this mixture of moods."

Barrault's interpretation of Alceste appears to be in line with Molière's original conception of the character. Furthermore, in a recently discovered play by Menander, the *Dyskolos* (*The Misanthrope*), the protagonist, Cnémon, "the hater of Mankind," is also treated humorously by the Greek dramatist; thus the comic treatment of such a serious figure is both ancient and well-founded. The *Dyskolos* was recently produced in Geneva, Switzerland, by actor-director François Simon, who believes that "Menander is closer to our time than Molière is, because modern audiences are better able to understand and appreciate the earthiness of the ancient writer than the formalism of the neoclassical one." Barrault, however, by the depth of his perception and the supreme power of his technique, was able to achieve the combination of these two seemingly disparate elements in his portrayal of Alceste.

SCENERY FOR *The Misanthrope*
An Interview with Pierre Delbée

Jean-Louis Barrault selected Pierre Delbée to design the set for *The Misanthrope* because of Delbée's intensive knowledge of seventeenth- and eighteenth-century décor. Delbée is the head of a celebrated Parisian firm of furniture dealers, which collects genuine antiques and also makes replicas of rare pieces in its own workshops. Barrault and Delbée had long preliminary discussions about the set, and Barrault admitted that he could not make up his mind whether to place the action in the drawing-room in Célimène's house, which would be an elegant, upper-class, seventeenth-century, Parisian interior; or in one of the rooms in the palace where the play was originally presented for the King, and which would represent a royal apartment.

Barrault asked Delbée to make two sketches, which the designer did. Each represented a single formal room, the walls of which were to be depicted on painted canvas. The room in Célimène's house, though done on a smaller scale, was a spacious private *salon,* with a door and two windows in the rear wall, and doors in each of the side walls. The room in the palace was done on a much grander scale, and in false perspective that gave it great height and depth; it had a large central door at the rear and a huge fireplace at one side; openings in the side walls led to other chambers.

Barrault studied the sketches carefully and still could not make up his mind as to which to use, so he had both interiors built and painted, and used them alternately at rehearsals. After a time he asked the actors which décor they preferred, and by a vote they chose the royal apartment, saying that its ornateness and spaciousness gave them more of the feeling of the grandeur of the period, so that they could act with greater freedom and breadth. The drawing-room set was stored away to be used later for another of Molière's plays.

The room in the palace, as designed by Delbée, resembled an old steel engraving; that is, it was painted entirely in black, white, and gray. The starkness of these neutral colors was relieved only by a very narrow border of red and gold near the ceiling. Every inch of wall space was covered with the ornate designs of the aristocratic baroque style; painted on the canvas were cupids in stucco relief, garlands, wreaths, and floral patterns, caryatids perched on fanciful scroll frames, and panels enclosed by columns and pilasters. The fireplace, too, was painted on the canvas.

The furniture was not actually antique although it appeared to be; it was specially designed for the production by Delbée and consisted of straight-backed chairs, armchairs, small stools, and side tables with mirrors above them; the mirrors were painted on the walls. A number of small "props" were on the tables. All of the furnishings were exact reproductions of those in the apartments of Louis XIII and Louis XIV and were made in Delbée's workshops, as were the upholstery fabrics, which suggested rich brocades although actually they were heavy muslin painted red, blue, and gold. The entire décor gave the impression of sumptuousness and formality.

Although the set appeared to be strong and solid, the canvas walls of the room could easily be taken off the pipes from which they were hung and off their frames, and rolled up for traveling. The floor, which represented marble in a black and gray checkerboard pattern, was also painted on canvas and could be rolled up like the walls. The large central door in the rear wall had a removable frame; there were no doors in the left and right walls, only arched openings. Painted backings were seen when the rear doors were opened and outside the openings in the side walls. As Barrault toured with this play in both North and South America, flexibility and ease of handling were major concerns in the basic design of the set, and yet, under lights (Barrault himself did the lighting), the room had great beauty, dignity, and urbanity.

"One of the greatest advantages of the use of neutral background tones in the scenery," said Delbée, "is the fact that it throws the emphasis upon the brilliant and subtle color combinations in the costumes. And yet, strange as it may seem, instead of being ignored, the scenery was singled out for praise by almost every critic who saw the play."

Costumes for *The Misanthrope*
An Interview with Marcel Escoffier

Marcel Escoffier created the costumes for many of the films of Jean Cocteau, working in close collaboration with Christian Berard who designed the sets. Escoffier won special praise for the costumes he did for *Orphée*, a highly imaginative and fantastic film; and when Cocteau was asked to provide the sketches for the Renaud-Barrault stage production of *Bacchus*, Escoffier was called upon to execute them. When Barrault decided to produce *The Misanthrope*, he offered the job of designing the costumes to Escoffier.

The production plans were worked out very quickly and simply. Delbée's idea to use only black and white as a background for the production gave Escoffier a free hand and made it possible for him to choose any color in the spectrum with the sure knowledge that it would not clash with the scenery. Costume designers usually have a difficult time matching clothing to sets, but this production was a delight to Escoffier, who could give his color sense free rein.

Although he can well afford a large wardrobe, Alceste, who is unpretentious by nature, was given the same costume throughout the play. The other characters, too, were provided with only one costume apiece. Célimène was the single exception; as a foil to Alceste, she was seen in two glorious gowns which provided a striking contrast to the drab colors and simple lines of his suit.

The first gown which Célimène wore was the color of sand or of light caramel and bathed her in a golden aura. It was Louis XIV in style but subtly adapted to the modern taste for *haute couture;* the dress was made of heavy satin, tulle, and organza, and was extremely smart. Escoffier's technique, and one which he has used very often, was to combine several related materials in a single costume. The skirt, for example, of heavy satin, was elaborately embroidered with organza to produce a luxurious and extravagant effect. "I believe in mixing materials," says Escoffier, "in order to emphasize the contrast in textures, to give each material a richness it would not have if it stood alone, and to cause the entire gown to glitter."

Célimène wore a blonde wig in which were fixed soft, curling plumes to match the golden gown, and with this costume she carried a fan made of feathers of bird-of-paradise, arranged like two crossed crescents, which added a note of frivolity. Her satin shoes matched her dress; her jewelry was scintillating; and she wore long white kid gloves.

The second costume in which Célimène appeared was pale blue and off-white, the combination producing a shimmery, watery effect; only white and pale blue lights were used to illuminate the stage. The costume, which was extremely stylized and sophisticated, had an overgown and an underdress. The bodice and the overskirt were a silvery white almost fading into blue and were made of heavy dull satin and faille silk, while the tulle underskirt was a pale and delicate shade of blue. Following the line of the overskirt was a margin, a few inches wide, of blue-white organza placed there to avoid a sharp contrast between the satin and the tulle but to create a soft blending, a sort of smoky fading of the one into the other; the three-quarter sleeves were great puffs of organza.

The ornamentation and accessories that set off the blue gown were masterful creations in themselves. The bodice was elaborately embroidered with beads and pearls, and a beaded bow with half a dozen strands of pendant pearls was affixed to the sleeve below the left shoulder. Rings, earrings, bracelet, and necklace of beads and pearls completed the fantasy.

In Célimène's hair was a diamond brooch in which was set a spray of egrets, according to Escoffier, "like that of a horse in a circus." At times she carried a large handkerchief with a wide border of delicate lace; at other times, a fan of curly plumes from the handle of which hung loops of satin ribbon. She wore long white kid gloves and blue-white satin shoes. From head to toe she sparkled like a blue-white diamond. "She was exciting but cold," says Escoffier, "the quintessence of Célimène!"

Although Escoffier is well aware of the fact that lace was used to excess on the clothing worn in Molière's day, he seldom uses it in his stage designs, even if it means departing from reality, since he does not think that it has much "theatrical" value. No lace was used on either of Célimène's gowns nor on any of the other costumes in this production.

Alceste wore a suit that combined black, gray, and green; a minor concession to fashion were the few loops of dark green ribbon at his right shoulder. The costume was made of wool, with touches of velvet in it; the materials were chosen to characterize a man who was extremely serious, stiff, and formal. The somberness of the costume was relieved only by the white shirt sleeves and cuffs secured with a ribbon at the wrist and by a plain white jabot. No ribbons or buckles enlivened Alceste's black shoes, and there were no decorations or adornments of any kind on his clothing or on his person. He wore a black wig that was uncurled, and to make it even flatter and more unattractive he kept smoothing it down with the palm of his hand.

Arsinoé, the hypocrite, wore a velvet gown of dark red and gray; the overskirt was plum-colored, suggesting subdued passion; while the underskirt was gray to symbolize the woman's false purity. Her hood, shoulder-length cape, long sleeves, and gloves were of royal blue organza; she wore a spray of rubies in her hair and ruby earrings. On her breast was a large, showy cross, but at the same time she had long, sharp, clawlike fingernails—the contrast of the hypocrite.

Philinte is a man of the world who understands the weaknesses of humanity and condones them. His colors were uncomplicated; he wore various shades of brown elegantly put together. His wig was long and curled, in the fashion approved by the Court; it was a chestnut color and matched his costume.

Eliante wore the most charming costume of all; it was light blue and pink, suggested the sweetness and brightness of an innocent young girl, and yet was extremely distinguée. The gown had a *"bateau"* neckline of stiff organza; on the bodice was a long, triangular bib with a row of buttons which descended from the breast to the waist. Eliante's hair was simply and softly arranged, and except for an oval locket she wore no jewelry; she carried a small handbag of *petit-point*.

Oronte, the poet, was dressed in flaming red, orange, and green and was meant to suggest a parrot. His enormous wig was reddish-blond and descended to his shoulders in a series of huge corkscrew curls; the wide brim of his large hat was encircled by plumes; and his green gloves were like gauntlets, the stiff cuffs ornamented with fringes. A large muff covered with loops of velvet ribbon was suspended from his neck on a silk cord and hung at his waist; enormous roses bloomed on his shoes; and he wore a great shiny ring on the gloved finger of his right hand.

The two marquises were similarly dressed in that they were both costumed to look like pretentious and ridiculous fools. Since both are exhibitionists and extremely extroverted, they wore shrill, screaming colors. Acaste, who was all in gold, had yards of organza at his wrists and knees, ribbons frothed and floated on his person, and huge rosettes smothered his shoes. Clitandre, in turquoise and blue, was adorned with yards of ribbon done in loops at his throat, shoulders, elbows, wrists, along the edges of his clothes, and on his shoes. Both courtiers had elaborately curled wigs and extravagant hats with enormous plumes. Their ostentatious and flamboyant costumes, all glitter and flutter, dazzled the spectator.

The minor characters, members of the working class, wore simple clothing which did not call attention to itself, since it was unadorned and done in neutral colors.

It is Escoffier's theory that the colors and lines of each costume should indicate clearly the character's psychology as well as his function in the play; if the costume does not fully express the character of its wearer, the designer has failed in his job.

〽 *The Misanthrope*

DONE INTO ENGLISH VERSE BY RICHARD WILBUR

CHARACTERS

ALCESTE, in love with Célimène
PHILINTE, Alceste's friend
ORONTE, in love with Célimène
CÉLIMÈNE, Alceste's beloved
ELIANTE, Célimène's cousin
ARSINOÉ, a friend of Célimène's
ACASTE ⎱
⎰ marquesses
CLITANDRE ⎰
BASQUE, Célimène's servant
A GUARD of the Marshalsea
DUBOIS, Alceste's valet

The scene throughout is in Célimène's house at Paris.

ACT ONE. SCENE ONE

PHILINTE, ALCESTE

Philinte. Now, what's got into you?
Alceste (*Seated*)   Kindly leave me alone.
Philinte. Come, come, what is it? This lugubrious tone . . .
Alceste. Leave me, I said; you spoil my solitude.
Philinte. Oh, listen to me, now, and don't be rude.

Alceste. I choose to be rude, Sir, and to be hard of hearing.   5
Philinte. These ugly moods of yours are not endearing;
Friends though we are, I really must insist . . .
Alceste (*Abruptly rising*) Friends? Friends, you say? Well, cross me off your list.
I've been your friend till now, as you well know;
But after what I saw a moment ago

I tell you flatly that our ways must part.   11
I wish no place in a dishonest heart.
Philinte. Why, what have I done, Alceste? Is this quite just?
Alceste. My God, you ought to die of self-disgust.
I call your conduct inexcusable, Sir,
And every man of honor will concur.   16
I see you almost hug a man to death,
Exclaim for joy until you're out of breath,
And supplement these loving demonstrations
With endless offers, vows, and protestations;   20
Then when I ask you "Who was that?", I find
That you can barely bring his name to mind!
Once the man's back is turned, you cease to love him,
And speak with absolute indifference of him!
By God, I say it's base and scandalous   25
To falsify the heart's affections thus;
If I caught myself behaving in such a way,
I'd hang myself for shame, without delay.
Philinte. It hardly seems a hanging matter to me;
I hope that you will take it graciously   30
If I extend myself a slight reprieve,
And live a little longer, by your leave.
Alceste. How dare you joke about a crime so grave?
Philinte. What crime? How else are people to behave?
Alceste. I'd have them be sincere, and never part   35

With any word that isn't from the heart.
Philinte. When someone greets us with a show of pleasure,
It's but polite to give him equal measure,
Return his love the best that we know how,
And trade him offer for offer, vow for vow.   40
Alceste. No, no, this formula you'd have me follow,
However fashionable, is false and hollow,
And I despise the frenzied operations
Of all these barterers of protestations,
These lavishers of meaningless embraces,   45
These utterers of obliging commonplaces,
Who court and flatter everyone on earth
And praise the fool no less than the man of worth.
Should you rejoice that someone fondles you,
Offers his love and service, swears to be true,   50
And fills your ears with praises of your name,
When to the first damned fop he'll say the same?
No, no: no self-respecting heart would dream
Of prizing so promiscuous an esteem;
However high the praise, there's nothing worse   55
Than sharing honors with the universe.
Esteem is founded on comparison:
To honor all men is to honor none.
Since you embrace this indiscriminate vice,

Your friendship comes at far too
   cheap a price;   60
I spurn the easy tribute of a heart
Which will not set the worthy man
   apart:
I choose, Sir, to be chosen; and in
   fine,
The friend of mankind is no friend of
   mine.
Philinte. But in polite society, custom
   decrees   65
That we show certain outward cour-
   tesies. . . .
Alceste. Ah, no! we should condemn
   with all our force
Such false and artificial intercourse.
Let men behave like men; let them
   display
Their inmost hearts in everything
   they say;   70
Let the heart speak, and let our senti-
   ments
Not mask themselves in silly compli-
   ments.
Philinte. In certain cases it would be
   uncouth
And most absurd to speak the naked
   truth;
With all respect for your exalted no-
   tions,   75
It's often best to veil one's true emo-
   tions.
Wouldn't the social fabric come un-
   done
If we were wholly frank with every-
   one?
Suppose you met with someone you
   couldn't bear;
Would you inform him of it then and
   there?   80
Alceste. Yes.
Philinte.   Then you'd tell old Emilie
   it's pathetic
The way she daubs her features with
   cosmetic

And plays the gay coquette at sixty-
   four?
Alceste. I would.
Philinte. And you'd call Dorilas a
   bore,
And tell him every ear at court is
   lame   85
From hearing him brag about his
   noble name?
Alceste. Precisely.
Philinte.   Ah, you're joking.
Alceste.   *Au contraire:*
In this regard there's none I'd choose
   to spare.
All are corrupt; there's nothing to be
   seen
In court or town but aggravates my
   spleen.   90
I fall into deep gloom and melan-
   choly
When I survey the scene of human
   folly,
Finding on every hand base flattery,
Injustice, fraud, self-interest, treach-
   ery. . . .
Ah, it's too much; mankind has
   grown so base,   95
I mean to break with the whole
   human race.
Philinte. This philosophic rage is a bit
   extreme;
You've no idea how comical you
   seem;
Indeed, we're like those brothers in
   the play
Called *School for Husbands,* one of
   whom was prey . . .   100
Alceste. Enough now! None of your
   stupid similes.
Philinte. Then let's have no more ti-
   rades, if you please.
The world won't change, whatever
   you say or do;
And since plain speaking means so
   much to you,

I'll tell you plainly that by being
frank   105
You've earned the reputation of a
crank,
And that you're thought ridiculous
when you rage
And rant against the manners of the
age.

Alceste. So much the better; just what
I wish to hear.
No news could be more grateful to
my ear.   110
All men are so detestable in my eyes,
I should be sorry if they thought me
wise.

Philinte. Your hatred's very sweeping,
is it not?

Alceste. Quite right: I hate the whole
degraded lot.

Philinte. Must all poor human creatures
be embraced,   115
Without distinction, by your vast dis-
taste?
Even in these bad times, there are
surely a few . . .

Alceste. No, I include all men in one
dim view:
Some men I hate for being rogues;
the others
I hate because they treat the rogues
like brothers,   120
And, lacking a virtuous scorn for
what is vile,
Receive the villain with a com-
plaisant smile.
Notice how tolerant people choose to
be
Toward that bold rascal who's at law
with me.
His social polish can't conceal his
nature;   125
One sees at once that he's a treacherous creature;
No one could possibly be taken in

By those soft speeches and that
sugary grin.
The whole world knows the shady
means by which
The low-brow's grown so powerful
and rich,   130
And risen to a rank so bright and high
That virtue can but blush, and merit
sigh.
Whenever his name comes up in con-
versation,
None will defend his wretched repu-
tation;
Call him knave, liar, scoundrel, and
all the rest,   135
Each head will nod, and no one will
protest.
And yet his smirk is seen in every
house,
He's greeted everywhere with smiles
and bows,
And when there's any honor that can
be got
By pulling strings, he'll get it, like as
not.   140
My God! It chills my heart to see the
ways
Men come to terms with evil nowadays;
Sometimes, I swear, I'm moved to
flee and find
Some desert land unfouled by hu-
mankind.

Philinte. Come, let's forget the follies
of the times   145
And pardon mankind for its petty
crimes;
Let's have an end of rantings and of
railings,
And show some leniency toward human failings.
This world requires a pliant rectitude;
Too stern a virtue makes one stiff and
rude;   150

Good sense views all extremes with
   detestation,
And bids us to be noble in modera-
   tion.
The rigid virtues of the ancient days
Are not for us; they jar with all our
   ways   154
And ask of us too lofty a perfection.
Wise men accept their times without
   objection,
And there's no greater folly, if you
   ask me,
Than trying to reform society.
Like you, I see each day a hundred
   and one
Unhandsome deeds that might be
   better done,   160
But still, for all the faults that meet
   my view,
I'm never known to storm and rave
   like you.
I take men as they are, or let them
   be,
And teach my soul to bear their
   frailty;
And whether in court or town, what-
   ever the scene,   165
My phlegm's as philosophic as your
   spleen.
Alceste. This phlegm which you so
   eloquently commend,
Does nothing ever rile it up, my
   friend?
Suppose some man you trust should
   treacherously
Conspire to rob you of your property,   170
And do his best to wreck your reputation?
Wouldn't you feel a certain indignation?
Philinte. Why, no. These faults of
   which you so complain
Are part of human nature, I maintain,   174

And it's no more a matter for disgust
That men are knavish, selfish and un-
   just,
Than that the vulture dines upon the
   dead,
And wolves are furious, and apes ill-
   bred.
Alceste. Shall I see myself betrayed,
   robbed, torn to bits,
And not . . . Oh, let's be still and
   rest our wits.   180
Enough of reasoning, now. I've had
   my fill.
Philinte. Indeed, you would do well,
   Sir, to be still.
Rage less at your opponent, and give
   some thought
To how you'll win this lawsuit that
   he's brought.
Alceste. I assure you I'll do nothing of
   the sort.   185
Philinte. Then who will plead your case
   before the court?
Alceste. Reason and right and justice
   will plead for me.
Philinte. Oh, Lord. What judges do
   you plan to see?
Alceste. Why, none. The justice of my
   cause is clear.
Philinte. Of course, man; but there's
   politics to fear. . . .   190
Alceste. No, I refuse to lift a hand.
   That's flat.
I'm either right, or wrong.
Philinte.   Don't count on that.
Alceste. No, I'll do nothing.
Philinte.   Your enemy's influence
   Is great, you know . . .
Alceste.   That makes no difference.
Philinte. It will; you'll see.
Alceste.   Must honor bow to guile?
If so, I shall be proud to lose the
   trial.   196
Philinte. Oh, really . . .
Alceste.   I'll discover by this case

Whether or not men are sufficiently
base
And impudent and villainous and
perverse   199
To do me wrong before the universe.
Philinte. What a man!
Alceste.   Oh, I could wish, whatever
the cost,
Just for the beauty of it, that my trial
were lost.
Philinte. If people heard you talking so,
Alceste,
They'd split their sides. Your name
would be a jest.
Alceste. So much the worse for jesters.
Philinte.   May I enquire 205
Whether this rectitude you so ad-
mire,
And these hard virtues you're en-
amored of
Are qualities of the lady whom you
love?
It much surprises me that you, who
seem
To view mankind with furious dis-
esteem,   210
Have yet found something to enchant
your eyes
Amidst a species which you so de-
spise.
And what is more amazing, I'm
afraid,
Is the most curious choice your heart
has made.   214
The honest Eliante is fond of you,
Arsinoé, the prude, admires you too;
And yet your spirit's been perversely
led
To choose the flighty Célimène in-
stead,
Whose brittle malice and coquettish
ways   219
So typify the manners of our days.
How is it that the traits you most
abhor

Are bearable in this lady you adore?
Are you so blind with love that you
can't find them?
Or do you contrive, in her case, not
to mind them?
Alceste. My love for that young widow's
not the kind   225
That can't perceive defects; no, I'm
not blind.
I see her faults, despite my ardent
love,
And all I see I fervently reprove.
And yet I'm weak; for all her falsity,
That woman knows the art of pleas-
ing me,   230
And though I never cease com-
plaining of her,
I swear I cannot manage not to love
her.
Her charm outweighs her faults; I
can but aim
To cleanse her spirit in my love's
pure flame.
Philinte. That's no small task; I wish
you all success.   235
You think then that she loves you?
Alceste.   Heavens, yes!
I wouldn't love her did she not love
me.
Philinte. Well, if her taste for you is
plain to see,
Why do these rivals cause you such
despair?
Alceste. True love, Sir, is possessive,
and cannot bear   240
To share with all the world. I'm here
today
To tell her she must send that mob
away.
Philinte. If I were you, and had your
choice to make,
Eliante, her cousin, would be the one
I'd take;
That honest heart, which cares for
you alone,   245

Would harmonize far better with
  your own.
Alceste. True, true: each day my reason
  tells me so;
But reason doesn't rule in love, you
  know.
Philinte. I fear some bitter sorrow is in
  store;
This love . . .   250

SCENE TWO

ORONTE, ALCESTE, PHILINTE

Oronte (*To* ALCESTE) The servants
  told me at the door
That Eliante and Célimène were
  out,
But when I heard, dear Sir, that you
  were about,
I came to say, without exaggeration,
That I hold you in the vastest ad-
  miration,   5
And that it's always been my dearest
  desire
To be the friend of one I so admire.
I hope to see my love of merit re-
  quited,
And you and I in friendship's bond
  united.
I'm sure you won't refuse—if I may
  be frank—   10
A friend of my devotedness—and
  rank.

(*During this speech of* ORONTE's,
ALCESTE *is abstracted, and seems unaware that he is being spoken to. He
only breaks off his reverie when*
ORONTE *says:*)

It was for you, if you please, that my
  words were intended.
Alceste. For me, Sir?
Oronte.   Yes, for you. You're not offended?
Alceste. By no means. But this much
  surprises me. . . .

The honor comes most unexpect-
  edly. . . .
Oronte. My high regard should not
  astonish you;
The whole world feels the same. It is
  your due.
Alceste. Sir . . .
Oronte.   Why, in all the State there
  isn't one
Can match your merits; they shine,
  Sir, like the sun.
Alceste. Sir . . .
Oronte.   You are higher in my esti-
  mation   20
Than all that's most illustrious in the
  nation.
Alceste. Sir . . .
Oronte.   If I lie, may heaven strike
  me dead!
To show you that I mean what I have
  said,
Permit me, Sir, to embrace you most
  sincerely,
And swear that I will prize our
  friendship dearly.   25
Give me your hand. And now, Sir, if
  you choose,
We'll make our vows.
Alceste.   Sir . . .
Oronte.   What! You refuse?
Alceste. Sir, it's a very great honor you
  extend:
But friendship is a sacred thing, my
  friend;   29
It would be profanation to bestow
The name of friend on one you
  hardly know.
All parts are better played when
  well-rehearsed;
Let's put off friendship, and get ac-
  quainted first.
We may discover it would be un-
  wise
To try to make our natures harmo-
  nize.   35

Oronte. By heaven! You're sagacious to the core;
This speech has made me admire you even more.
Let time, then, bring us closer day by day;
Meanwhile, I shall be yours in every way.
If, for example, there should be anything   40
You wish at court, I'll mention it to the King.
I have his ear, of course; it's quite well known
That I am much in favor with the throne.
In short, I am your servant. And now, dear friend,
Since you have such fine judgment, I intend   45
To please you, if I can, with a small sonnet
I wrote not long ago. Please comment on it,
And tell me whether I ought to publish it.
Alceste. You must excuse me, Sir; I'm hardly fit
To judge such matters.
Oronte.   Why not?
Alceste.   I am, I fear,   50
Inclined to be unfashionably sincere.
Oronte. Just what I ask; I'd take no satisfaction
In anything but your sincere reaction.
I beg you not to dream of being kind.
Alceste. Since you desire it, Sir, I'll speak my mind.   55
Oronte. Sonnet. It's a sonnet. . . .
Hope . . . The poem's addressed
To a lady who wakened hopes within my breast.
Hope . . . this is not the pompous sort of thing,

Just modest little verses, with a tender ring.
Alceste. Well, we shall see.
Oronte.   Hope . . . I'm anxious to hear   60
Whether the style seems properly smooth and clear,
And whether the choice of words is good or bad.
Alceste. We'll see, we'll see.
Oronte.   Perhaps I ought to add
That it took me only a quarter-hour to write it.
Alceste. The time's irrelevant, Sir: kindly recite it.   65
Oronte (*Reading*) *Hope comforts us awhile, t'is true,*
Lulling our cares with careless laughter,
And yet such joy is full of rue,
My Phyllis, if nothing follows after.
Philinte. I'm charmed by this already; the style's delightful.   70
Alceste (*Sotto voce, to* Philinte) How can you say that? Why, the thing is frightful.
Oronte. Your fair face smiled on me awhile,
But was it kindness so to enchant me?
'Twould have been fairer not to smile,
If hope was all you meant to grant me.   75
Philinte. What a clever thought! How handsomely you phrase it!
Alceste (*Sotto voce, to* Philinte) You know the thing is trash. How dare you praise it?
Oronte. If it's to be my passion's fate
Thus everlastingly to wait,
Then death will come to set me free: 80
For death is fairer than the fair;
Phyllis, to hope is to despair

When one must hope eternally.
Philinte. The close is exquisite—full of feeling and grace.
Alceste (*Sotto voce, aside*) Oh, blast the close; you'd better close your face   85
Before you send your lying soul to hell.
Philinte. I can't remember a poem I've liked so well.
Alceste (*Sotto voce, aside*) Good Lord!
Oronte (*To* PHILINTE)   I fear you're flattering me a bit.
Philinte. Oh, no!
Alceste (*Sotto voce, aside*)   What else d'you call it, you hypocrite?
Oronte (*To* ALCESTE) But you, Sir, keep your promise now: don't shrink   90
From telling me sincerely what you think.
Alceste. Sir, these are delicate matters; we all desire
To be told that we've the true poetic fire.
But once, to one whose name I shall not mention,
I said, regarding some verse of his invention,   95
That gentlemen should rigorously control
That itch to write which often afflicts the soul;
That one should curb the heady inclination
To publicize one's little avocation;
And that in showing off one's works of art   100
One often plays a very clownish part.
Oronte. Are you suggesting in a devious way
That I ought not . . .
Alceste.   Oh, that I do not say.
Further, I told him that no fault is worse

Than that of writing frigid, lifeless verse,   105
And that the merest whisper of such a shame
Suffices to destroy a man's good name.
Oronte. D'you mean to say my sonnet's dull and trite?
Alceste. I don't say that. But I went on to cite
Numerous cases of once-respected men   110
Who came to grief by taking up the pen.
Oronte. And am I like them? Do I write so poorly?
Alceste. I don't say that. But I told this person, "Surely
You're under no necessity to compose;
Why you should wish to publish, heaven knows.   115
There's no excuse for printing tedious rot
Unless one writes for bread, as you do not.
Resist temptation, then, I beg of you;
Conceal your pastimes from the public view;
And don't give up, on any provocation,   120
Your present high and courtly reputation,
To purchase at a greedy printer's shop
The name of silly author and scribbling fop."
These were the points I tried to make him see.
Oronte. I sense that they are also aimed at me;   125
But now—about my sonnet—I'd like to be told . . .
Alceste. Frankly, that sonnet should be pigeonholed.

You've chosen the worst models to imitate.

The style's unnatural. Let me illustrate:

For example, *Your fair face smiled on me awhile,*   130
Followed by, *'Twould have been fairer not to smile!*
Or this: *such joy is full of rue;*
Or this: *For death is fairer than the fair;*
Or, *Phyllis, to hope is to despair When one must hope eternally!*   135

This artificial style, that's all the fashion,
Has neither taste, nor honesty, nor passion;
It's nothing but a sort of wordy play,
And nature never spoke in such a way.
What, in this shallow age, is not debased?   140
Our fathers, though less refined, had better taste;
I'd barter all that men admire today
For one old love-song I shall try to say:

If the King had given me for my own Paris, his citadel,   145
And I for that must leave alone Her whom I love so well,
I'd say then to the Crown,
Take back your glittering town;
My darling is more fair, I swear,   150
My darling is more fair.

The rhyme's not rich, the style is rough and old,
But don't you see that it's the purest gold
Beside the tinsel nonsense now preferred,

And that there's passion in its every word?   155

If the King had given me for my own Paris, his citadel,
And I for that must leave alone Her whom I love so well,
I'd say then to the Crown,   160
Take back your glittering town;
My darling is more fair, I swear,
My darling is more fair.

There speaks a loving heart. (*To* PHILINTE) You're laughing, eh?
Laugh on, my precious wit. Whatever you say,   165
I hold that song's worth all the bibelots
That people hail today with ah's and oh's.

Oronte. And I maintain my sonnet's very good.

Alceste. It's not at all surprising that you should.
You have your reasons; permit me to have mine   170
For thinking that you cannot write a line.

Oronte. Others have praised my sonnet to the skies.

Alceste. I lack their art of telling pleasant lies.

Oronte. You seem to think you've got no end of wit.

Alceste. To praise your verse, I'd need still more of it.   175

Oronte. I'm not in need of your approval, Sir.

Alceste. That's good; you couldn't have it if you were.

Oronte. Come now, I'll lend you the subject of my sonnet;
I'd like to see you try to improve upon it.

Alceste. I might, by chance, write something just as shoddy;   180

But then I wouldn't show it to everybody.

Oronte. You're most opinionated and
conceited.

Alceste. Go find your flatterers, and be
better treated.

Oronte. Look here, my little fellow,
pray watch your tone.

Alceste. My great big fellow, you'd better watch your own.　　　　185

Philinte (*Stepping between them*) Oh,
please, please, gentlemen! This will
never do.

Oronte. The fault is mine, and I leave
the field to you.

I am your servant, Sir, in every
way.

Alceste. And I, Sir, am your most abject
valet.

SCENE THREE

PHILINTE, ALCESTE

Philinte. Well, as you see, sincerity in
excess

Can get you into a very pretty
mess;

Oronte was hungry for appreciation. . . .

Alceste. Don't speak to me.

Philinte.　　　　　　What?

Alceste.　　　No more conversation.

Philinte. Really, now . . .

Alceste.　　　　Leave me alone.

Philinte.　　　　If I . . .

Alceste.　　　　　Out of my sight!

Philinte. But what . . .　　　　6

Alceste.　　　I won't listen.

Philinte.　　　　　But . . .

Alceste.　　　　　　Silence!

Philinte.　　　Now, is it polite . . .

Alceste. By heaven, I've had enough.
Don't follow me.

Philinte. Ah, you're just joking. I'll keep
you company . . .

ACT TWO. SCENE ONE.

ALCESTE, CÉLIMÈNE

Alceste. Shall I speak plainly, Madam?
I confess

Your conduct gives me infinite distress,

And my resentment's grown too hot
to smother.

Soon, I foresee, we'll break with one
another.

If I said otherwise, I should deceive
you;　　　　5

Sooner or later, I shall be forced to
leave you,

And if I swore that we shall never
part,

I should misread the omens of my
heart.

Célimène. You kindly saw me home, it
would appear,　　　　9

So as to pour invectives in my ear.

Alceste. I've no desire to quarrel. But I
deplore

Your inability to shut the door

On all these suitors who beset you
so.

There's what annoys me, if you care
to know.

Célimène. Is it my fault that all these
men pursue me?　　　　15

Am I to blame if they're attracted to
me?

And when they gently beg an audience,

Ought I to take a stick and drive
them hence?

Alceste. Madam, there's no necessity
for a stick;

A less responsive heart would do the
trick.　　　　20

Of your attractiveness I don't complain;

But those your charms attract, you
then detain

By a most melting and receptive
   manner,
And so enlist their hearts beneath
   your banner.
It's the agreeable hopes which you
   excite   25
That keep these lovers round you
   day and night;
Were they less liberally smiled upon,
That sighing troop would very soon
   be gone.
But tell me, Madam, why it is that
   lately
This man Clitandre interests you so
   greatly?   30
Because of what high merits do you
   deem
Him worthy of the honor of your
   esteem?
Is it that your admiring glances
   linger
On the splendidly long nail of his
   little finger?
Or do you share the general deep
   respect   35
For the blond wig he chooses to af-
   fect?
Are you in love with his embroidered
   hose?
Do you adore his ribbons and his
   bows?
Or is it that this paragon bewitches
Your tasteful eye with his vast Ger-
   man breeches?   40
Perhaps his giggle, or his falsetto
   voice,
Makes him the latest gallant of your
   choice?
Célimène. You're much mistaken to
   resent him so.
Why I put up with him you surely
   know: 44
My lawsuit's very shortly to be tried,
And I must have his influence on my
   side.

Alceste. Then lose your lawsuit,
   Madam, or let it drop;
Don't torture me by humoring such a
   fop.
Célimène. You're jealous of the whole
   world, Sir.
Alceste.   That's true,
Since the whole world is well-re-
   ceived by you.   50
Célimène. That my good nature is so
   unconfined
Should serve to pacify your jealous
   mind;
Were I to smile on one, and scorn
   the rest,
Then you might have some cause to
   be distressed.
Alceste. Well, if I mustn't be jealous,
   tell me, then,   55
Just how I'm better treated than
   other men.
Célimène. You know you have my love.
   Will that not do?
Alceste. What proof have I that what
   you say is true?
Célimène. I would expect, Sir, that my
   having said it
Might give the statement a sufficient
   credit.   60
Alceste. But how can I be sure that you
   don't tell
The selfsame thing to other men as
   well?
Célimène. What a gallant speech! How
   flattering to me!
What a sweet creature you make me
   out to be!
Well then, to save you from the pangs
   of doubt,   65
All that I've said I hereby cancel out;
Now, none but yourself shall make a
   monkey of you:
Are you content?
Alceste.   Why, why am I doomed to
   love you?

I swear that I shall bless the blissful hour
When this poor heart's no longer in your power!   70
I make no secret of it: I've done my best
To exorcise this passion from my breast;
But thus far all in vain; it will not go;
It's for my sins that I must love you so.

Célimène. Your love for me is matchless, Sir; that's clear.   75

Alceste. Indeed, in all the world it has no peer;
Words can't describe the nature of my passion,
And no man ever loved in such a fashion.

Célimène. Yes, it's a brand-new fashion, I agree:
You show your love by castigating me,   80
And all your speeches are enraged and rude.
I've never been so furiously wooed.

Alceste. Yet you could calm that fury, if you chose.
Come, shall we bring our quarrels to a close?
Let's speak with open hearts, then, and begin . . .   85

Scene Two

CÉLIMÈNE, ALCESTE, BASQUE

Célimène. What is it?
Basque.   Acaste is here.
Célimène.   Well, send him in.

Scene Three

CÉLIMÈNE, ALCESTE

Alceste. What! Shall we never be alone at all?
You're always ready to receive a call,
And you can't bear, for ten ticks of the clock,
Not to keep open house for all who knock.

Célimène. I couldn't refuse him: he'd be most put out.   5

Alceste. Surely that's not worth worrying about.

Célimène. Acaste would never forgive me if he guessed
That I consider him a dreadful pest.

Alceste. If he's a pest, why bother with him then?

Célimène. Heavens! One can't antagonize such men;   10
Why, they're the chartered gossips of the court,
And have a say in things of every sort.
One must receive them, and be full of charm;
They're no great help, but they can do you harm,
And though your influence be ever so great,   15
They're hardly the best people to alienate.

Alceste. I see, dear lady, that you could make a case
For putting up with the whole human race;
These friendships that you calculate so nicely . . .

Scene Four

ALCESTE, CÉLIMÈNE, BASQUE

Basque. Madam, Clitandre is here as well.
Alceste. Precisely.
Célimène. Where are you going?
Alceste.   Elsewhere.
Célimène.   Stay.
Alceste.   No, no.
Célimène. Stay, Sir.

Alceste.   I can't.
Célimène.   I wish it.
Alceste.   No, I must go.
I beg you, Madam, not to press the matter;
You know I have no taste for idle chatter.   5
Célimène. Stay: I command you.
Alceste.   No, I cannot stay.
Célimène. Very well; you have my leave to go away.

SCENE FIVE

ELIANTE, PHILINTE, ACASTE, CLITANDRE,
  ALCESTE, CÉLIMÈNE, BASQUE

Eliante (*To* CÉLIMÈNE) The Marquesses have kindly come to call.
Were they announced?
Célimène.   Yes. Basque, bring chairs for all.

(BASQUE *provides the chairs, and exits.*)
(*To* ALCESTE)

You haven't gone?
Alceste.   No; and I shan't depart
Till you decide who's foremost in your heart.
Célimène. Oh, hush.
Alceste.   It's time to choose; take them, or me.   5
Célimène. You're mad.
Alceste.   I'm not, as you shall shortly see.
Célimène. Oh?
Alceste.   You'll decide.
Célimène.   You're joking now, dear friend.
Alceste. No, no; you'll choose; my patience is at an end.
Clitandre. Madam, I come from court, where poor Cléonte
Behaved like a perfect fool, as is his wont.   10

Has he no friend to counsel him, I wonder,
And teach him less unerringly to blunder?
Célimène. It's true, the man's a most accomplished dunce;
His gauche behavior strikes the eye at once;
And every time one sees him, on my word,   15
His manner's grown a trifle more absurd.
Acaste. Speaking of dunces, I've just now conversed
With old Damon, who's one of the very worst;
I stood a lifetime in the broiling sun
Before his dreary monologue was done.   20
Célimène. Oh, he's a wondrous talker, and has the power
To tell you nothing hour after hour:
If, by mistake, he ever came to the point,
The shock would put his jawbone out of joint.
Eliante (*To* PHILINTE) The conversation takes its usual turn,   25
And all our dear friends' ears will shortly burn.
Clitandre. Timante's a character, Madam.
Célimène.   Isn't he, though?
A man of mystery from top to toe,
Who moves about in a romantic mist
On secret missions which do not exist.   30
His talk is full of eyebrows and grimaces;
How tired one gets of his momentous faces;
He's always whispering something confidential
Which turns out to be quite inconsequential;

Nothing's too slight for him to mys-
    tify;   35
He even whispers when he says
    "good-by."
Acaste. Tell us about Géralde.
Célimène.   That tiresome ass.
    He mixes only with the titled class,
    And fawns on dukes and princes, and
        is bored
    With anyone who's not at least a
        lord.   40
    The man's obsessed with rank, and
        his discourses
    Are all of hounds and carriages and
        horses;
    He uses Christian names with all the
        great,
    And the word Milord, with him, is
        out of date.
Clitandre. He's very taken with Bélise,
    I hear.   45
Célimène. She is the dreariest company,
    poor dear.
    Whenever she comes to call, I grope
        about
    To find some topic which will draw
        her out,
    But, owing to her dry and faint re-
        plies,
    The conversation wilts, and droops,
        and dies.   50
    In vain one hopes to animate her face
    By mentioning the ultimate common-
        place;
    But sun or shower, even hail or frost
    Are matters she can instantly exhaust.
    Meanwhile her visit, painful though
        it is,   55
    Drags on and on through mute
        eternities,
    And though you ask the time, and
        yawn, and yawn,
    She sits there like a stone and won't
        be gone.
Acaste. Now for Adraste.

Célimène.   Oh, that conceited elf
    Has a gigantic passion for himself;
    He rails against the court, and cannot
        bear it   61
    That none will recognize his hidden
        merit;
    All honors given to others give of-
        fense
    To his imaginary excellence.
Clitandre. What about young Cléon?
    His house, they say,   65
    Is full of the best society, night and
        day.
Célimène. His cook has made him
    popular, not he:
    It's Cléon's table that people come to
        see.
Eliante. He gives a splendid dinner,
    you must admit.
Célimène. But must he serve himself
    along with it?   70
    For my taste, he's a most insipid
        dish
    Whose presence sours the wine and
        spoils the fish.
Philinte. Damis, his uncle, is admired
    no end.
    What's your opinion, Madam?
Célimène.   Why, he's my friend.
Philinte. He seems a decent fellow, and
    rather clever.   75
Célimène. He works too hard at clever-
    ness, however.
    I hate to see him sweat and struggle
        so
    To fill his conversation with bons
        mots.
    Since he's decided to become a wit
    His taste's so pure that nothing
        pleases it;   80
    He scolds at all the latest books and
        plays,
    Thinking that wit must never stoop
        to praise,
    That finding fault's a sign of intellect,

That all appreciation is abject,
And that by damning everything in
  sight   85
One shows oneself in a distinguished
  light.
He's scornful even of our conversa-
  tions:
Their trivial nature sorely tries his
  patience;
He folds his arms, and stands above
  the battle,
And listens sadly to our childish prat-
  tle.   90
Acaste. Wonderful, Madam! You've hit
  him off precisely.
Clitandre. No one can sketch a char-
  acter so nicely.
Alceste. How bravely, Sirs, you cut and
  thrust at all
  These absent fools, till one by one
    they fall:
  But let one come in sight, and you'll
    at once   95
  Embrace the man you lately called a
    dunce,
  Telling him in a tone sincere and
    fervent
  How proud you are to be his humble
    servant.
Clitandre. Why pick on us? Madame's
  been speaking, Sir,
  And you should quarrel, if you must,
    with her.   100
Alceste. No, no, by God, the fault is
  yours, because
  You lead her on with laughter and
    applause,
  And make her think that she's the
    more delightful
  The more her talk is scandalous and
    spiteful.
  Oh, she would stoop to malice far,
    far less   105
  If no such claque approved her
    cleverness.

It's flatterers like you whose foolish
  praise
Nourishes all the vices of these days.
Philinte. But why protest when some-
  one ridicules
  Those you'd condemn, yourself, as
    knaves or fools?   110
Célimène. Why, Sir? Because he loves
  to make a fuss.
  You don't expect him to agree with
    us,
  When there's an opportunity to ex-
    press
  His heaven-sent spirit of contrari-
    ness?
  What other people think, he can't
    abide;   115
  Whatever they say, he's on the other
    side;
  He lives in deadly terror of agreeing;
  'Twould make him seem an ordinary
    being.
  Indeed, he's so in love with contradic-
    tion,
  He'll turn against his most profound
    conviction   120
  And with a furious eloquence de-
    plore it,
  If only someone else is speaking for
    it.
Alceste. Go on, dear lady, mock me as
  you please;
  You have your audience in ecstasies.
Philinte. But what she says is true: you
  have a way   125
  Of bridling at whatever people say;
  Whether they praise or blame, your
    angry spirit
  Is equally unsatisfied to hear it.
Alceste. Men, Sir, are always wrong,
  and that's the reason
  That righteous anger's never out of
    season;   130
  All that I hear in all their conversa-
    tion

Is flattering praise or reckless con-
  demnation.
Célimène. But . . .
Alceste.　　No, no, Madam, I am
  forced to state
That you have pleasures which I
  deprecate,
And that these others, here, are much
  to blame　　　　　　　　　　135
For nourishing the faults which are
  your shame.
Clitandre. I shan't defend myself, Sir;
  but I vow
I'd thought this lady faultless until
  now.
Acaste. I see her charms and graces,
  which are many;
But as for faults, I've never noticed
  any.　　　　　　　　　　　　140
Alceste. I see them, Sir; and rather than
  ignore them,
I strenuously criticize her for them.
The more one loves, the more one
  should object
To every blemish, every least defect.
Were I this lady, I would soon get
  rid　　　　　　　　　　　　145
Of lovers who approved of all I
  did,
And by their slack indulgence and
  applause
Endorsed my follies and excused my
  flaws.
Célimène. If all hearts beat according
  to your measure,
The dawn of love would be the end
  of pleasure;　　　　　　　　150
And love would find its perfect con-
  summation
In ecstasies of rage and reprobation.
Eliante. Love, as a rule, affects men
  otherwise,
And lovers rarely love to criticize.
They see their lady as a charming
  blur,　　　　　　　　　　　155

And find all things commendable in
  her.
If she has any blemish, fault, or
  shame,
They will redeem it by a pleasing
  name.
The pale-faced lady's lily-white, per-
  force;
The swarthy one's a sweet brunette,
  of course;　　　　　　　　　160
The spindly lady has a slender grace;
The fat one has a most majestic pace;
The plain one, with her dress in dis-
  array,
They classify as *beauté négligée;*
The hulking one's a goddess in their
  eyes,　　　　　　　　　　165
The dwarf, a concentrate of Para-
  dise;
The haughty lady has a noble mind;
The mean one's witty, and the dull
  one's kind;
The chatterbox has liveliness and
  verve,　　　　　　　　　　169
The mute one has a virtuous reserve.
So lovers manage, in their passion's
  cause,
To love their ladies even for their
  flaws.
Alceste. But I still say . . .
Célimène.　　I think it would be nice.
To stroll around the gallery once or
  twice.
What! You're not going, Sirs?
Clitandre and Acaste.　　No, Madam,
  no.　　　　　　　　　　　175
Alceste. You seem to be in terror lest
  they go.
Do what you will, Sirs; leave, or
  linger on,
But I shan't go till after you are gone.
Acaste. I'm free to linger, unless I
  should perceive
Madame is tired, and wishes me to
  leave.　　　　　　　　　　180

THE MISANTHROPE 285

Clitandre. And as for me, I needn't go
today
Until the hour of the King's *coucher.*
Célimène (*To* ALCESTE) You're joking,
surely?
Alceste.   Not in the least; we'll see
Whether you'd rather part with
them, or me.

SCENE SIX

ALCESTE, CÉLIMÈNE, ELIANTE, ACASTE,
PHILINTE, CLITANDRE, BASQUE

Basque (*To* ALCESTE) Sir, there's a
fellow here who bids me state
That he must see you, and that it
can't wait.
Alceste. Tell him that I have no such
pressing affairs.
Basque. It's a long tailcoat that this
fellow wears,
With gold all over.
Célimène (*To* ALCESTE)   You'd best
go down and see.   5
Or—have him enter.

SCENE SEVEN

ALCESTE, CÉLIMÈNE, ELIANTE, ACASTE,
PHILINTE, CLITANDRE, A GUARD of the
Marshalsea

Alceste (*Confronting the* GUARD) Well,
what do you want with me?
Come in, Sir.
Guard.   I've a word, Sir, for your ear.
Alceste. Speak it aloud, Sir; I shall
strive to hear.
Guard. The Marshals have instructed
me to say
You must report to them without
delay.   5
Alceste. Who? Me, Sir?
Guard.   Yes, Sir; you.
Alceste.   But what do they want?
Philinte (*To* ALCESTE) To scotch your
silly quarrel with Oronte.

Célimène (*To* PHILINTE) What quar-
rel?
Philinte. Oronte and he have fallen out
Over some verse he spoke his mind
about;
The Marshals wish to arbitrate the
matter.   10
Alceste. Never shall I equivocate or
flatter!
Philinte. You'd best obey their sum-
mons; come, let's go.
Alceste. How can they mend our quar-
rel, I'd like to know?
Am I to make a cowardly retraction,
And praise those jingles to his satis-
faction?   15
I'll not recant; I've judged that son-
net rightly.
It's bad.
Philinte.   But you might say so more
politely. . . .
Alceste. I'll not back down; his verses
make me sick.
Philinte. If only you could be more
politic!   19
But come, let's go.
Alceste.   I'll go, but I won't unsay
A single word.
Philinte.   Well, let's be on our way.
Alceste. Till I am ordered by my lord
the King
To praise that poem, I shall say the
thing
Is scandalous, by God, and that the
poet
Ought to be hanged for having the
nerve to show it.   25
(*To* CLITANDRE *and* ACASTE, *who are
laughing*)
By heaven, Sirs, I really didn't know
That I was being humorous.
Célimène.   Go, Sir, go;
Settle your business.

Alceste. I shall, and when I'm through,
I shall return to settle things with you.

ACT THREE. SCENE ONE.

CLITANDRE, ACASTE

Clitandre. Dear Marquess, how contented you appear;
All things delight you, nothing mars your cheer.
Can you, in perfect honesty, declare
That you've a right to be so debonair?
Acaste. By Jove, when I survey myself, I find   5
No cause whatever for distress of mind.
I'm young and rich; I can in modesty
Lay claim to an exalted pedigree;
And owing to my name and my condition
I shall not want for honors and position.   10
Then as to courage, that most precious trait,
I seem to have it, as was proved of late
Upon the field of honor, where my bearing,
They say, was very cool and rather daring.
I've wit, of course; and taste in such perfection   15
That I can judge without the least reflection,
And at the theater, which is my delight,
Can make or break a play on opening night,
And lead the crowd in hisses or bravos,
And generally be known as one who knows.   20

I'm clever, handsome, gracefully polite;
My waist is small, my teeth are strong and white;
As for my dress, the world's astonished eyes
Assure me that I bear away the prize.
I find myself in favor everywhere,
Honored by men, and worshiped by the fair;   26
And since these things are so, it seems to me
I'm justified in my complacency.
Clitandre. Well, if so many ladies hold you dear,
Why do you press a hopeless courtship here?   30
Acaste. Hopeless, you say? I'm not the sort of fool
That likes his ladies difficult and cool.
Men who are awkward, shy, and peasantish
May pine for heartless beauties, if they wish,
Grovel before them, bear their cruelties,   35
Woo them with tears and sighs and bended knees,
And hope by dogged faithfulness to gain
What their poor merits never could obtain.
For men like me, however, it makes no sense
To love on trust, and foot the whole expense.   40
Whatever any lady's merits be,
I think, thank God, that I'm as choice as she;
That if my heart is kind enough to burn
For her, she owes me something in return;   44

And that in any proper love affair
The partners must invest an equal
   share.
Clitandre. You think, then, that our
   hostess favors you?
Acaste. I've reason to believe that that
   is true.
Clitandre. How did you come to such
   a mad conclusion?
   You're blind, dear fellow. This is
   sheer delusion. 50
Acaste. All right, then: I'm deluded
   and I'm blind.
Clitandre. Whatever put the notion in
   your mind?
Acaste. Delusion.
Clitandre.   What persuades you that
   you're right?
Acaste. I'm blind.
Clitandre.   But have you any proofs
   to cite?
Acaste. I tell you I'm deluded.
Clitandre.   Have you, then, 55
   Received some secret pledge from
   Célimène?
Acaste. Oh, no: she scorns me.
Clitandre.   Tell me the truth, I beg.
Acaste. She just can't bear me.
Clitandre.   Ah, don't pull my leg.
   Tell me what hope she's given you, I
   pray.
Acaste. I'm hopeless, and it's you who
   win the day. 60
   She hates me thoroughly, and I'm so
   vexed
   I mean to hang myself on Tuesday
   next.
Clitandre. Dear Marquess, let us have
   an armistice
   And make a treaty. What do you say
   to this?
   If ever one of us can plainly prove 65
   That Célimène encourages his love,
   The other must abandon hope, and
   yield.

And leave him in possession of the
   field.
Acaste. Now, there's a bargain that appeals to me;
   With all my heart, dear Marquess, I
   agree 70
   But hush.

SCENE TWO

CÉLIMÈNE, ACASTE, CLITANDRE

Célimène. Still here?
Clitandre.   T'was love that stayed
   our feet.
Célimène. I think I heard a carriage
   in the street.
   Whose is it? D'you know?

SCENE THREE

CÉLIMÈNE, ACASTE, CLITANDRE, BASQUE

Basque.   Arsinoé is here,
   Madame.
Célimène.   Arsinoé, you say? Oh,
   dear.
Basque. Eliante is entertaining her be-
   low.
Célimène. What brings the creature
   here, I'd like to know?
Acaste. They say she's dreadfully prud-
   ish, but in fact 5
   I think her piety . . .
Célimène.   It's all an act.
   At heart she's worldly, and her poor
   success
   In snaring men explains her prudish-
   ness.
   It breaks her heart to see the beaux
   and gallants
   Engrossed by other women's charms
   and talents, 10
   And so she's always in a jealous rage
   Against the faulty standards of the
   age.
   She lets the world believe that she's
   a prude
   To justify her loveless solitude,

And strives to put a brand of moral
    shame   15
On all the graces that she cannot
    claim.
But still she'd love a lover; and
    Alceste
Appears to be the one she'd love the
    best.
His visits here are poison to her
    pride;
She seems to think I've lured him
    from her side;   20
And everywhere, at court or in the
    town,
The spiteful, envious woman runs me
    down.
In short, she's just as stupid as can
    be,
Vicious and arrogant in the last de-
    gree,
And . . .   25

SCENE FOUR

ARSINOÉ, CÉLIMÈNE, CLITANDRE, ACASTE

Célimène. Ah! What happy chance has
    brought you here?
    I've thought about you ever so much,
      my dear.
Arsinoé. I've come to tell you some-
    thing you should know.
Célimène. How good of you to think of
    doing so!

    (CLITANDRE *and* ACASTE *go out,
    laughing.*)

SCENE FIVE

ARSINOÉ, CÉLIMÈNE

Arsinoé. It's just as well those gentle-
    men didn't tarry.
Célimène. Shall we sit down?
Arsinoé.   That won't be necessary.
    Madam, the flame of friendship
    ought to burn

Brightest in matters of the most con-
    cern,
And as there's nothing which con-
    cerns us more   5
Than honor, I have hastened to your
    door
To bring you, as your friend, some
    information
About the status of your reputation.
I visited, last night, some virtuous
    folk,
And, quite by chance, it was of you
    they spoke;   10
There was, I fear, no tendency to
    praise
Your light behavior and your dash-
    ing ways.
The quantity of gentlemen you see
And your by now notorious coquetry
Were both so vehemently criticized
By everyone, that I was much sur-
    prised.   16
Of course, I needn't tell you where I
    stood;
I came to your defense as best I
    could,
Assured them you were harmless,
    and declared
Your soul was absolutely unimpaired.
But there are some things, you must
    realize,   21
One can't excuse, however hard one
    tries,
And I was forced at last into con-
    ceding
That your behavior, Madam, is mis-
    leading,
That it makes a bad impression, giv-
    ing rise   25
To ugly gossip and obscene surmise,
And that if you were more *overtly*
    good,
You wouldn't be so much misunder-
    stood.

Not that I think you've been unchaste
  —no! no!
The saints preserve me from a
  thought so low!   30
But mere good conscience never did
  suffice:
One must avoid the outward show of
  vice.
Madam, you're too intelligent, I'm
  sure,
To think my motives anything but
  pure
In offering you this counsel—which
  I do   35
Out of a zealous interest in you.
Célimène. Madam, I haven't taken you
  amiss;
I'm very much obliged to you for
  this;
And I'll at once discharge the obliga-
  tion
By telling you about *your* reputa-
  tion.   40
You've been so friendly as to let me
  know
What certain people say of me, and
  so
I mean to follow your benign ex-
  ample
By offering you a somewhat similar
  sample.   44
The other day, I went to an affair
And found some most distinguished
  people there
Discussing piety, both false and true.
The conversation soon came round to
  you.
Alas! Your prudery and bustling
  zeal
Appeared to have a very slight ap-
  peal.   50
Your affectation of a grave demeanor,
Your endless talk of virtue and of
  honor,

The aptitude of your suspicious mind
For finding sin where there is none
  to find,
Your towering self-esteem, that pity-
  ing face   55
With which you contemplate the hu-
  man race,
Your sermonizings and your sharp
  aspersions
On people's pure and innocent diver-
  sions—
All these were mentioned, Madam,
  and, in fact,
Were roundly and concertedly at-
  tacked.   60
"What good," they said, "are all these
  outward shows,
When everything belies her pious
  pose?
She prays incessantly; but then, they
  say,
She beats her maids and cheats them
  of their pay;
She shows her zeal in every holy
  place,   65
But still she's vain enough to paint
  her face;
She holds that naked statues are immoral,
But with a naked *man* she'd have no
  quarrel."
Of course, I said to everybody there
That they were being viciously unfair;   70
But still they were disposed to criticize you,
And all agreed that someone should
  advise you
To leave the morals of the world
  alone,
And worry rather more about your
  own.
They felt that one's self-knowledge
  should be great   75

Before one thinks of setting others
  straight;
That one should learn the art of liv-
  ing well
Before one threatens other men with
  hell,
And that the Church is best
  equipped, no doubt,
To guide our souls and root our vices
  out.   80
Madam, you're too intelligent, I'm
  sure,
To think my motives anything but
  pure
In offering you this counsel—which I
  do
Out of a zealous interest in you.
Arsinoé. I dared not hope for gratitude,
  but I   85
Did not expect so acid a reply;
I judge, since you've been so ex-
  tremely tart,
That my good counsel pierced you to
  the heart.
Célimène. Far from it, Madam. Indeed,
  it seems to me
We ought to trade advice more fre-
  quently.   90
One's vision of oneself is so defec-
  tive
That it would be an excellent cor-
  rective.
If you are willing, Madam, let's ar-
  range
Shortly to have another frank ex-
  change
In which we'll tell each other, *entre
  nous,*   95
What you've heard tell of me, and I
  of you.
Arsinoé. Oh, people never censure you,
  my dear;
It's me they criticize. Or so I hear.
Célimène. Madam, I think we either
  blame or praise

According to our taste and length of
  days.   100
There is a time of life for coquetry,
And there's a season, too, for prudery.
When all one's charms are gone, it is,
  I'm sure,
Good strategy to be devout and
  pure:
It makes one seem a little less for-
  saken.   105
Some day, perhaps, I'll take the road
  you've taken:
Time brings all things. But I have
  time aplenty,
And see no cause to be a prude at
  twenty.
Arsinoé. You give your age in such a
  gloating tone
That one would think I was an an-
  cient crone;   110
We're not so far apart, in sober truth,
That you can mock me with a boast
  of youth!
Madam, you baffle me, I wish I knew
What moves you to provoke me as
  you do.
Célimène. For my part, Madam, I
  should like to know   115
Why you abuse me everywhere you
  go.
Is it my fault, dear lady, that your
  hand
Is not, alas, in very great demand?
If men admire me, if they pay me
  court   119
And daily make me offers of the sort
You'd dearly love to have them make
  to you,
How can I help it? What would you
  have me do?
If what you want is lovers, please feel
  free
To take as many as you can from me.
Arsinoé. Oh, come. D'you think the
  world is losing sleep   125

Over that flock of lovers which you
   keep,
Or that we find it difficult to guess
What price you pay for their de-
   votedness?
Surely you don't expect us to suppose
Mere merit could attract so many
   beaux?   130
It's not your virtue that they're
   dazzled by;
Nor is it virtuous love for which they
   sigh.
You're fooling no one, Madam; the
   world's not blind;
There's many a lady heaven has de-
   signed
To call men's noblest, tenderest feel-
   ings out,   135
Who has no lovers dogging her
   about;
From which it's plain that lovers
   nowadays
Must be acquired in bold and shame-
   less ways,
And only pay one court for such
   reward   139
As modesty and virtue can't afford.
Then don't be quite so puffed up, if
   you please,
About your tawdry little victories;
Try, if you can, to be a shade less
   vain,
And treat the world with somewhat
   less disdain.   144
If one were envious of your amours,
One soon could have a following like
   yours;
Lovers are no great trouble to collect
If one prefers them to one's self-
   respect.
Célimène. Collect them then, my dear;
   I'd love to see
You demonstrate that charming
   theory;   150
Who knows, you might . . .

Arsinoé.   Now, Madam, that will do;
   It's time to end this trying interview.
My coach is late in coming to your
   door,
Or I'd have taken leave of you be-
   fore.
Célimène. Oh, please don't feel that
   you must rush away;   155
I'd be delighted, Madam, if you'd
   stay.
However, lest my conversation bore
   you,
Let me provide some better company
   for you;
This gentleman, who comes most
   apropos,
Will please you more than I could
   do, I know.   160

Scene Six

ALCESTE, CÉLIMÈNE, ARSINOÉ

Célimène. Alceste, I have a little note
   to write
Which simply must go out before tonight;
Please entertain *Madame;* I'm sure
   that she
Will overlook my incivility.

Scene Seven

ALCESTE, ARSINOÉ

Arsinoé. Well, Sir, our hostess gra-
   ciously contrives
For us to chat until my coach ar-
   rives;
And I shall be forever in her debt
For granting me this little tête-à-tête.
We women very rightly give our
   hearts   5
To men of noble character and parts,
And your especial merits, dear Al-
   ceste,
Have roused the deepest sympathy
   in my breast.

Oh, how I wish they had sufficient
sense
At court, to recognize your excel-
lence!   10
They wrong you greatly, Sir. How it
must hurt you
Never to be rewarded for your vir-
tue!
Alceste. Why, Madam, what cause have
I to feel aggrieved?
What great and brilliant thing have
I achieved?
What service have I rendered to the
King   15
That I should look to him for any-
thing?
Arsinoé. Not everyone who's honored
by the State
Has done great services. A man must
wait
Till time and fortune offer him the
chance.   19
Your merit, Sir, is obvious at a glance,
And . . .
Alceste.   Ah, forget my merit; I'm
not neglected.
The court, I think, can hardly be
expected
To mine men's souls for merit, and
unearth
Our hidden virtues and our secret
worth.
Arsinoé. Some virtues, though, are far
too bright to hide;   25
Yours are acknowledged, Sir, on
every side.
Indeed, I've heard you warmly
praised of late
By persons of considerable weight.
Alceste. This fawning age has praise
for everyone,
And all distinctions, Madam, are un-
done.   30
All things have equal honor nowadays,

And no one should be gratified by
praise.
To be admired, one only need exist,
And every lackey's on the honors
list.
Arsinoé. I only wish, Sir, that you had
your eye   35
On some position at court, however
high;
You'd only have to hint at such a
notion
For me to set the proper wheels in
motion;
I've certain friendships I'd be glad to
use
To get you any office you might
choose.   40
Alceste. Madam, I fear that any such
ambition
Is wholly foreign to my disposition.
The soul God gave me isn't of the
sort
That prospers in the weather of a
court.
It's all too obvious that I don't pos-
sess   45
The virtues necessary for success.
My one great talent is for speaking
plain;
I've never learned to flatter or to
feign;
And anyone so stupidly sincere   49
Had best not seek a courtier's career.
Outside the court, I know, one must
dispense
With honors, privilege, and influ-
ence;
But still one gains the right, forego-
ing these,
Not to be tortured by the wish to
please.
One needn't live in dread of snubs
and slights,   55
Nor praise the verse that every idiot
writes,

Nor humor silly Marquesses, nor bestow
Politic sighs on Madam So-and-So.
Arsinoé. Forget the court, then; let the matter rest.
But I've another cause to be distressed   60
About your present situation, Sir.
It's to your love affair that I refer.
She whom you love, and who pretends to love you,
Is, I regret to say, unworthy of you.
Alceste. Why, Madam! Can you seriously intend   65
To make so grave a charge against your friend?
Arsinoé. Alas, I must. I've stood aside too long
And let that lady do you grievous wrong;
But now my debt to conscience shall be paid:
I tell you that your love has been betrayed.   70
Alceste. I thank you, Madam; you're extremely kind.
Such words are soothing to a lover's mind.
Arsinoé. Yes, though she *is* my friend, I say again
You're very much too good for Célimène.
She's wantonly misled you from the start.   75
Alceste. You may be right; who knows another's heart?
But ask yourself if it's the part of charity
To shake my soul with doubts of her sincerity.
Arsinoé. Well, if you'd rather be a dupe than doubt her,
That's your affair. I'll say no more about her.   80

Alceste. Madam, you know that doubt and vague suspicion
Are painful to a man in my position;
It's most unkind to worry me this way
Unless you've some real proof of what you say.
Arsinoé. Sir, say no more: all doubt shall be removed,   85
And all that I've been saying shall be proved.
You've only to escort me home, and there
We'll look into the heart of this affair.
I've ocular evidence which will persuade you
Beyond a doubt, that Célimène's betrayed you.   90
Then, if you're saddened by that revelation,
Perhaps I can provide some consolation.

ACT FOUR. SCENE ONE.

ELIANTE, PHILINTE

Philinte. Madam, he acted like a stubborn child;
I thought they never would be reconciled;
In vain we reasoned, threatened, and appealed;
He stood his ground and simply would not yield.
The Marshals, I feel sure, have never heard   5
An argument so splendidly absurd.
"No, gentlemen," said he, "I'll not retract.
His verse is bad: extremely bad, in fact.
Surely it does the man no harm to know it.
Does it disgrace him, not to be a poet?   10

A gentleman may be respected still,
Whether he writes a sonnet well or
   ill.
That I dislike his verse should not of-
   fend him;
In all that touches honor, I commend
   him;
He's noble, brave, and virtuous—but
   I fear   15
He can't in truth be called a son-
   neteer.
I'll gladly praise his wardrobe; I'll
   endorse
His dancing, or the way he sits a
   horse;
But, gentlemen, I cannot praise his
   rhyme.   19
In fact, it ought to be a capital crime
For anyone so sadly unendowed
To write a sonnet, and read the thing
   aloud."
At length he fell into a gentler mood
And, striking a concessive attitude,
He paid Oronte the following cour-
   tesies: 25
"Sir, I regret that I'm so hard to
   please,
And I'm profoundly sorry that your
   lyric
Failed to provoke me to a panegyric."
After these curious words, the two
   embraced,
And then the hearing was adjourned
   —in haste.   30
Eliante. His conduct has been very
   singular lately;
Still, I confess that I respect him
   greatly.
The honesty in which he takes such
   pride
Has—to my mind—its noble, heroic
   side.
In this false age, such candor seems
   outrageous;   35

But I could wish that it were more
   contagious.
Philinte. What most intrigues me in our
   friend Alceste
Is the grand passion that rages in his
   breast.
The sullen humors he's compounded
   of
Should not, I think, dispose his heart
   to love;   40
But since they do, it puzzles me still
   more
That he should choose your cousin to
   adore.
Eliante. It does, indeed, belie the
   theory
That love is born of gentle sympathy,
And that the tender passion must be
   based   45
On sweet accords of temper and of
   taste.
Philinte. Does she return his love, do
   you suppose?
Eliante. Ah, that's a difficult question,
   Sir. Who knows?
How can we judge the truth of her
   devotion?
Her heart's a stranger to its own emo-
   tion.   50
Sometimes it thinks it loves, when no
   love's there;
At other times it loves quite unaware.
Philinte. I rather think Alceste is in for
   more
Distress and sorrow than he's bar-
   gained for;
Were he of my mind, Madam, his
   affection   55
Would turn in quite a different direc-
   tion,
And we would see him more responsive to
The kind regard which he receives
   from you.

Eliante. Sir, I believe in frankness, and
  I'm inclined,
  In matters of the heart, to speak my
    mind.   60
  I don't oppose his love for her; in-
    deed,
  I hope with all my heart that he'll
    succeed,
  And were it in my power, I'd rejoice
  In giving him the lady of his choice.
  But if, as happens frequently enough
  In love affairs, he meets with a re-
    buff—   66
  If Célimène should grant some rival's
    suit—
  I'd gladly play the role of substitute;
  Nor would his tender speeches please
    me less
  Because they'd once been made with-
    out success.   70
Philinte. Well, Madam, as for me, I
    don't oppose
  Your hopes in this affair; and heaven
    knows
  That in my conversations with the
    man
  I plead your cause as often as I can.
  But if those two should marry, and
    so remove   75
  All chance that he will offer you his
    love,
  Then I'll declare my own, and hope
    to see
  Your gracious favor pass from him to
    me.
  In short, should you be cheated of
    Alceste,   79
  I'd be most happy to be second best.
Eliante. Philinte, you're teasing.
Philinte.   Ah, Madam, never fear;
  No words of mine were ever so
    sincere,
  And I shall live in fretful expectation
  Till I can make a fuller declaration.

Scene Two

ALCESTE, ELIANTE, PHILINTE

Alceste. Avenge me, Madam! I must
    have satisfaction,
  Or this great wrong will drive me to
    distraction!
Eliante. Why, what's the matter?
    What's upset you so?
Alceste. Madam, I've had a mortal,
    mortal blow.
  If Chaos repossessed the universe,   5
  I swear I'd not be shaken any worse.
  I'm ruined. . . . I can say no more.
  . . . My soul . . .
Eliante. Do try, Sir, to regain your self-
    control.
Alceste. Just heaven! Why were so
    much beauty and grace
  Bestowed on one so vicious and so
    base?   10
Eliante. Once more, Sir, tell us. . . .
Alceste.   My world has gone to
    wrack;
  I'm—I'm betrayed; she's stabbed me
    in the back:
  Yes, Célimène (who would have
    thought it of her?)
  Is false to me, and has another lover.
Eliante. Are you quite certain? Can
    you prove these things?   15
Philinte. Lovers are prey to wild im-
    aginings
  And jealous fancies. No doubt there's
    some mistake. . . .
Alceste. Mind your own business, Sir,
    for heaven's sake.

(*To* ELIANTE)

  Madam, I have the proof that you
    demand
  Here in my pocket, penned by her
    own hand.   20
  Yes, all the shameful evidence one
    could want

Lies in this letter written to Oronte—
Oronte! whom I felt sure she couldn't
    love,
And hardly bothered to be jealous of.
Philinte. Still, in a letter, appearances
    may deceive;   25
This may not be so bad as you be-
    lieve.
Alceste. Once more I beg you, Sir, to
    let me be;
Tend to your own affairs; leave mine
    to me.
Eliante. Compose yourself; this anguish
    that you feel . . .
Alceste. Is something, Madam, you
    alone can heal.   30
My outraged heart, beside itself with
    grief,
Appeals to you for comfort and re-
    lief,
Avenge me on your cousin, whose
    unjust
And faithless nature has deceived my
    trust;
Avenge a crime your pure soul must
    detest.   35
Eliante. But how, Sir?
Alceste.   Madam, this heart within
    my breast
Is yours; pray take it; redeem my
    heart from her,
And so avenge me on my torturer.
Let her be punished by the fond
    emotion,
The ardent love, the bottomless de-
    votion,   40
The faithful worship which this
    heart of mine
Will offer up to yours as to a
    shrine.
Eliante. You have my sympathy, Sir, in
    all you suffer;
Nor do I scorn the noble heart you
    offer;   44
But I suspect you'll soon be mollified,

And this desire for vengeance will
    subside.
When some beloved hand has done
    us wrong
We thirst for retribution—but not for
    long;
However dark the deed that she's
    committed,
A lovely culprit's very soon acquit-
    ted.   50
Nothing's so stormy as an injured
    lover,
And yet no storm so quickly passes
    over.
Alceste. No, Madam, no—this is no
    lovers' spat;
I'll not forgive her; it's gone too far
    for that;
My mind's made up; I'll kill myself
    before   55
I waste my hopes upon her any more.
Ah, here she is. My wrath intensifies.
I shall confront her with her tricks
    and lies,
And crush her utterly, and bring you
    then   59
A heart no longer slave to Célimène.

SCENE THREE

CÉLIMÈNE, ALCESTE

Alceste (*Aside*) Sweet heaven, help
    me to control my passion.
Célimène. (*Aside*) Oh, Lord. (*To* AL-
    CESTE) Why stand there staring in
    that fashion?
And what d'you mean by those dra-
    matic sighs,
And that malignant glitter in your
    eyes?
Alceste. I mean that sins which cause
    the blood to freeze   5
Look innocent beside your treach-
    eries;
That nothing Hell's or Heaven's
    wrath could do

Ever produced so bad a thing as you.
Célimène. Your compliments were al-
ways sweet and pretty.
Alceste. Madam, it's not the moment
to be witty.   10
No, blush and hang your head; you've
ample reason,
Since I've the fullest evidence of your
treason.
Ah, this is what my sad heart proph-
esied;
Now all my anxious fears are verified;
My dark suspicion and my gloomy
doubt   15
Divined the truth, and now the truth
is out.
For all your trickery, I was not de-
ceived;
It was my bitter stars that I believed.
But don't imagine that you'll go scot-
free;   19
You shan't misuse me with impunity.
I know that love's irrational and
blind;
I know the heart's not subject to the
mind,
And can't be reasoned into beating
faster;
I know each soul is free to choose its
master;
Therefore had you but spoken from
the heart,   25
Rejecting my attentions from the
start,
I'd have no grievance, or at any
rate
I could complain of nothing but my
fate.
Ah, but so falsely to encourage me—
That was a treason and a treachery
For which you cannot suffer too se-
verely,   31
And you shall pay for that behavior
dearly.
Yes, now I have no pity, not a shred;

My temper's out of hand; I've lost
my head;
Shocked by the knowledge of your
double-dealings,   35
My reason can't restrain my savage
feelings;
A righteous wrath deprives me of my
senses,
And I won't answer for the conse-
quences.
Célimène. What does this outburst
mean? Will you please explain?
Have you, by any chance, gone quite
insane?   40
Alceste. Yes, yes, I went insane the day
I fell
A victim to your black and fatal spell,
Thinking to meet with some sin-
cerity
Among the treacherous charms that
beckoned me.
Célimène. Pooh. Of what treachery can
you complain?   45
Alceste. How sly you are, how cleverly
you feign!
But you'll not victimize me any
more.
Look: here's a document you've seen
before.
This evidence, which I acquired to-
day,
Leaves you, I think, without a thing
to say.   50
Célimène. Is this what sent you into
such a fit?
Alceste. You should be blushing at the
sight of it.
Célimène. Ought I to blush? I truly
don't see why.
Alceste. Ah, now you're being bold as
well as sly;
Since there's no signature, perhaps
you'll claim . . .   55
Célimène. I wrote it, whether or not it
bears my name.

Alceste. And you can view with equa-
nimity
This proof of your disloyalty to me!
Célimène. Oh, don't be so outrageous
and extreme.
Alceste. You take this matter lightly, it
would seem.   60
Was it no wrong to me, no shame to
to you,
That you should send Oronte this
billet-doux?
Célimène. Oronte! Who said it was for
him?
Alceste.   Why, those
Who brought me this example of
your prose.
But what's the difference? If you
wrote the letter   65
To someone else, it pleases me no
better.
My grievance and your guilt remain
the same.
Célimène. But need you rage, and need
I blush for shame,
If this was written to a *woman*
friend?
Alceste. Ah! Most ingenious. I'm im-
pressed no end;   70
And after that incredible evasion
Your guilt is clear. I need no more
persuasion.
How dare you try so clumsy a decep-
tion?
D'you think I'm wholly wanting in
perception?
Come, come, let's see how brazenly
you'll try   75
To bolster up so palpable a lie:
Kindly construe this ardent closing
section
As nothing more than sisterly affec-
tion!
Here, let me read it. Tell me, if you
dare to,
That this is for a woman . . .

Célimène.   I don't care to. 80
What right have you to badger and
berate me,
And so highhandedly interrogate
me?
Alceste. Now, don't be angry; all I ask
of you
Is that you justify a phrase or
two . . .
Célimène. No, I shall not. I utterly
refuse,   85
And you may take those phrases as
you choose.
Alceste. Just show me how this letter
could be meant
For a woman's eyes, and I shall be
content.
Célimène. No, no, it's for Oronte;
you're perfectly right.
I welcome his attentions with de-
light,   90
I prize his character and his intellect,
And everything is just as you suspect.
Come, do your worst now; give your
rage free rein;
But kindly cease to bicker and com-
plain.
Alceste (*Aside*) Good God! Could any-
thing be more inhuman?   95
Was ever a heart so mangled by a
woman?
When I complain of how she has be-
trayed me,
She bridles, and commences to up-
braid me!
She tries my tortured patience to the
limit;
She won't deny her guilt; she glories
in it!   100
And yet my heart's too faint and
cowardly
To break these chains of passion, and
be free,
To scorn her as it should, and rise
above

This unrewarded, mad, and bitter
  love.

(*To* Célimène)

Ah, traitress, in how confident a
  fashion   105
You take advantage of my helpless
  passion,
And use my weakness for your faithless charms
To make me once again throw down
  my arms!
But do at least deny this black trans-
  gression;
Take back that mocking and perverse confession;   110
Defend this letter and your innocence,
And I, poor fool, will aid in your
  defense.
Pretend, pretend, that you are just
  and true,
And I shall make myself believe in
  you.
Célimène. Oh, stop it. Don't be such a
  jealous dunce,   115
Or I shall leave off loving you at
  once.
Just why should I *pretend?* What
  could impel me
To stoop so low as that? And kindly
  tell me
Why, if I loved another, I shouldn't
  merely
Inform you of it, simply and sincerely!   120
I've told you where you stand, and
  that admission
Should altogether clear me of suspicion;
After so generous a guarantee,
What right have you to harbor
  doubts of me?
Since women are (from natural
  reticence)   125

Reluctant to declare their sentiments,
And since the honor of our sex
  requires
That we conceal our amorous desires,
Ought any man for whom such laws
  are broken
To question what the oracle has
  spoken?   130
Should he not rather feel an obliga-
  tion
To trust that most obliging declara-
  tion?
Enough, now. Your suspicions quite
  disgust me;
Why should I love a man who doesn't
  trust me?   134
I cannot understand why I continue,
Fool that I am, to take an interest in
  you.
I ought to choose a man less prone to
  doubt,
And give you something to be vexed
  about.
Alceste. Ah, what a poor enchanted
  fool I am;
These gentle words, no doubt, were
  all a sham;   140
But destiny requires me to entrust
My happiness to you, and so I must.
I'll love you to the bitter end, and see
How false and treacherous you dare
  to be.
Célimène. No, you don't really love me
  as you ought.   145
Alceste. I love you more than can be
  said or thought;
Indeed, I wish you were in such
  distress
That I might show my deep devoted-
  ness.
Yes, I could wish that you were
  wretchedly poor,
Unloved, uncherished, utterly ob-
  scure;   150

That fate had set you down upon the
earth
Without possessions, rank, or gentle
birth;
Then, by the offer of my heart, I
might
Repair the great injustice of your
plight;
I'd raise you from the dust, and
proudly prove   155
The purity and vastness of my love.

Célimène. This is a strange benevolence
indeed!
God grant that I may never be in
need. . . .
Ah, here's Monsieur Dubois, in
quaint disguise.

Scene Four

CÉLIMÈNE, ALCESTE, DUBOIS

Alceste. Well, why this costume? Why
those frightened eyes?
What ails you?
Dubois.   Well, Sir, things are most
mysterious.
Alceste. What do you mean?
Dubois.   I fear they're very serious.
Alceste. What?
Dubois.   Shall I speak more loudly?
Alceste.   Yes; speak out.
Dubois. Isn't there someone here, Sir?
Alceste.   Speak, you lout!   5
Stop wasting time.
Dubois.   Sir, we must slip away.
Alceste. How's that?
Dubois.   We must decamp without
delay.
Alceste. Explain yourself.
Dubois.   I tell you we must fly.
Alceste. What for?
Dubois.   We mustn't pause to say
good-by.
Alceste. Now what d'you mean by all
of this, you clown?   10

Dubois. I mean, Sir, that we've got to
leave this town.
Alceste. I'll tear you limb from limb
and joint from joint
If you don't come more quickly to
the point.
Dubois. Well, Sir, today a man in a
black suit,
Who wore a black and ugly scowl to
boot,   15
Left us a document scrawled in such
a hand
As even Satan couldn't understand.
It bears upon your lawsuit, I don't
doubt;
But all hell's devils couldn't make it
out.
Alceste. Well, well, go on. What then?
I fail to see   20
How this event obliges us to flee.
Dubois. Well, Sir: an hour later, hardly
more,
A gentleman who's often called be-
fore
Came looking for you in an anxious
way.
Not finding you, he asked me to con-
vey   25
(Knowing I could be trusted with
the same)
The following message. . . . Now,
what *was* his name?
Alceste. Forget his name, you idiot.
What did he say?
Dubois. Well, it was one of your
friends, Sir, anyway.
He warned you to begone, and he
suggested   30
That if you stay, you may well be ar-
rested.
Alceste. What? Nothing more specific?
Think, man, think!
Dubois. No, Sir. He had me bring him
pen and ink,

And dashed you off a letter which,
I'm sure,
Will render things distinctly less ob-
scure.   35
Alceste. Well—let me have it!
Célimène.   What *is* this all about?
Alceste. God knows; but I have hopes
of finding out.
How long am I to wait, you blitherer?
Dubois (*After a protracted search for
the letter*) I must have left it on
your table, Sir.
Alceste. I ought to . . .
Célimène.   No, no, keep your self-
control;   40
Go find out what's behind his rig-
marole.
Alceste. It seems that fate, no matter
what I do,
Has sworn that I may not converse
with you;
But, Madam, pray permit your faith-
ful lover
To try once more before the day is
over.   45

ACT FIVE. SCENE ONE.

ALCESTE, PHILINTE

Alceste. No, it's too much. My mind's
made up, I tell you.
Philinte. Why should this blow, however hard, compel you . . .
Alceste. No, no, don't waste your breath
in argument;
Nothing you say will alter my intent;
This age is vile, and I've made up my
mind   5
To have no further commerce with
mankind.
Did not truth, honor, decency, and
the laws
Oppose my enemy and approve my
cause?

My claims were justified in all men's
sight;   9
I put my trust in equity and right;
Yet, to my horror and the world's dis-
grace,
Justice is mocked, and I have lost my
case!
A scoundrel whose dishonesty is
notorious
Emerges from another lie victorious!
Honor and right condone his brazen
fraud,   15
While rectitude and decency ap-
plaud!
Before his smirking face, the truth
stands charmed,
And virtue conquered, and the law
disarmed!
His crime is sanctioned by a court
decree!
And not content with what he's done
to me,   20
The dog now seeks to ruin me by
stating
That I composed a book now circu-
lating,
A book so wholly criminal and vi-
cious
That even to speak its title is sedi-
tious!
Meanwhile Oronte, my rival, lends
his credit   25
To the same libelous tale, and helps
to spread it!
Oronte! a man of honor and of rank,
With whom I've been entirely fair
and frank;
Who sought me out and forced me,
willy-nilly,
To judge some verse I found ex-
tremely silly;   30
And who, because I properly refused
To flatter him, or see the truth
abused,

Abets my enemy in a rotten slander!
There's the reward of honesty and
    candor!
The man will hate me to the end of
    time   35
For failing to commend his wretched
    rhyme!
And not this man alone, but all hu-
    manity
Do what they do from interest and
    vanity;
They prate of honor, truth, and
    righteousness,
But lie, betray, and swindle nonethe-
    less.   40
Come then: man's villainy is too
    much to bear;
Let's leave this jungle and this jackal's
    lair.
Yes! treacherous and savage race of
    men,
You shall not look upon my face
    again.
Philinte. Oh, don't rush into exile pre-
    maturely;   45
Things aren't as dreadful as you
    make them, surely.
It's rather obvious, since you're still
    at large,
That people don't believe your en-
    emy's charge.
Indeed, his tale's so patently untrue
That it may do more harm to him
    than you.   50
Alceste. Nothing could do that scoun-
    drel any harm:
His frank corruption is his greatest
    charm,
And, far from hurting him, a further
    shame
Would only serve to magnify his
    name.
Philinte. In any case, his bald prevari-
    cation   55

Has done no injury to your reputa-
    tion,
And you may feel secure in that
    regard.
As for your lawsuit, it should not be
    hard
To have the case reopened, and con-
    test   59
This judgment . . .
Alceste.   No, no, let the verdict rest.
Whatever cruel penalty it may
    bring,
I wouldn't have it changed for any-
    thing.
It shows the times' injustice with
    such clarity
That I shall pass it down to our
    posterity
As a great proof and signal demon-
    stration   65
Of the black wickedness of this gen-
    eration.
It may cost twenty thousand francs;
    but I
Shall pay their twenty thousand, and
    gain thereby
The right to storm and rage at hu-
    man evil,
And send the race of mankind to the
    devil.   70
Philinte. Listen to me. . . .
Alceste.   Why? What can you pos-
    sibly say?
Don't argue, Sir; your labor's thrown
    away.
Do you propose to offer lame ex-
    cuses
For men's behavior and the times'
    abuses?
Philinte. No, all you say I'll readily
    concede: 75
This is a low, conniving age indeed;
Nothing but trickery prospers now-
    adays,

And people ought to mend their
shabby ways.
Yes, man's a beastly creature; but
must we then
Abandon the society of men?   80
Here in the world, each human
frailty
Provides occasion for philosophy,
And that is virtue's noblest exercise;
If honesty shone forth from all men's
eyes,
If every heart were frank and kind
and just,   85
What could our virtues do but gather
dust
(Since their employment is to help
us bear
The villainies of men without de-
spair)?
A heart well-armed with virtue can
endure. . . .
Alceste. Sir, you're a matchless rea-
soner, to be sure;   90
Your words are fine and full of co-
gency;
But don't waste time and eloquence
on me.
My reason bids me go, for my own
good.
My tongue won't lie and flatter as it
should;
God knows what frankness it might
next commit,   95
And what I'd suffer on account of it.
Pray let me wait for Célimène's re-
turn
In peace and quiet. I shall shortly
learn,
By her response to what I have in
view,
Whether her love for me is feigned
or true.   100
Philinte. Till then, let's visit Eliante up-
stairs.

Alceste. No, I am too weighed down
with somber cares.
Go to her, do; and leave me with my
gloom
Here in the darkened corner of this
room.
Philinte. Why, that's no sort of company, my friend;   105
I'll see if Eliante will not descend.

SCENE TWO

CÉLIMÈNE, ORONTE, ALCESTE

Oronte. Yes, Madam, if you wish me to
remain
Your true and ardent lover, you must
deign
To give me some more positive as-
surance.
All this suspense is quite beyond
endurance.
If your heart shares the sweet de-
sires of mine,   5
Show me as much by some con-
vincing sign;
And here's the sign I urgently sug-
gest:
That you no longer tolerate Alceste,
But sacrifice him to my love, and
sever
All your relations with the man for-
ever.   10
Célimène. Why do you suddenly dis-
like him so?
You praised him to the skies not long
ago.
Oronte. Madam, that's not the point.
I'm here to find
Which way your tender feelings are
inclined.
Choose, if you please, between Al-
ceste and me,   15
And I shall stay or go accordingly.
Alceste (*Emerging from the corner*)

Yes, Madam, choose; this gentleman's demand
Is wholly just, and I support his
stand.
I too am true and ardent; I too am
here
To ask you that you make your feelings clear.   20
No more delays, now; no equivocation;
The time has come to make your
declaration.

Oronte. Sir, I've no wish in any way to
be
An obstacle to your felicity.

Alceste. Sir, I've no wish to share her
heart with you;   25
That may sound jealous, but at least
it's true.

Oronte. If, weighing us, she leans in
your direction . . .

Alceste. If she regards you with the
least affection . . .

Oronte. I swear I'll yield her to you
there and then.

Alceste. I swear I'll never see her face
again.   30

Oronte. Now, Madam, tell us what
we've come to hear.

Alceste. Madam, speak openly and
have no fear.

Oronte. Just say which one is to remain
your lover.

Alceste. Just name one name, and it
will all be over.

Oronte. What! Is it possible that you're
undecided?   35

Alceste. What! Can your feelings possibly be divided?

Célimène. Enough: this inquisition's
gone too far:
How utterly unreasonable you are!
Not that I couldn't make the choice
with ease;

My heart has no conflicting sympa-
thies;   40
I know full well which one of you I
favor,
And you'd not see me hesitate or
waver.
But how can you expect me to reveal
So cruelly and bluntly what I feel?
I think it altogether too unpleasant
To choose between two men when
both are present;   46
One's heart has means more subtle
and more kind
Of letting its affections be divined,
Nor need one be uncharitably plain
To let a lover know he loves in vain.

Oronte. No, no, speak plainly; I for one
can stand it.   51
I beg you to be frank.

Alceste.   And I demand it.
The simple truth is what I wish to
know,
And there's no need for softening the
blow.
You've made an art of pleasing everyone,   55
But now your days of coquetry are
done:
You have no choice now, Madam,
but to choose,
For I'll know what to think if you
refuse;
I'll take your silence for a clear admission
That I'm entitled to my worst suspicion.   60

Oronte. I thank you for this ultimatum,
Sir,
And I may say I heartily concur.

Célimène. Really, this foolishness is
very wearing:
Must you be so unjust and overbear-
ing?
Haven't I told you why I must
demur?   65

Ah, here's Eliante; I'll put the case to
her.

ELIANTE, PHILINTE, CÉLIMÈNE, ORONTE,
ALCESTE

Célimène. Cousin, I'm being persecuted
here
By these two persons, who, it would
appear,
Will not be satisfied till I confess
Which one I love the more, and
which the less,
And tell the latter to his face that
he   5
Is henceforth banished from my com-
pany.
Tell me, has ever such a thing been
done?
Eliante. You'd best not turn to me; I'm
not the one
To back you in a matter of this kind:
I'm all for those who frankly speak
their mind.   10
Oronte. Madam, you'll search in vain
for a defender.
Alceste. You're beaten, Madam, and
may as well surrender.
Oronte. Speak, speak, you must; and
end this awful strain.
Alceste. Or don't, and your position will
be plain.
Oronte. A single word will close this
painful scene.   15
Alceste. But if you're silent, I'll know
what you mean.

ARSINOÉ, CÉLIMÈNE, ELIANTE,
ALCESTE, PHILINTE,
ACASTE, CLITANDRE, ORONTE

Acaste (*To* CÉLIMÈNE) Madam, with
all due deference, we two
Have come to pick a little bone with
you.

Clitandre (*To* ORONTE *and* ALCESTE)
I'm glad you're present, Sirs; as
you'll soon learn,
Our business here is also your con-
cern.
Arsinoé (*To* CÉLIMÈNE) Madam, I visit
you so soon again   5
Only because of these two gentle-
men,
Who came to me indignant and ag-
grieved
About a crime too base to be be-
lieved.
Knowing your virtue, having such
confidence in it,
I couldn't think you guilty for a
minute,   10
In spite of all their telling evidence;
And, rising above our little difference,
I've hastened here in friendship's
name to see
You clear yourself of this great cal-
umny.
Acaste. Yes, Madam, let us see with
what composure   15
You'll manage to respond to this
disclosure.
You lately sent Clitandre this tender
note.
Clitandre. And this one, for Acaste, you
also wrote.
Acaste (*To* ORONTE *and* ALCESTE)
You'll recognize this writing, Sirs,
I think;   19
The lady is so free with pen and ink
That you must know it all too well, I
fear.
But listen: this is something you
should hear.

"How absurd you are to condemn
my lightheartedness in society, and
to accuse me of being happiest in the
company of others. Nothing could be
more unjust; and if you do not come

to me instantly and beg pardon for saying such a thing, I shall never forgive you as long as I live. Our big bumbling friend the Viscount . . ."

What a shame that he's not here. 32

"Our big bumbling friend the Viscount, whose name stands first in your complaint, is hardly a man to my taste; and ever since the day I watched him spend three-quarters of an hour spitting into a well, so as to make circles in the water, I have been unable to think highly of him. As for the little Marquess . . ." 41

In all modesty, gentlemen, that is I.

"As for the little Marquess, who sat squeezing my hand for such a long while yesterday, I find him in all respects the most trifling creature alive; and the only things of value about him are his cape and his sword. As for the man with the green ribbons . . ." 50

(*To* ALCESTE)
It's your turn now, Sir.

"As for the man with the green ribbons, he amuses me now and then with his bluntness and his bearish ill-humor; but there are many times indeed when I think him the greatest bore in the world. And as for the sonneteer . . ." 58

(*To* ORONTE)
Here's your helping.

"And as for the sonneteer, who has taken it into his head to be witty, and insists on being an author in the teeth of opinion, I simply cannot be bothered to listen to him, and his prose wearies me quite as much as his poetry. Be assured that I am not always so well-entertained as you suppose; that I long for your company, more than I dare to say, at all these entertainments to which people drag me; and that the presence of those one loves is the true and perfect seasoning to all one's pleasures." 74

Clitandre. And now for me.

"Clitandre, whom you mention, and who so pesters me with his saccharine speeches, is the last man on earth for whom I could feel any affection. He is quite mad to suppose that I love him, and so are you, to doubt that you are loved. Do come to your senses; exchange your suppositions for his; and visit me as often as possible, to help me bear the annoyance of his unwelcome attentions." 87

It's a sweet character that these letters show,
And what to call it, Madam, you well know.
Enough. We're off to make the world acquainted 90
With this sublime self-portrait that you've painted.
Acaste. Madam, I'll make you no farewell oration;
No, you're not worthy of my indignation.
Far choicer hearts than yours, as you'll discover,
Would like this little Marquess for a lover. 95

SCENE FIVE

CÉLIMÈNE, ELIANTE, ARSINOÉ, ALCESTE, ORONTE, PHILINTE

Oronte. So! After all those loving letters you wrote,

You turn on me like this, and cut my
    throat!
And your dissembling, faithless heart,
    I find,
Has pledged itself by turns to all
    mankind!
How blind I've been! But now I
    clearly see;   5
I thank you, Madam, for enlight-
    ening me.
My heart is mine once more, and I'm
    content;
The loss of it shall be your punish-
    ment.

(*To* ALCESTE)

Sir, she is yours; I'll seek no more to
    stand
Between your wishes and this lady's
    hand.   10

SCENE SIX

CÉLIMÈNE, ELIANTE, ARSINOÉ, ALCESTE,
PHILINTE

Arsinoé (*To* CÉLIMÈNE) Madam, I'm
    forced to speak. I'm far too stirred
To keep my counsel, after what I've
    heard.
I'm shocked and staggered by your
    want of morals.
It's not my way to mix in others'
    quarrels;
But really, when this fine and noble
    spirit,   5
This man of honor and surpassing
    merit,
Laid down the offering of his heart
    before you,
How *could* you . . .
Alceste.   Madam, permit me, I im-
    plore you,
To represent myself in this debate.
Don't bother, please, to be my ad-
    vocate.   10
My heart, in any case, could not af-
    ford

To give your services their due re-
    ward;
And if I chose, for consolation's
    sake,
Some other lady, t'would not be you
    I'd take.
Arsinoé. What makes you think you
    could, Sir? And how dare you   15
Imply that I've been trying to en-
    snare you?
If you can for a moment entertain
Such flattering fancies, you're ex-
    tremely vain.
I'm not so interested as you suppose
In Célimène's discarded gigolos.   20
Get rid of that absurd illusion, do.
Women like me are not for such as
    you.
Stay with this creature, to whom
    you're so attached;
I've never seen two people better
    matched.

SCENE SEVEN

CÉLIMÈNE, ELIANTE, ALCESTE, PHILINTE

Alceste (*To* CÉLIMÈNE) Well, I've been
    still throughout this exposé,
Till everyone but me has said his say.
Come, have I shown sufficient self-
    restraint?
And may I now . . .
Célimène.   Yes, make your just com-
    plaint.
Reproach me freely, call me what
    you will;   5
You've every right to say I've used
    you ill.
I've wronged you, I confess it; and
    in my shame
I'll make no effort to escape the
    blame.
The anger of those others I could
    despise;
My guilt toward you I sadly recog-
    nize.   10

Your wrath is wholly justified, I fear;
I know how culpable I must appear,
I know all things bespeak my treach-
ery,
And that, in short, you've grounds for
hating me.
Do so; I give you leave.
Alceste.   Ah, traitress—how, 15
How should I cease to love you, even
now?
Though mind and will were pas-
sionately bent
On hating you, my heart would not
consent.

(To Eliante *and* Philinte)

Be witness to my madness, both of
you;   19
See what infatuation drives one to;
But wait; my folly's only just begun,
And I shall prove to you before I'm
done
How strange the human heart is, and
how far
From rational we sorry creatures are.

(To Célimène)

Woman, I'm willing to forget your
shame,   25
And clothe your treacheries in a
sweeter name;
I'll call them youthful errors, instead
of crimes,
And lay the blame on these cor-
rupting times.
My one condition is that you agree
To share my chosen fate, and fly
with me   30
To that wild, trackless, solitary place
In which I shall forget the human
race.
Only by such a course can you atone
For those atrocious letters; by that
alone
Can you remove my present horror of
you,   35

And make it possible for me to love
you.
Célimène. What! *I* renounce the world
at my young age,
And die of boredom in some her-
mitage?
Alceste. Ah, if you really loved me as
you ought,
You wouldn't give the world a mo-
ment's thought;   40
Must you have me, and all the world
beside?
Célimène. Alas, at twenty one is ter-
rified
Of solitude. I fear I lack the force
And depth of soul to take so stern a
course.
But if my hand in marriage will con-
tent you,   45
Why, there's a plan which I might
well consent to,
And . . .
Alceste.   No, I detest you now. I
could excuse
Everything else, but since you thus
refuse
To love me wholly, as a wife should
do,
And see the world in me, as I in
you,   50
Go! I reject your hand, and disen-
thrall
My heart from your enchantments,
once for all.

Scene Eight

ELIANTE, ALCESTE, PHILINTE

Alceste (To Eliante) Madam, your
virtuous beauty has no peer;
Of all this world, you only are sincere;
I've long esteemed you highly, as you
know;
Permit me ever to esteem you so,

And if I do not now request your
hand,   5
Forgive me, Madam, and try to un-
derstand.
I feel unworthy of it; I sense that fate
Does not intend me for the married
state,
That I should do you wrong by offer-
ing you
My shattered heart's unhappy resi-
due,   10
And that in short . . .

Eliante.   Your argument's well
taken:
Nor need you fear that I shall feel
forsaken.
Were I to offer him this hand of
mine,
Your friend Philinte, I think, would
not decline.

Philinte. Ah, Madam, that's my heart's
most cherished goal,   15
For which I'd gladly give my life and
soul.

Alceste (*To* Eliante *and* Philinte)
May you be true to all you now
profess,
And so deserve unending happiness.
Meanwhile, betrayed and wronged
in everything,
I'll flee this bitter world where vice
is king,   20
And seek some spot unpeopled and
apart
Where I'll be free to have an honest
heart.

Philinte. Come, Madam, let's do everything we can
To change the mind of this unhappy
man.

St. Patrick's Day

\text{\textasciitilde} RICHARD BRINSLEY SHERIDAN

INTRODUCTION

Richard Brinsley Sheridan, the most accomplished writer of social comedy to appear in the two centuries that separated William Congreve from George Bernard Shaw, was born in Dublin on October 30, 1751. His grandfather, Thomas Sheridan, was a Doctor of Divinity, a celebrated wit, and a friend of Dean Swift, who said of him, "You cannot make him a greater compliment than by telling him before his face, how careless he was in any affair that related to his interest and his fortune." The Dean thought him a good-natured man, honest, and generous, but lacking in prudence and good judgment. Richard clearly inherited all of these characteristics from his grandfather.

His father, also named Thomas, was, as a young man, a successful actor in tragic parts, and appeared with David Garrick at the Drury Lane Theatre in London. While still only in his twenties, Thomas was offered the directorship of the Theatre Royal in Smock Alley, Dublin, and returned to his native city, where almost immediately he ran into trouble with actors and audiences. In a dictatorial and pedantic way he set out to improve the actors' speech, the taste of the public, conditions in the theater, and education in general. He devoted more attention to his reformatory ideas than to satisfying the wishes of his audience. Soon mutiny in the company and riots in the auditorium drove Thomas and his family out of Dublin. Thereafter he eked out a living by lecturing, writing on education, and compiling a dictionary that won him a small pension.

Thomas had married Frances Chamberlaine, a clever and beautiful woman who had begun to write at fifteen and later became a successful playwright and novelist; she bore four children who survived: Charles, Richard, Alicia, and Elizabeth. Charles was his father's favorite, Richard was shunted aside. He was put to school in Dublin when the other members of the family left for London, and did not rejoin them until 1759. Three years later he was sent to Harrow, a preparatory school for gentlemen's sons, while the rest of the family, to avoid paying their

\text{310}

debts, went to live in France. There, in 1766, Mrs. Sheridan died and was buried; Richard had hardly known his mother. Apparently forgotten by everyone, he felt rejected and suffered fits of depression, caused in part by the shabby clothes he was forced to wear. His good nature and wit masked his true feelings and won him friends among his classmates, and his teachers agreed that he was clever and talented, but he did poorly in his studies.

In 1769 he left Harrow and rejoined his father, brother, and sisters in London; a grown-up young man, he was almost a stranger in the family. At home, Thomas Sheridan talked incessantly about the theater and insisted upon giving his sons lessons in oratory. From these interests of his father, Richard apparently drew the motivation for his future activities. Thomas Sheridan suddenly decided that he required a more aristocratic arena for the display of his talents and removed the family to Bath, the most fashionable town of eighteenth century England, where he planned to instruct the polite world in the art of elocution.

Richard was nineteen years old when he was let loose in the Capital of Pleasure and Intrigue, and it became his university. His personal observations and experiences provided him with all the material he needed for such satirical comedies as *The Rivals* and *The School for Scandal*. He began by wooing and winning the most sought after beauty of the day, Elizabeth Ann Linley, a celebrated singer who had even caught the eye of George III. Among her many suitors was a Captain Mathews, a married man, who persisted in forcing his unwanted attentions upon her. Sheridan took it upon himself to engage the Captain in two duels and succeeded in driving him off. In the face of opposition from both their fathers, Richard and Elizabeth eloped to France where they went through a mock wedding, but their marriage was eventually solemnized at Marylebone Church in London in 1773. This affair became the talk of the town, a feast for scandalmongers.

Although Elizabeth had been earning thousands of pounds by her singing, Sheridan would not permit her to continue to perform in public after their marriage; he himself turned to the theater for a living. At the suggestion of Thomas Harris, owner of Covent Garden, Sheridan, in six to eight weeks during the summer of 1774, wrote *The Rivals*, a comedy based on the difficulties he had encountered in winning his wife. On opening night, January 18, 1775, the play was hissed; it was overwritten, and poorly acted by John Lee, in the rôle of the Irish Sir Lucius O'Trigger. Sheridan withdrew the play for revision, mainly cutting it, and for the part of Sir Lucius hired Lawrence Clinch, an Irish actor, who was a friend of his father. When it reopened ten days later, *The Rivals*, and especially Clinch, drew resounding applause.

Sheridan was grateful to Clinch for the brilliant performance he had turned in and, as a reward, wrote a two-act farce, *St. Patrick's Day, or The Scheming Lieutenant*, for him to star in on his "benefit night." It took Sheridan only forty-eight hours to compose the play, which was presented on May 2, 1775. This work, too, won immediate acclaim and was successfully performed a number of times during the season.

In November, 1775, four days before his opera, *The Duenna*, opened to equal success, Sheridan's son Tom was born. *The Duenna* for which his father-in-law, Thomas Linley, composed the music, played for seventy-five nights on its first run and became even more successful than *The Beggar's Opera*.

From three hits in one year, money was pouring in and Sheridan, who always found ways to get rid of it, decided to expand his activities. In 1776 he became part owner and sole manager of Drury Lane, which he acquired from David Garrick. For its acting company he wrote *A Trip to Scarborough*, adapted from the Restoration play, *The Relapse*, by Vanbrugh; and composed his masterpiece *The School for Scandal*, which was also in the mode of Restoration drama. Both plays were produced in 1777 and earned not only critical approval but great financial rewards. In 1779 Sheridan wrote *The Critic*, a satire on the drama; it was a sprightly work in the vein of *The Rehearsal*, a literary burlesque by the Duke of Buckingham. *The Critic*, which managed to drive *The Rehearsal* from the stage, was Sheridan's last original play. This period is known as "the Indian summer of the Restoration."

In only a half dozen years, Sheridan's genius had carried him to the peak of his profession; he had far surpassed his father's achievements in the theater, but did not consider this to be a serious career. He was twenty-nine and ready to turn his talents in another direction. He chose politics, and in 1780, by allying himself with the Whigs, was elected to the House of Commons, where he served with distinction for thirty-two years.

As Sheridan devoted his attention more and more to the affairs of government, his wife assumed many of his duties at the theatre; she read scripts, auditioned actors, kept accounts, and placated the members of the company when, as frequently happened, it was not possible to pay their salaries. Sheridan occasionally directed plays and revised scripts submitted for production, notably two translations from the German of August Kotzebue: *The Stranger* (1798) and *Pizarro* (1799), the latter a heroic tragedy that was so successful it almost put the house on a paying basis.

But Sheridan's major interest now lay in politics and his rise was rapid. In 1782 he became Under Secretary for Foreign Affairs, and the following year, Secretary to the Treasury. His parliamentary reputation dates from his great speeches in the impeachment of Warren Hastings (1787-1794). In 1794 he again electrified the House by a magnificent oration in denunciation of the French Revolution. He was a devoted friend and adherent of the Whig leader, Charles James Fox, and confidential adviser to the Prince of Wales (later George IV). On Fox's death, Sheridan was disappointed in not being made leader of the Whigs.

In 1792, his first wife died and three years later he married the daughter of the Dean of Winchester, Esther Jane Ogle, who bore him a son, Charles. The affairs of the theater were going badly. The old building had to be closed as unfit to hold large audiences, and a new one, opened in 1794, burned down in 1809. He was ousted from the management of the theater that took its place, and this put the finishing touches to his financial distress. In 1812 he lost his seat in parliament because he could not afford the election expenses. In 1813, he was arrested for debt, but was rescued by his friends. The remaining three years of his life were clouded by ill health and anxiety; he died impoverished on July 7, 1816. He was given, ironically, a magnificent funeral, attended by everyone from the members of the nobility down to the players of Drury Lane; the pall-bearers were lords of the realm. He wanted to be buried next to his political associate, Charles Fox, for, as Thomas Moore said, "He disliked any allusion to his being a dramatic writer." But he was placed where he actually belonged, beside David Garrick in the Poets' Corner in Westminster Abbey.

As a politician, Sheridan was independent, courageous, and incorruptible in a corrupt age; he opposed the war with America, and defended the liberty of the press. His oratorical powers, thanks to his father's training and his own natural gifts, were unmatched.

As a dramatist, he ranked in popularity next to Shakespeare; and has been surpassed by few in the creation of mirth-provoking situations, entertaining dialogue, and fascinating characters, among them Mrs. Malaprop, whose name has contributed a colorful noun to our language. Sheridan's reputation rests securely on the actability of his plays as well as on their brilliant wit, sharp repartee, and clever social satire, which continue to appeal strongly to modern audiences.

With his lively imagination, enormous vitality, and great verbal facility, Sheridan did not linger very long over the writing of his plays. *The Rivals*, his first effort, was turned out in a couple of weeks and reached the stage in record time. John Lee, an English actor, member of the company at Covent Garden, was hastily cast in the rôle of the Irishman, Sir Lucius O'Trigger. It did not take the audience long, on the opening night of the play, to realize that Lee could not handle the Irish dialect. They hissed loudly. Startled and offended, Lee went down to the footlights and asked, "Are you hissing me or the play?" "You," came the clear reply. But Sheridan did not place upon the actor the entire blame for the audience's dissatisfaction; he knew that the script was faulty and vastly overwritten. He withdrew the play and, within ten days, made the necessary cuts and revisions, offered the rôle of Sir Lucius to the Irish actor Lawrence Clinch, and, having closed a failure, reopened with a notable success.

Sheridan, with his usual generosity, credited Clinch with having saved *The Rivals* and decided to reward him in a practical way. Keeping in mind this actor's special gift for farce as well as his exaggerated, comic brogue, Sheridan, in two days, composed a short work for Clinch to star in, and in high spirits called it *St. Patrick's Day*. From the plot, which deals with the exploits of a scheming lieutenant, the playwright provided himself with a subtitle which more appropriately describes the play.

It is interesting to note Sheridan's devotion to Ireland though he had spent only the first eight years of his life there. For thirty years he was a member of the Benevolent Society of St. Patrick, established in 1784, for the education of poor Irish children in London. Each year, on St. Patrick's Day, the Society held a fund-raising dinner, which was faithfully attended by Sheridan, who not only delivered the keynote speech but contributed twenty pounds. The playwright, who was somewhat of a "joker," thought it would amuse Clinch to appear in a play named for their patron saint; and, since it was to be performed for the benefit of an Irishman who was the head of a large and needy family, Sheridan was in a sense inaugurating, in 1774, his own benevolent society ten years before the official one.

The original bill for the Covent Garden premiere announced that "For Mr. Clinch's Benefit on May 2, 1775," there would be "a new farce called St. Patrick's Day, or The Scheming Lieutenant." The play was well received on opening night and became a regular offering in the company's repertoire. The bustling, hilarious nature of the farce may be judged by a brief outline of the plot.

St. Patrick's Day opens on a street near Justice Credulous' house, where Lieutenant O'Connor has been loitering in the hope of catching a glimpse of his beloved Lauretta, the judge's daughter; here O'Connor is confronted by his sergeant, his corporal, and a delegation of soldiers, who have come to lodge a complaint against the inns in the town—the Two Magpies, the Angel, the Sun, and others—which have been treating them badly. O'Connor hears them out sympathetically, then sends them off with a treat in honor of St. Patrick's Day.

He next encounters Doctor Rosy, an eccentric friend, who is in perpetual mourning for Dolly, his long-dead wife. The doctor has been trying without success to intercede in behalf of O'Connor with Justice Credulous for the hand of the latter's daughter. But the Justice hates equally the Irish and the military, and wants his daughter to have nothing to do with O'Connor. The young lieutenant, however, is not put off so easily and with Dr. Rosy as co-conspirator he begins to play tricks on the Justice.

Dr. Rosy first introduces O'Connor as Humphrey Hum, a strong country fellow, with an enormous cudgel, who is hired by the Justice as a bodyguard to protect him and his daughter, Lauretta, from the military in general, and from a certain rascally Lieutenant O'Connor in particular. Humphrey, left alone with Lauretta, discloses his identity; the Justice unexpectedly enters at the very moment when the lieutenant is obeying, too literally, the old man's strict charge to "keep close" to his daughter. In a scuffle, O'Connor is recognized and the Justice becomes terrified; he sends for a blunderbuss, and the lieutenant beats a hasty retreat.

But the young man has a more successful scheme in reserve. The Justice receives a letter stating that O'Connor, though disappointed at not being permitted to woo Lauretta, has still the satisfaction of knowing that he is revenged on her unnatural father, by having that morning put a dose of poison in his chocolate. The Justice is petrified, he sees death staring him in the face; he loses his voice, grows dizzy, and is about to collapse. Dr. Rosy enters and increases his alarm. How the Justice has changed! There are black spots on his nose, a wild stare in his right eye, and his body swollen out of all proportion. His only hope is in a German quack, who is famous for his antidotes for poison, so the medical wonder-worker is introduced and his outlandish jargon, as translated by Dr. Rosy, sends the Justice into fresh fits of despair. Lauretta enters, and the quack is electrified at the sight of her beauty; he will cure the patient without fee or reward, if he is permitted to win the affections of the lady. The Justice, who has a passionate love of life, immediately accepts the terms; the miraculous prescription is handed over, and he finds himself cured by his affectionate son-in-law, Lieutenant O'Connor.

The critics were almost unanimous in their praise of the play, saying, "Its verbal felicities are many and delightful," it is "theatrically effective," and "it promises a high feast for the sons and daughters of fun"; at the same time they could not resist suggesting that its elements had been borrowed from Plautus, Molière, Wycherley, and Beaumarchais; one critic, however, wisely added, "But as Horace said, he 'rendered old things new by dexterous adaptation.'" If the situations in the play are traditional, and as ancient as those in Greek New Comedy or the primitive farces of Rome, Sheridan managed to revitalize them with his own fresh brand of humor; and with a sure theatrical touch, wrote every part, no matter how small, so as to give a competent performer a chance to make an effective appeal to the audience. *St. Patrick's Day*, as Louis Kronenberger observes, "did handsomely for Clinch, it enabled him, by virtue of some lightning quickchanges, to impersonate a lively Irish officer, an English booby, and a German quack." In addition, of course, it provided him with a good financial return on his "benefit" night.

One perceptive observer, writing about *St. Patrick's Day*, said, "Unpretentious as it is, it reproduces the distinguishing characteristics of *The Rivals* in its unforced gaiety, racy dialogue, and general air of sparkling spontaneity." He might have gone further and noted that the short farce is actually a spin-off from the full-length comedy. In both plays, what appear to be stock stage figures—the impatient young lover, the unhappy virgin, the talkative matron, the testy old father, and various other humorous and eccentric types—were actual personages in Sheridan's real-life drama; and in both plays, the efforts of a man to win the woman he loves and the difficulty of doing so form the basis of the plot. Sheridan comments on this situation obliquely and amusingly in the epilogue to *The Rivals*, spoken by the popular actress, Mrs. Bulkley:

> Ladies, for you—I heard our poet say—
> He'd try to coax some moral from his play:
> "One moral's plain," cried I, "without more fuss;
> Man's social happiness all rests on us. . . ."

Almost no eighteenth-century play was complete without both prologue and epilogue—written in verse, and delivered by a member of the cast—in which the playwright sought more often to instruct or to preach than to amuse. *St. Patrick's Day* had neither prologue nor epilogue, for Sheridan was no moralist; he did not find it necessary to sermonize. But in an offhand way, and in crackling dialogue, he managed to satirize the law in the figure of a prejudiced judge; medicine, in the guise of a vapid practitioner; the army, with its hit-and-miss recruitment system and starvation wages; and the trials of marriage, in a carping wife and a nubile, headstrong daughter.

St. Patrick's Day or, The Scheming Lieutenant was first published in a pirated edition in Dublin in 1788 and, though it is less familiar than Sheridan's "classic" comedies, *The Rivals* and *The School for Scandal*, has since been performed with great success on numerous occasions in various countries. Its chief drawback for professional production is its length; it is too long for a curtain-raiser, and too short for a full evening. It works ideally, however, on radio and television, and for dramatic clubs and groups, particularly in schools and colleges. In 1972, Harold Hobson, drama critic for the London *Sunday Times*, said of the play's most recent revival: "The Soho-Poly Lunchtime Theatre has revived Sheridan's *Scheming Lieutenant* with wit and finesse in a production by Frederick Proud."

PRODUCTION IN THE EIGHTEENTH-CENTURY THEATER

It is necessary to understand the change in man's thinking from the seventeenth century to our own in order to see how the drama has reflected it step by step.

The simple religious faith which had been the basis of the drama in the medieval period had sustained it through its flowering in the Renaissance. But during the reign of Charles I the Puritans, who were religious fanatics, rose to power under Oliver Cromwell, and in their zeal closed all the public theatres in 1642. They remained closed during the Commonwealth.

With the restoration of the British monarchy in 1660 under Charles II, theater activity in England started up once more. Life at Court was a coarse replica of that at pleasure-loving Versailles, and Charles lost no time in issuing licenses to Thomas Killigrew and William D'Avenant for the formation of new acting companies. A magnificent theater was built for each of these men. D'Avenant's house, Lincoln's Inn Fields, whose license later passed to Covent Garden, specialized in musical productions—opera, ballet, and musicalized versions of Shakespeare; while the Theatre Royal, Drury Lane, which was run by Killigrew, introduced the work of the new Restoration playwrights. The plays of the period were divided between cynical, witty, and immoral comedies of manners, and a long succession of bombastic and false heroic tragedies.

By the middle years of the eighteenth century, religious fervor had died out, and many were turning away from faith and relying instead upon the mind for guidance in worldly affairs. Reason and logic were valued above everything else. Men now came to believe that all human difficulties could be alleviated, if not completely eliminated, by the proper use of the intellect. The Age of Reason began in high spirits and the greatest optimism.

Under the influence of the Deists, men started to put their minds to work on social and economic problems and to take a special interest in the downtrodden, the exploited, and the poverty-stricken. This ushered in a procession of sentimental comedies and middle-class tragedies; these plays were highly moral, superficial, and didactic. Almost as an antidote to them there suddenly appeared, early in the eighteenth century, a great number of revivals and of adaptations, parodies, and burlesques—all filled with music, song, and dance; theatergoers, apparently, were now more interested in lively and spectacular entertainments than in uplifting dramas.

The Theater

The new theaters of the Restoration (1660-1700) did not resemble the old Elizabethan open-air playhouses that had been shut down eighteen years before.

Interior of Drury Lane Theatre, 1775. On May 2 of that year, *St. Patrick's Day* was performed there for the first time. In later years the theater was renovated and enlarged several times. (New York Public Library)

They were modeled instead on the opera houses of the Italian Renaissance, which were being imitated all over Europe and, later, in America. They also furnished the design for the eighteenth-century theater building, a structure with which we are still familiar.

Constructed of brick and faced with stone or plaster, the theater is two or more stories high. It is entered from the street, and the entryway is often decorated with sculptured figures, tall columns, or other architectural ornaments. The lobbies and foyers may be gilded, mirrored, and carpeted to appeal to the desire of the public for luxury. The entrance to the stage is at the back of the house, usually at the end of a dim passageway leading into a maze of stairways, stage scenery and machinery. The contrast between the gilt and brocades in the foyer and the beams and ropes backstage dramatizes the difference between illusion and reality.

The interior of the theater is shaped roughly like a horseshoe and is divided into two main parts, the auditorium and the stage. In the seventeenth and eighteenth centuries, balconies rose in tiers—sometimes as many as six in height—around the walls of the auditorium. These balconies were divided into private boxes, little cubicles reserved for the use of the royal family, the members of the nobility, and the upper classes. They were the most expensive seats in the house.

The seats in the orchestra, called "the pit," were less expensive and were occupied by members of the middle class. The working class, including servants, sat on benches in the cheapest location, above the boxes and just under the roof, in an undivided area called the gallery.

The stage of the traditional theater is separated from the auditorium by a proscenium arch, in which the front curtain hangs. The stage setting fills the entire proscenium opening. In the older theaters the set took up almost all the backstage area; and in the eighteenth-century buildings it was practically impossible to walk around behind the set as the wings and drops were close to the walls of the house. Toward the end of the century, when the backstage area was enlarged, it was filled with revolving and rolling platforms, as well as mechanical and lighting equipment. The stage floor had trap doors for special theatrical effects, and beneath the stage there might be rehearsal rooms, the wardrobe, and storage space. Above the stage, and behind the proscenium arch, was a space in which scenery and large properties were hung, and raised or lowered by means of a counterweight system, worked by hand. The actors' dressing rooms were ranged along corridors on various levels backstage.

Theater Management

The celebrated actor Colley Cibber, who was also a playwright, and co-manager of Drury Lane after 1710, complained of the long hours and arduous duties required of him. The theater manager, according to Cibber, had to read every play offered for production, though not one in twenty was worth presenting, and he had to deal with the authors of such plays. Then for two or three hours every morning he had to attend rehearsals of plays and other entertainments that were being readied for the stage; and be present at the performances every evening. He had to help choose the costumes for the actors, and to order them. There were about one hundred and fifty persons in his employ—actors, singers, dancers, painters, machinists, door-keepers, servants and officers—all of whom had to be kept in good temper and watched with care lest they neglect their duty and defraud the management.

Profits from theatrical production were not large, so every penny had to be watched. The "officers" at each performance counted the people in the house and checked the number against the cash in the box-office. The manager paid all the bills and kept the money left over. There was an extra income at the end of each season from the sale of the costumes, the candle ends, and the fruit and candy concessions. When David Garrick managed Drury Lane, he was considered parsimonious, because he paid attention to the smallest details; the collection of candle ends, for instance, became part of the housekeeper's salary. Garrick retired a wealthy man, all his bills paid. Sheridan, who followed Garrick in the management of Drury Lane, was known for his extravagance; he thought more of his political campaigns than of candle ends, and was often in debt to the actors and other employees at the theatre.

As the population and the interest in entertainment continued to grow during the eighteenth century, the playhouses in London, several times destroyed by fire, were always enlarged when rebuilt; and the government was forced to issue licenses for the building of theaters in other cities, among them Bath, Bristol, Birmingham, Liverpool, and Manchester, all of which supported excellent acting companies.

The Actors

The appearance of women on the Restoration stage had a significant effect on the actors' art, particularly in those scenes in which both sexes were involved. When boys had played the female parts—a convention that existed until the closing of the theaters in 1642—the love scenes had been more or less formal and stylized. With women on the stage, these scenes became more physical, sensual, and realistic. Realism, as we understand it, however, was unknown, and acting continued to be exaggerated and artificial for the next two centuries. When a performer was required to fall to the floor, a stagehand would suddenly appear and spread a cloth to keep the actor's costume from being soiled; and when a player completed an especially showy speech or scene, he was applauded, as are our opera singers today.

In the eighteenth century there was no dearth of theories concerning the relative merits of nature and art in acting. The great controversy then arose, and still goes on, as to whether actors should feel the emotions they portray or simply feign them. In a pamphlet titled *The Paradox of Acting*, Denis Diderot, the French philosopher and critic, spoke out strongly for external acting and the *imitation* of emotion. The opposite view was expressed by many theorists and actors in England. In his book *The Actor* (1750), John Hill objected to "imitation" as a mechanical art and recommended that the performer rely on his own feelings. Later in the century, John Walker, in a volume called *Elements of Elocution* (1781), foreshadowed Stanislavsky in urging the actor to use his own experience to arouse emotion. Walker wrote:

> Calling to mind such passages of our own life as are similar to those we read or speak of, will, if I am not mistaken, considerably assist us in gaining that fervour and warmth of expression, which, by a certain sympathy, is sure to affect those who hear us.

Among the stars on the English stage, there were advocates and practitioners of both the external and internal styles of acting. James Quin, a member of the former school, always spoke in deep sing-song tones with no variation of cadence, accompanied by a sawing kind of gesture, with stilted and artificial movements of his body. He excelled in such Shakespearean rôles as Brutus and King John. Thomas Sheridan, the playwright's father, is said to have performed, like Quin, in a stiff and pedantic manner. One critic said of his Macbeth, "Then the cold Sheridan half froze the part."

Another set of players, commencing with Charles Macklin, understood the importance of good diction, but aimed at a natural rather than a mannered style. An exponent of naturalism long before the term came into use, Macklin believed that the actor should completely identify with the character and feel his emotions.

Macklin trained young players, and described his system in *The Art and Duty of an Actor*. David Garrick, a friend of Macklin and possibly influenced by him, was the outstanding exponent of naturalistic acting in the eighteenth century. He avoided ranting, starts, and attitudes and communicated feeling by subtle tones of voice, telling looks, and emphatic gestures. No actor was more highly praised for his ability to arouse strong responses from the audience. In his last season at Drury Lane, he introduced into his company a provincial actress named Sarah Siddons. With her brother, John Philip Kemble, she dominated the stage in the last decades of the century and imposed new standards of simplicity and feeling upon acting.

Throughout the century, actors and actresses, as well as other workers in the theater, counted on a "benefit night" to augment their salaries. On this special night, in addition to the general public, personal friends and "fans" of the actor attended, and frequently gave him large gifts. Great hostesses would pay several hundred pounds for benefit boxes and were waited on by the principal actor or

A playbill issued by the Theatre Royal, Covent Garden, announcing for Thursday, March 17, 1831, a revival of *St. Patrick's Day* to be presented on a triple bill with *The Stranger* and *The Irishman in London*. (Theatre Collection/Victoria and Albert Museum)

actress. A proportion of the proceeds from the sale of tickets went to the management, but a smaller share might be taken. Sheridan not only wrote *St. Patrick's Day* for Clinch's benefit night, but allowed the actor to keep the major share of the profits.

One annoying convention of the period was that of allowing spectators to sit on the stage during the performance, particularly on benefit nights, when the auditorium was jammed. This increased the income of the actor, but also interfered with his playing, as many fops paraded around the stage just to show off their fine clothes. Thomas Sheridan had tried to drive the audience from the stage of the Smock Alley Theatre, Dublin, but they got rid of him instead. David Garrick was determined to clear the stage of viewers, but met with opposition from the actors, who feared a loss of income; a compromise was reached when Garrick agreed to increase the seating capacity of the auditorium, and the actors gave their approval for the removal of the troublesome spectators.

Direction

The theatrical director, as we know him today, first made his appearance less than a hundred years ago. Before that time the task of coordinating the various elements of a production was left to the playwright, the star, or a stage manager. There was no actual need for a director—the very title was unknown—in the Greek, medieval, Elizabethan, or neoclassical theater, in each of which dramatic presentations had more or less fixed forms, established by traditions that the actors observed and the audiences recognized.

The indoor playhouse had brought with it the picture-frame stage, on which the leading actor took over the pictorial arrangements, placing himself in the foreground center. The other actors learned their lines and the moves they would be required to make, and the production would remain unchanged over a long span of years. Rehearsals of revivals of familiar plays could safely be reduced, therefore, to a few run-throughs of the important scenes. Actors tended to rehearse by themselves, relying on stock attitudes and gestures, with no attempt to achieve unity of style or effect. General rehearsals concerned themselves with entrances, exists, and tableaux. The only unity in the production was supplied by the imposing personality of such stars as Thomas Betterton, Colley Cibber, James Quin, and John Philip Kemble, who drew attention entirely to themselves.

Some attempts were made in the eighteenth century to achieve more realistic effects in acting, costuming, and scenery and to integrate these arts in a unified production. Richard Brinsley Sheridan paid particular attention to the staging of his play, *The Camp*, which took place at a military establishment for army recruits. The scenery was painted by the brilliant Philippe Jacques de Loutherbourg, the backdrop depicting the site of an actual camp at Coxheath; the soldiers wore authentic uniforms; and when the drill sergeant gave intelligible commands, Sheridan stopped him and said, "That won't do at all, Mr. Bannister; it is very unsoldierlike—you speak to be understood; they never do that on the parade."

The most notable steps in the direction of a unified, realistic production—

though they did not proceed very far—were taken by Claire Hippolyte Clairon and Henri-Louis LeKain in France, Konrad Ekhof and Friedrich Schroeder in Germany, and Charles Macklin and David Garrick in England. These influential actors, most of whom were also managers, insisted upon the careful casting of minor parts, adequate readings and rehearsals, less posturing and declamation in the acting, and appropriate sets and costumes.

Scenery

Scenery in the modern sense of the word began to be used only after the withdrawal of the stage behind the proscenium; that is to say, in the time of the later Renaissance in Europe generally, and of the Restoration in England.

The painters of the Renaissance discovered the laws of perspective, and stage designers soon put them to use to create the illusion of space, size, and distance in the limited area at their disposal. The Restoration stage was two or three times the size of the auditorium (these proportions were reversed in the eighteenth century) and, framed by a proscenium arch, lent itself admirably to pictorial treatment. When the curtain went up, the audience was delighted by an eye-filling scene depicting a castle in the midst of a forest, a fleet of ships at sea, a town square, or whatever locale was called for by the text. These pictures were created by the use of "wing-and-drop" scenery.

The stage floor sloped up from the footlights to the rear wall and was covered with a green baize cloth. On either side of the stage and parallel to each other were six rows of side wings (painted flats of canvas stretched over wooden frames). These flats, representing buildings or trees rendered in perspective, diminished in size and converged toward each other as they neared the backdrop (a painted cloth that completed the stage picture), the wings and drop forming a visual unit. Two additional wings downstage, called shutters, could be brought together in the center to hide the changes of scene, though the scenery was often changed in full view of the audience to the accompaniment of music. This could be done very quickly as the wings ran on tracks and one set could be pulled in while another was being pushed out; or the wings formed three sides of a pyramid, which revolved on a central axis, and merely had to be turned; the drops meanwhile were raised and lowered from the flies. These sudden transformations gave the audience great pleasure.

Painted flats and cloths gradually replaced all solidly built scenery, though scene-painters themselves admitted that a painted representation could never achieve the realism of an architectural column or cornice. The interior of a castle, nevertheless, was painted in detail complete with paneled walls, mullioned windows, stags' antlers, and coats of arms, while the interiors of humbler homes showed rough plaster walls, bare tables, rickety chairs, and pots and pans around the hearth.

During the eighteenth century the size of the auditorium increased at the expense of the stage. Its shallowness forced the actor to stand closer to the painted drops, which showed up the false perspective and destroyed all illusion of reality. In the meantime, however, while painted scenery was still in vogue, members of the Bibiena family and other designers were creating scenes of such complexity and grandeur as to fill us to this day with admiration and wonder. But tentative efforts were being made to improve the stage picture by providing more authentic visual settings. To begin with, the privileged spectators who had for over a century been allowed to sit on the stage during the performance were driven off in order to increase the plausibility of the scene within the picture frame.

Garrick's stage designer, de Loutherbourgh, provided several scenic innovations. One was the introduction of "ground rows," which represented low walls, rocks, or distant mountains and could be placed anywhere on stage; another, the beginning of local color, was the reproduction of actual locales, which were familiar to the audience. Although backdrops were painted in minute detail, actual stage furnishings were rather meager, consisting simply of a bed, a table and chair, or a royal throne.

The scene designer, possibly as a result of de Loutherbourgh's influence, achieved a prominent place in the theater, but was nowhere so important as at Covent Garden, which specialized in the production of opera, ballet, pantomime, and other spectacles. Robert Clerici, one of Ferdinando Bibiena's pupils, and Giovanni Servandoni were outstanding among the many English designers, who provided eye-filling and breath-taking scenery for the productions at Covent Garden. Chariots, dragons, clouds, and witches on broomsticks all floated, flew, or rolled across the stage in continuous action, as scenes changed with amazing rapidity, worked by the ingenious machines invented by the designers. As the century wore on, theatergoers began to lose interest in the sentimental comedies and heroic tragedies then being offered as artistic dramatic fare, and flocked to the spectacular entertainments which Alexander Pope ridiculed in The Dunciad (1743):

> All sudden, Gorgons hiss, and Dragons glare,
> And ten horn'd fiends and Giants rush to war.
> Hell rises, Heav'n descends, and dance on Earth:
> Gods, imps, and monsters, music, rage and mirth,
> A fire, a jigg, a battle, and a ball,
> Till one wide conflagration swallows all.

The inventive skill of the scene designer, nevertheless, produced many technical advances not the least of which were improvements in lighting the stage.

Lighting

Lighting the stage of an indoor theater presented a problem in the seventeenth century because candles were the only source of illumination, though for special optical effects they burned various substances, such as moss, and set off fireworks. Candles, even in large quantities, did not shed much light, nor could the light be altered to suit a particular scene. Large chandeliers, containing hundreds of wax tapers, were suspended over the stage and auditorium and burned throughout the performance. Candles in tin sconces served as footlights, and sconces were also attached to the backs of the side wings to light the painted drop at the rear of the stage. Actors performed downstage, close to the footlights, so that their faces could be clearly seen. Lanterns directed from offstage, like primitive spotlights, cast a bit of extra light on certain characters and acting areas. Undoubtedly, there was more smoke, smell, and heat than light. The Restoration comedies, whose texts are so brilliant and glittering, were performed in a rather dim and flickering atmosphere.

By the eighteenth century, stage lighting was somewhat improved by the use of oil lamps, which could be controlled to a certain extent and enabled the designer to show changes in the time of day and in the weather, and to create such special effects as fire and storm. De Loutherbourgh was fascinated by lighting effects, and experimented with them in his model theater, the Eidophusikon. He used the Argand lamp for the first time, which gave a much more brilliant light than candles and oil lamps. At Drury Lane, he placed a row of lamps behind the proscenium, and by using various filters such as stained glass, colored silk, and oiled paper, was able to tint the scenes from above and in front, and show gradually changing light from cool dawn to glaring noon and ruddy sunset, with mists and moving clouds. Similar effects more precisely produced had to wait the coming of gas and electric light.

Costumes

From 1660 to about 1850, theatrical costumes were neither accurate nor consistent, so far as the period of the play or the individuality of the character was concerned. Each production showed a welter of styles in dress, which depended on the wardrobe of the performer or on a theatrical tradition. The actor usually wore the fashionable clothes of his own day; in the Restoration, for instance, Thomas Betterton played Hamlet in frilled lace, full-bottomed wig, and petticoat breeches, while in the eighteenth century David Garrick acted the rôle in the smallclothes of his day. Female performers, like their male counterparts, were generally attired in the height of current fashion; for almost two centuries women's dresses showed a number of variations of low-cut necklines, full sleeves, and narrow waists, though the silhouette of the skirt went from broad panniers to straight shift to huge hoops.

In addition to contemporary fashions, there were some conventional costumes, inherited from the Elizabethan theater, for warriors, for Orientals, and for other types. The actor impersonating a soldier, of whatever time or place, wore a fanciful costume that resembled a Roman military uniform, consisting of a tunic, breastplate, plumed helmet, high cross-gartered boots, and a shield, spear, or sword to complete the outfit. The costume for Orientals was distinguished by full pantaloons secured at the ankles and worn by both men and women, with a long robe, a plumed turban, and a scimitar or dagger for the actor, and an overskirt, an elaborate commode headdress, and flying streamers, for the actress. For Shakespearean rôles the actor sometimes wore approximations to the doublet and hose.

Acting companies continued well into the eighteenth century to follow the Elizabethan custom of using the cast-off clothing of members of the aristocracy though it did not always answer their needs. Eventually they bought their costumes or hired seamstresses to make them. Stage clothing was well constructed of the richest materials, sometimes trimmed with genuine silver and gold, and always in the latest style. The costumes were often very costly; the women's wardrobe at Covent Garden in 1769 was valued at almost three thousand pounds, and the men's clothing at only slightly less. Managers complained bitterly of the expense, but knew that the elegant upper classes were attracted to the theater as to a fashion show and expected to see a display of sumptuous costumes. The audience was not disturbed by historical inaccuracy, nor were the most serious and dedicated performers. But both John and Aaron Hill, and several other critics, suggested frequently that actors be attired in more authentic and appropriate clothing. The eighteenth century, however, saw no revolutionary improvement in stage costume.

Music and Dance

Beginning in the seventeenth century, incidental music and dance interludes were thrust into plays for no dramatic or logical reason except that they gave pleasure to the audience. William D'Avenant, the famous Restoration playwright and theater manager, staged *Macbeth* "with alterations, amendments, additions, and new songs and divertissement [short ballets or dance numbers]," which grew more elaborate from year to year until Shakespeare's play resembled a patchwork opera.

The custom of interpolating music and dance numbers into serious plays, with total disregard for their relevance, continued and grew in the eighteenth century. In 1747, Charles Macklin, who was celebrated for portraying Shylock as a serious, almost tragic, figure, did not hesitate, however, to offer a spectacular dance interlude, performed by the ballet stars of the day, in the midst of his production of *The Merchant of Venice*. The sentimental comedies and domestic tragedies then in vogue gave pleasure to their audiences by reducing them to tears, and counted heavily on incidental music of a melancholy kind to achieve the desired effect.

Early in the eighteenth century, Italian opera became a fashionable entertainment among the members of the English nobility; but the mass of the population scorned it for several reasons: it was sung in a foreign language, the singers were "Papists," and excessively high fees were paid to the celebrated *castrati* (men who sang in the female range). Audiences wanted operas in English sung by native singers, and English writers responded by creating so-called ballad operas, which resembled musical comedies. These works were satirical and farcical; in their complicated plots, the writer attacked Italian opera, fashionable society, and politics. The clever and charming lyrics were integrated with the story and dialogue, but the music was borrowed mainly from the popular tunes of the day.

The three most successful ballad operas were *The Beggar's Opera* (1728) by John Gay, *Love in a Village* (1762) by Isaac Bickerstaff, and *The Duenna* (1774) by Richard Brinsley Sheridan. *The Duenna* contained thirty-three songs for solo, duet, trio, and chorus, many of them composed by Thomas Linley, Sheridan's father-in-law, who also coached the singers and conducted the orchestra; but most of the songs were based on well-known tunes by other composers. At the end of Act II of *The Duenna*, there was offered "a new Spanish Dance by Signor and Signora Zucelli, Mr. Dagueville, Signora Vidini, etc"; it was given fourteen performances, then dropped.

Signor and Signora Zucelli, and many other French and Italian dancers, appeared in ballets, burlesques, and pantomimes, as well as between the acts and at the end of serious plays, and, as their art did not depend upon language, found acceptance with London audiences. Comic opera and comic dances were preferred to the more serious types of entertainment offered in the eighteenth century.

Audience and Playwright

John Dryden, the foremost poet, critic, and dramatist of the Restoration, asserting that "the drama's laws the drama's patrons give," recognized the importance of the audience and its influence on the playwright. The Restoration audience was a privileged group: aristocratic, wealthy, sophisticated, and pleasure-seeking. The witty, sexual comedies of such writers as Etherege, Congreve, Wycherley, and Dryden projected the audience's hedonistic views and lampooned its manners; and in the bombastic heroic tragedies, such as Nathaniel Lee's *The Rival Queens* and Thomas Otway's *Venice Preserved*, whose ostensible purpose was to instruct and elevate, there were great, declamatory parts for the performers and spine-tingling moments for the audience. In both comedy and tragedy, the Restoration playwright lost no opportunity to point an irreverent finger at cracks in the structure of the Establishment, for his new audience had a strong taste for social, political, and ecclesiastical satire.

The eighteenth century saw a growing interest in the theater among all classes of society, but it was the prosperous merchants who mainly filled the playhouses, and their middle-class morality dictated the taste and types in plays, which ran to sentimental comedies and domestic tragedies. Examples of the first genre may be found in Richard Steele's *The Consicous Lovers* and Hugh Kelly's *False Delicacy*; and of the second in George Lillo's *The London Merchant* and Edward Moore's *The Gamester*. Heroic tragedy had become by now only a subject for burlesque, as in Henry Fielding's *Tragedy of Tragedies; or, The Life and Death of Tom Thumb the Great*. The very concepts of "heroism" and "tragedy" seemed ridiculous, until revived in the romantic plays and melodramas of the next century.

At the patent theaters (those licensed by the Crown, such as Drury Lane and Covent Garden), a different program was presented every night of the week, so there were frequent repetitions of standard plays. Like modern operagoers, eighteenth-century audiences saw the same works again and again, with different after-pieces (short comedies), and different casts, and thus became expert at judging acting techniques. They often complained, however, that not enough new works were presented.

Playwrights had the same complaint; it was difficult to get a play produced. When a script was accepted, it was often because the manager saw in it a good part for himself, or could revise the play to furnish one. The play became the property of the company, but the author received the takings (less expenses) from the third, sixth, and ninth performances of his play, and could count on one hundred pounds for the publication rights.

In the large patent houses, the admission charges were one shilling for the upper gallery, two shillings for the gallery, three for the pit, and five for the boxes. Performances began at six or six-thirty, but the doors were open much earlier for those who wanted choice seats, as seats were not reserved. Footmen were often sent to keep places for their masters. Tradespeople, the professional classes, and the aristocracy had their preferred locations, but there were no hard and fast rules. Prostitutes and pickpockets favored those sections where the crowds were greatest, usually in the galleries.

The playgoer was extremely responsive and often unruly, laughing and applauding appreciatively, or hissing and pelting the actors with sucked oranges and apple cores when displeased. Such was the harsh treatment accorded John Lee on the opening night of *St. Patrick's Day*. Angry audiences went even further in expressing their displeasure at plays, players, or management, and did not hesitate to create disturbances in the theater, or to resort to such riotous behavior as tearing up benches, smashing scenery and chandeliers, and attempting to burn the house down. Whether or not what they demanded was proper or wise, in the long run the audience had its way.

A REVIEW OF A REVIVAL
London Times, August 1, 1938

Canterbury, July 31. (From our special correspondent)

Cricket Week in Canterbury opened yesterday with streets festooned, bright batting, and a bright, even ostentatious, sun; and after dark . . . the Old Stagers took to the boards again in a triple bill of appropriate colour and variety. . . . We had a peep at the theatrical history of three centuries—very proper in the oldest company of amateurs in the Empire. So Sheridan dropped in with a laugh from a vanished Covent Garden—a young and unpolitical Sheridan . . . and gilded amateurs gave us the jolliest of entertainments.

St. Patrick's Day is unmistakably a farce written by a wit. It has the right air of impromptu, as though it had indeed been dashed off before the author could tire of his own laughter; but the laughter has passed into the speeches, and only a voice is needed to bring to life the brilliant nonsense left over from Georgian supper-talk. "Hic jacet many years one of His Majesty's justices," moans Justice Credulous, when the last of the Lieutenant's schemes is in train, and prefers to expire rather than be saved by a quack.* But naturally it is marriage with Miss Credulous, not murder, that O'Connor desires. For this he masquerades as a bumpkin of a bodyguard presented to Credulous by Dr. Rosy, who is in on the young man's secret, cudgels his own recruiting men in the streets, and affably informs poor Credulous that his morning chocolate holds poison. It is a part that requires high spirits, and Mr. Humphrey Tilling [as Lt. O'Connor] gaily exchanges a smock for a quack's engaging patter, beats his soldiers' heads as soundly as if they were fast balls sent down the St. Lawrence [cricket] ground, and with a devilish innocence induced Lieutenant-Colonel Hawkes to reveal the Sergeant's grand pretentions.

* That was the advice of Mrs. Credulous; the critic is in error here.—*Ed.*

Mr. Ralph Alderson has a very good manner for Credulous, whose grim and testy outside covers a very passable heart; his quarrels with Lady Crutchley show that there is the best possible understanding between the Credulous parents, and his way with such lines as "I shall burst and no assistance" is superb. But the character who charms us is Rosy, whose departed spouse was a model of medical endowments and pharmaceutical accomplishment, and who can never recall her without tears, and if Major Clarke-Jervoise gives him the appearance of a real, and far more formidable, doctor, the incongruity is quite as charming.

St. Patrick's Day, or The Scheming Lieutenant

DRAMATIS PERSONAE

CORPORAL FLINT

SERGEANT TROUNCE

LIEUTENANT O'CONNOR

DOCTOR ROSY

LAURETTA

MRS. BRIDGET CREDULOUS

JUSTICE CREDULOUS

JOHN
SUSAN } SERVANTS

SOLDIERS, COUNTRYMEN, DRUMMER

SCENE.—A Town in England

ACT ONE

SCENE ONE

A STREET NEAR
JUSTICE CREDULOUS' HOUSE

(*Enter* SERGEANT TROUNCE, CORPORAL FLINT, *and four* SOLDIERS, *with shamrocks in their hats.*)

1st Soldier. I say you're wrong. We should all speak together, each for himself, and all at once, that we may be heard the better.

2nd Soldier. Right, Jack, we'll argue in platoons.

3rd Soldier. Ay, ay, let him have our grievances in a volley, or if we be to have a spokesman, there's our corporal is the lieutenant's countryman, and knows his humor.

Corporal. Let me alone for that. I served three years within a little bit, under his honour, in the Royal Inniskillins, and I never will see a sweeter-tempered officer, nor one more free with his purse. I put a great shamrock in his hat this morning, and I'll be bound for him he'll wear it, if it was as big as Stephen's Green.

4th Soldier. I say again then, you talk like youngsters, like militia striplings. There's a discipline, look'ee, in all things, whereof the sergeant must be our guide. He's a gentleman of words, he understands your foreign lingo; your figures, and such like auxiliaries in scoring. Confess now, for a reckoning, whether in chalk or writing, ben't he your only man?

Corporal. Why the sergeant is a scholar to be sure, and has the gift of reading.

Sergeant. Good soldiers, and fellow gentlemen, if you make me your spokesman, you will show the more judgment; and let me alone for the argument. I'll be as loud as a drum, and point blank from the purpose.

All. Agreed, agreed.

Corporal. Oh, faith, here comes the lieutenant. Now, Sergeant.

Sergeant. So then, to order. Put on your mutiny looks. Let every man grumble a little to himself, and some of you hum the Deserter's March.

(*Enter* LIEUTENANT O'CONNOR.)

O'Connor. Well, honest lads, what is it you have to complain of?

Soldiers. Ahem! Hem! Hem!

4th Soldier (*Aside*). There, damme, did you ever hear a better hem to begin with? The lieutenant is staggered already!

Sergeant. So please your honour, the grievance of the matter is this: Ever since your honour has differed with Justice Credulous here, our inn-keepers use us most scurvily. By my halbert, their treatment is such, that if your spirit was willing to put up with it, flesh and blood could by no means agree. So we humbly petition that your honour would make an end of the matter at once, by running away with the Justice's daughter, or else get us fresh quarters—Hem, hem!

O'Connor. Indeed! Pray which of the houses use you ill?

1st Soldier. There's the Red Lion ha'n't half the civility as the old Red Lion had.

2nd Soldier. Ay, and there's the White Horse, if he wasn't case hardened, ought to be ashamed to show his face.

O'Connor. Very well, the Horse and the Lion shall answer for it at the Quarter Sessions.

Sergeant. The Two Magpies are civil enough, but the Angel uses us like devils, and the Rising Sun refuses us light to go to bed by.

O'Connor. Indeed! Then, upon my word, I'll have the Rising Sun put down, and the Angel shall give security for his good behaviour. But are you sure you do nothing to quit scores with them?

Corporal. Nothing at all, your honour, unless now and then we happen to fling a cartridge into the kitchen fire, or put a spatterdash or so into the soup . . . and sometimes Ned drums a little up and down stairs of a night.

O'Connor. Oh, all that's fair. But hark'ee, lads, I must have no grumbling on St. Patrick's Day; so here, take this, and divide it amongst you. But observe me now: Show yourselves men of spirit, and don't spend a sixpence of it in drink.

Sergeant. Nay, hang it, your honour, soldiers should never bear malice. We must drink St. Patrick and your honour's health.

All. Oh, damn malice! St. Patrick and his honour, by all means.

Corporal. Come away, then, lads, and first we'll parade round the Market Cross, for the honour of King George.

All. Thank your honour! Come along. St. Patrick, his honour, and strong beer for ever!

(*Exeunt all but the* LIEUTENTANT.)

O'Connor. Get along you thoughtless vagabonds! Yet, upon my conscience, 'tis very hard these poor fellows should scarcely have bread from the soil they would die to defend.

(*Enter* DOCTOR ROSY.)

Ah, my little Doctor Rosy, my Galen abridged, what's the news?

Rosy. All things are as they were, my Alexander, the Justice is as violent as ever. I felt his pulse on the matter again, and, thinking his rage began to intermit, I wanted to throw in the bark of good advice, but it would not do. He says you and your cut-throats have a plot upon his life, and swears he had rather see his daughter in a scarlet fever than in the arms of a soldier.

O'Connor. Upon my word, the army is very much obliged to him. Well, then, I must marry the girl first, and ask his consent afterwards.

Rosy. So, then, the case of her fortune is desperate, that's given over, hey?

O'Connor. Oh, hang the fortune, let that take its chance. There is a beauty in Lauretta's manner, so pure a bloom upon her charms, something so interesting in her simplicity . . .

Rosy. So there is, so there is. I understand you. You are for loveliness as nature made her, hey? No artificial graces, no cosmetic varnish, no beauty in grain, hey, Lieutenant?

O'Connor. Upon my word, Doctor, you're right. The London ladies were always too handsome for me; then they are so defended, such a circumvallation of hoop, with a breastwork of whalebone, that would turn a pistol bullet, much less Cupid's arrows; then turret on turret on top, with store of concealed weapons, under pretense of black pins, and above all, a standard of feathers that would do honour to a Knight of the Bath. Upon my conscience, I could as soon embrace an Amazon, armed at all points.

Rosy. Right, right, my Alexander! My taste to a tittle.

O'Connor. Then, Doctor, though I admire modesty in women, I like to see their faces. I'm for the changeable rose; but with one of these quality Amazons, if their midnight dissipations had left them blood enough to raise a blush, they haven't room on their cheeks to show it. To be sure, bashfulness is a very pretty thing, but in my mind, there is nothing on earth so impudent as an everlasting blush.

Rosy. My taste, my taste, Lieutenant! Well, Lauretta is none of these. Ah, I never see her but she reminds me of my poor dear wife.

O'Connor. Ay, faith, and in my opinion she can't do a worse thing. (*Aside.*) Now he's going to bother me about an old fat hag, who has been dead these six years.

Rosy. Ah, poor Dolly! I never shall see her like again! Such an arm for a bandage . . . veins that seemed to invite the lancet; then her skin, smooth and white as a gallipot; her mouth, round and not larger than the mouth of a penny phial. Her lips, conserve of roses! Then her teeth—none of your sturdy fixtures—ache as they would, 'twas but a pull and out they came. I believe I've drawn half a score of her poor dear pearls . . . (*Weeps.*) But what avails her beauty? Death has no consideration —one must die as well as another.

O'Connor. (*Aside.*) Oh, if he begins to moralize . . . (*Takes out his snuff box.*)

Rosy. Fair or ugly . . . crooked or straight . . . rich or poor . . flesh is grass . . . flowers fade!

O'Connor. Here, Doctor, take a pinch, and keep up your spirits.

Rosy. True, true, my friend, grief can't mend the matter. All's for the best, but such a woman was a great loss, Lieutenant.

O'Connor. To be sure, for doubtless she had mental accomplishments equal to her beauty.

Rosy. Mental accomplishments! She could have stuffed an alligator, or pickled a lizard, with any apothecary's wife in the kingdom! Why, she could decipher a prescription, and invent the ingredients almost as well as myself. Then she was such a hand at making foreign waters! For Seltzer, Pyrmont, Islington, or Chalybeate, she never had her equal; and her Bath and Bristol springs exceeded the originals. King Bladud never dipped his toe in better. Ah. poor Dolly! She fell a martyr to her own discoveries.

O'Connor. How so, pray?

Rosy. Poor soul, her illness was all occasioned by her zeal in trying an improvement of her spa water by an infusion of rum and acid.

O'Connor. Ay, ay, spirits never agree with water drinkers.

Rosy. No, no, you mistake. The rum agreed with her well enough; 'twas the water that killed the dear creature, for she died of a dropsy. Well, she's gone, never to return, and has left no pledge of our loves behind, no little baby, to hang like a label round papa's neck. Well, we're all mortal . . . sooner or later . . . flesh is grass . . . flowers fade!

O'Connor (*Aside*). Oh, the devil! Again.

Rosy. Life's a shadow! The world's a stage! We strut an hour—

O'Connor. (*Offers snuff*). Here, Doctor.

Rosy. True, true, my friend. Well, grief can't mend it. All's for the best, hey, my Alexander!

O'Connor. Right, right! An apothecary should never be out of spirits. But come, faith, 'tis time honest Humphrey should wait on the Justice; that must be our first scheme.

Rosy. True, true. You should be ready. The clothes are at my house, and I have given you such a character, that he is impatient to have you. He swears you shall be his bodyguard. Well, I honour the army, or I should never do so much to serve you.

O'Connor. Indeed I'm bound to you forever, Doctor, and when once I'm possessed of my dear Lauretta, I'll endeavour to make work for you as fast as possible.

Rosy. Now you put me in mind of my poor wife again.

O'Connor. Ah, pray forget her a little. Faith, we shall be too late.

Rosy. Poor Dolly!

O'Connor. 'Tis past twelve.

Rosy. Inhuman dropsy!

O'Connor. The Justice will wait.

Rosy. Cropped in her prime.

O'Connor. For heaven's sake, come!

Rosy. Well, flesh is grass.

O'Connor. Oh, the Devil!

Rosy. We must all die—

O'Connor. Doctor, come along!

Rosy. Kings, lords, and common whores . . .

(*Exeunt,* O'CONNOR *forcing* ROSY *off*)

SCENE TWO

A ROOM IN
JUSTICE CREDULOUS' HOUSE

(*Enter* LAURETTA *and* MRS. BRIDGET CREDULOUS.)

Lauretta. I repeat it again, Mama, officers are the prettiest men in the world, and Lieutenant O'Connor is the prettiest officer I ever saw.

Mrs. Credulous. For shame, Laury, how can you talk so? Or if you must have a military man, there's Lieutenant Plough, or Captain Haycock, or Major Dray, the brewer, are all your admirers; and though they are peaceable, good kind of men, they have as large cockades, and become scarlet, as well as the fighting folks.

Lauretta. Psha! Mama! You know I hate the militia. Officers indeed! A set of dunghill cocks with spurs on; heroes scratched off a church door; clowns in military masquerade, wearing the dress without supporting the character. No, give me the bold, upright youth, who makes love one day, and has his head shot off the next. Dear! to think how the sweet fellows sleep on the ground, and fight in silk stockings and lace ruffles.

Mrs. Credulous. Oh, barbarous! to want a husband, who may wed you in the morning, and be sent the Lord knows where, before night. Then in a twelvemonth, perhaps, to have him come home like a Colossus, with one leg in New York, and the other in Chelsea Hospital.

Lauretta. Then I'd be his crutch, Mama.

Mrs. Credulous. No, give me a husband who knows where his limbs are, though he hasn't the use of 'em. And if he should take you with him, child, to sleep in a baggage-cart—what a scene! —and stroll about the camp like a gipsy, with a knapsack and two children at your back, then by way of entertainment in the evening, to make a party with the sergeant's wife to drink bohea tea, and play at all-fours on a drum-head . . . Oh, 'tis a precious life, to be sure!

Lauretta. Nay, Mama, you should not be against my lieutenant, for I heard him say you were the best natured and best looking woman in the world.

Mrs. Credulous. Why, child, I never said but that Lieutenant O'Connor was a very well-bred and discerning young man. 'Tis your papa is so violent against him.

Lauretta. Why, Mama, Cousin Sophy married an officer.

Mrs. Credulous. Ay, Laury, an officer in the militia.

Lauretta. No, indeed, Mama, he was in a marching regiment.

Mrs. Credulous. No, child, I tell you he was a major of militia.

Lauretta. Indeed, Mama, he wasn't.

(*Enter* JUSTICE CREDULOUS)

Credulous. Bridget, my lovey, I've had a message.

Lauretta. It was Cousin Sophy, Mama, told me so.

Credulous. I have had a message, my love.

Mrs. Credulous. No, child, she could say no such thing.

Credulous. A message, I say—

Lauretta. How could he be in the militia, when he was ordered abroad?

Credulous. Why, Laury—

Mrs. Credulous. Ay, girl, hold your tongue! Well, my dear?

Credulous. I have had a message, I say, from Doctor Rosy.

Mrs. Credulous. He wasn't ordered abroad, miss, he went abroad for his health.

Credulous. Why, Bridget!

Mrs. Credulous. Well, deary— Now hold your tongue, miss.

Credulous. A message I say from Doctor Rosy, and Doctor Rosy says—

Lauretta. I am sure, Mama, his regimentals—

Credulous. Damn his regimentals! Why don't you listen, hussy?

Mrs. Credulous. Ay, girl, how dare you interrupt your papa?

Lauretta. Well, Papa?

Credulous. Doctor Rosy says that he'll bring—

Lauretta. Were blue turned up with red, Mama.

Credulous. Laury! Says that he will bring the young man—

Mrs. Credulous. Red and yellow, if you please.

Credulous. Bridget! The young man to be hired.

Mrs. Credulous. Besides, miss, it is very unbecoming of you to want to have the last word with your Mama; you ought to know—

Credulous. Why, zounds! Will you hear me or no?

Mrs. Credulous. I'm listening, my love, I'm listening! But what signifies my silence, what good is my not speaking a word, if this girl will interrupt, and let her tongue run on, and try for the last word, and let nobody speak but herself? I don't wonder, my life, at your impatience; your poor dear lips quiver to speak, but I suppose she'll run on, and not let you put in a word. Ay, lovey, you may well be angry, there is nothing, to be sure, so provoking as a chattering, talking—

Lauretta. Nay, Mama, I'm sure 'tis you won't let papa speak now.

Mrs. Credulous. Why, you little provoking minx—

Credulous. Get out of the room directly, both of you—get out!

Mrs. Credulous. Ay, go, girl.

Credulous. Go, Bridget, you're worse than she, you old magpie. I wish you were both up to your necks in the canal, to argue there till I took you out.

(*Enter* SERVANT)

Servant. Doctor Rosy, sir.

Credulous. Show him up.

(*Exit* SERVANT)

Lauretta. Then, Mama, you admit he was in a marching regiment?

Mrs. Credulous. You're an obstinate fool; for if that had been the case—

Credulous. You won't go?

Mrs. Credulous. We're going, Mr. Surly. If that had been the case, I say, how could—

Lauretta. Nay, Mama, one proof—

Mrs. Credulous. How could Major—

Lauretta. And a full proof—

RICHARD BRINSLEY SHERIDAN

334

(JUSTICE CREDULOUS *drives them off, still arguing*)

Credulous. There they go, ding dong, in for the day. Good lack! a fluent tongue is the only thing a mother don't like her daughter to resemble her in.

(*Enter* DOCTOR ROSY)

Well, Doctor, Where's the lad? Where's Trusty?

Rosy. At hand. He'll be here in a minute. I'll answer for it, he's such a one as you ha'n't met with—brave as a lion, gentle as a saline draught.

Credulous. Ah, he comes in the place of a rogue, a dog that was corrupted by the lieutenant. But this is a sturdy fellow, is he, Doctor?

Rosy. A very Hercules, and the best back sword in the country. He'll make the redcoats keep their distance.

Credulous. Oh, those villains! This is St. Patrick's Day, and the rascals have been parading round my house all the morning. I know they have a design upon me, but I have taken all precautions. I have magazines of arms, and if this fellow proves faithful, I shall be more at ease.

Rosy. Doubtless he'll be a comfort to you.

(*Enter the* SERVANT)

Servant. There is a man below, sir, enquiring for Doctor Rosy.

Rosy. Show him up here.

Credulous. Hold, hold! A little caution. How does he look?

Servant. A country-looking fellow, your worship.

Credulous. Oh, well, well . . . for the doctor— The rascals try all ways to get in here.

Servant. Ay, please your worship, there

was one here this morning wanted to speak to you; he said his name was Corporal Breakbones.

Credulous. Corporal Breakbones! There, you see?

Servant. And Drummer Crackskull came again.

Rosy. Drummer Crackskull!

Credulous. Ay, did you ever hear of such a damned confounded crew? Well, show the lad in here.

(*Exit* SERVANT)

Rosy. Ay, he'll be your porter; he'll give such rogues their answer.

(*The* SERVANT *shows in* LIEUTENANT O'CONNOR *disguised in a countryman's clothes, then retires.*)

Credulous. So, a tall fellow, in faith! What, has he lost an eye?

Rosy. Only a bruise he got one day in taking seven or eight highwaymen.

Credulous. Hey, he has a damned wicked leer somehow with the other.

Rosy. Oh, no, he's bashful—a sheepish look—

Credulous. Well, my lad, what's your name?

O'Connor. Humphrey Hum.

Credulous. Humphrey Hum! I don't like Hum.

O'Connor. But I be mostly called Honest Humphrey.

Rosy. There, I told you so, of noted honesty.

Credulous. Well, Honest Humphrey, the doctor has told you my terms, and you're willing to serve, hey?

O'Connor. And it please your worship, I shall be well content.

Credulous. Well, then, hark'ye, honest Humphrey, you're sure now you'll never be a rogue, never take a bribe? Hey, honest Humphrey?

O'Connor. A bribe! What's that?

Credulous. A very ignorant fellow indeed.

Rosy. His worship hopes you will never part with your honesty for money, Humphrey.

O'Connor. Oh, noa, noa.

Credulous. Well, honest Humphrey, my chief business for you is to watch the motions of a rake-helly fellow here, one Lieutenant O'Connor.

Rosy. Ay! You don't value the soldiers, do you, Humphrey?

O'Connor. Not I. They are but swaggerers, and you'll see they'll be as much afraid of me as they would of their captain.

Credulous. And, in faith, Humphrey, you have a pretty cudgel there.

O'Connor. Ay, the switch is better than nothing, but I should be glad of a stouter. Ha' ye got such a thing in the house as an old coach pole, or a spare bedpost?

Credulous. Oons, what a dragon it is!

Well, Humphrey, come with me, I'll just show him to Bridget, Doctor, and then we'll agree. Come along, honest Humphrey. (CREDULOUS *goes out.*)

O'Connor. My dear Doctor, now remember to bring the justice presently to the walk; I have a scheme to get into his confidence at once.

Rosy. I will, I will. (*They shake hands.*)

(CREDULOUS *returns.*)

Credulous. Why, Humphrey, Humphrey —what the devil are you at?

Rosy. I was just giving him a little advice. Well, I must go for the present. Good morning to your worship. You need not fear the lieutenant, while he's in your house.

Credulous. Well, get in, Humphrey. Goodbye, Doctor. (*The* DOCTOR *leaves.*) Come along, Humphrey. Now I think I'm a match for the lieutenant. (*He laughs as they leave.*)

ACT TWO

SCENE ONE

A STREET

(*Enter* SERGEANT TROUNCE, *some* SOLDIERS, *and a* DRUMMER.)

Sergeant. Come, silence your drum. There is no valour stirring today. I thought St. Patrick would have given us a recruit or two.

1st Soldier. Mark, sergeant!

(*Enter a* BLACKSMITH *and an* IRISHMAN, *drunk.*)

Sergeant. Hey, my fine fellows! Come now, for the honour of St. Patrick, will ye be after serving his Majesty? And instead of drowsy beer, have

seas of punch, and shamrock islands all your lives after?

Irishman (*To* BLACKSMITH). Come, neighbor, what say you? Shall we make a friend of his Majesty? I feel as if I could handle a musket.

Blacksmith. Taddy, you're drunk, but I'm sober and I know better. Sometimes when I'm merry, I thinks how I could make a soldier, but when I'm sober, I knows that I'm fit for nothing but a civil employment.

Irishman. Ay, neighbor, but I feel bold at all times.

Blacksmith. Taddy, you're a fool, I tell ye. You're brave only when you're drunk; and if you were a general, 'twould cost his Majesty five shillings a day to keep you in courage, so, come along. Good liquor and a whole skin to put it in for ever . . .

(*Exeunt* IRISHMAN and BLACKSMITH)

Sergeant. Poltroons, by my halbert.

(*Enter two* COUNTRYMEN)

Oh, here are the lads I was looking for, they have the looks of gentlemen. A'n't you single, my lads?

1st Countryman. Yes, an't please you, I be quite single. Thank God, my relations be all dead, more or less. I have but one poor mother left in the world, and she's a helpless woman.

Sergeant. Indeed. A very extraordinary case. Quite your own master then; the fitter to serve his Majesty. Can you read?

1st Countryman. Noa. I was always too lively to take to my larning.

Sergeant. A good quality in a soldier . . . look for preferment.

1st Countryman. But John here is main clever at it.

Sergeant. So! What you're a scholar, friend?

2nd Countryman. I was born so, master. Fayther taught grammar school.

Sergeant. Lucky man! In a campaign or two, put yourself down chaplain to the regiment. And I warrant you have read of warriors and heroes?

2nd Countryman. Yes, that I have. I ha' read of Jack the Giant Killer, and the Dragon of Wantly, and the—Noa, I believe that's all in the hero way— except once a little about a comet.

Sergeant. Wonderful knowledge! Well, my warriors, I'll write word to the King directly of your good intentions, and meet me in half an hour at the Two Magpies.

Both. We will, your honour, we will.

Sergeant. But stay; for fear I shouldn't know you again in the crowd, clap these little bits of ribbon into your hats.

1st Countryman. Our hats are none of the best.

Sergeant. Well, meet me at the Magpies, and I'll give ye money to buy new ones.

Both. Bless your honour. Thank your honour.

1st Countryman. Come, John.

(*Exeunt* COUNTRYMEN.)

Sergeant (*Winking at* SOLDIERS). Jack!

(*Exeunt* SOLDIERS, *following the* COUNTRYMEN.)

So, here comes one would make a grenadier.

(*Enter* LIEUTENANT O'CONNOR, *disguised as* HUMPHREY HUM.)

Stop, friend, will you list?

O'Connor. Who shall I serve under?

Sergeant. Under me, to be sure.

O'Connor. Isn't Lieutenant O'Connor your officer?

Sergeant. He is, and I am commander over him.

O'Connor. What, be you sergeants greater than captains?

Sergeant. To be sure we are; 'tis our business to keep them in order. For instance, now, the general writes to me, Dear Sergeant, or Dear Trounce, or Dear Sergeant Trounce—according to his hurry—if your lieutenant does not demean himself accordingly, let me know. Yours to command, General Deluge.

O'Connor. And do you complain of him often?

Sergeant. Why, no, the lad is good-natured at bottom, so I pass over small things. But hark'ee, between ourselves, he is confoundedly given to wenching.

(*Enter* CORPORAL FLINT)

Corporal (*To* O'CONNOR). Please, your honour, the doctor is coming this way with his worship. We are all ready, and have our cues.

O'Connor. Then, my dear Sergeant, or dear Trounce, or dear Sergeant Trounce, take yourself away.

Sergeant. Oons. 'Tis the lieutenant! I smell the black hole already.

(*Exeunt* SERGEANT *and* CORPORAL; O'CONNOR *walks about whistling. Enter* JUSTICE CREDULOUS *and* DOCTOR ROSY.)

Credulous. I thought I saw some of the cut-throats.

Rosy. I fancy not; there's no one but honest Humphrey. Ha! Odds life, here comes some of them. We'll stay by these trees. and let them pass.

Credulous. Oh, the bloody looking dogs.

(CREDULOUS *and* ROSY *stand aside. Enter* CORPORAL FLINT *and two* SOLDIERS.)

Corporal (*To* O'CONNOR). Hello, friend, do you serve Justice Credulous?

O'Connor. I do.

Corporal. Are you rich?

O'Connor. Noa.

Corporal. Nor ever will be with that old stingy booby. (*Hands him a purse.*) Look here, take it.

O'Connor. What must I do for this?

Corporal. Mark me, our lieutenant is in love with the old rogue's daughter. Help us to break his worship's bones, and carry off the girl, and you are a made man.

O'Connor (*Flings down the purse*). I'll

see you hanged first, you pack of scurvy villains!

Corporal. What, sirrah, you mutiny? Lay hold of him.

O'Connor. Nay, then, I'll try your armour for you. (*He beats them.*)

Soldiers. Oh! Oh! Quarter! Quarter!

(O'CONNOR *drives them off.* CREDULOUS *and* ROSY *come forward.*)

Credulous. Trim them! Trounce them! Break all their bones, honest Humphrey. What a spirit he has, Doctor!

Rosy. Aqua fortis.

O'Connor. Betray my master, indeed!

Rosy. What a miracle of fidelity.

Credulous. Ay, and it sha'n't go unrewarded. I'll give him sixpence on the spot. Here, honest Humphrey, there's for yourself. As for this base bribe . . . (*He picks up the purse.*) Such trash, is best in the hands of justice. Now, then, Doctor, I think I may trust him to guard the women; while he is with them, I may go out with safety.

Rosy. Doubtless, you may. I'll answer for the lieutenant's good behaviour, while honest Humphrey is with your daughter.

Credulous. Ay, ay, she shall go nowhere without him. Come along, honest Humphrey. How rare it is to meet with such a servant.

(*Exeunt, the* DOCTOR *and* LIEUTENANT *making signs to each other.*)

SCENE TWO

THE GARDEN, WITH A SUMMER HOUSE

(LAURETTA *discovered seated on a bench, playing a guitar and singing. Enter* JUSTICE CREDULOUS *and* LIEUTENANT O'CONNOR.)

Credulous. Why, you little truant, how dare you leave the house without my permission? Do you want to invite that scoundrel lieutenant to scale the walls and carry you off?

Lauretta. Lud, Papa, you are so apprehensive about nothing.

Credulous. What, hussy!

Lauretta. Well, then, I can't bear to be shut up so all day long, like a nun. I'm sure 'tis enough to make one wish to be run away with—and I wish I was run away with—I do— I wish the lieutenant knew it.

Credulous. You do, do you, hussy? Well, I think I'll take pretty good care to prevent that. Here, Humphrey, I leave this lady in your care. Now you may walk about the garden, Miss Pert, but Humphrey shall go with you wherever you go. So mind, honest Humphrey, I am obliged to go abroad for a little while; let no one but yourself come near her. Don't be shame-faced, you booby, but keep close to her. And now, Miss, let your lieutenant, or any of his crew, come near you if they can. (*Exit* CREDULOUS.)

Lauretta. How this booby gapes after him! (*She sits down and begins to sing.*)

Beneath a green shade, a lovely young swain,
One evening reclined to discover his pain;
So sad, yet so sweetly, he warbled his woe,
The winds ceased to breathe, and the fountains to flow.
Rude winds with compassion could hear him complain,
Yet Chloe, less gentle, was deaf to his strain.

O'Connor. Lauretta!

Lauretta. Not so free, fellow. . . . (*Sings.*)

How happy, he cried, my moments once flew
Ere Chloe's bright charms first flashed in my view.
Those eyes then with pleasure the dawn could survey,
Nor smiled the fair morning more cheerful than they;
Now scenes of distress please only my sight,
I'm tortured in pleasure and languish in light.

O'Connor. Lauretta, look at me.

Lauretta. Don't interrupt me, booby. . . . (*Sings.*)

Through changes in vain relief I pursue,
All, all but conspire my griefs to renew.
From sunshine to zephyrs and shades we repair,
To sunshine we fly from too piercing an air;
But love's ardent fever burns always the same,
No winter can cool it, no summer inflame.

O'Connor. No recollection!

Lauretta. Honest Humphrey, be quiet. (*Sings.*)

But see the pale moon all clouded retire;
The breezes grow cold not Strephon's desire.
I fly from the dangers of tempest and wind,
Yet nourish the madness that preys on the mind.
Ah, wretch, how can life be worthy thy care?

The song sung by Miss Brown in the role of Lauretta in the original production, with words by Sheridan and music by James Hook. The piece became a popular favorite. (Theatre Collection/Victoria and Albert Museum)

To lengthen its moments but lengthens despair!

O'Connor. Have you forgot your faithful soldier?
Lauretta. Oh! preserve me!
O'Connor. 'Tis I, my soul! Your truest slave, passing in this disguise—
Lauretta. Well, now, I declare this is charming. You are so disguised, my dear Lieutenant, and you look so delightfully ugly, I'm sure no one will find you out— (*She begins to laugh.*) You know, I'm under your protection — (*Laughing.*) Papa charged you to keep close to me.
O'Connor. True, my angel, and thus let me fulfil—

Lauretta. Oh pray now, dear Humphrey—

O'Connor (*Struggling to kiss her*). Nay, 'tis but what old Mittimus commanded.

(*Enter* JUSTICE CREDULOUS)

Credulous. Stay, Laury, my— Hey! What the devil's here?

Lauretta. Well now, one kiss, and be quiet. Oh, mercy!

Credulous. Your humble servant, honest Humphrey! Don't mind me—pray don't let me interrupt you.

Lauretta. Lud, Papa— Now that's so good-natured—Indeed, there's no harm—You didn't mean any rudeness did you, Humphrey?

O'Connor. No, indeed, Miss. His worship knows it isn't in me.

Credulous. I know that you are a lying, canting, hypocritical scoundrel, and if you don't take yourself out of my sight—

Lauretta. Indeed, Papa, now I'll tell you how it was. I was somehow taken with a sudden giddiness, and Humphrey seeing me begin to totter, ran to my assistance, quite frightened, poor fellow, and took me in his arms.

Credulous. Oh, poor fellow, was that all—nothing but a little giddiness, hey?

O'Connor. That's all, indeed, your worship; for seeing Miss change colour, I ran up instantly.

Credulous. Oh, 'twas very kind of you!

O'Connor. And luckily recovered her.

Credulous. And who made you a doctor, you impudent scoundrel, hey? Get out, I say, this instant, or by all the statutes—

Lauretta. Oh now, Papa, you frighten me, and I'm giddy again. Oh, help!

O'Connor (*Catches her in his arms*). Oh, dear lady, she'll fall!

Credulous. Zounds! What, before my face! Why, you mirror of impudence! (*Seizes* O'CONNOR's *hair, the wig comes off, and he is discovered.*) Mercy on me! Who have we here? Murder! Robbery! Fire! Rape! John! Susan! Bridget!

O'Connor. Good sir, don't be so alarmed; I intend you no harm.

Credulous. Thieves! Robbers! Soldiers!

O'Connor. You know my love for your daughter—

Credulous. Fire! Cut-throats!

O'Connor. And that alone—

Credulous. Treason! Gunpowder!

(*Enter* SERVANTS *with Arms; the* JUSTICE *takes a blunderbuss.*)

Now, you scoundrel, let her go this instant.

Lauretta. Oh, papa, you'll kill me.

Credulous. Honest Humphrey, be advised. Ay, Miss, this way, if you please.

O'Connor. Nay, sir, but hear me—

Credulous. I'll shoot.

O'Connor. And you'll be convinced—

Credulous. I'll shoot.

O'Connor. How very injurious—

Credulous. I"ll shoot— (*To a* SERVANT.) Take her away . . . (*Points gun at* O'CONNOR.) And so, your humble servant, honest Humphrey Hum . . .

(O'CONNOR *dashes out in one direction, the others go out in the opposite direction.*)

SCENE THREE

A STREET

(*Enter* DOCTOR ROSY)

Rosy. Well, I think my friend is now in a fair way of succeeding. Ah! I warrant he's full of hope and fear, doubt and anxiety. Truly, he has the fever

The revival by the Old Stagers company for the 1938 Canterbury Festival. The players are Rosalie Crutchley as Lauretta, Humphrey Tilling as Lt. O'Connor, Nigel de Grey as a servant, and Ralph Alderson as Credulous. (London *Times*)

of love strong upon him; faint, peevish, languishing all day, with burning restless nights. Ah, just my case, when first I pined for my poor dear Dolly, when she used to have daily colics, that her little doctor might be sent for. Then I would interpret the language of her pulse, declare my own sufferings in my prescriptions for hers—send her a pearl necklace in a pill-box, or a cordial draught with an acrostic on the label. Well, those days are over. No happiness lasting! All's vanity—now sunshine, now cloudy! We are as we were made, king and beggar! Then what avails—

(*Enter* LIEUTENANT O'CONNOR)

O'Connor. Oh, Doctor! Ruined and undone!
Rosy. The pride of beauty—

O'Connor. I am discovered and—
Rosy. The gaudy palace—
O'Connor. The Justice is—
Rosy. The pompous wig—
O'Connor. Is more enraged than ever.
Rosy. The gilded cane—
O'Connor (*Slaps him on the shoulder*). Why, Doctor!
Rosy. Hey!
O'Connor. Confound your morals! I tell you I'm discovered, discomfited, disappointed, ruined!
Rosy. Indeed! Good lack! To think of the instability of human affairs! Nothing certain in this world—most deceived when most confident—fools of fortune all!
O'Connor. My dear Doctor, I want at present a little practical wisdom. I am resolved this instant to try the scheme we were going to put into ex-

ecution last week. I have the letter already written, and only want your assistance to recover my ground.

Rosy. With all my heart, I warrant I'll bear my part in it. But how the deuce were you discovered?

O'Connor. I'll tell you as we go. There's not a moment to be lost.

Rosy. Heaven send we succeed better at present, but there's no knowing.

O'Connor. Very true.

Rosy. We may, and we may not.

O'Connor. Right.

Rosy. Time must show.

O'Connor. Certainly.

Rosy. We are but blind guessers.

O'Connor. Nothing more.

Rosy. Thick-sighted mortals.

O'Connor. Remarkably.

Rosy. Wandering in error.

O'Connor. Even so.

Rosy. Futurity is dark.

O'Connor. As a cellar.

Rosy. Men are moles—

(*Exeunt* LIEUTENANT O'CONNOR, *forcing out the* DOCTOR, *who is still pondering.*)

SCENE FOUR

A ROOM IN JUSTICE CREDULOUS' HOUSE

(*Enter* JUSTICE CREDULOUS *and* MRS. CREDULOUS.)

Credulous. Odds life, Bridget, you are enough to make one mad! I tell you he would have deceived a chief justice. The dog seemed as ignorant as my clerk, and talked of honesty as if he had been a churchwarden.

Mrs. Credulous. Pho! Nonsense! Honesty, indeed! What had you to do, pray, with honesty! A fine business you've made of it with your Hum-

phrey Hum. And Miss, too! She must have been privy to it. Lauretta! Ay, you would have her called so; but for my part, I never knew any good come of giving girls these heathen Christian names. If you had called her Deborah, or Tabitha, or Ruth, or Rebecca, nothing of this would have happened; but I always knew Lauretta was a runaway name.

Credulous. Pshaw! You're a fool!

Mrs. Credulous. No, Mr. Credulous, 'tis you are the fool, and no one but such a simpleton would have been so imposed on.

Credulous. Why, zounds, madam, how dare you talk so? If you have no respect for your husband, I should think *unus quorum* might command a little deference.

Mrs. Credulous. Don't tell me—Unus fiddlestick!—you ought to be ashamed to show your face at the sessions. You'll be the laughing-stock of the bench, and a by-word with all the pig-tailed lawyers and bag-wigged attorneys about town.

Credulous. Is this language to his Majesty's representative? By the statutes, it's high treason and petty treason both at once!

(*Enter a* SERVANT)

Servant. A letter for your worship.

Credulous. Who brought it?

Servant. A soldier, your worship.

Credulous. Take it away, and bury it! Combustible stuff, I warrant it—A threatening letter: Put ten pounds under a stone! With damned inflammatory spelling, and the bloody hands of a dozen rogues at bottom.

Mrs. Credulous. Stay! Now you're in such a hurry. It's some canting scrawl from the lieutenant, I suppose. Here, let me see it. (*Takes the letter*.) Ay, 'tis signed Lieutenant O'Connor—

(*Exit* SERVANT)

Credulous. Well, come read it out.

Mrs. Credulous (*Reads*). "Revenge is sweet."

Credulous. It begins so, does it? I'm glad of that, and I'll let the dog know I'm of his opinion.

Mrs. Credulous (*Reads*). "And though disappointed in my designs on your daughter, I have still the satisfaction of knowing that I am revenged on her unnatural father; for this morning, in your chocolate, I had the pleasure of administering to you a dose of poison." Mercy on us!

Credulous. No tricks, Bridget. Come, now, you know it's not so. You know it's a lie.

Mrs. Credulous (*Crying*). Read it yourself—

Credulous (*Takes the letter; reads*). "Pleasure of administering . . . a dose of poison." Oh, horrible! Cut-throat villain! Bridget—

Mrs. Credulous (*Takes letter and examines it*). Lovey, stay, here's a postscript. (*Reads.*) "N. B. 'Tis not in the power of medicine to save you." Oh, oh!

Credulous. Odds life, Bridget, why don't you call for help? I've lost my voice. My brain is giddy. I shall burst, and no assistance. John! Laury! John!

(*Enter* JOHN)

John. Your worship!

Credulous. Stay, John! Did you perceive anything in my chocolate cup this morning?

John. Nothing, your worship, unless it was a little grounds.

Credulous. Ay, arsenic, black arsenic! 'Tis plain enough. Why don't you run for Doctor Rosy, you rascal?

John. Now, your worship?

Mrs. Credulous. Oh, lovey, you may be sure it's in vain. Let him go for the lawyer to witness your will, my life.

Credulous. Zounds! Go for the doctor, you scoundrel. You are all confederate murderers.

John. Oh, here he is, your worship!

Credulous. Now Bridget, hold your tongue, and let me see if my horrid situation is apparent.

(*Enter* DOCTOR ROSY)

Rosy. I have but just called in to inform—Hey, bless me, what's the matter with your worship?

Credulous. There, he sees it already! Poison in my face, in capitals! Yes, yes, I'm a sure job for the undertakers, indeed!

Mrs. Credulous. Oh! oh! Alas, Doctor!

Credulous. Peace, Bridget! Why, Doctor, my dear old friend, do you really . . . see any change in me . . . hey?

Rosy. Change? Never was a man so altered. How came those black spots on your nose?

Credulous. Spots on my nose!

Rosy. And that wild stare in your right eye?

Credulous. In my right eye?

Rosy. Ay—and— Oh, lack! Oh, lack! How you are swelled!

Credulous. Swelled!

Rosy. Ay, don't you think he is, Madam?

Mrs. Credulous. Oh, 'tis in vain to conceal it. Indeed, lovey, you are as big again as you were in the morning.

Credulous. Yes, I feel it now—I'm poisoned! Doctor, help me for the love of justice! Give me life to see my murderer hanged.

Rosy. What?

Credulous. I'm poisoned, I say!

Rosy. Speak out.

Credulous. What, can't you hear me?

Rosy. Your voice . . . is so low and hollow, as it were, I can't hear a word you say.

Credulous. I am gone, then. *Hic jacet,* many years one of his Majesty's justices.

Mrs. Credulous (*Gives* Doctor *the letter*). Read that, Doctor. Ah, lovey, the will. Consider, my life, how soon you'll be dead.

Credulous. No, Bridget, I shall die by inches.

Mrs. Credulous. Well, lovey, at twelve inches a day—and that's good slow dying—you'll be gone in five and a half days.

Credulous. 'Tis false, cockatrice! I'm five foot eight.

Rosy. I never heard of such monstrous iniquity. Ah, you are gone, indeed, my friend. The mortgage of your little bit of clay is up, and the sexton has nothing to do but foreclose. We must all go, sooner or later, high or low. Death's a debt . . . His mandamus binds all alike—no bail, no demurrer . . .

Credulous. Silence, Doctor Croaker! Will you cure me, or will you not?

Rosy. Alas, my friend, it is not in my power; but I'll certainly see justice done on your murderer.

Credulous. I thank you, my dear friend, but I had rather see it myself.

Rosy. Ay, but if you recover, the villain will escape.

Mrs. Credulous. Will he? Then, indeed, lovey, 'twould be a pity you should recover. I'm so enraged against the villain, I can't bear the thought of his escaping the halter.

Credulous. That's very kind, my dear,

but if it's all the same to you, I had as lief recover, notwithstanding. Well, Doctor, no assistance?

Rosy. In faith, I can do nothing, but there's the German quack, whom you wanted to send from the town; I met him at the next door, and I know that he has antidotes for all poisons.

Credulous. Fetch him, my dear friend, fetch him! I'll get him a diploma if he cures me.

Rosy. Well, there's no time to be lost; you continue to swell immensely. (*The* Doctor *exits.*)

Mrs. Credulous. What, my dear, will you submit to be cured by a quack, a nostrum-monger? For my part, as much as I love you, I had rather follow you to your grave than see you owe your life to any but a regular-bred physician.

Credulous. I'm sensible of your affection, dearest, and believe me, nothing consoles me in my present melancholy situation so much as the thought of leaving you behind, my angel.

(*Enter* Doctor Rosy, *and* Lieutenant O'Connor, *dressed as a physician in a wig and cloak. They salute.*)

Rosy. Great luck. I met him passing by the door.

O'Connor. Metto dowsi pulseum.

Rosy. He desires to feel your pulse.

Credulous. Can't he speak English?

Rosy. Not a word.

O'Connor. Palio vivem mortem soonem.

Rosy. He says you have not six hours to live.

Credulous. Oh, mercy! Does he know my distemper?

Rosy. I believe not.

Credulous. Tell him 'tis arsenic they have given me.

Rosy. Giveabant illi arsenica.

O'Connor. Poisonatus.

Credulous. What does he say?

Rosy. He says then, that you are poisoned!

Credulous. We know that—but what will be the effect?

Rosy. Quid effectum?

O'Connor. Diabit toutalar.

Rosy. He says you'll die presently.

Credulous. Oh, horrible! What, no antidote?

O'Connor. Curum benakere bono fullum.

Rosy. He says he'll undertake to cure you for three thousand pounds.

Mrs. Credulous. Three thousand pounds! Three thousand halters! No, lovey, you shall never submit to such an imposition. Die at once, my life, and be a customer to none of them.

Credulous. I won't die, Bridget. I don't like death.

Mrs. Credulous. Pshaw! There's nothing in it, a moment and it's over.

Credulous. Ay, but it leaves a numbness behind that lasts for a plaguy long time.

(*Enter* LAURETTA.)

Lauretta. Oh, my father, what is it I hear?

O'Connor. Quiddum seeo miram deos tollam rosum.

Rosy. The doctor is astonished at the sight of your daughter.

Credulous. How so?

O'Connor. Damsellum luvum even vislebani—

Rosy. He says that he has lost his heart to her, and that if you will give him leave to pay his addresses to the young lady, and promise your consent to their union, if he should gain her affections, he will, on those conditions, cure you instantly without fee or reward.

Credulous. The devil! Did he say all that in so few words? What a fine language it is! Well, I agree, if he can prevail on the girl . . . (*Aside.*) And that I am sure he never will.

Rosy. Greeeat!

O'Connor. Writum bothum.

Rosy. He says you must give this under your hand, while he writes you a miraculous recipe.

(O'CONNOR *and* CREDULOUS *both sit down to write at the table.*)

Lauretta. Do, Mama, tell me the meaning of all this.

Mrs. Credulous. Don't speak to me, girl. Unnatural parent!

Credulous. There, Doctor, that's what he requires.

Rosy. And here's your recipe. Read it yourself.

Credulous. Hey! What's here? Plain English!

Rosy. Read it out—a wondrous nostrum, I'll answer for it.

(*While* CREDULOUS *reads,* O'CONNOR *throws off his disguise, and kneels with* LAURETTA.)

Credulous (*Reads*). "On reading this, you are cured by your affectionate son-in-law, O'Connor."

Credulous. What the deuce is the meaning of all this?

Mrs. Credulous. Oh, monstrous imposition!

Credulous. In the name of Beelzebub, who have we here?

O'Connor. Lieutenant O'Connor, at your service, and your faithful servant, honest Humphrey.

Mrs. Credulous. So, so, another trick.

Credulous. Out of my sight, varlet. I'll be off the bargain, I'll be poisoned again—and you shall be hanged.

Rosy. Come, come, my dear friend, don't put yourself in a passion. A man just escaped from the jaws of death shouldn't be so violent. Come, make a merit of necessity, and let your blessing join those, whom nothing on earth can keep asunder.

Credulous. I'll not do it. I'd sooner die, and leave my fortune to Bridget.

Mrs. Credulous. To be sure, on my conscience, I'd rather you should die, and leave me ten estates, than consent to such a thing.

Credulous. You had, had you! Harkee, Bridget, you behaved so affectionately just now, that I'll never follow your advice again, while I live. So, Mr. Lieutenant—

(O'CONNOR *and* LAURETTA *rise.*)

O'Connor. Sir!

Credulous. You're an Irishman, and an officer, ar'n't you?

O'Connor. I am, sir, and proud of both.

Credulous. The two things in the world I hate most. So mark me, forswear your country, and quit the army, and I'll receive you as my son-in-law.

O'Connor. You, Mister Justice, if you were not the father of your daughter there, I'd pull your nose for mentioning the first, and break your bones for proposing the second.

Rosy. You're right, Lieutenant.

Credulous. Is he? Why, then, I must be wrong. Here, Lauretta, you're a sly, tricking, little baggage, and I believe there is no one so fit to manage you as my honest friend here, who is the most impudent dog I ever saw.

O'Connor. With such a gift as Lauretta, every word is a compliment.

Mrs. Credulous. Come, then, since everything's settled, I give my consent; and this day's adventure, lovey, will be a good subject for us to quarrel about for the next ten years.

Credulous. So it will, my dear, though we are never at a loss for that.

Rosy. Come, I insist on one day without wrangling. The captain shall give us a dinner at the Two Magpies, and your worship shall put every man in the stocks, who is sober at eight o'clock. (*To* LAURETTA) So, joy to you, my little favourite—and I wish you may make just such a wife as my poor dear Dolly.

(*Exeunt omnes.*)

FINIS

An Enemy of the People

!!!!!!!!!!!!!!!!!!!!!!!!!!!!!!!!! HENRIK IBSEN

INTRODUCTION

Henrik Ibsen, who has been called the Father of Modern Drama, was born on March 20, 1828, in Skien, a small town on the southeast coast of Norway. He was the eldest of five surviving children born to Mariechen and Knud Ibsen. At the time of Henrik's birth, Knud Ibsen was a prosperous merchant and a prominent member of local society, living extravagantly in a large house, called Stockmanns-gaarden, in the center of town. But in 1836 his business failed, and he was driven into bankruptcy, which in those days meant social disgrace. When friends began to shun the family, the Ibsens moved to a decrepit farm in the isolated country-side. Knud Ibsen never recovered in spirit or finances from this failure. Bitter and sharp-tongued, he browbeat his hard-working wife and the children.

Henrik's reaction to the cheerlessness of his home was to withdraw into himself. He refused to play outdoors with his brothers and sister, but sat in a little room off the kitchen, drawing, painting, reading, and playing with a toy theater he had built. Although silent and withdrawn, he was extremely observant and imaginative, and much that he read, thought, and experienced at this time later found its way into his plays. The future seemed bleak, but he came to feel that it was his responsibility to restore the family name and fortune, though the only means at his disposal were painting and poetry. His success was to depend largely on the strength of his will.

When he was fifteen, the family moved back to Skien, but Henrik, not wanting to be a burden to them any longer and thinking that he might like to be a doctor, took off for the little town of Grimstad, where he apprenticed himself to an apothecary. From that day to the end of his life, he was self-supporting and independent, though he suffered through many lean years. By choice, Ibsen cut himself off entirely from his birthplace, never setting foot in it after 1850, and severed all personal contact with his family. He never again communicated with his parents or relatives, except for a few notes to his sister Hedvig and a letter to his uncle at the time of Knud Ibsen's death in 1877. Yet he was to achieve his purpose: the family name, because of his efforts, became known far beyond Skien and Norway; long before his death his fame was world-wide.

At Grimstad, Ibsen read voluminously and began to write poetry in earnest. When he was eighteen, he fathered a child with a servant in the house, a woman ten years his senior, and for the next fifteen years had to contribute to the child's support. Before he was nineteen, he held strongly unorthodox views about marriage, morals, and religion. In 1849, at the age of twenty-one, Ibsen completed *Catiline*, his first full-length play in verse. The play was not produced, but a friend managed to have a small edition printed.

In 1850 Ibsen went to Christiania, the capital of Norway, intending to enter the university. After cramming for the stiff entrance examinations, he passed eight out of the eleven tests, but was not permitted to matriculate. He had already written an essay called "The Importance of Self-Knowledge," and so he turned independently to intensive reading and writing. He was interested at this time in Scandinavian folk tales and legends, and wrote a short play, *The Warrior's Grave*, based on native material; it inaugurated a period of historical and romantic verse dramas. The play was submitted to the Christiania Theatre, accepted, and given three performances. Ibsen, watching his work being performed, shrank back in his seat when he realized how little he knew about playwriting.

In 1851 the celebrated violinist Ole Bull, who had recently founded a theater in Bergen, on the west coast of Norway, came to Christiania to recruit talent for his playhouse. He met Ibsen and hired him as playwright-in-residence and assistant stage manager at a salary of about $22 a month. When it was discovered that Ibsen knew very little about the theater, he was sent off to Denmark and Germany to study theatrical production, with the understanding that upon his return, he would remain at Bergen for five years. At the theaters he visited, he gained a wealth of knowledge about stagecraft and was particularly impressed by a little pamphlet from Germany called "The Modern Drama." Its author, Hermann Hettner, who was a scholar and critic, made a strong plea for psychological truth in dramatic characters, even those in historical plays. Hettner's pamphlet called Ibsen's attention to the work of the German playwright Friedrich Hebbel, who had already made the transition from romantic, historical drama in verse to modern social drama in prose.

A very much wiser Ibsen returned to Bergen to assume the duties of stage manager, which included taking charge of costumes and properties; he was learning his business, both as technician and playwright, from the ground up. During his five years at Bergen, Ibsen had a chance to study closely all the plays produced there, including those of the French playwright Eugène Scribe, outstanding exponent of the "well-made play." Ibsen observed, "These works have mostly a perfected technique, and therefore they please the public; they have nothing to do with poetry, and therefore perhaps they please the public still more." Despite his apparent scorn for the French playwright, Ibsen was indebted to Scribe for a foundation upon which he could build. It was Ibsen's addition of psychologically observed characters and controversial social problems to the Scribean technique that later produced the celebrated Ibsenic drama.

Until 1864 the young playwright continued to turn out poetic, romantic, historical plays, most of which failed. These include *St. John's Night* (1853); *Lady Inger of Ostraat* (1855); *The Feast at Solhaug* (1856), Ibsen's first success; *Olaf Liljekrans* (1857); *The Vikings at Helgeland* (1857); *On the Uplands* (1859); *Love's Comedy* (1862); and *The Pretenders* (1864), his second success. Though each play showed an advance in style and power, his career as a writer had thus far brought him few financial returns. In 1857 he had left Bergen to become the director of the Norwegian Theatre in Christiania; in 1858 he married Suzannah Thoresen, and in 1859 their son, Sigurd, was born. When the Norwegian Theatre failed in 1862, Ibsen began to borrow money. In 1864, with the slim·profits from the production of *The Pretenders,* he left Norway, and for the next twenty-seven years lived in voluntary exile with his wife and child, mainly in Italy and Germany. The furniture he had left behind in Norway was sold to discharge his debts.

Although Ibsen spent more than half of his adult life outside his native land, Norway provided the locale for all but one of his plays. His physical distance from home enabled him to view his own country with greater objectivity, and to evaluate current events in Scandinavia with a sharper eye. Isolated, in a foreign environment, he also carefully explored his background and personality and poured his findings into his work. In a creative life that spanned half a century, Ibsen's unremitting dedication to his art is impressive. Seven days a week, Ibsen rose at six-thirty, had his tea at seven, wrote at his desk until one, lunched, walked and meditated from two until five, dined, then read late into the night.

During his first thirteen years abroad, Ibsen wrote four important plays, three of which were monumental verse dramas; the fourth, in prose, was a tentative step in the direction that was later to lead him to world renown. *Brand* (1866) was a character study of a young pastor with an indomitable will, who, in fulfilling his idealistic mission, did not hesitate to sacrifice his mother, wife, son, neighbors, and, finally, himself. Ibsen noted, however, that Brand might very well have been a scientist or an artist as well as a pastor; it was the character, not the calling, that was important. In his next play, *Peer Gynt* (1867), Ibsen drew a lying, irresponsible rascal, completely devoid of idealism or integrity, always ready to agree to half-measures and compromises, the very antithesis of Brand. The adventures of Peer are presented episodically and combine fantasy with frivolity; in its theatricalism, it is Ibsen's dream play.

His next play, *The League of Youth* (1869), was Ibsen's first excursion into photographic realism in prose. Its protagonist, Stensgaard, is a lawyer-politician, who proves to be a demagogue and opportunist. The play was produced successfully in Christiania in 1869, and was often mounted in the other Scandinavian countries during the next thirty years. The success of this prose work did not immediately encourage Ibsen to cut short his career as a dramatic poet. His next play, *Emperor and Galilean* (1873), dealt with Roman history and religion in ten acts; it was his greatest failure and the last play he was to write in verse. This work is almost never performed on the stage and is seldom read, yet it was Ibsen's favorite.

At the age of forty-nine, Ibsen was ready to turn away for good from historical and legendary material, episodic structure, and dialogue in verse and to develop the style of drama that was to take his name and bring him to the attention of the world. In subject matter Ibsenic drama dealt iconoclastically with contemporary social, moral, and political problems. In structure, it was a miracle of compression

and economy, surpassing even that of the French practitioners, for the main
events of the story have taken place long ago, while the drama concerns itself primarily with revelations and the consequences to the characters of their former
deeds. In style Ibsen the poet renounced verse dialogue for the poetry of mood, of
symbolism, and of dramatic metaphor.

In the thirteen years from 1877 to 1890, which constitute his realistic period,
Ibsen wrote eight masterful plays, so arranged as to present opposing points of
view. Earlier, in *The League of Youth*, he had been blamed for attacking the
political Left. In *Pillars of Society* (1877), the first of his truly modern plays and
an unalloyed triumph in Scandinavia, he openly assailed the Right. *A Doll's
House* (1879) explores an unhappy marital relationship, which ends with the
woman leaving her husband. This play brought Ibsen international notoriety and
fame. *Ghosts* (1881) deals with another unhappy marital relationship, in which a
woman who has *not* left her husband comes to grief. *An Enemy of the People*
(1882) portrays an idealist who is stoned and reviled when he attempts sincerely
to help his fellow men. *The Wild Duck* (1884) depicts an idealist who causes
only suffering when he puts his idealism into practice. *Rosmersholm* (1886) is the
portrait of an alienated and guilt-ridden man, who has lost his old faith but
cannot find a new one and settles for love and death. With this play, Ibsen had
begun to explore his characters in depth, exercising an intuitive kind of ego psychology. *The Lady from the Sea* (1888) concerns a neurotic woman whose husband helps her to find her identity. *Hedda Gabler* (1890) has for its protagonist a
neurotic woman who is unable to find her identity and destroys herself. "What
Ibsen insists on," says George Bernard Shaw in *The Quintessence of Ibsenism*, "is
that there is no golden rule; that conduct must justify itself by its effect upon life
and not by its conformity to any rule or ideal."

All of these plays, despite their deep seriousness, show a mixture of styles,
including irony, satire, and bitter humor; they are tragicomedies that verge on the
grotesque and thus forshadow many of the plays of that type in the contemporary
theater.

After completing *Hedda Gabler*, Ibsen returned to Norway, chiefly for the benefit of his son, Sigurd, who was in the Norwegian diplomatic service and who had
fallen in love with—and was soon to marry—the daughter of an old friend of
Ibsen's, and his rival in the theater, Björnstjerne Björnson. Ibsen, now well-to-do
and universally known, settled down in Oslo (formerly called Christiania), where
he composed his last four plays.

The works of the final period are moody, symbolic, mystical, and often enigmatic; they are personal and nostalgic enough to be considered the playwright's
spiritual autobiography. *The Master Builder* (1892) is a retrospective and somber
play about old age and its destruction by youth; Solness, the protagonist, has
already been stricken with an existential despair. *Little Eyolf* (1894) portrays a
rejected child who is destroyed by indifferent parents. *John Gabriel Borkman*
(1896) depicts the last days of a bankrupt, who is loveless and half mad. *When
We Dead Awaken* (1899), Ibsen's last play, has much in common with *Brand*, one
of his first, but here it is a sculptor rather than a preacher who, in his coldness in

human relations and unswerving pursuit of his ideal, dies alone on an icy mountaintop.

After writing *When We Dead Awaken*, Ibsen told a newspaper editor, "The play forms an epilogue to the series of plays which began with *A Doll's House* and which now ends with *When We Dead Awaken*. . . . It completes the cycle, and makes an entity of it, and now I am finished with it. If I write anything more, it will be in another context; perhaps, too, in another form."

Ibsen clearly realized that he had taken realism and naturalism as far as they could go and that now some completely new departure was called for in the drama. Symbolism, expressionism, and other forms of theatricalism had already made their appearance; Ibsen's work was finished. In 1900 he suffered the first of a series of paralytic strokes, which brought his life to an end on May 23, 1906.

Because he dealt with ideas then rarely discussed in public and because he questioned the validity of generally accepted moral and ethical beliefs, Ibsen was reviled as a vicious scandalmonger, sensationalist, and muckraker. In vain he protested that he was not a reformer but a poet. Yet as each new play appeared in country after country, hidebound critics, nurtured on sentimental, conventional, and romantic drama, let out howls of protest and torrents of vituperation. Strindberg and Chekhov, among others, acknowledged Ibsen's skill as a dramatist, though they disliked his plays. But Shaw, from the very first, praised Ibsen enthusiastically and, during the older playwright's lifetime, coined the terms Ibsenism and Ibsenite. Pirandello said, "After Shakespeare, without hesitation, I put Ibsen first. . . ."

To readers and audiences throughout the world, there came at length a recognition of Ibsen's clarity of thought, objectivity, psychological insight, poetic vision, and human and emotional impact—the end products of this master builder's consummate craftsmanship. As a result Ibsen's plays immediately recommended themselves to the European stage directors who were just then introducing realistic techniques of theatrical production. The Duke of Saxe-Meiningen, André Antoine, Otto Brahm, J. T. Grein, and Stanislavsky, among others, used Ibsen's plays as vehicles for the development of psychological acting, the handling of stage crowds, the creation of mood and atmosphere in stage settings, and the imaginativeness and aptness of stage business. The old playwright saw and applauded some of the modern productions his artistry had made possible.

Regrettably Ibsen's success, and the honors bestowed upon him in old age, did not bring him happiness; but his technical and artistic innovations won him scores of disciples among critics, playwrights, and directors, and have had a lasting effect upon modern drama.

An Enemy of the People was published on November 28, 1882. It was Ibsen's practice to have a play ready in November or December of each year for the Christmas trade, as a large share of a playwright's income depended on the sale of his work in book form; it was usually after publication that his plays were released for production in the theater.

Ibsen had actually begun to write *An Enemy of the People* in 1880 but interrupted the work in order to complete *Ghosts*, which made its appearance in November, 1881. Though the playwright had anticipated a strong reaction to *Ghosts*, he was stunned by the storm of protest it raised; he was accused of undermining the morality of the social order. Now he was engaged in writing a play in which the central figure, Thomas Stockmann, a small-town doctor, defies the Establishment when he discovers that the municipal baths, on which the town depends for a livelihood, are dangerously polluted. The doctor is congratulated at first, but when he advocates the closing of the baths for repairs—which would mean a loss of income to the town for an indefinite period—the entire community, prompted by the press, turns against him. When he calls a public meeting to discuss the issue, he is shouted down and branded an enemy of the people.

This play is probably one of Ibsen's most clearly autobiographical works. The resemblance between the playwright and his protagonist, Thomas Stockmann, is unmistakable. To begin with, the house in which Ibsen was born was called Stockmannsgaarden; and with his probing mind and interest in self-knowledge, he had already at the age of twenty been a freethinker in such matters as marriage, love, morality, and religion. At that time, 1848, revolutions were sweeping Europe, and Ibsen later remarked, "While a great age thundered outside, I found myself in a state of war with the little community within which, by the circumstances of my work, I sat imprisoned." So must Ibsen have imagined Stockmann's feelings as he fought a losing battle with the townspeople over the condition of the baths.

Ibsen never relinquished the idea that the claims of the gifted individual should supersede those of the state. Ten years before writing *An Enemy of the People*, in a letter to his friend, the critic Georg Brandes, he said, "The state is the curse of the individual. . . . The state must go! That revolution is one that I shall join." In later communications with Brandes he remarked in all seriousness, "the individual who stands alone is the strongest," and "the minority is always right."

By the time he came to write *An Enemy of the People*, however, Ibsen had won many honors, was well-to-do, and inclined to be cautious, particularly after the hostile reception given to *Ghosts*. He attempted, therefore, to dissociate himself partially from Stockmann. In a letter to his publisher, when submitting the manuscript of the play, he said, "Doctor Stockmann and I got on excellently together, we agree about so many things, but the Doctor is more muddle-headed than I am. . . ."

The "muddle-headed" Doctor Stockmann bears a close resemblance to Alceste in *The Misanthrope*, in his lack of respect for the hypocrisy, deception, and skullduggery commonly practised in politics, business affairs, and social intercourse. In his bitterness, Stockmann, like Alceste, contemplates going to some primeval forest or South Sea Island, but he settles instead for a show of heroics, and strikes a monumental pose in defiance of society.

If Stockmann were no more than a misguided idealist, he would not be the impressive and sympathetic character he surely is, for we do not doubt his sincerity and we approve of his aims. He is a human being of enormous complexity, drawn with great psychological insight and subtlety. There is evidence in the play that his reformatory zeal, his drive for attention, success, and appreciation, are motivated by a desire to prove his worth to his powerful brother, the mayor, and to his wealthy father-in-law. This suggests overcompensation for a feeling of inferiority, for, like Ibsen, Stockmann persisted in championing unpopular ideas in the face of the most brutal opposition.

When Ibsen was completing *An Enemy of the People*, he was uncertain as to whether to call it a comedy or a straight drama, for, as he informed his publisher, "There is much of the nature of comedy in it, but it is also based on a serious idea." He was not joking about his wish to castigate politicians, press, and public, but his attack was waged with the most powerful weapon in his arsenal—irony, which permeates this play from its title to its protagonist's last line. Ibsen admitted that he had "a lot of fun" working on this play, and his intention apparently was to spare no one. Stockmann's brother Peter, the mayor of the town, is shown to be overly concerned about his own health but totally indifferent to that of the summer visitors who would use the polluted baths. The members of the press who claim to be the servants of the public offer their columns for sale to the highest bidder. Stockmann's father-in-law, old Morton Kiil, the conniving businessman, manages to make a profit out of every turn of fortune, good or bad; and Stockmann, who considers these machinations disgraceful, is accused of being a party to the old man's stock manipulations. Finally, Stockmann, after his patients have left him, his daughter has been fired, his sons beaten, and his house stoned, announces dramatically that he is the strongest man in the world, for he is strongest who stands most alone! Here is Ibsen laughing at himself.

An Enemy of the People had a much better reception than *Ghosts*, and was widely performed. Critics with a political bent, however, were not overenthusiastic about the subject-matter, except for George Bernard Shaw, Ibsen's staunchest defender, who over and over again praised him for eliminating romantic claptrap from his plays and substituting the "terrible art of sharpshooting at the audience, trapping them, fencing with them, aiming always at the sorest spot in their consciences." A contemporary critic, Erik Bögh, who was impressed by the play, said that those who only read of it in the newspaper would ask, "But how can an audience's attention be held for an entire evening by a debate which rages for three acts about a drainage system, in the fourth act makes fun of demagoguery, and in the fifth is finished?" The answer Bögh provided was that no one but Ibsen could have constructed and written such a "masterpiece."

Though it was written about a century ago, *An Enemy of the People* is in no sense dated. It is, if anything, more pertinent today than it was in the year of its composition—not because human nature or social conditions are basically different, but because pollution, corruption, demagoguery, cover-ups, misinformation, lack of credibility, irresponsible leadership, and public indifference have grown to unconscionable proportions. This is generally acknowledged by a paralyzed electorate, which looks for an idealist to champion its cause. That expectation would have afforded endless amusement to Ibsen, who had the genius to laugh at himself for conceiving so ineffectual a creature as the reformer Thomas Stockmann.

The Vienna Burgtheater before 1945 *(above)** and in 1956 *(right)* †Before it was dam-
aged in a bombing, the theater was a typical nineteenth-century house with five tiers
of boxes and heavy rococo décor. It was rebuilt and remodeled in accordance with
modern concepts of functionalism; and partitions between the boxes were altered to
permit the audience to mingle more freely. (*Bildarchivs der Ost. Nationalbilbliotek/
†Roy Bernard)

PRODUCTION IN THE NINETEENTH-CENTURY THEATER

We have seen the religiosity of early drama gradually eroded, and transmuted
into the serious secular plays of succeeding eras. By the eighteenth century the
drama, in reaction to moralistic, sentimental, and didactic playwriting, had become
increasing frivolous. And, through the efforts of the pantheists and transcenden-
talists of the first half of the nineteenth century, orthodox religious feeling was
dissipated still further, giving way to a romantic and idealistic program for ethical
and moral behavior and universal love. This brought on a rash of windy "poetic"
works steeped in sentimentality and romanticism.

Toward the end of the century men were making gigantic strides in industry
and economics, social reforms and scientific discoveries; and the ideas of Darwin,
Marx, and Freud were beginning to make themselves felt. Darwin taught that
man is related to the animals; Marx, that "thinking" animals can arrange society
to suit their needs; and Freud, that the nervous mechanisms of these animals can

be repaired if they break down during the process of living. Realism reflected this thinking in the theater; the Duke of Saxe-Meiningen tried to create the effect of reality in the visual aspects of his productions and the dramatists of the period were striving for the same effect in their plays. The works of Ibsen, Chekhov, and Shaw mirror modern man thinking; social, scientific, philosophical, and even religious questions provided the themes for their dramas.

The Theater

In the nineteenth century the middle and upper classes, who had dominated audiences of the preceding period, were greatly augmented by members of the working class. To accommodate them many new theaters were built, and the seating capacities of Drury Lane and Covent Garden were enlarged until each eventually could hold about three thousand persons in the pit, boxes, and gallery, the boxes and gallery finally rising to a height of five tiers. The stage area too was widened, heightened, and deepened, with the introduction of illusionism and the attempt to achieve historical accuracy in the settings. The Romantic drama featured exotic and picturesque scenes, called *local color*, and the designers of the period vied with each other in providing elaborate, eye-filling sets, which were solidly built and required a great deal of space. In addition, elaborate machinery was installed both above and below the stage.

Toward the end of the century, with the introduction of realism that demanded a greater intimacy with the audience, the box set was introduced and an effort was made to reform the picture-frame stage and the horseshoe auditorium, which almost invariably had the disadvantage of providing a considerable number of seats at the gallery ends that had a poor view of the stage. The first attempts to design a more democratic type of theater occurred in Germany, where experiments were performed with the thrust stage and with the shape of the proscenium in an effort to improve the acoustics and lighting. Innovations in engineering and the introduction of steel construction made it possible to do away with pillars and posts. It was the beginning of the modern auditorium with its single bank of seats on a sloping floor, and perhaps a single balcony; the absence of boxes and often of the proscenium frame; and simple, unpretentious decoration.

Acting

The theoretical discussions concerning the relative merits of nature and art in acting had little effect on actual practice during most of the nineteenth century, for performers continued to use flamboyant gestures and to declaim to the point of ranting. It was the widespread interest in sociology and psychology that led late nineteenth century writers and actors to study human emotions, motivations, and relationships, as well as the effect of the environment on character and personality. Chekhov, Ibsen's contemporary, was foremost among the new school of writers, whose plays demanded realistic acting as we know it.

The great exponent of internal acting in modern drama was the man who directed Chekhov's plays, Constantin Stanislavsky. By the Stanislavsky method, the performer draws upon his own psyche to achieve emotional identification with the character he is portraying. To stimulate affective and sense memories and to achieve relaxation and concentration, the actor is required to do special exercises and improvisations. He attempts to awaken within himself emotions he has felt in the past in specific situations related or adaptable to the character or scene he is to play. Since each actor must draw on his own psychological and emotional equipment and must depend on a free flow of psychic energy from his unconscious, method acting is plastic and variable. At present there are many variations of the Stanislavsky method; no modern actor or teacher of acting ignores it completely, though some question its value. Acting is an evolving art; and as the present realistic phase seems to be waning, new techniques for external acting in theatricalist drama have been developed.

Direction

The passion for truth, for reform, and for historical authenticity spurred nineteenth-century actor-managers to ever greater efforts toward integration and accuracy in their productions. Before the day of the stage director, John Philip Kemble, William Charles Macready, Samuel Phelps, and several others attempted, by careful preparation, to bring order and harmony into the movement of their actors, and to their sets, costumes, and lighting. Charles Kean went beyond his contemporaries, insisting upon the historical accuracy of all the visual elements in his productions and upon the careful "blocking" (arrangement) of stage crowds as well as of featured players. Kean was assisted by a staff of stage managers and technical experts, including scholars and historians.

The stage director, as we know him—the person with full controlling force over a production—came late in theater history, only about one hundred years ago. The man who has been called the first modern stage director, and who surpassed all his predecessors in achieving a totally integrated production, was George II, Duke of Saxe-Meiningen (1826-1914), the ruler of a small state in central Germany. The Duke was a painter and draughtsman who had a passion for the theater and who designed and directed every detail that went into his meticulous productions. His wife, who had been an actress, and his stage manager, Ludwig Chronegk, worked under his orders.

The Duke realized that every aspect of a production must be related both to the script and to the actor; with iron discipline he forged all the theatrical elements required for the play into a unified work of art. From the very first rehearsal the actors used the sets, costumes, and properties designed for the play, so that they would be thoroughly familiar with them during the performance. The Duke himself conceived every gesture, movement, and position for the actor. He treated each extra in a crowd scene as an individual and rehearsed him separately. This took weeks and even months of intensive work, but the Duke set no limits on either time or money. The work of this inspired amateur revealed, according to Lee Simonson, "the necessity for a commanding director who could visualize an entire performance and give it unity as an interpretation by complete control of every moment of it; the interpretive value of the smallest details of lighting, costuming, makeup, stage setting; the immense discipline and the degree of organization needed before the performance was capable of expressing the 'soul of the play.'"

Between 1874 and 1890 the Duke's company traveled throughout Europe and gave some 2600 performances in such cities as Berlin, London, Brussels, Stockholm, Basel, and Moscow. Where they were seen, these productions created a sensation and set in motion a chain reaction of imitation and innovation. They had enormous influence on the work of André Antoine, Otto Brahm, and Constantin Stanislavsky, the great exponents of realism and naturalism among modern directors. Stanislavsky, taking his cue from Ludwig Chronegk, behaved at first like a drillmaster toward his actors, prescribing their every gesture, movement, and inflection, all of which he had worked out in advance and set down in detailed production notes. By his own admission, it took him about twenty-five years to realize that this technique would produce only an external realism. By throwing away his production notes, planning nothing in advance, working creatively with his actors step by step through a play, he was finally able to achieve an inner, or psychological, realism of greater validity.

Scenery

In the early part of the nineteenth century, the wing-and-drop system was still in use. Actual stage furnishings were rather meager, but backdrops were painted in minute detail. The great hall of a castle, for instance, showed paneled walls, mullioned windows, stags' antlers, coats of arms, a banquet table fully set, and rich rugs; while the interior of humbler homes had rough plaster walls, rickety tables and chairs, pots and pans around the hearth, and even trash on the floor. As stages became shallower, the actor was forced to stand closer to the painted drop, which showed up the false perspective and completely destroyed the illusion of reality.

The cult of realism brought with it a revolution in stage settings. The box set, a room with the "fourth wall" (the curtain) removed, became the standard interior. At first the walls of the room were entirely constructed of painted canvas, with openings for practical doors and windows; gradually such architectural elements as cornices, columns, and panels, and even some of the walls, came to be built of sturdier materials. To heighten the sense of reality, the rooms were elaborately furnished; for the set of his first production, André Antoine moved the furniture from his own home to the stage of the Théâtre Libre. The interiors in Ibsen's plays were fitted out with real curtains, pictures, rugs, plants, and bric-a-brac. Conventional, realistic plays still use this type of set.

Lighting

In the first quarter of the nineteenth century, oil lamps were replaced by gaslight. The bright new illumination showed up the tawdriness of painted drops and hastened the introduction of more realistic scenery. By 1850 a dimmer-switchboard, which regulated the flow of gas to all parts of the stage, made it possible to control the intensity of the light with some accuracy.

In 1846 an electric arc lamp had first been used at the Paris Opera House to create the illusion of sunlight; about fifteen years later the Paris Opera introduced the floodlight and follow spot. By the end of the century, electricity was in use in all the important theaters in Europe, and not long afterward in the United States as well. This made it possible for stage lighting to develop into a full-fledged art.

The principles of modern stage lighting were worked out by Adolphe Appia in the last years of the nineteenth century. He drew a distinction between two types of lighting: diffused or general illumination, floodlighting, which casts an even radiance over the stage; and focused, mobile light, spotlighting, which gives three-dimensionality to the actor. One effect of his theories was to change the concept of space onstage: an actor stepping out of a "hot" spot into the semidarkness just a few feet away appears to have moved farther than one who goes clear across the stage in bright and even light. Before Appia's principles could be fully worked out in practice, however, a great deal of sophisticated electrical equipment, such as lamps, lenses, projectors, and switchboards, had to be developed.

Costumes

During the first half of the nineteenth century, only sporadic efforts were made to achieve some degree of individuality and historical accuracy in theatrical costumes. But in 1850 Charles Kean began to dress the actors in his Shakespearean productions with scrupulous care, and the growing interest in realism extended that care from the plays of Shakespeare to those of contemporary writers. In the plays of Ibsen and Strindberg we have the introduction of costumes appropriate to time, place, character, and situation, which heightened the verisimilitude of the scene.

Music and Dance

The forerunners of musical comedy—ballet, opera, operetta, burletta, and pantomime—as well as modern musical plays and revues, have always depended upon music and dance. But from the seventeenth century to the early twentieth, music and dance also played an important, though impertinent, part in serious drama and even in tragedy. All theatrical productions were looked upon merely as "entertainments" and "shows," and those plays were considered most successful into which elaborate song and dance interludes were injected no matter how inappropriate they might be.

The characteristic features of the romantic and sentimental plays of the eighteenth century reached their full development in the melodramas of the nineteenth; the close connection between music and melodrama is clear from the very name of the genre, the music being of the kind that was referred to as "hearts and flowers" because of its maudlin sentimentality. From the Restoration right through the nineteenth century, all productions, including those of Shakespeare, were enlivened by the introduction of a great deal of incidental music—seldom appropriate to character or situation, but simply to give pleasure to the audience.

Toward the middle of the nineteenth century, Richard Wagner tried to integrate meaning, movement, and music in what he called "music drama," but the result was opera. The realistic playwrights and directors succeeded, however, in eliminating extraneous songs and dances from serious plays; they retained only those that were appropriate to the action or the characters.

Adolphe Appia and Gordon Craig were pioneers in the use of music and light as a unifying element in the drama. Appia wrote: "Music and music alone can coordinate all the elements of scenic presentation into a completely harmonious whole in a way which is utterly beyond the capacity of our unaided imagination. Without music the possibility of such harmony does not exist and therefore cannot be discovered. . . ." Craig was equally aware of the importance of wedding movement to music in the creation of drama; he experimented with the movement of actors, of scenery, and of lights to produce a kind of visual music.

Audience and Playwright

What had been theory in the seventeenth and eighteenth centuries became technology in the nineteenth. The growth of industry and its mechanization caused radical alterations in the life of the common man and in the drama. Men found themselves mere cogs in great machines, and grew more and more alienated from their work and from each other. Industrialization brought with it an intensification of capitalism, which subjected workers to such intangible external influences as the fluctuations in foreign markets and on the stock exchange. Before the middle of the century, Balzac had written a play in which a financial wheeler-dealer, Mercadet, put off his creditors with the alibi that his partner had

Fredric March as Dr. Stockmann and Florence Eldridge as Mrs. Stockmann comforting the children in the final scene of Arthur Miller's adaptation of the Ibsen play (1950). Notice the broken windows. (New York Public Library)

absconded with their funds but was sure to return and that he was simply "waiting for Godeau!"

Social revolt seemed the only way to restore the individual's power to act, and this became the theme and substance of many of the romantic plays of the period. The usual romantic protagonist was a larger-than-life hero, who was torn between love and duty to an ideal (social or political), and who doggedly pursued the good, the true, and the beautiful; he lived and died (and therein lay the tragedy) for an "impossible dream." The romantic play was, of course, the farthest removed from reality; it was written in verse, and dealt always with historical persons and places, never contemporary ones, which made it possible for the audience to preserve the fiction that man was a creature of free will with the attributes of a tragic hero. By this time, however, the average playgoer was a wage slave, a prisoner in a shop or factory.

The well-made play—a mechanical construction as serviceable as the other machine-made products of the time—was perfected by Eugène Scribe, who wrote over four hundred pieces of various sorts for the theater and turned playwriting into big business. He sacrificed thought and characterization to clever intrigue, which proved tremendously popular with the ever-growing audiences that flocked to the theater as a result of the spread of education and the growth of affluence and democracy. Following in Scribe's footsteps, Victorien Sardou produced mechanical art full of sensationalism and moral platitudes. Between them, Scribe and Sardou provided the transition from the airy, romantic fantasy to the minutiae of the commonplace.

Henrik Ibsen must be accounted the father of modern realism, for his work was a clear attack on the rigidity and rationalism of late nineteenth-century society, and the beginning of streamlined drama. Before the end of the century, Alfred Jarry wrote *Ubu Roi*, which is considered the first absurdist drama; it satirized the illogical nature of the world, but it had no immediate successors. It was August Strindberg who made the first effective break with realism. He found the tight, logical structure of the well-made play, which is based strictly on cause and effect, too inflexible to contain his mercurial and flamboyant thoughts and feelings. His material came from explosive, personal experiences and neurotic fantasies, and his creative genius provided dramatic styles in which he could portray the subjective, savage, and irrational side of man's nature.

A third of a century after the initial staging of *An Enemy of the People*, some play reviewers were still unable to accept the work of the naturalistic playwrights. William Winter, dramatic critic of the *New York Tribune* from 1865 to 1909, called such plays "odious and revolting," and referred to

> persons who derive satisfaction from the barren contemplation of depravities, and who like the assurance (liberally provided, for example, in certain plays by the late Mr. Ibsen) that human nature is utterly corrupt, human society rotten, mankind a failure, and the world a gigantic mistake.

He goes on:

> Determination to prevent an immoral use of the Theatre, whether made with brazen audacity or with pretence of right motive and "serious purpose" in the presentment of nasty "problem plays," should be sternly and effectively evinced if the Theatre, which, rightfully administered, is a public blessing, is to be saved from deterioration into a public nuisance.
>
> . . . one reason why so many obnoxious things have, of late, been imposed upon the stage is that they are so easily made, and that because of their vileness and effrontery they seem likely, being designated as "daring," to attract profit. . . .°

° From *Vagrant Memories* (New York: George H. Doran Co., 1915).

THE PRODUCTION RECORD

An Enemy of the People was first performed at the Christiania Theatre in Christiania (now Oslo), Norway, on January 13, 1883, and shortly thereafter was produced in all the important Scandinavian theater centers. Productions soon followed in Austria and Germany, where it "went like wild-fire with the house," as Scottish critic William Archer wrote to his brother from Munich. It was presented in London on June 14, 1893, and the English company, headed by Beerbohm Tree, then brought the play to America.

At the grand opening of the National Theatre in Oslo in November, 1899, *An Enemy of the People* was one of three plays to be presented (the others were by Björnson and Holberg). On September 1, 1924, the twenty-fifth anniversary of the event, the same bill was offered as had been at the opening. The play had been performed there many times in between.

An Enemy of the People has been presented by great stars and directors innumerable times in every corner of the globe, and has been adapted as well for radio and television.

Arthur Miller's version, which is a rather free adaptation of the play, opened at the Broadhurst Theatre in New York on December 28, 1950, with Fredric March, Florence Eldridge, and Morris Carnovsky in leading roles, directed by Robert Lewis, with sets and costumes by Aline Bernstein. Since then, Miller's adaptation has frequently been performed in the United States, and served as the basis for the film version of the play starring Steve McQueen.

IBSEN'S WRITING PROCESS*

Before I write down one word, I have to have the character in mind through and through. I must penetrate into the last wrinkle of his soul. I always proceed from the individual; the stage setting, the dramatic ensemble, all of that comes naturally and does not cause me any worry, as soon as I am certain of the individual in every aspect of his humanity. But I have to have his exterior in mind also, down to the last button, how he stands and walks, how he conducts himself, what his voice sounds like. Then I do not let him go until his fate is fulfilled.

As a rule, I make three drafts of my dramas which differ very much from each other in characterization, not in action. When I proceed to the first sketch of the material I feel as though I had the degree of acquaintance with my characters that one acquires on a railway journey; one has met and chatted about this or that. With the next draft I see everything more clearly, I know the characters just about as one would know them after a few weeks' stay in a spa; I have learned the fundamental traits in their characters as well as their little peculiarities; yet it is not impossible that I might make an error in some essential matter. In the last draft, finally, I stand at the limit of knowledge; I know my people from close and long association—they are my intimate friends, who will not disappoint me in any way; in the manner in which I see them now, I shall always see them.

MRS. STOCKMANN IN THE FILMS
An Interview with Bibi Andersson

"I was on holiday in Paris in July, 1976," said Bibi Andersson, "when I got a phone call from George Schaefer, who said he was preparing to direct a film version of *An Enemy of the People* with Steve McQueen, and they wanted me for the role of Mrs. Stockmann. They were to start filming in August. My agent met with Schaefer and McQueen and settled the business arrangements; and I arrived in Hollywood two weeks before the picture was to get under way.

* Quoted by A. E. Zucker in *Ibsen: The Master Builder* (New York: Henry Holt, 1929). Copyright 1929, Henry Holt and Company. Reprinted by permission of Holt, Rinehart and Winston, Inc.

Michael Cristofer as Hovstad, Bibi Andersson as Mrs. Stockmann, and Charles Durning as Peter Stockmann in a scene from the 1977 film version. (Rogers & Cowan, Inc.)

"We had three weeks of rehearsal, which Schaefer conducted as if we were doing a play for the stage. The action was continuous, not chopped up as is usual in movie-making. Most of the actors in the film had had theater experience, and Schaefer himself had directed many plays for the theater and for television. So I didn't have the feeling that film techniques were overpowering us. We had plenty of time to work with our parts. Anyway, I always learn my lines before we start rehearsal. I like to be prepared, but not too prepared, because you have to leave something open for improvisation and for what is going to happen when you are on the set.

"Rehearsals began with the company sitting down together and reading the play; then the scenes were blocked. Schaefer did not give us a long analysis for each character and situation, but if anyone had a question he was glad to discuss it. We worked in a studio on the MGM lot, while the scenery was being built in another one; then we moved to the actual set. It consisted of a complete apartment: living-room, dining-room, kitchen, and so on. A cameraman came in at this point, watched the rehearsals, and started to figure out camera setups.

"The film version was not 'opened up' or significantly altered as is usually the practice when a play is adapted for the movies. I was told they were trying to be as faithful to Ibsen's text as possible; most of the scenes took place in the indoor sets called for by the playwright. But if we had gone to Norway and lived for a month or two in a small fishing village in the south, the film, I'm sure, would have been different—better or worse. But certainly different, because you always absorb the atmosphere; you can get suggestions from reality. I like to shoot scenes on the spot; you never know what will happen to you. Things happen in a real place that no one could ever think up in a script. When you step outside there is a certain kind of cold. You can imagine cold on a set, but when it's really cold it's different.

"Working with Steve McQueen was an unusual experience. I finally liked it very much, but in the beginning he was a little overanxious. He was the producer and the star, and he was running from one thing to another. I'm not used to working, first, with an actor who is also the producer and, second, with a star everybody listens to and around whom you have to worry how you say things. But I found he was a very good-hearted and sensitive person, and also, I think, a very good actor. He is completely unpretentious, and wanted all the acting to be real and sincere.

"At first he was bothered by my accent, because everybody in the film was American and he was afraid my accent would stick out. He asked me to work on my speech, and I did have sessions with a coach. Somehow I don't feel I'm acting real if I try to imitate a way of talking that's not my own. I don't want to be conscious of it. I want to speak because things come out of my subconscious, and we're now talking about one of the absolutely basic problems of acting. In my own language I can trust my subconscious; but in English I don't know what my subconscious is coming up with, because I don't know what I imitate. Anyway, I feel my acting is more faithful if I stick to my own way of saying things in English. I can understand that McQueen was worried, but what could I do more than really work on it?

"So far as the role of Mrs. Stockmann is concerned, it's not very big, but it's important. When I read the play in the original Norwegian, I found her very strong, very humorous, and very earthy. She is a good-natured, good-hearted woman, not very worldly, in a way naive, but supportive of her husband. They have struggled along together, have suffered and been poor; so she is not happy about his reforms, because it means the loss of the security they have worked for. She doesn't oppose him; she has to be very careful with Dr. Stockmann, not to hurt his feelings, because he's childish. She is a typical woman of the period who knows how to handle her man. This is not a play about women's liberation, but about a husband-wife relationship in which each one's role has been defined for centuries. The Stockmanns, incidentally, are younger in the film than in the play; their ages have been made to conform to those of the performers.

"I have no idea how the character of Mrs. Stockmann will emerge in this film. The script was based mainly on Arthur Miller's adaptation of Ibsen's play, and the writer of the screenplay introduced ideas of his own. A supporting part can be made to come out very important. It depends on whether the director gives you a chance. If there's a close-up at the right moment, when something is going on around you, it can have a very strong effect. Sometimes a silent scene can be your scene. The actor is at the mercy of the director—or the cutter. They might choose to emphasize that Dr. Stockmann is childish and wild and has big fights with his brother. In such a scene the wife's presence could be neglected. But they could also see the scene from the wife's point of view and be slightly ironical toward the whole thing. It depends on their analysis of the scene.

"I really enjoyed working with this particular group of actors; they were not only very professional, but very nice human beings. When you play in ensemble with a company of actors you have known for a long time, you feel more secure. Still, people aren't so different from one another, whether it's here or abroad. You share the same experiences and the same problems. The actor by nature is able to adjust to new situations. But it's always sad to leave a company you liked working with, even if it was only for ten weeks. (There were three weeks of rehearsal, and seven in front of the cameras.)

"I wouldn't turn down a part because it's too small, or because the character is evil. But there can be roles that are reactionary in a bad way. And I don't want to add to something in the world I really don't approve of as a human being. On the other hand, I don't look for parts that fit me exactly. That would be too limiting. You can't refuse a role that is not obviously good for you. The important thing is to keep acting and to broaden your range.

"Acting on stage is not very different from acting in films, but several important adjustments have to be made. In the theater, projection is the important thing; the person in the last row is entitled to hear and see everything. The actor, therefore, uses his entire body and voice. In films, the camera enlarges everything enormously so the actor must underplay, mainly with his face, his eyes; and he speaks in a conversational tone. Stage and screen require the same amount of concentration and energy, but the focal point is different. The stage actor seems to be talking to someone in another room; the screen actor, to someone as close as the camera.

"The stage actor is comparatively free in his gestures and movements; the screen actor is rigidly hemmed in by the lights, microphones, and cameras. A day in front of the camera requires as much stamina and can be as exhausting as an evening behind the footlights. The screen actor's performance is continually interrupted for adjustments of lights, mike, camera, fluffed lines, ruined makeup, airplanes passing overhead, or many other reasons, so that there can be anywhere from two to fifteen takes of a scene. The average is from three to five takes; but all details must be right.

"*An Enemy of the People* has not as yet been released so I can't say what it's like, or what I am like in it. Whatever I see on the screen never looks like what I intended it to, anyway. Though I wish the part of Mrs. Stockmann had been more substantial, it was my job as an actress to breathe life into her and to make her believable. There are many attractive things about this film; it has a strong story, beautiful photography, excellent direction, and fine, naturalistic acting. But the audience, of course, will be the final judge of its success."

An Experimental Production*
By Michael Feingold

Nothing could be stuffier than Ibsen, and nothing could be drier than his one-dimensional political tract, *An Enemy of the People*, right? Wrong, by the standard of most people who take theater seriously, but all too often right in performance, unfortunately.

When Ibsen is not played for open melodramatics in this country, he tends to be performed with a ponderous, lip-biting understatement that is even worse, with the actors all busily graying out their voices and drawing their shoulders up to show the audience they are engaged in something Very Important. Naturally, everyone thinks Ibsen was a dull old bird who wrote plays about water pollution, in which most of the stage time is spent reporting things that happened to the characters five years earlier.

Not, however, audiences [in Minneapolis] at the Guthrie Theatre's current production of *An Enemy of the People*. Adrian Hall, a director best known for his phantasmagoric stagings of new works at the Trinity Square theatre in Providence (where he is artistic director), has been unleashed on the play, with results that, while imperfect, make for an exciting enough production to shake all the accrued dust and solemnity off Ibsen's reputation, and incidentally give a refresher course in the cunning satirical comedy *Enemy of the People* really is. . . .

In an overly solemn or one-sided production, *An Enemy of the People* can seem both obvious and unfunny. Adrian Hall's approach is blunt, cinematic, and off-the-cuff. Starting from the assumption that a modern audience can anticipate Ibsen's structure, if not every event in his script, Hall starts the performance with Act Four (the climactic public meeting at which Stockmann is deprived of his post at the baths) and intercuts the first three acts as flashbacks along the way, taking care to juxtapose scenes so that the ironic shifts in the characters' positions are heightened.

Even more daringly, the direction tilts the play's style toward Expressionism, presenting the action through the eyes of Stockmann's idealistic daughter Petra (ironically, named for her father's brother), who narrates the action in voice-overs and goes through a personal spiritual crisis in lines lifted from *Ghosts* and *Rosmersholm*, linking her to Ibsen's other tormented liberal ladies.

But the torment, like everything else, is handled off-the-cuff. Hall's staging is full of the bustle and informality normally associated with George Abbott comedies; the acting is in the nervous Actors Studio style, overlaid with stammers, tics, and naturalistic gestures—more Swedish-modern Minneapolis than gloomy 19th-century Norway.

If some nuances and some depths are missing from Hall's radically cut and jumbled text, the added freshness and energy easily make up for them. Ibsen's cracked and dusty fountain, in this production, has been cleaned, and sparkles once again.

* From "Adrian Hall Cleans Ibsen's Spring" in *The Village Voice*, New York, October 18, 1976. Reprinted by permission.

An Enemy of the People

ENGLISH VERSION BY RANDOLPH GOODMAN

CAST OF CHARACTERS

DR. THOMAS STOCKMANN, Doctor in charge of the Municipal Baths

MRS. KATHERINE STOCKMANN, his wife

PETRA, their daughter, a schoolteacher

EILIF
MORTEN } their sons, aged thirteen and ten

PETER STOCKMANN, the Doctor's elder brother; Mayor, Chief of Police, Chairman of the Board of the Baths.

MORTON KIIL, owner of a tannery; Mrs. Stockmann's foster-father.

HOVSTAD, editor of *The People's Messenger*

BILLING, his assistant editor

CAPTAIN HORSTER, a young seafaring man

ASLAKSEN, a printer

Men and women of various types and classes, and a number of schoolboys, who attend the public meeting

The action takes place in a town on the southern coast of Norway.

ACT ONE

SCENE: *It is evening.* DOCTOR STOCKMANN's *living room, simply but tastefully furnished. In the side wall, right, are two doors, the upstage door leading to the hall, and the one downstage to the doctor's study. In the opposite wall, and directly facing the hall door, a door leads to the other rooms in the house. In the center of the wall on the left is a stove and further downstage a sofa, with a mirror above it, and an oval table in front of it. On the table is a lighted lamp with a shade. In the back wall of the room, the double doors to the dining room stand open. A lighted lamp is on the table, which is set for supper.* BILLING *is seated at the supper table; he has a napkin tucked under his chin.* MRS. STOCKMANN *stands beside him and places a dish of cold roast beef before him. The other places at the table are empty, and the table is in disorder, as though a meal had recently been finished.*

Mrs. Stockmann. When you come an hour late, Mr. Billing, you just have to put up with cold meat.

Billing (*Eating*). That's all right. It's delicious—absolutely delicious.

Mrs. Stockmann. My husband insists

upon having his meals on time, you know—

Billing. Oh, it doesn't bother me a bit. In fact, I think I enjoy a meal better when I can sit down alone and eat undisturbed.

Mrs. Stockmann. Oh, well, as long as you enjoy it—(*Turns toward the hall door, listening*) That's probably Mr. Hovstad coming in.

Billing. Very likely.

(PETER STOCKMANN, *the* MAYOR, *enters the living room through the hall door. He wears an overcoat, and the insignia of his office on his hat. He carries a cane.*)

The Mayor. Good evening, Katherine.

Mrs. Stockmann (*Coming forward into the living room*). Oh, good evening. It's you, Peter, How nice of you to call!

The Mayor. I happened to be passing by, and I— (*Glancing toward the dining room*) Oh, you have company, I see.

Mrs. Stockmann (*Slightly embarrassed*). No, not really. He just dropped in and—(*Quickly*) Won't you join him for a bite to eat?

The Mayor. Who, me? No, thank you. I never eat hot food at night! Not with my digestion.

Mrs. Stockmann. Oh, just this once wouldn't hurt.

The Mayor. Thank you, no. I stick to my tea and bread and butter. It's much better for you—as well as being more economical.

Mrs. Stockmann (*Smiling*). I hope you don't think Thomas and I are extravagant.

The Mayor. Not *you*, my dear. I would never think that of *you*. (*Points to the Doctor's study.*) Isn't he at home?

Mrs. Stockmann. No, he went out for a little walk after supper—with the boys.

The Mayor. I wonder if that's good for one's health. (*Listens.*) I think I hear him coming now.

Mrs. Stockmann. No, I don't think it's Thomas. (*A knock at the door.*) Come in! (HOVSTAD *enters from the hall.*) Oh, it's Mr. Hovstad!

Hovstad. Yes, I hope you'll forgive me, but I was delayed at the printer's. Good evening, Mr. Mayor.

The Mayor (*Bowing rather stiffly*). Good evening. You are here on business, I imagine.

Hovstad. Partly. It's about an article for the paper.

The Mayor. So I thought. I hear my brother has become a prolific contributor to *The People's Messenger*.

Hovstad. Yes, he's good enough to write a piece for the *Messenger* whenever he wants to get something off his chest.

Mrs. Stockmann (*To* HOVSTAD). But wouldn't you like to— (*Points to the dining room.*)

The Mayor. Of course, of course. I quite understand that he would be eager to reach the people who are most sympathetic to his point of view. But I assure you I have no personal objection to your paper, Mr. Hovstad.

Hovstad. I'm sure you haven't.

The Mayor. After all, there's an excellent spirit of tolerance in our town—a fine cooperative spirit. And that's because a great common interest unites us—an interest that's important to every right-thinking citizen.

Hovstad. You mean the Baths.

The Mayor. Exactly—our fine, new Baths. Take my word for it, Mr. Hovstad—the prosperity of our town will come to depend more and more upon the Baths. There is no doubt of it!

Mrs. Stockmann. That's just what Thomas says.

The Mayor. The way the town has grown in the last year or two is extraordinary. Business is booming, people are growing prosperous, and the value of property is rising steadily. The town is alive!

Hovstad. And practically no unemployment.

The Mayor. Yes, that's another thing. It's a great relief for the property owners that the taxes for welfare have been reduced. And there will be further relief for them if we have a really good summer this year, and lots of visitors—plenty of invalids to give the Baths a reputation.

Hovstad. And there's a good chance of that, I hear.

The Mayor. Inquiries about living accommodations and such keep coming in every day. Things look very promising.

Hovstad. Then the Doctor's article will be appearing at the right time.

The Mayor. So he's written something recently, has he?

Hovstad. No, it's something he wrote during the winter . . . an article about the Baths—recommending them for their excellent sanitary conditions. But I didn't print it at the time. I've held on to it.

The Mayor. Why? Has he put some of his strange notions into it?

Hovstad. No, not at all. I thought it would be better to hold it over till the spring, when people start making their plans for the summer.

The Mayor. A good idea, Mr. Hovstad, a very good idea.

Hovstad. No one works harder than Thomas where the Baths are concerned.

The Mayor. Well, he is the Chief Medical Officer there.

Hovstad. And the Baths were his idea in the first place.

The Mayor. His idea? Really! Some people may think so, but it seems to me that I played a modest part in the enterprise.

Mrs. Stockmann. That's what Thomas always says.

Hovstad. Of course, you did, Mr. Mayor. You got the thing going on a practical basis, everyone knows that. I only meant that Dr. Stockmann had the original idea.

The Mayor. Oh, ideas—yes! My brother has had plenty of ideas in his time —unfortunately. But when it comes to putting an idea into practice and making it work, you need a different sort of man, Mr. Hovstad. And I certainly should have thought that the people in this house at least—

Mrs. Stockmann. My dear Peter—

Hovstad. You don't think that—?

Mrs. Stockmann. Won't you go in and have something to eat, Mr. Hovstad? My husband should be back very soon.

Hovstad. Thank you. Maybe I will have just a bite. (*He goes into the dining room.*)

The Mayor (*Lowering his voice*). Funny how these men brought up on a farm never seem to have any tact.

Mrs. Stockmann. Oh, don't let it upset you, Peter! You and Thomas are brothers—why shouldn't you share the credit?

The Mayor. It seems to me we should— but apparently some people are not satisfied with a share.

Mrs. Stockmann. What nonsense! You and Thomas get on so well together. (*Listening.*) I think he's come back. (*She goes out and opens the hall door.*)

Dr. Stockmann (*Laughing and shouting in the hall*). Look Katherine—here's another guest for you. Isn't this fun! Come in, Captain Horster. Hang up your coat—oh, you don't wear an overcoat, do you? Just think, Katherine, I met the Captain on the street, and he didn't want to come up. I had a hard time persuading him. (CAPTAIN HORSTER *comes into the room and bows to* MRS. STOCKMANN. *He is followed by* DR. STOCKMANN.) Hurry up, boys. They're starving again, Katherine. Come on, Captain Horster, you must try some of our roast beef. (*He pushes* CAPTAIN HORSTER *into the dining room.* EILIF *and* MORTEN *run in after him.*)

Mrs. Stockmann. But, Thomas, don't you see—?

Dr. Stockmann (*Turns in the doorway*). Oh, it's you, Peter! (*Goes to him and shakes his hand.*) Now this is really delightful!

The Mayor. Unfortunately, I can only stay a minute—

Dr. Stockmann. Nonsense! We are going to have some hot toddy in a little while. You haven't forgotten the toddy, have you, Katherine?

Mrs. Stockmann. Of course not! The water is boiling now. (*She goes into the dining room.*)

The Mayor. Toddy, too!

Dr. Stockmann. Yes, let's sit down and be comfortable.

The Mayor. Thanks, but I don't care for drinking parties.

Dr. Stockmann. But this isn't a party.

The Mayor. It seems to me—(*He glances towards the dining room.*) It's amazing how they can put away all that food.

Dr. Stockmann (*Rubbing his hands*). Yes, doesn't it make you feel good to see young people eat? They're always hungry! And that's the way it should be. Lots of food—to make them strong! They are the ones who need the energy to stir things up and build the future.

The Mayor. And what, may I ask, needs "stirring up" here, as you put it?

Dr. Stockmann. Oh, you'll have to ask the young people about that—when the time comes. We won't be around to see it, of course, a couple of old fogies, like us—

The Mayor. Well, really! I must say you have an odd way of expressing yourself.

Dr. Stockmann. Oh, don't take me too seriously, Peter. I'm so happy and contented. I think I'm lucky to be living in the middle of things that are growing and progressing. It's a great time to be alive! It's as if a whole new world were being created around us.

The Mayor. Do you really think so?

Dr. Stockmann. Of course, you can't appreciate it as I do. You've lived here all your life and take things for granted. But I was buried up there in the North, in the backwoods, without a soul to talk to—at least no one with a new idea. So I feel as though I've suddenly been set down in the heart of a big city.

The Mayor. I wouldn't call this a big city!

Dr. Stockmann. I know, I know. It's small compared to a lot of other places. But there's life here—something to look forward to—so many things to work and strive for, and that's what counts. (*Calls.*) Katherine, has the mailman been here?

Mrs. Stockmann (*From the dining room*). No, he hasn't.

Dr. Stockmann. And then to earn more money, Peter! That's something you appreciate after you've struggled along on starvation-wages, as we have—

The Mayor. Now, really!

Dr. Stockmann. We often had a very hard time up there making ends meet, believe me. And now we live like lords! Today, for instance, we had roast beef for dinner—and for supper, too. Wouldn't you like to have some? Let me show it to you, at least. Come here.

The Mayor. No, no—it's not necessary!

Dr. Stockmann. Well, come over here anyway. Look! Do you see, we have a new tablecloth?

The Mayor. Yes, I noticed it.

Dr. Stockmann. And we have a new lampshade, too. Katherine saved up for them! It makes the room look very cozy. Don't you think so? Just stand here for a minute—no, no, not there—here. That's it! Now look, when you see it altogether in this light—I think it looks very nice, doesn't it?

The Mayor. Yes, if you can afford such luxuries—

Dr. Stockmann. Oh, we can afford them now. Katherine tells me I earn almost as much as we spend.

The Mayor. Almost—!

Dr. Stockmann. But a man of science should live with a certain degree of style. I'll bet you the average government employee spends more in a year than I do.

The Mayor. Very likely. A government employee in a top position—!

Dr. Stockmann. Take any ordinary businessman, then. I'll bet you he spends two or three times as much as—

The Mayor. That all depends on the circumstances.

Dr. Stockmann. Anyway, I don't spend money foolishly, I assure you. But I can't deny myself the pleasure of entertaining my friends. I need something like that, you see. I've been out of it all for so long, it's essential that I have the company of intelligent, ambitious, liberal-minded men, like those young fellows who are enjoying their supper in there. I wish you knew Hovstad a bit better—

The Mayor. That reminds me, Hovstad was telling me that he is going to print another article of yours.

Dr. Stockmann. An article of mine?

The Mayor. Yes, about the Baths. An article you wrote during the winter.

Dr. Stockmann. Oh, that one! Well, I don't want it to be published right now.

The Mayor. Why not? It seems to me this is just the right time for it.

Dr. Stockmann. Yes, perhaps under ordinary circumstances. (*He paces about the room.*)

The Mayor (*Follows him with his eyes*). And what's so unusual about the present circumstances?

Dr. Stockmann (*Stands still*). I can't talk about it right now, Peter—not tonight, anyway. There might be a lot that's unusual about the present circumstances, and then again there might be nothing unusual at all—just something I'm imagining.

The Mayor. I must say it all sounds very mysterious. What's going on? Are you keeping something from me? It seems to me that as Chairman of the Board of the Baths, I have a right to—

Dr. Stockmann. And it seems to me that I have a right to—! Oh, don't let's come to blows, Peter.

The Mayor. What's that!? I'm not in the habit of coming to blows with people, as you put it. I tell you most emphatically that all matters concerning the Baths must be dealt with in a businesslike manner, through the proper channels, and by the appointed authorities. I won't stand for things being done behind my back in an underhanded way.

Dr. Stockmann. When have I ever done anything in an underhanded way?

The Mayor. You have an ingrained tendency to take matters into your own hands, but that cannot be tolerated in a well-ordered community. The individual must be willing to subordinate himself to the community—or, to put it more precisely, to those authorities who are responsible for the welfare of that community.

Dr. Stockmann. Perhaps so. But what the devil has all that got to do with me?

The Mayor. It's the very thing you are not willing to learn, my dear Thomas. But, mark my words, sooner or later you will suffer for it. I am warning you! Goodbye.

Dr. Stockmann. Have you gone out of your mind? You're on the wrong track altogether.

The Mayor. I am not usually on the wrong track. You must excuse me now — (*He calls into the dining room.*) Good night, Katherine. Good night, gentlemen. (*He goes out.*)

Mrs. Stockmann (*Coming into the living room.*) Has he gone?

Dr. Stockmann. Yes, and in a terrible temper.

Mrs. Stockmann. Thomas, dear, what did you say to him this time?

Dr. Stockmann. Nothing at all. Anyway, he can't expect me to turn in my report before it's ready.

Mrs. Stockmann. What sort of report do you have to make to him?

Dr. Stockmann. Well! Leave that to me, Katherine. (*Slight pause.*) It's very strange that the mailman hasn't come.

(HOVSTAD, BILLING, *and* HORSTER *have left the table and come into the living room.* EILIF *and* MORTEN *come in shortly after them.*)

Billing (*Stretching himself*). Ahh! A meal like that makes you feel like a new man.

Hovstad. The Mayor seemed to be in a bad mood tonight.

Dr. Stockmann. It's his stomach. He has trouble with his digestion.

Hovstad. I'm inclined to think it was the two of us from *The People's Messenger* that he couldn't digest.

Mrs. Stockmann. I thought you got on very well with him.

Hovstad. It was just a sort of armistice.

Billing. Yes, an armistice. That's the word for it.

Dr. Stockmann. Peter is a lonely man. Don't forget he's a bachelor with none of the joys of a home, and nothing to occupy his mind but business. And all that damned tea he pours into himself! Now then, fellows, bring your chairs up to the table. And what about that toddy, Katherine?

Mrs. Stockmann (*Going towards the*

dining room). You'll have it in a minute. (*She goes out.*)

Dr. Stockmann. Come sit here on the sofa with me, Captain Horster. We so seldom get a chance to see you. Sit down, men.

(*They sit down at the table.* Mrs. Stockmann *brings in a tray with a kettle, decanters, glasses, etc.*)

Mrs. Stockmann. There you are! This is palm liquor, this is rum, and this one is brandy. Now help yourselves.

Dr. Stockmann (*Taking a glass*). We will. (*The men help themselves to toddy.*) And let's have some cigars. Eilif, you know where the box is. And you, Morten, can get my pipe. (*The* Boys *go into the room on the right.*) I have a suspicion Eilif helps himself to a cigar now and then, but I pretend not to notice it. (*Calls out.*) And my smoking-cap too, Morten! Katherine, you can tell him where it is. Oh, he's found it. (*The* Boys *bring in the various things;* Dr. Stockmann *offers cigars.*) Here you are, my friends. I'll stick to my pipe. You know, this one has seen plenty of bad weather with me up there in the North. (*They clink glasses.*) Good health! I must say it's a whole lot better sitting here warm and snug among friends.

Mrs. Stockmann (*Sits in a chair near the sofa, knitting*). Are you sailing soon, Captain Horster?

Horster. We expect to be ready next week.

Mrs. Stockmann. Will you be going to America?

Horster. Yes, that's the plan.

Mrs. Stockmann. Then you won't be able to vote in the coming election.

Horster. Is there going to be an election?

Billing. Didn't you know?

Horster. No, I don't bother about such things.

Billing. You mean you have no interest in public affairs?

Horster. No, I don't know a thing about politics.

Billing. But one ought to vote, at least.

Horster. Even if you don't know what's going on?

Billing. Don't know what's going on! What do you mean by that? A community is like a ship; everyone ought to be ready to take the helm.

Horster. That may be all right on shore; but it would never work on a ship.

Hovstad. It beats me how little most sailors care about what happens on dry land.

Billing. Yes, it's amazing!

Dr. Stockmann. Sailors are like birds of passage, at home everywhere. And that's just another reason why we who stay here must do much more than we're doing. Will there be anything of public interest in tomorrow's paper, Hovstad?

Hovstad. No, nothing of local importance. But the day after tomorrow I thought I'd run your article—

Dr. Stockmann. Oh, damn it—my article! I'm afraid you'll have to hold on to it for a while.

Hovstad. Why? We happen to have the space for it, and I thought this would be the time—

Dr. Stockmann. Yes, I suppose you're right; but it will have to wait all the same. I'll explain it to you later.

(Petra, *in hat and coat, comes in from the hall, with a bundle of exercise books under her arm.*)

Petra. Good evening.

Dr. Stockmann. Oh, Petra, good evening.

(*Greetings all around.* PETRA *takes off her hat and coat and puts them, and the exercise books, on a chair near the door.*)

Petra. So while I was slaving away in the classroom, you've been sitting here and enjoying yourselves!

Dr. Stockmann. Well, come and join us and enjoy yourself too!

Billing. May I mix you a drink?

Petra (*Coming to the table*). Thanks, but I'll do it myself; you always make it too strong. Oh, Father, I almost forgot—I have a letter for you.

(*She goes to the chair where she has put her things.*)

Dr. Stockmann. A letter? From whom?

Petra (*Looking in her coat pocket*). The mailman gave it to me as I was going out—

Dr. Stockmann (*Rising and going towards her*). You should have given it to me before.

Petra. I really didn't have time to run upstairs again. Here it is!

Dr. Stockmann. (*Seizing the letter*). Let me see—let me see, child! Yes, this is it!

Mrs. Stockmann. Is it the one you've been expecting, Thomas?

Dr. Stockmann. Yes, it is. I must go to my room now and read it. Is there a light there, Katherine? I suppose there's no lamp in the room.

Mrs. Stockmann. Yes, there is; the lamp on your desk is already lit.

Dr. Stockmann. Good. Excuse me for a moment— (*He goes into his study.*)

Petra. What's going on, Mother?

Mrs. Stockmann. I don't know; but for the past few days he has constantly been on the lookout for the mailman.

Billing. It's probably from some patient out in the country.

Petra. Poor old dad! He's working himself to death. (*Mixes a drink for herself.*) There, this should taste good!

Hovstad. Were you teaching at night school this evening?

Petra (*Sipping her drink*). Yes, for two hours.

Billing. And four hours of school in the morning—

Petra. Five.

Mrs. Stockmann. And you've still got exercises to correct for tomorrow, I see.

Petra. Yes, lots of them.

Horster. You keep pretty busy yourself, it seems to me.

Petra. Yes—but that's good. I'm so deliciously tired afterwards.

Billing. Do you like that?

Petra. Yes, it makes me sleep so well.

Morten. You must be an awful sinner, Petra.

Petra. A sinner?

Morten. Yes, because you have to work so hard. Work is a punishment for our sins. That's what Mr. Rörlund always says.

Eilif. How can you be so stupid, believing a thing like that!

Mrs. Stockmann. Now, now, Eilif!

Billing (*Laughing*). That's really funny!

Hovstad. Don't you want to work hard, Morten?

Morten. No, I don't.

Hovstad. What do you want to be when you grow up?

Morten. I want to be a Viking.

Eilif. You'd have to be a heathen, then.

Morten. Well, I can be a heathen, can't I?

Billing. That's the idea, Morten! I feel the same way.

Mrs. Stockmann (Making signs to him). I'm sure you don't, Mr. Billing.

Billing. I swear I do! I'm a heathen, and I'm proud of it. And we'll all be heathens before long, just you wait and see.

Morten. And then we'll be allowed to do anything we like, won't we?

Billing. Well, I'm not so sure about that, Morten.

Mrs. Stockmann. Run along now, boys; I'm sure you have some homework to do for tomorrow.

Eilif. Can't *I* stay just a little bit longer—?

Mrs. Stockmann. No, you can't. Run along now, both of you.

(*The* Boys *say goodnight and go into the room, left.*)

Hovstad. Do you think it's bad for the boys to listen to such talk?

Mrs. Stockmann. I don't know; I just don't like it.

Petra. But, Mother, aren't you being too strict?

Mrs. Stockmann. Maybe, I am, but I don't like it—not in our own home.

Petra. Oh, there is so much hypocrisy! At home we mustn't speak our minds, and at school we have to stand there and lie to the children.

Horster. Lie to them?

Petra. Yes, of course. We have to teach them all sorts of things we don't believe in ourselves.

Billing. And that's the truth!

Petra. If only I had enough money, I'd start a school of my own—and I'd run things very differently.

Billing. Oh, always money—!

Horster. If you're really thinking of doing that, Miss Stockmann, I have the ideal place for a schoolroom. The great big old house my father left me is standing there practically empty, and there's an enormous dining room on the ground floor that—

Petra (Laughing). Oh, thanks very much, but I'm sure nothing will come of it.

Hovstad. It seems to me, Miss Petra is much more likely to go in for journalism. By the way, have you had a chance to do anything with that English story you promised to translate for us?

Petra. No, not yet; but you'll have it very soon.

(Dr. Stockmann *comes in from his room with the open letter in his hand.*)

Dr. Stockmann (Waving the letter). Well, here's some news that'll wake up the town!

Billing. News?

Mrs. Stockmann. What news?

Dr. Stockmann. A great discovery, Katherine.

Hovstad. Really?

Mrs. Stockmann. A discovery of yours?

Dr. Stockmann. Yes—of mine. (*Paces up and down.*) And I dare them to say, as they usually do, that it's all in my head, and just another one of my crazy ideas! They'll think twice about it this time, I'll bet!

Petra. But, Father, tell us what it is.

Dr. Stockmann. Just give me time, and I'll tell you all about it. I wish Peter were here now! It only goes to show how men form their opinions, and carry on their business, as blind as bats—

Hovstad. What are you driving at, Doctor?

Dr. Stockmann. Everybody believes

that our town is a very healthy place —isn't that so?

Hovstad. Yes, of course.

Dr. Stockmann. An exceptionally healthy place, in fact, a place that should be highly recommended not only for invalids, but for those who are well—

Mrs. Stockmann. Yes, but my dear Thomas—

Dr. Stockmann. And so we've been recommending and advertising it— and I myself have sung its praises, not only in the *Messenger*, but in a half a dozen pamphlets—

Hovstad. Well, what about it?

Dr. Stockmann. And these Baths that have been called "the main artery" of the town, its "nerve center"—and the devil only knows what else—

Hovstad. "The town's pulsating heart" —that's what I called them once on a happy occasion—

Dr. Stockmann. Oh, yes. Well, do you know what these Baths are? These great and glorious Baths, that have cost us so much money—do you know what they really are?

Hovstad. No, what are they?

Mrs. Stockmann. What are they, Thomas?

Dr. Stockmann. The Baths are nothing but a cesspool!

Petra. The Baths, Father?

Mrs. Stockmann (*At the same time*). Our Baths!

Hovstad. But, Doctor—

Billing. That's incredible!

Dr. Stockmann. The Baths are a whited sepulchre; they're poisonous, and a menace to the public health! All the waste matter from the tanneries up at Mill Valley, all that stinking filth, is seeping into the pipes that feed the Baths, and that same damned poison is pouring out onto the shore—

Horster. Where the people bathe?

Dr. Stockmann. Precisely.

Hovstad. How can you be so sure of all this, Doctor?

Dr. Stockmann. I've investigated the matter thoroughly. I'd suspected something of the kind for a long time. Last year I noticed there was an unusually large number of cases of illness among the visitors to the Baths—typhoid and gastric fever—

Mrs. Stockmann. Yes, so there were.

Dr. Stockmann. At first we were sure the visitors had brought the infection with them; but later on, during the winter, I began to have different ideas. So I carried out some tests on the water, as far as I could.

Mrs. Stockmann. So that's what's been keeping you so busy!

Dr. Stockmann. Yes, that's what I've been concentrating on, Katherine. But I didn't have the necessary equipment here; so I gathered samples of the water at the Baths and at the beach, and sent them to the University laboratories for a complete chemical analysis.

Hovstad. And you've gotten that?

Dr. Stockmann (*Showing the letter*). Yes—here it is! It proves without a doubt the presence of decaying organic matter in the water—it is teeming with infusoria. The water is so polluted it is dangerous to use it, either internally or externally.

Mrs. Stockmann. What a blessing you discovered it in time!

Dr. Stockmann. Yes, indeed.

Hovstad. Now what do you propose to do about it, Doctor?

Dr. Stockmann. See that the water is cleaned up, of course.

Hovstad. Can that be done?

Dr. Stockmann. It *must* be done. Otherwise the Baths will be useless, finished. But there's no need to worry about that. I know exactly how to remedy the situation.

Mrs. Stockmann. But, Thomas, why have you kept all this so secret?

Dr. Stockmann. What did you expect me to do, go running around town shooting my mouth off about it, before I had absolute proof? No, thanks. I'm not such a fool as all that.

Petra. Still, you might have told *us*—

Dr. Stockmann. I couldn't tell a living soul. But tomorrow you can run up to Mill Valley and tell the old Badger—

Mrs. Stockmann. Oh, Thomas!

Dr. Stockmann. Well, tell your grandfather, then. That'll shake the old boy up! I know he thinks I'm cracked—and a lot of other people think so too, I've noticed. But now they'll see—this time I'll show them! (*Walks back and forth, rubbing his hands.*) You can't imagine what an uproar there'll be in the town, Katherine, when they find out they have to dig up and re-lay all the waterpipes.

Hovstad (*Getting up*). All the waterpipes—?

Dr. Stockmann. Yes, of course. The intake is too low down; it will have to be moved much higher up. I told them that in the first place.

Petra. You were right after all, Father.

Dr. Stockmann. Yes—you remember, Petra? I opposed their plans and pointed out all the errors even before they started to work. Of course, no one would listen to me then. Well, now I'll let them have it! I've prepared a statement for the Board of Directors; it's been ready for a week. I was only waiting for this to come. (*Indicating the letter.*) I'll send it off at once. (*Goes into his room and comes back with a manuscript.*)

Look, here—four closely written pages—and this laboratory report will go with them. Do we have a large envelope, Katherine? (*She produces one from a drawer.*) Good. And now give this to—to—what the devil is that girl's name? To the maid! Tell her to deliver it to the Mayor immediately.

(Mrs. Stockmann *takes the envelope and goes out through the dining room.*)

Petra. What do you think Uncle Peter will say, Father?

Dr. Stockmann. What *can* he say? It seems to me he'll be very glad that such an important fact has come to light.

Hovstad. Do you mind if we put a little paragraph about your discovery in the *Messenger*?

Dr. Stockmann. I'd be very grateful if you would.

Hovstad. The sooner the public hears about this, the better.

Dr. Stockmann. Certainly.

Mrs. Stockmann (*Returning*). She's gone off with it.

Billing. Take my word for it, Doctor, you are going to be the most famous man in town!

Dr. Stockmann (*Pacing back and forth, joyfully*). Oh, nonsense! I only did my duty. I was just lucky enough to discover it—that's all. But still—

Billing. Hovstad, don't you think the town ought to arrange to honor Dr. Stockmann in some way?

Hovstad. I'll certainly suggest it.

Billing. And I'll talk it over with Aslaksen.

Dr. Stockmann. No, no, my dear friends! Let's have none of that nonsense. I won't hear of it. And if the Board of Directors decides to vote me a raise in salary—I won't accept it. Do you hear me, Katherine? I'll absolutely refuse it!

Mrs. Stockmann. Yes, Thomas, you are quite right.

Petra (*Raising her glass*). To your health, Father!

Hovstad and Billing. Your health! Good health, Doctor!

Horster (*Clinks glasses with* Dr. Stockmann). I hope it will bring you the best of luck!

Dr. Stockmann. Thank you, thank you, my dear friends! I can't tell you how happy I am! It's a wonderful thing to feel that you've been of some service to your fellow-citizens and to the town you live in. Katherine, let's dance!

(*He puts his arms round her and whirls her round the room. She screams and tries to free herself. The others laugh, clap their hands, and cheer the doctor. The two boys put their heads in at the door to see what is going on.*)

CURTAIN

Act Two

SCENE. *The Doctor's living room. Morning. The double doors to the dining room are closed.* Mrs. Stockmann, *with a sealed letter in her hand, comes in from the dining room, goes to the door of the doctor's study, and peeps in.*

Mrs. Stockmann. Are you in there, Thomas?

Dr. Stockmann (*From within*). Yes, I just got back.(*Enters.*) What is it?

Mrs. Stockmann (*Giving him the letter*). A letter from your brother.

Dr. Stockmann. Oh, let me see it. (*He opens the letter and reads.*) "I am returning herewith the report you sent me—" (*He reads on and mutters to himself.*) Hm—

Mrs. Stockmann. Well, what does he say?

Dr. Stockmann (*Putting the papers in his pocket*). He just says he'll stop in around noon.

Mrs. Stockmann. Well, try to remember to be at home then.

Dr. Stockmann. Don't worry, I will. I've made all my morning visits.

Mrs. Stockmann. I can't wait to hear what he has to say about it.

Dr. Stockmann. You'll see, he'll be angry because I made the discovery, and he didn't.

Mrs. Stockmann. Doesn't that make you nervous?

Dr. Stockmann. Oh, he'll really be glad, but he won't show it. Peter is always so damned upset when anyone but himself does something good for this town.

Mrs. Stockmann. Thomas, take my advice—be generous, and share the credit for this with him. Couldn't you pretend it was some hint he dropped that started you thinking?

Dr. Stockmann. I'm willing to do that —as long as we get this thing cleared up.

(Morten Kiil *sticks his head in at the hall door, glances around, and chuckles.*)

Kiil (*Slyly*). It is true? Is it?

Mrs. Stockmann. Father! Come in.

Dr. Stockmann. Good morning, good morning.

Mrs. Stockmann. Father, please come in.

Kiil. If it's true, I will; if not, goodbye.

Dr. Stockmann. If what's true?

Kiil. This crazy story about the water. Is it true?

Dr. Stockmann. Of course, it's true. But how did you find out about it?

Kiil. From Petra. She ran in to see me on her way to school—

Dr. Stockmann. Oh, did she?

Kiil. Yes, she did. I thought she was trying to make a fool of me, but Petra wouldn't do that.

Dr. Stockmann. Of course not. How could you think such a thing!

Kiil. Well, you can't trust anybody, and I don't like to be made a fool of. Anyway, is it true?

Dr. Stockmann. It is absolutely true. Here, why don't you sit down? (*He shows* KIIL *to the sofa.*) Well, it's a lucky thing for the town, isn't it?

Kiil (Trying to keep from laughing). A lucky thing for the town?!

Dr. Stockmann. Yes, that I made this discovery in time—

Kiil (Fighting his laughter). Oh, sure, sure—But I never thought you'd have the nerve to play tricks on your own brother!

Dr. Stockmann. Play tricks—!

Mrs. Stockmann. But, Father, he's not—!

Kiil (Rests his hands and chin on the handle of his cane and winks slyly at the doctor). Let's see now, what's the story? Some kind of little creature got into the waterpipes—is that it?

Dr. Stockmann. Infusoria—yes.

Kiil. And Petra said a lot of these little creatures got in—a whole lot—

Dr. Stockmann. Yes, millions, probably.

Kiil. But no one can see them—is that right?

Dr. Stockmann. Of course, no one can see them.

Kiil (Laughing quietly). I'll be damned if that isn't the best story I've ever heard!

Dr. Stockmann. What do you mean?

Kiil. You'll never get the Mayor to believe that one!

Dr. Stockmann. We shall see.

Kiil. You think he's as crazy as all that?

Dr. Stockmann. I hope the whole town will be as crazy as all that.

Kiil. The whole town! That's fine! It'll serve them right—yes, it will, and teach them a lesson. They think they're so much smarter than us old-timers. They booted me off the Town Council—kicked me out like a dog. Now I'll get even. Go ahead and play your tricks on them, Thomas!

Dr. Stockmann. Wait a minute, listen—

Kiil (Standing up). You trick them! And if you put this one over on the Mayor and his pals, I swear I'll give a hundred crowns to charity—on the spot!

Dr. Stockmann. That's very kind of you.

Kiil. You know, I don't have money to throw away, but you put this over and next Christmas I'll give fifty crowns to charity.

(HOVSTAD *enters from the hall.*)

Hovstad. Good morning! (*Seeing* KIIL.) Oh, pardon me—

Dr. Stockmann. That's all right; come in.

Kiil (Starts to chuckle). Oho! Is he in on this, too?

Hovstad. What do you mean?

Dr. Stockmann. Yes, of course he is.

Kiil. I might have known it! He has to put it in his paper. You know how to handle it, Thomas! You figure it out! I've got to go.

Dr. Stockmann. Why don't you stay a little while longer?

Kiil. No, I must go. I'll let *you* think up the tricks. You won't be sorry; it'll damn well be to your advantage!

(*He goes out, followed by* Mrs. Stockmann.)

Dr. Stockmann (*Laughing*). What do you think?—The old man doesn't believe a word of all this about the water—

Hovstad. Oh, is that what you were talking about?

Dr. Stockmann. Yes, and I suppose that's what brings *you* here.

Hovstad. Yes, it is. Can you spare me a few moments, Doctor?

Dr. Stockmann. Of course, as long as you like.

Hovstad. Have you heard anything from the Mayor yet?

Dr. Stockmann. No, not yet—only that he's coming over later.

Hovstad. Since I left here last night, I've given this matter a great deal of thought.

Dr. Stockmann. You have?

Hovstad. It seems to me that you, as a doctor and a scientist, view this business of the water-supply as an isolated problem. Perhaps you don't realize how many other things it may involve.

Dr. Stockmann. How do you mean? Let's sit down—(Hovstad *sits on the sofa,* Dr. Stockmann *on a chair on the other side of the table.*) Now then. What were you saying?

Hovstad. Last night you said that the pollution of the water comes from impurities in the soil.

Dr. Stockmann. Yes, I'm absolutely cer-

tain that it comes from the poisonous waste materials from the tanneries at Mill Valley.

Hovstad. Forgive me, Doctor, but I think it comes from an altogether different sort of poison.

Dr. Stockmann. What poison is that?

Hovstad. The poison that is polluting and contaminating the very life of this town.

Dr. Stockmann. What the devil are you talking about, Hovstad?

Hovstad. Little by little, the whole town has been taken over by a pack of bureaucrats.

Dr. Stockmann. Oh, come now. They're not all bureaucrats.

Hovstad. Maybe not—but if they aren't bureaucrats themselves, they're the friends and supporters of those who are. It's the well-to-do and the old established families, who have everything and everyone in this town sewed up.

Dr. Stockmann. Yes—but they are also men of ability and knowledge.

Hovstad. How much ability and knowledge did they show when they laid the waterpipes where they are now?

Dr. Stockmann. That, of course, was a tremendous piece of stupidity. But we'll soon clear that up.

Hovstad. Do you think it's going to be as easy as all that?

Dr. Stockmann. Easy or not, it's got to be done.

Hovstad. But you'll need the Press to back you up.

Dr. Stockmann. I don't think that'll be necessary; I'm sure that my brother—

Hovstad. Excuse me, Doctor, I feel bound to give this matter a great deal of publicity.

Dr. Stockmann. In the newspaper?

Hovstad. Yes. When I took over *The*

People's Messenger, it was my idea to drive out the gang of reactionary old fogies who control this town.

Dr. Stockmann. With the result that you almost lost the paper—you told me that yourself.

Hovstad. Yes, at that time we had to back down a bit, it's true. The whole project of the Baths was in danger of falling through, if they withheld their money. But now that the Baths are a going concern, we can do without those high and mighty gentlemen.

Dr. Stockmann. Do without them, yes; but we have a lot to thank them for.

Hovstad. Oh, we'll thank them, all right. But a journalist who considers himself a liberal, as I do, can't afford to let an opportunity like this go by. The myth of official infallibility must be exploded. That sort of superstition must be wiped out.

Dr. Stockmann. I agree with you entirely, Mr. Hovstad; if it's a superstition, I say away with it!

Hovstad. I hesitate to implicate the Mayor—since he's your brother; but I'm sure you agree with me that the truth comes first.

Dr. Stockmann. I certainly do. (*Strongly.*) Yes, but—

Hovstad. I don't want you to misjudge me. I'm no more self-centered or ambitious than most men.

Dr. Stockmann. My dear fellow— No one says you are!

Hovstad. I come from poor people, as you know, Doctor, and so from personal experience I am acquainted with the most pressing needs of the underprivileged. They want to have some say in the way the government is run, because that will allow them to develop their ability, their knowledge, and their self-respect—

Dr. Stockmann. That's very understandable—

Hovstad. Yes—and in my opinion a journalist is seriously to blame if he neglects the slightest opportunity to bring some measure of freedom to the masses—to the poor and the oppressed. I know very well that those in power will call me an agitator, and what not. But, let them—as long as my conscience is clear!

Dr. Stockmann. Absolutely! Absolutely right, Mr. Hovstad! But all the same—damn it! (*There is a knock at the door.*) Come in!

(ASLAKSEN *appears at the hall door. He is poorly but decently dressed in a black suit, with a slightly wrinkled white tie. He carries a felt hat and gloves.*)

Aslaksen (*Bowing*). Excuse me, Doctor, if I'm interrupting—

Dr. Stockmann (*Rising*). Well, well! It's Mr. Aslaksen!

Aslaksen. Yes, Doctor.

Hovstad (*Rising*). Do you want to see me, Aslaksen?

Aslaksen. No, I didn't even know you were here. It's the Doctor I—

Dr. Stockmann. What can I do for you?

Aslaksen. Is it true what Mr. Billing tells me, that you are planning to improve our water-system?

Dr. Stockmann. Yes, for the Baths.

Aslaksen. Oh, I see. Well, Doctor, I want you to know I'll do everything in my power to back you up.

Hovstad (*To the doctor*). You see!

Dr. Stockmann. Well, I'm very grateful to you, but—

Aslaksen. I think you'll find it helpful to have the small businessmen behind you. We form a solid majority in the town. And it's always a good thing to have the majority on your side, Doctor.

Dr. Stockmann. That's very true; but I don't see why such unusual measures are necessary. After all, it's a simple, straightforward matter—

Aslaksen. Well, it might be useful, all the same. I know the local authorities very well. Politicians are not usually very ready to act on suggestions that come from others. That's why I think it would be a good idea if we organized a little demonstration.

Hovstad. A fine idea!

Dr. Stockmann. A demonstration? What on earth are you going to demonstrate about?

Aslaksen. Your plan! Oh, we'll act with moderation, Doctor. That's always my aim—moderation. It's the citizen's greatest virtue—at least *I* think so.

Dr. Stockmann. You are well known for your moderation, I believe, Mr. Aslaksen.

Aslaksen. Yes, and I'm proud of it. And as to the matter of the water supply —that's of the utmost importance to us little businessmen. The Baths are getting to be a regular gold mine for the town. We'll all soon be making our living out of them, especially those of us who are home owners. That's why we'll support your plans for the Baths one hundred percent. And since I am the president of the Home Owners Association—

Dr. Stockmann. Yes—?

Aslaksen. And also the local secretary of the Temperance Society—you know, of course, Doctor, that I'm in favor of prohibition—?

Dr. Stockmann. Naturally.

Aslaksen. As a result, I come into contact with a great many people. And since I'm known to be a law-abiding and responsible citizen—like yourself, Doctor—I have a certain influence in this town—you might say, a bit of power.

Dr. Stockmann. I know that very well, Mr. Aslaksen.

Aslaksen. So you see, it would be an easy matter for me to get up some sort of testimonial in your behalf, if we had to.

Dr. Stockmann. A testimonial?

Aslaksen. Yes—a petition of thanks from the citizens for your share in a matter of such importance to the community. It goes without saying that it must be worded with the utmost moderation, so as not to offend the authorities, who run this town, after all. But, if we keep that in mind, I don't see how anyone can object!

Hovstad. Well, what if they do object—!

Aslaksen. No, no! We must do nothing to offend the authorities, Mr. Hovstad. We can't afford to antagonize the men who control our livelihood. I've seen enough of that in my time —and no good ever comes of it. But no one can object to a citizen who expresses his honest opinion in moderate terms.

Dr. Stockmann (*Shaking his hand*). My dear Mr. Aslaksen, I can't tell you how delighted I am to know that I can count on the support of my fellow-citizens. It makes me very happy —indeed, it does! And now, how about a glass of sherry?

Aslaksen. No, thank you; I never touch alcoholic beverages.

Dr. Stockmann. But, surely, a glass of beer?

Aslaksen. No, Doctor—many thanks, but I never drink anything so early in the day. Well, I'll be on my way now. I want to talk to some of the home owners in town and get their reactions.

Dr. Stockmann. That's very kind of you, Mr. Aslaksen; but I really don't understand the necessity for all these preparations. It seems to me this thing should move ahead under its own steam.

Aslaksen. You don't realize how slow the authorities are to act, Doctor. But far be it from me to blame them—!

Hovstad. We're going to stir them up in the paper tomorrow, Aslaksen.

Aslaksen. No incitement to violence, I hope, Mr. Hovstad. If you want results, proceed with caution. Take my advice; I speak from experience in the school of hard knocks. Well, I must say goodbye. Remember, Doctor, you have the little businessmen behind you like a stone wall. The solid majority are on your side.

Dr. Stockmann. Thank you very much, Mr. Aslaksen. (*They shake hands.*) Goodbye, goodbye!

Aslaksen. Are you going to the office now, Mr. Hovstad?

Hovstad. I'll be there in a little while. There are one or two things I want to discuss with the doctor.

Aslaksen. Very well.

(*He bows and goes out;* Dr. Stock-mann *follows him into the hall.*)

Hovstad (*As the doctor re-enters*). Well, what do you think of that, Doctor? Don't you agree it's about time we shook up these muddle-headed, timid, do-nothings?

Dr. Stockmann. Are you referring to Aslaksen?

Hovstad. Yes, I am. He's a stick-in-the-mud—not a bad fellow, otherwise;

but he's like most of the other people around here—wavering and floundering—can't make up their minds. They're so cautious and carping, they never dare to take a definite stand.

Dr. Stockmann. But Aslaksen seems to me to have good intentions.

Hovstad. Good intentions are all right; but it's more important for a man to be self-assured and reliable.

Dr. Stockmann. Yes—I agree with you there.

Hovstad. That's why I want to take this opportunity to stiffen the backbone of these people with good intentions. Their tendency to bow to authority has got to be rooted out. The gross and inexcusable blunder about the water system must be brought to the attention of every single voter . . . in a strong editorial.

Dr. Stockmann. Very well; if you think it's for the good of the community. But not a word till I've had a talk with my brother.

Hovstad. In the meantime, I'll write the editorial. But what if your brother refuses to take action—

Dr. Stockmann. That's inconceivable!

Hovstad. It is not entirely inconceivable. Then what?

Dr. Stockmann. Then I promise you— If he refuses, you may print my report, every word of it.

Hovstad. I may? I have your word for it?

Dr. Stockmann (*Giving him the manuscript*). Here it is; take it with you. It can't do any harm for you to read it, and you can give it back to me later on.

Hovstad. Very good; I shall do so. (*He puts the manuscript in his pocket.*) Goodbye for now, Doctor.

Dr. Stockmann. Goodbye. Everything

will go more smoothly than you think, Mr. Hovstad—just wait and see.

Hovstad. Well, we shall see. (*He bows and goes out.*)

Dr. Stockmann. (*Opens the dining room door, looks in, and calls.*) Katherine! Oh, you've come back, Petra!

Petra (*Coming into the living room*). Yes, I just got back from school.

Mrs. Stockmann (*Enters*). Hasn't he been here yet?

Dr. Stockmann. Peter? No. But I had a long talk with Hovstad. He's quite excited about my discovery. It seems to have much wider implications than I imagined at first. He's put his newspaper at my disposal, in case I should need it.

Mrs. Stockmann. Do you think you will?

Dr. Stockmann. Certainly not. Still, it's very flattering to know that his progressive, independent paper is on my side. Oh, yes—I've also had a visit from the president of the Home Owners Association!

Mrs. Stockmann. Really! What did he want?

Dr. Stockmann. He wanted to offer me his support as well. They will all stand by me, if I should need them. And do you know what I've got behind me, Katherine?

Mrs. Stockmann. Behind you? No, what have you got behind you?

Dr. Stockmann. The solid majority.

Mrs. Stockmann. Really? Is that a good thing for you, Thomas?

Dr. Stockmann. A good thing! Well, I should think so! (*He paces back and forth and rubs his hands.*) It's wonderful to feel like a brother to everyone in town!

Petra. And to be able to do so much that is good and useful, Father!

Dr. Stockmann. Especially when it's for your own home town, Petra!

(*The doorbell rings.*)

Mrs. Stockmann. That was the doorbell.

Dr. Stockmann. It must be Peter. (*He calls into the hall.*) Come in!

The Mayor (*Enters*). Good morning.

Dr. Stockmann. I'm glad to see you, Peter.

Mrs. Stockmann. Good morning, Peter. How are you today?

The Mayor. Just so-so, thank you. (*To the* Doctor.) Yesterday, after office-hours, I got your report dealing with the condition of the water at the Baths.

Dr. Stockmann. Have you read it?

The Mayor. Yes, I have.

Dr. Stockmann. Well, what do you have to say about it?

The Mayor (*Glances aside and clears his throat*). Hm—

Mrs. Stockmann. Come with me, Petra. (*She and* Petra *go into the room, left.*)

The Mayor (*After a pause*). Why did you find it necessary to make all these investigations behind my back?

Dr. Stockmann. Until I was absolutely sure about it, I—

The Mayor. Then you mean that now you are absolutely sure?

Dr. Stockmann. Didn't my report convince you of that?

The Mayor. Do you intend to submit this report to the Board of Directors as an official document?

Dr. Stockmann. Of course. Something's got to be done about it—at once.

The Mayor. You always use such strong expressions. In your report, you say, among other things, that we offer the visitors to our Baths a permanent case of poisoning.

Dr. Stockmann. Well, what would you call it, Peter? I tell you—whether you drink it or bathe in it—the water is poisonous! And that's what we offer the sick people who come here, trust us, pay exorbitant prices, and expect to be cured!

The Mayor. And that leads you to the conclusion that we must build a sewer to carry off the alleged impurities from Mill Valley, and construct an entirely new system of water-pipes.

Dr. Stockmann. Yes. Can you think of any other solution? I can't.

The Mayor. I found an excuse for going to see the Chief Engineer this morning, and half-jokingly mentioned that we might consider making these changes some time in the future.

Dr. Stockmann. Some time in the future!

The Mayor. He laughed at the proposal. Naturally, he thought it was my idea. Have you taken the trouble to find out what the alterations you suggest would cost? Well, he said it would probably come to several hundred thousand crowns.

Dr. Stockmann. As much as that?

The Mayor. Yes—but that's not the worst of it. The work would take at least two years.

Dr. Stockmann. Two years? Two whole years?

The Mayor. At least. And what would we do with the Baths in the meantime? Close them up? We'd have to. Do you think anyone would come near the place if it got out that the water was polluted?

Dr. Stockmann. But, Peter, that's just what it is.

The Mayor. And this has to happen now—just when the Baths are becoming popular. There are other towns around here that qualify as well as ours as a health resort. Don't you think they would do everything in their power to divert this stream of visitors to themselves? Of course they would; and where would that leave us? After investing all that money in the Baths, we'd probably have to close them up entirely. And the town would be ruined—thanks to you!

Dr. Stockmann. Ruined—thanks to me!

The Mayor. The only future the town has—the only future worth mentioning, that is—depends upon the Baths. You know that as well as I do.

Dr. Stockmann. Well, then, what do you think ought to be done?

The Mayor. Your report has not convinced me that the condition of the water at the Baths is as bad as you consider it to be.

Dr. Stockmann. If anything it's worse! Or it certainly will be with the summer coming on—and the hot weather.

The Mayor. I still think you are greatly exaggerating the matter. A competent physician ought to be able to find antidotes for the harmful substances—and effective remedies, if they persist.

Dr. Stockmann. Well, well. And what else?

The Mayor. The existing water supply for the Baths is an established fact, and has got to be treated as such. But the Board of Directors may be willing to consider making certain improvements if the financial expenditure is within reason.

Dr. Stockmann. Do you think I'd have anything to do with such trickery?

The Mayor. Trickery?

Dr. Stockmann. Yes—it would be a trick, a fraud, a cover-up, and a downright crime against the whole community!

The Mayor. As I said before, I am not convinced that there is actually any immediate danger.

Dr. Stockmann. I can't believe that you are not convinced. My report presents the facts exactly as they are; and you know that very well, Peter, but you won't acknowledge it. It was you who insisted that the Baths and the water supply be built where they are. It was your mistake, damn it! But now you won't admit it! Do you think I don't see through you?

The Mayor. And even if that were true? If I want to protect my reputation, it is for the good of the town. It would be impossible for me to direct public affairs for the general welfare, as I see it, if I were stripped of my moral authority. And for that reason—among others—it is imperative that you do not submit your report to the Board. In the best interests of the public, you must withhold it. Later on I'll bring up the question, and we will try to work it out quietly; but not a single word—not a hint—of this unfortunate situation must leak out.

Dr. Stockmann. I'm afraid it won't be possible to prevent that, my dear Peter.

The Mayor. It must and shall be prevented.

Dr. Stockmann. It's no use, I tell you. Too many people know of it already.

The Mayor. People know of it? Who? Surely not those fellows on the *Messenger*—?

Dr. Stockmann. Yes, they know about it. The progressive, independent press will see to it that you public officials do your duty.

The Mayor. You are an incredibly foolish man, Thomas. Haven't you thought about the serious consequences this may have for you?

Dr. Stockmann. Serious consequences—for me?

The Mayor. Yes, for you and your family.

Dr. Stockmann. What the devil do you mean by that?

The Mayor. I think I've always behaved in a brotherly way to you. I've always been ready and willing to help you.

Dr. Stockmann. Yes, you have—and I thank you for it.

The Mayor. Well, you needn't thank me. I was more or less forced to do it—for my own sake. By helping you to improve your finances, I hoped to be able to keep some sort of check on you.

Dr. Stockmann. What? You mean you only did it for your own sake?

The Mayor. To some extent, yes. It is extremely embarrassing for a public official when his closest relative continually involves himself in questionable situations.

Dr. Stockmann. And you think I do that, do you?

The Mayor. Yes, you do—unfortunately, and without even being aware of it. You have a restless, aggressive, rebellious nature, and you can't resist rushing into print regardless of the subject, so long as you have your say. The minute an idea pops into your head you must write an article for the newspaper, or a whole pamphlet, about it.

Dr. Stockmann. Well, don't you think it's a man's duty to share new ideas with the public?

The Mayor. No, the public doesn't need any new ideas. The public is better off with the good old ideas it already has.

Dr. Stockmann. And you really believe that?

The Mayor. Yes, and for once I must be frank with you. I've tried up till now to avoid it, because I know how irritable you are; but now I must tell you the truth, Thomas. You have no idea how you injure yourself by your rashness. You criticize the authorities, you even criticize the government—you are always finding fault. And then you complain of being ignored and persecuted. But what else can such a troublemaker as you expect?

Dr. Stockmann. What's that! A troublemaker, am I?

The Mayor. Yes, Thomas, you are an extremely difficult man to work with —as I know from experience. You disregard everyone you ought to consider. You seem to forget completely that you have me to thank for your appointment as Chief Medical Officer at the Baths—

Dr. Stockmann. I was entitled to that position—I had a better right to it than anyone else. It was I who first saw the possibility of turning this town into a health resort; and for many years it was I, and I alone, who fought for the idea. I wrote article after article—

The Mayor. There is no doubt about that! But the time wasn't right for the project then. You were living way up there in the North in those days, so of course you could not be a judge of that. But as soon as the appropriate moment came I—and the others—took the matter in hand—

Dr. Stockmann. Yes, took the matter in hand, and made a mess of it. Ruined my beautiful plan! It's pretty obvious now what clever fellows you were!

The Mayor. It seems to me that you are only looking for an outlet for your aggressiveness. You want to attack your superiors; that's an old habit of yours. You cannot submit to the slightest authority; you regard anyone above you as a personal enemy; and come what may, you will find a weapon to use against him. But now I have made it clear to you that the interests of the whole town are at stake—and, incidentally, my own interests as well. And so, Thomas, I want you to know that I shall be absolutely ruthless unless you comply with what I am going to ask you to do.

Dr. Stockmann. And what is that?

The Mayor. Since you have been so thoughtless as to speak of this matter to outsiders, when you should have treated it in an entirely official and confidential manner, it is too late to hush it up now. There will soon be all sorts of rumors going around and everybody who has a grudge against us will be sure to elaborate and spread them. Therefore it will be necessary for you to refute them publicly.

Dr. Stockmann. I? But how? I don't understand.

The Mayor. We shall expect you to come to the conclusion—after further investigation—that the situation is by no means as dangerous or as critical as you had at first imagined.

Dr. Stockmann. Oh! So that's what you expect, do you?

The Mayor. And, furthermore, we shall expect you to make a public statement expressing your confidence in the Board, and its readiness to study the matter fully and conscientiously, and to take whatever steps may be necessary to remedy any possible defects.

Dr. Stockmann. But you will never be able to correct the situation merely by patching and tinkering—never! Take my word for it, Peter; I know what I'm talking about. And that's my unalterable opinion!

The Mayor. As a member of the Board, you have no right to a personal opinion.

Dr. Stockmann (Amazed). No right?

The Mayor. Not as a member of the Board—no! As a private individual—that's an entirely different matter. But as a subordinate member of the staff of the Baths, you have no right to express publicly any opinion which runs contrary to that of your superiors.

Dr. Stockmann. This is too much! Do you mean to say that I, as a doctor and a scientist, have no right to—!

The Mayor. But this is not simply a matter of science. It is more complicated than that; there are economic and technical problems involved as well.

Dr. Stockmann. I don't give a damn about all that! No one can stop me from expressing my opinions freely on any and every subject!

The Mayor. You are free to speak on any subject you please—as long as it doesn't concern the Baths. We forbid you to mention them.

Dr. Stockmann (Shouting). You forbid me—! You and a bunch of—!

The Mayor. I forbid it—I, your superior, personally forbid it. And I expect you to obey.

Dr. Stockmann (Controlling himself). Peter—if you weren't my brother—

Petra (Throws open the door and runs in). Father, you mustn't stand for this!

Mrs. Stockmann (Coming in after her). Petra, Petra—!

The Mayor. What have you two been doing, eavesdropping?

Mrs. Stockmann. You were talking so loud, we couldn't help hearing.

Petra. No, I was eavesdropping.

The Mayor. Well, I am very glad you heard.

Dr. Stockmann (Going up to him). You were saying something about forbidding and obeying?

The Mayor. You compelled me to speak to you like that.

Dr. Stockmann. And now you want me to lie to the public for you?

The Mayor. It is absolutely necessary that you issue the sort of statement I have asked you for.

Dr. Stockmann. And if I refuse to—obey?

The Mayor. Then we shall issue a statement ourselves to reassure the public.

Dr. Stockmann. Very well; I'll fight you in the newspapers. I'll stick to what I've said, and prove that I am right and you are wrong. And what will you do then?

The Mayor. Then I simply won't be able to keep you from being dismissed.

Dr. Stockmann. What—?

Petra. Father—dismissed!

Mrs. Stockmann. Dismissed!

The Mayor. Yes, dismissed from the staff. I shall be obliged to advise the Board to give you your notice and prevent you from having any further connection with the Baths.

Dr. Stockmann. You wouldn't dare to do that!

The Mayor. You are forcing me to do it!

Petra. Uncle, this is a shameful way to treat a man like Father!

Mrs. Stockmann. Please be quiet, Petra!

The Mayor (Looking at PETRA*).* So we have our own opinions already, have we? Well, that's only natural!

(*To* MRS. STOCKMANN.) Katherine, you seem to be the most sensible member of the household. I wish you would use any influence you have over your husband, and make him understand what this will mean to his family and—

Dr. Stockmann. My family concerns me and nobody else!

The Mayor. I was saying—for his family and for the town he lives in.

Dr. Stockmann. I'm the one who has the good of this town at heart! And I intend to expose the faults that will sooner or later come to light. That will prove how much I love my native town.

The Mayor. You are so obstinate that to prove your love, you are willing to cut off the source of the town's prosperity!

Dr. Stockmann. But the source is poisoned, man! Are you mad? Do you want the town to grow rich by selling filth and corruption? Can't you see that our prosperity is based on a lie?

The Mayor. That's ridiculous—it's worse than that. Any man who can make such damaging insinuations about his native town is nothing but an enemy of the community.

Dr. Stockmann (*Going up to him*). How dare you say that!

Mrs. Stockmann (*Throwing herself between them*). Thomas!

Petra (*Seizing her father's arm*). Don't get excited, Father!

The Mayor. I will not expose myself to violence. You have been warned; now think about what you owe to yourself and your family. Goodbye. (*He goes out.*)

Dr. Stockmann. Am I supposed to take this lying down? And in my own home? What do you think of that, Katherine?

Mrs. Stockmann. It's a disgrace, Thomas —it really is—

Petra. I'd like to give Uncle Peter a piece of my mind!

Dr. Stockmann. I suppose it's my own fault. I should have stood up to him long ago—bared my teeth—bit back! He called me an enemy of the community! Me! No, I'll be damned if I take that lying down!

Mrs. Stockmann. But, Thomas dear, your brother has all the power on his side—

Dr. Stockmann. Yes, but I have the right on mine.

Mrs. Stockmann. Oh, yes, the right! What good is the right without might?

Petra. Mother! How can you say such a thing—

Dr. Stockmann. Don't be absurd, Katherine. Isn't it enough, in a free country, to have right on your side? Besides, haven't I got the progressive, independent press supporting me, and the solid majority as well, behind me? If that isn't might, what is?

Mrs. Stockmann. But, Thomas, you surely don't intend to—

Dr. Stockmann. Don't intend to what?

Mrs. Stockmann. To oppose your brother in public.

Dr. Stockmann. What the devil can I do? How else can I stand up for the right and the truth?

Petra. I was just going to ask the same question.

Mrs. Stockmann. But you know it's a useless battle. If they won't do it, they won't.

Dr. Stockmann. Oh, just you give me time, Katherine. I'll fight this thing to a finish—you'll see.

Mrs. Stockmann. Yes, and while you're fighting, you'll be dismissed—that's what.

Dr. Stockmann. In any case I shall have done my duty to the community— even though I'm supposed to be its enemy!

Mrs. Stockmann. But what about your family, Thomas? Those in your own home? Would you be doing your duty to us?

Petra. Oh, don't always think of us first, Mother.

Mrs. Stockmann. It's easy enough for you to talk; you can look after yourself, if need be. But what about the boys, Thomas? And yourself? And me?

Dr. Stockmann. You must be out of your mind, Katherine. If I were such a miserable coward as to go crawling to Peter and his damned gang, do you think I'd ever be happy again as long as I live?

Mrs. Stockmann. I don't know about that; but God preserve us from the kind of happiness we'll have if you insist upon defying them! You'll find yourself just where you were before —no job, no income. Didn't we have enough of that in the old days? Don't forget that, Thomas; think of the consequences.

Dr. Stockmann (*Struggling with him-self and clenching his fists*). And this is the sort of slavery that politicians can impose on a free and honorable man! Isn't it shocking, Katherine?

Mrs. Stockmann. Yes, they've treated you disgracefully, I must say that. But there is so much injustice in this world—one simply has to put up with it. Think of the boys, Thomas. Look at them! What's to become of them? Oh, you'd never have the heart to—

(*EILIF and MORTEN have come in while she was speaking; they carry their schoolbooks.*)

Dr. Stockmann. The boys—! (*Suddenly recovers himself.*) I don't care if the whole world goes to pieces, I won't be a slave to anyone! (*He goes to-ward his study.*)

Mrs. Stockmann (*Following him*). Thomas! What are you going to do?

Dr. Stockmann (*At the door*). When my sons are grown men, I want to be able to look them in the face! (*He goes into his room.*)

Mrs. Stockmann (*Bursting into tears*). God help us all!

Petra. Oh, Father is wonderful! He'll never give in.

(*The BOYS look at her questioningly; she motions to them not to speak.*)

CURTAIN

ACT THREE

SCENE. *The editorial office of* The People's Messenger. *The entrance from the street is in the rear wall on the left; on the right side is another door with glass panes through which the pressroom can be seen. There is another door in the wall right. In the middle of the room stands a large table covered with papers, newspapers, and books. Down left, a window, in front of which are a desk and a high stool. There are a couple of easy chairs by the table, and other chairs against the walls. The room is dingy and crowded; the furniture is old, the chairs stained and torn. In the pressroom some printers can be seen at work; one man is running a hand-press.*

HOVSTAD *is seated at the desk, writing. After a moment or two,* BILLING *enters through the door right, with Dr. Stockmann's manuscript in his hand.*

Billing. Well, I must say!

Hovstad (Still writing). Have you finished reading it?

Billing (Laying the manuscript on the desk). Yes, I have.

Hovstad. Don't you think the Doctor comes down on them pretty hard?

Billing. Hard? It's absolutely crushing! Every word is like the blow of a sledgehammer.

Hovstad. Yes, but they're not the sort of people who throw in the towel at the first blow.

Billing. That's very true; so we'll just have to keep walloping them until the whole damn bureaucracy falls apart. As I sat there reading that article, I could almost see a revolution in the making.

Hovstad (Turning around). Watch it! Don't let Aslaksen hear that.

Billing (Lowering his voice). Aslaksen is a chicken-hearted little coward. Who'd ever call him a man! But you'll insist on having your own way this time, won't you? You'll definitely use the Doctor's article?

Hovstad. Yes, and if the Mayor doesn't like it—

Billing. That would be a damned nuisance!

Hovstad. Well, fortunately, we can turn the situation to our own advantage, whatever happens. If the Mayor doesn't go along with the Doctor's plan, he'll have all the small businessmen down on him—the Home Owners Association and all the rest of them. And if he does go along, his chief supporters will turn on him—

that whole crowd of stockholders with big investments in the Baths—

Billing. Well, to make those alterations would cost them a pretty penny—

Hovstad. You can be damn sure it will! And once that gang of reactionaries is broken up, we can hammer away at the Mayor's inefficiency, and convince the public that the most trustworthy people, and those most capable of running the government, are the Liberals.

Billing. And that's the truth! I see it coming—I see it; it's a revolution!

(There is a knock at the door.)

Hovstad. Shh! *(Calls out.)* Come in! *(*DR. STOCKMANN *comes in by the street door.* HOVSTAD *goes to meet him.)* Ah, here's the Doctor, now. Well?

Dr. Stockmann. You may go ahead and print it, Mr. Hovstad!

Hovstad. So it's come to that, has it?

Billing. Hurrah!

Dr. Stockmann. Yes, it's come to that, so print away. They're looking for a fight, Billing, and they're going to get it!

Billing. A fight to the death, I hope! All-out war, Doctor!

Dr. Stockmann. This article is only the beginning. There are four or five others already taking shape in my head. Where is Aslaksen?

Billing (Calls into the pressroom). Aslaksen! Can you come here for a minute?

Hovstad. Four or five more articles, you say? On the same subject?

Dr. Stockmann. No, not at all. They'll

deal with several other things. But they're all related to the problem of the water supply and the sewer system. One thing leads to another, you know. It's exactly like trying to repair an old house.

Billing. By God, that's true! You fix it here and you fix it there, but the whole thing is so rotten, you end by tearing it down!

Aslaksen (*Entering from the press-room*). Tearing it down? Surely, Doctor, you're not thinking of tearing down the Baths!

Hovstad. No, of course not. Don't get alarmed!

Dr. Stockmann. We were talking about something entirely different. Well, what do you think of my article, Mr. Hovstad?

Hovstad. I must say, I think it's a masterpiece—

Dr. Stockmann. Do you really think so? Well, I'm glad of that, very glad.

Hovstad. It's so clear and to the point —you don't have to be a specialist to understand it. You'll have every intelligent man on your side.

Aslaksen. And every prudent man too, I hope.

Billing. Prudent and imprudent alike— practically the whole town.

Aslaksen. In that case, I think we might venture to print it.

Dr. Stockmann. Well, I should say so!

Hovstad. It'll be in the paper tomorrow morning.

Dr. Stockmann. That's good! We mustn't waste a single minute. And Mr. Aslaksen, I meant to ask you, would you set up the article yourself?

Aslaksen. I'd be glad to!

Dr. Stockmann. Treat it like a treasure! No misprints—every word is important. I'll stop in again a little later; perhaps you'll have a proof ready. I can't wait to see it in print—and watch it burst on the public—

Billing. Yes—burst like a bombshell!

Dr. Stockmann. I want every intelligent citizen to read it and make up his own mind. You have no idea what I've been through today—the pressures and the threats; they tried to rob me of my basic rights—

Billing. What! Your rights!

Dr. Stockmann. Yes! They tried to make me crawl, and lie, and put my personal interests before my most sacred beliefs—

Billing. That's going too far. I'll be damned if it isn't!

Hovstad. Oh, you mustn't be surprised at anything they do.

Dr. Stockmann. Well, I have a few surprises for them; they can rest assured of that. I'd like to set up my armory here at *The People's Messenger* and bombard them every single day with another article—

Aslaksen. Yes, but wait—

Billing. Hurrah! It's war—it's war!

Dr. Stockmann. I'll batter them to the ground—I'll smash them—I'll annihilate them! I'll make the public see them for what they really are! That's what I'll do!

Aslaksen. Yes, attack—with caution.

Billing. Yes, yes! Don't spare the dynamite!

Dr. Stockmann. It's not just a question of the water supply and the sewers now, it's the whole community we've got to clean up and disinfect—

Billing. Spoken like a warrior!

Dr. Stockmann. All the old incompetents must be drummed out of office —regardless of their rank! Today I had a vision of what things might be like. I don't see all the details clearly as yet, but I will in time. What we need, my friends, are young and vigorous leaders—new commanders at the outposts.

Billing. Hear, hear!

Dr. Stockmann. If we stand by one another, we're sure to win easily. The revolution will be launched smoothly—like a new ship sliding down the ways. Don't you think so?

Hovstad. I think there's a possibility now of putting some power into the hands of the right people.

Aslaksen. If we make sure to proceed with caution, I don't think we'll run into any trouble.

Dr. Stockmann. Who gives a damn about trouble—when you're doing something for the sake of truth and conscience!

Hovstad. You deserve everyone's support, Doctor.

Aslaksen. The Doctor is a true friend of the town—a real friend of the community, that's what he is.

Billing. Believe me, Aslaksen, Doctor Stockmann is a friend of the people.

Aslaksen. I imagine the Home Owners Association will soon be using that as a slogan.

Dr. Stockmann (*Touched*). Thank you, thank you, dear friends, for your encouragement. It does me good to listen to you; my brother called me something very different. But he'll be paid back—with interest! Now I must be off to see a patient who's expecting me—but I'll be back. Keep a sharp eye on the manuscript, Aslaksen, and be sure you don't leave out any of my exclamation marks! You may even add one or two if you like—that would be fine! Well, goodbye for now—goodbye, goodbye!

(*They say goodbye as they accompany him to the door; he goes out.*)

Hovstad. There's a man who could be very useful to us.

Aslaksen. Yes, as long as he sticks to this business of the Baths. But if he goes further than that, I don't think it would be wise to follow him.

Hovstad. Well, that all depends on—

Billing. You're always so damned scared, Aslaksen!

Aslaksen. Scared? Yes, when it comes to criticizing the local authorities, I am scared, Mr. Billing; I've learned that from experience, let me tell you. But just put me in high-level politics, even in opposition to the Government itself, and then see if I'm scared.

Billing. Maybe not. But you seem to be contradicting yourself.

Aslaksen. I happen to have a conscience where the town is concerned. If you attack the Government, you don't harm the community. Those fellows up there pay no attention to you; they do as they please, and you can't touch them. But the local authorities are different—they can be turned out of office. And the next bunch you get might be worse—a lot of ignorant incompetents who would do irreparable harm to the home owners and the entire community.

Hovstad. But what about educating the citizens by allowing them to govern themselves—don't you think that's important?

Aslaksen. When a man has his own interests to protect, he can't worry about everything, Mr. Hovstad.

Hovstad. Then I hope I never have interests of my own that need such careful protection!

Billing. Hear, hear!

Aslaksen (*With a smile*). Hm! (*Points to the desk.*) Mr. Stensgaard used to sit at that editor's desk where you are. Now he's the sheriff.

Billing (*Spitting*). Ppp! That turncoat!

Hovstad. Well, I'm not a weathercock —and never will be.

Aslaksen. Anyone involved with politics should never say "never," Mr. Hovstad. As for you. Mr. Billing, don't you think you ought to watch your step now that you've applied for the job of secretary to the Chief Justice?

Billing. I—!

Hovstad. Is that true, Billing?

Billing. Well, yes—it is. But I'm only doing it, you understand, to annoy the Bigwigs.

Aslaksen. Anyway, it's none of my business. You can accuse me of being timid and inconsistent, but my political record is an open book. I've never changed except to become a little more moderate, perhaps. But my heart is still with the people. I don't deny that my common sense has given me a certain bias towards the authorities—the local ones, I mean.

(*He goes into the pressroom.*)

Billing. Don't you think we ought to try to get rid of him, Hovstad?

Hovstad. Do you know of anyone else who'd be willing to pay our paper and printing bills?

Billing. It's a damned shame we don't have a little capital to work with.

Hovstad (*Sitting down at his desk*). Yes, if we only had that—!

Billing. How about asking Dr. Stockmann?

Hovstad (*Glancing through some papers*). What's the use of that? He has no money.

Billing. No, but he's got a well-heeled relative, old Morten Kiil—the "Badger," as they call him.

Hovstad (*Writing*). What makes you think *he's* got anything?

Billing. Good God, of course he has! And he'll be leaving some of it to the Stockmann family. Anyway, I'm sure he'll take care of the children.

Hovstad (*Half turning*). Can you count on that?

Billing. Count on it? Of course not, you can't count on anything.

Hovstad. That's right. And I wouldn't count on that job as secretary either, if I were you; I assure you, you won't get it.

Billing. Do you think I don't know that? That's why I applied for it—just to be rejected! A slap in the face like that will start my adrenalin flowing—put more fight in me. In this dead-end hole, where nothing ever happens, you need something like that to get you going.

Hovstad (*Continues writing*). Yes, yes —I know.

Billing. You'll see, they'll hear of me yet! Well, now I'll go in and write the appeal to the Home Owners Association.

(*He goes into the room on the right.*)

Hovstad (*Sits at his desk, bites his penholder, and says slowly*) Hm! So that's the way it is, is it? (*A knock at the door.*) Come in! (PETRA *comes in through the street door;* HOVSTAD *rises.*) Well, Petra! What are you doing here?

Petra. You must excuse me, but—

Hovstad (*Pulling a chair forward*). Won't you sit down?

Petra. No, thanks; I can only stay a minute.

Hovstad. Have you brought a message from your father?

Petra. No, it's about myself. (*Takes a book out of her coat pocket.*) I've brought back that English story.

Hovstad. Why have you brought it back?

Petra. Because I don't care to translate it.

Hovstad. But you gave me your promise—

Petra. Yes, I did, but I hadn't read it then. And you haven't read it either, have you?

Hovstad. You know very well I don't read English; but—

Petra. Well—I suggest that you find another story. (*Putting the book on the table.*) You certainly can't print this one in *The People's Messenger.*

Hovstad. Why not?

Petra. Because it's against everything you stand for.

Hovstad. Well, as far as that's concerned—

Petra. But you don't understand. The point of the story is that there's a supernatural power that looks after all the so-called good people in this world and continually rewards them —whereas all the so-called bad people are punished.

Hovstad. Well, that's all right. That's just what our readers want.

Petra. And are you going to be the one to give it to them? I think it's perfect nonsense, and so do you! You know very well that things don't happen that way in real life.

Hovstad. Of course, you're right; but an editor can't always do as he pleases. He's got to cater to the public in many little ways. But it's politics that's the most important thing for a newspaper. If I want to get my readers accustomed to more progressive ideas, I can't afford to scare them away. So I put a little moral tale like that on the back page of the paper to make them feel happy and secure, and then they'll be more inclined to accept what I print on the front page.

Petra. That's disgraceful! It's a trick! You couldn't be guilty of such a thing!

Hovstad (*Smiling*). Thank you for thinking so well of me. As a matter of fact, it's Billing's idea, not mine.

Petra. Billing's!

Hovstad. Yes; he held forth on that theory here the other day. It's Billing who wants me to print that story. I don't know anything about it.

Petra. But how can Mr. Billing, with his realistic views—

Hovstad. Oh, Mr. Billing is a man of many talents. He's applying for the position of secretary to the Chief Justice, I hear.

Petra. Oh, I don't believe that, Mr. Hovstad. How could he possibly want to get involved in courthouse politics?

Hovstad. I'm afraid you'll have to ask him that yourself.

Petra. I would never have thought that of him.

Hovstad (*Looking at her closely*). No? Does it really surprise you that much?

Petra. Well, yes—but maybe not altogether—Really, I don't know what to think—

Hovstad. We journalists are a pretty worthless lot, Miss Petra.

Petra. Do you really mean that?

Hovstad. Yes—sometimes I think so.

Petra. Perhaps in petty, everyday affairs—I can understand that. But now that you've undertaken an important cause—

Hovstad. You mean your father's crusade?

Petra. You can call it that, if you like! That ought to make you feel that you are worth more than the ordinary man.

Hovstad. Yes, I somehow feel a bit like that today.

Petra. Of course, you do—you must! You've chosen a splendid career! To be in the vanguard of those who defend the truth—and fight for new ideas. Why, you're not even afraid to come out in the open and support the cause of a man who's been wronged—

Hovstad. Especially when the wronged man is—I don't quite know how to put it—

Petra. When he's upright and decent, you mean?

Hovstad (*Quietly*). No, I mean—especially when he's *your* father.

Petra. My—! (*Taken aback*). Oh, you mean—?

Hovstad. Yes, Petra—Miss Petra.

Petra. Is that it? Is that what means most to you? Not the cause itself? Not the truth? Not my father's generous nature? All that means nothing to you?

Hovstad. That's not true—it does—that too.

Petra. Thank you, Mr. Hovstad. I understand you now. I shall never trust you again in anything.

Hovstad. Do you really think it's so improper, because it's mostly for your sake—?

Petra. What makes me angry is that you haven't been honest with my father.

Dallas Anderson as Hovstad "making a play" for Marie Adels as Petra in the Walter Hampden production of *An Enemy of the People* at the Hampden Theater, October 3, 1927. (New York Public Library)

You led him to believe that the truth about the Baths and the good of the community were most important to you, when really—! You've made fools of both of us, Mr. Hovstad. You're not the man you pretend to be. I shall never forgive you for that —never!

Hovstad. If I were you, Miss Petra, I wouldn't speak so sharply—at least, not right now.

Petra. Why not now?

Hovstad. Because your father can't do without my help.

Petra. Oh, that too! Is that the sort of man you are?

Hovstad. No, no, I'm not. I didn't know what I was saying, you must believe me.

Petra. I know very well what to believe. Goodbye.

Aslaksen (Enters from the pressroom, with an air of mystery). Damn it, Hovstad! *(Sees* PETRA.*)* Oh, forgive me—

Petra. There's the book. Get someone else to do it for you. *(Goes towards the door.)*

Hovstad (Following her). But Miss Petra—

Petra. Goodbye. *(She goes out.)*

Aslaksen. Listen—Hovstad—

Hovstad. What is it? What do you want?

Aslaksen. The Mayor—he's out in the pressroom—

Hovstad. The Mayor—here?

Aslaksen. Yes—and he wants to talk to you. He came in the back way— didn't want to be seen, obviously.

Hovstad. What does he want? Wait a minute. I'll go myself. *(He goes to the door of the pressroom, opens it, bows, and invites the* MAYOR *to come in.)* Take care, Aslaksen, and see that nobody—

Aslaksen. I understand. *(He goes into the pressroom.)*

The Mayor. I don't imagine you expected to see me here, Mr. Hovstad.

Hovstad. No, I can't say I did.

The Mayor (Looking around). You've got a comfortable place here—very nice.

Hovstad. Oh—

The Mayor. And I've dropped in, without any notice, and I'm taking up your time!

Hovstad. Oh, not at all, Mr. Mayor. I'm glad to be of service. Let me take your things—*(Takes the Mayor's hat and cane and puts them on a chair.)* Won't you sit down?

The Mayor (Sits by the table). Thank you. *(*HOVSTAD *sits down nearby.)* I've had to deal with an extremely troublesome matter today, Mr. Hovstad.

Hovstad. Really? But, of course—all the problems you have to attend to—

The Mayor. My brother is responsible for what happened today.

Hovstad. Dr. Stockmann?

The Mayor. Yes. He's written a report in which he alleges certain defects in the Baths, and he's sent copies of it to the Board of Directors.

Hovstad. Did he, really?

The Mayor. Hasn't he told you? I thought he said—

Hovstad. Oh, yes—that's right—he did mention something about—

Aslaksen (Enters from the pressroom). Where did I leave that manuscript—?

Hovstad (Angrily). There it is on the desk.

Aslaksen (Taking it). Right.

The Mayor. Look here! Isn't that—?

Aslaksen. It's Dr. Stockmann's article.

Hovstad. Oh, is *that* what you were talking about?

The Mayor. Yes, it is. What do you think of it?

Hovstad. I'm not an expert, of course— and I've only just glanced at it—

The Mayor. And yet you intend to print it?

Hovstad. I can't very well refuse a man in his position—

Aslaksen. I have nothing to do with editing the paper, Mr. Mayor—

The Mayor. I understand that.

Aslaksen. I'm a printer—I just print what they hand me.

The Mayor. Yes, of course.

Aslaksen. Now, if you'll excuse me— (*He goes towards the pressroom.*)

The Mayor. Just a moment, Mr. Aslaksen. With your permission, Mr. Hovstad?

Hovstad. Certainly, Mr. Mayor.

The Mayor. You are a discreet and sensible man, Mr. Aslaksen.

Aslaksen. I'm very glad you think so—

The Mayor. And a man with a great deal of influence.

Aslaksen. Mainly among the small businessmen, Your Honor.

The Mayor. It's the small taxpayers who are in the majority—here as everywhere else.

Aslaksen. That's very true.

The Mayor. And I have no doubt you know the general trend of their opinions, don't you?

Aslaksen. I think I may say I do, Mr. Mayor.

The Mayor. Well, since there's such a fine spirit of self-sacrifice among the middle-class citizens of our town—

Aslaksen. What do you mean?

Hovstad. Self-sacrifice?

The Mayor. It's evidence of their public spirit, extremely pleasing evidence; though I must say I find it rather surprising! But then, you're in closer touch with public opinion than I am.

Aslaksen. But, Mr. Mayor—

The Mayor. I must say, it is no small sacrifice that the town is going to make.

Hovstad. The town? A sacrifice?

Aslaksen. I don't understand. Does it concern the Baths?

The Mayor. Yes. At a conservative, preliminary estimate, the alterations Dr. Stockmann considers necessary will cost something like two hundred thousand crowns.

Aslaksen. That's a lot of money, but—

The Mayor. Of course, we'll have to arrange for a municipal loan.

Hovstad (*Getting up*). You surely don't mean that the town must pay—?

Aslaksen. Are you saying that the small businessmen will have to pay for this out of their own pockets?

The Mayor. My dear Mr. Aslaksen, where else should the money come from?

Aslaksen. It seems to me the owners of the Baths should take care of it.

The Mayor. But the owners are not in a position now to increase their investment.

Aslaksen. Are you sure of that, Mr. Mayor?

The Mayor. Yes, I'm satisfied on that score. So if the town wants these very expensive alterations, it will have to pay for them.

Aslaksen. But, damn it all, Mr. Hovstad! —I'm sorry, Your Honor—this makes a big difference!

Hovstad. It certainly does.

The Mayor. The worst part of it is that we'll have to close down the Baths for a couple of years.

Hovstad. Close them? Completely?

Aslaksen. For two years?

The Mayor. Yes, it will take at least two years to do the work.

Aslaksen. I'll be damned if the tax-payers will stand for that, Mr. Mayor. What are the small business-men to live on in the meantime?

The Mayor. That's a very difficult question to answer, Mr. Aslaksen. But what do you want us to do? Do you suppose anybody is going to come here if people go around making up stories about the water being polluted and the whole town being a cesspool—?

Aslaksen. Then you think it's just a made-up story?

The Mayor. Yes—try as I will, I can't see it as anything else.

Aslaksen. Then I must say it's irresponsible of Dr. Stockmann—if you'll forgive me, Mr. Mayor.

The Mayor. Unfortunately, that's very true, Mr. Aslaksen. My brother, I'm sorry to say, has always been a very impulsive man.

Aslaksen. And you still want to support him, Mr. Hovstad?

Hovstad. Do you think for a minute that I—?

The Mayor. I've written a brief account of the situation as anyone with common sense would view it. And I've indicated how any minor defects that may exist can be taken care of without putting a strain on the budget.

Hovstad. Do you happen to have it with you, Mr. Mayor?

The Mayor (*Fumbling in his pocket*). Yes, I brought it along in case you—

Aslaksen. Good God, there he is!

The Mayor. Who? My brother?

Hovstad. Where? Where?

Aslaksen. He went into the press-room.

The Mayor. That's too bad! I didn't want to meet him here, and I still have several things I'd like to talk to you about.

Hovstad (*Pointing to the door on the right*). Wait in there for a minute.

The Mayor. But—?

Hovstad. There's no one in there but Mr. Billing.

Aslaksen. Hurry, Mr. Mayor. I see him coming.

The Mayor. Very well; but see if you can get rid of him quickly.

(*He goes out through the door on the right, which* ASLAKSEN *opens for him and shuts after him.*)

Hovstad. Pretend to be doing something, Aslaksen.

(HOVSTAD *sits down and writes.* ASLAKSEN *looks through a pile of newspapers on a chair.*)

Dr. Stockmann (*Entering from the pressroom*). Well, here I am—back again. (*He puts down his hat and cane.*)

Hovstad. Already, Doctor? Hurry up with the job we were talking about, Aslaksen. We're running very late today.

Dr. Stockmann (*To* ASLAKSEN). No proofs for me yet, I hear.

Aslaksen (*Without turning around*). You can hardly expect them so soon, Doctor.

Dr. Stockmann. Of course, of course. It's just that I'm impatient, you understand. I won't be able to relax till I see the thing in print.

Hovstad. Well, it'll take quite a while yet, won't it, Aslaksen?

Aslaksen. Yes, I'm afraid so.

Dr. Stockmann. All right, my friends. I'll come back. I don't mind coming back twice if I have to. What's a little inconvenience, if it's for the good of the town! (*He starts to go, then stops and comes back.*) By the way, there's something else I want to talk to you about.

Hovstad. I'm sorry, Doctor, but can it wait till another time?

Dr. Stockmann. I'll be very brief. It's only this. When people read my article tomorrow morning and realize that I spent my whole winter working for the good of the town—

Hovstad. Yes, but, Doctor—

Dr. Stockmann. Oh, I know what you're going to say—it was only my duty as a citizen. Of course, it wasn't; you know that as well as I. But all the good people in this town think so highly of me—

Aslaksen. Yes, they've thought very highly of you up to now, Doctor.

Dr. Stockmann. I know; and that's why I'm afraid they might—Well, what I mean is—when they hear about this, especially when the poorer people get wind of it, they might wake up and decide to take things into their own hands from now on—

Hovstad (*Rising*). Well, Doctor, I think I ought to tell you—

Dr. Stockmann. Ah!—I knew there was something going on! But I won't hear of it. If they're planning anything like that—

Hovstad. Like what?

Dr. Stockmann. Oh, I don't know—a banquet, a plaque, a rally in my honor—whatever it is, you must promise me you'll put a stop to it. And you too, Mr. Aslaksen; do you understand?

Hovstad. Excuse me, Doctor, but sooner or later we'll have to tell you the plain truth—

(Mrs. STOCKMANN, *in hat and coat, enters through the street door.*)

Mrs. Stockmann (*Seeing the doctor*). Just as I thought!

Hovstad (*Going towards her*). You are here too, Mrs. Stockmann?

Dr. Stockmann. Katherine, what on earth do *you* want here?

Mrs. Stockmann. You know very well what I want.

Hovstad. Won't you sit down? Or perhaps—

Mrs. Stockmann. No, thank you; don't bother about me. And forgive my coming here to look for my husband. There are three children at home.

Dr. Stockmann. What's this nonsense? Everybody knows that!

Mrs. Stockmann. Well, you don't seem to be giving much thought to it—or you wouldn't be dragging us into this disaster.

Dr. Stockmann. Are you out of your mind, Katherine? Just because a man has a wife and children, can't he stand up for the truth?—can't he be a useful citizen?—can't he do something for the town he lives in?

Mrs. Stockmann. Yes, Thomas—with moderation.

Aslaksen. That's just what I say. Everything in moderation.

Mrs. Stockmann. I think it's very wrong of you, Mr. Hovstad, to lure my husband away from his home, involve him in all this, and make a fool of him.

Hovstad. I'm not making a fool of anyone—

Dr. Stockmann. A fool! Do you think I'd let anyone make a fool of me?

Mrs. Stockmann. Yes, Thomas, you would. I know that you have more brains than anyone in town, but

you're very easily fooled. (*To* Hovstad.) Don't you realize he'll lose his
position at the Baths if you print
what he's written—

Aslaksen. What!

Hovstad. You know, Doctor—

Dr. Stockmann (*Laughing*). Just let
them try to get rid of me! They
wouldn't dare! Not with the solid
majority behind me!

Mrs. Stockmann. Yes, that's the worst
of it. You'd be better off without
them.

Dr. Stockmann. That's ridiculous,
Katherine! Go home and look after
the house and leave the community
to me. Why should you be afraid,
when I'm so happy and confident?
(*He paces back and forth, rubbing
his hands.*) The truth will win out,
and all the people will join hands
and march forward—(*Stops suddenly
beside a chair.*) What the devil is
that doing here?

Aslaksen (*Turns to look*). Oh, Lord!

Hovstad. Oh!

Dr. Stockmann (*Picks up the Mayor's
hat carefully and holds it up in the
air*). Here we have the peak of authority!

Mrs. Stockmann. It's the Mayor's hat!

Dr. Stockmann (*Picks up the cane*).
And his staff of office too! What the
devil are they doing here?

Hovstad. Well, Doctor, you see—

Dr. Stockmann. Oh, yes, I see very well.
He came here to try to win you over.
Barking up the wrong tree, wasn't
he? Then he saw me in the pressroom—(*Bursts out laughing.*) And
he took off. Didn't he, Mr. Aslaksen?

Aslaksen (*Hurriedly*). Yes, Doctor, he
did!

Dr. Stockmann. Ran off without his
cane and his—Oh, no! Not if I know

Peter—he wouldn't leave anything
behind. Where is he? What the devil
have you done with him? (*Looking
around.*) Oh, he's in there, of course.
Now, Katherine, you're going to see
some fun.

Mrs. Stockmann. Thomas—please!

Aslaksen. Don't do anything rash, Doctor.

(Dr. Stockmann *has put on the
Mayor's hat and taken hold of his
cane. He goes up to the door, throws
it open, and stands there saluting.
The* Mayor *enters, red with anger.*
Billing *follows him.*)

The Mayor. What's the meaning of this
foolish behavior?

Dr. Stockmann. Show a little respect,
Peter, if you don't mind. (*Marches
up and down*). I'm the authority-in-
chief now!

Mrs. Stockmann (*Almost in tears*). Oh,
Thomas, really!

The Mayor (*Following him around*).
Give me my hat and cane!

Dr. Stockmann (*In the same mocking
tone*). You may be chief of police,
but I'm the mayor—I'm the boss of
the whole town, you understand?

The Mayor. Take that hat off, I tell
you. It's part of an official uniform.

Dr. Stockmann. Nonsense! Official uniforms aren't going to frighten the
people any more. They're awake,
they know their strength—there's
going to be a revolution in this town
tomorrow, I want you to know. You
thought you could fire me; well, now
I'm going to fire you—turn you out of
office. Don't you think I can do it?
You'll see. I have all the power on
my side. Hovstad and Billing will
train their guns on you in *The Peo-*

ple's Messenger, and Aslaksen will lead the entire Home Owners Association into battle—

Aslaksen. No, Doctor, I won't.

Dr. Stockmann. But, of course, you will—

The Mayor. Oh, I see! And I suppose Mr. Hovstad intends to join this rebellion, too?

Hovstad. No, Mr. Mayor.

Aslaksen. No, Mr. Hovstad is not so foolish as to go and ruin his paper and himself for the sake of an imaginary problem.

Dr. Stockmann (*Looks from one to the other*). What does this mean?

Hovstad. You've presented this matter in an entirely false light, Doctor, so it's impossible for me to give you my support.

Billing. And after the Mayor's kind explanation to me just now, I—

Dr. Stockmann. A false light, eh? I'll be responsible for that—you just print my article. I'm ready to demonstrate the truth of every word of it.

Hovstad. Well, I'm not going to print it. I can't—I won't—I don't dare!

Dr. Stockmann. Don't dare—? That's ridiculous! You're the editor, aren't you? Don't you control your own paper?

Aslaksen. No—the readers do.

The Mayor. Fortunately—yes.

Aslaksen. It's the public—the educated public—the home owners and people like that; they control the paper.

Dr. Stockmann (*Calmly*). And all those people would be against me?

Aslaksen. Yes, without a doubt. If your article were printed, it would mean total ruin for the town.

Dr. Stockmann. I see.

The Mayor. May I have my hat and cane? (DR. STOCKMANN *takes off the hat and puts it and the cane on the table. The* MAYOR *picks them up.*) Your authority as mayor has come to rather an abrupt end, hasn't it?

Dr. Stockmann. This is certainly not the end, I assure you. (*To* HOVSTAD) So you find it impossible to print my article in the *Messenger?*

Hovstad. Quite impossible—if for no other reason, out of consideration for your family—

Mrs. Stockmann. You needn't concern yourself about his family, thank you, Mr. Hovstad.

The Mayor (*Taking some sheets of paper from his pocket*). This contains all the information the public needs. It is an official statement. Do you wish to have it?

Hovstad (*Taking the papers*). Certainly. I'll see that it's printed immediately.

Dr. Stockmann. But not mine! Do you think you can silence me and suppress the truth? You won't find that so easy to do! Mr. Aslaksen, please take my manuscript and print it as a pamphlet—I'll publish it at my own expense. I want four hunderd copies —no, five—better make it six.

Aslaksen. I couldn't use my press for such a purpose, Doctor—not for any amount of money. It would be an out-and-out defiance of public opinion. And you won't get anybody else in this town to print it for you.

Dr. Stockmann. Then give it back to me.

Hovstad (*Handing it to him*). Here you are.

Dr. Stockmann (*Taking his hat and cane*). This will be heard all the same. I'll call a public meeting—and read it to the people myself. The citizens in this town are going to hear the truth!

The Mayor. There's no one in town who

would provide a hall for such a meeting.

Aslaksen. No one—I'm certain of that.

Billing. I'm damned sure there isn't!

Mrs. Stockmann. That's outrageous! Thomas, why has everyone turned against you?

Dr. Stockmann (*Angrily*). I'll tell you why. Because all the men in this town are a lot of old women. All they think about is themselves—never about the good of all.

Mrs. Stockmann. Then I'll show them there's one old woman who can act like a man. (*She puts her arm through his.*) I'll stand by you, Thomas!

Dr. Stockmann. Bravo, Katherine! People are going to hear about this—as sure as I live! If I can't hire a hall, I'll rent a drum and parade around town. I'll read my report on every street corner.

The Mayor. Surely you're not as raving mad as all that!

Dr. Stockmann. Yes, I am.

Aslaksen. You won't get a single person in the whole town to go with you!

Billing. I'm damned if you will.

Mrs. Stockmann. Don't give in, Thomas. I'll ask the boys to go with you.

Dr. Stockmann. That's a wonderful idea!

Mrs. Stockmann. Morten would be delighted; and Eilif will do whatever his big brother does.

Dr. Stockmann. Yes—and what about Petra? And you, too, Katherine?

Mrs. Stockmann. Oh, no, not that! But I'll tell you what I will do—I'll stand at the window and cheer you.

Dr. Stockmann (*Embraces and kisses her*). Thank you for that! Well, the battle is on, gentlemen! Now, we'll see who's stronger—a bunch of corrupt cowards, or a concerned citizen who wants to clean up the pollution in his town! Come, Katherine!

(*The* DOCTOR *and* MRS. STOCKMANN *go out by the street door.*)

The Mayor (*Shaking his head incredulously*). Now he's managed to make *her* as mad as *he* is!

CURTAIN

ACT FOUR

SCENE. *A large old-fashioned room in* CAPTAIN HORSTER's *house. In the rear wall there are double doors, which are open, and lead to an anteroom. In the wall on the left are three windows; against the right wall, opposite, a small platform has been erected. On the platform are a small table with candles, a pitcher of water, a glass, and a bell. The room is lit by lamps between the windows. Down left is a table with candles, and a chair beside it; down right, a door with some chairs near it.*

In the room there is a crowd of townspeople of various types, a few women and some schoolboys among them. People continue to stream in from the anteroom until the large room is almost full.

First Man (*Meeting another*). Hello, Lamstad! You here, too?

Second Man. I wouldn't miss a public meeting for anything!

Third Man. I bet you brought your whistle along!

Second Man. Of course. Didn't you?

Third Man. Absolutely! Old Evensen

said he was going to bring his bull-horn.

Second Man. You just leave it to Old Evensen!

(*Laughter among the crowd.*)

Fourth Man (*Joining them*). Hey, fellows, what's going on here tonight?

Second Man. Dr. Stockmann's going to make a speech attacking the Mayor.

Fourth Man. But the Mayor is his brother!

First Man. That doesn't matter; Doctor Stockmann's not afraid of anyone.

Third Man. But he's in the wrong—that's what it says in the *Messenger.*

Second Man. He must be in the wrong this time, because the Home Owners Association wouldn't let him use their hall for this meeting—neither would the Citizens' Club.

First Man. There's a hall at the Baths—but *they* turned him down, too.

Second Man. There must be a reason!

A Man (*In another group*). Tell me—whose side are you on, eh?

Another Man (*In the group*). Keep your eye on Aslaksen and do as he does.

Billing (*Pushing his way through the crowd; he has a briefcase under his arm*). Excuse me, gentlemen—do you mind letting me through? I'm a reporter on *The People's Messenger.* Thanks very much—thanks! (*He sits down at the table on the left.*)

A Workman. Who's that?

Second Workman. Don't you know him? That's Billing—he writes for Aslaksen's paper.

(CAPTAIN HORSTER *leads* MRS. STOCKMANN *and* PETRA *through the door on the right.* EILIF *and* MORTEN *follow them in.*)

Horster. I think this will be a good place for you to sit. You can slip out easily from here, if things get out of hand.

Mrs. Stockmann. Do you think there'll be a disturbance?

Horster. You never can tell—with a crowd like this. Just sit there quietly, and don't worry.

Mrs. Stockmann. It was so kind of you to let my husband use this room.

Horster. Well, since nobody else would, I—

Petra (*She has sat down beside her mother*). And it was brave of you, too, Captain Horster.

Horster. Oh, it didn't really take a great deal of bravery.

(HOVSTAD *and* ASLAKSEN *enter and make their way through the crowd in different directions.*)

Aslaksen (*Going up to* HORSTER). Isn't Doctor Stockmann here yet?

Horster (*Indicating the door down right*). He's waiting in there.

(*Movement in the crowd near the door at the back.*)

Hovstad (*To* BILLING). Look—here comes the Mayor!

Billing. Well, I'll be damned—he showed up after all!

(*The* MAYOR *makes his way slowly through the crowd, bowing to right and left, and stands finally near the wall on the left. A moment later* DR. STOCKMANN *enters through the door down right. He wears a black frock coat and a white tie. There is some feeble applause, and some hissing, then silence.*)

Dr. Stockmann (*Softly*). How do you feel, Katherine?

Mrs. Stockmann. I'm all right, dear. (*Whispers*) Don't lose your temper, Thomas.

Dr. Stockmann. Oh, I can control myself. (*Looks at his watch, steps onto the platform, and bows.*) It's a quarter past—I think we can begin—(*Takes out his manuscript.*)

Aslaksen. Wait a minute! I think we ought to elect a chairman first.

Dr. Stockmann. That won't be necessary!

Several Men (*Shout*). Yes—yes!

The Mayor. Certainly—I agree! We must have a chairman.

Dr. Stockmann. But I've called this meeting to make a statement, Peter.

The Mayor (*To the crowd*). Doctor Stockmann's statement may very possibly lead to a considerable difference of opinion.

Voices in the Crowd. Let's have a chairman! A chairman!

Hovstad. The audience thinks a chairman should be elected.

Dr. Stockmann (*Controlling himself*). Very well—let the audience have its way.

Aslaksen. Perhaps the Mayor would be so good as to lend his services?

Three Men (*Clapping*). Bravo! Bravo!

The Mayor. Thank you—but for obvious reasons, and there are many, I beg to be excused. However, we are fortunate to have among us a man who, I am sure, will be acceptable to all of you. I refer to the president of the Home Owners Association, Mr. Aslaksen.

Many Voices. Yes—Yes, Aslaksen! We want Aslaksen!

(Dr. Stockmann *picks up his manuscript and walks back and forth on the platform.*)

Aslaksen. Since my fellow-citizens honor me with this duty, I cannot refuse.

(*Loud applause.* Aslaksen *mounts the platform.*)

Billing (*Writing in his notebook*). Mr. Aslaksen elected unanimously—

Aslaksen. And now—since you've elected me chairman—I'd like to say a few brief words to you. I am a quiet and peace-loving man, and I've always been a champion of discreet moderation, that is of—of moderate discretion. Anybody who knows me will swear to that.

Several Voices. That's right! That's right, Aslaksen!

Aslaksen. I've learned from long experience in the school of life that the greatest virtue a citizen can have is moderation—

The Mayor. Hear! Hear!

Aslaksen. Moderation and discretion—that's what a man needs if he wants to serve his community. So I urge our respected fellow-citizen, who has called this meeting, to try to keep strictly within the bounds of moderation.

A Man (*Near the door*). I'll drink to that!

A Voice. Shut up!

Several Voices. Sh!—Sh!

Aslaksen. No interruptions, gentlemen, please! Does anyone wish to speak?

The Mayor. Mr. Chairman.

Aslaksen. Yes, Mr. Mayor.

The Mayor. Because of my close relationship to the present Medical Officer of the Baths, I should have preferred not to appear or to speak this evening. But my position as Chairman of the Board and my concern for the vital interests of the town, force me to put forward a motion. I venture to state that there is not a single person present who would approve of spreading derogatory and exaggerated rumors concerning the sanitary conditions of our Baths and of our town.

Several Voices. No, no! Certainly not! Never! We protest!

The Mayor. I move, therefore, that this meeting pass a resolution forbidding Doctor Stockmann to read or even to discuss his proposed report.

Dr. Stockmann (*Angrily*). Forbid me—! What do you mean?

Mrs. Stockmann (*Coughing*). Hm! Hm!

Dr. Stockmann (*Controlling himself*). Oh, I see! Another catch! Go on!

The Mayor. In my article in *The People's Messenger*, I have informed the public of the essential facts of the matter, so that every intelligent citizen can make up his own mind. I think I've shown clearly that the doctor's proposals—apart from censuring the leading men of the town—would saddle the taxpayers with a totally unnecessary expenditure of several hundred thousand crowns.

(*Shouts of protest, whistles, and catcalls.*)

Aslaksen (*Rings the bell*). Quiet, gentlemen! Please come to order! I second the Mayor's motion. I agree with him when he says there is something behind the agitation started by the doctor. He may talk about the Baths, but what he's really aiming at is a revolution—he wants to overthrow the men who are now in power. The doctor has the best of intentions, of course—no one can doubt that. I myself am a firm believer in self-government for the people, provided it's not at the cost of the taxpayers, which it would be in the present case. And that's why, damn it—oh, excuse me, gentlemen—I can't support Doctor Stockmann in this matter. Sometimes you can pay too much for a thing. Well, that's my opinion.

(*Loud applause on all sides.*)

Hovstad. I feel I ought to make my position clear, too. Doctor Stockmann's agitation seemed to be winning a certain amount of approval at first, so I was bound to support it as impartially as I could. But soon we discovered that we had been misled by a misrepresentation of the state of affairs—

Dr. Stockmann. Misrepresentation—!

Hovstad. Well, a not entirely trustworthy representation, let us say. The Mayor's statement leaves no doubt about that; and I hope no one here questions my liberal views. Everyone knows the position *The People's Messenger* takes on important political issues. But the advice of experienced and thoughtful men has convinced me that when it comes to purely local matters a newspaper ought to proceed with a certain amount of caution.

Aslaksen. I completely agree with the speaker.

Hovstad. And, in the matter before us, it now appears without doubt that public opinion is against Doctor Stockmann. Now, what's an editor's first and most obvious duty, gentlemen? Isn't it to work in harmony with his readers? Isn't he obligated—by a sort of tacit mandate—to work constantly and devotedly for the welfare of his fellow-citizens? Or am I possibly mistaken in that?

Many Voices. No, no! You're right!

Hovstad. I find it very difficult to break with a man in whose house I have been a frequent guest lately; a man who till today has enjoyed the thorough esteem of his fellow-citizens; a man whose only, or perhaps it would be better to say whose principal fault, is that he's governed by his heart rather than his head.

A Few Scattered Voices. That's true! Good old Doctor Stockmann!

Hovstad. But my duty to the community has forced me to break with him. And there's another consideration that impels me to oppose him, and, if possible, to turn him from the dangerous course he's pursuing—and that is, consideration for his family—

Dr. Stockmann. You stick to the water supply and the sewers!

Hovstad. —consideration, I repeat, for his wife and the children who depend upon him.

Morten. Does he mean us, Mother?

Mrs. Stockmann. Hush!

Aslaksen. I shall now put the Mayor's resolution to a vote.

Dr. Stockmann. That won't be necessary! I have no intention of speaking tonight about all the pollution and corruption at the Baths. No! I want to deal with something very different.

The Mayor (*Under his breath*). What are we in for now?

A Drunken Man (*Near the entrance door*). I'm a taxpayer! So I have a right to speak! And my entire—firm —and inconsequential opinion is—

Several Voices. Quiet! Quiet back there!

Others. He's drunk! Throw him out!

(*They push him out.*)

Dr. Stockmann. May I speak now?

Aslaksen (*Rings the bell*). Doctor Stockmann has the floor.

Dr. Stockmann. If anyone had tried gagging me—even a few days ago— as I've been gagged tonight, I'd have fought like a lion to defend my rights. But it doesn't matter to me now. I have something much more important to say. (*The people move closer to him;* MORTEN KIIL *stands out in the crowd. The doctor continues.*) I've done a great deal of thinking in the last few days—pondering over so many things it seemed my head was about to burst—

The Mayor (*Coughing*). Hm—!

Dr. Stockmann. —but finally I got everything straightened out, and then I saw the whole situation very clearly. That's why I'm here tonight. What I intend to reveal to you now, my friends, is a discovery of much greater significance than the trivial fact that the water supply is polluted and the Baths are no better than a cesspool.

Many Voices. Don't talk about the Baths! None of that! We don't want to hear it!

Dr. Stockmann. I've already said I want to speak about a discovery I've made only lately—and that is, that the very sources of our moral life are polluted and the whole community is a cesspool covered up with a fabric of lies.

Angry Voices. What's that? What's he saying?

The Mayor. How dare you insinuate—!

Aslaksen (*His hand on the bell*). I call upon the speaker to use more moderate language.

Dr. Stockmann. I've always loved my native town—this place where I spent my happy boyhood. I was a young man when I left here; and living in exile, my memory cast a special glow over this place and its people. (*Scattered applause and words of approval.*) And there I was, for many years, stuck in that horrible hole in the far North, tending the wretched people whose hovels were scattered among the rocks. I often thought it would have been better if a veterinarian had been sent to look after those half-starved creatures instead of a physician like myself.

(*Murmurs among the crowd.*)

Billing. I'll be damned if I ever heard such—!

Hovstad. That's an insult to hard-working citizens!

Dr. Stockmann. Wait a minute! No one can accuse me of neglecting my job, or of forgetting about my home town. All the time I was there, I brooded like an eider duck sitting on her eggs—and what I finally hatched was the plan for our Baths. (*Applause and protests.*) And at last when fate was kind enough to make it possible for me to come home—I thought that all my wishes had been fulfilled. There was only one thing more I wished for—fervently and sincerely—and that was to be able to serve my home town and my fellow-citizens.

The Mayor (*Looking at the ceiling*). You chose a strange way to do it—!

Dr. Stockmann. I was blind then to the real situation, and I was supremely happy. But yesterday morning—no, to be precise, it was yesterday afternoon—my eyes were suddenly wide open, and the first thing I saw was the colossal stupidity of the authorities—

(*General uproar—shouts and laughter;* MRS. STOCKMANN *coughs several times.*)

The Mayor. Mr. Chairman!

Aslaksen (*Ringing his bell*). By virtue of my authority—!

Dr. Stockmann. You're not going to interrupt me because of a word, Mr. Aslaksen. What I mean is that I suddenly saw it's our leaders we can thank for the unholy mess at the Baths. I'm sick of these so-called leaders—I've seen enough of them. They're like goats in a garden—ruining everything. They stand in the way of free men, and hinder them at every turn. If I had my way, they'd be exterminated like any other pest—

(*Another uproar follows.*)

The Mayor. Mr. Chairman—can we let this go unchallenged?

Aslaksen (*His hand on the bell*). Doctor—!

Dr. Stockmann. I can't understand why it's taken me so long to see though these gentlemen, when practically every day I've had a perfect specimen before my very eyes—my brother Peter—unimaginative, hidebound, and prejudiced—

(*Laughter, uproar, and hisses.* MRS. STOCKMANN *coughs several times.* ASLAKSEN *rings his bell violently.*)

The Drunken Man (*Who has come in again*). Is he talking about me? My name's Petersen, all right—But what the hell can I—

Angry Voices. Throw that drunk out! Throw him out! (*They throw him out again.*)

The Mayor. Who was that person?

A Man. I don't know him, Mr. Mayor.

Second Man. Never saw him before.

Third Man. I think he's a longshoreman from over at— (*The rest is inaudible.*)

Aslaksen. He's obviously had too much to drink.—Proceed, Doctor; but please be more moderate in your language.

Dr. Stockmann. Well, gentlemen, I won't say any more about our leaders. And if anyone thinks, after what I've just said, that my object in coming here tonight was to attack them, he's wrong—absolutely wrong. You see, I cherish the comforting conviction that these opportunists—these relics of a dying age—are managing very well to destroy themselves; they don't have to call in a doctor to hasten their end. And besides, they are not the ones who are most dangerous to the community, nor should they bear the greatest blame for polluting the sources of our moral life and infecting the very ground we stand on. They are not the worst enemies of truth and freedom!

Shouts from All Sides. Who are? Who? Name them! Name them!

Dr. Stockmann. Oh, I'll name them all right! Because that's the great discovery I made yesterday. (*Raising his voice.*) The most dangerous enemy of truth and freedom in society is the majority—yes, the damned, solid, liberal majority—that's who it is! There's your answer!

(*Tremendous uproar. Most of the crowd are shouting, stamping, and hissing. A few of the older men exchange knowing looks and seem to be enjoying the situation.* MRS. STOCKMANN *gets up; she appears to be nervous.* EILIF *and* MORTEN *move threateningly toward some schoolboys who are jumping and screaming.* ASLAKSEN *rings his bell and calls for order.* HOVSTAD *and* BILLING *both try to speak but are drowned out. At last quiet is restored.*)

Aslaksen. I call upon the speaker to withdraw the thoughtless remarks he has just made.

Dr. Stockmann. No, Mr. Aslaksen— never! It's the majority that's denying me my freedom and trying to keep me from speaking the truth.

Hovstad. The majority is always right.

Billing. I'll be damned if it isn't!

Dr. Stockmann. The majority is *never* right. Never, I tell you! That's one of those myths that independent, intelligent men have got to destroy. After all, who are in the majority—the wise men or the fools? I'm sure you won't dispute the fact that the fools are in the overwhelming majority all over the world. And you certainly don't think it's right that the clever men be ruled by fools! (*Uproar and shouts.*) You can shout me down if you like, but you can't deny what I say! The majority has *might* on its side—unfortunately; but the *right* is on the side of a few individuals like me. It's the minority that's always right! (*Renewed disturbance.*)

Hovstad. Aha! So Doctor Stockmann has turned aristocrat overnight!

Dr. Stockmann. I've already said I don't intend to waste any words on the puny, narrow-chested, short-winded men who are falling behind in this race. Life will move forward without them. I'm more interested in the rare few among us who are ready to accept new and vital ideas. Such men are in the vanguard—far ahead of the solid majority that's unable to keep up with them; they are fighting for ideas so advanced that not many people dare to adopt them as yet.

Hovstad. Now the Doctor wants to start a revolution!

Dr. Stockmann. Yes, by God, I do, Mr. Hovstad! I intend to lead a revolution against the lie that the majority has a monopoly on the truth. And what kind of truths does the majority usually believe in? Old, worn-out platitudes that have practically lost their meaning. And when a truth is as old as that, gentlemen, it's really no better than a lie. (*Laughter and jeers.*) You can believe me or not, as you like. But truths don't live as long as Methuselah, as some people think they do. The average age of a so-called truth is about seventeen or eighteen years—twenty at most, seldom longer. But truths as old as that are pretty thin fare; still the majority accepts them and recommends them as wholesome moral food. But there's not much nourishment in a diet of that kind, I assure you; and as a doctor, I ought to know. These tired old truths are as rancid and moldy as last year's meat; and they are the cause of the moral scurvy that's plaguing our community.

Aslaksen. It seems to me the speaker has wandered a long way from his subject.

The Mayor. I agree with you, Mr. Chairman.

Dr. Stockmann. Have you lost your mind, Peter? I am sticking very closely to my subject. I'm saying that it's the masses—the damned solid majority—that poison the sources of our moral life and corrupt the very ground we walk on.

Hovstad. And so you condemn the great majority of intelligent people who are wise enough to respect and defend the old and time-tested truths?

Dr. Stockmann. My dear Mr. Hovstad, don't talk about time-tested truths! That's nonsense! The truths that the masses defend nowadays were advanced by the fighters in our grandfathers' time; we in the vanguard today no longer approve of them. There is only one basic truth, in my opinion—and that is that a community cannot live a healthy life if it draws its nourishment only from old, anemic truths.

Hovstad. Instead of standing there and spouting all those vague generalities, you ought to give us a few examples of the old, anemic truths we're supposed to be living on.

(*Applause from various parts of the room.*)

Dr. Stockmann. Oh, I could give you a long list of them; but I'll confine myself to one accepted truth which is actually a filthy lie, but which you, Mr. Hovstad, and *The People's Messenger*, and all its readers feed on every day—

Hovstad. Which is—?

Dr. Stockmann. Which is a belief you inherited from your grandparents and thoughtlessly go on proclaiming far and wide—the belief that the common crowd, the masses, are the essential part of the population—are the People—that the great crowd of ignorant and undeveloped men have the same right to censure and praise, to advise and to govern, as the few intellectually superior individuals.

Billing. Well, I'll be damned if I ever—!

Hovstad (*Shouting simultaneously*). Listen to that, my friends!

Angry Voices. Oh, so we're not the people! We're stupid! You've got to be someone special!

A Workman. He's got his nerve! Throw him out!

Others. Throw him out!

A Man (*Shouts*). Evensen, your horn! Blow your horn!

(*The blare of the horn mingles with hisses, boos, and cat-calls.*)

Dr. Stockmann (*As the uproar subsides*). Use your heads! Can't you stand hearing the truth? I don't expect all of you to agree with me at once; but I thought Mr. Hovstad would back me up, after he got over his shock. He claims to be a freethinker—

Several Voices. (*Murmurs of astonishment*). A freethinker! Is that what he said? Is Hovstad a freethinker?

Hovstad (*Shouts*). I defy you to prove it, Doctor Stockmann! Did you ever see anything like that in my paper?

Dr. Stockmann (*Thinking*). No, damn it—you're right! You never had the courage. Well, I won't embarrass you. Then let's say I'm the freethinker. I'm going to prove to you scientifically, my friends, that *The People's Messenger* misleads you and pulls you by the nose when it tells you that you, the common people, the crowd, are the cream of the population. It's just one of the lies you usually find in the newspaper. The masses are only the raw material from which a People is made. (*Groans, laughter, and confusion.*) Well, isn't that so in every form of life? It's all a matter of breeding. Take animals, for instance. The com-

mon barnyard hen isn't the greatest for eating or for laying eggs; her eggs aren't very much better than those of a crow or a raven. But take a carefully bred Spanish or Japanese hen—or a pheasant or turkey—and you'll see the difference! Or in the case of dogs, with which we are so familiar; there's the ordinary common cur—one of those dirty, flea-bitten mongrels that runs through the streets and befouls the walls, the gutters, and the sidewalks. And compare one of those curs with a pedigreed poodle, bred for generations in private homes, where they've had the best food, and have gotten used to hearing quiet voices and soft music. Don't you think the poodle's brain would be vastly superior to the cur's? Of course it would. The puppies of such poodles can be taught to do the cleverest tricks—things that a common cur could never learn to do even if it stood on its head. (*Shouts and mocking cries.*)

A Man (*Calls out*). Now what are you trying to say—that we're dogs?

Another. We're not animals, Doctor!

Dr. Stockmann. Of course we are! We're the finest in the animal kingdom; but even among us some are more highly bred than others. There's a tremendous difference between poodle-men and mongrel-men! The funny part of it is that Mr. Hovstad agrees with me entirely as long as we are talking about four-legged animals—

Hovstad. Yes, it's all right for *them.*

Dr. Stockmann. All right. But as soon as I apply the principle to two-legged animals, Mr. Hovstad objects. He's afraid to think independently, or to follow his ideas to their logical conclusion; so he turns the principle upside down and proclaims in the *Messenger* that the barnyard hen and the common cur are the finest specimens in the menagerie. And that's the way it'll always be, as long as we stick with the crowd instead of trying to work our way up to some sort of intellectual distinction.

Hovstad. I don't claim any sort of distinction. I come from poor country people and I'm proud of it. I'm proud to be one of the common people you're insulting.

Several Voices. That's right, Hovstad! Good for you!

Dr. Stockmann. The kind of common people I'm talking about aren't necessarily found among the poor. They're crawling and swarming all around us—even on the highest levels of society. Just look at your fine, distinguished Mayor! He's about as ordinary as anyone who walks on two feet—

The Mayor. I protest against such personal remarks.

Dr. Stockmann. —and not because one of our ancestors was a rascally old pirate on the Baltic Sea—

The Mayor. An absurd story! I deny it!

Dr. Stockmann. —but because he thinks what his superiors think, and mouths their opinions. That's what the common people do; they're intellectually dependent. And that's why my brother Peter, who appears to be so magnificent, really lacks any sort of distinction, and consequently could never be a liberal.

The Mayor. Mr. Chairman—!

Hovstad. You mean you have to be a man of distinction to be a liberal? Well, we learn something new every day!

(*General laughter.*)

Dr. Stockmann. Yes, that's part of my new discovery too. And there's something else: I've discovered that liberalism and morality are almost precisely the same thing. That's why I consider it absolutely inexcusable for the *Messenger* to go on preaching day in and day out that it's the common crowd, the majority, that has a monopoly on liberalism and morality —and that vice, corruption, and depravity seep into our community as a result of culture, just as all the filth from the tanneries up at Mill Valley drains into our Baths! (*Uproar and interruptions; but* DR. STOCKMANN *continues unperturbed.*) And yet the *Messenger* keeps insisting that the masses ought to be raised to a higher level of culture! But if that were to happen, by God, it would be sending them right down the road to depravity! Fortunately, the idea that culture demoralizes is just another one of the lies inherited from our grandfathers! No, it's ignorance, poverty, and ugliness that demoralize men! And to live in a house where the windows are never opened and the floors are never swept—and my wife thinks they ought to be *scrubbed* every day, but that's a debatable point—is equally demoralizing! Lack of oxygen weakens the moral fiber. So there must be precious little oxygen in the houses around here, if the majority of our citizens have so little moral fiber as to be willing to build the town's prosperity on a cesspool of lies and deceit.

Aslaksen. That's an insult to the entire community! It's a disgraceful accusation!

A Man. Mr. Chairman, make him sit down.

Many Voices. Yes, yes! That's right! Sit down!

Dr. Stockmann (Losing his temper). Then I'll shout it on every street corner! I'll send it to the newspapers in other towns! I'll let the whole country know what's going on here!

Hovstad. It seems as if Dr. Stockmann is determined to ruin the town.

Dr. Stockmann. Yes, I love this town so much that I'd rather destroy it than see it grow rich on a lie.

Aslaksen. This is really serious.

(*Shouts and cat-calls.* Mrs. STOCK-MANN *tries to attract her husband's attention in vain.*)

Hovstad (Shouting above the din). Any man who wants to destroy a whole community must be a public enemy!

Dr. Stockmann (With growing excitement). A community based on lies deserves to be destroyed! I say, it ought to be razed to the ground—and all those who live on lies should be exterminated like vermin! It begins by infecting one town, and then the infection spreads until the entire country will deserve to be destroyed. And if things should ever reach that state, I'd say from the bottom of my heart: Let it be destroyed, and let all the people perish!

A Man (Shouts). He talks like a real enemy of the people!

Billing. I'll be damned if he doesn't!

The Whole Crowd (Screaming). Yes, yes! He hates his own people! He hates his country! He's an enemy of the people!

Aslaksen. As a citizen of this town and as a private individual, I'm deeply disturbed by what I've heard here to-night. Dr. Stockmann has betrayed himself in a way I should never have dreamed possible. I must therefore, regretfully, concur with the opinion of my fellow-citizens, which, I propose, should be formally expressed in a resolution, as follows: "This meeting hereby declares Dr. Thomas Stockmann, the former Medical Director of the Baths, to be an enemy of the people."

(*A storm of cheers and applause. A number of people surround the* Doc-tor *and boo him.* Mrs. Stockmann *and* Petra *have risen from their seats.* Morten *and* Eilif *are fighting the other schoolboys for hissing; some grownups separate them.*)

Dr. Stockmann (To the jeering crowd). Oh, you fools! Fools! I tell you that—

Aslaksen (Ringing his bell). We can't listen to you now, Doctor. We're about to take a formal vote; but out of regard for personal feelings, it will be by secret ballot. Have you any blank paper, Mr. Billing?

Billing. Yes, I have both blue and white here. Which do you want?

Aslaksen (Going up to him). We'll use both; we can do it quicker that way. Let's cut them up into small strips—yes, that's it. (*To the crowd.*) Blue means no, white means yes. I'll come around myself to collect the votes.

(The Mayor *leaves the hall.* Aslak-sen *and one or two others go around the room with the slips of paper in their hats.*)

First Man (To Hovstad*).* What's come over the Doctor? What do you make of it?

Hovstad. He always wants to have his own way.

Second Man (*To* BILLING). Billing, you go to his house—would you say he drinks?

Billing. I'll be damned if I know what to say! He always offers you a toddy.

Third Man. I think he's a little crazy sometimes.

First Man. I wonder if it runs in his family.

Billing. I wouldn't be surprised if it did.

Fourth Man. No, it's pure spite; he wants to get even with someone for something.

Billing. Well, I know he wanted a raise in salary—but he didn't get it.

All the Men (*In unison*). Oh, that's what it is!

The Drunken Man (*In the crowd*). Give me a blue one! And give me a white one too!

Several Voices. That drunk is here again! Get rid of him!

Morten Kiil (*Going up to* DR. STOCKMANN). Well, Stockmann! Do you see what your shenanigans have led to?

Dr. Stockmann. I've only done my duty.

Kiil. What was that you said about the tanneries at Mill Valley?

Dr. Stockmann. You heard me; I said that's where the filth comes from.

Kiil. From my place too?

Dr. Stockmann. Unfortunately, yours is the worst of all.

Kiil. And you're going to put that in the papers?

Dr. Stockmann. I'm not hiding anything.

Kiil. You'll pay dearly for that, Stockmann! (*He goes out.*)

Mr. Vik (*A stout man; goes up to* CAPTAIN HORSTER, *ignoring the women*). So, Captain Horster, you lend your house to enemies of the people?

Horster. It seems to me I can do as I please with my own property, Mr. Vik.

Vik. Certainly. Then you won't object if I do as I please with mine.

Horster. What do you mean by that?

Vik. You'll hear from me in the morning. (*He turns and goes out.*)

Petra. Captain Horster—wasn't that the owner of your ship?

Horster. Yes—Mr. Vik.

Aslaksen (*With the slips of paper in his hand, gets up on the platform, and rings the bell*). Gentlemen, allow me to announce the results of the voting. All the voters, except one—

A Young Man. That must be the drunk!

Aslaksen. By the votes of everyone here, except the man who is intoxicated, this meeting declares Dr. Thomas Stockmann an enemy of the people. (*Cheers and applause.*) Three cheers for our old and honorable community! (*Cheers.*) And three cheers for our able and energetic Mayor, who has so loyally set family feeling aside! (*Cheers.*) The meeting is adjourned. (*He steps down from the platform.*)

Billing. Let's have three cheers for the Chairman!

All. Three cheers for Aslaksen!

Dr. Stockmann. My hat and coat, Petra! Captain, do you have room on your ship for passengers to the New World?

Horster. There'll always be room for you and yours, Doctor.

Dr. Stockmann (*As* PETRA *helps him into his coat*). Very good. Come, Katherine! Come, boys!

Mrs. Stockmann (*Quietly*). Thomas, dear, let's go out the back way.

Dr. Stockmann. No back ways for me, Katherine. (*Raises his voice*) You'll hear more from this enemy of the people before he turns his back on you! I'm not as tolerant as a certain person you know of; you won't hear me say, "I forgive you, for you know not what you do."

Aslaksen (*Shouts*). That comparison is blasphemous, Dr. Stockmann!

Billing. Well, I'll be—it's not fit for a decent man's ears.

A Coarse Voice. Now he's threatening us, is he!

Others (*Angrily*). Let's go and smash his windows! Duck him in the fjord!

A Man (*In the crowd*). Blow your horn, Evensen! Blow it, man!

(*Horn-blowing, hisses, and shouts.* DR. STOCKMAN *goes out through the hall with his family,* HORSTER *clearing the way for them.*)

All (*Yelling after them as they go*). Enemy of the people! Enemy of the people!

Billing (*Gathering his papers*). Well, I'll be damned if I go and drink toddy at the Stockmanns' tonight!

(*The crowd pushes toward the door; as they leave, and outside the house, they continue to shout, "Enemy of the people! Enemy of the people!"*)

CURTAIN

ACT FIVE

SCENE. DR. STOCKMANN's *study. The walls are lined with bookcases and cabinets containing specimens and bottles of chemicals. In the back wall is a door leading to the hall; down left a door leading to the living room. In the right wall are two windows, all the glass panes of which have been smashed. The* DOCTOR'S *desk, covered with books and papers, stands in the center of the room, which is in great disorder. It is morning.* DR. STOCKMANN, *in dressing-gown, slippers, and skull-cap, is bending down and raking under one of the cabinets with an umbrella; finally he manages to rake out a stone.*

Dr. Stockmann (*Calling through the open door into the living room*). Katherine, I've found another one.

Mrs. Stockmann (*From the living room*). You'll find a lot more, I'm sure.

Dr. Stockmann (*Adds the stone to a pile of others on the table*). I'm going to keep these stones as mementoes—and leave them to Eilif and Morten. When the boys grow up I want them to look at these relics of the stone age every day. (*Rakes under a bookcase.*) By the way, have you sent—what *is* that girl's name?— have you sent her for the glazier?

Mrs. Stockmann (*Coming in*). Yes, but he said he didn't know if he could come today.

Dr. Stockmann. Of course, he's afraid to come.

Mrs. Stockmann. Well, that's just what Randina thinks—he's afraid of the neighbors. (*Calls into the living room.*) What is it, Randina? Oh, I see. (*Goes out and returns immediately.*) It's a letter for you, Thomas.

Dr. Stockmann. Let me see it. (*Opens and reads it.*) Oh—of course!

Mrs. Stockmann. Who is it from?

Dr. Stockmann. The landlord. He's giving us notice.

Mrs. Stockmann. Not really! But he's such a nice man—

Dr. Stockmann (*Glancing at the letter*). Says he can't help himself—doesn't like doing it, but on account of the neighbors—public opinion—He has to make a living and he doesn't want to offend certain influential men—

Mrs. Stockmann. There you see, Thomas!

Dr. Stockmann. Yes, of course, I see—nothing but a lot of cowards in this town. No one dares to do anything for fear of someone else. (*Throws the letter on the table.*) Well, what do we care, Katherine? We'll be leaving soon for the New World—

Mrs. Stockmann. But, Thomas, do you really think that's a wise move?

Dr. Stockmann. Do you expect me to stay here, where they call me an enemy of the people—spit on me—break my windows! And look at this, Katherine—somebody tore a big hole in my black trousers!

Mrs. Stockmann. Oh, dear! And they're the best ones you've got!

Dr. Stockmann. Yes. Well, you should never wear your best trousers when you go out to fight for truth and freedom! I don't care so much about the trousers—you can always sew them up for me. But what I can't swallow is that the common herd should attack me as if they were my equals—that turns my stomach!

Mrs. Stockmann. I know, Thomas; they've treated you very badly here. But does that mean that we have to leave the country for good?

Dr. Stockmann. If we went to any other town, we'd find the common people just as offensive as they are here. They're all alike. Well, let the dogs snap—that's not the worst of it! The worst of it is that all over the country men are nothing but pawns of the politicians. As far as that goes, I don't suppose it's any better anywhere else—even in America. The ignorant majority and the so-called liberal public, and all the other damned riff-raff, are the same the world over—but at least it's on a bigger scale over there. They may kill a man, but they don't put him to slow torture. They don't squeeze the living soul out of a free man, as they do here. Anyway, there's plenty of room to get away from it all. (*Walks back and forth.*) If only I knew where there was a virgin forest, or a little South Sea island up for sale, cheap—

Mrs. Stockmann. But, Thomas, what about the boys?

Dr. Stockmann (*Comes to a halt*). You amaze me, Katherine! Do you really want the boys to grow up in a society like this? Why, you saw for yourself last night that half the people in this town are out of their minds, and if the other half haven't lost their senses, it's only because they're such savages, they have no sense to lose.

Mrs. Stockmann. But, Thomas dear, perhaps the caustic things you said had something to do with it.

Dr. Stockmann. Well, isn't what I said perfectly true? Don't they turn every idea upside-down—and make right look wrong? The things I know are true, they call lies! And the craziest part of it all is that these full-grown men go around in a crowd calling themselves liberals and imagining they're enlightened. Isn't that ridiculous, Katherine?

Mrs. Stockmann. Yes, I suppose it is, but— (PETRA *comes in from the living room.*) Back from school already, Petra?

Petra. Yes. I've been dismissed.

Mrs. Stockmann. Dismissed?

Dr. Stockmann. You too!

Petra. Mrs. Busk gave me my notice—and I thought it best to leave at once.

Dr. Stockmann. You were perfectly right!

Mrs. Stockmann. That was an awful thing for Mrs. Busk to do!

Petra. No it wasn't, Mother. It hurt her to do it, but she said she had to—so she let me go.

Dr. Stockmann (Laughing and rubbing his hands). She had to! Afraid of the others! That's great!

Mrs. Stockmann. Well, after the terrible scenes last night—

Petra. It wasn't only that. Father—listen to this!

Dr. Stockmann. Well?

Petra. Mrs. Busk showed me three letters she received this morning—

Dr. Stockmann. Anonymous, of course!

Petra. Yes.

Dr. Stockmann. They didn't even dare to sign their names, Katherine!

Petra. Two of the letters said that someone, who had been our guest here, had mentioned at the Club last night that my views on various subjects were extremely radical—

Dr. Stockmann. Which I hope you didn't deny!

Petra. Of course not! Mrs. Busk has expressed some pretty radical views herself on occasion—when we were alone; but after these letters—openly spreading reports about me—she daren't keep me on.

Mrs. Stockmann. A guest in our house —just imagine! That's the thanks you get for your hospitality, Thomas!

Dr. Stockmann. We're not going to live in this stinking hole any longer. Pack up as fast as you can, Katherine; the sooner we get out of here, the better.

Mrs. Stockmann. Be quiet a moment—I think I hear someone in the hall. See who it is, Petra.

Petra (Opens the hall door). Oh, it's Captain Horster! Won't you come in?

Horster (Coming in). Good morning. I thought I'd just come over to see how you were.

Dr. Stockmann (Shaking his hand). Thanks. That's very kind of you.

Mrs. Stockmann. And thank you, Captain Horster, for helping us through the crowd last night.

Petra. How did you ever manage to get home?

Horster. Oh, I made it—with a little muscle. They were pretty noisy—but their bark is worse than their bite!

Dr. Stockmann. Astonishing, isn't it—what cowards they are! Come here, I want to show you something! Those are all the stones they tossed through the windows. Just look at them! There aren't two decent stones in the pile—just a lot of pebbles and gravel. And yet they stood out there yelling and screaming that they were going to break my bones. But when it comes to *doing* anything—they never go through with it.

Horster. Well, that's lucky for you, Doctor!

Dr. Stockmann. True enough. But it makes me angry all the same. Suppose it were a serious question of national importance that called for a fight, you'd see that public opinion would be in favor of turning tail, and the solid majority would scatter like a bunch of frightened sheep. That's what's so depressing to think about, Captain Horster; it actually worries me— But to hell with it—why should I bother my head about it! They call me an enemy of the people, so I might as well *be* an enemy of the people!

Mrs. Stockmann. You'll never be that, Thomas!

Dr. Stockmann. Don't swear to it, Katherine! An ugly name is like a sore that won't heal. And what they've called me is sticking in my gut, and eating into me like acid— and the biggest dose of magnesia won't stop it!

Petra. Oh, Father, why don't you just laugh at them!

Horster. One of these days they'll change their minds about you, Doctor.

Mrs. Stockmann. Yes, Thomas, I'm sure of that.

Dr. Stockmann. They may—when it's too late. A lot of good it will do them then! Let them wallow in their filth and curse the day when they drove a patriot into exile. When do you sail, Captain?

Horster. Hm! That's something else I must talk to you about—

Dr. Stockmann. Oh? Is something wrong with the ship?

Horster. No—only I'm not sailing with her.

Petra. Do you mean you've been dismissed?

Horster (With a smile). Yes, I have.

Petra. You, too.

Mrs. Stockmann. There, you see, Thomas!

Dr. Stockmann. And all because of the truth! Oh, if I had thought such a thing could happen—

Horster. Don't you worry about that; I'm sure to find a ship somewhere else.

Dr. Stockmann. So that's our Mr. Vik— a wealthy man, who can afford to be completely independent—! It's disgraceful!

Horster. He's a pretty decent fellow otherwise; he told me himself he'd like to keep me on, but he didn't dare—

Dr. Stockmann. He didn't dare! Of course not!

Horster. He said it wasn't so easy for a member of the party—

Dr. Stockmann. He told the truth that time! A party is like a sausage-machine; it mashes up all their brains into one hash—fatheads and blockheads, all strung together in the party!

Mrs. Stockmann. Oh, Thomas, really!

Petra (To Horster). If only you hadn't seen us home, this might not have happened.

Horster. I don't regret it.

Petra (Holds out her hand to him). Thank you!

Horster (To Dr. Stockmann). There's something else I want to say—if you're really determined to leave— I've worked out another plan—

Dr. Stockmann. Excellent! We want to get away at once.

Mrs. Stockmann. Listen! Wasn't that someone knocking?

Petra. It must be Uncle Peter.

Dr. Stockmann. Aha! (Calls.) Come in!

Mrs. Stockmann. Thomas dear, please promise me—

(The Mayor enters from the hall.)

The Mayor (In the doorway). Oh, you're busy! Then I'd better—

Dr. Stockmann. No, no. Come in.

The Mayor. I wanted to speak to you alone.

Mrs. Stockmann. We'll go into the living room.

Horster. I'll come back again later.

Dr. Stockmann. No, don't go away, Captain. I want to hear more about—

Horster. Very well—then I'll wait. (He

follows Mrs. Stockmann *and* Petra *into the living room.*)

Dr. Stockmann (*Notices* The Mayor *looking at the windows*). It's a bit drafty in here today, isn't it? You'd better put your hat on.

The Mayor. Thanks—if I may. (*He does so.*) I think I caught cold last night. I suddenly felt a chill—

Dr. Stockmann. Really! I found it warm enough!

The Mayor. I'm sorry I couldn't prevent that outbreak after the meeting.

Dr. Stockmann. Is that the only thing you've come to say to me?

The Mayor (*Taking an envelope from his pocket*). I have this letter for you from the directors of the Baths.

Dr. Stockmann. My dismissal, I suppose.

The Mayor. Yes—as of today. (*Lays the letter on the table.*) We regret this decision but, frankly, we didn't dare do otherwise—because of public opinion, you understand.

Dr. Stockmann. You didn't dare do otherwise! I seem to have heard those words several times today.

The Mayor. I think it ought to be clear to you that from now on you won't be able to practice in this town.

Dr. Stockmann. To hell with my practice! But why are you so sure of that?

The Mayor. The Home Owners Association is circulating a petition urging all its members to refrain from using your services—and I'm sure that everyone will sign it. They wouldn't dare to refuse.

Dr. Stockmann. I don't doubt that! Anything else?

The Mayor. If you take my advice, you'll leave town for a while—

Dr. Stockmann. Yes, I've been thinking of doing that.

The Mayor. Good. Then—after six months or so—when you've had time to think things over—you might bring yourself to write a few words of apology, admitting your mistake—

Dr. Stockmann. And then, you think, I might get my job back?

The Mayor. You might; it's not altogether impossible.

Dr. Stockmann. But what about public opinion? You wouldn't dare to defy that!

The Mayor. Opinions—both public and private—have a way of changing. And to be quite frank, it would be necessary for you to give us a statement to that effect in writing.

Dr. Stockmann. Oh, so that's what you want! I've already told you what I think of your dirty tricks!

The Mayor. You were in a different position then—when you thought you had the whole town at your back—

Dr. Stockmann. And now, it seems, I have the whole town *on* my back— (*Flaring up.*) I wouldn't do it if I had the devil himself on my back! Never, I tell you; never!

The Mayor. A man with a family has no right to behave the way you're behaving, Thomas. Absolutely no right!

Dr. Stockmann. Haven't I? There's only one thing in this world a free man has no right to do. Do you know what that is?

The Mayor. No.

Dr. Stockmann. Of course not, but I'll tell you. A free man has no right to cover himself with filth; he has no right to behave in such a foul way as to want to spit in his own face.

The Mayor. That might sound very convincing if there weren't another explanation for your stubbornness—. But then, of course, there is—

Dr. Stockmann. What do you mean?

The Mayor. You know very well what I mean. But, as your brother and as a man who knows the world, I advise you not to build your hopes and expectations too high—they might collapse.

Dr. Stockmann. What in the world are you talking about?

The Mayor. Don't try to tell me that you're ignorant of the terms of Morten Kiil's will!

Dr. Stockmann. I only know he's left what little he has to a home for poor old people. What's that got to do with me?

The Mayor. In the first place, what he has is not so little—it happens to be a great deal. Morten Kiil is a very wealthy man.

Dr. Stockmann. I had no idea of that!

The Mayor. Hm—really? Then I don't suppose you had any idea, either, that a large part of his fortune will go to your children, and that you and your wife will have the interest on the principal for life. Didn't he ever tell you that?

Dr. Stockmann. Never—believe me! It's just the opposite—he does nothing but plead poverty and complain about the high taxes he has to pay. Peter, are you sure of this?

The Mayor. My information is absolutely reliable.

Dr. Stockmann. Then, thank God, Katherine and the children are provided for. I must tell her this at once—(*Calls out.*) Katherine, Katherine!

The Mayor (Holding him back). No, wait! Don't tell her yet!

Mrs. Stockmann (Opens the door). What is it, dear?

Dr. Stockmann. It's nothing; never mind. (*She shuts the door. He paces back and forth.*) Just think of it—we're provided for—all of us—and for life. It's a wonderful feeling to know you have that security!

The Mayor. Yes, but that's exactly what you don't have. Morten Kiil can change his will whenever he likes.

Dr. Stockmann. Oh, but he wouldn't do that, Peter. The old badger was overjoyed when I attacked you and your high-and-mighty friends.

The Mayor (Starts and looks at him intently). Oh, that puts a new light on things.

Dr. Stockmann. What things?

The Mayor. The way the two of you worked it out. The violent attacks you made on the leading men of the town, pretending it was all in the name of truth—

Dr. Stockmann. What are you getting at?

The Mayor. It was just done to please that vindictive old man—in exchange for your share in his will!

Dr. Stockmann. Peter—you are the vilest creature I've ever met in my life!

The Mayor. I'm through with you for good. Your dismissal is final—we have the goods on you now. (*He goes out.*)

Dr. Stockmann. Why, of all the dirty, slimy—! (*Calls.*) Katherine, this floor has got to be scrubbed after him! Let that girl—what the devil's her name! —fumigate this room—

Mrs. Stockmann (In the doorway). Thomas, Thomas, calm down!

Petra (Also in the doorway). Father, grandfather is here. He wants to know if he can speak to you alone.

Dr. Stockmann. Of course, he can. (*Goes to the door.*) Come in, Mr. Kiil. (MORTEN KIIL *comes in.* DR.

STOCKMANN *closes the door behind him.*) What can I do for you, sir? Won't you sit down?

Kiil. No, thanks. *(He looks around.)* You all look very comfortable here today, Thomas.

Dr. Stockmann. Yes, don't we.

Kiil. Very comfortable—plenty of fresh air. It looks as if you've got a good supply of that oxygen you were talking about last night. Your moral fiber should be in excellent condition today.

Dr. Stockmann. It is.

Kiil. I'm sure of that. *(Taps his chest.)* Do you know what I've got here?

Dr. Stockmann. Strong moral fiber, too, I hope.

Kiil. Bah!—Something much better than that. *(He takes out a large wallet, opens it, and shows* DR. STOCKMANN *a bundle of papers.)*

Dr. Stockmann (Looks at him in amazement). They're shares of stock! In the Baths?

Kiil. They were very easy to get hold of today.

Dr. Stockmann. You mean you've been buying them up?

Kiil. As many as I could get my hands on.

Dr. Stockmann. But, my dear Mr. Kiil— with the condition the Baths are in—!

Kiil. If you listen to reason—you can put the Baths back on its feet.

Dr. Stockmann. Well, you can see for yourself I'm doing everything I can, but— They're all mad in this town!

Kiil. You said last night that the worst of this pollution comes from my tannery. If that's true, then my grandfather and my father before me, and I myself have been poisoning this town for years—like three devils of destruction. Do you think I'm going to sit back and listen to an accusation like that?

Dr. Stockmann. I'm afraid you'll have to.

Kiil. No, thank you. My good name and reputation mean a lot to me. Some people call me "the Badger," so I'm told. A badger is a kind of pig, isn't it? Well, that's got to be changed— while I live and after I die. It's got to be cleaned up!

Dr. Stockmann. And how are you going to manage that?

Kiil. You are going to clean it up for me, Stockmann.

Dr. Stockmann. I?

Kiil. Do you know whose money I used to buy these shares? No, of course, you don't—but I'll tell you. It's the money Katherine, Petra, and the boys will inherit from me. Because I did manage to put something aside, after all.

Dr. Stockmann (Flaring up). And you mean to tell me you've put Katherine's money into *this*!

Kiil. Yes—I've invested every penny in the Baths. Now I want to see what a madman you are, Stockmann! If you keep on insisting that those nasty little creatures, or whatever they are, crawl into the pipes from my tannery, you'll just be stripping the skin from the backs of Katherine and Petra and the boys. And no man would do that to his own family—unless he was mad.

Dr. Stockmann (Pacing back and forth). Yes, I am mad; I'm a madman, all right!

Kiil. Do you want to hurt your wife and children? You can't be as mad as all that!

Dr. Stockmann (Stopping in front of him). Why on earth didn't you talk it over with me, before you went and bought all that trash?

Kiil. What's done is done.

Dr. Stockmann (Walking up and down). If only I weren't so sure about it—! But I know I'm absolutely right.

Kiil (Weighing the wallet in his hand). If you stick to your crazy idea, these won't be worth very much, you know. *(Puts the wallet in his pocket.)*

Dr. Stockmann. Damn it! Science ought be able to come up with something to purify the water—some sort of chemical—

Kiil. To kill those little animals, you mean?

Dr. Stockmann. Yes—or at least to make them harmless.

Kiil. Why don't you try rat poison?

Dr. Stockmann. Oh, don't talk nonsense! They all say it's only my imagination—so let it go at that! They're just a lot of ignorant mongrels. They call me an enemy of the people, and they'd like to tear the clothes off my back—

Kiil. And they smashed all your windows!

Dr. Stockmann. Well, I do have a duty to my family. I must talk it over with Katherine; she's wiser about these things than I am.

Kiil. That's right—she'll give you good advice.

Dr. Stockmann (Moves towards him angrily). What ever made you do such a senseless thing? Gamble with Katherine's money, and put me through hell! What kind of devil are you, anyway!

Kiil. I think I'd better be going. But I've got to have an answer from you —yes or no—before two o'clock. If

the answer is "no"—I'm going to turn the stock over to charity—today.

Dr. Stockmann. And what will Katherine get?

Kiil. Not a damn cent! *(The hall door opens;* HOVSTAD *and* ASLAKSEN *stand in the doorway.)* Well, look who's here!

Dr. Stockmann (Staring at them). What the hell do you two want? You have the nerve to set foot in my house?

Hovstad. For a reason.

Aslaksen. There's something we want to talk to you about.

Kiil (In a whisper). Yes or no—before two o'clock.

Aslaksen (With a glance at HOVSTAD*).* Aha!

(MORTEN KIIL *goes out.)*

Dr. Stockmann. Well, what do you want? Make it short!

Hovstad. We can understand that you'd resent our attitude at the meeting last night—

Dr. Stockmann. Oh, you call it an attitude, do you? It was a charming attitude! You old women—you damned cowards!

Hovstad. Call us what you like, we couldn't do otherwise.

Dr. Stockmann. You didn't *dare* do otherwise—isn't that so?

Hovstad. Put it any way you please.

Aslaksen. But why didn't you say a word about it beforehand—just a hint to Mr. Hovstad or to me?

Dr. Stockmann. A hint? About what?

Aslaksen. About what you had in mind all the time.

Dr. Stockmann. I don't know what you're talking about.

Aslaksen (Nods confidentially). Oh, yes, you do, Dr. Stockmann.

Hovstad. There's no need to make a mystery of it any longer.

Dr. Stockmann (Looks from one to the other). What are you two getting at?

Aslaksen. Hasn't your father-in-law been going around town buying up shares in the Baths?

Dr. Stockmann. Yes, he has—what about it?

Aslaksen. It might have been wiser to get somebody else to do it—someone less closely related to you.

Hovstad. In fact, your name need not have been mentioned at all. The attack on the Baths could have been made by someone else. You should have discussed it with me, Dr. Stockmann.

Dr. Stockmann (Stares straight ahead, then a light dawns, and he says in amazement). This is unbelievable! Are such things possible?

Aslaksen (With a smile). Obviously they are. But they ought to be done with finesse, you know.

Hovstad. And it's much better for several people to be involved in such a thing, because that makes it easier for each one to disclaim responsibility.

Dr. Stockmann (Calmly). Come to the point, gentlemen. What is it you want?

Aslaksen. Perhaps Mr. Hovstad had better—

Hovstad. No; you explain it, Aslaksen.

Aslaksen. Well, it's just this: Now that we know what's going on, we think we might venture to put *The People's Messenger* at your disposal.

Dr. Stockmann. And now you feel it's safe? But what about public opinion? Aren't you afraid of stirring up a storm of protest?

Hovstad. We think we can weather it.

Aslaksen. But you must be ready to shift your ground quickly, Doctor. As soon as your attacks on the Baths have had the desired effect—

Dr. Stockmann. You mean, as soon as my father-in-law and I have bought up the shares at the lowest possible price?

Hovstad. It's mainly for scientific reasons, I assume, that you want to get control of the Baths.

Dr. Stockmann. Of course—it was only for scientific reasons that I was able to get the old badger to come in on this deal with me. We'll tinker with the pipes a bit, and dig around on the beach—and it won't cost the town a penny. Will that be all right, eh?

Hovstad. I think so—if you have the *Messenger* to back you up.

Aslaksen. In a free community the Press is powerful, Doctor.

Dr. Stockmann. Oh, there's no doubt about that. And so is public opinion. I suppose you speak for the Home Owners Association, Mr. Aslaksen?

Aslaksen. Yes—and for the Temperance Society, too. You can count on that.

Dr. Stockmann. Now, tell me, gentlemen—I'm almost ashamed to ask—but what do you expect to get out of this?

Hovstad. Believe me, Doctor, we'd like to support you without any thought of a return, but the *Messenger* is in a rather shaky condition at the moment. We're not doing very well; and I'd hate to see the paper go out of business, just now when there's so much to be done in the way of political reform.

Dr. Stockmann. Oh, yes, I see! That would be a great blow to such a friend of the people as you are! *(Flares up.)* But I'm an enemy of the people, remember! (*Paces back and forth*). Where's my stick? Where the devil's my stick?

Hovstad. What's that?

Aslaksen. Surely you're not going to—

Dr. Stockmann (Comes to a halt). And suppose I refuse to give you a single penny of the fortune I make from those shares? Don't forget that we rich people hate to part with our money!

Hovstad. And don't you forget that this business with the shares can be presented in a very bad light.

Dr. Stockmann. Yes, and you're just the man to do it! If I don't come to the aid of the *Messenger*, you'll be sure to take a dim view of the affair. You'll go after me—you'll be out for my blood—like a hound at the throat of a hare.

Hovstad. That's the law of nature. Every animal must fight for its own survival.

Aslaksen. And get its food where it can find it.

Dr. Stockmann. Then go and look for yours in the gutter. (*Pacing about the room.*) I'll show you who's the strongest animal around here! (*Picks up his umbrella and brandishes it at them.*) Now, look out—!

Hovstad. You wouldn't dare strike us!

Aslaksen. Watch what you're doing with that umbrella!

Dr. Stockmann. Out of the window with you, Mr. Hovstad!

Hovstad (Edging towards the hall door.) Are you raving mad!

Dr. Stockmann. Out of the window, Mr. Aslaksen. Jump, I tell you! Before it's too late!

Aslaksen (Runs around the desk). Moderation, Doctor—I'm not very strong —I can't stand the excitement— (*Shouts.*) Help, help!

(Mrs. Stockmann, Petra, *and* Horster *enter from the living room.*)

Mrs. Stockmann. Good heavens, Thomas! What are you doing?

Dr. Stockmann (Brandishing the umbrella). Jump! Into the gutter with you!

Hovstad. He's assaulting an innocent man! You're a witness, Captain Horster! (*He rushes out through the hall door.*)

Aslaksen (Confused). If only I knew how to get out of here— (*He slinks out through the living room.*)

Mrs. Stockmann (Restraining the doctor). Thomas, control yourself!

Dr. Stockmann (Throws down the umbrella). The two of them got away— damn them!

Mrs. Stockmann. But what did they want?

Dr. Stockmann. I'll tell you later. I have something else on my mind right now. (*He goes to his desk and writes on a visiting card.*) Look, Katherine; I want you to see what I wrote.

Mrs. Stockmann (Reading from the card) "No—no—no!" What does that mean?

Dr. Stockmann. That's something else I'll explain later. (*Giving* Petra *the card.*) Here, Petra; tell what's-her-name—that girl—to run over and hand this to the badger, as quick as she can. Hurry! (Petra *takes the card and goes out to the hall.*) I think every devil out of hell has paid me a visit today! Now I've got to sharpen my pen and spear them with the point; I'll dip it in gall and venom; and hurl my ink-pot at their vicious heads!

Mrs. Stockmann. But, Thomas, aren't we going away?

(PETRA *returns*.)

Dr. Stockmann. Well?

Petra. She's gone off with it.

Dr. Stockmann. Good!—Did you say going away? No, I'll be damned if we are! We're going to stay right here, Katherine!

Petra. Stay here?

Mrs. Stockmann. Here, in town?

Dr. Stockmann. Right here in town. This is the battlefield—and this is where the battle must be fought—and won! As soon as you've patched up my pants, I'll go out to look for a place to live. We've got to have a roof over our heads this winter.

Horster. You are welcome to share my house.

Dr. Stockmann. We'd be in the way.

Horster. Not at all. There's plenty of room, and I'm hardly ever at home.

Mrs. Stockmann. That's very kind of you, Captain Horster!

Petra. Thank you!

Dr. Stockmann. (*Shaking his hand*). Thank you, thank you! That's one thing less to worry about! Now I can get down to work in earnest. There's so much to do, Katherine! But I have plenty of free time now, which is just as well—oh, I forgot to mention it— I've been dismissed—

Mrs. Stockmann (*Sighing*). Oh, yes, I expected that.

Dr. Stockmann. And they want to take my practice away from me, too. Well, let them! There'll always be the poor people—who don't pay anything. They're the ones who need me most, anyway. But, by God, I'm not going to keep quiet. I'll preach to them "in season and out of season"— as somebody once said—and they'll have to listen to me.

Mrs. Stockmann. But, Thomas dear, you've already preached to them, and you see how much good that did!

Dr. Stockmann. Don't be ridiculous, Katherine! Do you think I'd let public opinion, the solid majority, and all the rest of those devils drive me from the field? No, thank you! Besides, what I want to do is so simple and straightforward! I just want to drum into the heads of those stupid mongrels that the so-called liberals are the worst enemies of freedom—that party politics takes every new and vital idea and stifles it—that morality and justice are turned upside-down by corruption and greed—and that if we allow this to go on, life won't even be worth living! Captain Horster, don't you think I ought to be able to make people understand that?

Horster. Perhaps; I don't know much about such things myself.

Dr. Stockmann. It's very simple—I'll explain it to you. It's corrupt politics! The party bosses are like wolves— and they've got to be exterminated! Those hungry wolves couldn't exist without lots of little victims—the masses—to prey on. Just look at Hovstad and Aslaksen!—Just think of how many people they've crippled and brain-washed until they're fit for nothing but to be homeowners, teetotalers, and subscribers to *The People's Messenger*! (*Sits down on the edge of the table.*) Come here, Katherine! Look at how brilliantly the sun is shining today! And take deep breaths of this delicious air!

Mrs. Stockmann. Yes, Thomas, if only we could live on sunshine and air!

Dr. Stockmann. Oh, you'll have to economize a bit—but we'll get along. I'm not worried. What really worries

A scene from the 1975 Chichester Festival production, with Donald Sinden and Barbara Jefford as Dr. and Mrs. Stockmann, Sue Jones-Davies as Petra, and (standing behind the boys) Julian Somers as Horster. (*Plays and Players;* Reg Wilson)

me is that I don't know where I'll find a man who is independent and courageous enough to carry on my work after me.

Petra. Why worry about that now, Father; you have lots of time ahead of you.—Oh, look here are the boys!

(EILIF *and* MORTEN *come in from the living room.*)

Mrs. Stockmann. Has school let out early? It's not a holiday!

Morten. No, but we were fighting with some of the boys—

Eilif. No, we weren't!—They were fight ing with us.

Morten. Well, then Mr. Rörlund said we'd better stay home for a few days.

Dr. Stockmann (*Snapping his fingers and getting up from the table*). I've got it! It's a great idea! You're never going to set foot in that school again!

The Boys. No more school!

Mrs. Stockmann. But, Thomas—!

Dr. Stockmann. Never again, I say! I'll be your teacher; that is, I won't teach you a thing—

Morten. Hooray!

Dr. Stockmann. —except to be decent, honest, high-minded men—the both of you. And you'll help me with that, won't you, Petra?

Petra. Yes—gladly, Father.

Dr. Stockmann. And we'll have the school in the very room where they called me an enemy of the people. But there ought to be a few more pupils—I'd like to have at least a dozen to begin with.

Mrs. Stockmann. You'll certainly never get that many in this town.

Dr. Stockmann. Wait and see. (*To the* Boys.) Don't you know any boys who just hang around the streets—?

Morten. Oh, yes, Father, I know lots of them!

Dr. Stockmann. Good! Then find a few specimens and bring them to me. I'm going to experiment with mongrels for a change; there ought to be some brainy ones among them.

Morten. Father, what are we going to do when we grow up to be decent, high-minded men?

Dr. Stockmann. You're going to drive all the wolves out of the country, my boys! Get rid of them!

(EILIF *looks puzzled;* MORTEN *jumps around and cheers.*)

Mrs. Stockmann. Let's hope the wolves don't drive you out of the country, Thomas.

Dr. Stockmann. Katherine, you don't know what you're talking about! Drive *me* out! Now—when I'm the strongest man in town!

Mrs. Stockmann. You—the strongest?

Dr. Stockmann. Yes!—and I'll even go so far as to say that I'm one of the strongest men in the whole world.

Morten. Really, Father?

Dr. Stockmann (*Lowering his voice*). Sh! You mustn't say anything about it yet; but I've made a great discovery.

Mrs. Stockmann. What, not another one?

Dr. Stockmann. Yes—another one. (*Gathers the family around him and says confidentially*). And I'll tell you what it is—The strongest man in the world is the man who stands alone.

Mrs. Stockmann (*Smiles and shakes her head*). Oh, Thomas, Thomas!

Petra (*Grasping his hands and looking at him admiringly*). Father!

CURTAIN

The Ghost Sonata

AUGUST STRINDBERG

INTRODUCTION

August Strindberg, the intense, fiery, and tortured genius, Sweden's greatest playwright, was, after Ibsen, the most influential figure in the development of modern drama. Strindberg was born in Stockholm, on January 22, 1849, to a merchant who claimed aristocratic ancestors and a woman who had been a servant. His mother bore his father three sons before she married him, just prior to August's birth, and several children afterward—eight in all survived. Soon after August was born, his father went into bankruptcy, and the lonely, sensitive boy grew up in an atmosphere of poverty and discord. He had a limitless need for affection, but his father was cold and severe, and his mother slighted him for her oldest and favorite son. August was tormented by the thought that he was the son of a servant and considered himself the victim of injustice, a grievance that persisted and grew throughout his life until it became a mania. Although his tubercular mother could not give August all the attention he craved, she did try to instill in him her deep interest in religion. During his youth he scorned religion and denied the existence of God; but when a mental crisis overtook him in middle age, he turned to religion in an effort to retain his sanity.

When August was thirteen, his mother died, and his father married the housekeeper. The boy was disturbed by sexual conflicts; in his fantasies he saw his mother and stepmother, on the one hand, as pure and virginal and, on the other, as promiscuous and destructive. It was the beginning of the alternation of attraction and repulsion that he felt for the feminine sex throughout his life. This ambivalence, which recurs as a theme in much of his writing, was to ruin his marriages, in which he sought mothers and comrades rather than wives.

August did not get along with his stepmother or with his teachers. Although his unusual abilities were recognized at school, he refused to submit to discipline and did poorly in his studies. He read widely, however, laying the foundation of the enormous knowledge of poetry, drama, philosophy, and the natural sciences that later revealed itself in his literary, scientific, and pseudoscientific pursuits. At the age of eighteen, he entered the University of Uppsala, which he attended intermittently for about five years without earning a degree, suffering all the while from poverty, minor neuroses, and the effects of a dissolute life. He tried teaching but gave that up and went to live in the home of Dr. Axel Lamm, where he hoped to learn something about medicine and to earn some money by tutoring the doc-

tor's young sons. In the Lamm home, Strindberg experimented with chemicals in
the doctor's laboratory, read omnivorously in the excellent library, and met the
professional writers and artists who were guests of the Lamms.

When he failed in chemistry at the entrance examinations for the study of medicine, Strindberg decided to become an actor. At the Dramatic Theatre, he was
given a small part but was advised to enroll at the Dramatic Academy for some
acting courses. Full of rage and frustration at the suggestion that he return to
school, Strindberg went back to the attic in which he lived, took an opium pill,
expecting to die; instead, he fell into a deep sleep. When he awoke, his mind was
seething with memories of his childhood and adolescence, which were as vivid as
a play in the theater. He arranged his thoughts feverishly and set them down in
dramatic form. In four days of furious writing, he completed a two-act comedy,
and he felt an enormous sense of release. It was then that he knew he would be a
writer.

Almost all of Strindberg's literary and dramatic work shows a close relationship
to his first play. Nearly everything he wrote was autobiographical, was written
feverishly, had the quality of hallucination, provided him with therapeutic relief,
or was motivated by rage, revenge, or the need to bolster his ego. Often during
his life, Stindberg was close to suicide and insanity; yet even when it appeared to
others that he had gone beyond the bounds of reason, he managed to retain his
hold on reality, with the aid of his remarkable powers of self-analysis and his
compulsion to write.

Although at twenty he was in a state of mental turmoil, Strindberg began to
write poetry and plays, which won him a measure of recognition but no money.
He tried to support himself by journalism but failed at that. Then he applied for a
civil service job and, in spite of not having a college degree, was the winning candidate for the position of assistant librarian at the Royal Library of Stockholm.
During eight years there [1874-1882], he read and wrote with great intensity and
began to publish stories and essays about Sweden and to gather the material he
made use of later in his historical plays. He had come under the influence of Darwin's theory of evolution, Schopenhauer's pessimism, Buckle's relativistic theory of
history, Kierkegaard's existentialism, and von Hartmann's *Philosophy of the
Unconscious*. In 1879 he wrote his first autobiographical novel, *The Red Room*.
This bitterly incisive and realistic attack upon his country's institutions won him
the name of the Swedish Zola, although at the time he knew nothing of that writer's work. The novel created an uproar and was a great success.

Four years earlier, in 1875, when Strindberg was twenty-six, he had met Siri
von Essen and had fallen in love with her. She was the wife of Baron Wrangel, a
man much older than herself, and the mother of a young daughter. As a frequent
visitor at the Wrangels' house, Strindberg began to regard Siri and the Baron as
his mother and father. The young writer was looking for a home and for a woman
to mother him; Siri found home life dull and had a desire to go on the stage. At
Strindberg's insistence, Siri left the Baron; their widely publicized divorce caused
a great scandal. As long as she had been the wife of the Baron, Siri had appeared
to Strindberg to be pure, ethereal, and desirable, but as soon as she married him

he began to find fault with her, accusing her of trying to compete with him, of flirting, drinking, bearing him another man's child, trying to drive him mad, and particularly of being a poor housekeeper. [One of Strindberg's compulsions was an excessive neatness and cleanliness.] The couple left Sweden and moved from place to place on the Continent; several times they quarreled, separated, and came together again. The marriage lasted sixteen years and ended in divorce; Siri was granted custody of their three children. Throughout his life, Strindberg was haunted by Siri, who figured in almost everything he wrote. In the early and "happier" years of their union, Strindberg wrote mainly nondramatic works, but as his marital relations worsened and his rage increased, he had a burst of dramatic creativity. This pattern was repeated in his later marriages.

In 1893 he met and married Frida Uhl, an Austrian journalist, who was twenty-three years his junior. Frida's sister, Maria, who met the playwright several times before the marriage, wrote a penetrating description of him, which reads, in part:

> He manages to remain absorbed in his thoughts for a quarter of an hour at a time, not saying a word and not hearing what is said to him. I can never shake off the fear of seeing him suddenly go insane. At the same time he more and more impresses me as a great genius. . . . He gave himself up to scientific experiments . . . he also paints; there, too, he is a law unto himself, naturalistic symbolism he calls it. . . . He is so full of talent that he doesn't seem to know what to do with it. But his is not a joyful way of creating. It is more like the savage impulse driving a murderer to his crime. To me he is uncanny. I cannot understand Frida, nor how she dares entrust her future to the hands of such a man.

In less than three months Frida had left him, but she returned and left him again several times after that. They had one child.

Living in Paris alone and in a state of frenzy, Strindberg began to suffer from mental aberrations and hallucinations. Severe "electric shocks" were passing through his body, and he was sure that hostile "Powers" were persecuting him. He became haggard and unkempt, and moved from place to place to avoid his "enemies." In the meantime, he was furiously engaged in chemical experiments designed to produce gold. In the process he burned his hands with sulfur and was hospitalized for several months. He wrote a number of scientific treatises, as well as the two autobiographical volumes *Inferno* and *Legends*, which described in detail the hellish period he had just lived through.

By this time he had begun to study occultism and the mysticism of the eighteenth-century philosopher and theologian Swedenborg. It was the ideas of Swedenborg that turned Strindberg's mind toward religion by suggesting to him that his suffering was a punishment for his sins—loving his mother to excess, taking Siri away from the Baron, deserting his children, and trying to make gold. Hereafter, he vowed, he would do penance; and this resolution helped to restore his mental balance.

In 1899 he returned to Sweden and in the following year saw Harriet Bosse, a beautiful, young Norwegian actress in the role of Puck in *A Midsummer Night's Dream*. To her he offered the leading part in his play *To Damascus* and, although she was twenty-nine years his junior, he married her in 1901. Violent dissensions set in at once, and both of them felt trapped; it was a repetition of his former experiences. Harriet left him and returned to him several times, moving out finally in 1903 and taking with her their child. She agreed, however, to appear in a production of *A Dream Play* in 1907, in the role of Indra's Daughter, which Strindberg had written with her in mind. The playwright hoped for a reconciliation, but in 1908 Harriet married the actor Gunnar Wingard. Thereafter Strindberg lived alone and, though his health was failing, wrote a number of books and articles. After a life of torment and suffering, mainly self-induced, Strindberg died at the age of sixty-three on May 14, 1912.

Strindberg's versatility and productivity were astounding. In addition to his dramatic works, he wrote novels, short stories, essays, fairy tales, and poems. He engaged in scientific experiments, wrote music, and painted; he studied Chinese and wrote in both German and French. He produced books on philology, religion, botany, geology, and economics.

The list of his dramatic works alone is impressive. He was the author of about seventy-five plays, composed at three distinct periods of time.

His apprentice work was done between 1869 and 1876. The plays of this period were imitative and unsuccessful, but attracted the attention of the directors of the Dramatic Theatre and of the public. Written in 1869, *A Name-Day Gift*, his first play, was a domestic comedy; in the same year he wrote *Hermione*, in the manner of Greek tragedy. Both plays were rejected by the Royal Theatre. *In Rome* [1870], a one-act play in verse about the painter Thorwaldsen, was accepted for production but passed almost unnoticed. *The Free-Thinker* [1870], a full-length prose play, concerns a school-teacher who is punished for having advanced ideas. This play was published but was criticized for its echoes of Kierkegaard and Ibsen. *The Outlaw* [1871] deals with the conflict between paganism and Christianity in old Sweden. The play was produced unsuccessfully, the critics again suggesting that the young playwright had borrowed from Ibsen. It should be noted, however, that both Ibsen and Strindberg had been influenced by the Danish dramatist Ohlenschläger and that both had drawn on material from the Icelandic sagas. *Master Olaf*, which Strindberg worked on for five years [1872-76], was an historical play about a religious rebel, set in medieval Sweden in the reign of Gustavus Vasa. The playwright had given up his belief in Kierkegaard's idea of Either/Or and depicted Olof, not with the resolute character of Ibsen's Brand, but as a vacillating human being. The play was originally written in prose, was rejected, and was rewritten in verse; but still no theater would put it on. Strindberg revised it again and again. It was published in its verse form in 1877 and, after nine years of effort, was finally produced in 1881 in its original prose.

In the early years of his marriage to Siri von Essen, Strindberg wrote *The Secret of the Guild* [1880] to provide a vehicle for his wife's debut on the stage. The subject matter was unusual for him, in that the play deals with the building of a medieval church in Uppsala and demonstrates the power of faith to hold two people together. Put into immediate production, the play proved a success for both dramatist and star. When Siri appeared in her husband's next play, *Herr*

Bengt's Wife [1882], she won even greater acclaim. This play, too, had a medieval setting and was a paean in praise of love, marriage, and parenthood. Written in two weeks, *Lucky Peter's Journey* [1882], a romantic fairy play, contained the same message as Strindberg's two previous efforts and drew large and approving audiences. Siri's services as an actress were now in great demand, and she went off to play *Jane Eyre* in Finland, leaving Strindberg to look after the children and the housekeeping.

Siri's success soon worked a change in Strindberg's mood. While she was away from home, he was resentful and suspicious; when she returned, he started bitter quarrels and made wild accusations. He no longer considered her a comrade but a competitor. As their relationship deteriorated during the next four years, Strindberg seemed to store up a charge of resentment, which he finally hurled forth in a bolt of dramatic works. In the period from 1886 to 1892, he explored every stratagem in the battle of the sexes and, with a pen dipped in vitriol, wrote four important full-length plays, a number of one-acters, and, before his fury was spent, an autobiographical novel containing a vicious attack on Siri.

The four long plays created from 1886 to 1888 represent Strindberg's attempt to write with "scientific truth" in the manner of Emile Zola, the founder of naturalism. But the playwright's bias against women and his passion for revenge are incompatible with the coldly rational objectivity of the naturalist; in their violence and exaggeration they are closer to the manner of the impressionist. In *Comrades* [1886] Bertha and Axel, husband and wife, are both artists, living apparently in great comradeship until Axel discovers that his wife is really a petty, jealous, and deceitful competitor and drives her away. *The Father* [1887], a brilliant study in abnormal psychology, displays Strindberg's uncanny ability to probe the human mind. It also shows clearly his interest in hypnosis and the power of suggestion, as Laura raises doubts in her husband's mind as to the paternity of their child. The heartlessness of this vampire finally drives the man mad. *Miss Julie* [1888] puts the battle of the sexes on a class basis: Jean is a servant, Julie an aristocrat. This situation reflects Strindberg's feelings about his own social status as against Siri's. In the duel between them, the chief weapon is sex. According to the dramatist, *Miss Julie* was a study of one aspect of evil though it offered no solution; it is Strindberg's most naturalistic play. *Creditors* [1888] introduces another vampire in Tekla, who has written a scurrilous novel about her first husband and is now undermining her second husband by her domination of him. The first husband returns to open the eyes of his successor and, in so doing, destroys him. *The Father* and *Miss Julie* are the authentic masterpieces of Strindberg's so-called naturalistic period.

In the one-act plays that followed, the central theme continues to be the love-hate conflict between men and women. But now we see the influnce of Friedrich Nietzsche and Edgar Allan Poe, a greater emphasis on hypnotic suggestion, cynicism, and the horror and futility of life. There is also a heightened use of symbolic and expressionistic techniques. The outstanding plays in this group include *Pariah, The Stronger, Simoom,* and *Playing with Fire.*

The year before *Creditors* appeared, Strindberg had published *A Madman's*

Defence [1887], an autobiographical novel written in French, in which he had portrayed Siri as a man-devouring monster. Like Tekla's novel [in *Creditors*], it was a vicious book, which Strindberg himself found disgusting, for he wrote that he was using "his own wife as a rabbit for his vivisections." He was to forbid his second and third wives ever to read this book. *A Madman's Defence* was one of seven autobiographies, written between 1886 and 1898, which reflected Strindberg's internal tensions and traced his bitter marital experiences. For the time being, Strindberg had written himself out.

During the next six years, after marrying Frida Uhl and breaking with her, Strindberg went through the Inferno crisis that took him perilously close to the brink of insanity. His return to Sweden and his third marriage brought forth another flood of dramas; between 1898 and 1909 he wrote thirty plays. Many of these were "dream" plays, heavy with mood and symbolism in the manner of the Belgian playwright Maurice Maeterlinck, and employed such experimental techniques as kaleidoscopic scenes, unnamed characters, lyrical dialogue, and non-naturalistic lighting and scenery. These plays were replete with Strindberg's own "creedless religion," with mystical and ritualistic visions, and with vague expressions of hope, although the dramatist still pictured the world as filled with hypocrisy and filth, meanness and suffering.

The strongly "spiritual" plays of this period include *To Damascus* [Parts I and II, 1898; Part III, 1904], *Advent* [1898], and *Easter* [1900].

Then came a series of plays dealing with medieval Swedish history. In *The Saga of the Folkungs, Gustavus Vasa,* and *Erik XIV,* all written in 1899, Strindberg completed the cycle he had begun years before with *Master Olof.*

In *The Dance of Death* [1901] he returned briefly to naturalism and to the old subject of the horrors of the marital relationship. Yet in that very year he married Harriet Bosse and wrote two of his happiest pieces, the fairy plays *The Bridal Crown* and *Swanwhite,* his only love story. In that year, too, he created one of his undisputed masterpieces, *A Dream Play.*

More historical plays followed. Then, early in 1907, the young actor-director August Falck conceived the idea of founding a Strindberg Theatre, which would be devoted entirely to the production of the dramatist's plays. It was to be an intimate playhouse, and Strindberg was immediately inspired to write a series of "chamber plays" intended as dramatic equivalents of chamber music. The plays were to be short, the casts small, the staging simple. When the Intimate Theatre, which seated 161 people, opened its doors in November, 1907, Strindberg, who had been working at furious speed, had ready for it *The Storm, The Burned Lot, The Ghost Sonata,* and *The Pelican.* Dealing with marital discord, sin, shame, guilt, and retribution, these plays resembled earlier works in themes and situations. In mood and tone they are harsh and somber; in form and style they impress us with the terseness and force of their dialogue and with the compression, distortion, and nightmarish atmosphere later to be identified with expressionism and avant-garde drama. *The Ghost Sonata,* the most inventive and poetic work in the group, is the actual forerunner of surrealism in the theater.

Strindberg's last play, *The Great Highway* [1909], was a pilgrimage into his past, a backward glance at the emotional highlights of his life. Because it did not meet with the approval of either the public or the critics, the play, produced at the Intimate Theatre, had only a single performance. The theater itself, which had long been in financial difficulties, closed in 1910. In the two years of life remaining to him, Strindberg wrote no more plays.

Though Strindberg lived the greater part of his life in the nineteenth century, his work identifies him as a modern, experimental playwright. Ibsen, who was his older contemporary, had taken realism as far as it could go and knew that the drama was ready for new forms and techniques. These Strindberg developed, crossing the old frontiers of both the romantic-poetic and the well-made play and advancing into the unknown territories of "naturalistic symbolism," expressionism, and surrealism. By the exploration of his dreams and the deep analysis of his hallucinatory states, and by his ability to transfer these experiences in aesthetic form to the stage, Strindberg initiated the Theatre of Cruelty, and theater as a weapon, as well as absurdist and avant-garde drama. The use of nonlogical structure, the shattering of human identity, ambiguity in motivation and dialogue, supersubjectivity in theme and subject matter, and grotesqueness in scenery, costumes, and lighting are the formal elements that Strindberg has bequeathed to the playwrights of our time. His influence is clearly discernible in the work of Luigi Pirandello, Eugene O'Neill, and Sean O'Casey, to name but a few of the masters. In more recent times such cynical social commentators as Brecht, Ionesco, Beckett, Pinter, and Genet have raised a superstructure of raucous laughter, of cabaret and farce, on the somber foundations laid down by August Strindberg.

The Ghost Sonata, Opus Three of the chamber plays was inspired by Beethoven's D-Minor piano sonata and especially written for production at Strindberg's Intimate Theatre; it was published in 1907 and first performed in 1908.

Strindberg wrote the play in a few weeks in a white heat of emotion, while living alone in the apartment he had shared with his third wife, Harriet Bosse. She had divorced him and was about to remarry, and he was suffering from powerful feelings of guilt and resentment, which could only find an outlet in creative expression. Among the literary productions that had resulted from the separation from Frida Uhl, a dozen years before, was the fictionalized autobiography, *Inferno*. This book described the frenzy that assailed him as a result of the breakup of that marriage—a frenzy he was now feeling in a lesser degree—and provided many details for *The Ghost Sonata*.

In addition to his mental and emotional distress, Strindberg was now suffering from a number of physical ailments, including the onset of cancer of the stomach. He was also trying unsuccessfully to cope with housekeepers and household tasks, difficulties that grew out of his obsessions with cleanliness, orderliness, and food.

It is little wonder then that in this "dream" play, which is a mixture of reality, fantasy, and symbolism, we have the nightmarish images that were seething in his fervid imagination and tormenting him. Concerning the composition of *The Ghost Sonata*, Strindberg wrote to his German translator, Emil Schering, "I suffered as if I were in Kama-Loka (Sheol) . . . and my hands bled (literally) . . . I hardly knew myself what I had written, but I felt something awesome in it that makes me shudder." Strindberg thought at one time of calling the play Kama-Loka, the theosophist's name for purgatory.

The Ghost Sonata, like a piece of chamber music, is complex, though short; it is divided into three scenes, or movements—the statement, development, and re-capitulation—of two contrasting themes from the sonata form. Scene One, the image of the house, and the people in it as they seem to be; Scene Two, their un-masking, and the stripping away of all artifice and lies; Scene Three, the presenta-tion of a doctrine that can make life on earth bearable. The two themes are the Student's love, represented as perfectionism, and the Old Man's hate, which takes the form of vampirism—both of which prove to be destructive.

Even in a bare outline of the action it would be quite clear that *The Ghost Sonata* has very little to do with reality as we experience it. The characters and situations, based admittedly on people and events familiar to him, are more nearly an expression of Strindberg's fantasies than an accurate representation of the external world. In his other dream plays, the playwright had dealt with similar material: the sin, suffering, disease, and filth on the earth; the need to unmask liars, hypocrites, and criminals; and the vague, visionary hope for the final salva-tion of man. In *The Ghost Sonata*, every value in life, even love, proves to be an illusion calling for prayers of mercy.

Strindberg's preoccupations and anxieties, ranging from the mundane details of housekeeping, food, and sexuality, to the mysteries of hypnotism, the occult, and Oriental religion, made their way into this play in phantasmagoric fashion. He had dealt with all of these subjects in the *Inferno*, and did not hesitate to borrow liberally from that work. The Young Lady's complaints, for example, about the imperfections of her room, echo Strindberg's, "A thousand tiny inconveniences, combining eventually to make life intolerable. . . . The floor boards rocked beneath my feet, the table wobbled. . . . The lamp smoked, the inkwell was too narrow, and the penholder got covered with ink. . . ." (*Inferno*, p.234f.) At another point in the book, Strindberg speaks of himself as "a laughingstock that believed itself a prophet and found itself unmasked as an imposter," (p.282) which sounds very much like a description of old Mr. Hummel.

To achieve his effects the playwright found the means to tap his unconscious and to accommodate it to the exterior life around him. Like a dream, the play is variously unbelievable, frightening, funny, and confusing. And the symbols are visible everywhere: the apartment house, which looks so ordinary, may represent the human body, concealing corruption and disease (as vengeance on Harriet Bosse, the playwright thought at one time of having the Young Lady die of cancer of the uterus); the Student, a truth-seeker, may represent those innocents or saints who risk their lives without reward to save others; the wall-clock, which ticks away during the ghost supper, suggests the relentless passage of time and the brevity of life—the pendulum serving as a sexual symbol; the Mummy, who has withdrawn from the world, possibly symbolizes those who wish to conceal fear, guilt, or shame, and prattle like parrots to avoid meaningful conversation; the Dead Man, with his concern for his obsequies, represents undying vanity; and the

Old Man in his wheelchair, is certainly a symbol of those gods of the materialistic world—the manipulators and exploiters—who find ways to control people's destinies.

As a forerunner of the surrealists, Strindberg practiced automatic art—following his instincts and improvising as he wrote, letting chance and the irrational dictate much of the work, to create an "extraordinary confusion of the conscious and the unconscious"—again, like a dream. And yet it is safe to say that the playwright had never read Sigmund Freud's *The Interpretation of Dreams*, which appeared in 1899. Strindberg was familiar, however, with the work of several of Freud's predecessors: Hartmann's studies of the unconscious, and the experiments with hypnotism carried out in the 1880s by Charcot and Bernheim. His keen intuitive faculty and merciless self-analysis enabled Strindberg, like Sophocles and Shakespeare, to achieve an understanding of human motivation and behavior and to dramatize the processes operative in "dream work." Such dream figures as the Student who can see phantoms, the Old Man and the Cook who can suck the soul from the body, and the Mummy who speaks like a parrot, viewed metaphorically, leave the strong impression that we have known their counterparts in waking life, though they are the product of a writer's hallucinations.

As early as 1884, in a letter to his brother, Strindberg wrote: "My best writing comes when I am suffering from hallucinations . . ."; and in 1887 he remarked to a young Swedish writer, "It seems to me as though I walk in my sleep—as though reality and imagination are one. . . . Through much writing my life has become a shadow play." After his Inferno crisis of 1896, he said, "Human beings have a double life—our fancies, fantasies, and dreams possess a kind of reality."

To express that special "kind of reality," Strindberg was forced to devise a new dramatic form for the plays of his last period. He was aware of what he had done, for he declared in a letter to Emil Schering that he had created "a new form, which is my invention." This form was later to become the chief influence in the aesthetic movement called expressionism, which flourished in Germany in the 1920s—where among its notable practitioners were Georg Kaiser, Ernst Toller, and Walter Hasenclever—and later made its innovative force felt in the art and drama of many other countries.

Expressionism represents a strong reaction against the naturalist's goal of scientific objectivity and, consequently, avoids the formal elements of the well-made play. The characteristic features of expressionistic drama, all of which are exemplified in *The Ghost Sonata*, include:

1. Autobiographical and subjective material, projecting the feelings and attitudes of the playwright;
2. Episodic structure and vagueness of time;
3. Characters who are types rather than individuals, and often bear labels rather than names, as in the medieval morality plays;
4. Dialogue which is brief and telegraphic, or poetic in tone or form;
5. A copious use of symbolism, and frequently of music;
6. Elements of religious dogma and ritual, including myths and legends, often fictitious;

7. An emphasis on humane and spiritual values;
8. And, finally, an attempt to reach the intellect through the emotions, aroused by a succession of exciting images.

Strindberg's expressionistic dream plays have exerted a powerful influence on the avant-garde dramatists of our day. In the opinion of Professor Walter Johnson, "Strindberg succeeded in depicting the workings of the inner life (the irrational, the disordered, the undisciplined, the senseless) and in revealing what the realistic method cannot reveal, and thereby provided the blueprint for the most advanced drama of the twentieth century."

THE PRODUCTION RECORD

The Ghost Sonata had its premiere performance at the Intimate Theatre in Stockholm on January 21, 1908; like *The Storm* and *The Pelikan*, the two chamber plays that preceded it, the new work proved to be too avant-garde for the audience, and met with the disapproval of the critics.

It was Max Reinhardt's production of the play, done at the Chamber Theatre in Berlin in October 17, 1916, that showed the power of the work. Reinhardt took his production to Sweden, where it was mounted first at the Lorensberg Theatre in Gothenburg and then, on May 3, 1917, at the Royal Opera House in Stockholm. With Paul Wegener as Hummel and Gertrud Eysoldt as the Mummy, the play was highly acclaimed by critics and public alike. This production became internationally famous and was subsequently seen in Munich, Vienna, and Frankfurt-am-Main; other Reinhardt versions of the play were done in many cities on the Continent as late as the 1920s.

In the fall of 1941, Ingmar Bergman, then twenty-three years old, directed the play at the Medborgarhuset in Stockholm; the production, though interesting and clever, did not entirely succeed. In the autumn of the following year, Olof Molander, who had devoted his life to producing the plays of Strindberg, offered *The Ghost Sonata* at the Royal Theatre in Stockholm, with Lars Hanson as Hummel and Märta Eckström as the Mummy; here Molander showed his sensitivity to the playwright's feelings and intentions. Molander mounted several other productions of the play after that, and as late as 1962 prepared a version for the Théâtres des Nations festival in Paris, that was a notable success. On May 5, 1954, Ingmar Bergman restaged the play for the Malmö State Theater with a brilliant cast including Benkt-Åke Benktsson as Hummel and Folke Sundquist as the Student. This was hailed as a definitive rendition of the work. Numerous productions of the play have been mounted, with varying degrees of success, in all the important theater capitals of Europe.

In 1926 the play was introduced to the English public by James B. Fagan at the Oxford Playhouse, and the following year was put on by him at the Globe and Strand Theatres in London. The play did not appeal to British audiences. It had been translated into English by Fagan in collaboration with Eric Palmstierna.

The first American production of the play took place at the Provincetown Play-

(*Left*) Mary Morris as the Lady in Black and James Light, wearing a mask, as Baron Skanskorg, in the Provincetown Playhouse 1924 production, designed by Robert Edmond Jones. Jones and Light co-directed the play. (*Right*) Elaine Bullis as the Young Girl and Frank Pacelli as the student in John Sydow's production in the Experimental Theater at the Yale Drama School in January, 1950. (Yale School of Drama Library)

house in New York, on January 3, 1924, under the title of *The Spook Sonata*, in Edwin Björkman's translation. The play was done at the suggestion of Eugene O'Neill, who said that the Mummy's behavior reminded him of his mother's reclusive existence during most of her married life. The cast included Clare Eames, Mary Blair, Mary Morris, and Walter Abel; but despite the excellent acting and stunning designs, the critics were brutally severe. Empty houses resulted, and the play closed after twenty-four performances.

There have been very few professional productions of the play in the United States, but it has proved to be extremely popular with experimental theater groups and with university drama departments. It was staged at the Pasadena Playhouse in California with film actors from Hollywood; and has also been mounted at the University of Wisconson, at Vassar, and at Yale. Two recent productions were done at Washington State College in Bellingham (1969), and at the Roman Catholic College, Seattle University (1972).

The play was turned into an opera with music by Julius Weissmann, and was performed in Munich in 1930, and in Duisburg and Dortmund in 1956. A television production of the play, in Michael Meyer's translation, was aired by the British Broadcasting Corporation on March 16, 1962; this program was subsequently seen in the United States and Australia. A brilliant cast was headed by Robert

Helpmann as Hummel, Jeremy Brett as the Student, and Beatrix Lehmann as the Mummy, under the direction of Stuart Burge.

On September 30, 1977, the fall season of the Yale Repertory Theatre in New Haven opened with a production of *The Ghost Sonata* under the direction of Andrei Serban.

THE SKELETON IN THE BOX[*]
By Maurice Richardson

I wonder whether Strindberg would have taken to television. In some ways it might have been specially designed to suit the prolific paranoid Swede's naturalistic style. He would have liked the close-ups because he was a great believer in facial expression rather than "gesture and noise." He also favoured experiments

[*] From *Observer*, London, March 18, 1962. Reprinted by permission.

Benkt-Åke Benktsson as Mr. Hummel, Folke Sundquist as the Student, and, in the background, the Lady in Black and the Janitress, in Ingmar Bergman's production of the play at the Malmö State Theater in 1954. (Skåne-Reportage)

with "powerful sidelights on a small stage," and keeping the spectator's eye above the level of the actor's knee.

The Ghost Sonata is one of his dream plays, but he put a lot of his theatrical naturalism into it, which is probably why it acts so vividly. He wrote it five years before his death in 1912 in—though you would hardly think so—a comparatively calm period when he wasn't feeling unduly persecuted.

There was reason, perhaps, to be mildly optimistic on Friday night; even so you couldn't have expected Stuart Burge's production for the B.B.C. to be quite so triumphant. It deserves a special advance guard brilliancy prize.

At the opening encounter between the clairvoyant student, with whom we identify, and the ghostly drowned milkmaid, the reality of the dream was firmly established. The cast was strong and sound. Robert Helpmann managed to be simultaneously evil, senile and puckish as old Hummel, who seems to be making them all dance to his tune at the spooks' tea-party in the house of horror and frustration, death and marriage. Jeremy Brett was an ideal student. Beatrix Lehmann as the mummy woman who lives in the cupboard and talks like a parrot managed to steer well clear of absurdity.

This is a very difficult and vital role, for although in a dream there are no holds barred, yet in a dream play there is always a danger that one sudden rush of banality may break the spell. A particularly dangerous moment here is when the mummy stops the clock and Hummel is denounced as arch-hypocrite, swindler and soul-stealer and crawls off on all fours to take her place in the cupboard.

Anyone who has any hopes of a happy ending at this point doesn't know their Strindberg. Having trumped the father figures he still has a malevolent mother to play. The wooing of the Colonel's daughter by the Student hardly gets started: he is sniffing at death along with those hyacinths in front of the Buddha. (The play originally had a theosophical title, "Kama-Loka.") And when that grim cook appears, she who drains the food of all goodness, it is obvious that death, with the possibility of a better deal in a new incarnation, is all we can hope for.

Strindberg, incidentally, was somewhat haunted by cooks and often suspected them of poisoning his food. He was also, as you can see, seldom able to forget that his mother had been a domestic servant. On top of which, quite apart from their symbolic significance as hostile mother figures, he had six real cook-housekeepers in as many weeks just about the time he was writing *The Ghost Sonata*.

Perhaps they should have introduced it with a little drumming up. Sean O'Casey reciting his panegyric: "Strindberg. Strindberg. Strindberg, the greatest of them all . . . Ibsen can sit serenely in his Doll's House while Strindberg is battling with his heaven and his hell." The trouble about a dream or nightmare play is that you need to follow it with rapt concentration, and even then you only know who is doing what to whom on the surface. Strindberg himself used to object that critics had no right to dismiss his dream plays which were put on at the Intimate Theatre in Stockholm on the strength of one performance. I wonder how many people switched on at ten and stayed till the end. As many as a million? Doubtful. Even so it was probably a larger audience than the total number of people who had ever seen it before.

Incidentally, the decor, so peculiarly important here, was superlatively good. The surrealist element was not overstressed. The drawing-room for the spooks' tea-party was marvellously rich in furniture—including, of course, the death screen. And for the final curtain they hadn't forgotten Strindberg's favourite picture, Böcklin's "Isle of the Dead."

DIRECTING *The Ghost Sonata*
    An Interview with Andrei Serban

Early in the summer of 1977, Andrei Serban joined the Yale Repertory Theatre as Associate Director, and it was decided that he would mount the first production of the fall season. He chose *The Ghost Sonata*.

"I had no preconceptions concerning the play," said Serban. "What was interesting to me was to find what was hidden in Strindberg's lines. They contain a whole world of sensations and vibrations, and feelings which provoke the words to be spoken. There is no doubt that this play is extremely autobiographical and subjective, and related to the immediate facts of Strindberg's life. It is up to the director, the actors, and the audience to discover what is hidden in the play. So this production was an attempt to penetrate the process of Strindberg's creation, and to ferret out, if possible, what the playwright had in mind.

"We tried to understand the difficult symbolism in the text and to interpret it in terms of living, human experience, as it undoubtedly reflects Strindberg's suffering. The whole of the third act is filled with images of torment. It seems to me that, as it is written, it is an impossible act to stage. Most directors, including Ingmar Bergman, cut the beginning of the act because the metaphor of the hyacinths is so abstract, so hard to 'physicalize' on stage. And the writing in this act is so symbolic that actors find it unreal and difficult to relate to. So I chose to stage the third act as a dance of life, introducing, as Strindberg did, an Eastern influence. The highly stylized movements, resembling those of T'ai Chi, which the Student and the Young Girl perform, are meant to suggest their life-or-death struggle. This concept was evoked by the presence of the statue of the Buddha, and by the dialogue which is saturated with Oriental religion and philosophy. These elements introduce quite a foreign vocabulary into the play.

"Another example of our attempt to make a symbol more concrete and yet preserve its unreality, was the manner in which we handled the sudden appearance of the Dead Man. Instead of entering through the front door of the house, as called for in the script, he descends from the balcony of his apartment by sliding down a rope, like a spirit coming to earth from above. Furthermore, he is not dressed in a shroud but in the formal clothes and the insignia of his office.

"So far as my conception of the main characters was concerned, I saw Mr. Hummel as a sort of chameleon, with many facets to his personality, like a frequent change of masks. He is constantly on the move, briskly turning this way and that, and expressing more than one self, so that it is hard to catch his essence. In spite of the fact that he is confined to a wheelchair, which is more or less static, he proves to be as dangerous as a fast-moving animal. And therefore I tried to portray him as exemplifying the whole range of human types.

"The Mummy at first appears to be a creature or freak, but ends up by revealing a very true and deep humanity. The actress who plays the part must have an enormous vocal range, from an extremely high to a very low register, and the ability to produce bird calls and raucous squawks. We were very fortunate to have an actress with such a vocal range in Priscilla Smith, who was able to portray a human being reduced by suffering to a subhuman, animal level.

"The Student is usually made to represent Strindberg, as if he were the only character in the play to embody the writer's ideas and feelings. But I don't think he is the only one to do that, because Hummel and several of the other characters are equally representative of the playwright. The Student, who begins by being naive and idealistic, ends up by destroying the Young Girl.

"The set, as described by Strindberg, is in a stiff, nineteenth century style; and although we used all the elements described in the script, we wanted to isolate them in some way in order to give the impression of fragments as from a dream. Together with Michael Yeargan, the scene designer, I worked out a way to break up the set and to put each room in a separate frame, a boxlike cell. These cells could be shifted and interrelated like a Chinese puzzle. During the first act, the cells were upstage, side by side, suggesting the windows of an apartment house. In front of them, downstage, was the street, represented by a park bench, a fountain, and a kiosk. For the second act, the street props were removed, and the cells brought downstage and arranged in a semicircle to suggest the Round Room, where all the revelations and attacks occur. The last act is played on a practically bare stage; the Hyacinth Room is an empty cell backed up by an enormous figure of the Buddha, and in this cell the Student and the Young Girl enact their furious struggle for air, for escape from the prison of life.

"Although the third act appears to be extremely abstract, it represented for me the extension of perception, something beyond the visible, something that reaches a part of us not normally called on in the theater. In *The Ghost Sonata* there are two plays, what we see and what we feel underneath. I wanted to present correctly not only what the author was expressing on the surface, but to delve into the deep and seething world beneath that. It seems to me that Strindberg, writing this play towards the end of his life, was trying to see through everyday reality to a reality of another sort so that, as in Shakespeare's final romances, the real and the unreal, the visible and the invisible are present simultaneously. Here there is a special concern for and inclination towards something spiritual, for music and for art; and just as these things interested the playwright so they interested us when we were working on the play.

"We rehearsed for five weeks, but I feel that if we had had a little more time we could have achieved greater technical perfection of several minor details. We did, however, say what we wanted to say. The evening is an invitation to a dream. If you accept the invitation, you enter that world, if you refuse the invitation, you stay outside and judge it."

FRAGMENTS OF A REHEARSAL LOG*
   by Colette Brooks

> Excerpts from the log kept by Colette Brooks, for the Yale Repertory
> Theatre's production of **The Ghost Sonata**. They are highly subjective
> impressions of the rehearsal period, during which the Company was
> probing the underpinnings of Strindberg's text.

August 29. Company meeting. The cast is incomplete, so this first rehearsal is
devoted to general introductions. Serban will use the next week to work with
actors in the fully-cast scenes while auditioning others for the open parts—the
Hyacinth Girl, servants, beggars.

Model of the set is presented by designer Michael Yeargan. Consists of tubular
boxes representing the rooms of the house as specified in the text—hyacinth room,
Colonel's study, Fiancée's boudoir, Mummy's closet. "Walls" can be created by
placing scrims on front faces of each box. These areas are portable and will be
rearranged during the two intermission breaks. The street is represented by a
bench, kiosk and fountain. A certain "spookiness" is already apparent in the
design itself; each box is like a separate stage, and the rooms (when inhabited)
remind me of Madame Tussaud's waxworks. Wouldn't necessarily want to be
alone onstage with these characters.

August 30. Act I script session. The act is read and minor changes in the translation are made when the sound or sense of a line can be improved. A rather free-
wheeling discussion of the play follows: general thoughts and responses to particular moments are solicited and exchanged. Everyone agrees that we need an air-
conditioned rehearsal room.

Set change: the rooms representing the house in Act II will now be arranged to
form a semicircle facing the audience. This creates the "round room" where the
action takes place (chairs and table, as before, placed down-center in open space).
Also suggests a sense of the house itself closing in upon the characters and, perhaps, the audience.

Serban reads aloud Artaud's short essay on **Ghost Sonata**; it offers an interesting additional view of the play. We talk briefly about different levels of reality as
they collide, merge, and shift throughout the play. Artaud: ". . . this play arouses
all kinds of prejudice. It gives the feeling of something which is a part of a certain inner reality, without it being either supernatural or inhuman. And that is its
attraction. It shows nothing but what is known, although hidden and out of the
way. In this play the real and unreal merge, as they do in the mind of someone
falling asleep, or someone suddenly waking up under a false illusion.

"We have lived and dreamed everything this play reveals, but we have forgotten it."

August 31. Act I. The cast concentrates on working up improvisations. The

* From "Fragments of a Dramaturg's Log" by Colette Brooks. © Colette Brooks, 1977.

"action" that precedes the play's opening is physicalized. Steve Rowe (playing the Student) is asked several questions: what has happened to the Student during the night? How can he physicalize the scene at the accident in order to experience it? How many possibilities can be found in his behavior? Steve and Dennie Gordon (an assistant director) do an extended improvisation: after constructing the burning house from chairs, benches, clothes, and odd props found in the rehearsal room, they recreate the episode in which it collapses (which is only referred to and not actually played out in the text).

Max Wright (playing the Old Man) is asked, for the purposes of improvisation, to break down his first scene into a series of fragments to which different "masks" are affixed. He is to adopt a bewildering variety of masks in rapid succession, to create a chameleon-like character. This work is exploratory.

September 1. Act I. Continuation of work begun in the improvs last night. The Old Man and the Student mime the action of Act I while the lines themselves are read aloud by the stage manager. This creates a very interesting effect; by removing the lines as an element in the actors' work, Steve and Max are able to concentrate on conveying the action as precisely as possible while listening to but not speaking the words. The situation becomes quite clear-cut, and Max seems to display the abrupt shifts of mood that Serban wants—appearing at turns to be watchful, predatory, fearful, frail, surprised . . . The exercise is abandoned after a bit and the two once again read. Rough blocking is mapped out.

September 2. Act I. An observer asks Serban why he is humanizing the Old Man, who speaks of his past and life's frustrations for a brief moment in the scene. This moment, as directed by Serban, is strangely moving: an uncharacteristic contrast to the bad temper and malice the Old Man displays elsewhere. Serban, in response, points out that there are very few "perfect villains" in dramatic literature—Iago and Edmund come immediately to mind. The Old Man will be more interesting if he is more complex, and should reflect in part Strindberg himself—who wrote the play when he too was an old man, looking back upon his life and putting a bit of himself into his characters. Parts of him are in both the Old Man and the Student.

September 3. The Hyacinth Girl has been cast. We talk about the third act, which is notoriously difficult to stage. Strindberg subtitled the play *Kama-Loka,* the "ghost or dream world where mortals must wander before they finally enter death's kingdom and find peace," and this idea is especially pertinent to Act III. It is also an apt description of the rehearsal process itself.

September 7. First meeting with the full cast (except Priscilla Smith, who is still on tour in Europe). Serban asks everyone to break into smaller groups (as suggested by various situations in the play) and work through the Byzantine permutations of the plot. These discussions help to clarify for the actors the chain of deceptions, lies, crimes, guilt, repentance—Strindbergian themes.

From this work nonverbal improvisations are created and presented. The Student, as a little boy, witnesses his father's painful, revelatory dinner; the Colonel, Old Man, Mummy, and Fiancée play out the seductions and couplings that occurred in the past; the Baron announces the divorce while the Lady in Black hovers nearby.

Serban then assigns individual exercises: each character is to write a letter to another character, a made-up person, or himself, revealing the face beneath the character's public mask. These letters are read aloud to the group and followed with a simple action that conveys the essence of the character. The exercise forces the actors to find the hidden qualities in their own characters, and is fascinating to watch. Example: the Lady in Black writes to herself, proclaiming her desire for respectability, sanction, an approved place in the house. Her action: to run around the periphery of the room, clinging to the walls. She seems to want to melt into the walls, afraid that she'll be pulled away at any moment.

Extremely close attention is being paid to the creation of these "secondary" characters, many of whom don't speak, or make only cameo appearances. Serban wants each one to make a vivid impression; they are less characters than colors or sounds, embodiments of fleeting moments and moods that must strongly register upon the audience. As he says, it's not all in the words but also in the gap in-between, and the dreamlike tone of the play is set in these abrupt, silent appearances and disappearances. This reminds me of what Artaud said about "the way language communicates with the invisible reality which it is supposed to express;" as the Old Man talks of these people in the first act they appear—in a sense summoned by his speech. Each is almost invisible, but a presence that haunts the entire play.

In his essay Artaud writes that "several people rove around this house like dead people attracted by their mortal remains." Interesting idea—the Mummy worships her own statue; the young lady tends her hyacinths (the flower that arose from the blood of Hyacinth, Apollo's murdered male lover in the myth); the dead man attends his own funeral; the Fiancée watches the outside world reflected in her mirror. Each room in the house should be sharply differentiated, acquiring the quality of the character who inhabits it. Those who "rove" always return to their rooms.

A recurring question in rehearsal: Why do these people remain in the house? All are ostensibly free to leave. They are drawn to the ghost house, perhaps as the Student is inexplicably drawn to the house that collapses before the play opens. Strindberg was plagued by noises that other tenants in his apartment house made, but he forced himself to endure the annoyance—felt it was a necessary affliction. Houses and the secrets they held fascinated him, and he had a certified fear of open spaces. All this is discussed in rehearsal, but no firm decisions are made.

September 10. Act III. Brenda (the Hyacinth Girl) and Steve have been working by themselves this week, and today they show Serban what they've been up to. They had shared an impulse to do the scene without speaking; yesterday they ran it once in the dark to discover what points of contact they could find by entering into a different domain—beyond the visible.

September 12. Further improvisatory work with the cast. Example: One character is to create the vision that another character has communicated nonverbally, by molding people in the room into poses, tableaux, living paintings. I make my debut as the Hyacinth Girl stand-in, to general cheers.

Evening work on Act III with Brenda and Steve. Serban breaks the scene down into tiny fragments and blocks a couple of pages—using very slow movements that are almost dancelike. This creates a pronounced sense of physical struggle in the scene—Student and Hyacinth Girl appear to be fighting their way through the room itself, meeting a resistance in the air that makes it very hard to move. Everything is weighted-down and oppressive; it almost takes too much energy to breathe. Seems to make the couple's paradisaical vision (as conveyed in the text) all the more fragile, if not unearthly, by comparison. Interesting side effect: the text, which is lyrical and quite abstract in this act, acquires a kind of tortuous quality itself, since it takes special effort to deliver lines while moving in this manner.

September 17. Michael Gross (who plays Bengtsson) places the Death Screen around me before rehearsal begins. It is soon removed, but the implications of the act are not lost upon me.

Act II. Priscilla Smith (playing the Mummy) acclimatizes herself to the closet in which she must sit for much of the second act. (Screens are placed around her to simulate the actual closet, which is still in the workshop.) Her character, according to the text, has spent twenty years in this small space—"to avoid seeing and being seen"—and Serban wants Priscilla to develop a kind of territorial affection for her "home." Much time is spent on the moment in which Bengtsson opens the doors and reveals the Mummy for the first time. She is interrupted in the midst of her daily labors, sweeping the floor and fixing her hair, and must work through a number of different reactions to the intrusion. Today she is petulant, angry, pleased.

Scene between the Old Man and the Mummy (as they meet for the first time in twenty years) is all the more grotesque because delicately played. Each seems like a maimed bird. Priscilla contorts her body and cocks her head at improbable angles, Max whirls and falters on his crutches while his cape billows behind him. As they stalk each other, precariously alighting upon the various chairs in the Round Room, they seem to be performing an odd aerial dance. Both actors have worked together before, with Serban, and this exploratory but very precise interplay reflects an obvious rapport.

September 19. Act II. The scene is reworked, bit by bit, and some blocking changes are made. Much attention is devoted to the development of different voices for the Mummy-Parrot. Priscilla experiments with a variety of screeches, cries, and whistles until she and Serban find a rough tonal range that satisfies

Brenda Currin as the Hyacinth Girl and Stephen Rowe as Arkenholz perform the "Dance of Life" in the Yale Repertory Theater production, directed by Andrei Serban. (Eugene Cook)

them both. The parrot sounds must convey the character's tenderness, harshness and regret. There are points at which the Mummy slips into her "natural" voice, and these are tentatively marked today.

September 21. Act III. Blocking change: the hyacinth plants that form the side "walls" of the Hyacinth Room in this act (eight pots in two rows, left and right) are now to be removed by the servants as the Student reveals the world's horror, thus "killing" the Hyacinth Girl. This change illuminates the moment in a remarkable manner, making it at once both concrete and abstract. Brenda is given a very specific danger to work against—as she loses her life-giving plants, she gasps for air and begins to shrivel up; but the removal of the hyacinths alters our sense of the space, which becomes more abstract—the room itself seems to vanish as its perimeters disappear. The Hyacinth Girl is killed, finally, by the force of the Student's speech.

Evening work on the Rep stage. Asante Scott (playing the Cook) is directed to stand, motionless, in front of the Buddha (UC) throughout the Hyacineth Girl's "drudgery of life" speech. Her impassive presence is rather chilling—she becomes a malevolent counterpart to Buddha.

September 22. Music is incorporated into the production. Liz Swados, the composer, arrives at rehearsal with an assortment of chimes, gongs, cymbals, wood blocks and mallets. Each of these instruments is tested at moments when a particular effect is needed, and the one that produces the desired quality of sound is selected as the play is scored. Liz and Andrei have already made certain decisions —a recurring harp motif will be played as various characters enter their rooms in

Act I, while the Hyacinth Girl's entrances will be marked by a special Oriental-like melody. An autoharp will be used to produce the sour, discordant notes of a "broken" harp that sound in Acts II and III. The wood blocks will punctuate the more sinister moments when characters such as the Lady in Black and the Dead Man appear later; in Act II, the blocks will be struck to mark the passing of time as the clock ticks. The Milkmaid's appearances will be accompanied by a continuous clank of bottles offstage; the bottles she carries in her basket make no sound at all.

September 23. Act I. Technical work with the lights. Serban and the lighting crew run through a formidable number of impromptu set-ups for each lighting change desired in the scene. The final light plot will not be determined for several days; this initial experimentation serves to test various possibilities—what's feasible, most effective, etc. We are now working with the actual set, and Serban requests that the still-unfinished set pieces (kiosk, fountain, statue) be brought from the shop to rehearsal. He wants to work with as many of the actual production elements as possible at this point; final lighting and blocking decisions are dependent upon seeing what the stage will look and feel like when everything is in place.

September 27. Work-through and tightening of Acts II and III. Change in Act III: the Colonel and the Mummy will now "witness" the scene between the Student and the Hyacinth Girl, sitting upstage in two empty rooms. At the end of the play the Mummy will cross down to the Hyacinth Room and recite the "Song of the Sun" while holding the Hyacinth Girl, who will repeat each line after her. (In the script, the Student speaks the poem.) At finish, the two women will slowly part as Böcklin's painting *The Isle of the Dead* appears on the scrim in front of them.

September 29. Preview tonight. Afternoon rehearsal is devoted to the first complete run-through of the play. Serban takes extensive notes and gives them to the cast afterwards; the blocking in Act III is altered slightly to facilitate the servants' handling of the more cumbersome props they must carry (writing desk, washbucket, baby crib).

Fortuitous accident: Asante (the Cook) was detained downstairs and was unable to enter on cue in Act III, as the Hyacinth Girl calls the Student's attention to her ("The cook is coming this way . . . Look at her, how big and fat she is!"). She did eventually appear, but Serban decides to incorporate her initial absence into the staging. This further contributes to the eeriness of the scene—the Hyacinth Girl now recoils from a menacing apparition that isn't yet visible. The Student is appropriately perplexed and apprehensive himself. The moment, as with many in the production, is disquieting.

September 30. *The Ghost Sonata* opens.

~~~ *The Ghost Sonata*

ENGLISH VERSION BY RANDOLPH GOODMAN

CHARACTERS

THE OLD MAN, Mr. Hummel

THE STUDENT, Arkenholz

THE MILKMAID, an apparition

THE JANITRESS

THE DEAD MAN, formerly a Consul

THE LADY IN BLACK, daughter of the Dead Man and the Janitress

THE COLONEL

THE MUMMY, the Colonel's wife

THE YOUNG LADY, called the daughter of the Colonel, actually the daughter of
the Old Man

BARON SKANSKORG, engaged to the Lady in Black

JOHANSSON, the Old Man's servant

BENGTSSON, the Colonel's servant

THE FIANCEE, a white-haired old woman, once engaged to the Old Man

THE COOK

A HOUSEMAID

BEGGARS

Scene 1. The façade of a modern apartment house in Stockholm
Scene 2. The Round Room
Scene 3. The Hyacinth Room

SCENE ONE

*The outside of a modern apartment house only part of which
is visible. On the ground floor, at the corner, is the Round Room;
on the floor above it, there is a balcony with a flagpole. Some of
the windows of the Round Room are at the front of the house,
others look out on a side street that runs off to the rear. At the
beginning of the play, the windows of the Round Room are
open but the shades are down. Later, when they are raised, we
see a white marble statue of a young woman surrounded by
palms and bathed in sunlight.*

*To the left of the Round Room is the Hyacinth Room, its win-
dows filled with pots of hyacinths, blue, white, and pink. Further
to the left are wide double doors, the main entrance to the house;*

on either side of the entrance is a tub of laurels. The doors stand open revealing a white marble staircase with bannisters of mahogany and brass. To the left of the front doors is another window with a mirror outside it; the mirror is set at an angle to afford a view of the street from inside the room. Over the railing of the balcony on the first floor hang a blue silk quilt and two white pillowcases. The windows to the left are draped with white sheets, indicating that someone has died.

On the street in front of the house is a green bench; to the right of it is a public drinking fountain, with a cup hanging alongside it; to the left, a pillar with posters pasted on it. When the curtain rises, church bells, some near, some distant, can be heard ringing. It is a bright Sunday morning.

Through the open doors of the house may be seen the LADY IN BLACK, *standing motionless on the staircase.*

The JANITRESS *sweeps the front doorstep, then polishes the brass on the door, and waters the laurels. The* OLD MAN, *sitting in a wheelchair near the pillar, is reading a newspaper. His hair and beard are white and he wears glasses. The* MILKMAID *comes around the corner on the right, carrying milk bottles in a wire basket; she is wearing a summer dress, brown shoes, black stockings, and a white cap. She takes off the cap, hangs it on the fountain, takes a drink from the cup, washes her hands, and arranges her hair, using the water in the fountain as a mirror.*

A steamship bell is heard, and every now and then the silence is broken by the deep notes of the organs in the nearby churches. The MILKMAID *rests beside the fountain; there are a few moments of silence; then the* STUDENT *enters from the left. He is unshaven and looks as if he hasn't slept all night; he goes straight to the fountain.*

Student (*After a pause*). May I borrow the cup? (*The* MILKMAID *holds on to it tightly.*) Haven't you finished using it? (*The* MILKMAID *looks at him with fear.*)

Old Man (*To himself*). Who is he talking to? I don't see anyone! Is he crazy? (*He continues to watch them in amazement.*)

Student (*To the* MILKMAID). What are you staring at? Do I look so terrible? Well, I haven't slept all night, and of course you think I've been out on a spree . . . (*The* MILKMAID *remains motionless.*) You think I've been drinking, don't you? Do I smell like it? (*The* MILKMAID *continues to stare.*) I know I need a shave . . . Give me a drink of water, girl. I think I've earned it! (*Pause.*) Oh, all right, I suppose I'll have to tell you all about it. I spent the whole night bandaging wounds and sitting up with the injured. You see, I was there when that house collapsed last night. Now, you know. (*The* MILKMAID *rinses the cup and hands him a drink.*) Thanks! (*The* MILKMAID *does not move. He speaks slowly.*) Will you do me a great favor? (*Pause.*) Well, the thing is, my eyes are inflamed, as you can see, but I've been touching so many wounds and dead bodies, I don't dare put my hands near my eyes. Would you take this clean handkerchief, dip it in the fresh water, and bathe my poor eyes? Would you do that? Will you be the Good Samaritan? (*The* MILKMAID *hesitates, but does as he asks.*) Thank you, my friend. (*He takes out his wallet, but she makes a gesture of refusal*). Oh, forgive my thoughtlessness, but I'm only half awake . . .

(*The* MILKMAID *disappears.*)

Old Man (*To the* STUDENT). Excuse me for addressing you, but I heard you say you were at the scene of the accident last night. I was just sitting here reading about it in the paper.

Student. Is it in the paper already?

Old Man. Yes, the whole story. And your picture, too. But they're sorry they weren't able to get the name of the brave young student who—

Student (*Glances at the paper*). Yes, that's me! How do you like that!

Old Man. Who was that you were talking to just now?

Student. Didn't you see her? (*Pause*)

Old Man. Would you think me nosey if I asked you . . . to tell me . . . your name?

Student. What purpose would that serve? I'm not looking for publicity. As soon as they praise you, they start to criticize you. Running people down is a fine art nowadays. Anyway, I'm not looking for a reward.

Old Man. Are you rich?

Student. Not at all. Just the opposite! I haven't got a cent.

Old Man. Listen! I think I've heard your voice before. When I was a young man I had a friend who couldn't say "window," he always said "winnow," the way you do. I've never met anyone else who spoke

that way. Only him, and you. Are you by any chance related to a wholesale merchant by the name of Arkenholz?

Student. He was my father.

Old Man. Fate works in strange ways. I saw you when you were a baby . . . it was under very painful circumstances . . .

Student. Yes, I understand I came into the world just as my father was going bankrupt.

Old Man. That's right.

Student. Do you mind telling me your name?

Old Man. My name is Hummel.

Student. So you are the—? I remember now . . .

Old Man. You've often heard my name mentioned by your family?

Student. Yes.

Old Man. And always with a certain amount of hostility? (*The* STUDENT *is silent.*) You were told, I suppose, that I was the man who ruined your father? Men who ruin themselves by foolish speculations always put the blame on the man they couldn't cheat. (*Pause.*) The truth of the matter is that your father swindled me out of seventeen thousand crowns— all my savings up to that time.

Student. It's amazing how the same story can be told in two completely opposite ways!

Old Man. You think I'm not telling you the truth?

Student. I don't know what to think! My father didn't tell lies.

Old Man. That's so true, one's father never tells lies . . . But I'm a father, too, so—

Student. What are you trying to say?

Old Man. I saved your father from disaster and he repaid me with all the hatred a man feels when he's obliged to be grateful. So he taught his family to speak ill of me.

Student. Maybe you made him ungrateful by poisoning your charity with unnecessary humiliations.

Old Man. All charity is humiliating, young man.

Student. What do you want of me?

Old Man. I'm not asking you to return the money, but if you would be willing to perform a few small services for me, I'd consider myself repaid. You see that I'm a cripple. Some say it's my own fault, others blame my parents. Personally I blame life itself with all its traps; if you avoid one, you fall head first into another. Anyway, I can't climb stairs or ring doorbells, and that's why I'm asking you to help me.

Student. What can I do?

Old Man. First of all, push my chair over there so I can read the posters. I want to see what's playing at the theaters tonight.

Student (*Pushing the wheelchair*). Don't you have a man to take care of you?

Old Man. Yes, but I sent him on an errand. He'll be back soon. Are you a medical student?

Student. No, I'm studying languages, but I haven't really decided yet what I'm going to do.

Old Man. Aha! Are you good at mathematics?

Student. Pretty good.

Old Man. That's fine. How would you like a job?

Student. Yes. Why not?

Old Man. Excellent! (*He studies the posters on the pillar.*) They're giving *The Valkyrie* at the matinée today. That means that the Colonel and his daughter will be there, and they always sit on the aisle in the sixth row. I'll put you next to him. You go into that telephone booth over there, and order a ticket for seat eighty-two in the sixth row.

Student. You expect me to go to the opera in the middle of the day?

Old Man. Yes, you just listen to me and you won't regret it. I want to see you happy, rich, and respected. Because of your brave deeds last night, you'll be a celebrity by tomorrow, and your name will be worth something.

Student (*Going toward the telephone booth*). This is a ridiculous adventure!

Old Man. Aren't you a gambler?

Student. Yes, but I'm always unlucky.

Old Man. Well, this will change your luck. Go and telephone!

(*The* STUDENT *goes out. The* OLD MAN *reads his paper. The* LADY IN BLACK *comes out into the street and talks to the* JANITRESS. *The* OLD MAN *eavesdrops, but the audience cannot hear what is being said. The* STUDENT *returns.*)

Old Man. All taken care of?

Student. It's all arranged.

Old Man. Do you see that house?

Student. Yes, I often stop and look at it. I passed it yesterday when the sun was shining on the window panes, and I imagined all the beauty and luxury in there. I said to my friend, "Just imagine living up there on the fourth floor, with a beautiful young wife, two pretty little children, and an income of twenty thousand a year."

Old Man. Is that what you said? You said that? Is that so? I'm very fond of that house myself.

Student. Do you speculate in houses?

Old Man. Well, yes. But not in the way you mean ...

Student. Do you know the people who live there?

Old Man. Every one of them. When you get to be my age you know everybody, and their fathers and their grandfathers too, and you find out you're related to all of them in some way or other. I've just turned eighty, but no one knows me, not really. I take an interest in people's destinies ...

(*The window shades in the Round Room are raised. The* COLONEL, *in civilian clothes, is seen looking at the thermometer outside one of the windows; then he turns back into the room and stands in front of the marble statue.*)

Look, there's the Colonel. You'll be sitting next to him this afternoon.

Student. Oh, is that—the Colonel? I don't understand a thing that's going on! It's like a fairy tale.

Old Man. My whole life is like a book of fairy tales, my boy. All the stories are different, but they are held together by a thread, a single theme that keeps recurring.

Student. Who is that marble statue in there?

Old Man. That's his wife, of course ...

Student. Was she so wonderful?

Old Man. Oh—yes.

Student. Tell me about her.

Old Man. Well, it's hard to judge people, young man. If I were to tell you that he beat her, that she left him, then came back and married him a second time, and now she sits in there like a mummy, worshipping her

own statue—you would think I was crazy.

Student. I don't understand!

Old Man. I didn't think you would. And over there we have the window with the hyacinths. That's where his daughter lives. She's out horseback riding, but she'll be home soon.

Student. And who is the lady in black who's talking to the janitress?

Old Man. Well, that's a bit complicated. It concerns the man who just died— up there where you see the white sheets.

Student. And who was he?

Old Man. A human being like us, except that he was unbelievably vain. Now if you were a Sunday child, you would see him come through that door in a few minutes to look at the consulate flag flying at half-mast. He was a consul, and all he thought about was crowns and lions, plumed hats and colored ribbons.

Student. Sunday child, did you say? They tell me I was born on a Sunday.

Old Man. Were you, really? I should have guessed it from the color of your eyes. So you can see what others can't see! Haven't you noticed that?

Student. I don't know what other people can see, but sometimes—Well, I'd rather not talk about it.

Old Man. I was sure of it. But you can talk to me about it. I understand— things like that ...

Student. Well, yesterday, for instance— I felt as if I just had to walk down that dark little street where the house was about to collapse. I went there and stood in front of that building, which I had never seen before. Then I noticed a crack in the wall, and I could hear the floor boards snapping. I rushed over and picked up a child that was walking close to the wall. A minute later the whole house caved in. I escaped, but in my arms, where I thought I had the child, there was nothing.

Old Man. That's amazing, but I believe it. Now tell me something. Why were you making all those gestures at the fountain a little while ago? And why were you talking to yourself?

Student. Didn't you see the milkmaid I was talking to?

Old Man (*With a look of horror*). Milkmaid?

Student. Yes, of course, she handed me the cup.

Old Man. Oh, so that's what it was. Well, I don't have second sight, but I have other gifts . . .

(*The* FIANCEE, *a white-haired old woman, sits down at the window with the street-view mirror.*)

Look at that old lady in the window! Do you see her? Good! She was my fiancée once, sixty years ago. I was twenty. Don't worry, she doesn't recognize me. We see each other every day but it doesn't mean a thing to me, although we once vowed to love each other eternally. Eternally!

Student. How silly people were in those days! We'd never think of saying anything like that to the girls nowadays.

Old Man. Forgive us, young man. We didn't know any better! But can you see that that old woman was once young and beautiful?

Student. Not really. Oh, yes, she has charming looks . . . but I can't see her eyes.

(*The* JANITRESS *comes out of the house with a basket of pine branches which she scatters on the sidewalk—a funeral custom in Sweden.*)

Old Man. There's the janitress! The lady in black is her daughter by the dead man up there. That's how her husband got the job of janitor. But the lady in black has a lover, a member of the nobility, who expects to be rich one day. He's getting a divorce from his present wife, who is making him a gift of a magnificent house just to be rid of him. This noble lover is the son-in-law of the dead man—you can see his bedclothes being aired up there on the balcony. It's complicated, isn't it?

Student. Terribly complicated!

Old Man. Oh, yes, so it is, inside and out, and yet the house looks so ordinary.

Student. But then who was the dead man?

Old Man. You just asked me that, and I told you. If you could look around the corner, where the service entrance is, you'd see a crowd of poor people, beggars, he used to help—when he felt like it.

Student. Then he was a kind man?

Old Man. Yes—sometimes.

Student. Not always?

Old Man. No! That's how people are! Listen, young man, will you push my chair a little, so that I can get some sun. I'm terribly cold. If you can't move around, your blood gets sluggish. I'm going to die soon. I know that, but there are a few things I want to clear up before I go. Take my hand—just feel how cold I am.

Student (*Takes his hand*). Oh, I can't believe it! (*He shrinks back, tries to free his hand, but cannot.*)

Old Man. Don't leave me. I'm tired and I'm lonely, but I haven't always been like this, you know. I've lived an enormously long time—enormously long. I've made people unhappy and people have made me unhappy—one cancels out the other—but before I die I want to make you happy. Because of your father—and for other reasons—our fates are interwoven . . .

Student. Let go of my hand. You're sapping my strength. You're freezing me. What is it you want?

Old Man (*Letting go*). Be patient. You'll see and understand. Here comes the young lady. (*She is not yet in sight.*)

Student. The Colonel's daughter?

Old Man. Yes! His daughter! Just look at her! Have you ever seen such a masterpiece?

Student. She looks like the marble statue in there.

Old Man. Well, after all, that's her mother!

Student. You are right. I've never seen a woman so like the woman who bore her. He will be a happy man who leads her to the altar and to his home.

Old Man. Oh, so you see that! Not everyone recognizes her beauty. Well, then, it's predestined!

(*The* YOUNG LADY *enters wearing an English riding habit with breeches. Without looking at anyone, she walks slowly to the front door of the apartment house, where she pauses and speaks a few words with the* JANITRESS. *Then she goes into the house. The* STUDENT *covers his eyes with his hands.*)

Are you crying?

Student. When one's desire seems hopeless, one can only despair.

Old Man. But I can open doors, and hearts, if only I can find an arm to do my will. Serve me, and you will succeed.

Student. Is this some sort of pact? Must I sell my soul?

Old Man. Sell nothing! Listen. All my life I have *taken*; now I want more than anything else to give—to give! But nobody will take what I have to offer. I am rich, very rich, but I have no heirs—only a good-for-nothing son who torments the life out of me. You could be my son! Be my heir while I'm still alive, enjoy life and let me watch, if only from a distance.

Student. What do you want me to do?

Old Man. First, go and hear *The Valkyrie*.

Student. I've already agreed to that. What else?

Old Man. This evening you'll be sitting in there—in the Round Room!

Student. How will I get in there?

Old Man. By going to *The Valkyrie*!

Student. Why did you choose me as your go-between? Did you know me before?

Old Man. Yes, of course, I've had my eye on you for a long time. . . . But look up there now at the balcony. The maid is raising the flag to half-mast for the consul. Now she's turning the bed-clothes. Do you see that blue quilt! That was made for two to sleep under. Now it will cover only one.

(*The* YOUNG LADY, *who has changed her clothes, appears at the window and begins to water the hyacinths.*)

There's my little girl. Just look at her, look! She's talking to the flowers. Isn't she like a blue hyacinth herself? She's giving them a drink—it's only water but they turn it into color and perfume. And here comes the Colonel with his newspaper. He's showing her the item about the house that collapsed. Now he's pointing to your picture. She's impressed . . . she's reading about your bravery. . . . It seems to be clouding over. If it rains, I'll be in a fine fix, unless Johansson gets back here pretty soon . . .

(*It begins to grow cloudy and dark. The* Fiancee *closes her window.*)

You see, my fiancée is closing the window. Seventy-nine years old. The only mirror she looks into nowadays is the window mirror, where she doesn't see herself, only the world outside from two directions. But the world can see her—she doesn't realize that—anyhow, she's a good-looking old lady.

(*The* Dead Man *in his shroud comes out of the house.*)

Student. Good God, what's that?
Old Man. What do you see?
Student. Can't *you* see? There—in the doorway—the dead man?
Old Man. No, I don't see anything—but I expected something like this! Tell me what you see . . .
Student. He's coming out into the street. (*Pause.*) Now he's turning his head and looking up at the flag.
Old Man. What did I tell you? Believe me, he'll count every wreath and read every calling card. God help anyone whose name is missing!
Student. Now he's going around the corner . . .
Old Man. To count the beggars at the back door. The more there are, the better it will look. "Followed to the grave by the blessings of the multi-

tude." Well, he won't have my blessing! Just between you and me, he was an awful scoundrel.
Student. But benevolent . . .
Old Man. A benevolent scoundrel, whose only aim in life was to have a magnificent funeral. When he knew the end was near, he swindled the state out of fifty thousand crowns. Now his daughter is having an affair with another woman's husband and is worrying about the will. That scoundrel can hear every word we're saying. Good, let him! Ah, here comes Johansson! (Johansson *enters from the left.*) Report! (Johansson *speaks inaudibly.*) Not at home? You're an idiot! A telegram? Nothing? Go on. Six o'clock this evening? That's good. A special edition? With his name in full. Arkenholz . . . a student . . . date of birth . . . parents . . . Excellent! I think it's starting to rain . . . What did he say about it? Really, really! He didn't want to? Well, he'll have to! Here comes the Baron. Push me around the corner, Johansson, I want to hear what the beggars are saying. And Arkenholz, you wait for me here. You understand? (*To* Johansson.) Come on, let's go!

(Johansson *pushes the wheelchair around the corner. The* Student *stands there watching the* Young Lady, *who is tending the hyacinths.* Baron Skanskorg *enters; he is dressed in mourning, and approaches the* Lady in Black, *who has been pacing back and forth in front of the house.*)

Baron. Well, what can we do about it? We'll just have to wait!
Lady. I can't wait.

Baron. You can't? Then you'd better go to the country.

Lady. I don't want to do that.

Baron. Come over here, or they'll hear what we're saying. (*They move towards the pillar and continue to speak inaudibly.*)

Johansson (*Returns and approaches the* STUDENT). My master asks you not to forget that other matter, sir.

Student. Listen . . . first tell me something about your master. Who is he?

Johansson. Oh, there's so much to tell . . . he's been everything and done everything!

Student. Is he sane?

Johansson. Just what does that mean? He says he's been looking for a Sunday child all his life, but maybe he just made that up.

Student. What does he want? Money?

Johansson. He wants power. All day long he rides around in his chariot like the great god Thor. He looks at houses, pulls them down, opens up new streets, builds public squares . . . But he breaks into houses, too, sneaks in through the windows, tampers with people's lives, kills his enemies . . . and never forgives anyone or anything. Would you believe it, sir, this little cripple was once a Don Juan . . . but the women always left him.

Student. Why was that?

Johansson. Well, he's tricky, you see; he makes the women leave him when he gets tired of them. Now he's more like a horse thief, only he steals human beings instead of horses. He controls people in all sorts of ways. He literally stole me out of the hands of the law. I made a little mistake, you understand, and he was the only one who knew about it; so instead of sending me to jail, he made me his slave. And all he gives me is my food, and that's far from the best . . .

Student. What is he up to? What does he want to do in this house?

Johansson. Well, I'd rather not go into that! It's too involved.

Student. I think I'd better clear out of here.

Johansson. Look, the young lady's dropped her bracelet out of the window . . .

(*The* STUDENT *goes slowly over, picks up the bracelet, and returns it to the* YOUNG LADY, *who thanks him stiffly. The* STUDENT *goes back to Jo-* HANSSON.)

So you're thinking of leaving . . . That's not so easy, once he's got you in his net. And he's not afraid of anything in heaven or earth . . . yes, there's only one thing . . . or rather, one person . . .

Student. Wait, don't tell me who it is! I think I know!

Johansson. How can you know?

Student. I'm just guessing! Is it . . . a little milkmaid he's afraid of?

Johansson. He looks the other way whenever a milk wagon goes by. And he talks in his sleep. It seems he was once in Hamburg—

Student. Can you trust what he says?

Johansson. You can trust him . . . to do anything!

Student. What's he doing now around the corner?

Johansson. He's listening to the beggars . . . dropping a word here, loosening a stone there, little by little, till the house falls down . . . figuratively speaking, of course . . . You see, I'm an educated man . . . I used to be a bookseller . . . Are you going away now?

Student. I don't want to be ungrateful.

He saved my father once, and now he's only asking a small service in return.

Johansson. What is that?

Student. He wants me to go and hear *The Valkyrie.*

Johansson. I can't figure that one out. But he's always got something new up his sleeve. Look, now he's talking to that policeman. He always keeps on good terms with the police. He uses them, gets them involved in his affairs, keeps them on the hook with false promises and hopes, while all the time he's pumping them for information. You just wait and see . . . before the night is over he'll be received in the Round Room.

Student. What does he want in there? What has he got to do with the Colonel?

Johansson. I have a vague idea, but I'm not sure. You'll see for yourself once you're in there.

Student. I'll never get in there . . .

Johansson. That depends on you! Go to *The Valkyrie* . . .

Student. Is that the way to do it?

Johansson. Yes, if he said so! Look. Look at him in his war chariot, drawn in triumph by the beggars, who won't get a thing for their trouble, except maybe a free meal at his funeral.

Old Man. (*Appears standing up in his wheelchair, which is drawn by a* Beggar *and followed by others*). Hail to the noble youth, the hero of yesterday's accident! He risked his own life to save the life of others. Three cheers for Arkenholz! (*The* Beggars *take off their hats but do not cheer. The* Young Lady *at the window waves her handkerchief. The* Colonel *looks on from the window of the Round Room. The* Fiancee *stands up at her window. The* Maid *on the balcony raises the flag to the top of the pole.*) Fellow citizens, applaud! It's Sunday, I know, but the donkey in the pit and the ears in the cornfield will absolve us. I may not be a Sunday child, but I can foretell the future and heal the sick. I once brought a drowning person back to life. Yes, that was in Hamburg on a Sunday morning just like this. . . .

(*The* Milkmaid *enters, seen only by the* Student *and the* Old Man. *She raises her arms like a person who is drowning and stares fixedly at the* Old Man. *He sits down suddenly, huddles together, and cries out in a terror-stricken voice.*)

Johansson! Take me away! Quick! Arkenholz, don't forget *The Valkyrie!*

Student. What's the meaning of all this?

Johansson. We shall see! We shall see!

Scene Two

The Round Room. Against the rear wall is a white porcelain stove; there are also a mirror, a pendulum clock, and candelabra. To the right of the stove is an entrance hall through which can be seen the Green Room with its mahogany desk. To the left of the stove is the door to a closet papered like the wall. The marble statue is shaded by palms; there is a curtain that can be drawn to conceal it. A door on the left leads into the Hyacinth Room where the Young Lady *sits reading. The* Colonel, *who sits at the desk in the Green Room with his back to the audience, is writing.*

BENGTSSON, *the* COLONEL's *servant, dressed in livery, enters from the hall followed by* JOHANSSON, *in a waiter's uniform.*

Bengtsson. Listen, Johansson. You'll do the serving while I take care of the coats. Have you ever done this before?

Johansson. I push his chariot around all day, you know, but in the evenings I work as a waiter at receptions. It's always been my dream to come into this house. Queer lot of people, aren't they?

Bengtsson. Well, yes. A bit strange, you might say.

Johansson. Will this be a musical party—or what?

Bengtsson. Just the usual ghost supper, as we call it. They drink tea . . . don't say a word . . . or the Colonel does all the talking. And they munch on their biscuits, all at the same time, so it sounds like rats in an attic.

Johansson. Why do you call it a ghost supper?

Bengtsson. Well, they look like a bunch of ghosts. And they've been doing this for twenty years, the same crowd saying the same things, or saying nothing at all for fear of giving themselves away.

Johansson. Isn't there a lady of the house?

Bengtsson. Oh, yes, but she's crazy. She sits in a closet because her eyes can't stand the light. (*He points to the papered door.*) In there.

Johansson. In there?

Bengtsson. Yes, I told you they were a bit strange.

Johansson. What does she look like?

Bengtsson. Like a mummy. Want to have a look at her? (*He opens the closet door.*) There she is.

(*The* COLONEL's *wife is seen, pale and shrivelled like a mummy.*)

Johansson. Oh, my God!

Mummy (*Squawking*). Why did you open the door? Didn't I tell you to keep it closed?

Bengtsson (*In baby-talk*). Ta, ta, ta, ta! Be a good little girly now, and you'll get something nice! Pretty Polly!

Mummy (*Speaks like a parrot*). Pretty Polly! Is that you, Jacob? Currrrr!

Bengtsson. She thinks she's a parrot, and maybe she is . . . (*To the* MUMMY.) Come on, Polly, whistle a little for us!

(*The* MUMMY *whistles.*)

Johansson. Well, I've seen a lot in my day, but this beats everything.

Bengtsson. You know, when a house is old it gets moldy, and when people live together too long and torment each other, they go mad. The lady of the house—shut up, Polly!—that mummy there, has been sitting here for forty years—same husband, same furniture, same relatives, same friends. (*Closing the door on the* MUMMY.) And the things that have happened in this house—even I don't know the whole story . . . Look at this statue . . . that's her when she was young!

Johansson. God Almighty! Is that the Mummy?

Bengtsson. Yes! It's enough to make you cry! But this woman took it into her head somehow that she was a parrot, so she talks that way . . . and she picked up some of its other little quirks . . . She hates cripples and sick people. She can't even stand the sight of her own daughter, because the girl is sick . . .

Johansson. Is that young lady sick?

Bengtsson. Didn't you know that?

Johansson. No. And the Colonel, what's he like?

Bengtsson. You'll see very soon.

Johansson (*Looking at the statue*). It's terrible to think that—How old is the lady now?

Bengtsson. Nobody knows. They say that when she was thirty-five she looked nineteen, and she convinced the Colonel that she was—right here in this house . . . You see that black Japanese screen, over there by the couch? Do you know what that's for? They call it the death screen! When someone is going to die, they put it around him, like in a hospital!

Johansson. What a horrible house! And that young student was longing to get in here, as if it were paradise.

Bengtsson. What student? Oh, yes, I know. The one that's coming here this evening. The Colonel and his daughter met him at the opera and took a great liking to him. Hm! But now it's my turn to ask questions. Who's your boss? That old man? The one in the wheelchair?

Johansson. Yes, that's right! Is he coming here too?

Bengtsson. He wasn't invited.

Johansson. Then he'll come uninvited— if necessary!

(*The* OLD MAN *appears in the hall on crutches. He wears a full-dress suit and top hat. He moves forward warily and listens.*)

Bengtsson. He's a regular old rascal, isn't he?

Johansson. One of the biggest!

Bengtsson. He looks like the devil himself!

Johansson. And he must be a magician, too; he can go through locked doors . . .

(*The* OLD MAN *has come up behind* JOHANSSON *and takes him by the ear.*)

Old Man. Scoundrel! Watch out! (*To* BENGTSSON) Tell the Colonel I'm here.

Bengtsson. Yes . . . but we're expecting company here . . .

Old Man. I know that. But my visit won't be a complete surprise, though he's not exactly looking forward to it . . .

Bengtsson. I see. What was the name? Mr. Hummel?

Old Man. Precisely! Yes. (BENGTSSON *goes through the hall into the Green Room, and closes the door behind him. The* OLD MAN *turns on* JO- HANSSON.) Disappear! (JOHANSSON *hesitates.*) Vanish! (JOHANSSON *goes out through the hall. The* OLD MAN *looks around the room, then stands in astonishment in front of the statue.*) Amelia! Yes, it's Amelia! (*He wanders around the room examining several objects, stops in front of the mirror to adjust his wig, then returns to the statue.*)

Mummy (*From the closet*). Prrrretty Polly!

Old Man (*Startled*). What was that? Is there a parrot in the room? But I don't see it!

Mummy. Jacob, are you there?

Old Man. It's a ghost!

Mummy. Jacob!

Old Man. It's frightening! So those are the kinds of secrets they've been keeping in this house! (*With his back to the closet, he stands looking at a portrait on the wall.*) There he is! That's the Colonel!

(*The* Mummy *comes out of the closet, goes up behind the* Old Man, *and tugs at his wig.*)

Mummy. Currr! Are you—? Currr!

Old Man (*Jumps with fright*). Holy God in heaven! Who's that?

Mummy (*Speaking in a normal voice*). Is that you, Jacob?

Old Man. Yes, my name is Jacob . . .

Mummy (*With emotion*). And my name is Amelia!

Old Man. No, no, no! Oh, my God!

Mummy. Yes, this is how I look now. (*Points to the statue.*) And that's how I used to look! Life teaches one a lot—I live most of my life in the closet, so I won't have to see anyone, and they won't see me. But you, Jacob, what are you looking for here?

Old Man. My child! Our child . . .

Mummy. She's sitting in there.

Old Man. Where?

Mummy. In there. In the Hyacinth Room!

Old Man (*Looking at the* young lady). Yes, there she is! (*Pause*) And what does her father know about her? I mean the Colonel—your husband?

Mummy. I was angry at him once, and I told him everything . . .

Old Man. Well?

Mummy. He didn't believe me. He said, "That's what all women say when they want to destroy their husbands." It was a terrible crime just the same. It falsifies his whole life and his family tree. I read his biography in the almanac of the peerage occasionally, and I think, "She's going around with a false birth certificate, like a servant girl, and you can go to jail for that."

Old Man. Lots of people lie about their birth. I seem to remember that you once gave a false date . . .

Mummy. My mother made me do it. I wasn't to blame. And you were mostly to blame for the crime we committed. . . .

Old Man. No, it was your husband who was the cause of the crime, when he took my sweetheart from me! I can't forgive anyone until I've punished him. . . . I was born that way. That to me was an absolute duty—and it still is!

Mummy. What are you looking for in this house? What do you want here? How did you get in? Does it in any way concern my daughter? If you so much as touch her, you'll die!

Old Man. I only wish her well.

Mummy. And you must spare her father!

Old Man. Never!

Mummy. Then you shall die—in this room—behind the screen . . .

Old Man. That may be. But once I get my teeth into something, I can't let go . . .

Mummy. You want to marry her to that student. Why? He is nothing—and he has nothing.

Old Man. He will be rich, thanks to me!

Mummy. Were you invited here to-night?

Old Man. No. I just decided to invite myself to your ghost supper!

Mummy. Do you know who's coming?

Old Man. Not exactly.

Mummy. The Baron, who lives upstairs, and whose father-in-law was buried this afternoon . . .

Old Man. Oh, yes, the man who's getting a divorce so that he can marry the daughter of the janitress. He was once your lover!

Mummy. Another guest will be your

former fiancée—whom my husband seduced ...

Old Man. A very distinguished gathering!

Mummy. Oh, God, if only we could die! Die!

Old Man. Why do you go on meeting?

Mummy. Our crimes, our secrets, and our guilt bind us together! We've split up and gone our separate ways many times, but we are always drawn back together again ...

Old Man. I think the Colonel is coming ...

Mummy. Then I'll go in to Adele . . . (*Pause*) Jacob, mind what you do! Spare him . . . (*Pause. She goes into the Hyacinth Room.*)

(*The* COLONEL *enters, a letter in his hand. He is cold and reserved.*)

Colonel. Please sit down. (*The* OLD MAN *sits down slowly. There is a pause during which the* COLONEL *stares at him.*) Did you write this letter?

Old Man. I did.

Colonel. And your name is Hummel?

Old Man. It is. (*Pause*)

Colonel. Since, as I see, you have bought up all my outstanding promissory notes, it follows that I am entirely at your mercy. Now what do you want?

Old Man. I want to be paid—in one way or another.

Colonel. In what way?

Old Man. A very simple way. Let's not talk about money. Just allow me to come and go in your house—as a guest!

Colonel. If such a small thing will satisfy you—

Old Man. Thank you!

Colonel. And what else?

Old Man. Dismiss Bengtsson.

Colonel. Why should I do that? He's a devoted servant, and he's been with me for a lifetime. He won a military medal for faithful service. Why should I dismiss him?

Old Man. He has all those fine qualities in your imagination. But he's not the man he appears to be!

Colonel. Who is?

Old Man (*Taken aback*). True! But Bengtsson must go!

Colonel. Are you going to give orders in my house?

Old Man. Yes, since I own everything here—furniture, curtains, silverware, linen—and much more!

Colonel. What do you mean by much more?

Old Man. Everything! Everything you see here—is mine!

Colonel. Very well, it's all yours. But my noble heritage, my title, and my good name will always be mine!

Old Man. No, not even those! (*Pause*) You are not a nobleman!

Colonel. How dare you!

Old Man (*Takes out a piece of paper*). If you read this extract from the *Guide to Heraldry*, you will see that the family whose name you've been using has been extinct for a hundred years.

Colonel (*Reads*). I've heard rumors to this effect, but I inherited the name from my father. (*Reads*) So it's true. You are right. I am not a nobleman! I've got no right to the name. I must give it up—and this ring with the coat of arms. (*He takes it off.*) It belongs to you. Here you are!

Old Man (*Takes the ring and puts it in his pocket*). Now let's continue. You're not a colonel, either!

Colonel. Not a colonel?

Old Man. No! You once held the temporary rank of colonel in the American Volunteer Corps, but after the war in Cuba and the reorganization of the Army, all such titles were abolished.

Colonel. Is that true?

Old Man (*Reaching into his pocket*). Would you like to read about it?

Colonel. No, it's not necessary. Who are you, and what right do you have to sit there and strip me like this?

Old Man. You'll soon see. And as far as stripping you goes—do you really want to know who you are?

Colonel. Have you no shame?

Old Man. Take off your wig, and look at yourself in the mirror. And while you're at it, take out your false teeth, shave off your moustache, and let Bengtsson help you off with your metal corset, then we'll see if a certain Mr. X will recognize himself as the footman who used to sponge off the maids in a certain kitchen . . . (*The* COLONEL *reaches for the bell on the table, but the* OLD MAN *stops him.*) Don't touch that bell—don't bring Bengtsson in here. If you do, I'll have him arrested . . . Now your guests are arriving. Just keep calm; we'll go on playing our old parts for a little while longer!

Colonel. Who are you? I seem to recognize your eyes . . . and your voice . . .

Old Man. Don't try to find out. Just keep your mouth shut and do as I say.

(*The* STUDENT *enters and bows to the* COLONEL.)

Student. How do you do, sir.

Colonel. Welcome to my house, young man. Because of your remarkable behavior at that great disaster, your name is on everyone's lips, and I consider it an honor to receive you in my home . . .

Student (*Shyly*). Colonel, my humble background . . . your illustrious name and noble birth . . .

Colonel (*To the* OLD MAN). May I introduce Mr. Arkenholz, a student . . . Mr. Hummel . . . Would you be so good as to join the ladies in there, Mr. Arkenholz? I'd like to finish my conversation with Mr. Hummel . . . (*He shows the* STUDENT *into the Hyacinth Room, where he remains visible, talking shyly to the* YOUNG LADY.) A fine young man . . . he likes music, sings, writes poetry. If only he were wellborn, equal to my station, I don't think I'd object to . . .

Old Man. To what?

Colonel. To letting my daughter—

Old Man. *Your* daughter! And speaking of her, why does she always sit in that room?

Colonel. She insists upon sitting in the Hyacinth Room whenever she's at home. It's a peculiarity of hers. Ah, here comes Miss Beata von Holsteinkrona—a charming woman, active in the church, with an income commensurate with her birth and position . . .

Old Man (*To himself*). My old flame!

(*The* FIANCEE *enters, looking slightly crazy.*)

Colonel. Miss Holsteinkrona . . . Mr. Hummel. (*The* FIANCEE *curtsies and takes a seat.* BARON SKANSKORG *enters and takes a seat. He is wearing mourning and looks mysterious.*) Baron Skanskorg . . .

Old Man (*Aside, without rising*). Well, if it isn't the jewel thief! (*To the*

COLONEL.) Now if you bring in the mummy, the party will be complete . . .

Colonel (*At the door of the Hyacinth Room*). Polly!

Mummy (*Entering*). Currrr!

Colonel. Shall I ask the young people to join us?

Old Man. No, not the young people. Let's spare them.

(*They all sit in a circle in silence.*)

Colonel. Shall I ring for the tea?

Old Man. What for? No one likes tea. Why pretend? (*Pause*)

Colonel. Then shall we talk?

Old Man (*Speaks slowly, often pausing*). Talk about the weather? We all know about that! Ask about each other's health? We know all about that, too! I prefer silence. Then you can hear your thoughts and see the past. Silence can't hide anything . . . but words can. I read the other day that differences of language originated among savage tribes who were trying to keep their secrets from the other tribes. So every language is a code, and if you can find the key you can understand all the languages in the world. But that doesn't mean that every secret needs a key, especially in those cases where paternity has to be proved. Legal proof is another matter—all you need are two false witnesses who can make their testimony agree. But for the sort of affair I'm thinking of, there are usually no witnesses. Nature has made us too modest for that, so we hide what should be hidden. Still and all, unintentional slips occur and the darkest secret comes to light, the mask is torn from the imposter's face and the scoundrel is exposed. (*Pause. All look at each other in silence.*) Every-

one is so silent! (*Long pause.*) Here, for example, in this respectable house, in this elegant home, where beauty, culture, and wealth are united . . . (*Long pause*) All of us sitting here . . . we know what we are, don't we? I don't have to tell you. And you know all about me, though you pretend ignorance . . . (*He points to the Hyacinth Room.*) Sitting in that room is my daughter. Yes, *mine*—you know that too. She had lost the desire to live, without knowing why. She was withering away because the air in this house was polluted with crime, deceit, and falsehood of every kind. That is why I had to find her a friend who would enable her to bask in the light and warmth of his noble deeds . . . (*Long pause.*) That's why I've come to this house: to pull up the weeds, to expose the crimes, and to settle all accounts, so that these young people might make a fresh start in this home, which is my gift to them! (*Long pause.*) And now I give you leave to withdraw, each of you in his time and turn. If anyone stays, I'll have him arrested! (*Another long pause.*) Listen to the clock ticking on the wall like a deathwatch beetle! Do you hear what it says? "It's time! It's time!" It will strike in a few minutes, and your time will be up. Then you may go, but not before. But the clock raises its arm before it strikes. Listen! It's warning you: "Clocks can strike." And I can strike too . . . (*He strikes the table with his crutch.*) Do you hear?

(*Silence. The* MUMMY *goes to the clock and stops the pendulum. Then she speaks in a normal voice, seriously.*)

Mummy. But I can stop time in its course. I can wipe out the past, and undo what is done. Not with bribes, not with threats, but with suffering and repentance. (*She draws close to the* OLD MAN.) We are miserable human beings—we know that. We have erred and we have sinned, like all mortals. We are not what we appear to be, but at bottom we are better than we appear, because we detest our sins. But when you, Jacob Hummel, with your false name, take it upon yourself to sit in judgment over us, you prove that you are the worst sinner of us all. You are no more what you appear to be than we are. You are an unrepentant thief of human souls. You stole mine once with false promises. You murdered the consul who was buried today— you strangled him with debts. And you seized on the soul of the student with a lie about having helped his father, who never owed you a cent. (*The* OLD MAN *attempts to rise and to speak, but he falls back in his chair and crumples up more and more as she goes on.*) There is one dark spot in your life that I can only guess about, but Bengtsson, I'm sure, has the facts. (*She rings the bell on the table.*)

Old Man. No, not Bengtsson! Not him!

Mummy. Oh, so he does know! (*She rings again. The* MILKMAID *appears in the doorway to the hall, but is seen only by the* OLD MAN, *who shrinks back in fear. The* MILKMAID *disappears, when* BENGTSSON *enters.*) Bengtsson, do you know this man?

Bengtsson. Yes, I know him and he knows me. Life has its ups and downs, you know. I have been in his service, and he was once in mine.

For two whole years he was a freeloader in my kitchen. He had to get to work at three, so the cook prepared dinner at two, and my family had to eat the warmed-over leavings of that ox. He even drank up the soup stock, so that the gravy had to be made out of water. He sat in the kitchen like a vampire sucking all the nourishment out of our home, till we looked like skeletons. And he almost had us put in prison, when we called the cook a thief. Later on I met this man in Hamburg; he was using another name. He was a loan-shark, a bloodsucker. And he was accused of having lured a young girl out on the ice in order to drown her, because she had seen him commit a crime and he was afraid of being discovered...

Mummy (*Passes her hand over the* OLD MAN's *face*). There you are— that's you! Now give me those promissory notes and your will.

(JOHANSSON *appears in the doorway to the hall and watches the scene with great interest, knowing it means his release from slavery. The* OLD MAN *takes out a bundle of papers, which he throws on the table. The* MUMMY *begins to stroke the* OLD MAN's *back.*)

Old Man (*Speaking like a parrot*). Jacob is here! Kakadora! Dora!

Mummy. Can the clock strike?

Old Man (*Clucks*). The clock can strike! (*He imitates a cuckoo clock.*) Cuckoo—cuckoo—cuckoo...

Mummy (*Opens the door to the closet*). Now the clock has struck! Stand up and go into the closet where I have sat for twenty years bemoaning our sin. You'll find a rope hanging in there—it will remind you of the one with which you strangled the consul, and planned to strangle your benefactor. Go! (*The* OLD MAN *goes into the closet. The* MUMMY *closes the door.*) Bengtsson! Put up the screen! The death screen! (BENGTSSON *places the screen in front of the door.*) It's finished! God have mercy on his soul!

All. Amen.

(*There is a long pause. In the Hyacinth Room, the* YOUNG LADY *is seen playing the harp, while the* STUDENT *recites.*)

Student. I saw the sun,
And I seemed to see the Hidden One.
A man shall reap what he has sown,
And holy is he whose deeds are good.
What you have done in anger,
Cannot be undone with evil.
Comfort him you have brought to grief;
Goodness earns a rich reward.
The righteous have no need to fear,
For blessèd are the pure in heart.

SCENE THREE

> The Hyacinth Room. The room is exotically furnished in Oriental style. Hyacinths of various colors are everywhere. On top of the porcelain stove is a large seated Buddha, in whose lap lies a bulb from which rises the stem of a shallot with its globe of white, star-shaped flowers.
>
> On the right is an open door, leading into the Round Room, where the COLONEL and the MUMMY are seated; they are silent and do not move. The death screen is partly visible. At the left is a door to the pantry and kitchen.
>
> The STUDENT and the YOUNG LADY (Adele) are beside the table; he is standing, she is seated at her harp.

Young Lady. Now sing to my flowers!

Student. Is this the flower of your soul?

Young Lady. The one and only. Don't you love hyacinths?

Student. I love them above all other flowers—the stem rises like a young girl, straight and slender, out of the bulb, which rests on the surface of the water, and sends its pure, white roots down into the crystalline stream. And I love it for its colors: the snow-white of purity and innocence, the sweetness of honey-yellow, the pink flush of youth, the red ripeness of maturity, but best of all the blue, like deepset, dewy eyes full of trust and faith. I love them all more than gold and pearls. I have loved them ever since I was a child, and worshipped them because they have everything I lack . . . And yet—

Young Lady. What?

Student. My love is not returned . . . these beautiful flowers hate me.

Young Lady. Why do you say that?

Student. Their fragrance, strong and pure as the first winds of spring that have passed over melting snow, confuses my senses, deafens me, blinds me, drives me out of my room, sends poisoned arrows into my heart, and sets my head on fire. Don't you know the legend of this flower?

Young Lady. Tell it to me.

Student. First, I'll tell you what it means. The bulb, which is cradled in the water or rests in the soil, is the earth. The stalk, as it rises straight up, is the axis of the world. And crowning it all are the six-pointed, starlike flowers.

Young Lady. Above the earth—the stars! Oh, how marvellous! Who told you that? What made you think of it?

Student. Well, let me see! I looked into your eyes. There I saw the whole world. And that's why Buddha always holds the earth-bulb in his lap, brooding, and watching it grow upward and outward, and transforming itself into a heaven. This poor earth will some day become a heaven. That is what Buddha is waiting for!

Young Lady. I see that now! And don't snowflakes have six points like the hyacinth?

Student. Yes, they do. Then snowflakes must be falling stars ...

Young Lady. And the snowdrop is a snow-star ... that grows out of the snow.

Student. And golden-red Sirius, the largest and most beautiful star in the heavens, is the narcissus, with its gold and red chalice and six white rays ...

Young Lady. Have you ever seen the shallot in bloom?

Student. Yes, of course, I have. It bears its blossoms in a globe—like the globe of heaven—studded with white stars ...

Young Lady. Oh, how beautiful! Whose idea was that?

Student. Yours!

Young Lady. Yours!

Student. Ours! We've given birth to something together. We are wedded.

Young Lady. Not yet ...

Student. What more?

Young Lady. Waiting, testing, patience!

Student. All right. Put me to the test! (*Pause*) Tell me. Why are your parents sitting in there in silence? They're not saying a single word!

Young Lady. Because they have nothing to say to each other, and because neither ever believes what the other says. The way my father puts it is, "What's the use of talking, when neither of us can fool the other."

Student. That's horrible! I hate to hear things like that!

Young Lady. Here comes the cook. Look at her—how big and fat she is.

(*They look in the direction of the kitchen; the* Cook *is not yet visible to the audience.*)

Student. What does she want?

Young Lady. She wants to ask me about the dinner. I've been looking after the house since my mother has been ill.

Student. What have we got to do with the kitchen?

Young Lady. We must eat, mustn't we? Just look at her. I can't stand the sight of her.

Student. Who is that monstrous woman?

Young Lady. She belongs to the Hummel family of vampires. She is eating us up.

Student. Why don't you fire her?

Young Lady. She won't go. We can't control her. She's a punishment for our sins. Can't you see that we are wasting away?

Student. Don't you get enough to eat?

Young Lady. Oh, yes. She cooks up a lot of dishes, but there is no nourishment in them. After she boils the meat, she drinks the stock and gives us the fibers and water. And when there's a roast, she cooks the marrow out of it, and drinks the gravy and broth herself. Everything she touches loses its flavor, as if she had sucked it dry with her eyes. She drinks the coffee and gives us the grounds, she guzzles the wine and fills the bottles with water.

Student. Get rid of her!

Young Lady. We can't.

Student. Why not?

Young Lady. We don't know. She won't leave. Here she comes! She'll ask me what we want for dinner. I'll tell her this and that. She'll make objections, and in the end she'll do as she pleases.

Student. Then let her decide herself!

Young Lady. She won't do that.

Student. This is the weirdest house! It's bewitched!

Young Lady. Yes. She turned away as soon as she saw you.

Cook (*Appears in the doorway*). No, that's not why! (*She grins, and shows all her teeth.*)

Student. Get out!

Cook. When I'm ready! (*Pause*) Now I am ready! (*She disappears.*)

Young Lady. Don't lose your temper. Have patience. She is one of the trials we have to endure in this house. We have a housemaid, too! And we have to clean up after her!

Student. This is getting me down! Heart in heaven! Let's have some music!

Young Lady. Wait!

Student. Music!

Young Lady. Patience! This room is called the testing room. It's beautiful to look at, but it's full of imperfections.

Student. That's unbelievable! Then we'll just have to overlook them. It's very beautiful, but a little chilly. Why don't you have a fire?

Young Lady. Because the room gets full of smoke.

Student. Can't you have the chimney cleaned?

Young Lady. It doesn't help! You see that writing table over there?

Student. It's a very handsome piece!

Young Lady. But it wobbles. Every day I put a piece of cork under the leg, and every day the maid sweeps it away, and I have to cut a new piece. Every morning the pen is covered with ink and so is the inkstand. So I have to clean up after her every single day. (*Pause*) What's the worst job you can think of?

Student. Sorting the dirty laundry! (*He makes a sound of disgust.*)

Young Lady. Well, that's what I have to do! (*She makes a similar sound.*)

Student. What else?

Young Lady. Be awakened in the middle of the night by a rattling window, and have to get up and fix it because the maid forgot to.

Student. What else?

Young Lady. I have to climb up on a ladder and put a new cord on the damper, after the maid has torn it off . . .

Student. What else?

Young Lady. I have to sweep up after her, dust after her, and light the fire in the stove after her—all she does is throw in some wood. I have to check the damper, dry the glasses, set the table over again, open the wine bottles, see that the rooms are aired, remake my bed, rinse the green sediment out of the water carafes, buy matches and soap which we're always out of, clean the lamps and trim the wicks so they won't smoke, and fill them myself to be sure they won't go out when we have company . . .

Student. Let's have some music!

Young Lady. Wait! First comes the

drudgery . . . the drudgery of keeping the filth of life away from us.

Student. But you're rich . . . you've got two servants!

Young Lady. That's no help! Even if we had three! Living means hard work, and sometimes I get very tired . . . (*Pause*) Just imagine if there were a nursery as well!

Student. The greatest of joys. . .

Young Lady. And the dearest. Is life worth that much trouble?

Student. That all depends on the reward you expect for your efforts. I would do anything to win your hand.

Young Lady. Don't say that! You can never have me!

Student. Why not?

Young Lady. You mustn't ask. (*Pause*)

Student. You dropped your bracelet out of the window—

Young Lady. Because my hand has grown so thin . . . (*Pause*)

(*The* Cook *appears with a Japanese bottle in her hand.*)

She's the one who is devouring me, and all of us.

Student. What has she got in her hand?

Young Lady. It's the bottle of coloring fluid, with letters on it like scorpions. It's soy sauce. It turns water into soup and takes the place of gravy. It makes cabbage soup, and mock turtle soup, and . . .

Student (*To the* Cook). Get out!

Cook. You suck the marrow from us, and we suck it from you. We take the blood and give you back water— with some coloring added. (*She holds up the bottle.*) This is the coloring! I'm going now, but I'll stay on in this house, as long as I please. (*She goes out.*)

Student. What did Bengtsson get a medal for?

Young Lady. For his great merits.

Student. Doesn't he have any faults?

Young Lady. Oh, yes, many great ones. But you don't get a medal for them. (*They smile.*)

Student. You have so many secrets in this house . . .

Young Lady. As in all houses. Allow us to keep ours! (*Pause*)

Student. Do you approve of frankness?

Young Lady. Yes, within reason.

Student. Sometimes there comes over me a furious desire to say everything I'm thinking. But I know the world would collapse if everyone were completely honest. (*Pause*) I went to a funeral the other day . . . in church. It was very solemn and beautiful.

Young Lady. Mr. Hummel's funeral?

Student. For my false benefactor . . . yes! At the head of the coffin stood an old friend of the deceased. He carried the mace. I was deeply impressed by the dignified manner and moving words of the minister. I cried. We all cried. And afterwards, we went to a tavern, and there I learned that the man who had carried the mace had been in love with Hummel's son . . . (*The* Young Lady *looks at him, trying to understand.*) And that Hummel had borrowed some money from his son's admirer. (*Pause.*) The day after that, they arrested the minister for embezzling church funds! A pretty story, isn't it?

Young Lady. Oh! (*Pause.*)

Student. Do you know what I'm thinking about you now?

Young Lady. Don't tell me, or I'll die!

Student. I must, or I'll die!

Young Lady. In asylums people say everything they think.

Student. Exactly! My father ended up in an asylum.

Young Lady. Was he sick?

Student. No, he was pretty healthy, but he was insane. It came on very suddenly, and under the strangest circumstances. Like most of us, he had his circle of acquaintances—he called them his friends, for convenience sake. They were a lot of worthless characters, like most people, but he had to have some sort of companionship . . . he couldn't bear to sit around all alone. You know, you don't usually tell people what you think of them, and he didn't either. He knew very well how false they were, he could see clear through their deceit, but he was a clever man, and well brought up, so he was always polite. Then one day he gave a big party; it was in the evening. He was worn out after a hard day's work, and with the strain of wanting to hold his tongue while having to talk rubbish with his guests. (*The* YOUNG LADY *is frightened.*) Well, while they were at the dinner table, he rapped for silence, raised his glass, and got up to speak. Then something pulled the trigger, and he made a tremendous speech in which he stripped the whole company naked, one after the other, and told them what hypocrites they were. Then he sat right down in the middle of the table, and told them all to go to hell!

Young Lady. Oh!

Student. I was there, and I shall never forget what happened then. My father and mother began to fight, the guests rushed for the door . . . and father was taken to the asylum, where he died (*Pause*) If you keep quiet too long, it's like water that stands still—it gets putrid; that's what happened in this house. There is something putrid here! And I thought it was paradise when I saw you coming in here that first time. There I stood on that Sunday morning, outside looking in. I saw a Colonel who wasn't a Colonel; I had a generous benefactor who turned out to be a bandit and had to hang himself; I met a mummy who wasn't one, and a virgin who . . . and speaking of that, where can one find virginity? Or where is beauty to be found? In nature, and in my mind when I am dressed in my Sunday clothes. And where does one find honor and faithfulness? In fairy tales and in children's fantasies! Where can I find anything that fulfills its promise? Only in my imagination! You see, your flowers have poisoned me, and now I am poisoning you. I asked you to be my wife and share my home . . . we sang and played and made poetry . . . and then the cook came in. Lift up our hearts! Try once more to pluck fire and glory from your golden harp. Try, I beg you, I implore you on my knees . . . (*She does not move.*) Well then, I shall do it myself (*He plucks the strings, but no sound comes from the harp.*) It is silent and deaf. To think that the most beautiful flowers are so poisonous, are the most poisonous! A curse hangs over the whole of creation, over all of life . . . Why won't you be my wife? Because your life was poisoned at its source. Now I feel that vampire in the kitchen beginning to suck the life out of me. She must be one of those lamias who live on the blood of children. It's always in the kitchen that the child is nipped in the bud, if it hasn't already happened in the bedroom. There are poisons that blind and poisons that open the eyes. I must have been born with the latter kind, because I can't call what is ugly beautiful, or what is evil good. I cannot! They say that Jesus Christ descended into hell . . . but that was really His pilgrimage on earth: to this madhouse, this prison, this tomb we call earth. And the inmates killed Him when He tried to set them free, but they let the thief go. The thief gets all the sympathy! Woe! Woe to us all! Savior of the world, save us! We are perishing!

(*The* Young Lady *has been drooping in her chair, and appears to be dying. She rings.* Bengtsson *enters.*)

Young Lady. Bring the screen! Quickly! I'm dying!
(Bengtsson *returns with the screen, opens it, and places it in front of the* Young Lady.)

Student. Your Liberator is coming! Welcome, pale and gentle one! Now sleep, you lovely, innocent, unhappy creature, suffering for no fault of your own. Sleep without dreaming, and when you wake again, may you be greeted by a sun that doesn't burn, in a home without dust, by friends without guile, and by a love that is pure. You wise and gentle Buddha, who sit there waiting for a heaven to grow out of this earth, grant us purity of will and patience in our time of trial, so that your hope may not be in vain!

(*The strings of the harp hum softly, and a white light fills the room.*)

I saw the sun,
And I seemed to see the Hidden One.
A man shall reap what he has sown,
And holy is he whose deeds are good.
What you have done in anger,
Cannot be undone with evil.
Comfort him you have brought to
    grief;
Goodness earns a rich reward.
The righteous have no need to fear,
For blesséd are the pure in heart.

(*A faint moaning sound comes from behind the screen.*)

You poor little child . . . child of this word of illusion, of guilt, suffering, and death . . . this world of never-ending change, of disappointment, and pain! May the Lord of Heaven be merciful to you on your journey . . .

(*The room vanishes. Böcklin's painting* The Island of the Dead *appears in the background. Soft, peaceful, melancholy music comes from the island.*)

Cat on a Hot Tin Roof

TENNESSEE WILLIAMS

INTRODUCTION

Thomas Lanier Williams was born on March 26, 1911, in the rectory of the Episcopal church in Columbus, Mississippi. His mother, Edwina, was the daughter of the Reverend Walter E. Dakin; his father, Cornelius Coffin Williams, a descendant of Tennessee pioneers, was a loud and energetic man who worked as a traveling salesman for the International Shoe Company and was often absent from home. The boy spent the first eight years of his life with his mother and sister Rose, who was two years his senior, in the rather sheltered and literary atmosphere of his maternal grandparents' home. He suffered from a number of childhood illnesses and was very much pampered; he became a hypochondriac, extremely delicate and sensitive; he did not take part in the ordinary boys' activities, but read a great deal, played games with his sister, and had a rich imaginative life.

Just before the end of World War I, the family moved to St. Louis. The sensitive boy regarded this as a tragic event, for he found it almost impossible to adjust himself to life in the midwestern city. He hated the Eugene Field School where the boys made fun of him and beat him because he was small and weak for his age, and had a Southern accent. He hated the succession of small and dingy apartments in which the family was forced to live mainly because of his father's niggardliness. In one such apartment, to make his sister's dark little room livable, the boy helped her to paint the walls and furniture white and to install her collection of glass animals, "making a place of white and crystal in the midst of squalor." This collection of tiny glass creatures years later provided the material and title for Williams's first successful play.

The birth of a brother, named Walter Dakin for his grandfather, did not particularly please the boy, and the illness of his mother, who was stricken with influenza which weakened her lungs and brought on a slight case of tuberculosis, frightened him; these occurrences fostered feelings of anxiety and insecurity in Williams. "At the age of fourteen," he says, "I discovered writing as an escape from a world of reality in which I felt acutely uncomfortable. It immediately became my place of retreat, my cave, my refuge. From what? From being called a sissy by the neighborhood kids, and Miss Nancy by my father, because I would rather read books . . . than play marbles and baseball and other normal kid games."

While he had lived with his grandparents, he had never been aware of any privation, but in St. Louis it was forcibly impressed upon his mind that there were two distinct social classes—the rich and the poor. He had only to walk to that part of the city where there were many magnificent homes surrounded by beautiful gardens and then return to his own jungle of grimy tenements to have this inequality forced upon his consciousness and to arouse his resentment. "It produced a shock and a rebellion," says Williams, "that has grown into an inherent part of my work. It was the beginning of the social-consciousness which I think has marked most of my writing."

Reaching college age at the time of the depression, Williams continued to face unsettled and unsettling conditions which disrupted his formal education. He entered the University of Missouri in 1931 and quit in 1933 to go to work for the shoe company that employed his father. Although he was temperamentally unsuited to the job, he kept it for two years until he suffered a nervous breakdown. Upon his recovery, he was more of a hypochondriac than ever, but he had decided that he was going to be a writer and that he would finish his education. He attended Washington University from 1936 to 1937 and finally put himself through the University of Iowa, which granted him a B. A. degree in 1938. Whether he was attending school or not, he continued to write poems, essays, short stories, and plays; at the time of his graduation he had two full-length plays and innumerable one-acters to his credit.

After receiving his degree, Williams left St. Louis for New Orleans, arriving there at the end of the summer of 1938, a proper young man called Thomas Lanier, neatly dressed in a conservative suit, white shirt, tie, and polished shoes; when he left the French Quarter, at the beginning of the summer of 1939, he was the complete bohemian in sport shirt and sandals, carrying a typewriter, phonograph, a volume of Hart Crane's poetry, and the name of Tennessee.

It was in New Orleans that Williams discovered that all his material as a writer would henceforth be cut from the fabric of his own life. In the French Quarter he waited on table for little more than room and board, and wrote in his spare time; he read a great deal, too, his favorite writers being Hart Crane, D. H. Lawrence, Anton Chekhov, and Rainer Maria Rilke. One day he learned that the Group Theater in New York was holding a contest for writers of full-length plays, but he sent in his one-act pieces—four plays collectively titled *American Blues*. He was awarded a prize of one hundred dollars and came to the attention of Audrey Wood, who shortly afterward became his agent and represented him for many years.

Williams's first recognition came in 1940 when, through the efforts of Miss Wood, he received a Rockefeller grant for playwriting and completed the script of *Battle of Angels*, which was produced by the Theater Guild under the direction of Margaret Webster, with Miriam Hopkins in the leading role. The play opened in Boston on December 30, 1940, and closed during its tryout there; it was banned by that city's Watch and Ward Society. "I never heard of an audience getting so infuriated," said Williams, and added by way of explanation, "The thing is, you can't mix up sex and religion, as I did in *Battle of Angels*." His total income from this play was two hundred dollars.

The Rockefeller grant was renewed; then the Institute of Arts and Letters awarded him a thousand dollars, and Williams set out on a roving writing career. He traveled all over the country working as a bellhop, elevator operator, waiter, teletype clerk, reciter of verses in a Greenwich Village nightclub, and usher in a Broadway movie-house. "I lived carefully," says Williams, "and whenever I'd saved enough to go some place else, I'd get a bus ticket and go." Gradually he became known in theatrical circles as his plays were presented by Little Theater and community groups in different parts of the country. Suddenly Miss Wood summoned him to New York, and then shipped him off to Hollywood to write screen plays for Metro-Goldwyn-Mayer under a contract that called for a salary of $250 a week, but he lasted on the job only six months. During that time he wrote an original screen play, *The Gentleman Caller*, which did not interest the studio. He proceeded to turn the script into a stage play called *The Glass Menagerie*. When his contract expired, he left Hollywood.

The Glass Menagerie opened in Chicago on December 26, 1944, to critical acclaim but an indifferent public. The critics refused to let the play die, and before long people were flocking to see it; it ran for three months and then moved to the Playhouse in New York on March 31, 1945. The play was co-directed by Margo Jones and Eddie Dowling, and the cast of four consisted of Laurette Taylor, Julie Haydon, Eddie Dowling, and Anthony Ross. The play won the Drama Critics' Circle Award as the best American work produced in New York during the season 1944-45, and chalked up a run of 563 performances, closing in early August, 1946. Two road companies, one with the original cast, toured with the play in the fall of 1946. "I was snatched out of virtual oblivion," said Williams, "and thrust into sudden prominence."

You Touched Me!, a play based on a story by D. H. Lawrence, was written by Williams in collaboration with Donald Windham; it had been produced at the Cleveland Playhouse and the Pasadena Playhouse before opening in New York on September 25, 1946, but it failed to catch on.

A year later, on December 3, 1947, Williams won enormous acclaim and the Pulitzer Prize for *A Streetcar Named Desire*, a play that made its author a figure of international as well as national importance in the theater.

Summer and Smoke, which followed on October 6, 1948, had proved highly successful when staged by Margo Jones in her arena theater in Dallas; transferred to the proscenium stage of the Music Box Theater in New York the play failed despite an excellent production. When it was done in 1952 at the Circle-in-the-Square, an arena theater in Greenwich Village, it not only attracted enthusiastic audiences but brought stardom to Geraldine Page and plaudits to its director José Quintero.

To prove that he was capable of dealing with subjects other than neurotic Southern women, Williams wrote *The Rose Tattoo*, whose heroine is the living embodiment of elemental sexuality. The play opened at the Martin Beck Theater,

New York, on February 3, 1951, and enjoyed a moderate success, but it received a much warmer reception in Europe.

The dramatist's next work was a theatricalist and symbolist drama; the play, called *Camino Real,* which dealt with the dreams and defeat of modern man, failed on Broadway in 1953 but was revived off-Broadway in 1960.

On March 27, 1955, three days after the opening of *Cat on a Hot Tin Roof,* Williams's father died in Knoxville, Tennessee, at the age of 77. Although the playwright had not been on good terms with him for many years, he attended his father's funeral. Williams, Sr. had served as the model for the father in *The Glass Menagerie* and also for Big Daddy in *Cat on a Hot Tin Roof.*

Cat on a Hot Tin Roof, presented at the Morosco Theater, New York, on March 24, 1955, won for its author his second Pulitzer Prize. Despite the unpleasantness of its subject matter (homosexuality and cancer), the play was a resounding success and led to Williams' exploitation of ever more perverse and violent themes.

Orpheus Descending (1958), a revision of Williams's earlier play, *Battle of Angels,* ends with a lynching; *Suddenly Last Summer,* the more important of two one-act plays presented under the title of *Garden District* (1959), concerns itself with homosexuality and cannibalism; and *Sweet Bird of Youth* (1959) deals with castration both symbolically and actually.

Concerning his tendency to deal with lurid material in an exacerbated manner, Williams said not long ago: "All my life I have been haunted by the obsession that to desire a thing or to love a thing intensely is to place yourself in a vulnerable position, to be a possible, if not a probable, loser of what you most want. . . . Having always to contend with this adversary of fear, which was sometimes terror, gave me a certain tendency toward an atmosphere of hysteria and violence in my writing, an atmosphere that has existed in it since the beginning. What surprises me is the degree to which both critics and audience have accepted this barrage of violence." More recently he announced: "I'm through with what have been called my 'black' plays. Maybe analysis has helped me to get them out of my system. . . . Bestiality still exists, but I don't want to write about it any more. . . . From now on I want to be concerned with the kinder aspects of life."

Williams considered his next play "brighter" than those that had gone before; it was a comedy dealing with the problems of newlyweds, called *Period of Adjustment,* which opened on Broadway in the fall of 1960. This was followed by *The Night of the Iguana* (1961), a full-length version of a one-act play that had been presented in the summer of 1959 at the Festival of Two Worlds in Spoleto, Italy. This play proved to be a critical as well as a popular success. Later plays fared less well, though Williams continued to write uninterruptedly and to create characters and situations that were sensational and grotesque for such works as *The Milk Train Doesn't Stop Here Any More* (1963), *Slapstick Tragedy* (1965); *The Two-Character Play* (1967), *The Seven Descents of Myrtle* (1968); *In the Bar of a Tokyo Hotel* (1969), *Small Craft Warning* (1972); *Outcry* (1975, a rewrite of *The Two-Character Play*), *The Red Devil Battery Sign* (1975), *The Eccentricities of the Nightingale* (1976, a rewrite of *Summer and Smoke*), and, most recently, *Vieux Carré* (1977), a play which returns to the locale and period of *A Streetcar Named Desire*.

Tennesee Williams has written more than two dozen one-act plays, several film scenarios, six volumes of prose (short stories and novels), several volumes of poetry, and the libretto for an opera. He has had an unmistakable influence on the American theater. His personal, poetic expression and his free and unrestrained treatment of "untouchable" themes have broadened the horizons of playgoers as well as of other playwrights. Besides personally helping to bring into the theater such excellent writers as William Inge and Carson McCullers, Williams has played a part in creating a renewed interest in the work of Eugene O'Neill (who had been neglected in the late '30s and '40s); and has also prepared American audiences to accept and appreciate the works of such nonnaturalistic and avant-garde writers as Giraudoux, Anouilh, Beckett, Ionesco, and Genet. That Williams takes his playwriting seriously (his aim is: Not to deceive and not to bore) and that he continues to work with unabated imagination and energy augurs well for American drama.

The failure of his play *Camino Real* in 1953, according to his friend Gilbert Maxwell, left Tennesee Williams "morbidly wary and pessimistic." It was in this mood that Williams started to think about a new work that was to become *Cat on a Hot Tin Roof*. From his short story, "Three Players of a Summer Game," which had appeared in *The New Yorker* magazine in 1952, Williams took the central characters, Margaret and Brick Pollitt. In the story, Brick, a handsome young man, with an unspecified sexual maladjustment in his marriage, becomes an alcoholic and lapses deeper and deeper into his liquor. He tries to get hold of himself, but his disintegration continues while his wife grows stronger. She eventually takes over the management of their plantation and of Brick. In the play, the motive for Brick's alcoholism is made clearer. Maggie, fiercely jealous of Brick's devotion to his best friend, Skipper, manages to get Skipper drunk and attempts to seduce him, and, when he proves incapable, charges him with being a homosexual. Skipper takes to drugs and liquor, and dies. Brick in disgust at what Maggie has done, and disconsolate at the loss of his friend, becomes an alcoholic, and refuses to sleep with her.

The other members of the Pollitt family, Big Daddy, Big Mama, Gooper, Mae, and their brood of children, were conceived for the play. Big Daddy, a representation of Williams' father, Cornelius, is a coarse, boisterous man, with a passion for life. Cornelius, Williams said, relished poker and liquor and the companionship of men in hotel rooms far more than the family at home. One of his father's favorite expressions was "jumpy as a cat on a hot tin roof."

"Big Daddy became a sublimation of Cornelius," according to J. William Miller, and was "far more understanding toward his favorite son, Brick, than Cornelius ever was toward Williams. Emerging as a kind of purgation of Williams' one time hatred of his father, Big Daddy seems Williams' wish-fulfillment of what he would have liked his own father to have been. Big Daddy intimates that homosexuality is latent in Brick; Brick, like a loving but revengeful Williams, then turns on Big Daddy and tells him a terrible truth in turn—Big Daddy is dying of cancer, and the family has kept the news from him. So in a way, Williams was also expressing his death-wish for Cornelius."

By a strange coincidence, the playwright's father died three days after the opening of *Cat on a Hot Tin Roof*. At the front of the printed version of the play, which appeared later, Williams inserted a quotation from Dylan Thomas, suggesting that despite his lifelong hostility toward his father, he was dedicating this work to him. Big Daddy is a monumental character who associates the word mendacity with church, with clubs, and with his unloved wife; he leaves so powerful an impression as almost to make the play his own. The violence in his nature, as well as in other aspects of the play, exemplifies what has come to be known as the "Southern Gothic" school of writing.

Big Mama seems foolish and pathetic at times, but she loves Big Daddy, and when she learns of his fatal illness, she rises to the occasion with strength and dignity. Mildred Dunnock, the original Big Mama, interviewed by Mike Steen for his book, *A Look at Tennessee Williams*, said, "I was dying to be in that play. I asked the producer if there was anything for me and he said there wasn't. I said, 'Well, if there's any chance of my reading, I'd like to read.' I don't know whether anybody remembers the original script of *Cat on a Hot Tin Roof* but Big Mama was described as a short, squat woman with big feet, looking like a boxer dog or a Japanese wrestler. Well! That's kind of a hard description to live up to! Women spend their lives trying *not* to look like that, particularly actresses. . . . There just wasn't anybody of that description. I kept nagging away asking for a chance to read for her. And so I read for it. I got the part. I had a friend in college whose mother had a strange, husky, whiskey voice. It was just one of those rasping voices. And when I started to read for the part I guess I felt, 'I've got to compensate for not having big feet or looking like a Japanese wrestler.' And so those descriptive words somehow or other gave me a picture of the grotesquerie which I found in my voice.

"I did do Big Mama and I adored her. She had an element of women in her that I feel is so real. . . . She knew all about Brick, and she knew all about Big Daddy. But she never wanted to look at its harsh reality. . . . Well, I think a great many women are like that and that's what appealed to me about Big Mama. She bore the brunt of all of Big Daddy's jokes and hideosities but she never chose to see them, so that she never was annihilated by them. She had guts of her own, which matched those of Big Daddy."

Maggie the cat is a clever and aggressive woman, not entirely unmotivated by greed, who was born on the wrong side of the tracks. She is determined to claw her way to sexual and financial security, and has no intention of letting go of Brick or the plantation. The uncertainty of her situation makes her tense and jumpy, and causes her to lie about her pregnancy. Brick, handsome and weak, resembles Blanche DuBois of *A Streetcar Named Desire;* he is sensitive, overcome by guilt and self-disgust, verging on neuroticism, and a subject for psychoanalysis. His sexual makeup remains a mystery. Gooper and Mae, Brick's brother and his wife, are crass connivers who think only of themselves and what they might possibly

inherit after Big Daddy's death; the minor characters, Doctor Baugh and Reverend Tooker, are petty, ineffectual weaklings—the butt of Williams' satire.

Williams worked on *Cat on a Hot Tin Roof* during the summer of 1954, and in
the autumn had a completed script. In that first version, Big Daddy appears only
in Act Two; Maggie is depicted as sharp-tongued and less than charming; and
Brick is not won over by her in the end. Williams showed this first typed version
of the play to his director, Elia Kazan, who was excited by it but had reservations
about the third act. Kazan felt that Big Daddy was too vivid and important a
character to disappear from the play after the second act; he also thought that
Brick should undergo some "apparent mutation" toward masculinity after the confrontation with his father; and, finally, he wanted the character of Maggie to be
made more clearly sympathetic to an audience. Against his will, Williams revised
the play in accordance with Kazan's suggestions: Big Daddy returned in the third
act and told a story about an elephant, which the censor called obscene and
caused to be removed from the play (Williams later explained, "I had nothing for
him to say, so I had him tell a joke."); Maggie was made a softer and more attractive person; and Brick appeared at the end to be a compliant husband ready to
perform his conjugal duty. Having to make these revisions proved a traumatic
experience for Williams. In an interview in the *Saturday Review* (4/29/72), he
said: ". . . It was a deep psychic violation. I was very disturbed after that experience with *Cat*. In fact, I couldn't write for several months after that. I went to
Rome and simply could not write. Kazan's the only one I would do it for, though.
He is a man of such enormous talent. He did make the difference between success
and failure in a lot of cases, you know."

When the play was ready for production, Audrey Wood, Willaims' agent at the
time, offered it to Cheryl Crawford; she liked the script, but had one main objection. In a letter to Williams she said: "All the people seem monstrous except Big
Daddy . . . I don't think an audience can take such an unrelieved attack." Miss
Crawford, usually a rather astute producer, turned the play down, and later admitted her mistake.

Cat on a Hot Tin Roof opened in New York in March, 1955, under the banner
of the Playwrights' Company, and immediately became a resounding success. But
the critics too had reservations, mainly about the playwright's handling of Brick's
and Skipper's sexuality. One sexual failure, it was maintained, does not prove that
Skipper was a homosexual; and the sexual encounter between Maggie and Brick,
after the fall of the curtain, might also fail. The plot was thus seen to be weak and
inconclusive. Eric Bentley and Walter Kerr accused Williams of not having faced
up squarely to the pivotal theme of homosexuality. The scene between Brick and
Big Daddy in the second act, which should reveal the "truth" to both, approaches
a climax, then blows up into explanatory prose, evading the issue about Brick, and
creating a "mystery."

When Williams revised the play for production at the American Shakespeare
Theatre in 1974, he allowed Big Daddy to return in the third act with his ineffectual elephant story, but he kept Brick in a state of "spiritual disrepair." There is
no hint of a happy ending; Brick cannot bring himself to play the role of a hetero-

sexual male. Brick's catastrophe is his suspicion of his own inadequacy and the inadequacy of his best friend. The female is the aggressor in this sexual relationship, but there is no real assurance that Maggie's scheme will work. "Three Players of a Summer Game," the short story that served in part as the inception for the play might serve equally well as the play's sequel, for there we have the final disintegration of Brick and the triumph of Maggie.

Williams, in all his plays, has shown a mastery of dialogue, and nowhere is that so clearly apparent as in *Cat on a Hot Tin Roof*. The speech of the characters is natural and idiomatic, an amalgam of cliché and originality, often stylized, pompous, and rhetorical but eminently believable when the nature and motivation of the speaker is taken into consideration.

Tennessee Williams has said that his major influence as a playwright was Chekhov, with Strindberg a close second. Williams' plays are Chekhovian mainly in their creation of mood and locale, and Strindbergian in their psychological and theatrical effects. Like Strindberg, Williams makes frequent use of autobiographical material, and bases his characters on people he has met, merged, transmuted, altered by shading of memory, imagination, experience, and understanding. Also like Strindberg, he attempts to make use of every theatrical possibility— music, lighting, stylization, and symbolism. *Camino Real*, Williams' "dream play," was written entirely in expressionistic style. *Cat on a Hot Tin Roof*, which appears to be a more naturalistic and "well-made" play, still contains a number of expressionistic elements. Specific time and location, for instance, dissolve into space; the playwright's directions to the designer state in part: "The set should be far less realistic than I have so far implied in this description of it. I think the walls below the ceiling should dissolve mysteriously into air; the set should be roofed by the sky; stars and moon suggested by traces of milky pallor, as if they were observed through a telescope lens out of focus." And, as in expressionistic drama, there is a great deal of talk about Life, Death, Truth, and Hypocrisy as abstractions.

What is not at all obvious at first glance, because of Williams' enormous gift for assimilation, are the parallels between *Cat on a Hot Tin Roof* and Strindberg's play, *The Ghost Sonata*. Both are primarily concerned with the process of unmaking, of exposing the truth which the characters have attempted to keep hidden. The action in both plays takes place in a house that looks ordinary from the outside but encloses disease, guilt, vengeance, hypocrisy, malice, and vilification. Big Daddy like Mr. Hummel is a manipulator and tryant; Big Daddy speaks of his "kingdom," the imperial note often sounded by Hummel. Both men have been everywhere and seen and done everything. Both complain of the lies and pretenses of forty years polluting the house; both have sons who are thought to be homosexual. Big Daddy's last will and testament, like Hummel's, is a source of contention. Big Daddy's birthday party is the equivalent of the ghost supper where everything comes to a head. Sookey, the maid, calls Big Mamma Mizz Polly, for Mrs. Pollitt often prates like a parrot. The crutches in both plays are symbolic, providing moral as well as literal support, and prop up men whose façades belie their true natures; the crutches in both plays also are used as a threat and a weapon. The wall clock, which is like a death beetle in *The Ghost Sonata*, has its counterpart in the clock that chimes the hour during the confrontation scene between Brick and Big Daddy, underscoring the brevity of life and presaging death. When Maggie inveighs against "Poisons. Venomous thoughts and words . . . in hearts and minds . . . ," we seem to hear echoes of The Student's words in the final scene of *The Ghost Sonata*. Strindberg's play is more brutal and unrelenting than Williams'; the Swedish playwright leaves us with only the vaguest hope of salvation in the distant future, while Williams introduces a strong strain of sentimentality and, in a play whose theme seems to be the value of truth-telling, allows his protagonist to achieve her "happy ending" by resorting to a lie.

Tennessee Williams has said that *Cat on a Hot Tin Roof* is his favorite play, mainly because it observes the classical unities of place and time—a feat of art and craft difficult to achieve. The set never changes and the play's running time is exactly the time of the action; one act follows directly on the other. In his *Memoirs*, Williams says, "I believe that in *Cat* I reached beyond myself, in the second act, to a kind of crude eloquence of expression in Big Daddy that I have managed to give no other character of my creation."

PRODUCTION IN THE TWENTIETH-CENTURY THEATER

In the twentieth century, after a depression and two world wars, the outlook of the average man had become materialistic, nihilistic, and cynical. The increasing tension, violence, and nausea in the individual and the world are mirrored in the plays of Eugene O'Neill, Tennessee Williams, Jean-Paul Sartre, Albert Camus, and Friedrich Duerrenmatt. The utter despair of life in an atomic age is depicted in its most revolting aspects in the avant-garde dramas of Eugène Ionesco (where men, in their endeavor to conform, turn into rhinoceroses), of Jean Genet (where the world is seen as a brothel in which men live fantasy lives), and of Samuel Beckett (where we all end up in garbage cans, or communicate with ourselves via tape recorders).

In desperation men had begun to concede, though reluctantly, that they could not live by reason alone. A random playwright here and there—T. S. Eliot, Graham Greene, Christopher Fry—tried to start a religious revival, but faith cannot be imposed from above; it must flower in the hearts of the people. Since this is an eclectic age and there is no single conventional form in which a modern play must be cast, even our most accomplished playwrights have produced works imitative of those of earlier traditions. O'Neill's *Mourning Becomes Electra* looks back to a Greek model; Eliot's *Murder in the Cathedral*, to a medieval one; Anderson's *Elizabeth and Essex*, in form, subject-matter, and title, to the English Renaissance; S. N. Behrman's *Amphitryon 38* to French neoclassical style; and Lillian Hellman's *The Little Foxes*, to Ibsen. These five plays alone constitute a mini-history of Western drama.

In the last quarter of the twentieth century, realism and the well-made play seem to have lost their supremacy, for the newer examples of dramatic art have tended to be episodic and unstructured in form and decadent in content. Along with the introduction of multimedia presentation, the lines of demarcation between the various genres of art seem to be fading—ballet is intermixed with drama, and drama with mime, declamation, graphics, and film. Modern drama does not hesitate to flaunt its unabashed eclecticism.

The Theater

Since the 1920s architects, designers, and producers have attempted to vary the shape of the theater both outside and in. The most notable change has been made in the relative position of auditorium to stage. Many of these theaters, which have a seating capacity of only 300 to 500, are specially designed for open staging, of which there are two main types: the arena stage, where the actors are completely surrounded by the audience; and the thrust stage, where the actors are surrounded on three sides. These theaters have eliminated front curtains in order to reduce the elements separating actor from audience and to increase communication between them. The advantages of theater-in-the-round are the intimate relationship it establishes between performer and audience, its economy of operation, and its ease of management. It has been most effectively handled by college and community groups, and by semiprofessional and off-Broadway companies.

The avant-garde producer looks upon the traditional playhouse as an antiquated building, where classic and contemporary texts can only be recited in a routine and stultifying manner. For his productions he wants no stage, no sharp line of demarcation between the player and the playgoer. The actor must be able to move freely around the spectator, speak to him directly, touch him, and startle him by frequent surprise effects. The primary intention is to create a physical and emotional response in the audience. The place of performance, even if it is a conventional theater, is often made to appear unconventional by letting the "innards" of the stage—the pipes, the lights, the counterweight system—show. But what is generally preferred is something like a converted warehouse or even a rooftop. These various locations in which the spectators and actors intermix are environments.

The Director

The social, political, and economic upheavals attendant upon the revolution in Russia and on World War I liberated the generation of directors that came after Stanislavsky, and had an unsettling effect on those who were trying to achieve unity and stability in their productions. If a play is a microcosm of the world, and the world is shattered, looking at the stage would be like looking into a broken mirror. This accounts for the great variety of nonnaturalistic and expressionistic techniques that the more innovative directors began to adopt in the 1920s. One of the more creative of the experimentalists was Vsevolod Meyerhold, who attempted to reflect the mechanistic world in his sets and in the movements of his actors. Meyerhold's directorial ideas were based on the art of improvisation. A script was merely a springboard for his conceptions, and the actors were his puppets. Ideas similar to Meyerhold's were later expressed by Antonin Artaud, Jerzy Grotowski, and other theatricalist directors. One of Meyerhold's students, Nikolai Okhlopkov, founded the Realistic Theatre in Moscow and abolished the fixed stage; this was an early attempt to force actors and audience to mingle.

In this age of fragmented traditions, such talented and original directors as Tyrone Guthrie, Jean-Louis Barrault, Elia Kazan, José Quintero, Peter Brook, Roger Blin, and Judith Malina have had to impose their personal visions on both realistic and theatricalist plays; and contemporary directors will be forced to work in an individualistic manner until plays are once again able to mirror the "form and pressure" of a cohesive culture.

Jerzy Grotowski, a Polish director, using his own system of nonnaturalistic acting, trains the members of his company in gymnastics, acrobatics, breathing, rhythmic dance, plastic action, concentration, mask composition, and pantomime. The actors use no makeup, but control their facial muscles to give the impression that they are wearing masks. Their gestures and movements are grotesque; their speech is a series of whispers, shouts, chants, grunts, sighs, and groans. They depend on the elements of primitive ritual: fascination, suggestion, magic words and signs. The actors perform in a room without a stage and completely surround the spectators, who very often are treated as characters in the play. The texts they use, including the classics, are cut or altered to suit their point of view and style of acting. Each actor plays many parts, regardless of age or sex, and the parts are interchangeable—Romeo becomes Juliet; and Juliet, Romeo. These techniques have produced unusual and exciting results.

The Living Theatre, the Open Theatre, and other modern companies have for a long time been using methods like Grotowski's to a similar end: as a process of self-discovery for both actor and audience. Such an aim is not surprising in view of the depersonalization of man in our society, which is reflected in the dehumanization of the theatricalist actor and in many of the characters which the realistic actor is now called on to portray. Depersonalization is largely responsible, too, for the prevalence of nudity and obscenity on the stage—shock treatments for audience and actor alike. It is impossible to predict what the acting of the future will be like, for as the aims and ideas of a culture change so do its art forms.

The Actors

The Stanislavsky method (described on page 356), aimed at preparing a performer to create dramatic characterizations of great realism and psychological truth; as Lee Strasberg, a celebrated teacher of the "method," explains it: "It does not give the actor rules, but tools." At present there are many variations of the Stanislavsky method in use, and no modern actor or teacher of acting ignores it completely, though some question its value. In combination with the photographic accuracy of costumes and settings, and many refinements in makeup and stage lighting, "internal" acting has produced the most realistic theatrical representation the stage has ever known. In America, this style of acting has superseded every other; at the present time, we cannot match the beautiful stylization of period acting which the British achieve nor the extraordinary mime and movement of the French. Acting is a plastic and evolving art. The realistic phase is as much of a convention as were the masks and robes of Greece.

Erwin Piscator and his disciple Bertolt Brecht were among those who rejected the realism of Stanislavsky. They adopted instead the methods of the younger

Russian directors Meyerhold and Tairov. Epic Theatre, in which these techniques were used, sought to create an "alienation effect," by constantly reminding the audience that it was watching a play and not reality.

Acting, as an occupation, seems so colorful and exciting that it attracts many young people who are under the impression that great and immediate financial rewards are to be gained in this field. Nothing could be further from the truth; according to the statistics of Actors' Equity Association, the trade union of the profession, the great majority of its members are totally unemployed in the theater; those who do get more or less regular work earn rather small annual salaries; while the comparatively few who achieve great fame earn the large salaries we read about. Stage employment has actually decreased sharply in recent years; many actors have turned to motion pictures, radio, and television in search of jobs. Recently, too, there has grown up in the entertainment world a cult of "personality" which requires a performer to possess highly individualistic talents or unusual physical characteristics, which are exploited in the manner of a commercial commodity. Still, no actor may hope to reach the highest levels of his art unless that art is founded on sound discipline and fostered by unswerving dedication.

The Costumes

In the twentieth century there have been three main types of costume: historical, contemporary, and theatricalist.

Designers of historical costumes strive for authenticity of silhouette, texture, and color. Before embarking on a project, the designer will study the records and pictures of the period in which he is interested in order to reproduce the clothing with a high degree of reality. The stage costume will not be identical to the real one; it will merely appear to be so. It may be necessary to make minor modifications in the structure of the clothing to enable the actor to move with greater ease or to speed the change from one costume to another; and certain materials, such as satin brocades, may be too expensive to buy or too difficult to handle, but the clever designer is able to treat a cheaper and lighter fabric in such a way as to create a luxurious impression. Properties and makeup are also designed with an eye for archeological accuracy.

Contemporary clothing is designed to create a realistic effect, but stage costumes are usually done more broadly than those ordinarily worn at home. This is necessary so that they will be visible from the stage; to achieve the desired effect the lines of the costume are exaggerated and certain elements are emphasized. Colors are frequently modified and cover larger areas; and fabrics are specially selected for ease of handling and to facilitate the movement of the actor. Modern clothes may heighten the actor's characterization, as in the case of Stanley Kowalski's torn shirt and Blanche DuBois's fluffy dresses, or intensify the mood and tone of the entire play, the effect created by the homespun clothing in *Desire Under the Elms* and by Claire Zachanassian's magnificent wardrobe, befitting the "richest woman in the world," in *The Visit*.

A rather recent development in stage costuming is the practice of calling in a

famous fashion designer, not ordinarily connected with the theater, to provide
the dresses for the wealthy heroine of the play. Mainbocher, Schiaparelli, Val-
entina, Castillo, and Dior are some of the couturiers whose gowns have been seen
on Broadway stages.

Theatricalist costumes are the stylized or fantastic creations used in non-
naturalistic plays. In Rostand's *Chanticleer,* for example, the characters are dressed
to resemble barnyard animals. Roger Furse combined historical and theatricalist
costumes in his production of *Macbeth;* the Scotsmen were attired in clothing
patterned on that actually worn in the period, while the witches were dressed in
fantastic creations. Many expressionist, constructivist, and theatricalist plays use
highly stylized costumes for the purpose of symbolism and allegory.

Scenery

Two leaders in the revolt against naturalistic settings were Gordon Craig and
Adolphe Appia. These influential theoreticians objected to papier-mâché buildings, painted canvas, and cluttered stages; they advocated instead the use of
simple platforms, screens, and draperies to which light—the unifying element—
would give mass, line, and color. It was a form of theatrical impressionism which,
when accompanied by music, would appeal primarily to the emotions. These ideas
strongly influenced such American designers as Robert Edmond Jones, Norman
Bel Geddes, Lee Simonson, and Jo Mielziner. In 1952 Sheldon Cheney wrote,
"Today the setting is flat, perspectiveless, simplified almost to bareness; surface
reality no longer is pictured, but only faintly suggested, the 'atmosphere' is caught
in color and light. Progress today seems all in the direction of space stages and
honestly architectural stages. Painting on the stage seems to have gone into almost
complete eclipse."

The newer styles in scene design, which include expressionism, constructivism,
and other forms of theatricalism, range from the sculptural and the architectural
to the symbolic, antirealistic, and fantastic; happenings and events, whether presented indoors or out, use more props than scenery, not arranged formally but as
if by chance.

Lighting

The creative lighting designer today is able, by a sensitive control of the intensity,
color, distribution, and movement of light, to achieve enormous plasticity, the
most subtle psychological effects, and the exact mood called for by each moment
of the play. Modern stage lighting has become so flexible and expressive that
changes in the level of the illumination may go unnoticed by the spectator and yet
intensify his emotional reactions to the performance. One advanced instrument
that makes such precise control possible is the electronic switchboard, which per-
mits the presetting of hundreds of light cues in the most complicated combinations.

A light-plot is a very important part of every modern production; scene by
scene throughout the play, it is a visual comment on the action. It is a part of the
stage manager's prompt-book, and the work plan for the stage electrician. There

are special light rehearsals, and for a complicated production several days may be consumed while the lighting designer refines the lighting, sets the instruments and the readings.

Lighting, like acting and scenery, may be naturalistic, symbolic, stylized, or theatricalist. Happenings, Events, and other forms of avant-garde theater, either because of their artistic principles or their limited budgets, have not made use of sophisticated lighting equipment but seem to favor general illumination or simple spotlighting; for their outdoor performances they only require, as did the ancient Greeks, the natural light of day.

Music and Dance

Incidental music may or may not be called for by the dramatist but it is specially composed to accompany the action and is intended to enhance the emotional impact of the play. Edvard Grieg's score for *Peer Gynt* and Alex North's for *Death of a Salesman* are examples of this type of musical accompaniment. Incidental music was used frequently in the theater, even in the present century, until the arrival of motion pictures, radio, and television, which adopted the practice of "sneaking-in" mood music behind the action in the manner of the nineteenth-century melodrama. At present, incidental music serves to indicate moments of unreality in realistic plays, or as accompaniment to nonnaturalistic drama.

Irrelevant music is still occasionally heard in contemporary theaters, where it serves as an overture to the play and as entertainment during intermissions; its use appears to be declining.

Nonnaturalistic drama leans much more heavily upon music and dance than does drama that attempts to create the illusion of reality. In *The Visit,* a mixed choir begins to sing an ancient folk song to greet Claire Zachanassian when she arrives in Güllen, but the voices are drowned out by a passing express train; this is a dramatic and symbolic use of music, as it foreshadows the fact that the voices of the townspeople will later be silenced when Claire demands the death of Anton. The Epic theater of Bertolt Brecht, the expressionism of Ernst Toller, and the theatricalism of the Habima make extensive use of choreographic movement that resembles dance, chanted speech that approaches song, and specially composed musical scores. These newer styles of production have had a noticeable influence on modern musical comedies and revues, which often contain allegorical and symbolic elements expressed in abstract movement and atonal music. Avant-garde drama has also introduced electronic music, sound effects, and dissonant sounds to accompany abstract movement and acrobatics, and has achieved stirring and startling effects.

Playwright and Audience

The average playgoer's increasing interest in sociology and psychology, which developed in the middle of the nineteenth century, was maintained into the twentieth; and naturalism, expressionism, and symbolism followed in regular order. Writers were allowed ever greater freedom to explore sexual themes and sordid situations, and many plays were frankly polemical and reformatory. Dramatized case histories of abnormal people vied with spectacular musical comedies for the attention of materialistic, cynical, and generally bored audiences.

In today's theater, realism is no longer considered adequate for an in-depth portrayal of the absurdity and meaninglessness of our lives. Various avant-garde styles—grouped under the heading of theatricalism and exemplified by the plays of Ionesco, Beckett, Genet, and of many younger more experimental writers—seem better able to reflect the volatile and fragmented nature of our culture. Serious playwrights have not fared as well in our day, be it noted, as have writers of comedies, farces, and musicals, which offer escape and relaxation to audiences suffering from the malaise and tensions of modern life.

Audience moods are reflected in theatergoing behavior and dress. Nowadays a relatively small number of people in each audience wear dinner jackets and evening gowns to the theater; the average playgoer appears in informal attire. John Chapman, the drama critic, complained bitterly in his columns because audiences were turning up at the theater in "drab business suits" instead of "dressing" for the occasion. For despite the high price of tickets and the difficulty of obtaining them, theatergoing is no longer considered an event, and turtlenecks and jeans are seen more often than formal attire.

The behavior of the average Broadway playgoer is reserved and subdued. There are few outbursts of enthusiasm and fewer of resentment; no riots have occurred because of artistic principles or personal partisanships in over a century. If displeased, audiences are inclined to be contemptuous rather than indignant. A very bad play will send them into fits of laughter; a very dull one will send them home.

Because of the current theater shortage, plays which are not immediate hits disappear quickly from the scene. This creates an abnormally heavy demand for tickets to popular plays. Immediately upon the announcement of a play that seems likely to be a success, though the opening date is months in the future, people send checks to the producers' offices with orders for seats. On the day after the opening of a play that has received good notices, long lines form at the box-office; tickets are bought three to six months in advance of the actual performance. Theatergoers also buy tickets at set fees above the box-office price from legal brokers, at high premiums through charitable organizations, and at exorbitant prices from speculators. There are preview clubs, play-of-the-month clubs, and other ticket-supplying organizations. Out-of-towners have all of these devices and several others at their disposal; they may buy tickets to plays through travel agencies as part of a tour of New York, or book passage on a show-train or show-plane which makes a special excursion from some distant city to Broadway, providing dinner, a play, and transportation in a neat little package.

In addition to Broadway audiences there are, in America, at least six other categories of playgoers for semiprofessional and amateur theaters: audiences who attend the many little theaters off-Broadway; audiences in the eighteen or twenty cities throughout the nation where commercial theater is presented more or less regularly during the year; audiences for summer and winter stock companies; community theater audiences; college and university theater audiences, a growing

(Left) Ben Gazzara as Brick and Barbara Bel Geddes as Maggie in the original production of the play at the Morosco Theater, New York, March 1955, directed by Elia Kazan and designed by Jo Mielziner. (New York Public Library at Lincoln Center) *(Right)* Elizabeth Taylor and Paul Newman in a scene from the 1958 film version, adapted and directed by Richard Brooks and produced by Metro-Goldwyn-Mayer. (Courtesy Metro-Goldwyn-Mayer)

and discriminating brotherhood; and finally, a very special and important group, juvenile audiences—the audience of the future. The Ticketron, a device installed in suburban agencies throughout the country, obtains instantaneous information, via telephone wires, on the availability of theater tickets in the region's major cities.

In every age, playwrights, playhouses, and productional arts have undergone notable transformations, and certainly will continue to do so; and twenty-five hundred years of experience offer a clear intimation that audiences will retain a strong predilection for drama on stage.

The Production Record

Cat on a Hot Tin Roof opened at the Morosco Theatre in New York on March 24, 1955, with Barbara Bel Geddes as Maggie, Ben Gazzara as Brick, Burl Ives as Big Daddy, and Mildred Dunnock as Big Mama; the play was directed by Elia Kazan, with scenery and lighting by Jo Mielziner, and costumes by Lucinda Ballard. The newspaper reviewers were unanimous in their praise, Brooks Atkinson going so far as to say *"Cat on a Hot Tin Roof* is Mr. Williams' finest drama." The play ran for 694 performances on Broadway, and an additional 268 performances on the road in the United States and Canada. It won for Tennessee Williams his second Pulitzer Prize and his third Drama Critics' Circle Award.

TENNESSEE WILLIAMS

Banned from the commercial theaters in London, the play was presented there in 1956 at the New Watergate Theatre Club, with the American actress Kim Stanley as Maggie, and Paul Massie as Brick. Londoners saw the third act as originally written and still preferred by Williams. The reviews were "mixed," one critic objecting to the violence in the work.

The screen rights were bought by MGM for Grace Kelly, but when the film was made Elizabeth Taylor was seen as Maggie, Paul Newman as Brick, Burl Ives in his original role as Big Daddy, and Judith Anderson as Big Mama. The screenplay was written by James Poe and Richard Brooks; Brooks directed, and removed all references to homosexuality from the film, which became the story of Brick growing up, "maturing," learning to face life and his conjugal responsibilities. This adaptation weakened and muddled the play, but the picture proved to be a "blockbuster" and earned more than ten million dollars. It had its premiere at the Radio City Music Hall, New York, in September, 1958.

Williams revised the third act once more, and made a number of other changes in the play, which was tried out at Stage West, in West Springfield, Massachusetts, in 1973. The following year, on July 10, 1974, the new version was presented by the American Shakespeare Theatre at Stratford, Connecticut, with Elizabeth Ashley as Maggie, Keir Dullea as Brick, Fred Gwynne as Big Daddy, and Kate Reid as Big Mama. With these players intact, the company moved to the ANTA Theatre in New York on September 24. Both 1974 productions were directed by Michael Kahn, with scenery by John Conklin, lighting by Marc B. Weiss, and costumes by Jane Greenwood. The reaction of the critics was highly favorable, with special praise for Elizabeth Ashley's acting and Michael Kahn's direction. Harold Clurman, in *The Nation*, called the play a hit, and added, "It has Williams' stage canniness and power, euphonious writing of American tang and humor."

Laurence Olivier had the idea of appearing in a play on television as a tribute to America in its bicentennial year. He approached Granada, a British television company, which, in conjunction with NBC, agreed to sponsor the production. The play Olivier selected was *Cat on a Hot Tin Roof*. Olivier would coproduce with Derek Granger and would himself play Big Daddy. He chose as his costars Natalie Wood and her husband Robert Wagner, for the roles of Maggie and Brick, and Maureen Stapleton for the part of Big Mama. Robert Moore was chosen as director. The program was aired, after an enormous amount of publicity, on NBC-TV, Monday evening, December 6, 1976, from 9 to 11 P.M. EST. In an interview with Rex Reed (*Sunday News*, 11/28/76), which was part of the build-up, Natalie Wood said, "It was a lucky break for us. . . . We rehearsed for four weeks in London, blocked it just like a play, we could have gone on stage and played it. The whole thing was taped in nine days." The Wagners said that they had played southerners before, so the accent was no problem; and speaking of Olivier, they commented, "He chose not to do any suggestion of Burl Ives. He didn't play up the bigness of Big Daddy. His power as an actor does all of that. He took his direction just like everyone else and never interfered with Bob Moore's staging. It was probably the best working experience we've ever had." The critics, however, called it a disappointing and embarrassing production not only because the script had been cut and bungled—it was done in six scenes with many commercial interruptions—but because it was completely miscast, despite the expertise of the performers. Olivier played Big Daddy as though he were a gentleman farmer instead of the Mississippi redneck Williams calls for; Natalie Wood acted like a high-born lady; and Robert Wagner's performance was too low-key and listless; only Maureen Stapleton, who made Big Mama believable, won praise for her work. What the critics thought of the production that was to serve as a British tribute to America may be judged by the titles of two of the reviews: "A Dish of Southern Fried Turkey" (*The Observer*, London), and "Turkey on a Hot Tin Roof" (*The Village Voice*, New York).

Cat on a Hot Tin Roof has been produced in Germany, France, England, Portugal, Japan, and in many other countries, to great acclaim as well as to bitter criticism. It has been performed innumerable times by college groups and community theaters in the United States. In the summer of 1977, for instance, a group of dedicated young people, who call themselves the Throgs Neck Community Players, put on a spirited and creditable production of the play in a hospital auditorium located in the outer reaches of the Bronx!

THE WORLD I LIVE IN
Tennessee Williams Interviews Himself *

Question. Can we talk frankly?
Answer. There's no other way we can talk.
Q. Perhaps you know that when your first successful play, *The Glass Menagerie*, was revived early this season, a majority of the reviewers felt that it was still the best play you have written, although it is now twelve years old?
A. Yes, I read all my play notices and criticisms, even those that say that I write for money and that my primary appeal is to brutal and ugly instincts.
Q. Where there is so much smoke—!
A. A fire smokes the most when you start pouring water on it.
Q. But surely you'll admit that there's been a disturbing note of harshness and coldness and violence and anger in your more recent works?
A. I think, without planning to do so, I have followed the developing tension and anger and violence of the world and time that I live in through my own steadily increasing tension as a writer and person.
Q. Then you admit that this "developing tension," as you call it, is a reflection of a condition in yourself?
A. Yes.
Q. A morbid condition?
A. Yes.
Q. Perhaps verging on the psychotic?
A. I guess my work has always been a kind of psychotherapy for me.

* *The Observer*, London, April 7, 1957. Reprinted by permission.

Q. But how can you expect audiences to be impressed by plays and other writings
  that are created as a release for the tensions of a possible or incipient madman?

A. It releases their own.

Q. Their own what?

A. Increasing tensions, verging on the psychotic.

Q. You think the world's going mad?

A. Going? I'd say nearly gone! As the Gipsy said in *Camino Real,* the world is a
  funny paper read backwards. And that way it isn't so funny.

Q. How far do you think you can go with this tortured view of the world?

A. As far as the world can go in its tortured condition, maybe that far, but no
  further.

Q. You don't expect audiences and critics to go along with you, do you?

A. No.

Q. Then why do you push and pull them that way?

A. I go that way. I don't push or pull anyone with me.

Q. Yes, but you hope to continue to have people listen to you, don't you?

A. Naturally I hope to.

Q. Even if you throw them off by the violence and horror of your works?

A. Haven't you noticed that people are dropping all around you, like moths out
  of season, as the result of the present plague of violence and horror in this
  world and time that we live in?

Q. But you're an entertainer, with artistic pretensions, and people are not entertained any more by cats on hot tin roofs and Baby Dolls and passengers on
  crazy streetcars!

A. Then let them go to the musicals and the comedies. I'm not going to change
  my ways. It's hard enough for me to write what I want to write without me
  trying to write what you say they want me to write which I don't want to
  write.

Q. Do you have any positive message, in your opinion?

A. Indeed I do think that I do.

Q. Such as what?

A. The crying, almost screaming, need of a great worldwide human effort to know
  ourselves and each other a great deal better, well enough to concede that no
  man has a monopoly on right or virtue any more than any man has a corner
  on duplicity and evil and so forth. If people, and races and nations, would
  start with that self-manifest truth, then I think that the world could sidestep
  the sort of corruption which I have involuntarily chosen as the basic, allegorical theme of my plays as a whole.

Q. You sound as if you felt quite detached and superior to this process of corruption in society.

A. I have never written about any kind of vice which I can't observe in myself.

Q. But you accuse society, as a whole, of succumbing to a deliberate mendacity,
  and you appear to find yourself separate from it as a writer.

A. As a writer, yes, but not as a person.

Q. Do you think this is a peculiar virtue of yours as a writer?

A. I'm not sentimental about writers. But I'm inclined to think that most writers, and most other artists, too, are primarily motivated in their desperate vocation by a desire to find and to separate truth from the complex of lies and evasions they live in, and I think that this impulse is what makes their work not so much a profession as a vocation, a true "calling."

Q. Why don't you write about nice people? Haven't you ever known any nice people in your life?

A. My theory about nice people is so simple that I am embarrassed to say it.

Q. Please say it!

A. Well, I've never met one that I couldn't love if I completely knew him and understood him, and in my work I have at least tried to arrive at knowledge and understanding.

I don't believe in "original sin." I don't believe in "guilt." I don't believe in villains or heroes—only in right or wrong ways that individuals have taken, not by choice but by necessity or by certain still-uncomprehended influences in themselves, their circumstances and their antecedents.

This is so simple I'm ashamed to say it, but I'm sure it's true. In fact, I would bet my life on it! And that's why I don't understand why our propaganda machines are always trying to teach us, to persuade us, to hate and fear other people on the same little world that we live in.

Why don't we meet these people and get to know them as I try to meet and know people in my plays? This sounds terribly vain and egotistical.

I don't want to end on such a note. Then what shall I say? That I know that I am a minor artist who has happened to write one or two major works? I can't even say which they are. It doesn't matter. I have said my say. I may still say it again, or I may shut up now. It doesn't depend on you, it depends entirely on me, and the operation of chance or Providence in my life.

(The interview ends.)

DIRECTING *Cat on a Hot Tin Roof*

An Interview with Michael Kahn

In 1973, Michael Kahn, then the Artistic Director of the American Shakespeare Theatre in Stratford, Connecticut, was seeking a play by a major American writer; he was particularly interested in directing a realistic work of some stature and significance. His choice fell on *Cat on a Hot Tin Roof*, but when he sought permission to do the play he was informed that it was not then available for production. Several months later, however, Kahn got a call from Tennessee Williams' agent, who granted him the right to mount the work.

"What attracted me to *Cat* in the first place," Kahn said, "was that I felt that the play contained a metaphor for America. The conflict in the family seemed to be a microcosm of what was going on in the country at that time, post-Watergate:

Donna Donaldson and John Fox in the Throgs Neck Community Players production, in the auditorium of Jacobi Hospital, Bronx, N.Y., August 1977. (Aidala)

the struggle for power, the uncertain sexuality, the lies, and the cover-ups. In addition to that, the dialogue is a beautiful example of poetic realism because Tennessee is a poet as well as a playwright. And the play has an epic quality; the characters are larger than life—*Big* Daddy, *Big* Mama, Maggie the Cat, and Brick —all epic figures.

"How was I to deal with this play in 1974? In 1955, when it was done for the first time, it was considered a shocker. It achieved a great deal of notoriety. The Elephant Story was banned by the censor, and the audience expected to be titillated. Kazan, who is one of my idols, concentrated on sex and violence, but I feel that the play contains other themes which are equally, if not more, important.

Elizabeth Ashley and Keir Dullea in the American Shakespeare Theatre production at Stratford, Connecticut, July 1974, and at the ANTA Theater, New York, in September of the same year. Both productions were directed by Michael Kahn. (Martha Swope)

Mendacity, for one thing, truth-telling, and greed, these ideas concern us deeply today and should be stressed. Lillian Hellman dealt with them in *The Little Foxes*, I put a special emphasis on them, and I believe they came through.

"The original production was more stylized than mine, at least insofar as the set was concerned. Jo Mielziner, Kazan's designer, created a platform on which the bed was the object of central importance; I wanted more furnishings in the room in order to heighten the sense of reality, and to provide objects for Maggie to move among as she delivered her aria-like monologues.

"My casting also differed greatly from Kazan's, though I understand what he was aiming at. Ben Gazzara, the original Brick, was a macho type, and Barbara Bel Geddes, who played Maggie, was sweet and wholesome. Mildred Dunnock, a slight, delicate woman, seemed to me to be totally miscast as Big Mama, but Burl Ives was perfect as Big Daddy. In fact, he made such a deep impression upon me that I could hardly get him out of my mind. But I cast the play in line with my own conception of the characters. I wanted a Maggie who was not only physically attractive but also passionate by nature, and shrewd. I was lucky to find in Elizabeth Ashley an actress who could project all of those qualities. Ashley is a Southern woman, and Southern actresses play Southern women best. They have the remarkable ability to fight and flirt at the same time.

"My choice of Keir Dullea, for Brick, aroused a great deal of controversy, as he projects a rather aesthetic image. But I thought the usual stud version of the character—played by strong, muscular actors—was wrong. Brick, in my view, is extremely sensitive and, as Maggie says, is 'a weak, beautiful' person. Brick is suffering from what I call homosexual panic, and Dullea, through his own masculinity, was able to project the sensitive, hysterical qualities of Brick.

"Fred Gwynne was a member of the acting company at Stratford but I could not at first envision him in the role of Big Daddy. The image of a Big Daddy, as obese as Burl Ives, lingered in my mind; and it seemed as if I would not be able to erase it. But after much persuasion from other members of the company, who were urging me to use Fred, I took time out to think the problem through. Big Daddy was dying of cancer, and the memory of my mother, who had died of that wasting disease, came into my mind; at the last she was painfully thin, emaciated. So there was no reason why Big Daddy had to be corpulent. And there was Fred Gwynne, a fine actor, extremely tall and rather gaunt, and really a much more believable physical specimen as a terminal case than a fat man would be. So I finally got over my Burl Ives 'hangup' and chose Gwynne.

"The role of Big Mama is so written as to suggest a female rhinoceros; the part is a mixture of comedy and pathos, as the woman is vulgar, overstuffed, and overdressed, yet at the same time deeply devoted and loyal to Big Daddy. Kate Reid's performance was excellent, and Tennessee liked it very much.

"He came to several rehearsals and approved of some of the 'ad libs' the members of the cast had put in, and of some of my suggestions. In the script, for example, Doctor Baugh leaves the morphine for Big Daddy on a table, and no further mention is made of it. I had the Doctor hand the package to Maggie and, later, had Big Mama come in for it, in order to show that she had finally accepted the idea of administering sedation to Big Daddy. Tennessee allowed the change."

Tennessee Williams had said that the two modern playwrights whose work has impressed him most are Strindberg and Chekhov. Kahn was asked if he saw any indication of the influence of those writers on *Cat on a Hot Tin Roof*. He replied, "The play is Strindbergian in that it deals with the conflict between men and women and the hell it becomes, and also because of the obsessive nature of the characters. It is Chekhovian in mood and setting, and in the poetic quality of its language. I consider Williams as great a playwright as Strindberg or Chekhov, and I think that his work will last as long as theirs.

"I feel that my special contribution to *Cat* was to balance the themes of mendacity, greed, and sex, and to arrive at an equation of thought and emotion that is right for our time. At any rate, people seemed to think it was a better play the second time around. It certainly was one of the most satisfying experiences I have ever had in the theater, and is a production I am very proud of."

Cat on a Hot Tin Roof

And you, my father, there on the sad height,
Curse, bless, me now with your fierce tears, I pray.
Do not go gentle into that good night.
Rage, rage against the dying of the light!

DYLAN THOMAS

Cat on a Hot Tin Roof was first presented by the Playwrights' Company at the Morosco Theatre, New York City, on March 24, 1955, with the following cast:

MARGARET	*Barbara Bel Geddes*
BRICK	*Ben Gazzara*
BIG MAMA	*Mildred Dunnock*
BIG DADDY	*Burl Ives*
MAE, sometimes called Sister Woman	*Madeleine Sherwood*
GOOPER, sometimes called Brother Man	*Pat Hingle*
REVEREND TOOKER	*Fred Stewart*
DOCTOR BAUGH, pronounced "Baw"	*R. G. Armstrong*
LACEY,* a servant	*Maxwell Glanville*
SOOKEY, another	*Musa Williams*
CHILDREN	*Pauline Hahn, Darryl Richard, Seth Edwards, Janice Dunn*
FIELD-HANDS*	*Eva Vaughan Smith, Sonny Terry, Brownie McGhee*

* These parts were eliminated in later productions.

Staged by Elia Kazan, setting and lighting by Jo Mielziner, costumes by Lucinda Ballard.

NOTES FOR THE DESIGNER

The set is the bed-sitting-room of a plantation home in the Mississippi Delta. It is along an upstairs gallery which probably runs around the entire house; it has two pairs of very wide doors opening onto the gallery, showing white balustrades against a fair summer sky that fades into dusk and night during the course of the play, which occupies precisely the time of its performance, excepting, of course, the fifteen minutes of intermission.

Perhaps the style of the room is not what you would expect in the home of the Delta's biggest cotton-planter. It is Victorian with a touch of the Far East. It hasn't changed much since it was occupied by the original owners of the place, Jack Straw and Peter Ochello, a pair of old bachelors who shared this room all their lives together. In other words, the room must evoke some ghosts; it is gently and poetically haunted by a relationship that must have involved a tenderness which was uncommon. This may be irrelevant or unnecessary, but I once saw a reproduction of a faded photograph of the verandah of Robert Louis Stevenson's home on that Samoan island where he spent his last years, and there was a quality of tender light on weathered wood, such as porch furniture made of bamboo and wicker, exposed to tropical suns and tropical rains, which came to mind when I thought about the set for this play, bringing also to mind the grace and comfort of light, the reassurance it gives, on a late and fair afternoon in summer, the way that no matter what, even dread of death, is gently touched and soothed by it. For the set is the background for a play that deals with human extremities of emotion, and it needs that softness behind it.

The bathroom door, showing only pale-blue tile and silver towel racks, is in one side wall; the hall door in the opposite wall. Two articles of furniture need mention: a big double bed which staging should make a functional part of the set as often as suitable, the surface of which should be slightly raked to make figures on it seen more easily; and against the wall space between the two huge double doors upstage: a monumental monstrosity peculiar to our times, a *huge* console combination of radio-phonograph (hi-fi with three speakers), TV set *and* liquor cabinet, bearing and containing many glasses and bottles, all in one piece, which is a composition of muted silver tones, and the opalescent tones of reflecting glass, a chromatic link, this thing, between the sepia (tawny gold) tones of the interior and the cool (white and blue) tones of the gallery and sky. This piece of furniture (?!), this monument, is a very complete and compact little shrine to virtually all the comforts and illusions behind which we hide from such things as the characters in the play are faced with. . . .

The set should be far less realistic than I have so far implied in this description of it. I think the walls below the ceiling should dissolve mysteriously into air; the set should be roofed by the sky; stars and moon suggested by traces of milky pallor, as if they were observed through a telescope lens out of focus.

Anything else I can think of? Oh, yes, fanlights (transoms shaped like an open glass fan) above all the doors in the set, with panes of blue and amber, and above all, the designer should take as many pains

to give the actors room to move about freely (to show their restless-
ness, their passion for breaking out) as if it were a set for a ballet.

An evening in summer. The action is continuous, with two intermissions.

ACT ONE

*At the rise of the curtain someone is taking a shower in the
bathroom, the door of which is half open. A pretty young woman,
with anxious lines in her face, enters the bedroom and crosses to
the bathroom door.*

Margaret (*Shouting above roar of
water*). One of those no-neck monsters hit me with a hot buttered bis-
cuit so I have t' change!

(MARGARET's *voice is both rapid and
drawling. In her long speeches she
has the vocal tricks of a priest delivering a liturgical chant, the lines are
almost sung, always continuing a little beyond her breath so she has to
gasp for another. Sometimes she in-
tersperses the lines with a little
wordless singing, such as "Da-da-
daaaa!"*)
(*Water turns off and* BRICK *calls out
to her, but is still unseen. A tone of
politely feigned interest, masking indifference, or worse, is characteristic
of his speech with* MARGARET.)
Brick. Wha'd you say, Maggie? Water
was on s' loud I couldn't hearya. . . .
Margaret. Well, I!—just remarked that!
—one of th' no-neck monsters messed
up m' lovely lace dress so I got t'—
cha-a-ange. . . .

(*She opens and kicks shut drawers of
the dresser.*)
Brick. Why d'ya call Gooper's kiddies
no-neck monsters?
Margaret. Because they've got no necks!
Isn't that a good enough reason?
Brick. Don't they have any necks?
Margaret. None visible. Their fat little

heads are set on their fat little bodies
without a bit of connection.
Brick. That's too bad.
Margaret. Yes, it's too bad because you
can't wring their necks if they've got
no necks to wring! Isn't that right,
honey?

(*She steps out of her dress, stands in
a slip of ivory satin and lace.*)

Yep, they're no-neck monsters, all
no-neck people are monsters . . .

(CHILDREN *shriek downstairs.*)

Hear them? Hear them screaming? I
don't know where their voice boxes
are located since they don't have
necks. I tell you I got so nervous at
that table tonight I thought I would
throw back my head and utter a
scream you could hear across the Ar-
kansas border an' parts of Louisiana
an' Tennessee. I said to your charming sister-in-law, Mae, honey,
couldn't you feed those precious little
things at a separate table with an oil-
cloth cover? They make such a mess
an' the lace cloth looks *so* pretty! She
made enormous eyes at me and said,
"Ohhh, noooooo! On Big Daddy's
birthday? Why, he would never forgive me!" Well, I want you to know,
Big Daddy hadn't been at the table
two minutes with those five no-neck

monsters slobbering and drooling over their food before he threw down his fork an' shouted, "Fo' God's sake, Gooper, why don't you put them pigs at a trough in th' kitchen?" —Well, I swear, I simply could have di-ieed!

Think of it, Brick, they've got five of them and number six is coming. They've brought the whole bunch down here like animals to display at a county fair. Why, they have those children doin' tricks all the time! "Junior, show Big Daddy how you do this, show Big Daddy how you do that, say your little piece fo' Big Daddy, Sister. Show your dimples, Sugar. Brother, show Big Daddy how you stand on your head!"—It goes on all the time, along with constant little remarks and innuendos about the fact that you and I have not produced any children, are totally childless and therefore totally useless!—Of course it's comical but it's also disgusting since it's so obvious what they're up to!

Brick (Without interest). What are they up to, Maggie?
Margaret. Why, you know what they're up to!
Brick (Appearing). No, I don't know what they're up to.

(*He stands there in the bathroom doorway drying his hair with a towel and hanging onto the towel rack because one ankle is broken, plastered and bound. He is still slim and firm as a boy. His liquor hasn't started tearing him down outside. He has the additional charm of that cool air of detachment that people have who have given up the struggle. But now*

and then, when disturbed, something flashes behind it, light lightning in a fair sky, which shows that at some deeper level he is far from peaceful. Perhaps in a stronger light he would show some signs of deliquescence, but the fading, still warm, light from the gallery treats him gently.)

Margaret. I'll tell you what they're up to, boy of mine!—They're up to cutting you out of your father's estate, and—

(*She freezes momentarily before her next remark. Her voice drops as if it were somehow a personally embarrassing admission.*)

—Now we know that Big Daddy's dyin' of—*cancer.* . . .

(*There are voices on the lawn below: long-drawn calls across distance.* MARGARET *raises her lovely bare arms and powders her armpits with a light sigh.*

(*She adjusts the angle of a magnifying mirror to straighten an eyelash, then rises fretfully saying:*)

There's so much light in the room it—
Brick (Softly but sharply). Do we?
Margaret. Do we what?
Brick. Know Big Daddy's dyin' of cancer?
Margaret. Got the report today.
Brick. Oh . . .
Margaret (Letting down bamboo blinds which cast long, gold-fretted shadows over the room). Yep, got th' report just now . . . it didn't surprise me, Baby. . . .

(*Her voice has range, and music; sometimes it drops low as a boy's and you have a sudden image of her playing boy's games as a child.*)

I recognized the symptoms soon's we got here last spring and I'm willin' to bet you that Brother Man and his wife were pretty sure of it, too. That more than likely explains why their usual summer migration to the coolness of the Great Smokies was passed up this summer in favor of—hustlin' down here ev'ry whipstitch with their whole screamin' tribe! And why so many allusions have been made to Rainbow Hill lately. You know what Rainbow Hill is? Place that's famous for treatin' alcoholics an' dope fiends in the movies!

Brick. I'm not in the movies.

Margaret. No, and you don't take dope. Otherwise you're a perfect candidate for Rainbow Hill, Baby, and that's where they aim to ship you—over my dead body! Yep, over my dead body they'll ship you there, but nothing would please them better. Then Brother Man could get a-hold of the purse strings and dole out remittances to us, maybe get power of attorney and sign checks for us and cut off our credit wherever, whenever he wanted! Son-of-a-bitch!—How'd you like that, Baby?—Well, you've been doin' just about ev'rything in your power to bring it about, you've just been doin' ev'rything you can think of to aid and abet them in this scheme of theirs! Quittin' work, devoting yourself to the occupation of drinkin'!—Breakin' your ankle last night on the high school athletic field: doin' what? Jumpin' hurdles? At two or three in the morning? Just fantastic! Got in the paper. *Clarksdale Register* carried a nice little item about it, human interest story about a well-known former athlete stagin' a one-man track meet on the

Glorious Hill High School athletic field last night, but was slightly out of condition and didn't clear the first hurdle! Brother Man Gooper claims he exercised his influence t' keep it from goin' out over AP or UP or every goddam "P."

But, Brick? You still have one big advantage!

(*During the above swift flood of words,* BRICK *has reclined with contrapuntal leisure on the snowy surface of the bed and has rolled over carefully on his side or belly.*)

Brick (*Wryly*). Did you *say* something, Maggie?

Margaret. Big Daddy dotes on you, honey. And he can't stand Brother Man and Brother Man's wife, that monster of fertility, Mae. Know how I know? By little expressions that flicker over his face when that woman is holding fo'th on one of her choice topics such as—how she refused twilight sleep!—when the twins were delivered! Because she feels motherhood's an experience that a woman ought to experience fully!—in order to fully appreciate the wonder and beauty of it! HAH!—and how she made Brother Man come in an' stand beside her in the delivery room so he would not miss out on the "wonder and beauty" of it either!—producin' those no-neck monsters. . . .

(*A speech of this kind would be antipathetic from almost anybody but* MARGARET; *she makes it oddly funny, because her eyes constantly twinkle and her voice shakes with laughter which is basically indulgent.*)

—Big Daddy shares my attitude toward those two! As for me, well—I give him a laugh now and then and he tolerates me. In fact!—I sometimes suspect that Big Daddy harbors a little unconscious "lech" fo' me. . . .

Brick. What makes you think that Big Daddy has a lech for you, Maggie?

Margaret. Way he always drops his eyes down my body when I'm talkin' to him, drops his eyes to my boobs an' licks his old chops! Ha ha!

Brick. That kind of talk is disgusting.

Margaret. Did anyone ever tell you that you're an ass-aching Puritan, Brick?

I think it's mighty fine that that ole fellow, on the doorstep of death, still takes in my shape with what I think is deserved appreciation!

And you wanta know something else? Big Daddy didn't know how many little Maes and Goopers had been produced! "How many kids have you got?" he asked at the table, just like Brother Man and his wife were new acquaintances to him! Big Mama said he was jokin', but that ole boy wasn't jokin'. Lord, no!

And when they infawmed him that they had five already and were turning out number six!—the news seemed to come as a sort of unpleasant surprise . . .

(CHILDREN yell below.)

Scream, monsters!

(Turns to BRICK with a sudden gay, charming smile which fades as she notices that he is not looking at her but into fading gold space with a troubled expression.)

(It is constant rejection that makes her humor "bitchy.")

Yes, you should of been at that supper-table, Baby.

(Whenever she calls him "baby" the word is a soft caress.)

Y'know, Big Daddy, bless his ole sweet soul, he's the dearest ole thing in the world, but he does hunch over his food as if he preferred not to notice anything else. Well, Mae an' Gooper were side by side at the table, direckly across from Big Daddy, watchin' his face like hawks while they jawed an' jabbered about the cuteness an' brilliance of th' no-neck monsters!

(She giggles with a hand fluttering at her throat and her breast and her long throat arched.)

(She comes downstage and recreates the scene with voice and gesture.)

And the no-neck monsters were ranged around the table, some in high chairs and some on th' Books of Knowledge, all in fancy little paper caps in honor of Big Daddy's birthday, and all through dinner, well, I want you to know that Brother Man an' his partner never once, for one moment, stopped exchanging pokes an' pinches an' kicks an' signs an' signals!—Why, they were like a couple of cardsharps fleecing a sucker.— Even Big Mama, bless her ole sweet soul, she isn't th' quickest an' brightest thing in the world, she finally noticed, at last, an' said to Gooper, "Gooper, what are you an' Mae makin' all these signs at each other about?"—I swear t' goodness, I nearly choked on my chicken!

(MARGARET, back at the dressing table, still doesn't see BRICK. He is *watching her with a look that is not quite definable—Amused? shocked? contemptuous?—part of those and part of something else.*)

Y'know—your brother Gooper still cherishes the illusion he took a giant step up on the social ladder when he married Miss Mae Flynn of the Memphis Flynns.

But I have a piece of Spanish news for Gooper. The Flynns never had a thing in this world but money and they lost that, they were nothing at all but fairly successful climbers. Of course, Mae Flynn came out in Memphis eight years before I made my debut in Nashville, but I had friends at Ward-Belmont who came from Memphis and they used to come to see me and I used to go to see them for Christmas and spring vacations, and so I know who rates an' who doesn't rate in Memphis society. Why, y'know ole Papa Flynn, he barely escaped doing time in the Federal pen for shady manipulations on th' stock market when his chain stores crashed, and as for Mae having been a cotton carnival queen, as they remind us so often, lest we forget, well, that's one honor that I don't envy her for!—Sit on a brass throne on a tacky float an' ride down Main Street, smilin', bowin', and blowin' kisses to all the trash on the street—

(*She picks out a pair of jeweled sandals and rushes to the dressing table.*)

Why, year before last, when Susan McPheeters was singled out fo' that honor, y' know what happened to her? Y'know what happened to poor little Susie McPheeters?

Brick (*Absently*). No. What happened to little Susie McPheeters?

Margaret. Somebody spit tobacco juice in her face.

Brick (*Dreamily*). Somebody spit tobacco juice in her face?

Margaret. That's right, some old drunk leaned out of a window in the Hotel Gayoso and yelled, "Hey, Queen, hey, hey, there, Queenie!" Poor Susie looked up and flashed him a radiant smile and he shot out a squirt of tobacco juice right in poor Susie's face.

Brick. Well, what d'you know about that.

Margaret (*Gaily*). What do I know about it? I was there, I saw it!

Brick (*Absently*). Must have been kind of funny.

Margaret. Susie didn't think so. Had hysterics. Screamed like a banshee. They had to stop th' parade an' remove her from her throne an' go on with—

(*She catches sight of him in the mirror, gasps slightly, wheels about to face him. Count ten.*)

—Why are you looking at me like that?

Brick (*Whistling softly, now*). Like what, Maggie?

Margaret (*Intensely, fearfully*). The way y' were lookin' at me just now, befo' I caught your eye in the mirror and you started t' whistle! I don't know how t' describe it but it froze my blood!—I've caught you lookin' at me like that so often lately. What are you thinkin' of when you look at me like that?

Brick. I wasn't conscious of lookin' at you, Maggie.

Margaret. Well, I was conscious of it! What were you thinkin'?

Brick. I don't remember thinking of anything, Maggie.

Margaret. Don't you think I know that—? Don't you—?—Think I know that—?

Brick (*Coolly*). Know *what*, Maggie?

Margaret (*Struggling for expression*). That I've gone through this—hideous!—*transformation*, become—hard! Frantic!

(*Then she adds, almost tenderly:*)

—cruel! !

That's what you've been observing in me lately. How could y' help but observe it? That's all right. I'm not—thin-skinned any more, can't afford t' be thin-skinned any more.

(*She is now recovering her power.*)

—But Brick? Brick?

Brick. Did you say something?

Margaret. I was *goin'* t' say something: that I get—lonely. Very!

Brick. Ev'rybody gets that . . .

Margaret. Living with someone you love can be lonelier—than living entirely *alone!*—if the one that y' love doesn't love you. . . .

(*There is a pause.* BRICK *hobbles downstage and asks, without looking at her:*)

Brick. Would you like to live alone, Maggie?

(*Another pause: then—after she has caught a quick, hurt breath:*)

Margaret. No!—God!—I wouldn't!

(*Another gasping breath. She forcibly controls what must have been an impulse to cry out. We see her deliberately, very forcibly, going all the way back to the world in which you can talk about ordinary matters.*)

Did you have a nice shower?

Brick. Uh-huh.

Margaret. Was the water cool?

Brick. No.

Margaret. But it made y' feel fresh, huh?

Brick. Fresher. . . .

Margaret. I know something would make y' feel *much* fresher!

Brick. What?

Margaret. An alcohol rub. Or cologne, a rub with cologne!

Brick. That's good after a workout but I haven't been workin' out, Maggie.

Margaret. You've kept in good shape, though.

Brick (*Indifferently*). You think so, Maggie?

Margaret. I always thought drinkin' men lost their looks, but I was plainly mistaken.

Brick (*Wryly*). Why, thanks, Maggie.

Margaret. You're the only drinkin' man I know that it never seems t' put fat on.

Brick. I'm gettin' softer, Maggie.

Margaret. Well, sooner or later it's bound to soften you up. It was just beginning to soften up Skipper when—

(*She stops short.*)

I'm sorry. I never could keep my fingers off a sore—I wish you *would* lose your looks. If you did it would make the martyrdom of Saint Maggie a little more bearable. But no such goddam luck. I actually believe you've gotten better looking since you've gone on the bottle. Yeah, a person who didn't know you would think you'd never had a tense nerve in your body or a strained muscle.

(*There are sounds of croquet on the lawn below: the click of mallets, light voices, near and distant.*)

Of course, you always had that detached quality as if you were playing a game without much concern over whether you won or lost, and now that you've lost the game, not lost but just quit playing, you have that rare sort of charm that usually only happens in very old or hopelessly sick people, the charm of the defeated.—You look so cool, so cool, so enviably cool.

Reverend Tooker (*Off stage right*). Now looka here, boy, lemme show you how to get outa that!

Margaret. They're playing croquet. The moon has appeared and it's white, just beginning to turn a little bit yellow. . . .

You were a wonderful lover. . . .

Such a wonderful person to go to bed with, and I think mostly because you were really indifferent to it. Isn't that right? Never had any anxiety about it, did it naturally, easily, slowly, with absolute confidence and perfect calm, more like opening a door for a lady or seating her at a table than giving expression to any longing for her. Your indifference made you wonderful at lovemaking —*strange?*—but true. . . .

Reverend Tooker. Oh! That's a beauty.

Doctor Baugh. Yeah. I got you boxed.

Margaret. You know, if I thought you would never, never, *never* make love to me again—I would go downstairs to the kitchen and pick out the longest and sharpest knife I could find and stick it straight into my heart, I swear that I would!

Reverend Tooker. Watch out, you're gonna miss it.

Doctor Baugh. You just don't know me, boy!

Margaret. But one thing I don't have is

the charm of the defeated, my hat is still in the ring, and I am determined to win!

(*There is the sound of croquet mallets hitting croquet balls.*)

Reverend Tooker. Mmm—You're too slippery for me.

Margaret. —What is the victory of a cat on a hot tin roof?—I wish I knew. . . .

Just staying on it, I guess, as long as she can. . . .

Doctor Baugh. Jus' like an eel, boy, jus' like an eel!

(*More croquet sounds.*)

Margaret. Later tonight I'm going to tell you I love you an' maybe by that time you'll be drunk enough to believe me. Yes, they're playing croquet. . . .

Big Daddy is dying of cancer. . . .

What were you thinking of when I caught you looking at me like that? Were you thinking of Skipper?

(BRICK *takes up his crutch, rises.*)

Oh, excuse me, forgive me, but laws of silence don't work! No, laws of silence don't work. . . .

(BRICK *crosses to the bar, takes a quick drink, and rubs his head with a towel.*)

Laws of silence don't work. . . .

When something is festering in your memory or your imagination, laws of silence don't work, it's just like shutting a door and locking it on a house on fire in hope of forgetting that the house is burning. But not facing a fire doesn't put it out. Silence about a thing just magnifies it. It grows and festers in silence, becomes malignant. . . .

(*He drops his crutch.*)

Brick. Give me my crutch.

(*He has stopped rubbing his hair dry but still stands hanging onto the towel rack in a white towel-cloth robe.*)

Margaret. Lean on me.
Brick. No, just give me my crutch.
Margaret. Lean on my shoulder.
Brick. *I don't want to lean on your shoulder, I want my crutch!*

(*This is spoken like sudden lightning.*)

Are you going to give me my crutch or do I have to get down on my knees on the floor and—
Margaret. *Here, here, take it, take it!*

(*She has thrust the crutch at him.*)

Brick (*Hobbling out*). Thanks . . .
Margaret. We mustn't scream at each other, the walls in this house have ears. . . .

(*He hobbles directly to liquor cabinet to get a new drink.*)

—but that's the first time I've heard you raise your voice in a long time, Brick. A crack in the wall?—Of composure?

—I think that's a good sign. . . .

A sign of nerves in a player on the defensive!

(BRICK *turns and smiles at her coolly over his fresh drink.*)

Brick. It just hasn't happened yet, Maggie.
Margaret. What?
Brick. The click I get in my head when

I've had enough of this stuff to make me peaceful. . . .

Will you do me a favor?
Margaret. Maybe I will. What favor?
Brick. Just, just keep your voice down!
Margaret (*In a hoarse whisper*). I'll do you that favor, I'll speak in a whisper, if not shut up completely, if *you* will do *me* a favor and make that drink your last one till after the party.
Brick. What party?
Margaret. Big Daddy's birthday party.
Brick. Is this Big Daddy's birthday?
Margaret. You know this is Big Daddy's birthday!
Brick. No, I don't, I forgot it.
Margaret. Well, I remembered it for you. . . .

(*They are both speaking as breathlessly as a pair of kids after a fight, drawing deep exhausted breaths and looking at each other with faraway eyes, shaking and panting together as if they had broken apart from a violent struggle.*)

Brick. Good for you, Maggie.
Margaret. You just have to scribble a few lines on this card.
Brick. You scribble something, Maggie.
Margaret. It's got to be your handwriting; it's your present, I've given him my present; it's got to be your handwriting!

(*The tension between them is building again, the voices becoming shrill once more.*)

Brick. I didn't get him a present.
Margaret. I got one for you.
Brick. All right. You write the card, then.
Margaret. And have him know you didn't remember his birthday?
Brick. I didn't remember his birthday.

Margaret. You don't have to prove you didn't!

Brick. I don't want to fool him about it.

Margaret. Just write "Love, Brick!" for God's—

Brick. No.

Margaret. You've *got* to!

Brick. I don't have to do anything I don't want to do. You keep forgetting the conditions on which I agreed to stay on living with you.

Margaret (Out before she knows it). I'm not living with you. We occupy the same cage.

Brick. You've got to remember the conditions agreed on.

Sonny (Off stage). Mommy, give it to me. I had it first.

Mae. Hush.

Margaret. They're impossible conditions!

Brick. Then why don't you—?

Sonny. I want it, I want it!

Mae. Get away!

Margaret. HUSH! Who is out there? Is somebody at the door?

(There are footsteps in hall.)

Mae (Outside). May I enter a moment?

Margaret. Oh, *you!* Sure. Come in, Mae.

(MAE enters bearing aloft the bow of a young lady's archery set.)

Mae. Brick, is this thing yours?

Margaret. Why, Sister Woman—that's my Diana Trophy. Won it at the intercollegiate archery contest on the Ole Miss Campus.

Mae. It's a mighty dangerous thing to leave exposed round a house full of nawmal rid-blooded children attracted t'weapons.

Margaret. "Nawmal rid-blooded children attracted t'weapons" ought t'be taught to keep their hands off things that don't belong to them.

Mae. Maggie, honey, if you had children of your own you'd know how funny that is. Will you please lock this up and put the key out of reach?

Margaret. Sister Woman, nobody is plotting the destruction of your kiddies. —Brick and I still have our special archers' license. We're goin' deer-huntin' on Moon Lake as soon as the season starts. I love to run with dogs through chilly woods, run, run leap over obstructions—

(She goes into the closet carrying the bow.)

Mae. How's the injured ankle, Brick?

Brick. Doesn't hurt. Just itches.

Mae. Oh, my! Brick—Brick, you should've been downstairs after supper! Kiddies put on a show. Polly played the piano, Buster an' Sonny drums, an' then they turned out the lights an' Dixie an' Trixie puhfawmed a toe dance in fairy costume with *spahkluhs!* Big Daddy just beamed! He just beamed!

Margaret (From the closet with a sharp laugh). Oh, I bet. It breaks my heart that we missed it!

(She reenters.)

But Mae? Why did y'give dawgs' names to all your kiddies?

Mae. Dogs' names?

Margaret (Sweetly). Dixie, Trixie, Buster, Sonny, Polly! —Sounds like four dogs and a parrot . . .

Mae. Maggie?

(MARGARET turns with a smile.)

Why are you so catty?

Margaret. Cause I'm a cat! But why can't *you* take a joke, Sister Woman?

Mae. Nothin' pleases me more than a joke that's funny. You know the real names of our kiddies. Buster's real name is Robert. Sonny's real name is Saunders. Trixie's real name is Marlene and Dixie's—

(GOOPER *downstairs calls for her.* "Hey, Mae! Sister Woman, intermission is over!" —*She rushes to door, saying:*)

Intermission is over! See ya later!
Margaret. I wonder what Dixie's real name is?
Brick. Maggie, being catty doesn't help things any . . .
Margaret. I know! WHY—Am I so catty?—Cause I'm consumed with envy an' eaten up with longing? — Brick, I'm going to lay out your beautiful Shantung silk suit from Rome and one of your monogrammed silk shirts. I'll put your cuff links in it, those lovely star sapphires I get you to wear so rarely. . . .
Brick. I can't get trousers on over this plaster cast.
Margaret. Yes, you can, I'll help you.
Brick. I'm not going to get dressed, Maggie.
Margaret. Will you just put on a pair of white silk pajamas?
Brick. Yes, I'll do that, Maggie.
Margaret. Thank you, thank you so *much!*
Brick. Don't mention it.
Margaret. Oh, Brick! How long does it have t' go on? This punishment? Haven't I done time enough, haven't I served my term, can't I apply for a —pardon?
Brick. Maggie, you're spoiling my liquor. Lately your voice always sounds like you'd been running upstairs to warn somebody that the house was on fire!

Margaret. Well, no wonder, no wonder. Y'know what I feel like, Brick? *I feel all the time like a cat on a hot tin roof!*
Brick. Then jump off the roof, jump off off it, cats can jump off roofs and land on their four feet uninjured!
Margaret. Oh, yes!
Brick. Do it!—fo' God's sake, do it . . .
Margaret. Do what?
Brick. Take a lover!
Margaret. I can't see a man but you! Even with my eyes closed, I just see you! Why don't you get ugly, Brick, why don't you please get fat or ugly or something so I could stand it?

(*She rushes to hall door, opens it, listens.*)

The concert is still going on! Bravo, no-necks, bravo!

(*She slams and locks door fiercely.*)

Brick. What did you lock the door for?
Margaret. To give us a little privacy for a while.
Brick. You know better, Maggie.
Margaret. No, I don't know better. . . .

(*She rushes to gallery doors, draws the rose-silk drapes across them.*)

Brick. Don't make a fool of yourself.
Margaret. I don't mind makin' a fool of myself over you!
Brick. I mind, Maggie. I feel embarrassed for you.
Margaret. Feel embarrassed! But don't continue my torture. I can't live on and on under these circumstances.
Brick. You agreed to—
Margaret. I know but—
Brick. —Accept that condition!
Margaret. I CAN'T! CAN'T! CAN'T!

(*She seizes his shoulder.*)

Brick. Let go!

(*He breaks away from her and seizes the small boudoir chair and raises it like a lion-tamer facing a big circus cat.*)

(*Count five. She stares at him with her fist pressed to her mouth, then bursts into shrill, almost hysterical laughter. He remains grave for a moment, then grins and puts the chair down.*)

(BIG MAMA *calls through closed door.*)

Big Mama. Son? Son? Son?
Brick. What is it, Big Mama?
Big Mama (*Outside*). Oh, son! We got the most wonderful news about Big Daddy. I just had t'run up an' tell you right this—

(*She rattles the knob.*)

—What's this door doin', locked, faw? You all think there's robbers in the house?
Margaret. Big Mama, Brick is dressin', he's not dressed yet.
Big Mama. That's all right, it won't be the first time I've seen Brick not dressed. Come on, open the door!

(MARGARET, *with a grimace, goes to unlock and open the hall door, as* BRICK *hobbles rapidly to the bathroom and kicks the door shut.* BIG MAMA *has disappeared from the hall.*)

Margaret. Big Mama?
(BIG MAMA *appears through the opposite gallery doors behind* MARGARET, *huffing and puffing like an old bulldog. She is a short, stout woman; her sixty years and 170 pounds have left her somewhat breathless most of* the time; she's always tensed like a boxer, or rather, a Japanese wrestler. Her "family" was maybe a little superior to BIG DADDY's, but not much. She wears a black or silver lace dress and at least half a million in flashy gems. She is very sincere.)

Big Mama (*Loudly, startling* MARGARET.) Here—I come through Gooper's and Mae's gall'ry door. Where's Brick? *Brick*—Hurry on out of there, son, I just have a second and want to give you the news about Big Daddy. —I hate locked doors in a house. . . .
Margaret. (*With affected lightness.*) I've noticed you do, Big Mama, but people have got to have *some* moments of privacy, don't they?
Big Mama. No, ma'am, not in *my* house. (*without pause*) Whacha took off you' dress faw? I thought that little lace dress was so sweet on yuh, honey.
Margaret. I thought it looked sweet on me, too, but one of m' cute little table-partners used it for a napkin so—!
Big Mama (*Picking up stockings on floor*). What?
Margaret. You know, Big Mama, Mae and Gooper's so touchy about those children—thanks, Big Mama . . .

(BIG MAMA *has thrust the picked-up stockings in* MARGARET's *hand with a grunt*).

—that you just don't dare to suggest there's any room for improvement in their—
Big Mama. Brick, hurry out!—Shoot, Maggie, you just don't like children.
Margaret. I do SO like children! Adore them!—well brought up!
Big Mama (*Gentle—loving*). Well, why don't you have some and bring them

up well, then, instead of all the time pickin' on Gooper's an' Mae's?

Gooper (*Shouting up the stairs*). Hey, hey, Big Mama, Betsy an' Hugh got to go, waitin' t' tell yuh g'by!

Big Mama. Tell 'em to hold their hawses, I'll be right down in a jiffy!

Gooper. Yes ma'am!

(*She turns to the bathroom door and calls out.*)

Big Mama. Son? Can you hear me in there?

(*There is a muffled answer.*)

We just got the full report from the laboratory at the Ochsner Clinic, completely negative, son, ev'rything negative, right on down the line! Nothin' a-tall's wrong with him but some little functional thing called a spastic colon. Can you hear me, son?

Margaret. He can hear you, Big Mama.

Big Mama. Then why don't he say something? God Almighty, a piece of news like that should make him shout. It made *me* shout, I can tell you. I shouted and sobbed and fell right down on my knees!—Look!

(*She pulls up her skirt.*)

See the bruises where I hit my kneecaps? Took both doctors to haul me back on my feet!

(*She laughs—she always laughs like hell at herself.*)

Big Daddy was furious with me! But ain't that wonderful news?

(*Facing bathroom again, she continues:*)

After all the anxiety we been through to git a report like that on Big Dad-

dy's birthday? Big Daddy tried to hide how much of a load that news took off his mind, but didn't fool *me*. He was mighty close to crying about it *himself*!

(*Goodbyes are shouted downstairs, and she rushes to door.*)

Gooper. Big Mama!

Big Mama. *Hold those people down there, don't let them go!*—Now, git dressed, we're all comin' up to this room fo' Big Daddy's birthday party because of your ankle.—How's his ankle, Maggie?

Margaret. Well, he broke it, Big Mama.

Big Mama. I know he broke it.

(*A phone is ringing in hall. A* NEGRO *voice answers: "Mistuh Polly's residence."*)

I mean does it hurt him much still.

Margaret. I'm afraid I can't give you that information, Big Mama. You'll have to ask Brick if it hurts much still or not.

Sookey (*In the hall*). It's Memphis, Mizz Polly, it's Miss Sally in Memphis.

Big Mama. Awright, Sookey.

(BIG MAMA *rushes into the hall and is heard shouting on the phone:*)

Hello, Miss Sally. How are you, Miss Sally?—Yes, well, I was just gonna call you about it. *Shoot!*—

(BIG MAMA *raises her voice to a bellow.*)

Big Mama. *Miss Sally? Don't ever call me from the Gayoso Lobby, too much talk goes on in that hotel lobby, no wonder you can't hear me!* Now listen, Miss Sally. They's nothin' serious wrong with Big Daddy. We got the report just now, they's nothin' wrong but a thing called a—spastic! SPASTIC!—colon . . .

(*She appears at the hall door and calls to* MARGARET.)

—Maggie, come out here and talk to that fool on the phone. I'm shouted breathless!

Margaret (*Goes out and is heard sweetly at phone*). Miss Sally? This is Brick's wife, Maggie. So nice to hear your voice. Can you hear *mine*? Well, *good!*—Big Mama just wanted you to know that they've got the report from the Ochsner Clinic and what Big Daddy has is a spastic colon. Yes. Spastic colon, Miss Sally. That's right, spastic colon. *G'bye, Miss Sally, hope I'll see you real soon!*

(*Hangs up a little before* MISS SALLY *was probably ready to terminate the talk. She returns through the hall door.*)

She heard me perfectly. I've discovered with deaf people the thing to do is not shout at them but just enunciate clearly. My rich old Aunt Cornelia was deaf as the dead but I could make her hear me just by sayin' each word slowly, distinctly, close to her ear. I read her the *Commercial Appeal* ev'ry night, read her the classfied ads in it, even, she never missed a word of it. But was she a mean ole thing! Know what I got when she died? Her unexpired subscriptions to five magazines and the Book-of-the-Month Club and a LIBRARY full of ev'ry dull book ever written! All else went to her hellcat

of a sister . . . meaner than she was, even!

(BIG MAMA *has been straightening things up in the room during this speech.*)

Big Mama (*Closing closet door on discarded clothes*). *Miss Sally sure is a case!* Big Daddy says she's always got her hand out fo' something. He's not mistaken. That poor ole thing always has her hand out fo' somethin'. I don't think Big Daddy gives her as much as he should.

Gooper. Big Mama! Come on now! Betsy and Hugh can't wait no longer!

Big Mama (*Shouting*). I'm comin'!

(*She starts out. At the hall door, turns and jerks a forefinger, first toward the bathroom door, then toward the liquor cabinet, meaning: "Has Brick been drinking?"* MARGARET *pretends not to understand, cocks her head and raises her brows as if the pantomimic performance was completely mystifying to her.*)

(BIG MAMA *rushes back to* MARGARET:)

Shoot! Stop playin' so dumb!—I mean has he been drinkin' that stuff much yet?

Margaret (*With a little laugh*). Oh, I think he had a highball after supper.

Big Mama. Don't laugh about it!—Some single men stop drinkin' when they git married and others start! Brick never touched liquor before he—!

Margaret (*Crying out*). THAT'S NOT FAIR!

Big Mama. Fair or not fair I want to ask you a question, one question: D'you make Brick happy in bed?

Margaret. Why don't you ask if he makes *me* happy in bed?
Big Mama. Because I know that—
Margaret. *It works both ways!*
Big Mama. Something's not right. You're childless and my son drinks!
Gooper. Come on, Big Mama!

(GOOPER *has called her downstairs and she has rushed to the door on the line above. She turns at the door and points at the bed.*)

—When a marriage goes on the rocks, the rocks are *there,* right *there!*

Margaret. *That's—*

(BIG MAMA *has swept out of the room and slammed the door.*)

—not—*fair . . .*

(MARGARET *is alone, completely alone, and she feels it. She draws in, hunches her shoulders, raises her arms with fists clenched, shuts her eyes tight as a child about to be stabbed with a vaccination needle. When she opens her eyes again, what she sees is the long oval mirror and she rushes straight to it, stares into it with a grimace and says: "Who are you?"—Then she crouches a little and answers herself in a different voice which is high, thin, mocking: "I am Maggie the Cat!"—Straightens quickly as bathroom door opens a little and* BRICK *calls out to her.*)
Brick. Has Big Mama gone?
Margaret. She's gone.

(*He opens the bathroom door and hobbles out, with his liquor glass now empty, straight to the liquor cabinet. He is whistling softly.* MAR-GARET's *head pivots on her long, slender throat to watch him.*)

(*She raises a hand uncertainly to the base of her throat, as if it was difficult for her to swallow, before she speaks:*)

You know, our sex life didn't just peter out in the usual way, it was cut off short, long before the natural time for it to, and it's going to revive again, just as sudden as that. I'm confident of it. That's what I'm keeping myself attractive for. For the time when you'll see me again like other men see me. Yes, like other men see me. They still see me, Brick, and they like what they see. Uh-huh. Some of them would give their— Look, Brick!

(*She stands before the long oval mirror, touches her breast and then her hips with her two hands.*)

How high my body stays on me!— Nothing has fallen on me—not a fraction. . . .

(*Her voice is soft and trembling: a pleading child's. At this moment as he turns to glance at her—a look which is like a player passing a ball to another player, third down and goal to go—she has to capture the audience in a grip so tight that she can hold it till the first intermission without any lapse of attention.*)

Other men still want me. My face looks strained, sometimes, but I've kept my figure as well as you've kept yours, and men admire it. I still turn heads on the street. Why, last week in Memphis everywhere that I went men's eyes burned holes in my clothes, at the country club and in restaurants and department stores, there wasn't a man I met or walked by that didn't just eat me up with his eyes and turn around when I passed him and look back at me. Why, at Alice's party for her New York cousins, the best-lookin' man in the crowd —followed me upstairs and tried to force his way in the powder room with me, followed me to the door and tried to force his way in!

Brick. Why didn't you let him, Maggie?

Margaret. Because I'm not that common, for one thing. Not that I wasn't almost tempted to. You like to know who it was? It was Sonny Boy Maxwell, that's who!

Brick. Oh, yeah, Sonny Boy Maxwell, he was a good end-runner but had a little injury to his back and had to quit.

Margaret. He has no injury now and has no wife and still has a lech for me!

Brick. I see no reason to lock him out of a powder room in that case.

Margaret. And have someone catch me at it? I'm not that stupid. Oh, I might sometime cheat on you with someone, since you're so insultingly eager to have me do it!—But if I do, you can be damned sure it will be in a place and a time—where no one but me and the man could possibly know. Because I'm not going to give you any excuse to divorce me for being unfaithful or anything else. . . .

Brick. Maggie, I wouldn't divorce you for being unfaithful or anything else. Don't you know that? Hell. I'd be relieved to know that you'd found yourself a lover.

Margaret. Well, I'm taking no chances. No, I'd rather stay on this hot tin roof.

Brick. A hot tin roof's 'n uncomfo'table place t' stay on. . . .

(He starts to whistle softly.)

Margaret (Through his whistle). Yeah, but I can stay on it just as long as I have to.

Brick. You could leave me, Maggie.

(He resumes whistle. She wheels about to glare at him.)

Margaret. Don't want to and will not! Besides if I did, you don't have a cent to pay for it but what you get from Big Daddy and he's dying of cancer!

(For the first time a realization of BIG DADDY's *doom seems to penetrate to* BRICK's *consciousness, visibly, and he looks at* MARGARET.)

Brick. Big Mama just said he *wasn't,* that the report was okay.

Margaret. That's what she thinks because she got the same story that they gave Big Daddy. And was just as taken in by it as he was, poor ole things. . . .

But tonight they're going to tell her the truth about it. When Big Daddy goes to bed, they're going to tell her that he is dying of cancer.

(She slams the dresser drawer.)

—It's malignant and it's terminal.

Brick. Does Big Daddy know it?

Margaret. Hell, do they *ever* know it? Nobody says, "You're dying." You have to fool them. They have to fool *themselves.*

Brick. Why?

Margaret. Why? Because human beings dream of life everlasting, that's the reason! But most of them want it on earth and not in heaven.

(*He gives a short, hard laugh at her touch of humor.*)

Well. . . . (*She touches up her mascara.*) That's how it is, anyhow. . . . (*She looks about.*) Where did I put down my cigarette? Don't want to burn up the home-place, at least not with Mae and Gooper and their five monsters in it!

(*She has found it and sucks at it greedily. Blows out smoke and continues:*)

So this is Big Daddy's last birthday. And Mae and Gooper, they know it, oh, *they* know it, all right. They got the first information from the Ochsner Clinic. That's why they rushed down here with their no-neck monsters. Because. Do you know something? Big Daddy's made no will? Big Daddy's never made out any will in his life, and so this campaign's afoot to impress him, forcibly as possible, with the fact that you drink and I've borne no children!

(*He continues to stare at her a moment, then mutters something sharp but not audible and hobbles rather rapidly out onto the long gallery in the fading, much faded, gold light.*)

Margaret. (*Continuing her liturgical chant*). Y'know, I'm *fond* of Big Daddy, I am genuinely fond of that old man, I really *am*, you know. . . .

Brick (*Faintly, vaguely*). Yes, I know you are. . . .

Margaret. I've always sort of admired him in spite of his coarseness, his four-letter words and so forth. Because Big Daddy *is* what he *is*, and he makes no bones about it. He

hasn't turned gentleman farmer, he's still a Mississippi redneck, as much of a redneck as he must have been when he was just overseer here on the old Jack Straw and Peter Ochello place. But he got hold of it an' built it into th' biggest an' finest plantation in the Delta.—I've always *liked* Big Daddy. . . .

(*She crosses to the proscenium.*)

Well, this is Big Daddy's last birthday. I'm sorry about it. But I'm facing the facts. It takes money to take care of a drinker and that's the office that I've been elected to lately.

Brick. You don't have to take care of me.

Margaret. Yes, I do. Two people in the same boat have got to take care of each other. At least you want money to buy more Echo Spring when this supply is exhausted, or will you be satisfied with a ten-cent beer?

Mae an' Gooper are plannin' to freeze us out of Big Daddy's estate because you drink and I'm childless. But we can defeat that plan. We're *going* to defeat that plan!

Brick, y'know, I've been so God damn disgustingly poor all my life!— That's the *truth*, Brick!

Brick. I'm not sayin' it isn't.

Margaret. Always had to suck up to people I couldn't stand because they had money and I was poor as Job's turkey. You don't know what that's like. Well, I'll tell you, it's like you would feel a thousand miles away from Echo Spring!—And had to get back to it on that broken ankle . . . without a crutch!

That's how it feels to be as poor as Job's turkey and have to suck up to relatives that you hated because they had money and all you had was a bunch of hand-me-down clothes and a few old moldy three-per-cent government bonds. My daddy loved his liquor, he fell in love with his liquor the way you've fallen in love with Echo Spring!—And my poor Mama, having to maintain some semblance of social position, to keep appearances up, on an income of one hundred and fifty dollars a month on those old government bonds!

When I came out, the year that I made my debut, I had just two evening dresses! One Mother made me from a pattern in *Vogue*, the other a hand-me-down from a snotty rich cousin I hated!

—The dress that I married you in was my grandmother's weddin' gown. . . . So that's why I'm like a cat on a hot tin roof!

(BRICK *is still on the gallery. Someone below calls up to him in a warm* NEGRO *voice, "Hiya, Mistuh Brick, how yuh feelin'?"* BRICK *raises his liquor glass as if that answered the question.*)

Margaret. You can be young without money, but you can't be old without it. You've got to be old *with* money because to be old without it is just too awful, you've got to be one or the other, either *young* or *with money*, you can't be old and *without* it.— That's the *truth*, Brick. . . .

(BRICK *whistles softly, vaguely.*)

Well, now I'm dressed, I'm all dressed, there's nothing else for me to do.

(*Forlornly, almost fearfully*).

I'm dressed, all dressed, nothing else for me to do. . . .

(*She moves about restlessly, aimlessly, and speaks, as if to herself.*)

What am I—? Oh!—my bracelets. . . .

(*She starts working a collection of bracelets over her hands onto her wrists, about six on each, as she talks.*)

I've thought a whole lot about it and now I know when I made my mistake. Yes, I made my mistake when I told you the truth about that thing with Skipper. Never should have confessed it, a fatal error, tellin' you about that thing with Skipper.

Brick. Maggie, shut up about Skipper. I mean it, Maggie; you got to shut up about Skipper.

Margaret. You ought to understand that Skipper and I—

Brick. You don't think I'm serious, Maggie? You're fooled by the fact that I am saying this quiet? Look, Maggie. What you're doing is a dangerous thing to do. You're—you're—you're—foolin' with something that nobody ought to fool with.

Margaret. This time I'm going to finish what I have to say to to you. Skipper and I made love, if love you could call it, because it made both of us feel a little bit closer to you. You see, you son of a bitch, you asked too much of people, of me, of him, of all the unlucky poor damned sons of bitches that happen to love you, and there was a whole pack of them, yes, there was a pack of them besides me and Skipper, you asked too goddam much of people that loved you, you

—superior creature!—you godlike being!—And so we made love to each other to dream it was you, both of us! Yes, yes, yes! Truth, truth! What's so awful about it? I like it, I think the truth is—yeah! I shouldn't have told you. . . .

Brick (*Holding his head unnaturally still and uptilted a bit*). It was Skipper that told me about it. Not you, Maggie.

Margaret. I told you!

Brick. After he told me!

Margaret. What does it matter who—?

Dixie. I got your mallet, I got your mallet.

Trixie. Give it to me, give it to me. It's mine.

(BRICK *turns suddenly out upon the gallery and calls*:)

Brick. Little girl! Hey, little girl!

Little Girl (*At a distance*). What, Uncle Brick?

Brick. Tell the folks to come up!—Bring everybody upstairs!

Trixie. It's mine, it's mine.

Margaret. I can't stop myself! I'd go on telling you this in front of them all, if I had to!

Brick. Little girl! Go on, go on, will you? Do what I told you, call them!

Dixie. Okay.

Margaret. Because it's got to be told and you, you!—you never let me!

(*She sobs, then controls herself, and continues almost calmly.*)

It was one of those beautiful, ideal things they tell about in the Greek legends, it couldn't be anything else, you being you, and that's what made it so sad, that's what made it so awful, because it was love that never could be carried through to anything

satisfying or even talked about plainly.

Brick. Maggie, you gotta stop this.

Margaret. Brick, I tell you, you got to believe me, Brick, I *do* understand all about it! I—I think it was—*noble!* Can't you tell I'm sincere when I say I respect it? My only point, the only point that I'm making, is life has got to be allowed to continue even after the *dream* of life is—all—over. . . .

(BRICK *is without his crutch. Leaning on furniture, he crosses to pick it up as she continues as if possessed by a will outside herself:*)

Why I remember when we double-dated at college, Gladys Fitzgerald and I and you and Skipper, it was more like a date between you and Skipper. Gladys and I were just sort of tagging along as if it was necessary to chaperone you!—to make a good public impression—

Brick (*Turns to face her, half lifting his crutch*). Maggie, you want me to hit you with this crutch? Don't you know I could kill you with this crutch?

Margaret. Good Lord, man, d' you think I'd care if you did?

Brick. One man has one great good true thing in his life. One great good thing which is true!—I had friendship with Skipper.—You are naming it dirty!

Margaret. I'm not naming it dirty! I am naming it clean.

Brick. Not love with you, Maggie, but friendship with Skipper was that one great true thing, and you are naming it dirty!

Margaret. Then you haven't been listenin', not understood what I'm saying! I'm naming it so damn clean that it killed poor Skipper!—You two had something that had to be kept on ice, yes, incorruptible, yes!—and death was the only icebox where you could keep it. . . .

Brick. I married you, Maggie. Why would I marry you, Maggie, if I was—?

Margaret. Brick, let me finish!—I know, believe me I know, that it was only Skipper that harbored even any *unconscious* desire for anything not perfectly pure between you two!—Now let me skip a little. You married me early that summer we graduated out of Ole Miss, and we were happy, weren't we, we were blissful, yes, hit heaven together ev'ry time that we loved! But that fall you an' Skipper turned down wonderful offers of jobs in order to keep on bein' football heroes—pro-football heroes. You organized the Dixie Stars that fall, so you could keep on bein' teammates forever! But somethin' was not right with it!—*Me included!*—between you. Skipper began hittin' the bottle . . . you got a spinal injury—couldn't play the Thanksgivin' game in Chicago, watched it on TV from a traction bed in Toledo. I joined Skipper. The Dixie Stars lost because poor Skipper was drunk. We drank together that night all night in the bar of the Blackstone and when cold day was comin' up over the Lake an' we were comin' out drunk to take a dizzy look at it, I said, "SKIPPER! STOP LOVIN' MY HUSBAND OR TELL HIM HE'S GOT TO LET YOU ADMIT IT TO HIM!"—one way or another!

HE SLAPPED ME HARD ON THE MOUTH!—then turned and ran without stopping once, I am sure, all the way back into his room at the Blackstone. . . .

—When I came to his room that night, with a little scratch like a shy little mouse at his door, he made that pitiful, ineffectual little attempt to prove that what I had said wasn't true. . . .

(BRICK *strikes at her with crutch, a blow that shatters the gemlike lamp on the table.*)

—In this way, I destroyed him, by telling him truth that he and his world which he was born and raised in, yours and his world, had told him could not be told?

—From then on Skipper was nothing at all but a receptacle for liquor and drugs. . . .

—*Who shot cock robin? I with my*—

(*She throws back her head with tight shut eyes.*)

—*merciful arrow!*

(BRICK *strikes at her; misses.*)

Missed me!—Sorry, I'm not tryin' to whitewash my behavior, Christ, no! Brick, I'm not good. I don't know why people have to pretend to be good, nobody's good. The rich or the well-to-do can afford to respect moral patterns, conventional moral patterns, but I could never afford to, yeah, but—I'm honest! Give me credit for just that, will you *please?*—Born poor, raised poor, expect to die poor unless I manage to get us something out of what Big Daddy leaves when he dies of cancer! But Brick?!—*Skipper is dead! I'm alive!* Maggie the cat is—

(BRICK *hops awkwardly forward and strikes at her again with his crutch.*)

—alive! I am alive, alive! I am . . .

(*He hurls the crutch at her, across the bed she took refuge behind, and pitches forward on the floor as she completes her speech.*)

—alive!

(*A little girl,* DIXIE, *bursts into the room, wearing an Indian war bonnet and firing a cap pistol at* MARGARET *and shouting: "Bang, bang, bang!"*)

(*Laughter downstairs floats through the open hall door.* MARGARET *had crouched gasping to bed at child's entrance. She now rises and says with cool fury:*)

Little girl, your mother or someone should teach you—(*gasping*)—to knock at a door before you come into a room. Otherwise people might think that you—lack—good breeding. . . .

Dixie. Yanh, yanh, yanh, what is Uncle Brick doin' on th' floor?

Brick. I tried to kill your Aunt Maggie, but I failed—and I fell. Little girl, give me my crutch so I can get up off th' floor.

Margaret. Yes, give your uncle his crutch, he's a cripple, honey, he broke his ankle last night jumping hurdles on the high school athletic field!

Dixie. What were you jumping hurdles for, Uncle Brick?

Brick. Because I used to jump them, and people like to do what they used to do, even after they've stopped being able to do it. . . .

Margaret. That's right, that's your answer, now go away, little girl.

(DIXIE *fires cap pistol at* MARGARET *three times.*)

Stop, you stop that, monster! You little no-neck monster!

(*She seizes the cap pistol and hurls it through gallery doors.*)

Dixie (*with a precocious instinct for the cruelest thing*). You're *jealous!*—You're just jealous because you can't have babies!

(*She sticks out her tongue at* MARGARET *as she sashays past her with her stomach stuck out, to the gallery.* MARGARET *slams the gallery doors and leans panting against them. There is a pause.* BRICK *has replaced his spilt drink and sits, faraway, on the great four-poster bed.*)

Margaret. You see?—they gloat over us being childless, even in front of their five little no-neck monsters!

(*Pause.* VOICES *approach on the stairs.*)

Brick?—I've been to a doctor in Memphis, a—a gynecologist. . . .
I've been completely examined, and there is no reason why we can't have a child whenever we want one. And this is my time by the calendar to conceive. Are you listening to me? Are you? Are you LISTENING TO ME!

Brick. Yes, I hear you, Maggie.

(*His attention returns to her inflamed face.*)

—But how in hell on earth do you imagine—that you're going to have a child by a man that can't stand you?

Margaret. That's a problem that I will have to work out.

(*She wheels about to face the hall door.*)

Mae. (*Off stage left*). Come on, Big Daddy. We're all goin' up to Brick's room.

(*From off stage left, voices:* REVEREND TOOKER, DOCTOR BAUGH, MAE.)

Margaret. Here they come!

(*The lights dim.*)

CURTAIN

ACT TWO

There is no lapse of time. Margaret and Brick are in the same positions they held at the end of Act I.

Margaret (*At door*). Here they come!

(BIG DADDY *appears first, a tall man with a fierce, anxious look, moving carefully not to betray his weakness even, or especially, to himself.*)

Gooper. I read in the *Register* that you're getting a new memorial window.

(*Some of the people are approaching through the hall, others along the gallery: voices from both directions.* GOOPER *and* REVEREND TOOKER *become visible outside gallery doors, and their voices come in clearly.*)

(*They pause outside as* GOOPER *lights a cigar.*)

Reverend Tooker (*Vivaciously*). Oh, but St. Paul's in Grenada has three memorial windows, and the latest one is a Tiffany stained-glass window that cost twenty-five hundred dollars, a picture of Christ the Good Shepherd with a Lamb in His arms.

Margaret. Big Daddy.

Big Daddy. Well, Brick.

Brick. Hello Big Daddy. —Congratulations!

Big Daddy. —Crap. . . .

Gooper. Who give that window, Preach?

Reverend Tooker. Clyde Fletcher's widow. Also presented St. Paul's with a baptismal font.

Gooper. Y'know what somebody ought t' give your church is a *coolin'* system, Preach.

Mae (*Almost religiously*).—Let's see now, they've had their *tyyy*-phoid shots, and their tetanus shots, their diphtheria shots and their hepatitis shots and their polio shots, they got *those* shots every month from May through September, and—Gooper? Hey! Gooper!—What all have the kiddies been shot faw?

Reverend Tooker. Yes, siree, Bob! And y' know what Gus Hamma's family gave in his memory to the church at Two Rivers? A complete new stone parish-house with a basketball court in the basement and a—

Big Daddy. (*Uttering a loud barking laugh which is far from truly mirthful*). Hey, Preach! What's all this talk about memorials, Preach? Y' think somebody's about t' kick off around here? 'S that it?

(*Startled by this interjection,* REVEREND TOOKER *decides to laugh at the question almost as loud as he can.*)

(*How he would answer the question we'll never know, as he's spared that*

embarrassment by the voice of GOOP-
ER's *wife,* MAE, *rising high and clear
as she appears with* "DOC" BAUGH,
*the family doctor, through the hall
door.*)

Margaret (*Overlapping a bit*). Turn on
the hi-fi, Brick! Let's have some
music t' start off th' party with!
Brick. You turn it on, Maggie.

(*The talk becomes so general that
the room sounds like a great aviary
of chattering birds. Only* BRICK *remains unengaged, leaning upon the
liquor cabinet with his faraway
smile, an ice cube in a paper napkin
with which he now and then rubs his
forehead. He doesn't respond to*
MARGARET's *command. She bounds
forward and stoops over the instrument panel of the console.*)

Gooper. We gave 'em that thing for a
third anniversary present, got three
speakers in it.

(*The room is suddenly blasted by
the climax of a Wagnerian opera or a
Beethoven symphony.*)

Big Daddy. *Turn that damn thing off!*

(*Almost instant silence, almost instantly broken by the shouting
charge of* BIG MAMA, *entering
through hall door like a charging
rhino.*)

Big Mama. *Wha's my Brick, wha's mah
precious baby!!*
Big Daddy. *Sorry! Turn it back on!*

(*Everyone laughs very loud.* BIG
DADDY *is famous for his jokes at* BIG
MAMA's *expense, and nobody laughs
louder at these jokes than* BIG MAMA
herself, though sometimes they're

pretty cruel and BIG MAMA *has to
pick up or fuss with something to
cover the hurt that the loud laugh
doesn't quite cover.*)

(*On this occasion, a happy occasion
because the dread in her heart has
also been lifted by the false report on*
BIG DADDY's *condition, she giggles,
grotesquely, coyly, in* BIG DADDY's
direction and bears down upon
BRICK, *all very quick and alive.*)

Big Mama. Here he is, here's my precious baby! What's that you've got in
your hand? You put that liquor
down, son, your hand was made fo'
holdin' somethin' better than that!
Gooper. Look at Brick put it down!

(BRICK *has obeyed* BIG MAMA *by
draining the glass and handing it to
her. Again everyone laughs, some
high, some low.*)

Big Mama. Oh, you bad boy, you,
you're my bad little boy. Give Big
Mama a kiss, you bad boy, you!—
Look at him shy away, will you?
Brick never liked bein' kissed or
made a fuss over, I guess because
he's always had too much of it!
Son, you turn that thing off!

(BRICK *has switched on the TV set.*)

I can't stand TV, radio was bad
enough but TV has gone it one better, I mean—(*plops wheezing in
chair*)—one worse, ha ha! Now
what'm I sittin' down here faw? I
want t' sit next to my sweetheart on
the sofa, hold hands with him and
love him up a little!

(BIG MAMA *has on a black and white
figured chiffon. The large irregular
patterns, like the markings of some
massive animal, the luster of her*

great diamonds and many pearls, the brilliants set in the silver frames of her glasses, her riotous voice, booming laugh, have dominated the room since she entered. BIG DADDY *has been regarding her with a steady grimace of chronic annoyance.*)

Big Mama (*Still louder*). Preacher, Preacher, hey, Preach! Give me you' hand an' help me up from this chair!

Reverend Tooker. None of your tricks, Big Mama!

Big Mama. What tricks? You give me you' hand so I can get up an'—

(REVEREND TOOKER *extends her his hand. She grabs it and pulls him into her lap with a shrill laugh that spans an octave in two notes.*)

Ever seen a preacher in a fat lady's lap? Hey, hey, folks! Ever seen a preacher in a fat lady's lap?

(BIG MAMA *is notorious throughout the Delta for this sort of inelegant horseplay.* MARGARET *looks on with indulgent humor, sipping Dubonnet "on the rocks" and watching* BRICK, *but* MAE *and* GOOPER *exchange signs of humorless anxiety over these antics, the sort of behavior which* MAE *thinks may account for their failure to quite get in with the smartest young married set in Memphis, despite all. One of the Negroes,* LACY *or* SOOKEY, *peeks in, crackling. They are waiting for a sign to bring in the cake and champagne. But* BIG DADDY'S *not amused. He doesn't understand why, in spite of the infinite mental relief he's received from the doctor's report, he still has these same old fox teeth in his guts. "This spastic condition is something else,"*

he says to himself, but aloud he roars at BIG MAMA:)

Big Daddy. BIG MAMA, WILL YOU QUIT HORSIN'?—You're too old an' too fat fo' that sort of crazy kid stuff an' besides a woman with your blood pressure—she had two hundred last spring!—is riskin' a stroke when you mess around like that. . . .

(MAE *blows on a pitch pipe.*)

Big Mama. Here comes Big Daddy's birthday!

(NEGROES *in white jackets enter with an enormous birthday cake ablaze with candles and carrying buckets of champagne with satin ribbons about the bottle necks.*)

(MAE *and* GOOPER *strike up song, and everybody, including the* NEGROES *and* CHILDREN, *joins in. Only* BRICK *remains aloof.*)

Everyone. Happy birthday to you.
Happy birthday to you.
Happy birthday, Big Daddy—

(*Some sing: "Dear, Big Daddy!"*)

Happy birthday to you.

(*Some sing: "How old are you?"*)

(MAE *has come down center and is organizing her children like a chorus. She gives them a barely audible: "One, two, three!" and they are off in the new tune.*)

Children. Skinamarinka—dinka—dink
Skinamarinka—do
We love you.
Skinamarinka—dinka—dink
Skinamarinka—do.

(*All together, they turn to* BIG DADDY.)

Big Daddy, you!

(*They turn back front, like a musical comedy chorus.*)

We love you in the morning;
We love you in the night.
We love you when we're with you,
And we love you out of sight.
Skinamarinka—dinka—dink
Skinamarinka—do.

(MAE *turns to* BIG MAMA.)

Big Mama, too!

(BIG MAMA *bursts into tears. The* NEGROES *leave.*)

Big Daddy. Now Ida, what the hell is the matter with you?
Mae. She's just so happy.
Big Mama. I'm just so happy, Big Daddy, I have to cry or something.

(*Sudden and loud in the hush:*)

Brick, do you know the wonderful news that Doc Baugh got from the clinic about Big Daddy? Big Daddy's one hundred per cent!
Margaret. Isn't that wonderful?
Big Mama. He's just one hundred per cent. Passed the examination with flying colors. Now that we know there's nothing wrong with Big Daddy but a spastic colon, I can tell you something. I was worried sick, half out of my mind, for fear that Big Daddy might have a thing like—

(MARGARET *cuts through this speech, jumping up and exclaiming shrilly:*)

Margaret. Brick, honey, aren't you going to give Big Daddy his birthday present?

(*Passing by him, she snatches his liquor glass from him.*)

(*She picks up a fancily wrapped package.*)

Here it is, Big Daddy, this is from Brick!

Big Mama. This is the biggest birthday Big Daddy's ever had, a hundred presents and bushels of telegrams from—
Mae (*At same time*). What is it, Brick?
Gooper. I bet 500 to 50 that Brick don't *know* what it is.
Big Mama. The fun of presents is not knowing what they are till you open the package. Open your present, Big Daddy.
Big Daddy. Open it you'self. I want to ask Brick somethin! Come here, Brick.
Margaret. Big Daddy's callin' you, Brick.

(*She is opening the package.*)

Brick. Tell Big Daddy I'm crippled.
Big Daddy. I see you're crippled. I want to know how you got crippled.

Margaret (*Making diversionary tactics*). Oh, look, oh, look, why, it's a cashmere robe!

(*She holds the robe up for all to see.*)

Mae. You sound surprised, Maggie.
Margaret. I never saw one before.
Mae. That's funny.—Hah!
Margaret (*turning on her fiercely, with a brilliant smile*). Why is it funny? All my family ever had was family— and luxuries such as cashmere robes still surprise me!
Big Daddy (*Ominously*). Quiet!
Mae. (*Heedless in her fury*). I don't see how you could be so surprised when you bought it yourself at Loewen-

stein's in Memphis last Saturday. You know how I know?

Big Daddy. I said, Quiet!

Mae. —I know because the salesgirl that sold it to you waited on me and said, Oh, Mrs. Pollitt, your sister-in-law just bought a cashmere robe for your husband's father!

Margaret. Sister Woman! Your talents are wasted as a housewife and mother, you really ought to be with the FBI or—

Big Daddy. QUIET!

(REVEREND TOOKER's *reflexes are slower than the others'. He finishes a sentence after the bellow.*)

Reverend Tooker (*To Doc Baugh*).— the Stork and the Reaper are running neck and neck!

(*He starts to laugh gaily when he notices the silence and* BIG DADDY's *glare. His laugh dies falsely.*)

Big Daddy. Preacher, I hope I'm not butting in on more talk about memorial stained-glass windows, am I, Preacher?

(REVEREND TOOKER *laughs feebly, then coughs dryly in the embarrassed silence.*)

Preacher?

Big Mama. Now, Big Daddy, don't you pick on Preacher!

Big Daddy (*Raising his voice*). You ever hear that expression all hawk and no spit? You bring that expression to mind with that little dry cough of yours, all hawk an' no spit. . . .

(*The pause is broken only by a short startled laugh from* MARGARET, *the*

only one there who is conscious of and amused by the grotesque.)

Mae (*Raising her arms and jangling her bracelets*). I wonder if the mosquitoes are active tonight?

Big Daddy. What's that, Little Mama, Did you make some remark?

Mae. Yes, I said I wondered if the mosquitoes would eat us alive if we went out on the gallery for a while.

Big Daddy. Well, if they do, I'll have your bones pulverized for fertilizer!

Big Mama (*Quickly*). Last week we had an airplane spraying the place and I think it done some good, at least I haven't had a—

Big Daddy (*Cutting her speech*). Brick, they tell me, if what they tell me is true, that you done some jumping last night on the high school athletic field?

Big Mama. Brick, Big Daddy is talking to you, son.

Brick (*Smiling vaguely over his drink*). What was that, Big Daddy?

Big Daddy. They said you done some jumping on the high school track field last night.

Brick. That's what they told me, too.

Big Daddy. Was it jumping or humping that you were doing out there? What were you doing out there at three A.M., layin' a woman on that cinder track?

Big Mama. Big Daddy, you are off the sick-list, now, and I'm not going to excuse you for talkin' so—

Big Daddy. Quiet!

Big Mama. —nasty in front of Preacher and—

Big Daddy. QUIET!—I ast you, Brick, if you was cuttin' you'self a piece o' poon-tang last night on that cinder track? I thought maybe you were chasin' poon-tang on that track an' tripped over something in the heat of the chase—'sthat it?

(GOOPER *laughs, loud and false, others nervously following suit.* BIG MAMA *stamps her foot, and purses her lips, crossing to* MAE *and whispering something to her as* BRICK *meets his father's hard, intent, grinning stare with a slow, vague smile that he offers all situations from behind the screen of his liquor.*)

Brick. No, sir, I don't think so. . . .
Mae (*At the same time, sweetly*). Reverend Tooker, let's you and I take a stroll on the widow's walk.

(*She and the preacher go out on the gallery as* BIG DADDY *says:*)

Big Daddy. Then what the hell were you doing out there at three o'clock in the morning?
Brick. Jumping the hurdles, Big Daddy, runnin' and jumpin' the hurdles, but those high hurdles have gotten too high for me, now.
Big Daddy. Cause you was drunk?
Brick (*His vague smile fading a little*). Sober I wouldn't have tried to jump the *low* ones. . . .
Big Mama (*Quickly*). Big Daddy, blow out the candles on your birthday cake!
Margaret (*At the same time*). I want to propose a toast to Big Daddy Pollitt on his sixty-fifth birthday, the biggest cotton planter in—
Big Daddy (*Bellowing with fury and disgust*). *I told you to stop it, now stop it, quit this—!*
Big Mama (*Coming in front of* BIG DADDY *with the cake*). Big Daddy, I will not allow you to talk that way, not even on your birthday, I—
Big Daddy. I'll talk like I want to on

my birthday, Ida, or any other goddam day of the year and anybody here that don't like it knows what they can do!
Big Mama. You don't mean that!
Big Daddy. What makes you think I don't mean it?

(*Meanwhile various discreet signals have been exchanged and* GOOPER *has also gone out on the gallery.*)

Big Mama. I just know you don't mean it.
Big Daddy. You don't know a goddam thing and you never did!
Big Mama. Big Daddy, you don't mean that.
Big Daddy. Oh, yes, I do, oh, yes, I do, I mean it! I put up with a whole lot of crap around here because I thought I was dying. And you thought I was dying and you started taking over, well, you can stop taking over now, Ida, because I'm not gonna die, you can just stop now this business of taking over because you're not taking over because I'm not dying, I went through the laboratory and the goddam exploratory operation and there's nothing wrong with me but a spastic colon. And I'm not dying of cancer which you thought I was dying of. Ain't that so? Didn't you think that I was dying of cancer, Ida?

(*Almost everybody is out on the gallery but the two old people glaring at each other across the blazing cake.*)

(BIG MAMA's *chest heaves and she presses a fat fist to her mouth.*)

(BIG DADDY *continues, hoarsely.*)

Ain't that so, Ida? Didn't you have an idea I was dying of cancer and now you could take control of this place and everything on it? I got that impression, I seemed to get that impression. Your loud voice everywhere, your fat old body butting in here and there!

Big Mama. Hush! The Preacher!

Big Daddy. Rut the goddam preacher!

(BIG MAMA *gasps loudly and sits down on the sofa which is almost too small for her.*)

Did you hear what I said? I said rut the goddam preacher!

(*Somebody closes the gallery doors from outside just as there is a burst of fireworks and excited cries from the* CHILDREN.)

Big Mama. I never seen you act like this before and I can't think what's got in you!

Big Daddy. I went through all that laboratory and operation and all just so I would know if you or me was boss here! Well, now it turns out that I am and you ain't—and that's my birthday present—and my cake and champagne!—because for three years now you been gradually taking over. Bossing. Talking. Sashaying your fat old body around the place I made! I made this place! I was overseer on it! I was the overseer on the old Straw and Ochello plantation. I quit school at ten! I quit school at ten years old and went to work like a nigger in the fields. And I rose to be overseer of the Straw and Ochello plantation. And old Straw died and I was Ochello's partner and the place got bigger and bigger and bigger and bigger and bigger! I did all that myself with no goddam help from you, and now you think you're just about to take

over. Well, I am just about to tell you that you are not just about to take over, you are not just about to take over a God damn thing. Is that clear to you, Ida? Is that very plain to you, now? Is that understood completely? I been through the laboratory from A to Z. I've had the goddam exploratory operation, and nothing is wrong with me but a spastic colon—made spastic, I guess, by *disgust!* By all the goddam lies and liars that I have had to put up with, and all the goddam hypocrisy that I lived with all these forty years that we been livin' together!

Hey! Ida! Blow out the candles on the birthday cake! Purse up your lips and draw a deep breath and blow out the goddam candles on the cake!

Big Mama. Oh, Big Daddy, oh, oh, oh, Big Daddy!

Big Daddy. What's the matter with you?

Big Mama. *In all these years you never believed that I loved you??*

Big Daddy. Huh!

Big Mama. *And I did, I did so much, I did love you!—I even loved your hate and your hardness, Big Daddy!*

(*She sobs and rushes awkwardly out onto the gallery.*)

Big Daddy (*To himself*). *Wouldn't it be funny if that was true. . . .*

(*A pause is followed by a burst of light in the sky from the fireworks.*)

BRICK! HEY, BRICK!

(*He stands over his blazing birthday cake.*)

(*After some moments,* BRICK *hobbles in on his crutch, holding his glass.*)

(MARGARET *follows him with a bright, anxious smile.*)

I didn't call you, Maggie. I called Brick.

Margaret. I'm just delivering him to you.

(*She kisses* BRICK *on the mouth which he immediately wipes with the back of his hand. She flies girlishly back out.* BRICK *and his father are alone.*)

Big Daddy. Why did you do that?
Brick. Do what, Big Daddy?
Big Daddy. Wipe her kiss off your mouth like she'd spit on you.
Brick. I don't know. I wasn't conscious of it.
Big Daddy. That woman of yours has a better shape on her than Gooper's but somehow or other they got the same look about them.
Brick. What sort of look is that, Big Daddy?
Big Daddy. I don't know how to describe it but it's the same look.
Brick. They don't look peaceful, do they?
Big Daddy. No, they sure in hell don't.
Brick. They look nervous as cats?
Big Daddy. That's right, they look nervous as cats.
Brick. Nervous as a couple of cats on a hot tin roof?
Big Daddy. That's right, boy, they look like a couple of cats on a hot tin roof. It's funny that you and Gooper being so different would pick out the same type of woman.
Brick. Both of us married into society, Big Daddy.
Big Daddy. Crap . . . I wonder what gives them both that look?
Brick. Well. They're sittin' in the middle of a big piece of land, Big Daddy,

twenty-eight thousand acres is a pretty big piece of land and so they're squaring off on it, each determined to knock off a bigger piece of it than the other whenever you let it go.
Big Daddy. I got a surprise for those women. I'm not gonna let it go for a long time yet if that's what they're waiting for.
Brick. That's right, Big Daddy. You just sit tight and let them scratch each other's eyes out. . . .
Big Daddy. You bet your life I'm going to sit on it and let those sons of bitches scratch their eyes out, ha ha ha. . . .

But Gooper's wife's a good breeder, you got to admit she's fertile. Hell, at supper tonight she had them all at the table and they had to put a couple of extra leafs in the table to make room for them, she's got five head of them, now, and another one's comin'.
Brick. Yep, number six is comin'. . . .
Big Daddy. Six hell, she'll probably drop a litter next time. Brick, you know, I swear to God, I don't know the way it happens?
Brick. The way what happens, Big Daddy?
Big Daddy. You git you a piece of land, by hook or crook, an' things start growin' on it, things accumulate on it, and the first thing you know it's completely out of hand, completely out of hand!
Brick. Well, they say nature hates a vacuum, Big Daddy.
Big Daddy. That's what they say, but sometimes I think that a vacuum is a hell of a lot better than some of the stuff that nature replaces it with.
Is someone out there by that door?
Gooper. Hey Mae.
Brick. Yep.

Big Daddy. Who?

(*He has lowered his voice.*)

Brick. Someone int'rested in what we say to each other.
Big Daddy. Gooper?——*GOOPER!*

(*After a discreet pause,* MAE *apears in the gallery door.*)

Mae. Did you call Gooper, Big Daddy?
Big Daddy. Aw, it was you.
Mae. Do you want Gooper, Big Daddy?
Big Daddy. No, and I don't want you. I want some privacy here, while I'm having a confidential talk with my son Brick. Now it's too hot in here to close them doors, but if I have to close those ruttin' doors in order to have a private talk with my son Brick, just let me know and I'll close 'em. Because I hate eavesdroppers, I don't like any kind of sneakin' an' spyin'.
Mae. Why, Big Daddy—
Big Daddy. You stood on the wrong side of the moon, it threw your shadow!
Mae. I was just—
Big Daddy. You was just nothing but *spyin'* an' you *know* it!
Mae (*Begins to sniff and sob*). Oh, Big Daddy, you're so unkind for some reason to those that really love you!
Big Daddy. Shut up, shut up, shut up! I'm going to move you and Gooper out of that room next to this! It's none of your goddam business what goes on in here at night between Brick an' Maggie. You listen at night like a couple of ruttin' peekhole spies and go and give a report on what you hear to Big Mama an' she comes to me and says they say such and such and so and so about what they heard goin' on between Brick

an' Maggie, and Jesus, it makes me sick. I'm goin' to move you an' Gooper out of that room, I can't stand sneakin' an' spyin', it makes me puke. . . .

(MAE *throws back her head and rolls her eyes heavenward and extends her arms as if invoking God's pity for this unjust martyrdom; then she presses a handkerchief to her nose and flies from the room with a loud swish of skirts.*)

Brick (*Now at the liquor cabinet*). They listen, do they?
Big Daddy. Yeah. They listen and give reports to Big Mama on what goes on in here between you and Maggie. They say that—

(*He stops as if embarrassed.*)

—You won't sleep with her, that you sleep on the sofa. Is that true or not true? If you don't like Maggie, get rid of Maggie!—What are you doin' there now?
Brick. Fresh'nin' up my drink.
Big Daddy. Son, you know you got a real liquor problem?
Brick. Yes, sir, yes, I know.
Big Daddy. Is that why you quit sports-announcing, because of this liquor problem?
Brick. Yes, sir, yes, sir, I guess so.

(*He smiles vaguely and amiably at his father across his replenished drink.*)

Big Daddy. Son, don't guess about it, it's too important.
Brick (*Vaguely*). Yes, sir.
Big Daddy. And listen to me, don't look at the damn chandelier. . . .

(*Pause.* BIG DADDY's *voice is husky.*)

—Somethin' else we picked up at th' big fire-sale in Europe.

(*Another pause.*)

Life is important. There's nothing else to hold onto. A man that drinks is throwing his life away. Don't do it, hold onto your life. There's nothing else to hold onto. . . .

Sit down over here so we don't have to raise our voices, the walls have ears in this place.

Brick (*Hobbling over to sit on the sofa beside him*). All right, Big Daddy.

Big Daddy. Quit!—how'd that come about? Some disappointment?

Brick. I don't know. Do you?

Big Daddy. I'm askin' you, God damn it! How in hell would I know if you don't.

Brick. I just got out there and found that I had a mouth full of cotton. I was always two or three beats behind what was goin' on on the field and so I—

Big Daddy. Quit!

Brick (*Amiably*). Yes, quit.

Big Daddy. Son?

Brick. Huh?

Big Daddy (*Inhales loudly and deeply from his cigar; then bends suddenly a little forward, exhaling loudly and raising a hand to his forehead*). — Whew!—ha ha!—I took in too much smoke, it made me a little light-headed. . . .

(*The mantel clock chimes.*)

Why is it so damn hard for people to talk?

Brick. Yeah. . . .

(*The clock goes on sweetly chiming till it has completed the stroke of ten.*)

—Nice peaceful-soundin' clock, I like to hear it all night. . . .

(*He slides low and comfortable on the sofa;* BIG DADDY *sits up straight and rigid with some unspoken anxiety. All his gestures are tense and jerky as he talks. He wheezes and pants and sniffs through his nervous speech, glancing quickly, shyly, from time to time, at his son.*)

Big Daddy. We got that clock the summer we wint to Europe, me an' Big Mama on that damn Cook's Tour, never had such an awful time in my life, I'm tellin' you, son, those gooks over there, they gouge your eyeballs out in their grand hotels. And Big Mama bought more stuff than you could haul in a couple of boxcars, that's no crap. Everywhere she wint on this whirlwind tour, she bought, bought, bought. Why, half that stuff she bought is still crated up in the cellar, under water last spring!

(*He laughs.*)

That Europe is nothin' on earth but a great big auction, that's all it is, that bunch of old worn-out places, it's just a big fire-sale, the whole ruttin' thing, an' Big Mama wint wild in it, why, you couldn't hold that woman with a mule's harness! Bought, bought, bought!—lucky I'm a rich man, yes siree, Bob, an' half that stuff is mildewin' in th' basement. It's lucky I'm a rich man, it sure is lucky, well, I'm a rich man, Brick, yep, I'm a mighty rich man.

(*His eyes light up for a moment.*)

Y'know how much I'm worth? Guess, Brick! Guess how much I'm worth!

(BRICK *smiles vaguely over his drink.*)

Close on ten million in cash an' blue-chip stocks, outside, mind you, of twenty-eight thousand acres of the richest land this side of the valley Nile!

But a man can't buy his life with it, he can't buy back his life with it when his life has been spent, that's one thing not offered in the Europe fire-sale or in the American markets or any markets on earth, a man can't buy his life with it, he can't buy back his life when his life is finished. . . . That's a sobering thought, a very sobering thought, and that's a thought that I was turning over in my head, over and over and over— until today. . . .

I'm wiser and sadder, Brick, for this experience which I just gone through. They's one thing else that I remember in Europe.

Brick. What is that, Big Daddy?

Big Daddy. The hills around Barcelona in the country of Spain and the children running over those bare hills in their bare skins beggin' like starvin' dogs with howls and screeches, and how fat the priests are on the streets of Barcelona, so many of them and so fat and so pleasant, ha ha!—Y'know I could feed that country? I got money enough to feed that goddam country, but the human animal is a selfish beast and I don't reckon the money I passed out there to those howling children in the hills around Barcelona would more than upholster the chairs in this room, I mean pay to put a new cover on this chair!

Hell, I threw them money like you'd scatter feed corn for chickens, I threw money at them just to get rid of them long enough to climb back into th' car and—drive away. . . .

And then in Morocco, them Arabs, why, I remember one day in Marrakech, that old walled Arab city, I set on a broken-down wall to have a cigar, it was fearful hot there and this Arab woman stood in the road and looked at me till I was embarrassed, she stood stock still in the dusty hot road and looked at me till I was embarrassed. But listen to this. She had a naked child with her, a little naked girl with her, barely able to toddle, and after a while she set this child on the ground and give her a push and whispered something to her.

This child come toward me, barely able t' walk, come toddling up to me and—

Jesus, it makes you sick t' remember a thing like this!

It stuck out its hand and tried to unbutton my trousers!

That child was not yet five! Can you believe me? Or do you think that I am making this up? I wint back to the hotel and said to Big Mama, Git packed! We're clearing out of this country. . . .

Brick. Big Daddy, you're on a talkin' jag tonight.

Big Daddy (*Ignoring this remark*). Yes, sir, that's how it is, the human animal is a beast that dies but the fact that he's dying don't give him pity for others, no, sir, it—
—Did you say something?

Brick. Yes.

Big Daddy. What?

Brick. Hand me over that crutch so I can get up.

Big Daddy. Where you goin'?
Brick. I'm takin' a little short trip to Echo Spring.
Big Daddy. To where?
Brick. Liquor cabinet. . . .
Big Daddy. Yes, sir, boy—

(*He hands* BRICK *the crutch.*)

—the human animal is a beast that dies and if he's got money he buys and buys and buys and I think the reason he buys everything he can buy is that in the back of his mind he has the crazy hope that one of his purchases will be life everlasting!— Which it never can be. . . . The human animal is a beast that—
Brick (*At the liquor cabinet*). Big Daddy, you sure are shootin' th' breeze here tonight.

(*There is a pause and voices are heard outside.*)

Big Daddy. I been quiet here lately, spoke not a word, just sat and stared into space. I had something heavy weighing on my mind but tonight that load was took off me. That's why I'm talking.—The sky looks diff'rent to me. . . .
Brick. You know what I like to hear most?
Big Daddy. What?
Brick. Solid quiet. Perfect unbroken quiet.
Big Daddy. Why?
Brick. Because it's more peaceful.
Big Daddy. Man, you'll hear a lot of that in the grave.

(*He chuckles agreeably.*)

Brick. Are you through talkin' to me?
Big Daddy. Why are you so anxious to shut me up?
Brick. Well, sir, ever so often you say to me, Brick, I want to have a talk with you, but when we talk, it never materializes. Nothing is said. You sit in a chair and gas about this and that and I look like I listen. I try to look like I listen, but I don't listen, not much. Communication is—awful hard between people an'—somehow between you and me, it just don't— happen.
Big Daddy. Have you ever been scared? I mean have you ever felt downright terror of something?

(*He gets up.*)

Just one moment.

(*He looks off as if he were going to tell an important secret.*)

Big Daddy. Brick?
Brick. What?
Big Daddy. Son, I thought I had it!
Brick. Had what? Had what, Big Daddy?
Big Daddy. Cancer!
Brick. Oh . . .
Big Daddy. I thought the old man made out of bones had laid his cold and heavy hand on my shoulder!
Brick. Well, Big Daddy, you kept a tight mouth about it.
Big Daddy. A pig squeals. A man keeps a tight mouth about it, in spite of a man not having a pig's advantage.
Brick. What advantage is that?
Big Daddy. Ignorance—of mortality— is a comfort. A man don't have that comfort, he's the only living thing that conceives of death, that knows what it is. The others go without knowing which is the way that anything living should go, go without knowing, without any knowledge of it, and yet a pig squeals, but a man sometimes, he can keep a tight mouth about it. Sometimes he—

TENNESSEE WILLIAMS

(There is a deep, smoldering ferocity in the old man.)

—can keep a tight mouth about it. I wonder if—

Brick. What, Big Daddy?

Big Daddy. A whiskey highball would injure this spastic condition?

Brick. No, sir, it might do it good.

Big Daddy *(Grins suddenly, wolfishly).* Jesus, I can't tell you! The sky is open! Christ, it's open again! It's open, boy, it's open!

(Brick looks down at his drink.)

Brick. You feel better, Big Daddy?

Big Daddy. Better? Hell! I can breathe! —All of my life I been like a doubled up fist. . . .

(He pours a drink.)

—Poundin', smashin', drivin'!—now I'm going to loosen these doubled-up hands and touch things *easy* with them. . . .

(He spreads his hands as if caressing the air.)

You know what I'm contemplating?

Brick *(Vaguely).* No, sir. What are you contemplating?

Big Daddy. Ha ha!—*Pleasure!*—pleassure with *women!*

(Brick's smile fades a little but lingers.)

—Yes, boy. I'll tell you something that you might not guess. I still have desire for women and this is my sixty-fifth birthday.

Brick. I think that's mighty remarkable, Big Daddy.

Big Daddy. Remarkable?

Brick. *Admirable,* Big Daddy.

Big Daddy. You're damn right it is, remarkable and admirable both. I re-alize now that I never had me enough. I let many chances slip by because of scruples about it, scruples, convention—crap. . . . All that stuff is bull, bull, bull! —It took the shadow of death to make me see it. Now that shadow's lifted, I'm going to cut loose and have, what is it they call it, have me a—ball!

Brick. A ball, huh?

Big Daddy. That's right, a ball, a ball! Hell!—I slept with Big Mama till, let's see, five years ago, till I was sixty and she was fifty-eight, and never even liked her, never did!

(The phone has been ringing down the hall. BIG MAMA enters, exclaiming:)

Big Mama. Don't you men hear that phone ring? I heard it way out on the gall'ry.

Big Daddy. There's five rooms off this front gall'ry that you could go through. Why do you go through this one?

(BIG MAMA makes a playful face as she bustles out the hall door.)

Hunh!—Why, when Big Mama goes out of a room, I can't remember what that woman looks like—

Big Mama. Hello.

Big Daddy.—But when Big Mama comes back into the room, boy, then I see what she looks like, and I wish I didn't!

(Bends over laughing at this joke till it hurts his guts and be straightens with a grimace. The laugh subsides to a chuckle as he puts the liquor glass a little distrustfully down on the table.)

Big Mama. Hello, Miss Sally.

(BRICK *has risen and hobbled to the gallery doors.*)

Big Daddy. Hey! Where you goin'?
Brick. Out for a breather.
Big Daddy. Not yet you ain't. Stay here till this talk is finished, young fellow.
Brick. I thought it was finished, Big Daddy.
Big Daddy. It ain't even begun.
Brick. My mistake. Excuse me. I just wanted to feel that river breeze.
Big Daddy. Set back down in that chair.

(BIG MAMA's *voice rises, carrying down the hall.*)

Big Mama. You're a case! You're a caution, Miss Sally.
Big Daddy. Jesus, she's talking to my old maid sister again.
Big Mama. Why didn't you give me a chance to explain it to you?
Big Daddy. Brick, this stuff burns me.
Big Mama. Well, goodbye, now, Miss Sally. You come down real soon. Big Daddy's dying to see you.
Big Daddy. Crap!
Big Mama. Yaiss, goodbye, Miss Sally. . . .

(*She hangs up and bellows with mirth.* BIG DADDY *groans and covers his ears as she approaches.*)

(*Bursting in:*)

Big Daddy, that was Miss Sally callin' from Memphis again! You know what she done, Big Daddy? She called her doctor in Memphis to git him to tell her what that spastic thing is! Ha-*HAAAA!*—And called back to tell me how relieved she was that—Hey! Let me in!

(*Big Daddy has been holding the door half closed against her.*)

Big Daddy. Naw I ain't. I told you not to come and go through this room. You just back out and go through those five other rooms.
Big Mama. Big Daddy? Big Daddy? Oh, Big Daddy!—You didn't mean those things you said to me, did you?

(*He shuts door firmly against her but she still calls.*)

Sweetheart? Sweetheart? Big Daddy? You didn't mean those awful things you said to me?—I know you didn't. I know you didn't mean those things in your heart. . . .

(*The childlike voice fades with a sob and her heavy footsteps retreat down the hall.* BRICK *has risen once more on his crutches and starts for the gallery again.*)

Big Daddy. All I ask of that woman is that she leave me alone. But she can't admit to herself that she makes me sick. That comes of having slept with her too many years. Should of quit much sooner but that old woman she never got enough of it—and I was good in bed . . . I never should of wasted so much of it on her. . . . They say you got just so many and each one is numbered. Well, I got a few left in me, a few, and I'm going to pick me a good one to spend 'em on! I'm going to pick me a choice one, I don't care how much she costs, I'll smother her in—minks! Ha ha! I'll strip her naked and smother her in minks and choke her with diamonds! Ha ha! I'll strip her naked and choke her with diamonds and smother her with minks and hump her from hell to breakfast. *Ha aha ha ha ha!*
Mae (*Gaily at door*). Who's that laughin' in there?

Gooper. Is Big Daddy laughin' in there?

Big Daddy. Crap!—them two—*drips.*
. . .

(*He goes over and touches* BRICK's *shoulder.*)

Yes, son. Brick boy.—I'm—*happy!* I'm happy, son, I'm happy!

(*He chokes a little and bites his under lip, pressing his head quickly, shyly against his son's head and then, coughing with embarrassment, goes uncertainly back to the table where he set down the glass. He drinks and makes a grimace as it burns his guts.* BRICK *sighs and rises with effort.*)

What makes you so restless? Have you got ants in your britches?

Brick. Yes, sir . . .

Big Daddy. Why?

Brick. —Something—hasn't—happened. . . .

Big Daddy. Yeah? What is that!

Brick (*Sadly*).—the click. . . .

Big Daddy. Did you say click?

Brick. Yes, click.

Big Daddy. What click?

Brick. A click that I get in my head that makes me peaceful.

Big Daddy. I sure in hell don't know what you're talking about, but it disturbs me.

Brick. It's just a mechanical thing.

Big Daddy. What is a mechanical thing?

Brick. This click that I get in my head that makes me peaceful. I got to drink till I get it. It's just a mechanical thing, something like a—like a—like a—

Big Daddy. Like a—

Brick. Switch clicking off in my head, turning the hot light off and the cool night on and—

(*He looks up, smiling sadly.*)

—all of a sudden there's—peace!

Big Daddy (*Whistles long and soft with astonishment, he goes back to Brick and clasps his son's two shoulders*). Jesus! I didn't know it had gotten that bad with you. Why, boy, you're —alcoholic!

Brick. That's the truth, Big Daddy. I'm alcoholic.

Big Daddy. This shows how I—let things go!

Brick. I have to hear that little click in my head that makes me peaceful. Usually I hear it sooner than this, sometimes as early as—noon, but— —Today it's—dilatory. . . . —I just haven't got the right level of alcohol in my bloodstream yet!

(*This last statement is made with energy as he freshens his drink.*)

Big Daddy. Uh—huh. Expecting death made me blind. I didn't have no idea that a son of mine was turning into a drunkard under my nose.

Brick (*Gently*). Well, now you do, Big Daddy, the news has penetrated.

Big Daddy. UH-huh, yes, now I do, the news has—penetrated. . . .

Brick. And so if you'll excuse me—

Big Daddy. No, I won't excuse you.

Brick.—I'd better sit by myself till I hear that click in my head, it's just a mechanical thing but it don't happen except when I'm alone or talking to no one. . . .

Big Daddy. You got a long, long time to sit still, boy, and talk to no one, but now you're talkin' to me. At least I'm talking to you. And you set there and listen until I tell you the conversation is over!

Brick. But this talk is like all the others we've ever had together in our lives! It's nowhere, nowhere!—it's—it's *painful,* Big Daddy. . . .

Big Daddy. All right, then let it be painful, but don't you move from that chair!—I'm going to remove that crutch. . . .

(*He seizes the crutch and tosses it across room.*)

Brick. I can hop on one foot, and if I fall, I can crawl!

Big Daddy. If you ain't careful you're gonna crawl off this plantation and then, by Jesus, you'll have to hustle your drinks along Skid Row!

Brick. That'll come, Big Daddy.

Big Daddy. Naw, it won't. You're my son and I'm going to straighten you out; now that *I'm* straightened out, I'm going to straighten out you!

Brick. Yeah?

Big Daddy. Today the report come in from Ochsner Clinic. Y'know what they told me?

(*His face glows with triumph.*)

The only thing that they could detect with all the instruments of science in that great hospital is a little spastic condition of the colon! And nerves torn to pieces by all that worry about it.

(*A little girl bursts into room with a sparkler clutched in each fist, hops and shrieks like a monkey gone mad and rushes back out again as* BIG DADDY *strikes at her.*)

(*Silence. The two men stare at each other. A woman laughs gaily outside.*)

I want you to know I breathed a sigh of relief almost as powerful as the Vicksburg tornado!

(*There is laughter outside, running footsteps, the soft plushy sound and light of exploding rockets.*)

(BRICK *stares at him soberly for a long moment; then makes a sort of startled sound in his nostrils and springs up on one foot and hops across the room to grab his crutch, swinging on the furniture for support. He gets the crutch and flees as if in horror for the gallery. His father seizes him by the sleeve of his white silk pajamas.*)

Stay here, you son of a bitch!—till I say go!

Brick. I can't.

Big Daddy. You sure in hell will, God damn it.

Brick. No, I can't. We talk, you talk, in —circles! We get no where, no where! It's always the same, you say you want to talk to me and don't have a ruttin' thing to say to me!

Big Daddy. Nothin' to say when I'm tellin' you I'm going to live when I thought I was dying?!

Brick. Oh—*that!*—Is that what you have to say to me?

Big Daddy. Why, you son of a bitch! Ain't that, ain't that—*important?!*

Brick. Well, you said that, that's said, and now I—

Big Daddy. Now you set back down.

Brick. You're all balled up, you—

Big Daddy. I ain't balled up!

Brick. You are, you're all balled up!

Big Daddy. Don't tell me what I am, you drunken whelp! I'm going to tear this coat sleeve off if you don't set down!

Brick. Big Daddy—

Big Daddy. Do what I tell you! I'm the boss here, now! I want you to know I'm back in the driver's seat now!

(BIG MAMA *rushes in, clutching her great heaving bosom.*)

Big Mama. Big Daddy!

Big Daddy. What in hell do you want in here, Big Mama?

Big Mama. Oh, Big Daddy! Why are you shouting like that? I just cain't stainnnnnnd—it. . . .

Big Daddy (*Raising the back of his hand above his head*). GIT!—outa here.

(*She rushes back out, sobbing.*)

Brick (*Softly, sadly*). Christ. . . .

Big Daddy (*Fiercely*). Yeah! Christ—is right. . . .

(BRICK *breaks loose and hobbles toward the gallery.*)

(BIG DADDY *jerks his crutch from under* BRICK *so he steps with the injured ankle. He utters a hissing cry of anguish, clutches a chair and pulls it over on top of him on the floor.*)

Son of a—tub of—hog fat. . . .

Brick. Big Daddy! Give me my crutch.

(BIG DADDY *throws the crutch out of reach.*)

Give me that crutch, Big Daddy.

Big Daddy. Why do you drink?

Brick. Don't know, give me my crutch!

Big Daddy. You better think why you drink or give up drinking!

Brick. Will you please give me my crutch so I can get up off this floor?

Big Daddy. First you answer my question. Why do you drink? Why are you throwing your life away, boy, like somethin' disgusting you picked up on the street?

Brick (*Getting onto his knees*). Big Daddy, I'm in pain, I stepped on that foot.

Big Daddy. Good! I'm glad you're not too numb with the liquor in you to feel some pain!

Brick. You—spilled my—drink . . .

Big Daddy. I'll make a bargain with you. You tell me why you drink and I'll hand you one. I'll pour you the liquor myself and hand it to you.

Brick. Why do I drink?

Big Daddy. Yeah! Why?

Brick. Give me a drink and I'll tell you.

Big Daddy. Tell me first!

Brick. I'll tell you in one word.

Big Daddy. What word?

Brick. DISGUST!

(*The clock chimes softly, sweetly.* BIG DADDY *gives it a short, outraged glance.*)

Now how about that drink?

Big Daddy. What are you disgusted with? You got to tell me that, first. Otherwise being disgusted don't make no sense!

Brick. Give me my crutch.

Big Daddy. You heard me, you got to tell me what I asked you first.

Brick. I told you, I said to kill my disgust!

Big Daddy. DISGUST WITH WHAT!

Brick. You strike a hard bargain.

Big Daddy. What are you disgusted with?—an' I'll pass you the liquor.

Brick. I can hop on one foot, and if I fall, I can crawl.

Big Daddy. You want liquor that bad?

Brick (*Dragging himself up, clinging to bedstead*). Yeah, I want it that bad.

Big Daddy. If I give you a drink, will you tell me what it is you're disgusted with, Brick?

Brick. Yes, sir, I will try to.

(*The old man pours him a drink and solemnly passes it to him.*

(*There is silence as* BRICK *drinks.*)

Have you ever heard the word "mendacity"?

Big Daddy. Sure. Mendacity is one of them five-dollar words that cheap politicians throw back and forth at each other.

Brick. You know what it means?

Big Daddy. Don't it mean lying and liars?

Brick. Yes, sir, lying and liars.

Big Daddy. Has someone been lying to you?

Children (*Chanting in chorus offstage*). We want Big Dad-dee! We want Big Dad-dee!

(GOOPER *appears in the gallery door.*)

Gooper. Big Daddy, the kiddies are shouting for you out there.

Big Daddy (*Fiercely*). Keep out, Gooper!

Gooper. 'Scuse *me!*

(BIG DADDY *slams the doors after* GOOPER.)

Big Daddy. Who's been lying to you, has Margaret been lying to you, has your wife been lying to you about something, Brick?

Brick. Not her. That wouldn't matter.

Big Daddy. Then who's been lying to you, and what about?

Brick. No single person and no one lie. . . .

Big Daddy. Then what, what then, for Christ's sake?

Brick.—The whole, the whole—thing. . . .

Big Daddy. Why are you rubbing your head? You got a headache?

Brick. No, I'm tryin' to—

Big Daddy.—Concentrate, but you can't because your brain's all soaked with liquor, is that the trouble? Wet brain!

(*He snatches the glass from* BRICK'S *hand.*)

What do you know about this mendacity thing? Hell! I could write a book on it! Don't you know that? I could write a book on it and still not cover the subject? Well, I could, I could write a goddam book on it and still not cover the subject anywhere near enough!!—Think of all the lies I got to put up with!—Pretenses! Ain't that mendacity? Having to pretend stuff you don't think or feel or have any idea of? Having for instance to act like I care for Big Mama!—I haven't been able to stand the sight, sound, or smell of that woman for forty years now!—even when I *laid* her!—regular as a piston. . . .

Pretend to love that son of a bitch of a Gooper and his wife Mae and those five same screechers out there like parrots in a jungle? Jesus! Can't stand to look at 'em!

Church!—it bores the bejesus out of me but I go!—I go an' sit there and listen to the fool preacher!

Clubs!—Elks! Masons! Rotary!—crap!

(*A spasm of pain makes him clutch his belly. He sinks into a chair and his voice is softer and hoarser.*)

You I *do* like for some reason, did always have some kind of real feeling for—affection—respect—yes, always. . . .

You and being a success as a planter is all I ever had any devotion to in my whole life!—and that's the truth. . . .

I don't know why, but it is!

I've lived with mendacity!—Why can't *you* live with it? Hell, you *got* to live with it, there's nothing *else* to *live* with except mendacity, is there?

Brick. Yes, sir. Yes, sir, there is something else that you can live with!

Big Daddy. What?

Brick (*Lifting his glass*). This!—Liquor. . . .

Big Daddy. That's not living, that's dodging away from life.

Brick. I want to dodge away from it.

Big Daddy. Then why don't you kill yourself, man?

Brick. I like to drink. . . .

Big Daddy. Oh, God, I can't talk to you. . . .

Brick. I'm sorry, Big Daddy.

Big Daddy. Not as sorry as I am. I'll tell you something. A little while back when I thought my number was up—

(*This speech should have torrential pace and fury.*)

—before I found out it was just this —spastic—colon. I thought about you. Should I or should I not, if the jig was up, give you this place when I go—since I hate Gooper an' Mae an' know that they hate me, and since all five same monkeys are little Maes an' Goopers.—And I thought, No!—Then I thought, Yes!—I couldn't make up my mind. I hate Gooper and his five same monkeys and that bitch Mae! Why should I turn over twenty-eight thousand acres of the richest land this side of the valley Nile to not my kind?—But why in hell, on the other hand, Brick—should I subsidize a goddam fool on the bottle?—Liked or not liked, well, maybe even—*loved!* —Why should I do that?—Subsidize worthless behavior? Rot? Corruption?

Brick (*Smiling*). I understand.

Big Daddy. Well, if you do, you're smarter than I am, God damn it, because I don't understand. And this I will tell you frankly. I didn't make up my mind at all on that question and still to this day I ain't made out no will!—Well, now I don't *have* to. The pressure is gone. I can just wait and see if you pull yourself together or if you don't.

Brick. That's right, Big Daddy.

Big Daddy. You sound like you thought I was kidding.

Brick (*Rising*). No, sir, I know you're not kidding.

Big Daddy. But you don't care—?

Brick (*Hobbling toward the gallery door*). No, sir, I don't care. . . .

(*He stands in the gallery doorway as the night sky turns pink and green and gold with successive flashes of light.*)

Big Daddy. WAIT!—Brick. . . .

(*His voice drops. Suddenly there is something shy, almost tender, in his restraining gesture.*)

Don't let's—leave it like this, like them other talks we've had, we've always—talked around things, we've— just talked around things for some ruttin' reason, I don't know what, it's always like something was left not spoken, something avoided because neither of us was honest enough with the—other. . . .

Brick. I never lied to you, Big Daddy.

Big Daddy. Did I ever to *you?*

Brick. No, sir. . . .

Big Daddy. Then there is at least two people that never lied to each other.

Brick. But we've never *talked* to each other.

Big Daddy. We can *now.*

Brick. Big Daddy, there don't seem to be anything much to say.

Big Daddy. You say that you drink to kill your disgust with lying.

Brick. You said to give you a reason.

Big Daddy. Is liquor the only thing that'll kill this disgust?

Brick. Now. Yes.

Big Daddy. But not once, huh?

Brick. Not when I was still young an' believing. A drinking man's someone who wants to forget he isn't still young an' believing.

Big Daddy. Believing what?

Brick. Believing. . . .

Big Daddy. Believing *what?*

Brick (*Stubbornly evasive*). Believing.

Big Daddy. I don't know what the hell you mean by believing and I don't think you know what you mean by believing, but if you still got sports in your blood, go back to sports announcing and—

Brick. Sit in a glass box watching games I can't play? Describing what I can't do while players do it? Sweating out their disgust and confusion in contests I'm not fit for? Drinkin' a coke, half bourbon, so I can stand it? That's no goddam good any more, no help—time just outran me, Big Daddy—got there first . . .

Big Daddy. I think you're passing the buck.

Brick. You know many drinkin' men?

Big Daddy (*With a slight, charming smile*). I have known a fair number of that species.

Brick. Could any of them tell you why he drank?

Big Daddy. Yep, you're passin' the buck to things like time and disgust with "mendacity" and—crap!—if you got to use that kind of language about a thing, it's ninety-proof bull, and I'm not buying any.

Brick. I had to give you a reason to get a drink!

Big Daddy. You started drinkin' when your friend Skipper died.

(*Silence for five beats. Then* BRICK *makes a startled movement, reaching for his crutch.*)

Brick. What are you suggesting?

Big Daddy. I'm suggesting nothing.

(*The shuffle and clop of* BRICK's *rapid hobble away from his father's steady, grave attention.*)

—But Gooper an' Mae suggested that there was something not right exactly in your—

Brick (*Stopping short downstage as if backed to a wall*). "Not right"?

Big Daddy. Not, well, exactly *normal* in your friendship with—

Brick. They suggested that, too? I thought that was Maggie's suggestion.

(BRICK's *detachment is at last broken through. His heart is accelerated; his forehead sweat-beaded; his breath becomes more rapid and his voice hoarse. The thing they're discussing, timidly and painfully on the side of* BIG DADDY, *fiercely, violently on* BRICK's *side, is the inadmissible thing that* SKIPPER *died to disavow between them. The fact that if it existed it had to be disavowed to "keep face" in the world they lived in, may be at the heart of the "mendacity" that* BRICK *drinks to kill his disgust with. It may be the root of his collapse. Or maybe it is only a single manifestation of it, not even the most important. The bird that I hope to catch in the net of this play is not the solution of one man's psychological problem. I'm trying to catch the true quality of experience in a group of people, that cloudy, flickering, evanescent—fiercely charged!—interplay of live human beings in the thundercloud of a common crisis. Some mys-*

tery should be left in the revelation of character in a play, just as a great deal of mystery is always left in the revelation of character in life, even in one's own character to himself. This does not absolve the playwright of his duty to observe and probe as clearly and deeply as he legitimately can: but it should steer him away from "pat" conclusions, facile definitions which make a play just a play, not a snare for the truth of human experience.)

(The following scene should be played with great concentration, with most of the power leashed but palpable in what is left unspoken.)

Who else's suggestion is it, is it yours? How many others thought that Skipper and I were—

Big Daddy (*Gently*). Now, hold on, hold on a minute, son.—I knocked around in my time.

Brick. What's that got to do with—

Big Daddy. I said "Hold on!"—I bummed, I bummed this country till I was—

Brick. Whose suggestion, who else's suggestion is it?

Big Daddy. Slept in hobo jungles and railroad Y's and flophouses in all cities before I—

Brick. Oh, *you* think so, too, you call me your son and a queer. Oh! Maybe that's why you put Maggie and me in this room that was Jack Straw's and Peter Ochello's, in which that pair of old sisters slept in a double bed where both of 'em died!

Big Daddy. Now just don't go throwing rocks at—

(Suddenly REVEREND TOOKER *appears in the gallery doors, his head slightly, playfully, fatuously cocked, with a practised clergyman's smile, sincere as a bird call blown on a hunter's whistle, the living embodiment of the pious, conventional lie.)*

*(*BIG DADDY *gasps a little at this perfectly timed, but incongruous, apparition.)*

—What're you lookin' for Preacher?

Reverend Tooker. The gentleman's lavatory, ha ha!—heh, heh . . .

Big Daddy (*With strained courtesy*).—Go back out and walk down to the other end of the gallery, Reverend Tooker, and use the bathroom connected with my bedroom, and if you can't find it, ask them where it is!

Reverend Tooker. Ah, thanks.

(He goes out with a deprecatory chuckle.)

Big Daddy. It's hard to talk in this place . . .

Brick. Son of a—!

Big Daddy (*Leaving a lot unspoken*).—I seen all things and understood a lot of them, till 1910. Christ, the year that—I had worn my shoes through, hocked my—I hopped off a yellow dog freight car half a mile down the road, slept in a wagon of cotton outside the gin—Jack Straw an' Peter Ochello took me in. Hired me to manage this place which grew into this one.—When Jack Straw died—why, old Peter Ochello quit eatin' like a dog does when its master's dead, and died, too!

Brick. Christ!

Big Daddy. I'm just saying I understand such—

Brick (*Violently*). Skipper is dead. I have not quit eating!

Big Daddy. No, but you started drinking.

(BRICK *wheels on his crutch and hurls his glass across the room shouting.*)

Brick. YOU THINK SO, TOO?

(*Footsteps run on the gallery. There are women's calls.*)

(BIG DADDY *goes toward the door.*)

(BRICK *is transformed, as if a quiet mountain blew suddenly up in volcanic flame.*)

Brick. You think so, too? You think so, too? You think me an' Skipper did, did, did!—*sodomy!*—together?

Big Daddy. Hold—!

Brick. That what you—

Big Daddy.—ON—a minute!

Brick. You think we did dirty things between us, Skipper an'—

Big Daddy. Why are you shouting like that? Why are you—

Brick.—Me, is that what you think of Skipper, is that—

Big Daddy.—so excited? I don't think nothing. I don't know nothing. I'm simply telling you what—

Brick. You think that Skipper and me were a pair of dirty old men?

Big Daddy. Now that's—

Brick. Straw? Ochello? A couple of—

Big Daddy. Now just—

Brick.—friggin' sissies? Queers? Is that what you—

Big Daddy. Shhh.

Brick.—think?

(*He loses his balance and pitches to his knees without noticing the pain. He grabs the bed and drags himself up.*)

Big Daddy. Jesus!—Whew. . . . Grab my hand!

Brick. Naw, I don't want your hand. . . .

Big Daddy. Well, I want yours, Git up!

(*He draws him up, keeps an arm about him with concern and affection.*)

You broken out in a sweat! You're panting like you'd run a race with—

Brick (*Freeing himself from his father's hold*). Big Daddy, you shock me, Big Daddy, you, you—*shock* me! Talkin' so—

(*He turns away from his father.*)

—casually! about a—thing like that . . .

—Don't you know how people *feel* about things like that? How, how *disgusted* they are by things like that? Why, at Ole Miss when it was discovered a pledge to our fraternity, Skipper's and mine, did a, *attempted* to do a, unnatural thing with—

We not only dropped him like a hot rock!—We told him to git off the campus, and he did, he got!—All the way to—

(*He halts, breathless.*)

Big Daddy.—Where?

Brick.—North Africa, last I heard!

Big Daddy. Well, I have come back from further away than that, I have just now returned from the other side of the moon, death's country, son, and I'm not easy to shock by anything here.

(*He comes downstage and faces out.*)

Always, anyhow, lived with too much space around me to be infected by ideas of other people. One thing you can grow on a big place more important than cotton!—is *tolerance!*—I grown it.

(*He returns toward* BRICK.)

Brick. Why can't exceptional friendship, *real, real, deep, deep friendship!* between two men be respected as something clean and decent without being thought of as—

Big Daddy. It can, it is, for God's sake.

Brick.—Fairies. . . .

(*In his utterance of this word, we gauge the wide and profound reach of the conventional mores he got from the world that crowned him with early laurel.*)

Big Daddy. I told Mae an' Gooper—

Brick. Frig Mae and Gooper, frig all dirty lies and liars!—Skipper and me had a clean, true thing between us! —had a clean friendship, practically all our lives, till Maggie got the idea you're talking about. Normal? No!—It was too rare to be normal, any true thing between two people is too rare to be normal. Oh, once in a while he put his hand on my shoulder or I'd put mine on his, oh, maybe even, when we were touring the country in profootball an' shared hotel-rooms we'd reach across the space between the two beds and shake hands to say goodnight, yeah, one or two times we
—

Big Daddy. Brick, nobody thinks that that's not normal!

Brick. Well, they're mistaken, it was! It was a pure an' true thing an' that's not normal.

Mae (*Off stage*). Big Daddy, they're startin' the fireworks.

(*They both stare straight at each other for a long moment. The tension breaks and both turn away as if tired.*)

Big Daddy. Yeah, it's—hard t'—talk. . . .

Brick. All right, then, let's—let it go. . . .

Big Daddy. Why did Skipper crack up? Why have you?

(*BRICK looks back at his father again. He has already decided, without knowing that he has made this decision, that he is going to tell his father that he is dying of cancer. Only this could even the score between them: one inadmissible thing in return for another.*)

Brick (*Ominously*). All right. You're asking for it, Big Daddy. We're finally going to have that real true talk you wanted. It's too late to stop it, now, we got to carry it through and cover every subject.

(*He hobbles back to the liquor cabinet.*)

Uh-huh.

(*He opens the ice bucket and picks up the silver tongs with slow admiration of their frosty brightness.*)

Maggie declares that Skipper and I went into pro-football after we left Ole Miss because we were scared to grow up . . .

(*He moves downstage with the shuffle and clop of a cripple on a crutch. As MARGARET did when her speech became "recitative," he looks out into the house, commanding its attention by his direct, concentrated gaze—a broken, "tragically elegant" figure telling simply as much as he knows of "the Truth."*)

—Wanted to—keep on tossing— those long, long!—high, high!— passes that—couldn't be intercepted except by time, the aerial attack that made us famous! And so we did, we did, we kept it up for one season, that aerial attack, we held it high!—Yeah, but—that summer, Maggie, she laid the law down to me, said. Now or never, and so I married Maggie. . . .

Big Daddy. How was Maggie in bed?

Brick (*Wryly*). Great! the greatest!

(BIG DADDY *nods as if he thought so.*)

She went on the road that fall with the Dixie Stars. Oh, she made a great show of being the world's best sport. She wore a—wore a—tall bearskin cap! A shako, they call it, a dyed moleskin coat, a moleskin coat dyed red!—Cut up crazy! Rented hotel ballrooms for victory celebrations, wouldn't cancel them when it—turned out—defeat. . . .

MAGGIE THE CAT! Ha ha!

(BIG DADDY *nods.*)

—But Skipper, he had some fever which came back on him which doctors couldn't explain and I got that injury—turned out to be just a shadow on the X-ray plate—and a touch of bursitis. . . .

I lay in a hospital bed, watched our games on TV, saw Maggie on the bench next to Skipper when he was hauled out of a game for stumbles, fumbles!—Burned me up the way she hung on his arm!—Y'know, I think that Maggie had always felt sort of left out because she and me never got any closer together than two people just get in bed, which is not much closer than two cats on a—fence humping. . . .

So! She took this time to work on poor dumb Skipper. He was a less than average student at Ole Miss, you

know that, don't you?!—Poured in his mind the dirty, false idea that what we were, him and me, was a frustrated case of that ole pair of sisters that lived in this room. Jack Straw and Peter Ochello!—He, poor Skipper, went to bed with Maggie to prove it wasn't true, and when it didn't work out, he thought it *was* true!—Skipper broke in two like a rotten stick—nobody ever turned so fast to a lush—or died of it so quick. . . .

—Now are you satisfied?

(BIG DADDY *has listened to this story, dividing the grain from the chaff. Now he looks at his son.*)

Big Daddy. Are *you* satisfied?

Brick. With what?

Big Daddy. That half-ass story!

Brick. What's half-ass about it?

Big Daddy. Something's left out of that story. What did you leave out?

(*The phone has started ringing in the hall.*)

Gooper (*Off stage*). Hello.

(*As if it reminded him of something,* BRICK *glances suddenly toward the sound and says:*)

Brick. Yes!—I left out a long-distance call which I had from Skipper—

Gooper. Speaking, go ahead.

Brick.—In which he made a drunken confession to me and on which I hung up!

Gooper. No.

Brick.—Last time we spoke to each other in our lives . . .

Gooper. No, sir.

Big Daddy. You musta said something to him before you hung up.

Brick. What could I say to him?

Big Daddy. Anything. Something.

Brick. Nothing.

Big Daddy. Just hung up?

Brick. Just hung up.

Big Daddy. Uh-huh. Anyhow now!—we have tracked down the lie with which you're disgusted and which you are drinking to kill your disgust with, Brick. You been passing the buck. This disgust with mendacity is disgust with yourself.

You!—dug the grave of your friend and kicked him in it!—before you'd face truth with him!

Brick. *His* truth, not *mine!*

Big Daddy. His truth, okay! But you wouldn't face it with him!

Brick. Who *can* face truth? Can *you?*

Big Daddy. Now don't start passin' the rotten buck again, boy!

Brick. How about these birthday congratulations, these many, many happy returns of the day, when ev'rybody knows there won't be any except you!

(GOOPER, *who has answered the hall phone, lets out a high, shrill laugh; the voice becomes audible saying:* "No, no, you got it all wrong! Upside down! Are you crazy?")

(BRICK *suddenly catches his breath as he realizes that he has made a shocking disclosure. He hobbles a few paces, then freezes, and without looking at his father's shocked face, says:*)

Let's, let's—go out, now, and—watch the fireworks. Come on, Big Daddy.

(BIG DADDY *moves suddenly forward and grabs hold of the boy's crutch like it was a weapon for which they were fighting for possession.*)

Big Daddy. Oh, no, no! No one's going out! What did you start to say?

Brick. I don't remember.

Big Daddy. "Many happy returns when they know there won't be any"?

Brick. Aw, hell, Big Daddy, forget it. Come on out on the gallery and look at the fireworks they're shooting off for your birthday. . . .

Big Daddy. First you finish that remark you were makin' before you cut off. "Many happy returns when they know there won't be any"?—Ain't that what you just said?

Brick. Look, now. I can get around without that crutch if I have to but it would be a lot easier on the furniture an' glassware if I didn' have to go swinging along like Tarzan of th'—

Big Daddy. FINISH! WHAT YOU WAS SAYIN'!

(*An eerie green glow shows in sky behind him.*)

Brick (*Sucking the ice in his glass, speech becoming thick*). Leave th' place to Gooper and Mae an' their five little same little monkeys. All I want is—

Big Daddy. "LEAVE TH' PLACE," did you say?

Brick (*Vaguely*). All twenty-eight thousand acres of the richest land this side of the valley Nile.

Big Daddy. Who said I was "leaving the place" to Gooper or anybody? This is my sixty-fifth birthday! I got fifteen years or twenty years left in me! I'll outlive *you!* I'll bury you an' have to pay for your coffin!

Brick. Sure. Many happy returns. Now let's go watch the fireworks, come on, let's—

Big Daddy. Lying, have they been lying? About the report from th'—

clinic? Did they, did they—find something?—*Cancer.* Maybe?

Brick. Mendacity is a system that we live in. Liquor is one way out an' death's the other. . . .

(*He takes the crutch from Big Daddy's loose grip and swings out on the gallery leaving the doors open.*

(*A song, "Pick a Bale of Cotton," is heard.*)

Mae (*appearing in door*). Oh, Big Daddy, the field hands are singin' fo' you!

Brick. I'm sorry, Big Daddy. My head don't work any more and it's hard for me to understand how anybody could care if he lived or died or was dying or cared about anything but whether or not there was liquor left in the bottle and so I said what I said without thinking. In some ways I'm no better than the others, in some ways worse because I'm less alive. Maybe it's being alive that makes them lie, and being almost *not* alive makes me sort of accidentally truthful—I don't know but anyway— we've been friends . . .

—And being friends is telling each other the truth. . . .

(*There is a pause.*)

You told *me!* I told *you!*

Big Daddy (*Slowly and passionately*). CHRIST—DAMN—

Gooper (*Off stage*). Let her go!

(*Fireworks off stage right.*)

Big Daddy.—ALL—LYING SONS OF —LYING BITCHES!

(*He straightens at last and crosses to the inside door. At the door he turns and looks back as if he had some desperate question he couldn't put into words. Then he nods reflectively and says in a hoarse voice:*)

Yes, all liars, all liars, all lying dying liars!

(*This is said slowly, slowly, with a fierce revulsion. He goes on out.*)

—Lying! Dying! Liars!

(BRICK *remains motionless as the lights dim out and the curtain falls.*)

CURTAIN

ACT THREE

There is no lapse of time. BIG DADDY *is seen leaving as at the end of ACT II.*

Big Daddy. ALL LYIN'—DYIN'!— LIARS! LIARS!—LIARS!

(MARGARET *enters.*)

Margaret. Brick, what in the name of God was goin' on in this room?

(DIXIE *and* TRIXIE *enter through the doors and circle around* MARGARET

shouting. MAE *enters from the lower gallery window.*)

Mae. Dixie, Trixie, you quit that!

(GOOPER *enters through the doors.*)

Gooper, will y' please get these kiddies to bed right now!

Gooper. Mae, you seen Big Mama?

Mae. Not yet.

(Gooper *and kids exit through the doors.* Reverend Tooker *enters through the windows.*)

Reverend Tooker. Those kiddies are so full of vitality. I think I'll have to be starting back to town.

Mae. Not yet, Preacher. You know we regard you as a member of this family, one of our closest an' dearest, so you just got t' be with us when Doc Baugh gives Big Mama th' actual truth about th' report from the clinic.

Margaret. Where do you think you're going?

Brick. Out for some air.

Margaret. Why'd Big Daddy shout "Liars"?

Mae. Has Big Daddy gone to bed, Brick?

Gooper (*Entering*). Now where is that old lady?

Reverend Tooker. I'll look for her.

(*He exits to the gallery.*)

Mae. Cain'tcha find her, Gooper?
Gooper. She's avoidin' this talk.
Mae. I think she senses somethin'.

Margaret (*Going out on the gallery to* Brick). Brick, they're goin' to tell Big Mama the truth about Big Daddy and she's goin' to need you.

Doctor Baugh. This is going to be painful.

Mae. Painful things caint always be avoided.

Reverend Tooker. I see Big Mama.
Gooper. Hey, Big Mama, come here.
Mae. Hush, Gooper, don't holler.

Big Mama (*Entering*). Too much smell of burnt fireworks makes me feel a little bit sick at my stomach.—Where is Big Daddy?

Mae. That's what I want to know, where has Big Daddy gone?

Big Mama. He must have turned in, I reckon he went to baid . . .

Gooper. Well, then, now we can talk.
Big Mama. What *is* this talk, *what* talk?

(Margaret *appears on the gallery, talking to* Doctor Baugh.)

Margaret (*Musically*). My family freed their slaves ten years before abolition. My great-great-grandfather gave his slaves their freedom five years before the War between the States started!

Mae. Oh, for God's sake! Maggie's climbed back up in her family tree!

Margaret (*Sweetly*). What, Mae?

(*The pace must be very quick: great Southern animation.*)

Big Mama (*Addressing them all*). I think Big Daddy was just worn out. He loves his family, he loves to have them around him, but it's a strain on his nerves. He wasn't himself tonight, Big Daddy wasn't himself, I could tell he was all worked up.

Reverend Tooker. I think he's remarkable.

Big Mama. Yaiss! Just remarkable. Did you all notice the food he ate at that table? Did you all notice the supper he put away? Why he ate like a hawss!

Gooper. I hope he doesn't regret it.

Big Mama. What? Why that man—ate a huge piece of cawn bread with molasses on it! Helped himself twice to hoppin' John.

Margaret. Big Daddy loves hoppin' John.—We had a real country dinner.

Big Mama (*Overlapping Margaret*). Yaiss, he simply adores it! an' candied yams? Son? That man put away enough food at that table to stuff a *field* hand!

Gooper (*With grim relish*). I hope he don't have to pay for it later on . . .

Big Mama (*fiercely*). What's *that*, Gooper?

Mae. Gooper says he hopes Big Daddy doesn't suffer tonight.

Big Mama. Oh, shoot, Gooper says, Gooper says! Why should Big Daddy suffer for satisfying a normal appetite? There's nothin' wrong with that man but nerves, he's sound as a dollar! And now he knows he is an' that's why he ate such a supper. He had a big load off his mind, knowin' he wasn't doomed t'—what he thought he was doomed to . . .

Margaret (*Sadly and sweetly*). Bless his old sweet soul . . .

Big Mama (*Vaguely*). Yais, bless his heart, where's Brick?

Mae. Outside.

Gooper.—Drinkin' . . .

Big Mama. I know he's drinkin'. Cain't I see he's drinkin' without you continually tellin' me that boy's drinkin'?

Margaret. Good for you, Big Mama!

(*She applauds.*)

Big Mama. Other people *drink* and *have* drunk an' will *drink*, as long as they make that stuff an' put it in bottles.

Margaret. That's the truth. I never trusted a man that didn't drink.

Big Mama. Brick? Brick!

Margaret. He's still on the gall'ry. I'll go bring him in so we can talk.

Big Mama (*Worriedly*): I don't know what this mysterious family conference is about.

(*Awkward silence.* BIG MAMA *looks from face to face, then belches slightly and mutters, "Excuse me . . ."*

She opens an ornamental fan suspended about her throat. A black lace fan to go with her black lace gown, and fans her wilting corsage, sniffing nervously and looking from face to face in the uncomfortable silence as MARGARET *calls "Brick?" and* BRICK *sings to the moon on the gallery.*)

Margaret. Brick, they're gonna tell Big Mama the truth an' she's gonna need you.

Big Mama. I don't know what's wrong here, you all have such long faces! Open that door on the hall and let some air circulate through here, will you please, Gooper?

Mae. I think we'd better leave that door closed, Big Mama, till after the talk.

Margaret. Brick!

Big Mama. Reveren' Tooker, will *you* please open that door?

Reverend Tooker. I sure will, Big Mama.

Mae. I just didn't think we ought t' take any chance of Big Daddy hearin' a word of this discussion.

Big Mama. *I swan!* Nothing's going to be said in Big Daddy's house that he caint hear if he want to!

Gooper. Well, Big Mama, it's—

(MAE *gives him a quick, hard poke to shut him up. He glares at her fiercely as she circles before him like a burlesque ballerina, raising her skinny bare arms over her head, jangling her bracelets, exclaiming:*)

Mae. *A breeze! A breeze!*

Reverend Tooker. I think this house is the coolest house in the Delta.—Did you all know that Halsey Banks's widow put air-conditioning units in the church and rectory at Friar's Point in memory of Halsey?

(*General conversation has resumed; everybody is chatting so that the stage sounds like a bird cage.*)

Gooper. Too bad nobody cools your church off for you. I bet you sweat in that pulpit these hot Sundays, Reverened Tooker.

Reverend Tooker. Yes, my vestments are drenched. Last Sunday the gold in my chasuble faded into the purple.

Gooper. Reveren', you musta been preachin' hell's fire last Sunday.

Mae (*At the same time to* DOCTOR BAUGH). You reckon those vitamin B12 injections are what they're cracked up t' be, Doc Baugh?

Doctor Baugh. Well, if you want to be stuck with something I guess they're as good to be stuck with as anything else.

Big Mama (*At the gallery door*). Maggie, Maggie, aren't you comin' with Brick?

Mae (*Suddenly and loudly, creating a silence*). I have a strange feeling, I have a peculiar feeling!

Big Mama (*Turning from the gallery*). What feeling?

Mae. That Brick said somethin' he shouldn't of said t'Big Daddy.

Big Mama. Now what on earth could Brick of said t' Big Daddy that he shouldn't say?

Gooper. Big Mama, there's somethin'—

Mae. NOW, WAIT!

(*She rushes up to* BIG MAMA *and gives her a quick hug and kiss.* BIG MAMA *pushes her impatiently off.*)

Doctor Baugh. In my day they had what they call the Keeley cure for heavy drinkers.

Big Mama. Shoot!

Doctor Baugh. But now I understand they just take some kind of tablets.

Gooper. They call them "Annie Bust" tablets.

Big Mama. Brick don't need to take nothin'.

(BRICK *and* MARGARET *appear in gallery doors,* BIG MAMA *unaware of his presence behind her.*)

That boy is just broken up over Skipper's death. You know how poor Skipper died. They gave him a big, big dose of that sodium amytal stuff at his home and then they called the ambulance and give him another big, big dose of it at the hospital and that and all of the alcohol in his system fo' months an' months just proved too much for his heart . . . I'm scared of needles! I'm more scared of a needle than the knife . . . I think more people have been needled out of this world than—

(*She stops short and wheels about.*)

Oh—here's Brick! My precious baby—

(*She turns upon* BRICK *with short, fat arms extended, at the same time uttering a loud, short sob, which is both comic and touching.* BRICK *smiles and bows slightly, making a burlesque gesture of gallantry for* MARGARET *to pass before him into the room. Then he hobbles on his crutch directly to the liquor cabinet and there is absolute silence, with everybody looking at Brick as everybody has always looked at Brick when he spoke or moved or appeared. One by one he drops ice cubes in his glass, then suddenly, but*

*not quickly, looks back over his
shoulder with a wry, charming smile,
and says:*)

Brick. I'm sorry! Anyone else?

Big Mama (*Sadly*). No, son. I *wish* you
wouldn't!

Brick. I wish I didn't have to, Big
Mama, but I'm still waiting for that
click in my head which makes it all
smooth out!

Big Mama. Ow, Brick, you—BREAK
MY HEART!

Margaret (*At same time*). Brick, go sit
with Big Mama!

Big Mama. I just cain't staiiiiii-nnnnnd-
it . . .

(*She sobs.*)

Mae. Now that we're all assembled—

Gooper. We kin talk . . .

Big Mama. Breaks my heart . . .

Margaret. Sit with Big Mama, Brick,
and hold her hand.

(Big Mama *sniffs very loudly three
times, almost like three drumbeats in
the pocket of silence.*)

Brick. You do that, Maggie. I'm a restless cripple. I got to stay on my
crutch.

(Brick *hobbles to the gallery door;
leans there as if waiting.*)

(Mae *sits beside* Big Mama, *while*
Gooper *moves in front and sits on
the end of the couch, facing her.*
Reverend Tooker *moves nervously
into the space between them; on the
other side,* Doctor Baugh *stands
looking at nothing in particular and
lights a cigar.* Margaret *turns away.*)

Big Mama. Why're you all *surroundin'*
me—like this? Why're you all starin'

at me like this an' makin' signs at
each other?

(Reverend Tooker *steps back startled.*)

Mae. Calm yourself, Big Mama.

Big Mama. Calm you'self, *you'self*, Sister Woman. How could I calm my-
self with everyone starin' at me as if
big drops of blood had broken out on
m'face? What's this all about, annh!
What?

(Gooper *coughs and takes a center
position.*)

Gooper. Now, Doc Baugh.

Mae. Doc Baugh?

Gooper. Big Mama wants to know the
complete truth about the report we
got from the Ochsner Clinic.

Mae (*Eagerly*).—on Big Daddy's condition!

Gooper. Yais, on Big Daddy's condition,
we got to face it.

Doctor Baugh. Well . . .

Big Mama (*Terrified, rising*). Is there?
Something? Something that I? Don't
—know?

(*In these few words, this startled,
very soft, question,* Big Mama *reviews the history of her forty-five
years with* Big Daddy, *her great, almost embarrassingly true-hearted
and simple-minded devotion to* Big
Daddy, *who must have had something* Brick *has, who made himself
loved so much by the "simple expedient" of not loving enough to disturb
his charming detachment, also once
coupled, like* Brick, *with virile
beauty.*)

(Big Mama *has a dignity at this moment; she almost stops being fat.*)

Doctor Baugh (*After a pause, uncomfortably*). Yes?—Well—

Big Mama. I!!!—want to—knowww . . .

(*Immediately she thrusts her fist to her mouth as if to deny that statement. Then for some curious reason, she snatches the withered corsage from her breast and hurls it on the floor and steps on it with her short, fat feet.*)

Somebody must be lyin'!—I want to know!

Mae. Sit down, Big Mama, sit down on this sofa.

Margaret. Brick, go sit with Big Mama.

Big Mama. What is it, what is it?

Doctor Baugh. I never have seen a more thorough examination than Big Daddy Pollitt was given in all my experience with the Ochsner Clinic.

Gooper. It's one of the best in the country.

Mae. It's THE best in the country—bar *none!*

(*For some reason she gives* GOOPER *a violent poke as she goes past him. He slaps at her hand without removing his eyes from his mother's face.*)

Doctor Baugh. Of course they were ninety-nine and nine-tenths per cent sure before they even started.

Big Mama. Sure of what, sure of what, sure of—*what?*—*what?*

(*She catches her breath in a startled sob.* MAE *kisses her quickly. She thrusts* MAE *fiercely away from her, staring at the* DOCTOR.)

Mae. Mommy, be a brave girl!

Brick (*In the doorway, softly*). "By the light, by the light, Of the sil-ve-ry mo-oo-n . . ."

Gooper. Shut up!—Brick.

Brick. Sorry . . .

(*He wanders out on the gallery.*)

Doctor Baugh. But now, you see, Big Mama, they cut a piece off this growth, a specimen of the tissue and—

Big Mama. Growth? You told Big Daddy—

Doctor Baugh. Now wait.

Big Mama (*Fiercely*). You told me and Big Daddy there wasn't a thing wrong with him but—

Mae. Big Mama, they always—

Gooper. Let Doc Baugh talk, will yuh?

Big. Mama.—little spastic condition of—

(*Her breath gives out in a sob.*)

Doctor Baugh. Yes, that's what we told Big Daddy. But we had this bit of tissue run through the laboratory and I'm sorry to say the test was positive on it. It's—well—malignant . . .

(*Pause*)

Big Mama.—Cancer?! Cancer?!

(*Doctor Baugh nods gravely. Big Mama gives a long gasping cry.*)

Mae and Gooper. Now, now, now. Big Mama, you had to know . . .

Big Mama. WHY DIDN'T THEY CUT IT OUT OF HIM? HANH? HANH?

Doctor Baugh. Involved too much, Big Mama, too many organs affected.

Mae. Big Mama, the liver's affected and so's the kidneys, both! It's gone way past what they call a—

Gooper. A surgical risk.

Mae.—Uh-huh . . .

(*Big Mama draws a breath like a dying gasp.*)

Reverend Tooker. Tch, tch, tch, tch, tch!

Doctor Baugh. Yes it's gone past the knife.

Mae. That's why he's turned yellow, Mommy!

Big Mama. Git away from me, git away from me, Mae!

(*She rises abruptly.*)

I want Brick! Where's Brick? Where is my only son?

Mae. Mama! Did she say "only son"?

Gooper. What does that make *me*?

Mae. A sober responsible man with five precious children!—Six!

Big Mama. I want Brick to tell me! Brick! Brick!

Margaret (*Rising from her reflections in a corner*). Brick was so upset he went back out.

Big Mama. Brick!

Margaret. Mama, let *me* tell you!

Big Mama. No, no, leave me alone, you're not my blood!

Gooper. Mama, I'm your son! Listen to *me*!

Mae. Gooper's your son, he's your first-born!

Big Mama. Gooper never liked Daddy.

Mae (*As if terribly shocked*). That's not TRUE!

(*There is a pause. The minister coughs and rises.*)

Reverend Tooker (*To Mae*). I think I'd better slip away at this point.

(*Discreetly.*)

Good night, good night, everybody, and God bless you all . . . on this place . . .

(*He slips out.*)

(MAE *coughs and points at* BIG MAMA.)

Well, Big Mama . . .

(*She sighs.*)

Big Mama. It's all a mistake, I know it's just a bad dream.

Doctor Baugh. We're gonna keep Big Daddy as comfortable as we can.

Big Mama. Yes, it's just a bad dream, that's all it is, it's just an awful dream.

Gooper. In my opinion Big Daddy is having some pain but won't admit that he has it.

Big Mama. Just a dream, a bad dream.

Doctor Baugh. That's what lots of them do, they think if they don't admit they're having the pain they can sort of escape the fact of it.

Gooper (*With relish*). Yes, they get sly about it, they get real sly about it.

Mae. Gooper and I think—

Gooper. Shut up, Mae! Big Mama, I think—Big Daddy ought to be started on morphine.

Big Mama. Nobody's going to give Big Daddy morphine.

Doctor Baugh. Now, Big Mama, when that pain strikes it's going to strike mighty hard and Big Daddy's going to need the needle to bear it.

Big Mama. I tell you, nobody's going to give him morphine.

Mae. Big Mama, you don't want to see Big Daddy suffer, you know you—

(GOOPER, *standing beside her, gives her a savage poke.*)

Doctor Baugh (*Placing a package on the table*). I'm leaving this stuff here, so if there's a sudden attack you all won't have to send out for it.

Mae. I know how to give a hypo.

Big Mama. Nobody's gonna give Big Daddy morphine.

Gooper. Mae took a course in nursing during the war.

Margaret. Somehow I don't think Big Daddy would want Mae to give him a hypo.

Mae. You think he'd want *you* to do it?

Doctor Baugh. Well . . .

(DOCTOR BAUGH *rises.*)

Gooper. Doctor Baugh is goin'.

Doctor Baugh. Yes, I got to be goin'. Well, keep your chin up, Big Mama.

Gooper (*With jocularity*). She's gonna keep *both* chins up, aren't you, Big Mama?

(BIG MAMA *sobs.*)

Now stop that, Big Mama.

Gooper (*At the door with* DOCTOR BAUGH). Well, Doc, we sure do appreciate all you done. I'm telling you, we're surely obligated to you for—

(DOCTOR BAUGH *has gone out without a glance at him.*)

—I guess that doctor has got a lot on his mind but it wouldn't hurt him to act a little more human . . .

(BIG MAMA *sobs.*)

Now be a brave girl, Mommy.

Big Mama. It's not true, I know that it's just not true!

Gooper. Mama, those tests are infallible!

Big Mama. Why are you so determined to see your father daid?

Mae. Big Mama!

Margaret (*Gently*). I know what Big Mama means.

Mae (*Fiercely*). Oh, do you?

Margaret (*Quietly and very sadly*). Yes, I think I do.

Mae. For a newcomer in the family you sure do show a lot of understanding.

Margaret. Understanding is needed on this place.

Mae. I guess you must have needed a lot of it in your family, Maggie, with your father's liquor problem and now you've got Brick with his!

Margaret. Brick does not have a liquor problem at all. Brick is devoted to Big Daddy. This thing is a terrible strain on him.

Big Mama. Brick is Big Daddy's boy, but he drinks too much and it worries me and Big Daddy, and, Margaret, you've got to co-operate with us, you've got to co-operate with Big Daddy and me in getting Brick straightened out. Because it will break Big Daddy's heart if Brick don't pull himself together and take hold of things.

Mae. Take hold of *what* things, Big Mama?

Big Mama. The place.

(*There is a quick violent look between* MAE *and* GOOPER.)

Gooper. Big Mama, you've had a shock.

Mae. Yais, we've all had a shock, but . . .

Gooper. Let's be realistic—

Mae.—Big Daddy would never, would *never*, be foolish enough to—

Gooper.—put this place in irresponsible hands!

Big Mama. Big Daddy ain't going to leave the place in anybody's hands; Big Daddy is *not* going to die. I want you to get that in your heads, all of you!

Mae. Mommy, Mommy, Big Mama, we're just as hopeful an' optimistic as you are about Big Daddy's prospects, we have faith in *prayer*—but nevertheless there are certain matters that have to be discussed an' dealt with, because otherwise—

Gooper. Eventualities have to be considered and now's the time . . . Mae, will you please get my brief case out of our room?

Mae. Yes, honey.

(*She rises and goes out through the hall door.*)

Gooper (*Standing over* BIG MAMA). Now, Big Mom. What you said just now was not at all true and you know it. I've always loved Big Daddy in my own quiet way. I never made a show of it, and I know that Big Daddy has always been fond of me in a quiet way, too, and he never made a show of it neither.

(MAE *returns with* GOOPER's *brief case.*)

Mae. Here's your brief case, Gooper honey.

Gooper (*Handing the brief case back to her*). Thank you . . . Of cou'se, my relationship with Big Daddy is different from Brick's.

Mae. You're eight years older'n Brick an' always had t' carry a bigger load of th' responsibilities than Brick ever had t' carry. He never carried a thing in his life but a football or a highball.

Gooper. Mae, will y' let me talk, please?

Mae. Yes, honey.

Gooper. Now, a twenty-eight-thousand-acre plantation's a mighty big thing t' run.

Mae. Almost singlehanded.

(MARGARET *has gone out onto the gallery and can be heard calling softly to* BRICK.)

Big Mama. You never had to run this place! What are you talking about? As if Big Daddy was dead and in his grave, you had to run it? Why, you just helped him out with a few business details and had your law practice at the same time in Memphis!

Mae. Oh, Mommy, Mommy, Big Mommy! Let's be fair!

Margaret. Brick!

Mae. Why, Gooper has given himself body and soul to keeping this place up for the past five years since Big Daddy's health started failing.

Margaret. Brick!

Mae. Gooper won't say it, Gooper never thought of it as a duty, he just did it. And what did Brick do? Brick kept living in his past glory at college! Still a football player at twenty-seven!

Margaret (*Returning alone*). Who are you talking about now? Brick? A football player? He isn't a football player and you know it. Brick is a sports announcer on T.V. and one of the best-known ones in the country!

Mae. I'm talking about what he was.

Margaret. Well, I wish you would just stop talking about my husband.

Gooper. I've got a right to discuss my brother with other members of MY OWN family, which don't include *you*. Why don't you go out there and drink with Brick?

Margaret. I've never seen such malice toward a brother.

Gooper. How about his for me? Why, he can't stand to be in the same room with me!

Margaret. This is a deliberate campaign of vilification for the most disgusting and sordid reason on earth, and I know what it is! It's *avarice, avarice, greed, greed!*

Big Mama. Oh, I'll scream! I will scream in a moment unless this stops!

(GOOPER *has stalked up to* MARGARET *with clenched fists at his sides as if he would strike her.* MAE *distorts her face again into a hideous grimace behind* MARGARET's *back.*)

Big Mama (*Sobs*). Margaret. Child. Come here. Sit next to Big Mama.

Margaret. Precious Mommy. I'm sorry, I'm sorry, I—!

(*She bends her long graceful neck to press her forehead to* BIG MAMA's *bulging shoulder under its black chiffon.*)

Mae. How beautiful, how touching, this display of devotion! Do you know why she's childless? She's childless because that big beautiful athlete husband of hers won't go to bed with her!

Gooper. You jest won't let me do this in a nice way, will yah? Aw right—I don't give a goddam if Big Daddy likes me or don't like me or did or never did or will or will never! I'm just appealing to a sense of common decency and fair play. I'll tell you the truth. I've resented Big Daddy's partiality to Brick ever since Brick was born, and the way I've been treated like I was just barely good enough to spit on and sometimes not even good enough for that. Big Daddy is dying of cancer, and its spread all through him and it's attacked all his vital organs including the kidneys and right now he is sinking into uremia, and you all know what uremia is, it's poisoning of the whole system due to the failure of the body to eliminate its poisons.

Margaret (*To herself, downstage, hissingly*). Poisons, poisons! Venomous thoughts and words! In hearts and minds!—That's poisons!

Gooper (*Overlapping her*). I am asking for a square deal, and, by God, I expect to get one. But if I don't get one, if there's any peculiar shenanigans going on around here behind my back, well, I'm not a corporation lawyer for nothing, I know how to protect my own interests.

(BRICK *enters from the gallery with a tranquil, blurred smile, carrying an empty glass with him.*)

Brick. Storm coming up.

Gooper. Oh! A late arrival!

Mae. Behold the conquering hero comes!

Gooper. The fabulous Brick Pollitt! Remember him?—Who could forget him!

Mae. He looks like he's been injured in a game!

Gooper. Yep, I'm afraid you'll have to warm the bench at the Sugar Bowl this year, Brick!

(MAE *laughs shrilly.*)

Or was it the Rose Bowl that he made that famous run in?—

(*Thunder*)

Mae. The punch bowl, honey. It was in the punch bowl, the cut-glass punch bowl!

Gooper. Oh, that's right, I'm getting the bowls mixed up!

Margaret. Why don't you stop venting your malice and envy on a sick boy?

Big Mama. Now you two hush, I mean it, hush, all of you, hush!

Daisy, Sookey. Storm! Storm comin'! Storm! Storm!

Lacey. Brightie, close them shutters.

Gooper. Lacey, put the top up on my Cadillac, will yuh?

Lacey. Yes, suh, Mistah Pollitt!

Gooper (*At the same time*). Big Mama, you know it's necessary for me t' go back to Memphis in th' mornin' t' represent the Parker estate in a lawsuit.

(*Mae sits on the bed and arranges papers she has taken from the brief case.*)

Big Mama. Is it, Gooper?

Mae. Yaiss.

Gooper. That's why I'm forced to—to bring up a problem that—

Mae. Somethin' that's too important t' be put off!

Gooper. If Brick was sober, he ought to be in on this.

Margaret. Brick is present; we're present.

Gooper. Well, good. I will now give you this outline my partner, Tom Bullitt, an' me have drawn up—a sort of dummy—trusteeship.

Margaret. Oh, that's it! You'll be in charge an' dole out remittances, will you?

Gooper. This we did as soon as we got the report on Big Daddy from th' Ochsner Laboratories. We did this thing, I mean we drew up this dummy outline with the advice and assistance of the Chairman of the Boa'd of Directors of th' Southern Plantahs Bank and Trust Company in Memphis, C. C. Bellowes, a man who handles estates for all th' prominent fam'lies in West Tennessee and th' Delta.

Big Mama. Gooper?

Gooper (*Crouching in front of* Big Mama). Now this is not—not final, or anything like it. This is just a preliminary outline. But it does provide a basis—a design—a—possible, feasible—*plan!*

Margaret. Yes, I'll bet it's a plan.

(*Thunder*)

Mae. It's a plan to protect the biggest estate in the Delta from irresponsibility an'—

Big Mama. Now you listen to me, all of you, you listen here! They's not goin' to be any more catty talk in my house! And Gooper, you put that away before I grab it out of your hand and tear it right up! I don't know what the hell's in it, and I don't want to know what the hell's in it. I'm talkin' in Big Daddy's language now; I'm his *wife*, not his *widow*, I'm still his *wife!* And I'm talkin' to you in his language an'—

Gooper. Big Mama, what I have here is—

Mae (*At the same time*). Gooper explained that it's just a plan . . .

Big Mama. I don't care what you got there. Just put it back where it came from, an' don't let me see it again, not even the outside of the envelope of it! Is that understood? Basis! Plan! Preliminary! Design! I say—what is it Big Daddy always says when he's disgusted?

Brick (*From the bar*). Big Daddy says "crap" when he's disgusted.

Big Mama (*Rising*). That's right— CRAP! I say CRAP too, like Big Daddy!

(*Thunder*)

Mae. Coarse language doesn't seem called for in this—

Gooper. Somethin' in me is *deeply outraged* by hearin' you talk like this.

Big Mama. *Nobody's goin' to take nothin'!*—till Big Daddy lets go of it —maybe, just possibly, not—not even then! No, not even then!

(*Thunder*)

Mae. Sookey, hurry up an' git that po'ch furniture covahed; want th' paint to come off?

Gooper. Lacey, put mah car away!

Lacey. Caint, Mistah Pollitt, you got the keys!

Gooper. Naw, you got 'em, man. Where th' keys to th' car, honey?

Mae. You got 'em in your pocket!

Brick. "You can always hear me singin' this song, Show me the way to go home."

(*Distant thunder.*)

Big Mama. Brick! Come here, Brick, I need you. Tonight Brick looks like he used to look when he was a little boy, just like he did when he played wild games and used to come home when I hollered myself hoarse for him, all sweaty and pink cheeked and sleepy, with his—red curls shining . . .

(BRICK *draws aside as he does from all physical contact and continues the song in a whisper, opening the ice bucket and dropping in the ice cubes one by one as if he were mixing some important chemical formula.*)

(*Distant thunder.*)

Time goes by so fast. Nothin' can outrun it. Death commences too early—almost before you're half acquainted with life—you meet the other . . . Oh, you know we just got to love each other an' stay together, all of us, just as close as we can, especially now that such a *black* thing has come and moved into this place without invitation.

(*Awkwardly embracing* BRICK, *she presses her head to his shoulder.*)

(*A dog howls off stage.*)

Oh, Brick, son of Big Daddy, Big Daddy does so love you. Y'know what would be his fondest dream come true? If before he passed on, if Big Daddy has to pass on . . .

(*A dog howls.*)

. . . you give him a child of yours, a grandson as much like his son as his son is like Big Daddy . . .

Margaret. I know that's Big Daddy's dream.

Big Mama. That's his dream.

Mae. Such a pity that Maggie and Brick can't oblige.

Big Daddy (*Off down stage right on the gallery*). Looks like the wind was takin' liberties with this place.

Servant (*Off stage*). Yes, sir, Mr. Pollitt.

Margaret (*Crossing to the right door*). Big Daddy's on the gall'ry.

(BIG MAMA *has turned toward the hall door at the sound of* BIG DADDY's *voice on the gallery.*)

Big Mama. I can't stay here. He'll see somethin' in my eyes.

(BIG DADDY *enters the room from up stage right.*)

Big Daddy. Can I come in?

(*He puts his cigar in an ash tray.*)

Margaret. Did the storm wake you up, Big Daddy?

Big Daddy. Which stawm are you talkin' about—th' one outside or th' hullabaloo in here?

(GOOPER *squeezes past* BIG DADDY.)

Gooper. 'Scuse me.

(MAE *tries to squeeze past* BIG DADDY *to join* GOOPER, *but* BIG DADDY *puts his arm firmly around her.*)

Big Daddy. I heard some mighty loud talk. Sounded like somethin' important was bein' discussed. What was the powwow about?

Mae (*Flustered*). Why—nothin', Big Daddy . . .

Big Daddy (*Crossing to extreme left center, taking* MAE *with him*). What is that pregnant-lookin' envelope you're puttin' back in your brief case, Gooper?

Gooper (*At the foot of the bed, caught, as he stuffs papers into envelope.*) That? Nothin', suh—nothin' much of anythin' at all . . .

Big Daddy. Nothin'? It looks like a whole lot of nothin'!

(*He turns up stage to the group.*)

You all know th' story about th' young married couple—

Gooper. Yes, sir!

Big Daddy. Hello, Brick—

Brick. Hello, Big Daddy.

(*The group is arranged in a semicircle above* BIG DADDY, MARGARET *at the extreme right, then* MAE *and* GOOPER, *then* BIG MAMA, *with* BRICK *at the left.*)

Big Daddy. Young married couple took Junior out to th' zoo one Sunday, inspected all of God's creatures in their cages with satisfaction.

Gooper. Satisfaction.

Big Daddy (*Crossing to up stage center, facing front*). This afternoon was a warm afternoon in spring an' that ole elephant had somethin' else on his mind which was bigger'n peanuts. You know this story, Brick?

(GOOPER *nods.*)

Brick. No, sir, I don't know it.

Big Daddy. Y'see in th' cage adjoinin' they was a young female elephant in heat!

Big Mama (*At* BIG DADDY's *shoulder*). Oh, Big Daddy!

Big Daddy. What's the matter, preacher's gone, ain't he? All right. That female elephant in the next cage was permeatin' the atmosphere about her with a powerful and excitin' odor of female fertility! Huh! Ain't that a nice way to put it, Brick?

Brick. Yes, sir, nothin' wrong with it.

Big Daddy. Brick says th's nothin' wrong with it!

Big Mama. Oh, Big Daddy!

Big Daddy (*Crossing to down stage center*). So this ole bull elephant still had a couple of fornications left in him. He reared back his trunk an' got a whiff of that elephant lady next door!—began to paw at the dirt in his cage an' butt his head against the separatin' partition and, first thing y'know, there was a conspicuous change in his *profile*—very *conspicuous*! Ain't I tellin' this story in decent language, Brick?

Brick. Yes, sir, too ruttin' decent!

Big Daddy. So, the little boy pointed at it and said, "What's that?" His mama said, "Oh, that's—nothin'!"—His papa said, "She's spoiled!"

(BIG DADDY *crosses to* BRICK *at left.*)

You didn't laugh at that story, Brick.

(BIG MAMA *crosses to down stage right crying.* MARGARET *goes to her.* MAE *and* GOOPER *hold up stage right center.*)

Brick. No, sir, I didn't laugh at that story.

Big Daddy. What is the smell in this room? Don't you notice it, Brick? Don't you notice a powerful and obnoxious odor of mendacity in this room?

Brick. Yes, sir, I think I do, sir.

Gooper. Mae, Mae . . .

Big Daddy. There is nothing more powerful. Is there, Brick?

Brick. No, sir. No, sir, there isn't, an' nothin' more obnoxious.

Big Daddy. Brick agrees with me. The odor of mendacity is a powerful and obnoxious odor an' the stawm hasn't blown it away from this room yet. You notice it, Gooper?

Gooper. What, sir?

Big Daddy. How about you, Sister Woman? You notice the unpleasant odor of mendacity in this room?

Mae. Why, Big Daddy, I don't even know what that is.

Big Daddy. You can smell it. Hell it smells like death!

(Big Mama *sobs.* Big Daddy *looks toward her.*)

What's wrong with that fat woman over there, loaded with diamonds? Hey, what's-your-name, what's the matter with you?

Margaret (*Crossing toward* Big Daddy). She had a slight dizzy spell, Big Daddy.

Big Daddy. You better watch that, Big Mama. A stroke is a bad way to go.

Margaret (*Crossing to* Big Daddy *at center*). Oh, Brick, Big Daddy has on your birthday present to him, Brick, he has on your cashmere robe, the softest material I have ever felt.

Big Daddy. Yeah, this is my soft birthday, Maggie . . . Not my gold or my silver birthday, but my soft birthday, everything's got to be soft for Big Daddy on this soft birthday.

(Maggie *kneels before* Big Daddy *at center.*)

Margaret. Big Daddy's got on his Chinese slippers that I gave him, Brick. Big Daddy, I haven't given you my big present yet, but now I will, now's the time for me to present it to you! I have an announcement to make!

Mae. What? What kind of announcement?

Gooper. A sports announcement, Maggie?

Margaret. Announcement of life beginning! A child is coming, sired by Brick, and out of Maggie the Cat! I have Brick's child in my body, an' that's my birthday present to Big Daddy on this birthday!

(Big Daddy *looks at* Brick *who crosses behind* Big Daddy *to down stage portal, left.*)

Big Daddy. Get up, girl, get up off your knees, girl.

(Big Daddy *helps* Margaret *to rise. He crosses above her, to her right, bites off the end of a fresh cigar, taken from his bathrobe pocket, as he studies* Margaret.)

Uh-huh, this girl has life in her body, that's no lie!

Big Mama. BIG DADDY'S DREAM COME TRUE!

Brick. JESUS!

Big Daddy (*Crossing right below wicker stand*). Gooper, I want my lawyer in the mornin'.

Brick. Where are you goin', Big Daddy?

Big Daddy. Son, I'm goin' up on the roof, to the belvedere on th' roof to look over my kingdom before I give up my kingdom—twenty-eight thousand acres of th' richest land this side of the valley Nile!

(*He exits through right doors, and down right on the gallery.*)

Big Mama (*Following*). Sweetheart, sweetheart, sweetheart—can I come with you?

(*She exits down stage right.*)

(MARGARET *is down stage center in the mirror area.* MAE *has joined* GOOPER *and she gives him a fierce poke, making a low hissing sound and a grimace of fury.*)

Gooper (*Pushing her aside*). Brick, could you possibly spare me one small shot of that liquor?

Brick. Why, help yourself, Gooper boy.

Gooper. I will.

Mae (*Shrilly*). Of course we know that this is—a lie.

Gooper. *Be still, Mae.*

Mae. I won't be still! I know she's made this up!

Gooper. Goddam it, I said shut up!

Margaret. Gracious! I didn't know that my little announcement was going to provoke such a storm!

Mae. *That* woman isn't *pregnant!*

Gooper. Who said she was?

Mae. *She* did.

Gooper. The doctor didn't. Doc Baugh didn't.

Margaret. I haven't gone to Doc Baugh.

Gooper. Then who'd you go to, Maggie?

Margaret. One of the best gynecologists in the South.

Gooper. Uh huh, uh huh!—I see . . .

(*He takes out a pencil and note-book.*)

—May we have his name, please?

Margaret. No, you may not, Mister Prosecuting Attorney!

Mae. He doesn't have any name, he doesn't exist!

Margaret. Oh, he exists all right, and so does my child, Brick's baby!

Mae. You can't conceive a child by a man that won't sleep with you unless you think you're—

(BRICK *has turned on the phonograph. A scat song cuts* MAE's *speech.*)

Gooper. Turn that off!

Mae. We know it's a lie because we hear you in here; he won't sleep with you, we hear you! So don't imagine you're going to put a trick over on us, to fool a dying man with a—

(*A long drawn cry of agony and rage fills the house.* MARGARET *turns the phonograph down to a whisper. The cry is repeated.*)

Mae. Did you hear that, Gooper, did you hear that?

Gooper. Sounds like the pain has struck. Come along and leave these lovebirds together in their nest!

(*He goes out first.* MAE *follows but turns at the door, contorting her face and hissing at* MARGARET.)

Mae. Liar!

(*She slams the door.*)

(MARGARET *exhales with relief and moves a little unsteadily to catch hold of* BRICK's *arm.*)

Margaret. Thank you for—keeping still . . .

Brick. O.K., Maggie.

Margaret. It was gallant of you to save my face!

(*He now pours down three shots in quick succession and stands waiting, silent. All at once he turns with a smile and says:*)

Brick. *There!*

Margaret. What?

Brick. The *click* . . .

(His gratitude seems almost infinite as he hobbles out on the gallery with a drink. We hear his crutch as he swings out of sight. Then, at some distance, he begins singing to himself a peaceful song. MARGARET *holds her big pillow forlornly as if it were her only companion, for a few moments, then throws it on the bed. She rushes to the liquor cabinet, gathers all the bottles in her arms, turns about undecidedly, then runs out of the room with them, leaving the door ajar on the dim yellow hall.* BRICK *is heard hobbling back along the gallery, singing his peaceful song. He comes back in, sees the pillow on the bed, laughs lightly, sadly, picks it up. He has it under his arm as* MARGARET *returns to the room.* MARGARET *softly shuts the door and leans against it, smiling softly at* BRICK.*)*

Margaret. Brick, I used to think that you were stronger than me and I didn't want to be overpowered by you. But now, since you've taken to liquor—you know what?—I guess it's bad, but now I'm stronger than you and I can love you more truly! Don't move that pillow. I'll move it right back if you do!—Brick?

(She turns out all the lamps but a single rose-silk-shaded one by the bed.)

I really have been to a doctor and I know what to do and—Brick?—this is my time by the calendar to conceive.

Brick. Yes, I understand, Maggie. But how are you going to conceive a child by a man in love with his liquor?

Margaret. By locking his liquor up and making him satisfy my desire before I unlock it!

Brick. Is that what you've done, Maggie?

Margaret. Look and see. That cabinet's mighty empty compared to before!

Brick. Well, I'll be a son of a—

(He reaches for his crutch but she beats him to it and rushes out on the gallery, hurls the crutch over the rail and comes back in, panting.)

Margaret. And so tonight we're going to make the lie true, and when that's done, I'll bring the liquor back here and we'll get drunk together, here, tonight, in this place that death has come into . . .—What do you say?

Brick. I don't say anything. I guess there's nothing to say.

Margaret. Oh, you weak people, you weak, beautiful people!—who give up with such grace. What you want is someone to—

(She turns out the rose-silk lamp.)

—take hold of you.—Gently, gently with love hand your life back to you, like somethin' gold you let go of. I *do* love you, Brick, I *do*!

Brick (Smiling with charming sadness). Wouldn't it be funny if that was true?

THE END

The Visit

〰〰〰〰〰〰〰〰〰〰〰 FRIEDRICH DUERRENMATT

INTRODUCTION

Friedrich Duerrenmatt was born on January 5, 1921, in Konolfingen, in the canton of Bern, Switzerland, the son of Reinhold and Hulda (Zimmermann) Duerrenmatt; his father was a Lutheran minister and his grandfather, Ulrich Duerrenmatt, was a well-known satirist and political poet. The boy's thinking was shaped by a fusion of the two strains: moral rectitude and social criticism intermixed and cemented with his own special brand of wit and irony. "My grandfather was once sent to prison for ten days because of a poem he wrote," says Duerrenmatt. "I haven't been honored in that way yet. Maybe it's my fault, or maybe the world has gone so far to the dogs that it doesn't even feel insulted any more if it's criticized most severely."

As a boy, Duerrenmatt, like the young Ibsen, wanted to be a painter; he was especially interested in the dramatic moments of history and drew many bloody battle scenes. He still owns the notebook containing his drawings of the Battle of the Nibelungen. At the age of twelve, he entered a drawing competition with a picture called "Swiss Battle," and won a watch—his first prize. At thirteen the boy moved with his family to the city of Bern, where he was enrolled in the free high school. From there he went to the University of Bern and took courses in literature, theology, philosophy, and science. He first became interested in the theater in Bern and attended the operettas there regularly. He spent one semester at the University of Zurich, going to lectures in philosophy and art, when suddenly his interest in painting waned and he had a fervent desire to write. He withdrew from the University without taking a degree, and his painting became merely a hobby. "The things we like best are not always the things we do best," says Duerrenmatt. "For me writing is far more difficult than painting."

He completed his military service and began to read seriously; among his favorite authors were the expressionist poet Georg Heym, Kierkegaard, Aristophanes, and Thornton Wilder. He tried his hand at playwriting at this time; while on an excursion to Wallis, in the fall of 1943, he completed *Comedy*, a lyrical and apocalyptic work. At twenty-two he was already leveling serious criticisms against society, for in a preface to this play he said, in part, "The State, Religion, and Art are only related to themselves, they are not related to each other; they are abstract, immersed in technicalities, the symbols of unreality." The play remained unpublished and unproduced.

Duerrenmatt's first play to reach the stage was written during 1945 and 1946 and was called *Es steht geschrieben* (*It Is Decreed*); the author describes it as "a wild story of German Anabaptists during the Reformation." It had its premiere at the Schauspielhaus in Zurich on April 19, 1947, and created a mild furor because of its unorthodox religious sentiments; after the excitement died down, it won a prize for the playwright.

In 1947 Duerrenmatt married the actress Lotti Geissler and moved to Basel. Then followed several difficult years for the playwright; in order to earn money, he turned to the writing of short stories, mystery novels, and radio plays. Friends helped out with loans and even total strangers made small donations. He continued to write for the theater, however; two plays, *The Blind Man* and *Romulus the Great*, were produced at the Stadttheater, Basel, in 1948 and 1949 respectively, but they caused no great stir.

What Duerrenmatt calls his "breakthrough" came in 1952 with the production of his comedy *Die Ehe des Herrn Mississippi* (*The Marriage of Mr. Mississippi*), which was directed by Hans Schweikart at the Munich Chamber Theater. Boos and hisses greeted the play, but the applauders won out. This work established Duerrenmatt as one of the most gifted of contemporary European dramatists; his style, with its peculiar mixture of the serious and the grotesque, was recognized as a unique and distinguishing feature of his work. An unusual setting was required for this play; as the action progressed, a splendidly furnished middle-class interior was to disintegrate slowly into a veritable slum in order to reflect visually the course of events and the degeneration of the characters. Under the title *Fools Are Passing Through,* this play was given in English at the Jan Hus House, an off-Broadway theater in New York, for a brief run starting on April 2, 1958.

Two other plays were produced at the Munich Chamber Theater: *Nocturnal Conversation with a Scorned Man,* a one-acter, opened on July 25, 1952; and *Ein Engel kommt nach Babylon* (*An Angel Comes to Babylon*), a comedy in three acts, had its premiere on December 22, 1953.

To accommodate a growing family—there were now three children, Peter, Barbara, and Ruth—Duerrenmatt moved into larger living quarters, a house in Neuchâtel, high up on the mountainside overlooking the lake. He prefers to live at some distance from Bern, Basel, and Zurich because friends and relatives disturb a writer's routine. He takes little part in community life and is known to his neighbors only through the articles about him which appear in the newspapers from time to time. It was in Neuchâtel that Duerrenmatt wrote his "tragic comedy" *Der Besuch der alten Dame* (*The Old Lady's Visit*) and his even more bitter satire *Frank V.*

Der Besuch der alten Dame had its premiere at the Zurich Schauspielhaus in 1956, and was an immediate success. This play brought international fame to its author. When *The Visit* (its title shortened from the original) opened in New York, the critics agreed almost to a man that the play was a brilliant theatrical work, but they, and many playgoers as well, took note of the author's cynicism and wondered about his central meaning. "People should accept my fancies and ignore the deeper meanings," says Duerrenmatt. "Claire Zachanassian symbolizes neither Justice, nor the Marshall Plan, nor the Apocalypse; she is just what she is supposed to be—the richest woman in the world. With her fortune she is in a position to behave like the heroine of a Greek tragedy, arbitrarily, dreadfully, like Medea."

The dramatist's next play, *Frank V—Oper einer Privatbank* (*Frank the Fifth—Opera about a Private Bank*), another furious attack upon modern society, opened at the Zurich Schauspielhaus on March 20, 1959, with Therese Giehse and Maria Becker, that theater's foremost actresses, in leading roles. The play presents a ruthless picture of the hopelessly racket-ridden and ruthless business world from which there can be no escape, depicted in the manner of a gangster comic. Duerrenmatt indulged in as much exaggeration as possible, but enlisted the cooperation of composer Paul Burkhard to set this horror comic to the kind of music that would tone down his overstatement so that it might seem "like the heartless flippancy of a limerick engraved on a tombstone." Not as yet translated into English, *Frank V* has been produced by several theaters in Germany.

With an increasingly heavy writing schedule, Duerrenmatt seldom takes time out to travel, but in April, 1959, he went to New York to receive the Drama Critics' Circle Award for *The Visit,* and in July of the same year, he went to Mannheim, Germany, where in a public ceremony he was awarded the renowned Schiller Prize of ten thousand German marks (about $2500). His play, *The Visit,* had been performed seventeen times to great acclaim in the repertory of the Mannheim National Theater during the 1958-1959 season.

In 1962 Duerrenmatt wrote *The Physicists,* which helped to strengthen his international reputation; the play takes place in an insane asylum, where three scientists live in anonymity because they consider it "the only place where we are still allowed to think with impunity." This satire met with worldwide success. His next play, *The Meteor* (1966), was a fantasy concerning a Nobel prize-winner, a writer who cannot die but who watches everyone around him succumb. This work was seen in London and in various cities on the Continent but has not had a professional production in the United States. In 1968 Duerrenmatt produced an adaptation of Shakespeare's *King John*; and the following year turned Strindberg's *The Dance of Death,* which deals with the incessant quarrels of a husband and wife, into a farce resembling a boxing match in twelve rounds. *Play Strindberg,* as the work was called, was received with laughter and applause both here and abroad. *The Conformer* (1975), a political "thriller," in which a man fired from his job during an economic recession becomes a member of an underworld gang, is an attack upon society reminiscent of Duerrenmatt's earlier play *Frank the Fifth.* The work has been produced abroad but not in the United States.

The dramatist occasionally attends performances of his plays in various cities in Germany, but he spends most of his time at his writing table. His method of work is unusual and exhausting; he rewrites and re-edits his plays endlessly—revising them completely after almost every production—probably because of the experimental nature of his work. "His plays, though realistic on the surface, transcend reality in many ways," according to critic, H. F. Garten. "But this surrealism is far removed from the symbolism of neoromantic drama or the abstractions of expressionism. It has the oppressive quality of a dream in which every detail stands out with glaring clarity while the whole remains unfathomable and obscure. The characters are frighteningly real, though often distorted into carica-ture. The fundamental mood is one of profound pessimism, reflecting the fear and insecurity of our present world. But against this background there is a sense of the grotesque, a readiness to laugh, which turns tragedy as if by magic into comedy." In a long critical essay called *Problems of the Theater* (1955), Duerrenmatt argued that the time for writing tragedies has passed. Tragedy, he contended, presupposes a well-ordered cosmos with established standards of guilt and retri-bution. Our disintegrating world, however, in which we live "like Gulliver amongst the giants," powerless to resist the course of events bigger than ourselves, calls for comedy—a comedy born not of despair, but of courage. The playwright also has very definite views concerning theater management. He has said: "A director should not be a star, but a worker. The modern theatre needs an adminis-trator who will provide the most favorable terms of employment for the artists."

Friedrich Duerrenmatt (wearing glasses), author of *The Visit*, and Teo Otto, scene designer, con-ferring during rehearsals of the original produc-tion in Zurich. (Swiss Information Service)

Duerrenmatt, personally, is a tall, heavy-set man, who weighs over 225 pounds; he is witty and genial and much given to smoking long black cigars. When he smiles, the twinkle in his blue eyes and the dimples in his face belie his probing intellect and his horrendous view of life. This man has said, "The world, for me, stands as something monstrous, an enigma of calamity that has to be ac-cepted but to which there must be no surrender." Later, he added: "Long ago I learned from my grandfather that writing can be a form of fighting!"

Duerrenmatt's interests of his university days—theology, philosophy, science, literature, and art—have carried over into his work as a novelist and playwright, and are nowhere more manifest than in *The Visit*.

Although he is the son of a minister of the Protestant faith, he does not feel obligated to any religious dogma; he satirizes orthodox beliefs as well as men of the cloth. In *The Visit*, the Pastor is shown to be as weak a vessel and as corrupt a man as the Policeman. Despite an avowed belief in the existence of God, Duerrenmatt sees the world as empty and meaningless; only great material wealth and worldly power, he feels, can give certain individuals the semblance of divinity. Claire Zachanassian, who controls such a large share of the world's goods, moves, according to the playwright, "outside of the human order; she has become fixed and immutable, incapable of growth, unless it be to turn into stone, to become an idol." Only self-discipline, love, and mercy, says Duerrenmatt, can assure the salvation of man.

Duerrenmatt's philosophy shows the strong influence of the existentialism of Kierkegaard; in this hollow, hopeless world, a man's character is his fate. Man is free to choose his path but once the first step is taken everything that follows is inevitable. Claire Zachanassian points this out to Anton Schill. Schill is even given a second chance: offered a gun with which to destroy himself, he prefers to let the town punish him for his guilt. This choice signifies the distinction between cowardice and courage.

The branch of science that interests Duerrenmatt above all others is psychology. His stories and plays deal extensively with the minds and motivations of his characters; most of his dramatic situations depend for their effectiveness upon the psychological tensions inherent in them. The second act of *The Visit* provides an excellent example of the manner in which the playwright has explored the psychology of fear in all its nuances. A brilliant psychological touch occurs at the railroad station where Schill is confronted by the natives of Güllen; not a threatening word is uttered and yet he behaves like a man possessed, betrayed by his own fear.

A man's relationship to his God, to other men, and to himself are like the interwoven threads of a tapestry which cannot be separated out; as an impartial, almost Olympian, observer of life, Duerrenmatt has noted this and has said:

"I was able to see that there were Germans who took no part in the atrocities, but who nonetheless felt guilty. True justice is tied to conscience and, as such, it too is capable of guilt. In *The Visit*, the villagers desperately want money, which they consider their just due. Accordingly, they seek to buy justice for themselves by killing the guilty man among them. The fact that the man, Anton Schill, is guilty of a crime provides their justification, but this, of course, is not justice. Schill's justice is a personal matter between himself and God. Because of his guilt, however, the whole community is in danger. This is the central problem of the play. The theater for me is a totality like the world and has many facets. The playwright's job is to show these facets no matter how depressing they may be, for they do exist and are real."

Duerrenmatt has given a great deal of serious thought to the ways in which other genres differ from drama and has arrived at workable conclusions for himself. When he writes a story or novel he sets the action in Switzerland and describes the locale with absolute literalness, but when he writes a play he creates a world of his own and counts on active collaboration from the theatergoer.

"Güllen, as presented on the stage, does not exist," says the playwright, "except in the imagination of the audience. Just as it is impossible to have theater without spectators, so it is senseless to treat a play as if it were a kind of ode. A piece written for the theater becomes living theater when it is played, when it can be seen, heard, felt, and thus experienced immediately. This immediacy is one of the most essential aspects of the theater; a play is an event, is something that happens. In the theater everything must be transformed into the visible and sensible, and must seem to be happening at the present moment."

Dialogue, of course, is the life-blood of the drama; but it must be brief and of a very special kind. In describing dramatic dialogue, Duerrenmatt has given a clear and concise summary of the art of playwriting. He has said:

"The human being of the drama is, after all, a talking individual, and speech is his limitation. The action only serves to force this human being on the stage to talk in a certain way. The action is the crucible in which the human being is melted into words. This, of course, means that I, as the playwright, have to get the people in my drama into situations which force them to speak. If I merely show two people sitting together and drinking coffee while they talk about the weather, politics, or the latest fashions, then I provide neither a dramatic situation nor dramatic dialogue, no matter how clever their talk. Some other ingredient must be added to their conversation, something to cause wounds, conflicts, double meanings. If the audience knows that there is some poison in one of the coffee cups, or perhaps even in both, so that the conversation is really one between two poisoners, then an innocuous tête-à-tête over a coffee table is transformed by this technical device into a dramatic situation, out of which dramatic dialogue can develop. The tension in the situation creates dialogue which causes conflict and produces new situations and dialogue, and so on throughout the play."

But the art of drama is also the dramatist's total view of life as expressed in an individual style. Duerrenmatt's uncommon imagination and biting wit lend themselves naturally to nonrealistic treatment. In his plays, as in many of his paintings, there is a conscious mixture of styles; *The Visit*, for instance, is predominantly realistic with a strong intermingling of symbolism and expressionism. It is Duerrenmatt's wish to avoid literal statement and a photographic representation of life; he attempts by the use of theatricalist techniques to intensify the spectator's interest and excitement and to achieve a degree of universality. Although symbolism is the tool of the poet rather than of the playwright, Duerrenmatt often uses it to heighten the mood and mystery of his work. One eloquent symbol in *The Visit* is the panther, which, in representing Schill, not only expresses the destructive power of the young seducer but also prefigures his eventual fate. A more important element in the author's style was supplied by expressionism, which is the escape from literal reality into broader forms that embrace allegory, symbolism, fantasy, or any other expression of the dramatist's free-roving mind. From expressionism Duerrenmatt has taken the short scenes, terse dialogue, unnamed characters, "space" staging, stylized acting, interpolated songs, and sinister poetic atmosphere which are to be found in all plays of this genre from August Strindberg's to Thornton Wilder's. Having Claire Zachanassian sit on the balcony of The Golden Apostle while life goes on in the town below her as if within her purview is an expressionistic device; and the same is true of the terrifying panther hunt with armed men stalking across the stage from opposite directions like automata with highly stylized movements.

What has not been previously noticed is the strong similarity which a basic element of the plot of The Visit bears to that in An Enemy of the People. In both plays a highly respected member of the community becomes the central figure in a situation involving the financial solvency of the town. Dr. Stockmann condemns the Baths on which the community depends for its livelihood, and Anton Schill attempts to prevent his fellow-citizens from accepting Claire Zachanassian's gift of a billion marks which will put the town back in business. The townspeople, in both plays, become so hostile and threatening to the man who thwarts them, that he decides to leave the place, but later changes his mind, and, adamantly, remains to confront his adversaries and to suffer the consequences: for Stockmann it means stoning and ostracism; for Schill, condemnation and death. Such was the treatment accorded the archetypal scapegoat, the man who was loaded, by curses and incantations, with the sins and guilt of the community, then driven out or destroyed, to insure the purification of the tribe. Ibsen and Duerrenmatt satirize this ritual in their plays; the older playwright with heavy irony, the younger, with more grotesque and brutal effects; but both manifestly sympathize with the scapegoat over the morally lax, hypocritical, and corrupt members of the tribe.

It has been noted by almost all critics that Duerrenmatt takes special delight in the grotesque; many of his characters and situations are absurd, exaggerated, or bizarre. Maurice Valency felt that it was necessary to alter or omit the most fantastic aspects of The Visit to suit the tastes of English-speaking audiences. Duerrenmatt gave the semblance of an explanation for the presence of the grotesque in his plays when he said:

"Man expresses his need by crying and his freedom by laughing. Our task today is to demonstrate freedom. The tyrants of this planet are not moved by the works of poets. They yawn at a poet's lamentations. For them heroic epics are silly fairy tales and religious poetry puts them to sleep. Tyrants fear only one thing: a writer's mockery. For this reason, then, parody has crept into all literary genres, into the novel, into lyric poetry, into drama. Much of painting, even of music, has been invaded by parody, and the grotesque has followed, often well-camouflaged, on the heels of parody: all of a sudden the grotesque is there."

Duerrenmatt's concern with the effect of his plays upon "tyrants" marks him as a moralist, and The Visit becomes thereby an elaborate exemplum.

The plot of The Visit is basically uncomplicated and relatively unadorned; it has the simplicity and directness characteristic of classical drama. There are no involved subplots, and the numerous and varied incidents are all completely integrated into the main line of the action. The story unfolds in a small and impoverished provincial town "somewhere in Europe," to which an old woman returns after an absence of many years. Now fabulously wealthy, she has come back to get revenge on the man who had seduced her many years before.

Gradually and relentlessly she buys up the entire town, corrupting even the most respected citizens, until they accede to her wishes and cold-bloodedly execute her former lover. Her mission accomplished, she leaves the town.

The characterization, except for that of Anton Schill, is one-dimensional. The townspeople are not individually explored in depth, and even Claire Zachanassian has a singleness of purpose that does not permit us to see very deeply into her character. We are presented, in her case, with a wealth of biographical details which help us to understand the facets of her personality rather than those of her psyche. Schill, on the other hand, is brilliantly depicted as step by step he makes the lacerating journey to his Gethsemane. He begins as a poor, insignificant shopkeeper, an unsuspecting victim, guilty, of course, but certain that life itself has canceled the debt. He is the image of the simple, thoughtless man upon whom it slowly dawns, through fear, horror, and personal suffering, that justice is being meted out and that he will have to pay for his guilt. It is in this recognition and in the acceptance of his fate that he becomes great in his death, if he was not great in his life; by his insight and resignation he achieves, as it were, a certain monumentality.

The play's dialogue is sharp, mordant, contemporary; it crackles with wit and irony. It not only presents the characters in clear outline, but carries the action forward at breakneck pace. Its subtlety includes a hint, beyond the artlessness of the various speeches, of the author's cynical comment on what is being said.

The theme of *The Visit* is difficult to pinpoint; some critics have seen it as the mercilessness of revenge, others as the ravaging force of greed, and still others as the brutalizing effect of grinding poverty; it is all of these things and, like life, much more, including the dire results of frustrated love, the ruthless drive for power, the fruitless search for justice, and the importance of human dignity. Concerning didacticism in art, Duerrenmatt has said:

"When you write a play you don't do it to teach a lesson or prove a point or build a philosophy, because you can never force art to prove anything. The fault of most critics is that they think a play, or a novel, must be based on a thesis. I don't work that way. I write something, and then there may or may not be a thesis in it."

The element of spectacle plays a much more important part in *The Visit* than it does in most modern plays. Probably because of his visualmindedness as well as his special training in art, Duerrenmatt integrates scenery and action in such a way as to make each serve his dramatic purpose more effectively. When we first see the town of Güllen, for instance, it is drab, ramshackle, and wretched; with the arrival of Claire Zachanassian, the natives begin to paint and refurbish the buildings, tend their gardens, buy typewriters, television sets, and new church bells; when the town's benefactor is finally ready to depart, her generosity is clearly visible in the bright and beautiful buildings and other civic improvements that fill the stage. Güllen (the name is a variation of the word Gülle, Swiss dialect for excrement) is resurrected, in an unobstrusive but constant crescendo, from the shabbiest poverty and neglect to the most sparkling opulence—worthy, indeed, of a happier ending.

Therese Giehse as Claire and Gustav Knuth as Anton; the man holding branches represents a tree. (Swiss Information Service)

THE PRODUCTION RECORD

Friedrich Duerrenmatt's *Der Besuch der alten Dame* (*The Visit*) was performed for the first time at the Zurich Schauspielhaus on January 29, 1956. The press said the play was "full of original ideas, uncommon imagination, and a new type of wit," and hailed the work of the director, Oskar Wälterlin, of the scene designer, Teo Otto, and of the stars, Therese Giehse and Gustav Knuth. Almost immediately after its premiere, the play was performed in half a dozen cities in Switzerland, Austria, and Germany.

Maurice Valency's English version of the play, called at first *Time and Again* and later renamed *The Visit,* opened in Brighton, England, on December 24, 1957. It then went on a tour of the English provinces and also was seen in Scotland and Ireland, but it was not taken to London. The explanation offered for this was that British critics and audiences were so shocked by the harshness and horror of the play that the producers hesitated to take it to London, in spite of the fact that Valency's adaptation had subdued much of "the macabre gallows-humor of the original" and had heightened the romantic elements.

The play opened at the Lunt-Fontanne Theater on Broadway on May 5, 1958, and after a run of nine weeks, suspended for the summer. It reopened on August 20 at the Morosco Theater and remained there until November 29, 1958. *The Visit* received the Drama Critics' Circle Award as the best foreign play on Broadway for the season 1958-1959.

After an interval of ten months, the Lunts, under the joint sponsorship of the American Theater Society and the Council of the Living Theater, took *The Visit* on a tour of the United States and Canada that included seventeen cities and lasted from September, 1959, to March, 1960. The engagement concluded with two weeks at the City Center in New York (March 8 to March 20) where the attraction played to completely sold out houses. The New York critics were more enthusiastic about the play on this occasion than they had been at its premiere two years before. Lewis Funke, of the New York *Times*, wrote in part: "To see Friedrich Duerrenmatt's *The Visit* again is to understand why it has lingered so powerfully in memory. It happens to be one of the more trenchant and mordant plays of our time. . . . *The Visit* reminds us what a temple the theater actually can be."

From a financial point of view, too, *The Visit* was phenomenally successful in America; in fifty-four weeks of interrupted playing time from the start of its pre-Broadway tryout in April, 1958, to the closing of its post-Broadway tour in March, 1960, the play grossed over two million dollars and broke the box-office records for straight dramatic plays at the Biltmore Theater, Los Angeles; the National Theater, Washington; the Forrest Theater, Philadelphia; and the City Center, New York.

During the fourth season of the International Theater Festival which opened in Paris on March 15, 1960, Peter Brook mounted a new production of *La Visite de la Vieille Dame;* and on June 23, 1960, the Lunts had the honor of opening a new theater in London, The Royalty, where they appeared in *The Visit* for an engagement, scheduled for eight weeks, that actually stretched out to twenty.

At last report, the play has been translated into more than fifteen languages and has been produced in over twenty-five countries, including Japan and Israel.

CONCEIVING *The Visit*
An Interview with Friedrich Duerrenmatt

Duerrenmatt first thought of writing *The Visit* in the form of a short novel. Originally, there was no Claire Zachanassian in the story. The central figure was a man who returned to his home town after he had made a great fortune. He offered a huge sum of money to the townspeople if they would kill an old enemy of his, the rival who had won his boyhood sweetheart away from him. The townspeople objected and, feeling offended, evolved a plan to thwart the millionaire. It was midwinter, deep snows were on the ground; they were felling trees in the forest and managed to arrange to kill the "visitor" by having him struck by a falling tree.

Duerrenmatt was not satisfied with the idea. It seemed to him that the story would be more interesting if a woman were more prominently involved in it. He mulled over the idea for a long time and finally decided to have a wealthy woman return to her native town for the purpose of revenge. The models Duerrenmatt kept in mind while creating the background and character of Claire were the reputations and careers of the internationally famous millionaires Zacharoff, Onassis, and Gulbenkian, and from their names he concocted his heroine's— Zacha-nass-ian. Her money gave Claire the status and power that royal birth had given to Medea and to the other heroines of classical tragedy.

As he began to envision the action centered in a single locale, Duerrenmatt thought of it more and more in theatrical terms and decided that it would be more effective as a play than as a novel. It is his opinion that, on the stage, *place* is more important than character, and that it is the function of the dramatist to create a world that is palpable and entire. In this play the conflict takes a tri-angular form—the man, the woman, and the people of Güllen are pitted against each other—and the Town must therefore have the force and concreteness of each of the other protagonists.

Contrary to the belief of the critics, Duerrenmatt did not start his play with a theme, and he never does, since he is convinced that although a problem may be inherent in a play it should not be the primary element. The problem should emerge as a "by-product" created by the interrelationship of the characters and the situations. If a play has real depth and value, moreover, it usually concerns itself with more than one problem; it suggests all sorts of problems—a whole "spindle" of them. In Duerrenmatt's imagination, the play actually started with the town. It must be shown to be very poor. How? The men of the town are unemployed and have nothing better to do than to sit around the railroad station and watch the trains go by. The railroad station itself is rundown, shabby, neg-lected. What are the men waiting for? A rich and charitable woman who will come and help them out of their distress. But if she is so rich, why does she come by train? She ought to arrive in her own chauffeur-driven limousine. But she has been in many accidents and no longer travels by plane or by motor car. She has lost a hand and a leg, but these mutilations do not immobilize her. She has a will of steel and is unswerving in the pursuit of her goal; her powerful ag-gressiveness contains an element of the superhuman.

Claire Zachanassian turns up in Güllen with a coffin prepared for her former lover, whom in her youth she called her "black panther"; she also travels with a black panther which she keeps as a pet; and to complete the collection of gro-tesqueries, she has, in the original version of the play, a wooden leg. It was pointed out to Duerrenmatt that these three identical circumstances resemble actual details in the life of Sarah Bernhardt. Bernhardt owned a rosewood coffin with which she traveled and in which she often slept; she kept a pet panther; and at the age of seventy-one, she underwent an operation for the amputation of her leg, but this did not deter her from appearing on the stage and in films. Duerren-matt declared that he was completely unaware of these facts in the life of Bern-hardt, and that his choice of them was purely coincidental, but he could not vouch for the part that his unconscious had played in the process. "To make his characters interesting and theatrical," said the playwright, "the writer thinks of many things, but these things must be unified and consistent; they must be true for the character. It is for that reason that a play is much more complicated and demanding than a novel; on the stage the personalities of the characters should have a startling and grotesque quality."

It is Duerrenmatt's opinion that a play is not entirely written by the playwright; the director and the actors make important contributions to both characterization and plot. Alfred Lunt, for example, wanted a more pointed climax than had originally been written for the railroad scene at the end of the second act, so a brand-new character was introduced at this point, one whom the playwright had never thought of during the process of composition: the man who stopped for a pail of water and casually offered Anton a lift in his truck; he added greatly to both plot and characterization. Duerrenmatt has no objection to making changes, whether minor or drastic ones, if they will serve the good of the play; he feels that professional directors and actors, if they are genuine artists, know instinctively what makes good theater. He has tremendous respect for both Peter Brook and Alfred Lunt as creative technicians; before the English version of his play was done, the dramatist talked the script through scene by scene with Peter Brook and made many changes in accordance with Brook's views. And yet Duerrenmatt does not feel that there is only one way to mount a play; the text is merely a plan for a production, it is the unfulfilled "possibility" of a theatrical presentation. He liked the forest scene, for instance, when it was done in Zurich with men representing trees expressionistically, and he liked it just as well when it was done by the Lunts on an absolutely bare stage. Each actor creates a role differently and an author is often amazed to see things he never dreamed of emerge from his work; but he is not always pleased, he may quite often be disappointed or dismayed.

To Duerrenmatt, Anton Schill is the more important of the two central figures in the play, since he starts out as a small and insignificant human being and develops as the action progresses into a person with a strong and courageous character. The playwright feels that Lunt did a brilliant job in showing this development. Claire Zachanassian, on the other hand, remains unchanged throughout, but Fontanne played the part with such a strong undercurrent of wit and humor that she gave it enormous variety.

The original version of *The Visit* was thought to be too fantastic and grotesque to suit the tastes of American audiences, so the most extreme examples of these elements were removed from the play by the director and the adaptor. But Duerrenmatt says, "I do not understand why Broadway is so realistic and naturalistic when the greatest figures in American literature and American films were masters of fantasy and the grotesque." To prove his point, the playwright named Mark Twain—(a strong resemblance has been noted between the Twain story "The Man Who Corrupted Hadleyburg" and *The Visit*). In his enthusiasm for Mark Twain, the playwright compared him to Aristophanes and Swift in the manner in which he satirized politics and democracy. "Mark Twain's stories are written in every conceivable style, including surrealism," says Duerrenmatt. "If modern literature can do it, why can't the stage?" Duerrenmatt also mentioned Poe, Hawthorne, Melville, and Faulkner, whom he admires tremendously, and also Chaplin, whose best work was a magnificent tissue of odd, whimsical, and startling conceits. It is only in the theater, apparently, that English-speaking audiences seem to be afraid of nonrealistic work, but Duerrenmatt would like to be influential in introducing a freer use of the imagination to British and American stages; European audiences accept his work unaltered.

Duerrenmatt also remarked about other differences between European and American theatrical conditions which affect the playwright. When *The Visit* and his later play, *Frank V*, were done in Zurich, the critics had some harsh things to say about them, but they also offered many constructive suggestions. Duerrenmatt pondered the reviewers' advice, then changed, rewrote, and improved the scripts, which were subsequently mounted in many cities in Switzerland, Germany, and Austria. He saw many productions of these plays and continued to make changes over a long period of time. The same system proved to be of invaluable aid to Ionesco and Beckett, who came out of the little theaters of Paris and looked upon each production as an opportunity to make further improvements; a failure in Europe is not considered a calamity. But the American theater is so highly financed that Broadway cannot afford to take a chance on the serious, young, experimental writer and will only produce the young writer's work if it happens to fall into a fairly conventional mold. Broadway is more daring, but still full of trepidation, if the "odd-ball" play happens to come from the pen of an internationally famous writer. On the American stage, said Duerrenmatt, we see pictures of the South and of the Bronx, but we don't see America; that is because the realistic style has a tendency to emphasize the local rather than the universal, or world, view.

Duerrenmatt insists that he will continue to be antinaturalistic, will put anything into his plays that occurs to him because all things are possible on the stage. In *The Visit*, for instance, it delighted him to think that Claire Zachanassian was so rich that she could do her shopping all over the world: She got her sedan-chair from the Louvre and then bought two gangsters in America to serve as chair-bearers.

DIRECTING *The Visit*
An Interview with Peter Brook

"Everyone may not like this play," says Peter Brook, "because it shows so vividly that people will do absolutely anything for money. It has a simple, direct story but it takes a certain amount of sophistication on the part of the audience to appreciate its cynicism." He feels that the play is written in epic and fabulous terms. It is interesting to note that the productions of the play done in Germany and France differ vastly from those done in England and America because of the different cultural and theatrical traditions in each country.

Brook's interpretation of the play differed from both the German and the French in that he was not trying for a detached alienation from the audience but wanted to tell the story in heightened human terms. He wanted the audience to feel that Claire Zachanassian and Anton Schill were two comprehensible human beings whose actions were real and motivated, and he could only achieve this effect by dramatizing their human traits.

The continental actresses who had undertaken the part invariably stressed Claire's grossness, coarseness, and physical disfigurement. Brook felt, however, that to portray Claire as a dazzling, impersonal beauty would be more vivid and effective and would cast a mythical aura about her, while Anton was to be presented with the utmost realism, since he was utterly a creature of the ter-restrial plane. It worked out as planned; Lynn Fontanne had the cool imper-sonality of a goddess, while Alfred Lunt was torn by the conflicts in the common man.

In the strong feelings he has against the purely "theatrical" approach, Brook is anti-Brechtian; he believes that the interest of the audience is, and should be, caught by the imagination, and that the stimulation of the imagination is one of the great social and artistic functions performed by the theater. Teo Otto's scenery was exciting because it built up feeling by impressionistic means and demanded the creative cooperation of the audience. The Lunts, too, alone on a bare stage, just sitting on a bench, had a deeper and more intimate relationship than they would have had if they had been surrounded by a clutter of scenery.

Brook tried to bring out the subtle mood of each scene and so he minimized the broadly stylized and exaggerated elements in the original script. Out and out expressionism, he felt, would have had very little meaning for Anglo-Saxon audiences.

Peter Brook came to direct *The Visit* by a series of international arrangements. He was working on *Cat on a Hot Tin Roof* at the Théâtre Antoine in Paris, when he learned that a play called *The Visit* by a new Swiss dramatist was being presented at the Théâtre Marigny. He stopped in to see it, was impressed enough to read it in French, and then learned that Maurice Valency had done a version in English. Shortly afterwards, in London, Brook had a discussion with Roger Stevens, who owned the American production rights to the play, and both agreed that if the play were to be done, the Lunts would have to do it; but Stevens had already offered the play to them and they had turned it down. Later, while Brook was on tour in Belgrade, with his production of *Titus Andronicus*, Hugh Beaumont informed him that the Lunts had agreed to do the play. Brook re-turned from Belgrade, Valency came on from New York, and Duerrenmatt from Switzerland, and the three men met in Paris. There they worked on the script together, retranslating and rewriting. Alfred Lunt turned up at one of these meetings and immediately began to talk about his costumes; he said that Lynn Fontanne, too, had begun to think of her gowns and had decided that she wanted Castillo, whose studio is in Paris, to design them. Brook was delighted, since it is his feeling that the better the actor the more thought he gives to his stage-clothes.

Brook then went to Switzerland with Duerrenmatt to continue work on the play. The dramatist suggested that Teo Otto, who had provided the scenery for the original production, be engaged for the English version. Brook was discon-certed; he had always begun a play with his own pictorial "vibration"—a visual solution which came to him in the form of a definite image; *Titus Andronicus,* for example, evoked a barbaric décor in which architectural columns served as trees. It was for that reason that he had reservations about Otto; he did not think that he could work with someone else's designs. He began to brood about the problem. One day he noticed four sketches for stage settings which had been framed and hung on the walls in Duerrenmatt's home, and he became terribly excited by them. When he learned that they were the work of Teo Otto, Brook immediately agreed that this artist was the man to design *The Visit.*

Working with Otto was a pleasure, Brook discovered, because, being more highly creative than imaginative, Otto was extremely amenable to suggestions. When Brook proposed that certain of the details in his designs be altered, Otto promptly consented. It was not necessary, Brook felt, to have men masquerade as trees; the Lunts and a simple wooden bench were sufficient to transform a bare stage into a forest. Brook believes that all forms of theater are related to specific social and cultural conditions, and that one change in a production determines many others. In the last scene of the play as it was done in Switzerland a gilded, rococo proscenium, with a scarlet front-curtain, was dropped in from the "flies," and the murder of Anton Schill took place behind the curtain; this scene provided a great contrast to the style of the rest of the production, but its intention was to give an unreal and "theatrical" quality to the brutal act. Hugh Beaumont objected to the set because, although it suggested the stage of a local municipal theater which is a familiar sight to all European playgoers it would mean nothing to English and American audiences. It occurred to Brook that a Gothic hall with hanging lamps in a dark and somber mood would be more appropriate for the scene, and that is the set that Otto provided, with such skill that many critics singled it out for special praise.

Rehearsals of *The Visit* were held at the Lyric Theater in the West End, London. At the first rehearsal, Brook usually delivers a long talk so that the actors will have some idea about the play, the sets, and the costumes. Then the actors read the script aloud; Brook never reads to the actors because he considers it boring. In France it is regarded as revolutionary to allow the actors to read, but Brook observes the practice even in that country. He believes that reading serves no purpose but a social one for the first meeting, since it is a way of breaking the ice for the members of the company who are to work together.

"My method of directing is like painting a picture in oils," says Brook. "First I make a large free sketch, then I put in more and more details, but I keep changing and adding throughout the rehearsal period. I give the actors rough positions but each day I make changes until exactly the right places are found. Old-school actors want the very thing that should be most insulting to them, that is, to be told what to do, when to do it, and where to do it." An actor often asks a direct question but instead of replying Brook works with him in rehearsals and it is sometimes three weeks later that the question will be answered. The director considers this sort of cooperative creation the only way that he can work. It results in choreographic patterns without endless planning in ad-

vance. Brook makes very few notes and preserves nothing on paper. Even the
crowd scenes are worked out slowly and experimentally to get richness and
complexity. In Duerrenmatt's original script, the townsmen echo every line that
Lunt speaks at the railroad station. This did not seem to play properly and Brook
wanted to change it; he tried many variations until it finally occurred to him
to have all the men suddenly speak in chorus at one point, then have one speak
alone, and at another time allow them all to remain silent, and this gave him
the variety and effect that he wanted.

"If you plan too precisely in advance," says Brook, "you get parental, possessive, and proprietary; if you don't plan, you don't mind scrapping what you've
done. The danger in the latter technique, however, is that in continually revising you sometimes scrap something that is excellent and ought to be retained.
The Lunts were able to hold me down. They would say, 'You've done something good, let's save it.' Lynn has great stability; Alfred is mercurial. In Stratford, we introduced a completely new version of the play with much less text
and more action; Lynn went on trembling, but came off convinced that the new
version was better than the old."

In the original play, the schoolteacher is depicted as a weak man who suddenly comes to the forefront of those who denounce Schill at the public trial.
Duerrenmatt did not hesitate to exaggerate or to use unmotivated reversals of
character, but Brook thought that it would be more effective to show the teacher
breaking down slowly rather than changing suddenly. Brook tried several
approaches; in England, the teacher's final speech was a total denunciation, but
in New York it was the expression of a man without moral courage who finally
did not dare to act upon his convictions. Duerrenmatt had also put a heavy
layer of farce and "cabaret" humor over his serious play, and these had to be
removed along with many grotesque elements. The author, for instance, had
conceived of Claire as a spitting, biting, ugly, and hard old witch, but that did
not accord with either the director's or the American actress's conception. Lynn
Fontanne played her twenty percent witch, eighty percent other qualities:
success in life, attractive to men, and so on. "Lynn thinks Claire is mad," says
Brook, "so in order to give her some 'balance' she added the attributes of tenderness, grace, and style." It was Duerrenmatt's idea that the part of the pastor
ought to be played by a physically heavy man who had a worldly heartiness;
Brook adopted the suggestion and a big, genial man created the role in England,
but it did not work. "In New York," says Brook, "I used William Hansen, who
is short and slight, quiet and serious, and whose performance was remarkable
for its understanding."

The most difficult act to direct, Brook found, was Act II. Act I was sheer
story-telling; and Act III simply had to be trimmed so that it would move more
quickly and more starkly to its conclusion. In Act II, however, Schill starts out
by being self-satisfied and ends up by being submissive and it is necessary to
show this slow and subtle development; but many of the scenes in this act are
repetitious and all are in the same tone and are predictable. There were, in
addition, too many scenes on the balcony of the hotel that added nothing to the

play. What was to be done? Maurice Valency wrote a big scene for the Lunts in order to bring the principals on, but the scene was finally discarded. Another scene was added in which Claire visited a tailor and ordered her funeral clothes; the scene ended with a monologue specially written by Duerrenmatt. That too was dropped. The problem was solved mainly by judicious cutting. The scene in which Claire stands on the balcony and confronts Anton as he levels a gun at her was an inspiration; somehow Lynn Fontanne was impelled to point her finger at Alfred Lunt at the very moment that he was pointing the gun at her. This simultaneous action is followed by Claire's long speech during which Anton is called upon to react in silence. Lunt found this particularly exciting because he enjoys communicating ideas in pantomime. Brooks Atkinson has called Alfred Lunt "the master of wordless eloquence."

"Directing Lunt is a revelation," says Brook. "You can't imagine the countless tiny details that Alfred puts into a performance. This may sound like finicky acting but these painstaking details make up an enormous conception. It is like one of Seurat's pointillist paintings. Each little dot is not art, but the whole is magnificent. Alfred and Lynn start by getting a broad outline of what they're going to do and then they fill in the details. It's absolutely like somebody making a mosaic. They work endlessly from one detail to the next—fine, fine points— one after another. They're deep and flexible people and they have lightning speed and great artistic glory."

Peter Brook called on his stage manager, Mary Lynn, to help select English actors for the New York production because he did not want two different speech patterns in the same play, but when he heard the entire cast speaking in English accents he felt that it was wrong and suggested that they all adopt a slightly American accent.

"It is important for every aspiring stage director to possess several special attributes," says Peter Brook; "prominent among them are imagination, patience, and the ability to deal with seemingly infinite details."

STAGE MANAGING *The Visit*
    An Interview with Mary Lynn

The job of the stage manager is the most complex of all those connected with a theatrical presentation. It entails intensive and detailed work before and during the production. Functioning primarily as a coordinator, the stage manager must see that the various elements of the production are properly organized and integrated; he works closely, therefore, with the artists—author, actors, director; with the technicians—property, electrical, and carpentry departments; and with the producer's office—accounting, legal, and publicity divisions.

Mary Lynn, one of the few women to hold the position of professional stage manager, has had a varied career in the theater. She began as a dancer in the celebrated revues of André Charlot and remained with his company for two and a half years. She then joined Ivor Novello, the star and producer of elaborate operettas, and for four years at the Drury Lane Theater served as ballet mistress and organizer of the road companies of the plays that were sent on tour. In about 1939, Miss Lynn became connected with the H. M. Tennent producing organization, one of the most important in London, in the dual capacities of ballet mistress and second assistant stage manager. She rose to the position of first assistant stage manager, a post she also held for John Gielgud's productions of *Macbeth*, *Love for Love*, and *Hamlet*. For the last five years, she has not only been a full-fledged stage manager but a company manager as well, which means that she concerns herself with the business end of the production.

"Long before the opening of the play," says Miss Lynn, "the stage manager sends out calls for the audition of actors, takes charge of the readings, and books the halls for the rehearsals." On the first day of rehearsal, she arranges the chairs in a semicircle on the stage for the actors and sets up a table and chair facing them for the director. She introduces the actors to each other and holds a copy of the script as they read through the play. She attends all readings and rehearsals and makes a note of everything needed for the production; this includes all line changes, positions and movements of actors, light and sound cues, and any other special notes given by the director. At the end of each rehearsal, she finds out from the director which actors he will want to see the following day and when and where they will meet.

In England, a small model of the set is made for every production and the ground plan is painted to scale on a cloth which is put on the stage floor during rehearsals for the guidance of the actors; it is the stage manager's duty to attend to both the model and the cloth.

Because *The Visit* was played on a practically bare stage, the properties were not only numerous but were extremely important; Miss Lynn had a complete list of the properties needed for the play and checked them at every rehearsal and performance. During the rehearsals in England, every property was used from the very first day, since benches, ladders, and streamers, as well as many other items, had to be handled with extreme precision. In this play, the actors themselves brought on and removed the various properties and pieces of furniture needed for each scene. That meant that the movement of the actors had to be organized; but "since actors are notoriously careless," says Miss Lynn, "they had to be drilled like soldiers so that they would enter and exit precisely on cue." Because of the union rules in New York, actors are not permitted to handle actual props during the rehearsal period; Miss Lynn conceived the idea of making rehearsal props out of newspaper and cardboard. Many products used on the stage, including foods and beverages, are supplied by the manufacturer in exchange for program credit, but most properties are rented or bought; large and expensive items which can serve for many productions are even bought on the installment plan. It is the job of the stage manager to secure the needed properties in good time.

When the director is absent, the stage manager is in charge of rehearsals, and it is always his special job to rehearse the understudies. Miss Lynn takes this task seriously and makes sure that the understudies are letter perfect before opening night. On two occasions involving productions with which she was connected, the stars were absent during the very first week but the understudies stepped in without any difficulty.

The final week of rehearsal is the most difficult one for the stage manager for then he must prepare all the "plots"—the costume, property, lighting, sound, and music cues. The complete script of the play including all of these cues must be ready at this time. And it is then that the stage manager works most closely with the property master and the chief carpenter.

The Visit had about fifty-six light cues and forty-eight sound cues. "All stage managers should know something about music, should have a sense of rhythm and timing," Miss Lynn believes, "because all plays contain many sound cues, and it may even be necessary to raise or lower the curtain on a certain bar of music." For the English production, the sounds were supplied by records and a panatrope machine, but in New York the sound was put on tape. Peter Brook wanted the growling panther to sound authentic, and Miss Lynn tried several experiments. She is able to make a snarling sound and she put this noise on record; then she enlisted the two Siamese cats owned by the New York stage manager, Fritz de Wilde, when she noticed that these animals made a rumbling growl when they were hungry. The two sounds—Miss Lynn's snarl and the cats' growl—recorded together gave the impression of an angry jungle beast. Then Miss Lynn went to the Boston Zoo and recorded the growling of a real panther; both tapes were played for Peter Brook who, without knowing the source of either, selected the one featuring Miss Lynn and the two cats, and that was used for the play.

The original opening of the play in Brighton, England, fell on a Tuesday night. Dress rehearsals were held on the previous Saturday night and all day Sunday to perfect the lighting. Two dress rehearsals were held on Monday and one on Tuesday. In addition to her regular dressing room, Lynn Fontanne had a portable dressing room just off-stage in the wings, where she made several quick changes. The stage manager allots dressing rooms to the members of the cast and sees that the house staff keeps them clean. The theater in Dublin did not have adequate dressing room space so Alfred Lunt was forced to use a little closet which did not even have a sink in it.

During the run of the play, the stage manager is in complete charge of the show. Since he has the final responsibility for the smooth running of the performance, he must check every item involved, from the personal props of the stars to the furniture markings on the stage. He makes sure that everything is shipshape before he takes up his post at the switchboard. One evening Lynn Fontanne sat beside Mary Lynn at the switchboard, watching the stage manager marshal her forces before the curtain went up, and said, "I wouldn't have your job for anything." "Miss Fontanne," says Miss Lynn, "was always completely relaxed and ready to go on. She has a superstition which she calls her Green Umbrella. When she has fixed on the right thing to do, she says she has "found her green umbrella."

Since the stage manager works more closely with the director than with anyone

else connected with the production, Mary Lynn had ample opportunity to observe closely the methods of Peter Brook and to develop a great admiration for
him. According to Miss Lynn, Brook is especially adept at casting a play. He
never selects an actor primarily on the basis of "type" or looks, but on the
affinity of the actor's character for the role.

On the first day of rehearsal, the company got together in the morning and
began to read the play; they sat around a table and Brook interrupted the
reading to talk about the theme of the work, the town in which the action
takes place, and what the people are like. After a break for lunch, the reading
continued until the play was completed. On the second day the actors were
on their feet; Brook does not believe in long discussion sessions. He starts at
the beginning of the script and blocks it out, scene by scene, straight through
to the end. He is very soft-spoken, and uses his hands a great deal while he
speaks to give the actors the mood and meaning of each scene; he often communicates more clearly with his hands than he does with words. Although he
adopts many suggestions made by the actors, producers, or writer, he knows
what he wants and will not budge an inch when he feels that he is right. Many
evening rehearsals were held in the ballet room under the stage at the Drury
Lane Theater. After Brook had roughly blocked out the play from beginning
to end, he broke it down into individual scenes and worked separately with the
actors involved. The rehearsals went on for a month before the opening, but
after the opening Brook kept changing and perfecting the play; then he went
away for a fortnight and came back to take a fresh look at it.

Because his style of directing is basically improvisational, Brook continues
to make changes as new thoughts and insights strike him. This often drives the
actors mad but they go along with him because they realize that the changes
are usually for the better. In the English production, the small set-pieces of
scenery were backed by a velvet drop and there were three returns (drops
serving as wings) on each side of the stage. All of these curtains were covered
with multicolored paint in bright colors such as orange and green; when Brook
arrived in America he had an inspiration concerning the curtains. In Boston,
where the play was trying out before its New York opening, Brook suddenly
decided to have the curtains sprayed with a thin coating of black paint so that
all the colors would be toned down and muted which not only gave them a
sad, old, and poverty-stricken look but also made the brilliant costumes of Lynn
Fontanne stand out against them in striking contrast. In the same way Brook
thought spontaneously of individualizing the properties and costumes of the
men who sat around the railroad station in Güllen; one was to be smoking an
old German pipe, another was to wear worn and raveling mittens, and so on.

Seven members of the English cast went with the Lunts to America where
innumerable alterations were made in both the play and the characterizations.
In the English version, for instance, Peter Woodthorpe, who is only in his
twenties, was made up as an old man for the role of the Schoolteacher; he
shaved off part of his own hair, donned a gray wig, and behaved in a patriarchal
manner. Brook had one of his flashes of intuition and when the play went into

rehearsal in New York, Woodthorpe emerged as a young, energetic, and passionate figure, whose confrontation of Claire Zachanassian and stubbornness in resisting the arguments of the other townspeople were perfect expressions of the intransigence of youth, and took audiences by storm.

After the New York cast had been selected, Brook worked with the company for a week in the little theater atop the New Amsterdam in Forty-second Street. There were about twenty-seven new people involved and Brook continued his practice of reworking and reshaping the play both in structure and in dialogue as he went along. A scene in which the Schill family went for a drive originally followed a family scene in the grocery store; the automobile was created by simply turning the shop counter around and pulling out two drawers, which served as the front seats of the car. These were occupied by the son and the daughter, while Anton and his wife stood behind them. Brook then decided to do away with the car scene so the grocery counter was removed along with the shelves; the family went off-stage to where the car was parked and Anton was left to walk into the forest alone; a few lines of dialogue were cut and the scenes flowed smoothly together.

Even the Lunts made constant changes in their roles always seeking improvements. Lynn Fontanne's scenes involving the panther were tried in many ways; in one of them the blind men were beaten; in another, when it was announced that the animal had been killed, Miss Fontanne cried like a panther; and in still another, she stated proudly that the panther had originally been ferocious, had killed more than two hundred men, but she had tamed him and slept with him. All of these "bits," which were tried out at one time or another, were eventually omitted.

The scene at the railroad station, during which Anton Schill attempts to run away, had fewer men threatening him as it was played in England and yet the effect was quite terrifying; in New York, more actors were added but their threats were psychological rather than physical and Alfred Lunt consequently reacted differently; he added the retching and vomiting which he had not done in England. In the strangling scene, as performed in England, however, he not only thrashed his feet about but also made unearthly gurgling sounds in his throat; while in America, he used only the beating of the feet. To express his fear of death Lunt uttered the words, "Oh, God . . . oh, God!" with great depth and fervency, and once told Miss Lynn that he remembered hearing his mother utter those words in just that way as she lay dying.

During the play's first week of tryout in Brighton, England, at the Saturday matinee, while Lunt was gurgling and kicking his feet as he was being strangled, an elderly woman sitting in the orchestra made a gurgling noise in her throat and people sitting near her thought she was snoring; when the house emptied out at the end of the play, the woman continued to sit in her seat and it was found that she was dead. The manager of the Theater Royal knew the woman, as she had attended the Saturday matinee regularly for many years, and during the intermission of *The Visit* she had gone up to him and told him how much she was enjoying the play; it was his unpleasant duty to notify her relatives and

Alfred Lunt, as Schill, pleads for his life at the feet of the inflexible Lynn Fontanne, as Claire. John Wyse and Eric Porter look on. (Vandamm)

then have a coffin brought round to the front of the house so that her body could be removed to a chapel. In the very same week, Miss Lynn recalled, a man in the audience had suffered a heart attack during the performance. These occurrences had a demoralizing effect upon some of the members of the company; the assistant stage manager almost had a nervous breakdown because of the "wickedness" of the play, and a female member of the cast announced, "This is an evil play; it will never get to London." It seemed for a time as if that prediction would come true, for after its tour of the provinces, *The Visit* went to New York.

Costumes for Lynn Fontanne
An Interview with Antonio del Castillo

Antonio Canovas del Castillo, of the house of Lanvin-Castillo, Paris, created Lynn Fontanne's costumes for *The Visit*. Because of his experience as the designer for some of the wealthiest women in international society, Castillo was especially suited to do the costumes for Claire Zachnassian, "the richest woman in the world." The play impressed the designer as being "modern Shakespeare . . . bloody," but he thought it would be "great fun to do" because it allowed him imaginative scope with "its capes, its veils, and even a wedding dress."

After reading the script, Castillo invited Alfred Lunt, Lynn Fontanne, and Peter Brook to dinner at his flat in Paris, and during the evening the play was discussed in minute detail. It was decided that Lynn Fontanne was to have six gowns: a traveling costume for her first entrance, an evening gown for the restaurant scene at the end of Act I, a hostess gown for the balcony scenes in the second act, a wedding gown for the barn scene, a peasant dress for the forest scene in the third act, and widow's weeds for her final scene and exit. One particular accessory, which, in addition to being decorative, was symbolic of Claire's wealth and power, was to be worn throughout the play regardless of the costume; that was an elaborate pearl necklace, its design suggested to Castillo by a famous old piece of jewelry which had formerly belonged to the Queen of France.

Peter Brook suggested that it would be interesting if the peasant dress for the third act were done in genuine Hungarian style, full of gold thread and decorative embroidery. Castillo objected; the "peasant" costumes he has been making for rich women for years are always the last word in simplicity. This was the keynote adopted by Castillo as the basis for all of Miss Fontanne's clothes; the designer started by asking himself, "What sort of clothes would a woman as rich as Claire Zachanassian order if she were going on such a trip?" Castillo then made preliminary sketches of the gowns; it is interesting to note that in all of these original drawings the skirts are so long that the hems touch the floor. The designer explained that he was attempting to conceal the wooden leg that this character had in the original version of the play, but after Peter Brook changed his conception of Claire and decided that she was to be as attractive as possible, all mention of the wooden leg was removed from the script and the gowns were altered to various lengths. The peasant dress was shortest, the dresses for arrival and departure were of street length, the evening, hostess, and wedding gowns were long.

Castillo draped materials in various colors and textures on Miss Fontanne before a final selection was made. The actress's measurements were taken, and the first patterns were turned out in muslin. Miss Fontanne had only two fittings; then the gowns were made in the final fabrics. The designer and his assistants went to London twice to complete the fittings and to attend early rehearsals of the play. Castillo was particularly concerned about a difficult change from street dress to evening gown in the first act; he was convinced, however, that the gowns worked very well. And he came away speaking in glowing terms of the actress. "She is wonderful to work with," said Castillo, "very easygoing and extremely clever, but most important of all, she carries herself magnificently, with tremendous awareness, and has a sense of real elegance." Castillo added, "One reason why Miss Fontanne's clothes look so effective on stage is that she takes such good care of them; she wears and handles them with tenderness, and she even wraps her gloves in cellophane between performances."

When creating costumes for a play, Castillo always works very closely with the scene designer; *The Visit* provided an unusual experience as he did not see the scenery until long after the play's opening. In their preliminary talks, Brook described the sets in detail, but the principle that guided Castillo in his designs was that Miss Fontanne had to be seen in contrast to everyone else on stage at all times. Throughout, the natives of Güllen were plainly dressed while Claire appeared in rich attire; they were drab and she was bright. In the last act, however, the contrast was reversed when all the townspeople turned out in gay clothing, their Sunday best, and Claire Zachanassian moved among them in funereal black.

Although it did not take Castillo very long either to create or to complete the costumes, the quality of the materials and the workmanship brought their cost to between six hundred and one thousand dollars apiece.

For her first appearance in the play, Miss Fontanne was dressed in a single shade of red. With a red woolen dress and cape, she wore a red felt cloche hat, a long red chiffon scarf, red shoes, and carried a red umbrella. Her red hair was streaked with white and her make-up was extremely pale. The panels affixed to the shoulders of the dress appeared to be "wings" but were described by Castillo as "three large petals." The actress carried no handbag with this outfit, since a woman of Claire's wealth and position would be presumed to travel with attendants who paid the bills, carried the keys, and so on. Claire did carry a cane, not because of any obvious infirmity but rather as a symbol of authority.

Because of the demands of the action of the play, Miss Fontanne had to change from the red dress into her most elaborate evening costume for the restaurant scene in just twenty-two seconds. This change was made in the portable dressing room just off-stage in the wings, and in darkness. The red hat had a large button at the back which a dresser could undo in a second; the hat then opened out like a belt and came off easily without disturbing the actress's hairdo. The red dress was zipped off; Miss Fontanne stepped into the gown, put her hands through the armholes, the gown was zipped up the back—and the change was made. The long gown was of apricot velvet with matching apricot gloves. The dress appeared to be extremely complicated because the entire bodice was embroidered in pearls and rubies, and pendants of pearls fell from the shoulder straps, but these jewels were actually attached to the gown and though they gave an extremely elaborate effect they did not require separate handling; the basic idea behind the design was ease of management for the quick change. With this costume Miss Fontanne wore dangling earrings of rubies and pearls.

The yellow hostess gown worn in the balcony scenes in the second act, was, from the point of view of materials and workmanship, the most intricate and expensive of the six dresses created by Castillo. It was made of cloth of silver and gold and of brocaded satin of a very unusual pattern. Miss Fontanne hesitated to approve it because of the price, but Peter Brook thought it was worth it because of the effect it would create. When Alfred Lunt saw the gown, he said jokingly to Castillo: "What have you done to me? If she is dressed so beautifully during that scene, no one will look at or listen to *me*."

The wedding gown was of white satin moiré, brocaded with water lilies to make the fabric heavier and richer. The veil, topped by a coronet of white flowers and pearls, was fastened under the chin and formed a free floating panel behind, and billows of veiling were draped carefully around the actress before each performance. A macabre note in this scene was that the bride smoked a cigar and sent up clouds of smoke that mingled with and seemed to augment the veiling. She wore, of course, the ubiquitous pearl necklace. As Miss Fontanne sat in the sedan-chair, waiting for the curtain to go up and the performance to begin, other members of the company would stand around and talk to her, always at a distance so as not to disarrange her gown.

The colors in the peasant dress were mainly brown, black, and white, and were meant to be slightly reminiscent of those worn by the peasants in Castillo's native Spain; but the designer made sure that the dress would give the impression of wealth rather than of poverty by combining several rich materials: brown wool, black velvet, and a blouse of white organza. Black vertical stripes in the bodice enhanced Miss Fontanne's slim, young look. At first it was thought that for this scene the actress should wear her hair loose or in braids over her shoulders, but that seemed too coy; instead, the hair was swept up from her ears in a very attractive arrangement. Castillo pointed out that the red wig worn by Miss Fontanne in this production was specially made for her in London; it was a beautiful creation whose three-part construction assured that it would fit perfectly, and its luxuriant hair could be dressed like one's own.

The black dress worn in the final scenes was done in a heavy silk known as widow's crepe; the ensemble was completed by black shoes and a black circular hat. The hat was covered by a black veil that fell to the waist in front and below the skirt in back. "Miss Fontanne thought the hat so becoming," said Castillo, "that she ordered one for her personal use in private life for street wear." The identical pattern was used for the red dress at the beginning and the black dress at the end of the play, except that the cape was omitted from the latter.

"The gowns were made in Paris and sent to Brighton, England, for the opening," said Castillo, "but I could not attend the opening, unfortunately, because I was ill at the time. Several months later, I went to New York and saw the play for the first time in a rehearsal hall on the roof of the New Amsterdam Theater. The company went through the action without scenery or adequate lighting, but I felt that the costumes were what I had planned. Later, when I saw the play in its own theater under proper conditions, I was satisfied that the costumes were right."

After the New York opening, *Vogue* Magazine published photographs of Miss Fontanne's costumes, and Castillo's creations caused a great stir in the world of high fashion.

The final scene of the Norwegian production in Oslo, showing Claire Zachanassian, played by Lillebil Ibsen, leaving Güllen in her sedan chair. (Oslo National Theater)

PUBLICIZING *The Visit*
An Interview with Barry Hyams

Barry Hyams has spent over twenty-five years in the theater as press agent for some of the most important productions to reach Broadway. He has publicized ballet and opera attractions as well as the drama and says that the press agent's basic job is "selling the show to the public." He has three main avenues of approach for bringing his play to the notice of the potential theatergoer: media publicity, advertising, and promotion and exploitation.

Newspapers, magazines, television, and radio comprise the media to which the press agent sends news items, feature stories, and photographs, and with which he arranges interviews for the personalities connected with the play. Editors and program directors are willing to make space and time in their media available free of charge because of the reader's and listener's appetite for human interest and news stories concerning the theater.

Advertising differs from publicity in that, although the same media are used, the space and time are paid for; "ads" range in size from the half-inch single-column notice in the local newspaper to the monster billboard on the public highway and include one-minute spots on radio or television, window cards, three-sheet posters, and the display materials seen in such public places as railroad and subway stations, airport terminals, and trains.

The field of promotion and exploitation is so complex that it almost defies description; it includes but is not limited to circulation by mail, preparation of heralds, flyers, and leaflets of many sorts, window display tie-ups with department stores and individual shops, advertising tie-ups with the manufacturers of various products, and preparation of the signs and photographs displayed in theater lobbies and elsewhere.

A press agent's "campaign" is a plan whereby the various channels—publicity, advertising, promotion—are combined in the best way to sell a particular play; campaigns differ, of course, from production to production, depending upon the nature of the play, the stature of the author, stars, director, and upon many other significant factors. "But there are really only two basic ways to run a campaign," says Barry Hyams, "and these accomplish the same purpose, although they start from opposite directions. According to one plan, a detailed announcement is sent to the press far in advance of the opening of the production; then day by day the various aspects of the story are developed in more elaborate form. This approach, going from the general to the particular, as it were, was used to announce the arrival of the Sadler's Wells Ballet on its first visit to America; the initial release acquainted the American public with the history, techniques, traditions, and aims of the English company; then followed news and features of its personnel, while the repertory schedule was withheld until the public had been warmed with anticipation and had become eager to purchase tickets. The second, and more 'classic,' approach works from the particular to the general; the idea is to start the campaign with a small announcement and to increase the size and importance of the releases as time goes on, allowing the information to take root and flourish. The ideal campaign, whichever system is adopted, is based on good material astutely used."

The publicity campaign for *The Visit* emerged as a perfect example of the "classic" type; the event evolved and "built" like a well-constructed drama in three acts with a clearly defined beginning, middle, and end. The strongest elements in the "plot" were the refurbishing and renaming of an old theater, the return of the Lunts in a serious play, and a brand new playwright; among the important "subplots" were a brilliant director, and a fabulous set of costumes for the feminine star.

In May, 1957, an announcement was sent to the newspapers concerning the purchase of the Globe Theater on Broadway by Robert W. Dowling, Roger L. Stevens, and Robert Whitehead, the directors of the Producers' Theater. The Globe had been built in 1910 for legitimate drama but had been serving since 1931 as a movie-house; it was the intention of its new owners to restore the old playhouse to its original glory by transmuting it into a model of ease and beauty and initiating its reclamation with a dramatic offering of distinction.

Instantly the drama reporters and gossip columnists let loose a succession of conjectures as to who the first tenant of the new Globe would be. Meanwhile, work had begun on the theater and the plans and progress of its transformation were detailed regularly to the press; the completion date was predicted for March 1, 1958. In February, the Producers' Theater released the news that the Lunts would open the Globe in *The Visit*.

It was a freezing Sunday morning when the members of the press were invited to a conference in the drafty unfinished cellar of the theater where they huddled in a makeshift cubicle in front of electric heaters, while technicians hurried to set up a two-way radio hookup to Dublin. At eleven o'clock, the three executives of the Producers' Theater, in the presence of the reporters, took turns speaking with the Lunts in Ireland where they were then performing *The Visit*, and announced that the new playhouse on West 46th Street, directly opposite the Helen Hayes Theater, would thereafter be known as the Lunt-Fontanne.

The naming of the new theater for the stars who were to open the house with their latest play provided an exciting climax to the first act of the publicity campaign. The Lunts are the most celebrated pair in the American Theater, and their uninterrupted joint career of the preceding three decades, representing the quintessence of acting art, has always made excellent copy. Now every nugget of information, every anecdote dealing with the couple was mined and immediately minted into journalistic currency. Their public and private lives, beginning professionally in 1905 and maritally in 1922, were reviewed in text and photos. Among the data that most fascinated the chroniclers of the coming event was that *Thé Visit* would provide the Lunts' twenty-eighth joint appearance in New York, and would be the first serious drama they had acted since Robert E. Sherwood's *There Shall Be No Night*. To spice the occasion, the *New York Times* reported that *The Visit* might well be the Lunts' farewell.

When the date of the theater opening was moved ahead to April 14th, wagers were made as to whether the event would take place on schedule. One look at the heaps of unfinished masonry, acres of unlaid carpet, miles of wiring awaiting installation, and the odds rose. Postponement was inevitable, and a bulletin was issued designating Monday, May 5th, as the definite opening day.

The press fed on the features of the theater's design and made copy of everything from the fact that the audience in the mezzanine and balcony would enjoy smoking privileges, to the novelty of the tickets being colored red, white, and blue for easier identification of seat locations.

Simultaneously with this publicity program, its practical goal, the sale of seats, was proceeding with the aid and stimulation of advertising. *The Visit* played a pre-Broadway engagement in Boston in mid-April and was greeted with cheers. Several days later a demure advertisement was inserted in New York's papers simply quoting a statement made by the drama critic of the *Boston Traveler*: "The Lunts are superb! If they really mean it—that *The Visit* is their last play—they couldn't take their final curtain in a greater glory." A few days later this was repeated along with excerpts from the other Boston reviews. As the New York opening approached, further advertising of a more formal character began to appear. It stressed the names of the stars, of the new theater, of the play, and made a point of the fact that the engagement was limited to nine weeks.

The race to finish the theater on time was a neck-and-neck affair until the very end of April. The Lunts and a group of supporting players arrived on the 27th and the following day in the *New York Times* Meyer Berger described the sounds of "hammers pounding, sprayers hissing and vacuum cleaners droning," attesting to the management's doggedness to meet the deadline.

On the Friday before the official opening of the theater, a dedication ceremony was held in the mezzanine foyer. The splendors of the design and décor were unveiled before the press and a crowd of glamorous guests. The Lunt-Fontanne Theater was christened. Helen Hayes, the "neighbor from across the street," presented the couple with a "housewarming" gift, after which they were photographed under the marquee bearing their names.

At this point, the publicity which had been launched shortly after the theater campaign had got well under way, began to make itself felt. Just prior to the premiere, in addition to articles such as the *World-Telegram and Sun* published in its weekend magazine under the headline: "All That Glitters Is Gold, Blue, and Lunt-Fontanne," the newspapers treated in detail the serious values inherent in the play, the new playwright, and the style of the production. For this, the stage designs of Teo Otto, the costumes Castillo fashioned for Miss Fontanne, the return of director Peter Brook, and the introduction of a new young Swiss playwright, all provided fertile fields for feature writers on the art, fashion, and drama pages. Duerrenmatt, obscure in New York until then, became capital. Maurice Valency wrote an article on the playwright for *Theatre Arts Magazine,* as well as a briefer piece that was featured on the first page of the drama section of the Sunday *Times;* and shortly afterward, the *Times* printed an interview with the dramatist under the by-line of their foreign correspondent Joseph Morgenstern. Thus, the weekend prior to opening night was the climax of the second act of the publicity campaign.

The third act of the campaign began with the first performance of *The Visit* and the public opening of the Lunt-Fontanne Theater. It was a brilliant occasion; a superb play was magnificently acted. The final curtain was the signal for an ovation from Broadway celebrities and luminaries of the business, political, and industrial worlds. Following the performance, a grand fete was held in the ballroom of the Hotel Astor in honor of Alfred Lunt and Lynn Fontanne, and the next morning pictures of the event made most of the newspapers, while laudatory reviews and "word-of-mouth" started long lines at the box office. The succeeding weeks' strategy was more akin to a mopping-up action. The national magazines moved in to complete their photo and text assignments. Wire services, local and out-of-town correspondents were scheduled for interviews, all sorts of promotional tie-ups were arranged, and before long the nine weeks had passed and the job was done.

The entire engagement was sold out and the demand for tickets was so insistent and widespread that the Lunts returned after a holiday for fourteen additional weeks on Broadway, terminating on November 29th. They then set out on a na-

Two scenes from the German production of *The Visit* at the State Theater, Münster, Germany. *(Above)* The restaurant scene. Note the beer and water glasses, and compare the shabby appearance of the table and guests with the lavishness of the American production. *(Below)* The death scene, after which Claire hands her check to the townspeople. (Koschinski — Roy Bernard)

tional tour lasting until March, 1960, followed it with a two-week run in New York, and a production in London. The question whether *The Visit* was their farewell play was never answered during the entire campaign.

ᨁᨁᨁ *The Visit* ADAPTED BY MAURICE VALENCY

Presented by the Producers' Theater at the Lunt-Fontanne Theater, New York City, on May 5, 1958, with the following cast:

HOFBAUER (FIRST MAN)	KENNETH THORNETT
HELMESBERGER (SECOND)	DAVID CLARKE
WECHSLER (THIRD)	MILTON SELZER
VOGEL (FOURTH)	HARRISON DOWD
PAINTER	CLARENCE NORDSTROM
STATION MASTER	JOSEPH LEBERMAN
BURGOMASTER	ERIC PORTER
TEACHER	PETER WOODTHORPE
PASTOR	WILLIAM HANSEN
ANTON SCHILL	ALFRED LUNT
CLAIRE ZACHANASSIAN	LYNN FONTANNE
CONDUCTOR	JONATHAN ANDERSON
PEDRO CABRAL	MYLES EASON
BOBBY	JOHN WYSE
POLICEMAN	JOHN RANDOLPH
FIRST GRANDCHILD	LESLEY HUNT
SECOND GRANDCHILD	LOIS McKIM
MIKE	STANLEY ERICKSON
MAX	WILLIAM THOURLBY
FIRST BLIND MAN	VINCENT GARDENIA
SECOND BLIND MAN	ALFRED HOFFMAN
ATHLETE	JAMES MacAARON
FRAU BURGOMASTER	FRIEDA ALTMAN
FRAU SCHILL	DAPHNE NEWTON
DAUGHTER	MARLA ADAMS
SON	KEN WALKEN
DOCTOR NÜSSLIN	HOWARD FISCHER
FRAU BLOCK (FIRST WOMAN)	GERTRUDE KINNELL

TRUCK DRIVER	JOHN KANE
REPORTER	EDWARD MOOR
TOWNSMAN	ROBERT DONLEY
TOWNSMAN	KENT MONTROY

Directed by Peter Brook, designed by Teo Otto, supervision and lighting by Paul Morrison, Miss Fontanne's clothes by Castillo, incidental music arranged by James Stevens.

PROGRAM CREDITS

Miss Fontanne's dresses executed by Lanvin-Castillo of Paris. Shoes for Miss Fontanne by Delman. Miss Fontanne's gloves by Wear-Right. Stockings by Phoenix Hosiery. Lighting by Duwico. Sound Equipment by Masque Sound Company. Television set courtesy of General Electric. Lightweight baggage by Daisy Products. Hats by John B. Stetson Co. Luggage by Lee Fordin Co. Cosmetics by Diedre.

ACT ONE

A railway-crossing bell starts ringing. Then is heard the distant sound of a locomotive whistle. The curtain rises.

The scene represents, in the simplest possible manner, a little town somewhere in Central Europe. The time is the present. The town is shabby and ruined, as if the plague had passed there. Its name, Güllen, is inscribed on the shabby signboard which adorns the façade of the railway station. This edifice is summarily indicated by a length of rusty iron paling, a platform parallel to the proscenium, beyond which one imagines the rails to be, and a baggage truck standing by a wall on which a torn timetable, marked "Fahrplan," is affixed by three nails. In the station wall is a door with a sign: "Eintritt Verboten." This leads to the STATION MASTER's office.

Left of the station is a little house of gray stucco, formerly whitewashed. It has a tile roof, badly in need of repair. Some shreds of travel posters still adhere to the windowless walls. A shingle hanging over the entrance, left, reads: "Männer." On the other side the shingle reads: "Damen." Along the wall of the little house there is a wooden bench, backless, on which four men are lounging cheerlessly, shabbily dressed, with cracked shoes. A fifth man is busied with paintpot and brush. He is kneeling on the ground, painting a strip of canvas with the words: "Welcome, Clara."

The warning signal rings uninterruptedly. The sound of the approaching train comes closer and closer. The STATION MASTER issues from his office, advances to the center of the platform and salutes.

The train is heard thundering past in a direction parallel to the footlights, and is lost in the distance. The men on the bench follow its passing with a slow movement of their heads, from left to right.

First Man. The "Emperor." Hamburg-Naples.

Second Man. Then comes the "Diplomat."

Third Man. Then the "Banker."

Fourth Man. And at eleven twenty-seven the "Flying Dutchman." Venice-Stockholm.

First Man. Our only pleasure—watching trains.

(The station bell rings again. The STATION MASTER *comes out of his office and salutes another train. The men follow its course, right to left)*

Fourth Man. Once upon a time the "Emperor" and the "Flying Dutchman" used to stop here in Güllen. So did the "Diplomat," the "Banker" and the "Silver Comet."

Second Man. Now it's only the local from Kaffigen and the twelve-forty from Kalberstadt.

Third Man. The fact is, we're ruined.

First Man. What with the Wagonworks shut down . . .

Second Man. The Foundry finished . . .

Fourth Man. The Golden Eagle Pencil Factory all washed up . . .

First Man. It's life on the dole.

Second Man. Did you say life?

Third Man. We're rotting.

First Man. Starving.

Second Man. Crumbling.

Fourth Man. The whole damn town.

(The station bell rings)

Third Man. Once we were a center of industry.

Painter. A cradle of culture.

Fourth Man. One of the best little towns in the country.

First Man. In the world.

Second Man. Here Goethe slept.

Fourth Man. Brahms composed a quartet.

Third Man. Here Berthold Schwarz invented gunpowder.

Painter. And I once got first prize at the Dresden Exhibition of Contemporary Art. What am I doing now? Painting signs.

(The station bell rings. The STATION MASTER *comes out. He throws away a cigarette butt. The men scramble for it)*

First Man. Well, anyway, Madame Zachanassian will help us.

Fourth Man. If she comes . . .

Third Man. If she comes.

Second Man. Last week she was in France. She gave them a hospital.

First Man. In Rome she founded a free public nursery.

Third Man. In Leuthenau, a bird sanctuary.

Painter. They say she got Picasso to design her car.

First Man. Where does she get all that money?

Second Man. An oil company, a shipping line, three banks and five railways—

Fourth Man. And the biggest string of geisha houses in Japan.

(From the direction of the town come the BURGOMASTER, *the* PASTOR, *the* TEACHER *and* ANTON SCHILL. *The* BURGOMASTER, *the* TEACHER *and* SCHILL *are men in their fifties. The* PASTOR *is ten years younger. All four are dressed shabbily and are sad-*

590   F R I E D R I C H   D U E R R E N M A T T

looking. The Burgomaster *looks official.* Schill *is tall and handsome, but graying and worn; nevertheless a man of considerable charm and presence. He walks directly to the little house and disappears into it)*

Painter. Any news, Burgomaster? Is she coming?

All. Yes, is she coming?

Burgomaster. She's coming. The telegram has been confirmed. Our distinguished guest will arrive on the twelve-forty from Kalberstadt. Everyone must be ready.

Teacher. The mixed choir is ready. So is the children's chorus.

Burgomaster. And the church bell, Pastor?

Pastor. The church bell will ring. As soon as the new bell ropes are fitted. The man is working on them now.

Burgomaster. The town band will be drawn up in the market place and the Athletic Association will form a human pyramid in her honor—the top man will hold the wreath with her initials. Then lunch at the Golden Apostle. I shall say a few words.

Teacher. Of course.

Burgomaster. I had thought of illuminating the town hall and the cathedral, but we can't afford the lamps.

Painter. Burgomaster—what do you think of this?

(He shows the banner)

Burgomaster *(Calls).* Schill! Schill!

Teacher. Schill!

*(*Schill *comes out of the little house)*

Schill. Yes, right away. Right away.

Burgomaster. This is more in your line. What do you think of this?

Schill *(Looks at the sign).* No, no, no. That certainly won't do, Burgomas-

ter. It's much too intimate. It shouldn't read: "Welcome, Clara." It should read: "Welcome, Madame . . ."

Teacher. Zachanassian.

Burgomaster. Zachanassian.

Schill. Zachanassian.

Painter. But she's Clara to us.

First Man. Clara Wäscher.

Second Man. Born here.

Third Man. Her father was a carpenter. He built this.

(All turn and stare at the little house)

Schill. All the same . . .

Painter. If I . . .

Burgomaster. No, no, no. He's right. You'll have to change it.

Painter. Oh, well, I'll tell you what I'll do. I'll leave this and I'll put "Welcome, Madame Zachanassian" on the other side. Then if things go well, we can always turn it around.

Burgomaster. Good idea. *(To* Schill*)* Yes?

Schill. Well, anyway, it's safer. Everything depends on the first impression.

(The train bell is heard. Two clangs. The Painter *turns the banner over and goes to work)*

First Man. Hear that? The "Flying Dutchman" has just passed through Leuthenau.

Fourth Man. Eleven twenty.

Burgomaster. Gentlemen, you know that the millionairess is our only hope.

Pastor. Under God.

Burgomaster. Under God. Naturally. Schill, we depend entirely on you.

Schill. Yes, I know. You keep telling me.

Burgomaster. After all, you're the only one who really knew her.

Schill. Yes, I knew her.

Pastor. You were really quite close to one another, I hear, in those days.

Schill. Close? Yes, we were close, there's no denying it. We were in love. I was young—good-looking, so they said—and Clara—you know, I can still see her in the great barn coming toward me—like a light out of the darkness. And in the Konradsweil Forest she'd come running to meet me—barefooted—her beautiful red hair streaming behind her. Like a witch. I was in love with her, all right. But you know how it is when you're twenty.

Pastor. What happened?

Schill (*Shrugs*). Life came between us.

Burgomaster. You must give me some points about her for my speech.

(*He takes out his notebook*)

Schill. I think I can help you there.

Teacher. Well, I've gone through the school records. And the young lady's marks were, I'm afraid to say, absolutely dreadful. Even in deportment. The only subject in which she was even remotely passable was natural history.

Burgomaster. Good in natural history. That's fine. Give me a pencil.

(*He makes a note*)

Schill. She was an outdoor girl. Wild. Once, I remember, they arrested a tramp, and she threw stones at the policeman. She hated injustice passionately.

Burgomaster. Strong sense of justice. Excellent.

Schill. And generous . . .

All. Generous?

Schill. Generous to a fault. Whatever little she had, she shared—so good-hearted. I remember once she stole a bag of potatoes to give to a poor widow.

Burgomaster (*Writing in notebook*). Wonderful generosity—

Teacher. Generosity.

Burgomaster. That, gentlemen, is something I must not fail to make a point of.

Schill. And such a sense of humor. I remember once when the oldest man in town fell and broke his leg, she said, "Oh, dear, now they'll have to shoot him."

Burgomaster. Well, I've got enough. The rest, my friend, is up to you.

(*He puts the notebook away*)

Schill. Yes, I know, but it's not so easy. After all, to part a woman like that from her millions—

Burgomaster. Exactly. Millions. We have to think in big terms here.

Teacher. If she's thinking of buying us off with a nursery school—

All. Nursery school!

Pastor. Don't accept.

Teacher. Hold out.

Schill. I'm not so sure that I can do it. You know, she may have forgotten me completely.

Burgomaster (*He exchanges a look with the* TEACHER *and the* PASTOR). Schill, for many years you have been our most popular citizen. The most respected and the best loved.

Schill. Why, thank you . . .

Burgomaster. And therefore I must tell you—last week I sounded out the political opposition, and they agreed. In the spring you will be elected to succeed me as Burgomaster. By unanimous vote.

(*The others clap their hands in approval*)

Schill. But, my dear Burgomaster—!

Burgomaster. It's true.

Teacher. I'm a witness. I was at the meeting.

Schill. This is—naturally, I'm terribly flattered— It's a completely unexpected honor.

Burgomaster. You deserve it.

Schill. Burgomaster! Well, well—! (*Briskly*) Gentlemen, to business. The first chance I get, of course, I shall discuss our miserable position with Clara.

Teacher. But tactfully, tactfully—

Schill. What do you take me for? We must feel our way. Everything must be correct. Psychologically correct. For example, here at the railway station, a single blunder, one false note, could be disastrous.

Burgomaster. He's absolutely right. The first impression colors all the rest. Madame Zachanassian sets foot on her native soil for the first time in many years. She sees our love and she sees our misery. She remembers her youth, her friends. The tears well up into her eyes. Her childhood companions throng about her. I will naturally not present myself like this, but in my black coat with my top hat. Next to me, my wife. Before me, my two grandchildren all in white, with roses. My God, if it only comes off as I see it! If only it comes off. (*The station bell begins ringing*) Oh, my God! Quick! We must get dressed.

First Man. It's not her train. It's only the "Flying Dutchman."

Pastor (*Calmly*). We have still two hours before she arrives.

Schill. For God's sake, don't let's lose our heads. We still have a full two hours.

Burgomaster. Who's losing their heads?

(*To* SECOND *and* FOURTH MAN) When her train comes, you two, Helmesberger and Vogel, will hold up the banner with "Welcome Madame Zachanassian." The rest will applaud.

Third Man. Bravo!

(*He applauds*)

Burgomaster. But, please, one thing—no wild cheering like last year with the government relief committee. It made no impression at all and we still haven't received any loan. What we need here is a feeling of genuine sincerity. That's how we greet with full hearts our beloved sister who has been away from us so long. Be sincerely moved, my friends, that's the secret; be sincere. Remember you're not dealing with a child. Next a few brief words from me. Then the church bell will start pealing—

Pastor. If he can fix the ropes in time.

(*The station bell rings*)

Burgomaster.—Then the mixed choir moves in. And then—

Teacher. We'll form a line down here.

Burgomaster. Then the rest of us will form in two lines leading from the station—

(*He is interrupted by the thunder of the approaching train. The men crane their heads to see it pass. The* STATION MASTER *advances to the platform and salutes. There is a sudden shriek of air brakes. The train screams to a stop. The four men jump up in consternation*)

Painter. But the "Flying Dutchman" never stops!

First Man. It's stopping.

Second Man. In Güllen!

Third Man. In the poorest—

First Man. The dreariest—

Second Man. The lousiest—
Fourth Man. The most God-forsaken hole between Venice and Stockholm.
Station Master. It cannot stop!

(*The train noises stop. There is only the panting of the engine*)
Painter. It's stopped!

(*The* STATION MASTER *runs out*)
Offstage Voices. What's happened? Is there an accident?

(*A hubbub of offstage voices, as if the passengers on the invisible train were alighting*)
Claire (*Offstage*). Is this Güllen?
Conductor (*Offstage*). Here, here, what's going on?
Claire (*Offstage*). Who the hell are you?
Conductor (*Offstage*). But you pulled the emergency cord, madame!
Claire (*Offstage*). I always pull the emergency cord.
Station Master (*Offstage*). I must ask you what's going on here.
Claire (*Offstage*). And who the hell are you?
Station Master (*Offstage*). I'm the Station Master, madame, and I must ask you—
Claire (*Enters*). No!

(*From the right* CLAIRE ZACHANASSIAN *appears. She is an extraordinary woman. She is in her fifties, red-haired, remarkably dressed, with a face as impassive as that of an ancient idol, beautiful still, and with a singular grace of movement and manner. She is simple and unaffected, yet she has the haughtiness of a world power. The entire effect is striking to the point of the unbelievable. Behind her comes her fiancé,* PEDRO CABRAL, *tall, young, very handsome,*

and completely equipped for fishing, with creel and net, and with a rod case in his hand. An excited CONDUCTOR *follows*)
Conductor. But, madame, I must insist! You have stopped "The Flying Dutchman." I must have an explanation.
Claire. Nonsense. Pedro.
Pedro. Yes, my love?
Claire. This is Güllen. Nothing has changed. I recognize it all. There's the forest of Konradsweil. There's a brook in it full of trout, where you can fish. And there's the roof of the great barn. Ha! God! What a miserable blot on the map.

(*She crosses the stage and goes off with* PEDRO)
Schill. My God! Clara!
Teacher. Claire Zachanassian!
All. Claire Zachanassian!
Burgomaster. And the town band? The town band! Where is it?
Teacher. The mixed choir! The mixed choir!
Pastor. The church bell! The church bell!
Burgomaster (*To the* FIRST MAN). Quick! My dress coat. My top hat. My grandchildren. Run! Run! (FIRST MAN *runs off. The* BURGOMASTER *shouts after him*) And don't forget my wife!

(*General panic. The* THIRD MAN *and* FOURTH MAN *hold up the banner, on which only part of the name has been painted: "Welcome Mad—"* CLAIRE *and* PEDRO *re-enter, right*)
Conductor (*Mastering himself with an effort*). Màdame. The train is waiting. The entire international railway schedule has been disrupted. I await your explanation.

Claire. You're a very foolish man. I wish to visit this town. Did you expect me to jump off a moving train?

Conductor (*Stupefied*). You stopped the "Flying Dutchman" because you wished to visit the town?

Claire. Naturally.

Conductor (*Inarticulate*). Madame!

Station Master. Madame, if you wished to visit the town, the twelve forty from Kalberstadt was entirely at your service. Arrival in Güllen, one seventeen.

Claire. The local that stops at Loken, Beisenbach and Leuthenau? Do you expect me to waste three-quarters of an hour chugging dismally through this wilderness?

Conductor. Madame, you shall pay for this!

Claire. Bobby, give him a thousand marks.

(BOBBY, *her butler, a man in his seventies, wearing dark glasses, opens his wallet. The townspeople gasp*)

Conductor (*Taking the money in amazement*). But, madame!

Claire. And three thousand for the Railway Widows' Relief Fund.

Conductor (*With the money in his hands*). But we have no such fund, madame.

Claire. Now you have.

(*The* BURGOMASTER *pushes his way forward*)

Burgomaster (*He whispers to the* CONDUCTOR *and* TEACHER). The lady is Madame Claire Zachanassian!

Conductor. Claire Zachanassian? Oh, my God! But that's naturally quite different. Needless to say, we would have stopped the train if we'd had the slightest idea. (*He hands the*

money back to BOBBY) Here, please. I couldn't dream of it. Four thousand. My God!

Claire. Keep it. Don't fuss.

Conductor. Would you like the train to wait, madame, while you visit the town? The administration will be delighted. The cathedral porch. The town hall—

Claire. You may take the train away. I don't need it any more.

Station Master. All aboard!

(*He puts his whistle to his lips.* PEDRO *stops him*)

Pedro. But the press, my angel. They don't know anything about this. They're still in the dining car.

Claire. Let them stay there. I don't want the press in Güllen at the moment. Later they will come by themselves. (*To* STATION MASTER) And now what are you waiting for?

Station Master. All aboard!

(*The* STATION MASTER *blows a long blast on his whistle. The train leaves. Meanwhile, the* FIRST MAN *has brought the* BURGOMASTER'S *dress coat and top hat. The* BURGOMASTER *puts on the coat, then advances slowly and solemnly*)

Conductor. I trust madame will not speak of this to the administration. It was a pure misunderstanding.

(*He salutes and runs for the train as it starts moving*)

Burgomaster (*Bows*). Gracious lady, as Burgomaster of the town of Güllen, I have the honor—

(*The rest of the speech is lost in the roar of the departing train. He continues speaking and gesturing, and at last bows amid applause as the train noises end*)

Claire. Thank you, Mr. Burgomaster.

(*She glances at the beaming faces, and lastly at* Schill, *whom she does not recognize. She turns upstage*)

Schill. Clara!

Claire (*Turns and stares*). Anton?

Schill. Yes. It's good that you've come back.

Claire. Yes. I've waited for this moment. All my life. Ever since I left Güllen.

Schill (*A little embarrassed*). That is very kind of you to say, Clara.

Claire. And have you thought about me?

Schill. Naturally. Always. You know that.

Claire. Those were happy times we spent together.

Schill. Unforgettable.

(*He smiles reassuringly at the* Burgo-master)

Claire. Call me by the name you used to call me.

Schill (*Whispers*). My kitten.

Claire. What?

Schill (*Louder*). My kitten.

Claire. And what else?

Schill. Little witch.

Claire. I used to call you my black panther. You're gray now, and soft.

Schill. But you are still the same, little witch.

Claire. I am the same? (*She laughs*) Oh, no, my black panther, I am not at all the same.

Schill (*Gallantly*). In my eyes you are. I see no difference.

Claire. Would you like to meet my fiancé? Pedro Cabral. He owns an enormous plantation in Brazil.

Schill. A pleasure.

Claire. We're to be married soon.

Schill. Congratulations.

Claire. He will be my eighth husband. (Pedro *stands by himself downstage, right*) Pedro, come here and show your face. Come along, darling—come here! Don't sulk. Say hello.

Pedro. Hello.

Claire. A man of few words! Isn't he charming? A diplomat. He's interested only in fishing. Isn't he handsome, in his Latin way? You'd swear he was a Brazilian. But he's not—he's a Greek. His father was a White Russian. We were betrothed by a Bulgarian priest. We plan to be married in a few days here in the cathedral.

Burgomaster. Here in the cathedral? What an honor for us!

Claire. No. It was my dream, when I was seventeen, to be married in Güllen cathedral. The dreams of youth are sacred, don't you think so, Anton?

Schill. Yes, of course.

Claire. Yes, of course. I think so, too. Now I would like to look at the town. (*The mixed choir arrives, breathless, wearing ordinary clothes with green sashes*) What's all this? Go away. (*She laughs*) Ha! Ha! Ha!

Teacher. Dear lady—(*He steps forward, having put on a sash also*) Dear lady, as Rector of the high school and a devotee of that noble muse, Music, I take pleasure in presenting the Güllen mixed choir.

Claire. How do you do?

Teacher. Who will sing for you an ancient folk song of the region, with specially amended words—if you will deign to listen.

Claire. Very well. Fire away.

(*The* Teacher *blows a pitch pipe. The mixed choir begins to sing the ancient folk song with the amended words. Just then the station bell starts ringing. The song is drowned in the roar of the passing express. The* STATION MASTER *salutes. When the train has passed, there is applause*)

Burgomaster. The church bell! The church bell! Where's the church bell?

(*The* PASTOR *shrugs helplessly*)

Claire. Thank you, Professor. They sang beautifully. The little blond bass—no, not that one—the one with the big Adam's apple—was most impressive. (*The* TEACHER *bows. The* POLICEMAN *pushes his way professionally through the mixed choir and comes to attention in front of* CLAIRE ZACHANASSIAN) Now, who are you?

Policeman (*Clicks heels*). Police Chief Schultz. At your service.

Claire (*She looks him up and down*) I have no need of you at the moment. But I think there will be work for you by and by. Tell me, do you know how to close an eye from time to time?

Policeman. How else could I get along in my profession?

Claire. You might practice closing both.

Schill (*Laughs*). What a sense of humor, eh?

Burgomaster (*Puts on the top hat*) Permit me to present my grandchildren, gracious lady. Hermine and Adolphine. There's only my wife still to come.

(*He wipes the perspiration from his brow, and replaces the hat. The little girls present the roses with elaborate curtsies*)

Claire. Thank you, my dears. Congrat-

ulations, Burgomaster. Extraordinary children.

(*She plants the roses in* PEDRO'S *arms. The* BURGOMASTER *secretly passes his top hat to the* PASTOR, *who puts it on*)

Burgomaster. Our pastor, madame.

(*The* PASTOR *takes off the hat and bows*)

Claire. Ah. The pastor. How do you do? Do you give consolation to the dying?

Pastor (*A bit puzzled*). That is part of my ministry, yes.

Claire. And to those who are condemned to death?

Pastor. Capital punishment has been abolished in this country, madame.

Claire. I see. Well, it could be restored, I suppose.

(*The* PASTOR *hands back the hat. He shrugs his shoulders in confusion*)

Schill (*Laughs*). What an original sense of humor!

(*All laugh, a little blankly*)

Claire. Well, I can't sit here all day— I should like to see the town.

(*The* BURGOMASTER *offers his arm*)

Burgomaster. May I have the honor, gracious lady?

Claire. Thank you, but these legs are not what they were. This one was broken in five places.

Schill (*Full of concern*). My kitten!

Claire. When my airplane bumped into a mountain in Afghanistan. All the others were killed. Even the pilot. But as you see, I survived. I don't fly any more.

Schill. But you're as strong as ever now.

Claire. Stronger.

Burgomaster. Never fear, gracious lady. The town doctor has a car.

Claire. I never ride in motors.

Burgomaster. You never ride in motors?

Claire. Not since my Ferrari crashed in Hong Kong.

Schill. But how do you travel, then, little witch? On a broom?

Claire. Mike—Max! (*She claps her hands. Two huge bodyguards come in, left, carrying a sedan chair. She sits in it*) I travel this way—a bit antiquated, of course. But perfectly safe. Ha! Ha! Aren't they magnificent? Mike and Max. I bought them in America. They were in jail, condemned to the chair. I had them pardoned. Now they're condemned to my chair. I paid fifty thousand dollars apiece for them. You couldn't get them now for twice the sum. The sedan chair comes from the Louvre. I fancied it so much that the President of France gave it to me. The French are so impulsive, don't you think so, Anton? Go!

(MIKE *and* MAX *start to carry her off*)

Burgomaster. You wish to visit the cathedral? And the old town hall?

Claire. No. The great barn. And the forest of Konradsweil. I wish to go with Anton and visit our old haunts once again.

The Pastor. Very touching.

Claire (*To the butler*) Will you send my luggage and the coffin to the Golden Apostle?

Burgomaster. The coffin?

Claire. Yes. I brought one with me. Go!

Teacher. Hip-hip—

All. Hurrah! Hip-hip, hurrah! Hurrah!

(*They bear her off in the direction of the town. The* TOWNSPEOPLE *burst into cheers. The church bell rings*)

Burgomaster. Ah, thank God—the bell at last.

(*The* POLICEMAN *is about to follow the others, when the two* BLIND MEN *appear. They are not young, yet they seem childish—a strange effect. Though they are of different height and features, they are dressed exactly alike, and so create the effect of being twins. They walk slowly, feeling their way. Their voices, when they speak, are curiously high and flutelike, and they have a curious trick of repetition of phrases*)

First Blind Man. We're in—

Both Blind Men. Güllen.

First Blind Man. We breathe—

Second Blind Man. We breathe—

Both Blind Men. We breathe the air, the air of Güllen.

Policeman (*Startled*). Who are you?

First Blind Man. We belong to the lady.

Second Blind Man. We belong to the lady. She calls us—

First Blind Man. Kobby.

Second Blind Man. And Lobby.

Policeman. Madame Zachanassian is staying at the Golden Apostle.

First Blind Man. We're blind.

Second Blind Man. We're blind.

Policeman. Blind? Come along with me, then. I'll take you there.

First Blind Man. Thank you, Mr. Policeman.

Second Blind Man. Thanks very much.

Policeman. Hey! How do you know I'm a policeman, if you're blind?

Both Blind Men. By your voice. By your voice.

First Blind Man. All policemen sound the same.

Policeman. You've had a lot to do with the police, have you, little men?

First Blind Man. Men he calls us!

Both Blind Men. Men!

Policeman. What are you then?

Both Blind Men. You'll see. You'll see.

(*The* Policeman *claps his hands suddenly. The* Blind Men *turn sharply toward the sound. The* Policeman *is convinced they are blind*)

Policeman. What's your trade?

Both Blind Men. We have no trade.

Second Blind Man. We play music.

First Blind Man. We sing.

Second Blind Man. We amuse the lady.

First Blind Man. We look after the beast.

Second Blind Man. We feed it.

First Blind Man. We stroke it.

Second Blind Man. We take it for walks.

Policeman. What beast?

Both Blind Men. You'll see—you'll see.

Second Blind Man. We give it raw meat.

First Blind Man. And she gives us chicken and wine.

Second Blind Man. Every day—

Both Blind Men. Every day.

Policeman. Rich people have strange tastes.

Both Blind Men. Strange tastes—strange tastes. (*The* Policeman *puts on his helmet*)

Policeman. Come along, I'll take you to the lady.

(*The two* Blind Men *turn and walk off*)

Both Blind Men. We know the way—we know the way.

(*The station and the little house*

vanish. *A sign representing the Golden Apostle descends. The scene dissolves into the interior of the inn. The Golden Apostle is seen to be in the last stages of decay. The walls are cracked and moldering, and the plaster is falling from the ancient lath. A table represents the café of the inn. The* Burgomaster *and the* Teacher *sit at this table, drinking a glass together. A procession of* Townspeople, *carrying many pieces of luggage, passes. Then comes a coffin, and, last, a large box covered with a canvas. They cross the stage from right to left*)

Burgomaster. Trunks. Suitcases. Boxes. (*He looks up apprehensively at the ceiling*) The floor will never bear the weight. (*As the large covered box is carried in, he peers under the canvas, then draws back*) Good God!

Teacher. Why, what's in it?

Burgomaster. A live panther. (*They laugh. The* Burgomaster *lifts his glass solemnly*) Your health, Professor. Let's hope she puts the Foundry back on its feet.

Teacher (*Lifts his glass*). And the Wagonworks.

Burgomaster. And the Golden Eagle Pencil Factory. Once that starts moving, everything else will go. *Prosit.*

(*They touch glasses and drink*)

Teacher. What does she need a panther for?

Burgomaster. Don't ask me. The whole thing is too much for me. The Pastor had to go home and lie down.

Teacher (*Sets down his glass*). If you want to know the truth, she frightens me.

Burgomaster (*Nods gravely*). She's a strange one.

Teacher. You understand, Burgomaster, a man who for twenty-two years has been correcting the Latin compositions of the students of Güllen is not unaccustomed to surprises. I have seen things to make one's hair stand on end. But when this woman suddenly appeared on the platform, a shudder tore through me. It was as though out of the clear sky all at once a fury descended upon us, beating its black wings—

(*The* POLICEMAN *comes in. He mops his face*)

Policeman. Ah! Now the old place is livening up a bit!

Burgomaster. Ah, Schultz, come and join us.

Policeman. Thank you. (*He calls*) Beer!

Burgomaster. Well, what's the news from the front?

Policeman. I'm just back from Schiller's barn. My God! What a scene! She had us all tiptoeing around in the straw as if we were in church. Nobody dared to speak above a whisper. And the way she carried on! I was so embarrassed I let them go to the forest by themselves.

Burgomaster. Does the fiancé go with them?

Policeman. With his fishing rod and his landing net. In full marching order. (*He calls again*) Beer!

Burgomaster. That will be her seventh husband.

Teacher. Her eighth.

Burgomaster. But what does she expect to find in the Konradsweil forest?

Policeman. The same thing she expected to find in the old barn, I suppose. The—the—

Teacher. The ashes of her youthful love.

Policeman. Exactly.

Teacher. It's poetry.

Policeman. Poetry.

Teacher. Sheer poetry! It makes one think of Shakespeare, of Wagner. Of Romeo and Juliet.

(*The* SECOND MAN *comes in as a waiter. The* POLICEMAN *is served his beer*)

Burgomaster. Yes, you're right. (*Solemnly*) Gentlemen, I would like to propose a toast. To our great and good friend, Anton Schill, who is even now working on our behalf.

Policeman. Yes! He's really working.

Burgomaster. Gentlemen, to the best-loved citizen of this town. My successor, Anton Schill!

(*They raise their glasses. At this point an unearthly scream is heard. It is the black panther howling off-stage. The sign of the Golden Apostle rises out of sight. The lights go down. The inn vanishes. Only the wooden bench, on which the four men were lounging in the opening scene, is left on the stage, downstage right. The procession comes on upstage. The two bodyguards carry in* CLAIRE's *sedan chair. Next to it walks* SCHILL. PEDRO *walks behind, with his fishing rod. Last come the two* BLIND MEN *and the butler.* CLAIRE *alights*)

Claire. Stop! Take my chair off somewhere else. I'm tired of looking at you. (*The bodyguards and the sedan chair go off*) Pedro darling, your brook is just a little further along down that path. Listen. You can hear it from here. Bobby, take him and show him where it is.

Both Blind Men. We'll show him the way—we'll show him the way.

(*They go off, left.* PEDRO *follows.* BOBBY *walks off, right*)

Claire. Look, Anton. Our tree. There's the heart you carved in the bark long ago.

Schill. Yes. It's still there.

Claire. How it has grown! The trunk is black and wrinkled. Why, its limbs are twice what they were. Some of them have died.

Schill. It's aged. But it's there.

Claire. Like everything else. (*She crosses, examining other trees*) Oh, how tall they are. How long it is since I walked here, barefoot over the pine needles and the damp leaves! Look, Anton. A fawn.

Schill. Yes, a fawn. It's the season.

Claire. I thought everything would be changed. But it's all just as we left it. This is the seat we sat on years ago. Under these branches you kissed me. And over there under the hawthorn, where the moss is soft and green, we would lie in each other's arms. It is all as it used to be. Only we have changed.

Schill. Not so much, little witch. I remember the first night we spent together, you ran away and I chased you till I was quite breathless—

Claire. Yes.

Schill. Then I was angry and I was going home, when suddenly I heard you call and I looked up, and there you were sitting in a tree, laughing down at me.

Claire. No. It was in the great barn. I was in the hayloft.

Schill. Were you?

Claire. Yes. What else do you remember?

Schill. I remember the morning we went swimming by the waterfall, and afterwards we were lying together on the big rock in the sun, when suddenly we heard footsteps and we just had time to snatch up our clothes and run behind the bushes when the old pastor appeared and scolded you for not being in school.

Claire. No. It was the schoolmaster who found us. It was Sunday and I was supposed to be in church.

Schill. Really?

Claire. Yes. Tell me more.

Schill. I remember the time your father beat you, and you showed me the cuts on your back, and I swore I'd kill him. And the next day I dropped a tile from a roof top and split his head open.

Claire. You missed him.

Schill. No!

Claire. You hit old Mr. Reiner.

Schill. Did I?

Claire. Yes. I was seventeen. And you were not yet twenty. You were so handsome. You were the best-looking boy in town.

(*The two* BLIND MEN *begin playing mandolin music offstage, very softly*)

Schill. And you were the prettiest girl.

Claire. We were made for each other.

Schill. So we were.

Claire. But you married Mathilde Blumhard and her store, and I married old Zachanassian and his oil wells. He found me in a whorehouse in Hamburg. It was my hair that entangled him, the old golden beetle.

Schill. Clara!

Claire (*She claps her hands*). Bobby! A cigar.

(BOBBY *appears with a leather case*

He selects a cigar, puts it in a holder, lights it, and presents it to CLAIRE)

Schill. My kitten smokes cigars!

Claire. Yes. I adore them. Would you care for one?

Schill. Yes, please. I've never smoked one of those.

Claire. It's a taste I acquired from old Zachanassian. Among other things. He was a real connoisseur.

Schill. We used to sit on this bench once, you and I, and smoke cigarettes. Do you remember?

Claire. Yes. I remember.

Schill. The cigarettes I bought from Mathilde.

Claire. No. She gave them to you for nothing.

Schill. Clara—don't be angry with me for marrying Mathilde.

Claire. She had money.

Schill. But what a lucky thing for you that I did!

Claire. Oh?

Schill. You were so young, so beautiful. You deserved a far better fate than to settle in this wretched town without any future.

Claire. Yes?

Schill. If you had stayed in Güllen and married me, your life would have been wasted, like mine.

Claire. Oh?

Schill. Look at me. A wretched shopkeeper in a bankrupt town!

Claire. But you have your family.

Schill. My family! Never for a moment do they let me forget my failure, my poverty.

Claire. Mathilde has not made you happy?

Schill. (*Shrugs*). What does it matter?

Claire. And the children?

Schill. (*Shakes his head*). They're so completely materialistic. You know,

they have no interest whatever in higher things.

Claire. How sad for you.

(*A moment's pause, during which only the faint tinkling of the music is heard*)

Schill. Yes. You know, since you went away my life has passed by like a stupid dream. I've hardly once been out of this town. A trip to a lake years ago. It rained all the time. And once five days in Berlin. That's all.

Claire. The world is much the same everywhere.

Schill. At least you've seen it.

Claire. Yes. I've seen it.

Schill. You've lived in it.

Claire. I've lived in it. The world and I have been on very intimate terms.

Schill. Now that you've come back, perhaps things will change.

Claire. Naturally. I certainly won't leave my native town in this condition.

Schill. It will take millions to put us on our feet again.

Claire. I have millions.

Schill. One, two, three.

Claire. Why not?

Schill. You mean—you will help us?

Claire. Yes.

(*A woodpecker is heard in the distance*)

Schill. I knew it—I knew it. I told them you were generous. I told them you were good. Oh, my kitten, my kitten.

(*He takes her hand. She turns her head away and listens*)

Claire. Listen! A woodpecker.

Schill. It's all just the way it was in the days when we were young and full of courage. The sun high above the pines. White clouds, piling up on one another. And the cry of the cuckoo in the distance. And the wind rustling the leaves, like the sound of surf on a beach. Just as it was years ago. If only we could roll back time and be together always.

Claire. Is that your wish?

Schill. Yes. You left me, but you never left my heart. (*He raises her hand to his lips*) The same soft little hand.

Claire. No, not quite the same. It was crushed in the plane accident. But they mended it. They mend everything nowadays.

Schill. Crushed? You wouldn't know it. See, another fawn.

Claire. The old wood is alive with memories.

(*Pedro appears, right, with a fish in his hand*)

Pedro. See what I've caught, darling. See? A pike. Over two kilos.

(*The Blind Men appear onstage*)

Both Blind Men (*Clapping their hands*). A pike! A pike! Hurrah! Hurrah!

(*As the Blind Men clap their hands, Claire and Schill exit, and the scene dissolves. The clapping of hands is taken up on all sides. The Townspeople wheel in the walls of the café. A brass band strikes up a march tune. The door of the Golden Apostle descends. The Townspeople bring in tables and set them with ragged tablecloths, cracked china and glassware. There is a table in the center, upstage, flanked by two tables perpendicular to it, right and left. The Pastor and the Burgomaster come in. Schill enters. Other Townspeople filter in, left and right. One, the Athlete, is in gym-*

nastic costume. The applause continues)

Burgomaster. She's coming! (*Claire enters upstage, center, followed by Bobby*) The applause is meant for you, gracious lady.

Claire. The band deserves it more than I. They blow from the heart. And the human pyramid was beautiful. You, show me your muscles. (*The Athlete kneels before her*) Superb. Wonderful arms, powerful hands. Have you ever strangled a man with them?

Athlete. Strangled?

Claire. Yes. It's perfectly simple. A little pressure in the proper place, and the rest goes by itself. As in politics.

(*The Burgomaster's wife comes up, simpering*)

Burgomaster (*Presents her*). Permit me to present my wife, Madame Zachanassian.

Claire. Annette Dummermuth. The head of our class.

Burgomaster. (*He presents another sour-looking woman*) Frau Schill.

Claire. Mathilde Blumhard. I remember the way you used to follow Anton with your eyes, from behind the shop door. You've grown a little thin and dry, my poor Mathilde.

Schill. My daughter, Ottilie.

Claire. Your daughter . . .

Schill. My son, Karl.

Claire. Your son. Two of them!

(*The town Doctor comes in, right. He is a man of fifty, strong and stocky, with bristly black hair, a mustache, and a saber cut on his cheek. He is wearing an old cutaway*)

Doctor. Well, well, my old Mercedes

got me here in time after all!

Burgomaster. Dr. Nüsslin, the town physician. Madame Zachanassian.

Doctor. Deeply honored, madame.

(*He kisses her hand.* CLAIRE *studies him*)

Claire. It is you who signs the death certificates?

Doctor. Death certificates?

Claire. When someone dies.

Doctor. Why certainly. That is one of my duties.

Claire. And when the heart dies, what do you put down? Heart failure?

Schill (*Laughing*). What a golden sense of humor!

Doctor. Bit grim, wouldn't you say?

Schill (*Whispers*). Not at all, not at all. She's promised us a million.

Burgomaster (*Turns his head*). What?

Schill. A million!

All (*Whisper*). A million!

(CLAIRE *turns toward them*)

Claire. Burgomaster.

Burgomaster. Yes?

Claire. I'm hungry. (*The girls and the waiter fill glasses and bring food. There is a general stir. All take their places at the tables*) Are you going to make a speech?

(*The* BURGOMASTER *bows.* CLAIRE *sits next to the* BURGOMASTER. *The* BURGOMASTER *rises, tapping his knife on his glass. He is radiant with good will. All applaud*)

Burgomaster. Gracious lady and friends. Gracious lady, it is now many years since you first left your native town of Güllen, which was founded by the Elector Hasso and which nestles in the green slope between the forest of Konradsweil and the beautiful valley of Pückenried.

Much has taken place in this time, much that is evil.

Teacher. That's true.

Burgomaster. The world is not what it was; it has become harsh and bitter, and we too have had our share of harshness and bitterness. But in all this time, dear lady, we have never forgotten our little Clara. (*Applause*) Many years ago you brightened the town with your pretty face as a child, and now once again you brighten it with your presence. (*Polite applause*) We haven't forgotten you, and we haven't forgotten your family. Your mother, beautiful and robust even in her old age—(*He looks for his notes on the table*)—although unfortunately taken from us in the bloom of her youth by an infirmity of the lungs. Your respected father, Siegfried Wäscher, the builder, an example of whose work next to our railway station is often visited—(SCHILL *covers his face*)—that is to say, admired—a lasting monument of local design and local workmanship. And you, gracious lady, whom we remember as a golden-haired—(*He looks at her*)—little red-headed sprite romping about our peaceful streets—on your way to school—which of us does not treasure your memory? (*He pokes nervously at his notebook*) We well remember your scholarly attainments—

Teacher. Yes.

Burgomaster. Natural history . . . Extraordinary sense of justice . . . And, above all, your supreme generosity. (*Great applause*) We shall never forget how you once spent the whole of your little savings to buy a sack of potatoes for a poor starving widow who was in need of food. Gracious lady, ladies and gentlemen, today, our little Clara has become the world-famous Claire Zachanassian who has founded hospitals, soup kitchens, charitable institutes, art projects, libraries, nurseries and schools, and now that she has at last once more returned to the town of her birth, sadly fallen as it is, I say in the name of all her loving friends who have sorely missed her: Long live our Clara!

All. Long live our Clara!

(*Cheers. Music. Fanfare. Applause.* CLAIRE *rises*)

Claire. Mr. Burgomaster. Fellow townsmen. I am greatly moved by the nature of your welcome and the disinterested joy which you have manifested on the occasion of my visit to my native town. I was not quite the child the Burgomaster described in his gracious address . . .

Burgomaster. Too modest, madame.

Claire. In school I was beaten—

Teacher. Not by me.

Claire. And the sack of potatoes which I presented to Widow Boll, I stole with the help of Anton Schill, not to save the old trull from starvation, but so that for once I might sleep with Anton in a real bed instead of under the trees of the forest. (*The* TOWNSPEOPLE *look grave, embarrassed*) Nevertheless, I shall try to deserve your good opinion. In memory of the seventeen years I spent among you, I am prepared to hand over as a gift to the town of Güllen the sum of one billion marks. Five hundred million to the town, and five hundred million to be divided per capita among the citizens.

(*There is a moment of dead silence*)

Burgomaster. A billion marks?

Claire. On one condition.

(*Suddenly a movement of uncontrollable joy breaks out. People jump on chairs, dance about, yell excitedly. The* ATHLETE *turns handsprings in front of the speaker's table*)

Schill. Oh, Clara, you astonishing, incredible, magnificent woman! What a heart! What a gesture! Oh—my little witch!

(*He kisses her hand*)

Burgomaster (*Holds up his arms for order*). Quiet! Quiet, please! On one condition, the gracious lady said. Now, madame, may we know what that condition is?

Claire. I will tell you. In exchange for my billion marks, I want justice.

(*Silence*)

Burgomaster. Justice, madame?

Claire. I wish to buy justice.

Burgomaster. But justice cannot be bought, madame.

Claire. Everything can be bought.

Burgomaster. I don't understand at all.

Claire. Bobby, step forward.

(*The butler goes to the center of the stage. He takes off his dark glasses and turns his face with a solemn air*)

Bobby. Does anyone here present recognize me?

Frau Schill. Hofer! Hofer!

All. Who? What's that?

Teacher. Not Chief Magistrate Hofer?

Bobby. Exactly. Chief Magistrate Hofer. When Madame Zachanassian was a girl, I was presiding judge at the criminal court of Güllen. I served there until twenty-five years ago, when Madame Zachanassian offered me the opportunity of entering her service as butler. I accepted. You may consider it a strange employment for a member of the magistracy, but the salary—

(CLAIRE *bangs the mallet on the table*)

Claire. Come to the point.

Bobby. You have heard Madame Zachanassian's offer. She will give you a billion marks—when you have undone the injustice that she suffered at your hands here in Güllen as a girl.

(*All murmur*)

Burgomaster. Injustice at our hands? Impossible!

Bobby. Anton Schill . . .

Schill. Yes?

Bobby. Kindly stand.

(SCHILL *rises. He smiles, as if puzzled. He shrugs*)

Schill. Yes?

Bobby. In those days, a bastardy case was tried before me. Madame Claire Zachanassian, at that time called Clara Wäscher, charged you with being the father of her illegitimate child. (*Silence*) You denied the charge. And produced two witnesses in your support.

Schill. That's ancient history. An absurd business. We were children. Who remembers?

Claire. Where are the blind men?

Both Blind Men. Here we are. Here we are.

(MIKE *and* MAX *push them forward*)

Bobby. You recognize these men, Anton Schill?

Schill. I never saw them before in my life. What are they?

Both Blind Men. We've changed. We've changed.

Bobby. What were your names in your former life?

First Blind Man. I was Jacob Hueblein. Jacob Hueblein.

Second Blind Man. I was Ludwig Sparr. Ludwig Sparr.

Bobby (*To* SCHILL). Well?

Schill. These names mean nothing to me.

Bobby. Jacob Hueblein and Ludwig Sparr, do you recognize the defendant?

First Blind Man. We're blind.

Second Blind Man. We're blind.

Schill. Ha-ha-ha!

Bobby. By his voice?

Both Blind Men. By his voice. By his voice.

Bobby. At that trial, I was the judge. And you?

Both Blind Men. We were the witnesses.

Bobby. And what did you testify on that occasion?

First Blind Man. That we had slept with Clara Wäscher.

Second Blind Man. Both of us. Many times.

Bobby. And was it true?

First Blind Man. No.

Second Blind Man. We swore falsely.

Bobby. And why did you swear falsely?

First Blind Man. Anton Schill bribed us.

Second Blind Man. He bribed us.

Bobby. With what?

Both Blind Men. With a bottle of schnapps.

Bobby. And now tell the people what happened to you. (*They hesitate and whimper*) Speak!

First Blind Man (*In a low voice*). She tracked us down.

Bobby. Madame Zachanassian tracked them down. Jacob Hueblein was found in Canada. Ludwig Sparr in Australia. And when she found you, what did she do to you?

Second Blind Man. She handed us over to Mike and Max.

Bobby. And what did Mike and Max do to you?

First Blind Man. They made us what you see.

(*The* BLIND MEN *cover their faces.* MIKE *and* MAX *push them off*)

Bobby. And there you have it. We are all present in Güllen once again. The plaintiff. The defendant. The two false witnesses. The judge. Many years have passed. Does the plaintiff have anything further to add?

Claire. There is nothing to add.

Bobby. And the defendant?

Schill. Why are you doing this? It was all dead and buried.

Bobby. What happened to the child that was born?

Claire (*In a low voice*). It lived a year.

Bobby. And what happened to you?

Claire. I became a whore.

Bobby. Why?

Claire. The judgment of the court left me no alternative. No one would trust me. No one would give me work.

Bobby. So. And now, what is the nature of the reparation you demand?

Claire. I want the life of Schill.

(FRAU SCHILL *springs to Anton's side. She puts her arms around him.*

The children rush to him. He breaks away)

Frau Schill. Anton! No! No!

Schill. No— No— She's joking. That happened long ago. That's all forgotten.

Claire. Nothing is forgotten. Neither the mornings in the forest, nor the nights in the great barn, nor the bedroom in the cottage, nor your treachery at the end. You said this morning that you wished that time might be rolled back. Very well—I have rolled it back. And now it is I who will buy justice. You bought it with a bottle of schnapps. I am willing to pay one billion marks.

(*The* BURGOMASTER *stands up, very pale and dignified*)

Burgomaster. Madame Zachanassian, we are not in the jungle. We are in Europe. We may be poor, but we are not heathens. In the name of the town of Güllen, I decline your offer. In the name of humanity. We shall never accept.

(*All applaud wildly. The applause turns into a sinister rhythmic beat. As* CLAIRE *rises, it dies away. She looks at the crowd, then at the* BURGOMASTER)

Claire. Thank you, Burgomaster. (*She stares at him a long moment*) I can wait.

(*She turns and walks off*)

Curtain

ACT TWO

The façade of the Golden Apostle, with a balcony on which chairs and a table are set out. To the right of the inn is a sign which reads: "ANTON SCHILL, HANDLUNG." Under the sign the shop is represented by a broken counter. Behind the counter are some shelves with tobacco, cigarettes and liquor bottles. There are two milk cans. The shop door is imaginary, but each entrance is indicated by a doorbell with a tinny sound.

It is early morning.

SCHILL *is sweeping the shop. The* SON *has a pan and brush and also sweeps. The* DAUGHTER *is dusting. They are singing "The Happy Wanderer."*

Schill. Karl—

(KARL *crosses with a dustpan.* SCHILL *sweeps dust into the pan. The doorbell rings. The* THIRD MAN *appears, carrying a crate of eggs*)

Third Man. 'Morning.

Schill. Ah, good mornnig, Wechsler.

Third Man. Twelve dozen eggs, medium brown. Right?

Schill. Take them, Karl. (*The* SON *puts the crate in a corner*) Did they deliver the milk yet?

Son. Before you came down.

Third Man. Eggs are going up again, Herr Schill. First of the month.

(*He gives* SCHILL *a slip to sign*)

Schill. What? Again? And who's going to buy them?

Third Man. Fifty pfennig a dozen.

Schill. I'll have to cancel my order, that's all.

Third Man. That's up to you, Herr Schill.

(SCHILL *signs the slip*)

Schill. There's nothing else to do. (*He hands back the slip*) And how's the family?

Third Man. Oh, scraping along. Maybe now things will get better.

Schill. Maybe.

Third Man (*Going*). 'Morning.

Schill. Close the door. Don't let the flies in. (*The children resume their singing*) Now, listen to me, children. I have a little piece of good news for you. I didn't mean to speak of it yet awhile, but well, why not? Who do you suppose is going to be the next Burgomaster? Eh? (*They look up at him*) Yes, in spite of everything. It's settled. It's official. What an honor for the family, eh? Especially at a time like this. To say nothing of the salary and the rest of it.

Son. Burgomaster!

Schill. Burgomaster. (*The* SON *shakes him warmly by the hand. The* DAUGHTER *kisses him*) You see, you don't have to be entirely ashamed of your father. (*Silence*) Is your mother coming down to breakfast soon?

Daughter. Mother's tired. She's going to stay upstairs.

Schill. You have a good mother, at least. There you are lucky. Oh, well, if she wants to rest, let her rest. We'll have breakfast together, the three of us. I'll fry some eggs and open a tin of the American ham. This morning we're going to breakfast like kings.

Son. I'd like to, only—I can't.

Schill. You've got to eat, you know.

Son. I've got to run down to the station. One of the laborers is sick. They said they could use me.

Schill. You want to work on the rails in all this heat? That's no work for a son of mine.

Son. Look, Father, we can use the money.

Schill. Well, if you feel you have to.

(*The* Son *goes to the door. The* Daughter *moves toward* Schill)

Daughter. I'm sorry, Father. I have to go too.

Schill. You too? And where is the young lady going, if I may be so bold?

Daughter. There may be something for me at the employment agency.

Schill. Employment agency?

Daughter. It's important to get there early.

Schill. All right. I'll have something nice for you when you get home.

Son and Daughter (*Salute*). Good day, Burgomaster.

(*The* Son *and* Daughter *go out. The* First Man *comes into* Schill's *shop. Mandolin and guitar music are heard offstage*)

Schill. Good morning, Hofbauer.

First Man. Cigarettes. (Schill *takes a pack from the shelf*) Not those. I'll have the green today.

Schill. They cost more.

First Man. Put it in the book.

Schill. What?

First Man. Charge it.

Schill. Well, all right, I'll make an exception this time—seeing it's you, Hofbauer.

(Schill *writes in his cash book*)

First Man (*Opening the pack of cigarettes*). Who's that playing out there?

Schill. The two blind men.

First Man. They play well.

Schill. To hell with them.

First Man. They make you nervous? (Schill *shrugs. The* First Man *lights a cigarette*) She's getting ready for the wedding, I hear.

Schill. Yes. So they say.

(*Enter the* First *and* Second Woman. *They cross to the counter*)

First Woman. Good morning, good morning.

First Man. Good morning.

Second Woman. Good morning.

Schill. Good morning, ladies.

First Woman. Good morning, Herr Schill.

Second Woman. Good morning.

First Woman. Milk please, Herr Schill.

Schill. Milk.

Second Woman. And milk for me too.

Schill. A liter of milk each. Right away.

First Woman. Whole milk, please, Herr Schill.

Schill. Whole milk?

Second Woman. Yes. Whole milk, please.

Schill. Whole milk, I can only give you half a liter each of whole milk.

First Woman. All right.

Schill. Half a liter of whole milk here, and half a liter of whole milk here. There you are.

First Woman. And butter please, a quarter kilo.

Schill. Butter, I haven't any butter. I can give you some very nice lard?

First Woman. No. Butter.

Schill. Goose fat? (*The* First Woman *shakes her head*) Chicken fat?

First Woman. Butter.

Schill. Butter. Now, wait a minute, though. I have a tin of imported butter here somewhere. Ah. There you are. No, sorry, she asked first, but I can order some for you from Kalberstadt tomorrow.

Second Woman. And white bread.

Schill. White bread.

(*He takes a loaf and a knife*)

Second Woman. The whole loaf.

Schill. But a whole loaf would cost . . .

Second Woman. Charge it.

Schill. Charge it?

First Woman. And a package of milk chocolate.

Schill. Package of milk chocolate—right away.

Second Woman. One for me, too, Herr Schill.

Schill. And a package of milk chocolate for you, too.

First Woman. We'll eat it here, if you don't mind.

Schill. Yes, please do.

Second Woman. It's so cool at the back of the shop.

Schill. Charge it?

Women. Of course.

Schill. All for one, one for all.

(*The* SECOND MAN *enters*)

Second Man. Good morning.

The Two Women. Good morning.

Schill. Good morning, Helmesberger.

Second Man. It's going to be a hot day.

Schill. Phew!

Second Man. How's business?

Schill. Fabulous. For a while no one came, and now all of a sudden I'm running a luxury trade.

Second Man. Good!

Schill. Oh, I'll never forget the way you all stood by me at the Golden Apostle in spite of your need, in spite of everything. That was the finest hour of my life.

First Man. We're not heathens, you know.

Second Man. We're behind you, my boy; the whole town's behind you.

First Man. As firm as a rock.

First Woman (*Munching her chocolate*). As firm as a rock, Herr Schill.

Both Women. As firm as a rock.

Second Man. There's no denying it—you're the most popular man in town.

First Man. The most important.

Second Man. And in the spring, God willing, you will be our Burgomaster.

First Man. Sure as a gun.

All. Sure as a gun.

(*Enter* PEDRO *with fishing equipment and a fish in his landing net*)

Pedro. Would you please weigh my fish for me?

Schill (*Weighs it*). Two kilos.

Pedro. Is that all?

Schill. Two kilos exactly.

Pedro. Two kilos!

(*He gives* SCHILL *a tip and exits*)

Second Woman. The fiancé.

First Woman. They're to be married this week. It will be a tremendous wedding.

Second Woman. I saw his picture in the paper.

First Woman (*Sighs*). Ah, what a man!

Second Man. Give me a bottle of schnapps.

Schill. The usual?

Second Man. No, cognac.

Schill. Cognac? But cognac costs twenty-two marks fifty.

Second Man. We all have to splurge a little now and again—

Schill. Here you are. Three Star.

Second Man. And a package of pipe tobacco.

Schill. Black or blond?

Second Man. English.

Schill. English! But that makes twenty-three marks eighty.

Second Man. Chalk it up.

Schill. Now, look. I'll make an exception this week. Only, you will have to pay me the moment your unemployment check comes in. I don't want to be kept waiting. (*Suddenly*) Helmesberger, are those new shoes you're wearing?

Second Man. Yes, what about it?

Schill. You too, Hofbauer. Yellow shoes! Brand new!

First Man. So?

Schill (*To the women*). And you. You all have new shoes! New shoes!

First Woman. A person can't walk around forever in the same old shoes.

Second Woman. Shoes wear out.

Schill. And the money. Where does the money come from?

First Woman. We got them on credit, Herr Schill.

Second Woman. On credit.

Schill. On credit? And where all of a sudden do you get credit?

Second Man. Everybody gives credit now.

First Woman. You gave us credit yourself.

Schill. And what are you going to pay with? Eh? (*They are all silent.* SCHILL *advances upon them threateningly*) With what? Eh? With what? With what?

(*Suddenly he understands. He takes his apron off quickly, flings it on the counter, gets his jacket, and walks off with an air of determination. Now the shop sign vanishes. The shelves are pushed off. The lights go up on the balcony of the Golden Apostle, and the balcony unit itself moves forward into the optical center.* CLAIRE *and* BOBBY *step out on the balcony.* CLAIRE *sits down.* BOBBY *serves coffee*)

Claire. A lovely autumn morning. A silver haze on the streets and a violet sky above. Count Holk would have liked this. Remember him, Bobby? My third husband?

Bobby. Yes, madame.

Claire. Horrible man!

Bobby. Yes, madame.

Claire. Where is Monsieur Pedro? Is he up yet?

Bobby. Yes, madame. He's fishing.

Claire. Already? What a singular passion!

(PEDRO *comes in with the fish*)

Pedro. Good morning, my love.

Claire. Pedro! There you are.

Pedro. Look, my darling. Four kilos!

Claire. A jewel! I'll have it grilled for your lunch. Give it to Bobby.

Pedro. Ah—it is so wonderful here! I like your little town.

Claire. Oh, do you?

Pedro. Yes. These people, they are all so—what is the word?

Claire. Simple, honest, hard-working, decent.

Pedro. But, my angel, you are a mind reader. That's just what I was going to say—however did you guess?

Claire. I know them.

Pedro. Yet when we arrived it was all so dirty, so—what is the word?

Claire. Shabby.

Pedro. Exactly. But now everywhere you go, you see them busy as bees, cleaning their streets—

Claire. Repairing their houses, sweeping—dusting—hanging new curtains in the windows—singing as they work.

Pedro. But you astonishing, wonderful woman! You can't see all that from here.

Claire. I know them. And in their gardens—I am sure that in their gardens they are manuring the soil for the spring.

Pedro. My angel, you know everything. This morning on my way fishing I said to myself, look at them all manuring their gardens. It is extraordinary—and it's all because of you

Your return has given them a new—what is the word?

Claire. Lease on life?

Pedro. Precisely.

Claire. The town was dying, it's true. But a town doesn't have to die. I think they realize that now. People die, not towns. Bobby! (BOBBY *appears*) A cigar.

(*The lights fade on the balcony, which moves back upstage. Somewhat to the right, a sign descends. It reads: "Polizei." The* POLICEMAN *pushes a desk under it. This, with the bench, becomes the police station. He places a bottle of beer and a glass on the desk, and goes to hang up his coat offstage. The telephone rings*)

Policeman. Schultz speaking. Yes, we have a couple of rooms for the night. No, not for rent. This is not the hotel. This is the Güllen police station.

(*He laughs and hangs up.* SCHILL *comes in. He is evidently nervous*)

Schill. Schultz.

Policeman. Hello, Schill. Come in. Sit down. Beer?

Schill. Please.

(*He drinks thirstily*)

Policeman. What can I do for you?

Schill. I want you to arrest Madame Zachanassian.

Policeman. Eh?

Schill. I said I want you to arrest Madame Zachanassian.

Policeman. What the hell are you talking about?

Schill. I ask you to arrest this woman at once.

Policeman. What offense has the lady committed?

Schill. You know perfectly well. She offered a billion marks—

Policeman. And you want her arrested for that?

(*He pours beer into his glass*)

Schill. Schultz! It's your duty.

Schultz. Extraordinary! Extraordinary idea!

(*He drinks his beer*)

Schill. I'm speaking to you as your next Burgomaster.

Policeman. Schill, that's true. The lady offered us a billion marks. But that doesn't entitle us to take police action against her.

Schill. Why not?

Policeman. In order to be arrested, a person must first commit a crime.

Schill. Incitement to murder.

Policeman. Incitement to murder is a crime. I agree.

Schill. Well?

Policeman. And such a proposal—if serious—constitutes an assault.

Schill. That's what I mean.

Policeman. But her offer can't be serious.

Schill. Why?

Policeman. The price is too high. In a case like yours, one pays a thousand marks, at the most two thousand. But not a billion! That's ridiculous. And even if she meant it, that would only prove she was out of her mind. And that's not a matter for the police.

Schill. Whether she's out of her mind or not, the danger to me is the same. That's obvious.

Policeman. Look, Schill, you show us where anyone threatens your life in any way—say, for instance, a man points a gun at you—and we'll be there in a flash.

Schill (*Gets up*). So I'm to wait till someone points a gun at me?

Policeman. Pull yourself together, Schill. We're all for you in this town.

Schill. I wish I could believe it.

Policeman. You don't believe it?

Schill. No. No, I don't. All of a sudden my customers are buying white bread, whole milk, butter, imported tobacco. What does it mean?

Policeman. It means business is picking up.

Schill. Helmesberger lives on the dole; he hasn't earned anything in five years. Today he bought French cognac.

Policeman. I'll have to try your cognac one of these days.

Schill. And shoes. They all have new shoes.

Policeman. And what have you got against new shoes? I'm wearing a new pair myself.

(*He holds out his foot*)

Schill. You too?

Policeman. Why not?

(*He pours out the rest of his beer*)

Schill. Is that Pilsen you're drinking now?

Policeman. It's the only thing.

Schill. You used to drink the local beer.

Policeman. Hogwash.

(*Radio music is heard offstage*)

Schill. Listen. You hear?

Policeman. "The Merry Widow." Yes.

Schill. No. It's a radio.

Policeman. That's Bergholzer's radio.

Schill. Bergholzer!

Policeman. You're right. He should close his window when he plays it. I'll make a note to speak to him.

(*He makes a note in his notebook*)

Schill. And how can Bergholzer pay for a radio?

Policeman. That's his business.

Schill. And you, Schultz, with your new shoes and your imported beer—how are you going to pay for them?

Policeman. That's my business. (*His telephone rings. He picks it up*) Police Station, Güllen. What? What? Where? Where? How? Right, we'll deal with it.

(*He hangs up*)

Schill (*He speaks during the* POLICE-MAN's *telephone conversation*) Schultz, listen. No. Schultz, please—listen to me. Don't you see they're all . . . Listen, please. Look, Schultz. They're all running up debts. And out of these debts comes this sudden prosperity. And out of this prosperity comes the absolute need to kill me.

Policeman (*Putting on his jacket*) You're imagining things.

Schill. All she has to do is to sit on her balcony and wait.

Policeman. Don't be a child.

Schill. You're all waiting.

Policeman (*Snaps a loaded clip into the magazine of a rifle*). Look, Schill, you can relax. The police are here for your protection. They know their job. Let anyone, any time, make the slightest threat to your life, and all you have to do is let us know. We'll do the rest . . . Now, don't worry.

Schill. No, I won't.

Policeman. And don't upset yourself. All right?

Schill. Yes. I won't. (*Then suddenly, in a low tone*) You have a new gold tooth in your mouth!

Policeman. What are you talking about?

Schill (*Taking the* POLICEMAN's *head in his hands, and forcing his lips open*). A brand new, shining gold tooth.

Policeman (*Breaks away and involuntarily levels the gun at* SCHILL). Are you crazy? Look, I've no time to waste. Madame Zachanassian's panther's broken loose.

Schill. Panther?

Policeman. Yes, it's at large. I've got to hunt it down.

Schill. You're not hunting a panther and you know it. It's me you're hunting!

(*The* POLICEMAN *clicks on the safety and lowers the gun*)

Policeman. Schill! Take my advice. Go home. Lock the door. Keep out of everyone's way. That way you'll be safe. Cheer up! Good times are just around the corner!

(*The lights dim in this area and light up on the balcony.* PEDRO *is lounging in a chair.* CLAIRE *is smoking*)

Pedro. Oh, this little town oppresses me.

Claire. Oh, does it? So you've changed your mind?

Pedro. It is true, I find it charming, delightful—

Claire. Picturesque.

Pedro. Yes. After all, it's the place where you were born. But it is too quiet for me. Too provincial. Too much like all small towns everywhere. These people—look at them. They fear nothing, they desire nothing, they strive for nothing. They have everything they want. They are asleep.

Claire. Perhaps one day they will come to life again.

Pedro. My God—do I have to wait for that?

Claire. Yes, you do. Why don't you go back to your fishing?

Pedro. I think I will.

(PEDRO *turns to go*)

Claire. Pedro.

Pedro. Yes, my love?

Claire. Telephone the president of Hambro's Bank. Ask him to transfer a billion marks to my current account.

Pedro. A billion? Yes, my love.

(*He goes. The lights fade on the balcony. A sign is flown in. It reads: "Rathaus." The* THIRD MAN *crosses the stage, right to left, wheeling a new television set on a hand truck. The counter of* SCHILL's *shop is transformed into the* BURGOMASTER's *office. The* BURGOMASTER *comes in. He takes a revolver from his pocket, examines it and sets it down on the desk. He sits down and starts writing.* SCHILL *knocks*)

Burgomaster. Come in.

Schill. I must have a word with you, Burgomaster.

Burgomaster. Ah, Schill. Sit down, my friend.

Schill. Man to man. As your successor.

Burgomaster. But of course. Naturally.

(SCHILL *remains standing. He looks at the revolver*)

Schill. Is that a gun?

Burgomaster. Madame Zachanassian's black panther's broken loose. It's been seen near the cathedral. It's as well to be prepared.

Schill. Oh, yes. Of course.

Burgomaster. I've sent out a call for all able-bodied men with firearms. The streets have been cleared. The children have been kept in school. We don't want any accidents.

Schill (*Suspiciously*). You're making quite a thing of it.

Burgomaster (*Shrugs*). Naturally. A panther is a dangerous beast. Well?

What's on your mind? Speak out. We're old friends.

Schill. That's a good cigar you're smoking, Burgomaster.

Burgomaster. Yes. Havana.

Schill. You used to smoke something else.

Burgomaster. Fortuna.

Schill. Cheaper.

Burgomaster. Too strong.

Schill. A new tie? Silk?

Burgomaster. Yes. Do you like it?

Schill. And have you also bought new shoes?

Burgomaster (*Brings his feet out from under the desk*). Why, yes. I ordered a new pair from Kalberstadt. Extraordinary! However did you guess?

Schill. That's why I'm here.

(*The* THIRD MAN *knocks*)

Burgomaster. Come in.

Third Man. The new typewriter, sir.

Burgomaster. Put it on the table. (*The* THIRD MAN *sets it down and goes*) What's the matter with you? My dear fellow, aren't you well?

Schill. It's you who don't seem well, Burgomaster.

Burgomaster. What do you mean?

Schill. You look pale.

Burgomaster. I?

Schill. Your hands are trembling. (*The* BURGOMASTER *involuntarily hides his hands*) Are you frightened?

Burgomaster. What have I to be afraid of?

Schill. Perhaps this sudden prosperity alarms you.

Burgomaster. Is prosperity a crime?

Schill. That depends on how you pay for it.

Burgomaster. You'll have to forgive me, Schill, but I really haven't the slightest idea what you're talking about. Am I supposed to feel like a criminal every time I order a new typewriter?

Schill. Do you?

Burgomaster. Well, I hope you haven't come here to talk about a new typewriter. Now, what was it you wanted?

Schill. I have come to claim the protection of the authorities.

Burgomaster. Ei! Against whom?

Schill. You know against whom.

Burgomaster. You don't trust us?

Schill. That woman has put a price on my head.

Burgomaster. If you don't feel safe, why don't you go to the police?

Schill. I have just come from the police.

Burgomaster. And?

Schill. The chief has a new gold tooth in his mouth.

Burgomaster. A new—? Oh, Schill, really! You're forgetting. This is Güllen, the town of humane traditions. Goethe slept here. Brahms composed a quartet. You must have faith in us. This is a law-abiding community.

Schill. Then arrest this woman who wants to have me killed.

Burgomaster. Look here, Schill. God knows the lady has every right to be angry with you. What you did there wasn't very pretty. You forced two decent lads to perjure themselves and had a young girl thrown out on the streets.

Schill. That young girl owns half the world.

(*A moment's silence*)

Burgomaster. Very well, then, we'll speak frankly.

Schill. That's why I'm here.

Burgomaster. Man to man, just as you said. (*He clears his throat*) Now—

after what you did, you have no moral right to say a word against this lady. And I advise you not to try. Also—I regret to have to tell you this—there is no longer any question of your being elected Burgomaster.

Schill. Is that official?

Burgomaster. Official.

Schill. I see.

Burgomaster. The man who is chosen to exercise the high post of Burgomaster must have, obviously, certain moral qualifications. Qualifications which, unhappily, you no longer possess. Naturally, you may count on the esteem and friendship of the town, just as before. That goes without saying. The best thing will be to spread the mantle of silence over the whole miserable business.

Schill. So I'm to remain silent while they arrange my murder?

(*The* Burgomaster *gets up*)

Burgomaster (*Suddenly noble*). Now, who is arranging your murder? Give me the names and I will investigate the case at once. Unrelentingly. Well? The names?

Schill. You.

Burgomaster. I resent this. Do you think we want to kill you for money?

Schill. No. You don't want to kill me. But you want to have me killed.

(*The lights go down. The stage is filled with men prowling about with rifles, as if they were stalking a quarry. In the interval the* Police-man's *bench and the* Burgomaster's *desk are shifted somewhat, so that they will compose the setting for the sacristy. The stage empties. The lights come up on the balcony.* Claire *appears*)

Claire. Bobby, what's going on here?

What are all these men doing with guns? Whom are they hunting?

Bobby. The black panther has escaped, madame.

Claire. Who let him out?

Bobby. Kobby and Lobby, madame.

Claire. How excited they are! There may be shooting?

Bobby. It is possible, madame.

(*The lights fade on the balcony. The* Sacristan *comes in. He arranges the set, and puts the altar cloth on the altar. Then* Schill *comes on. He is looking for the* Pastor. *The* Pastor *enters, left. He is wearing his gown and carrying a rifle*)

Schill. Sorry to disturb you, Pastor.

Pastor. God's house is open to all. (*He sees that* Schill *is staring at the gun*) Oh, the gun? That's because of the panther. It's best to be prepared.

Schill. Pastor, help me.

Pastor. Of course. Sit down. (*He puts the rifle on the bench*) What's the trouble?

Schill (*Sits on the bench*). I'm frightened.

Pastor. Frightened? Of what?

Schill. Of everyone. They're hunting me down like a beast.

Pastor. Have no fear of man, Schill. Fear God. Fear not the death of the body. Fear the death of the soul. Zip up my gown behind, Sacristan.

Schill. I'm afraid, Pastor.

Pastor. Put your trust in heaven, my friend.

Schill. You see, I'm not well. I shake. I have pains around the heart. I sweat.

Pastor. I know. You're passing through a profound psychic experience.

Schill. I'm going through hell.

Pastor. The hell you are going through

exists only within yourself. Many years ago you betrayed a girl shamefully, for money. Now you think that we shall sell you just as you sold her. No, my friend, you are projecting your guilt upon others. It's quite natural. But remember, the root of our torment lies always within ourselves, in our hearts, in our sins. When you have understood this, you can conquer the fears that oppress you; you have weapons with which to destroy them.

Schill. Siemethofer has bought a new washing machine.

Pastor. Don't worry about the washing machine. Worry about your immortal soul.

Schill. Stockers has a television set.

Pastor. There is also great comfort in prayer. Sacristan, the bands. (SCHILL *crosses to the altar and kneels. The* SACRISTAN *ties on the* PASTOR's *bands*) Examine your conscience, Schill. Repent. Otherwise your fears will consume you. Believe me, this is the only way. We have no other. (*The church bell begins to peal.* SCHILL *seems relieved*) Now I must leave you. I have a baptism. You may stay as long as you like. Sacristan, the Bible, Liturgy and Psalter. The child is beginning to cry. I can hear it from here. It is frightened. Let us make haste to give it the only security which this world affords.

Schill. A new bell?

Pastor. Yes. Its tone is marvelous, don't you think? Full. Sonorous.

Schill (*Steps back in horror*). A new bell! You too, Pastor? You too?

(*The* PASTOR *clasps his hands in horror. Then he takes* SCHILL *into his arms*)

Pastor. Oh, God, God forgive me. We are poor, weak things, all of us. Do not tempt us further into the hell in which you are burning. Go, Schill, my friend, go, my brother, go while there is time.

(*The* PASTOR *goes.* SCHILL *picks up the rifle with a gesture of desperation. He goes out with it. As the lights fade, men appear with guns. Two shots are fired in the darkness. The lights come up on the balcony, which moves forward*)

Claire. Bobby! What was that shooting? Have they caught the panther?

Bobby. He is dead, madame.

Claire. There were two shots.

Bobby. The panther is dead, madame.

Claire. I loved him. (*Waves* BOBBY *away*) I shall miss him.

(*The* TEACHER *comes in with two little girls, singing. They stop under the balcony*)

Teacher. Gracious lady, be so good as to accept our heartfelt condolences. Your beautiful panther is no more. Believe me, we are deeply pained that so tragic an event should mar your visit here. But what could we do? The panther was savage, a beast. To him our human laws could not apply. There was no other way— (SCHILL *appears with the gun. He looks dangerous. The girls run off, frightened. The* TEACHER *follows the girls*) Children—children—children!

Claire. Anton, why are you frightening the children?

(*He works the bolt, loading the chamber, and raises the gun slowly*)

Schill. Go away, Claire—I warn you. Go away.

Claire. How strange it is, Anton! How

clearly it comes back to me! The day we saw one another for the first time, do you remember? I was on a balcony then. It was a day like today, a day in autumn without a breath of wind, warm as it is now—only lately I am always cold. You stood down there and stared at me without moving. I was embarrassed. I didn't know what to do. I wanted to go back into the darkness of the room, where it was safe, but I couldn't. You stared up at me darkly, almost angrily, as if you wished to hurt me, but your eyes were full of passion. (SCHILL *begins to lower the rifle involuntarily*) Then, I don't know why, I left the balcony and I came down and stood in the street beside you. You didn't greet me, you didn't say a word, but you took my hand and we walked together out of the town into the fields, and behind us came Kobby and Lobby, like two dogs, sniveling and giggling and snarling. Suddenly you picked up a stone and hurled it at them, and they ran yelping back into the town, and we were alone. (SCHILL *has lowered the rifle completely. He moves toward her, as close as he can come*) That was the beginning, and everything else had to follow. There is no escape.

(*She goes in and closes the shutters.* SCHILL *stands immobile. The* TEACHER *tiptoes in. He stares at* SCHILL, *who doesn't see him. Then he beckons to the children*)

Teacher. Come, children, sing. Sing.

(*They begin singing. He creeps behind* SCHILL *and snatches away the the rifle.* SCHILL *turns sharply. The* PASTOR *comes in*)

Pastor. Go, Schill—go!

(SCHILL *goes out. The children continue singing, moving across the stage and off. The Golden Apostle vanishes. The crossing bell is heard. The scene dissolves into the railway-station setting, as in Act One. But there are certain changes. The time-table marked "Fahrplan" is now new, the frame freshly painted. There is a new travel poster on the station wall. It has a yellow sun and the words: "Reist in den Süden." On the other side of the Fahrplan is another poster with the words: "Die Passionsspiele Oberammergau." The sound of passing trains covers the scene change.* SCHILL *appears with an old valise in his hand, dressed in a shabby trench coat, his hat on his head. He looks about with a furtive air, walking slowly to the platform. Slowly, as if by chance, the* TOWNS-PEOPLE *enter, from all sides.* SCHILL *hesitates, stops*)

Burgomaster (*From upstage, center*). Good evening, Schill.

Schill. Good evening.

Policeman. Good evening.

Schill. Good evening.

Painter (*Enters*). Good evening.

Schill. Good evening.

Doctor. Good evening.

Schill. Good evening.

Burgomaster. So you're taking a little trip?

Schill. Yes. A little trip.

Policeman. May one ask where to?

Schill. I don't know.

Painter. Don't know?

Schill. To Kalberstadt.

Burgomaster (*With disbelief, pointing to the valise*). Kalberstadt?

Schill. After that—somewhere else.

Painter. Ah. After that somewhere else.

(*The* FOURTH MAN *walks in*)

Schill. I thought maybe Australia.

Burgomaster. Australia!

All. Australia!

Schill. I'll raise the money somehow.

Burgomaster. But why Australia?

Policeman. What would you be doing in Australia?

Schill. One can't always live in the same town, year in, year out.

Painter. But Australia—

Doctor. It's a risky trip for a man of your age.

Burgomaster. One of the lady's little men ran off to Australia . . .

All. Yes.

Policeman. You'll be much safer here.

Painter. Much!

(SCHILL *looks about him in anguish, like a beast at bay*)

Schill (*Low voice*). I wrote a letter to the administration at Kaffigen.

Burgomaster. Yes? And?

(*They are all intent on the answer*)

Schill. They didn't answer.

(*All laugh*)

Doctor. Do you mean to say you don't trust your old friends? That's not very flattering, you know.

Burgomaster. No one's going to do you any harm here.

Doctor. No harm here.

Schill. They didn't answer because our postmaster held up my letter.

Painter. Our postmaster? What an idea.

Burgomaster. The postmaster is a member of the town council.

Policeman. A man of the utmost integrity.

Doctor. He doesn't hold up letters. What an idea!

(*The crossing bell starts ringing*)

Station Master (*Announces*). Local to Kalberstadt!

(*The* TOWNSPEOPLE *all cross down to see the train arrive. Then they turn, with their backs to the audience, in a line across the stage.* SCHILL *cannot get through to reach the train*)

Schill (*In a low voice*). What are you all doing here? What do you want of me?

Burgomaster. We don't like to see you go.

Doctor. We've come to see you off.

(*The sound of the approaching train grows louder*)

Schill. I didn't ask you to come.

Policeman. But we have come.

Doctor. As old friends.

All. As old friends.

(*The* STATION MASTER *holds up his paddle. The train stops with a screech of brakes. We hear the engine panting offstage*)

Voice (*Offstage*). Güllen!

Burgomaster. A pleasant journey.

Doctor. And long life!

Painter. And good luck in Australia!

All. Yes, good luck in Australia.

(*They press around him jovially. He stands motionless and pale*)

Schill. Why are you crowding me?

Policeman. What's the matter now?

(*The* STATION MASTER *blows a long blast on his whistle*)

Schill. Give me room.

Doctor. But you have plenty of room.

(*They all move away from him*)

Policeman. Better get aboard, Schill.

Schill. I see. I see. One of you is going to push me under the wheels.

Policeman. Oh, nonsense. Go on, get aboard.

Schill. Get away from me, all of you.

Burgomaster. I don't know what you want. Just get on the train.

Schill. No. One of you will push me under.

Doctor. You're being ridiculous. Now, go on, get on the train.

Schill. Why are you all so near me?

Doctor. The man's gone mad.

Station Master. 'Board!

(*He blows his whistle. The engine bell clangs. The train starts*)

Burgomaster. Get aboard, man. Quick.

(*The following speeches are spoken all together until the train noises fade away*)

Doctor. The train's starting.

All. Get aboard, man. Get aboard. The train's starting.

Schill. If I try to get aboard, one of you will hold me back.

All. No, no.

Burgomaster. Get on the train.

Schill (*In terror, crouches against the wall of the* STATION MASTER's *office*). No—no—no. No. (*He falls on his knees. The others crowd around him. He cowers on the ground, abjectly.*

The train sounds fade away) Oh, no —no—don't push me, don't push me!

Policeman. There. It's gone off without you.

(*Slowly they leave him. He raises himself up to a sitting position, still trembling. A* TRUCK DRIVER *enters with an empty can*)

Truck Driver. Do you know where I can get some water? My truck's boiling over. (SCHILL *points to the station office*) Thanks. (*He enters the office, gets the water and comes out. By this time,* SCHILL *is erect*) Missed your train?

Schill. Yes.

Truck Driver. To Kalberstadt?

Schill. Yes.

Truck Driver. Well, come with me. I'm going that way.

Schill. This is my town. This is my home. (*With strange new dignity*) No, thank you. I've changed my mind. I'm staying.

Truck Driver (*Shrugs*). All right.

(*He goes out.* SCHILL *picks up his bag, looks right and left, and slowly walks off*)

Curtain

ACT THREE

Music is heard. Then the curtain rises on the interior of the old barn, a dim, cavernous structure. Bars of light fall across the shadowy forms, shafts of sunlight from the holes and cracks in the walls and roof. Overhead hang old rags, decaying sacks, great cobwebs. Extreme left is a ladder leading to the loft. Near it, an old haycart. Left, CLAIRE ZACHANASSIAN *is sitting in her gilded sedan chair, motionless, in her magnificent bridal gown and veil. Near the chair stands an old keg.*

Bobby (*Comes in, treading carefully*). The doctor and the teacher from the high school to see you, madame.

Claire (*Impassive*). Show them in.

(Bobby *ushers them in as if they were entering a hall of state. The two grope their way through the litter. At last they find the lady, and bow. They are both well dressed in new clothes, but are very dusty*)

Bobby. Dr. Nüsslin and Professor Müller.

Doctor. Madame.

Claire. You look dusty, gentlemen.

Doctor (*Dusts himself off vigorously*). Oh, forgive us. We had to climb over an old carriage.

Teacher. Our respects.

Doctor. A fabulous wedding.

Teacher. Beautiful occasion.

Claire. It's stifling here. But I love this old barn. The smell of hay and old straw and axle grease—it is the scent of my youth. Sit down. All this rubbish—the haycart, the old carriage, the cask, even the pitchfork—it was all here when I was a girl.

Teacher. Remarkable place.

(*He mops his brow*)

Claire. I thought the pastor's text was very appropriate. The lesson a trifle long.

Teacher. I Corinthians 13.

Claire. Your choristers sang beautifully, Professor.

Teacher. Bach. From the *St. Matthew Passion*.

Doctor. Güllen has never seen such magnificence! The flowers! The jewels! And the people.

Teacher. The theatrical world, the world of finance, the world of art, the world of science . . .

Claire. All these worlds are now back in their Cadillacs, speeding toward the capital for the wedding recep-

tion. But I'm sure you didn't come here to talk about them.

Doctor. Dear lady, we should not intrude on your valuable time. Your husband must be waiting impatiently.

Claire. No, no. I've packed him off to Brazil.

Doctor. To Brazil, madame?

Claire. Yes. For his honeymoon.

Teacher and Doctor. Oh! But your wedding guests?

Claire. I've planned a delightful dinner for them. They'll never miss me. Now what was it you wished to talk about?

Teacher. About Anton Schill, madame.

Claire. Is he dead?

Teacher. Madame, we may be poor. But we have our principles.

Claire. I see. Then what do you want?

Teacher (*He mops his brow again*). The fact is, madame, in anticipation of your well-known munificence, that is, feeling that you would give the town some sort of gift, we have all been buying things. Necessities . . .

Doctor. With money we don't have.

(*The* Teacher *blows his nose*)

Claire. You've run into debt?

Doctor. Up to here.

Claire. In spite of your principles?

Teacher. We're human, madame.

Claire. I see

Teacher. We have been poor for a long time. A long, long time.

Doctor (*He rises*). The question is, how are we going to pay?

Claire. You already know.

Teacher (*Courageously*). I beg you, Madame Zachanassian, put yourself in our position for a moment. For twenty-two years I've been cudgeling my brains to plant a few seeds of knowledge in this wilderness. And all this time, my gallant colleague, Dr. Nüsslin, has been rattling around in his ancient Mercedes, from patient to patient, trying to keep these wretches alive. Why? Why have we spent our lives in this miserable hole? For money? Hardly. The pay is ridiculous.

Doctor. And yet, the professor here has declined an offer to head the high school in Kalberstadt.

Teacher. And Dr. Nüsslin has refused an important post at the University of Erlangen. Madame, the simple fact is, we love our town. We were born here. It is our life.

Doctor. That's true.

Teacher. What has kept us going all these years is the hope that one day the community will prosper again as it did in the days when we were young.

Claire. Good.

Teacher. Madame, there is no reason for our poverty. We suffer here from a mysterious blight. We have factories. They stand idle. There is oil in the valley of Pückenried.

Doctor. There is copper under the Konradsweil Forest. There is power in our streams, in our waterfalls.

Teacher. We are not poor, madame. If we had credit, if we had confidence, the factories would open, orders and commissions would pour in. And our economy would bloom together with our cultural life. We would become once again like the towns around us, healthy and prosperous.

Doctor. If the Wagonworks were put on its feet again—

Teacher. The Foundry.

Doctor. The Golden Eagle Pencil Factory.

Teacher. Buy these plants, madame. Put them in operation once more, and I swear to you, Güllen will flourish and it will bless you. We don't need a billion marks. Ten million, properly invested, would give us back our life, and incidentally return to the investor an excellent dividend. Save us, madame. Save us, and we will not only bless you, we will make money for you.

Claire. I don't need money.

Doctor. Madame, we are not asking for charity. This is business.

Claire. It's a good idea . . .

Doctor. Dear lady! I knew you wouldn't let us down.

Claire. But it's out of the question. I cannot buy the Wagonworks. I already own them.

Doctor. The Wagonworks?

Teacher. And the Foundry?

Claire. And the Foundry.

Doctor. And the Golden Eagle Pencil Factory?

Claire. Everything. The valley of Pückenried with its oil, the forest of Konradsweil with its ore, the barn, the town, the streets, the houses, the shops, everything. I had my agents buy up this rubbish over the years, bit by bit, piece by piece, until I had it all. Your hopes were an illusion, your vision empty, your self-sacrifice a stupidity, your whole life completely senseless.

Teacher. Then the mysterious blight—

Claire. The mysterious blight was I.

Doctor. But this is monstrous!

Claire. Monstrous. I was seventeen when I left this town. It was winter. I was dressed in a sailor suit and my red braids hung down my back. I was in my seventh month. As I walked down the street to the station, the boys whistled after me, and someone threw something. I sat freezing in my seat in the Hamburg Express. But before the roof of the great barn was lost behind the trees, I had made up my mind that one day I would come back . . .

Teacher. But, madame—

Claire (*She smiles*). And now I have. (*She claps her hands*) Mike. Max. Take me back to the Golden Apostle. I've been here long enough.

(MIKE *and* MAX *start to pick up the sedan chair. The* TEACHER *pushes* MIKE *away*)

Teacher. Madame. One moment. Please. I see it all now. I had thought of you as an avenging fury, a Medea, a Clytemnestra—but I was wrong. You are a warm-hearted woman who has suffered a terrible injustice, and now you have returned and taught us an unforgettable lesson. You have stripped us bare. But now that we stand before you naked, I know you will set aside these thoughts of vengeance. If we made you suffer, you too have put us through the fire. Have mercy, madame.

Claire. When I have had justice. Mike!

(*She signals to* MIKE *and* MAX *to pick up the sedan chair. They cross the stage. The* TEACHER *bars the way*)

Teacher. But, madame, one injustice cannot cure another. What good will it do to force us into crime? Horror succeeds horror, shame is piled on shame. It settles nothing.

Claire. It settles everything.

(*They move upstage toward the exit. The* TEACHER *follows*)

Teacher. Madame, this lesson you have taught us will never be forgotten. We will hand it down from father to son. It will be a monument more lasting than any vengeance. Whatever we have been, in the future we shall be better because of you. You have pushed us to the extreme. Now forgive us. Show us the way to a better life. Have pity, madame— pity. That is the highest justice.

(*The sedan chair stops*)

Claire. The highest justice has no pity. It is bright and pure and clear. The world made me into a whore; now I make the world into a brothel. Those who wish to go down, may go down. Those who wish to dance with me, may dance with me. (*To her porters*) Go.

(*She is carried off. The lights black out. Downstage, right, appears* SCHILL's *shop. It has a new sign, a new counter. The doorbell, when it rings, has an impressive sound.* FRAU SCHILL *stands behind the counter in a new dress. The* FIRST MAN *enters, left. He is dressed as a prosperous butcher, a few bloodstains on his snowy apron, a gold watch chain across his open vest*)

First Man. What a wedding! I'll swear the whole town was there. Cigarettes.

Frau Schill. Clara is entitled to a little happiness after all. I'm happy for her. Green or white?

First Man. Turkish. The bridesmaids! Dancers and opera singers. And the dresses! Down to here.

Frau Schill. It's the fashion nowadays.

First man. Reporters! Photographers! From all over the world! (*In a low voice*) They will be here any minute.

Frau Schill. What have reporters to do with us? We are simple people, Herr Hofbauer. There is nothing for them here.

First Man. They're questioning everybody. They're asking everything. (*The* First Man *lights a cigarette. He looks up at the ceiling*) Footsteps.

Frau Schill. He's pacing the room. Up and down. Day and night.

First Man. Haven't seen him all week.

Frau Schill. He never goes out.

First Man. It's his conscience. That was pretty mean, the way he treated poor Madame Zachanassian.

Frau Schill. That's true. I feel very badly about it myself.

First Man. To ruin a young girl like that—God doesn't forgive it. (Frau Schill *nods solemnly with pursed lips. The butcher gives her a level glance*) Look, I hope he'll have sense enough to keep his mouth shut in front of the reporters.

Frau Schill. I certainly hope so.

First Man. You know his character.

Frau Schill. Only too well, Herr Hofbauer.

First Man. If he tries to throw dirt at our Clara and tell a lot of lies, how she tried to get us to kill him, which anyway she never meant—

Frau Schill. Of course not.

First Man. —Then we'll really have to do something! And not because of the money— (*He spits*) But out of ordinary human decency. God knows Madame Zachanassian has suffered enough through him already.

Frau Schill. She has indeed.

(*The* Teacher *comes in. He is not quite sober*)

Teacher (*Looks about the shop*). Has the press been here yet?

First Man. No.

Teacher. It's not my custom, as you know, Frau Schill—but I wonder if I could have a strong alcoholic drink?

Frau Schill. It's an honor to serve you, Herr Professor. I have a good Steinhäger. Would you like to try a glass?

Teacher. A very small glass.

(Frau Schill *serves bottle and glass. The* Teacher *tosses off a glass*)

Frau Schill. Your hand is shaking, Herr Professor.

Teacher. To tell the truth, I have been drinking a little already.

Frau Schill. Have another glass. It will do you good.

(*He accepts another glass*)

Teacher. Is that he up there, walking?

Frau Schill. Up and down. Up and down.

First Man. It's God punishing him.

(*The* Painter *comes in with the* Son *and the* Daughter)

Painter. Careful! A reporter just asked us the way to this shop.

First Man. I hope you didn't tell him.

Painter. I told him we were strangers here.

(*They all laugh. The door opens. The* Second Man *darts into the shop*)

Second Man. Look out, everybody! The press! They are across the street in your shop, Hofbauer.

First Man. My boy will know how to deal with them.

Second Man. Make sure Schill doesn't come down, Hofbauer.

First Man. Leave that to me.

(*They group themselves about the shop*)

Teacher. Listen to me, all of you. When the reporters come I'm going to speak to them. I'm going to make a statement. A statement to the world on behalf of myself as Rector of Güllen High School and on behalf of you all, for all your sakes.

Painter. What are you going to say?

Teacher. I shall tell the truth about Claire Zachanassian.

Frau Schill. You're drunk, Herr Professor; you should be ashamed of yourself.

Teacher. I should be ashamed? You should all be ashamed!

Son. Shut your trap. You're drunk.

Daughter. Please, Professor—

Teacher. Girl, you disappoint me. It is your place to speak. But you are silent and you force your old teacher to raise his voice. I am going to speak the truth. It is my duty and I am not afraid. The world may not wish to listen, but no one can silence me. I'm not going to wait—I'm going over to Hofbauer's shop now.

All. No, you're not. Stop him. Stop him.

(*They all spring at the* Teacher. *He defends himself. At this moment,* Schill *appears through the door upstage. In contrast to the others, he is dressed shabbily in an old black jacket, his best*)

Schill. What's going on in my shop? (*The* Townsmen *let go of the* Teacher *and turn to stare at* Schill) What's the trouble, Professor?

Teacher. Schill, I am speaking out at last! I am going to tell the press everything.

Schill. Be quiet, Professor.

Teacher. What did you say?

Schill. Be quiet.

Teacher. You want me to be quiet?

Schill. Please.

Teacher. But, Schill, if I keep quiet, if you miss this opportunity—they're over in Hofbauer's shop now . . .

Schill. Please.

Teacher. As you wish. If you too are on their side, I have no more to say.

(*The doorbell jingles. A* Reporter *comes in*)

Reporter. Is Anton Schill here? (*Moves to* Schill) Are you Herr Schill?

Schill. What?

Reporter. Herr Schill.

Schill. Er—no. Herr Schill's gone to Kalberstadt for the day.

Reporter. Oh, thank you. Good day.

(*He goes out*)

Painter (*Mops his brow*). Whew! Close shave.

(*He follows the* Reporter *out*)

Second Man (*Walking up to* Schill). That was pretty smart of you to keep your mouth shut. You know what to expect if you don't.

(*He goes*)

First Man. Give me a Havana. (Schill *serves him*) Charge it. You bastard!

(*He goes.* Schill *opens his account book*)

Frau Schill. Come along, children—

(Frau Schill, *the* Son *and the* Daughter *go off, upstage*)

Teacher. They're going to kill you. I've known it all along, and you too, you must have known it. The need is too strong, the temptation too great. And now perhaps I too will join against you. I belong to them and, like them, I can feel myself hardening into something that is not human —not beautiful.

Schill. It can't be helped.

Teacher. Pull yourself together, man. Speak to the reporters; you've no time to lose.

(SCHILL *looks up from his account book*)

Schill. No. I'm not going to fight any more.

Teacher. Are you so frightened that you don't dare open your mouth?

Schill. I made Claire what she is, I made myself what I am. What should I do? Should I pretend that I'm innocent?

Teacher. No, you can't. You are as guilty as hell.

Schill. Yes.

Teacher. You are a bastard.

Schill. Yes.

Teacher. But that does not justify your murder. (SCHILL *looks at him*) I wish I could believe that for what they're doing—for what they're going to do —they will suffer for the rest of their lives. But it's not true. In a little while they will have justified everything and forgotten everything.

Schill. Of course.

Teacher. Your name will never again be mentioned in this town. That's how it will be.

Schill. I don't hold it against you.

Teacher. But I do. I will hold it against myself all my life. That's why—

(*The doorbell jingles. The* BURGO-MASTER *comes in. The* TEACHER *stares at him, then goes out without another word*)

Burgomaster. Good afternoon, Schill. Don't let me disturb you. I've just dropped in for a moment.

Schill. I'm just finishing my accounts for the week.

(*A moment's pause*)

Burgomaster. The town council meets tonight. At the Golden Apostle. In the auditorium.

Schill. I'll be there.

Burgomaster. The whole town will be there. Your case will be discussed and final action taken. You've put us in a pretty tight spot, you know.

Schill. Yes. I'm sorry.

Burgomaster. The lady's offer will be rejected.

Schill. Possibly.

Burgomaster. Of course, I may be wrong.

Schill. Of course.

Burgomaster. In that case—are you prepared to accept the judgment of the town? The meeting will be covered by the press, you know.

Schill. By the press?

Burgomaster. Yes, and the radio and the newsreel. It's a very ticklish situation. Not only for you—believe me, it's even worse for us. What with the wedding, and all the publicity, we've become famous. All of a sudden our ancient democratic institutions have become of interest to the world.

Schill. Are you going to make the lady's condition public?

Burgomaster. No, no, of course not. Not directly. We will have to put the matter to a vote—that is unavoidable. But only those involved will understand.

Schill. I see.

Burgomaster. As far as the press is concerned, you are simply the intermediary between us and Madame Zachanassian. I have whitewashed you completely.

Schill. That is very generous of you.

Burgomaster. Frankly, it's not for your sake, but for the sake of your family.

They are honest and decent people.

Schill. Oh—

Burgomaster. So far we've all played fair. You've kept your mouth shut and so have we. Now can we continue to depend on you? Because if you have any idea of opening your mouth at tonight's meeting, there won't be any meeting.

Schill. I'm glad to hear an open threat at last.

Burgomaster. We are not threatening you. You are threatening us. If you speak, you force us to act—in advance.

Schill. That won't be necessary.

Burgomaster. So if the town decides against you?

Schill. I will accept their decision.

Burgomaster. Good. (*A moment's pause*) I'm delighted to see there is still a spark of decency left in you. But—wouldn't it be better if we didn't have to call a meeting at all? (*He pauses. He takes a gun from his pocket and puts it on the counter*) I've brought you this.

Schill. Thank you.

Burgomaster. It's loaded.

Schill. I don't need a gun.

Burgomaster (*He clears his throat*). You see? We could tell the lady that we had condemned you in secret session and you had anticipated our decision. I've lost a lot of sleep getting to this point, believe me.

Schill. I believe you.

Burgomaster. Frankly, in your place, I myself would prefer to take the path of honor. Get it over with, once and for all. Don't you agree? For the sake of your friends! For the sake of our children, your own children —you have a daughter, a son—Schill, you know our need, our misery.

Schill. You've put me through hell, you and your town. You were my friends, you smiled and reassured me. But day by day I saw you change—your shoes, your ties, your suits—your hearts. If you had been honest with me then, perhaps I would feel differently toward you now. I might even use that gun you brought me. For the sake of my friends. But now I have conquered my fear. Alone. It was hard, but it's done. And now you will have to judge me. And I will accept your judgment. For me that will be justice. How it will be for you, I don't know. (*He turns away*) You may kill me if you like. I won't complain, I won't protest, I won't defend myself. But I won't do your job for you either.

Burgomaster (*Takes up his gun*). There it is. You've had your chance and you won't take it. Too bad. (*He takes out a cigarette*) I suppose it's more than we can expect of a man like you. (SCHILL *lights the* BURGOMASTER's *cigarette*) Good day.

Schill. Good day. (*The* BURGOMASTER *goes,* FRAU SCHILL *comes in, dressed in a fur coat. The* DAUGHTER *is in a new red dress. The* SON *has a new sports jacket*) What a beautiful coat, Mathilde!

Frau Schill. Real fur. You like it?

Schill. Should I? What a lovely dress, Ottilie!

Daughter. C'est très chic, n'est-ce-pas?

Schill. What?

Frau Schill. Ottilie is taking a course in French.

Schill. Very useful. Karl—whose automobile is that out there at the curb?

Son. Oh, it's only an Opel. They're not expensive.

Schill. You bought yourself a car?

Son. On credit. Easiest thing in the world.

Frau Schill. Everyone's buying on credit now, Anton. These fears of yours are ridiculous. You'll see. Clara has a good heart. She only means to teach you a lesson.

Daughter. She means to teach you a lesson, that's all.

Son. It's high time you got the point, Father.

Schill. I get the point. (*The church bells start ringing*) Listen. The bells of Güllen. Do you hear?

Son. Yes, we have four bells now. It sounds quite good.

Daughter. Just like Gray's Elegy.

Schill. What?

Frau Schill. Ottilie is taking a course in English literature.

Schill. Congratulations! It's Sunday. I should very much like to take a ride in your car. Our car.

Son. You want to ride in the car?

Schill. Why not? I want to ride through the Konradsweil Forest. I want to see the town where I've lived all my life.

Frau Schill. I don't think that will look very nice for any of us.

Schill. No—perhaps not. Well, I'll go for a walk by myself.

Frau Schill. Then take us to Kalberstadt, Karl, and we'll go to a cinema.

Schill. A cinema? It's a good idea.

Frau Schill. See you soon, Anton.

Schill. Good-bye, Ottilie. Good-bye, Karl. Good-bye, Mathilde.

Family. Good-bye.

(*They go out*)

Schill. Good-bye. (*The shop sign flies off. The lights black out. They come up at once on the forest scene*)

Autumn. Even the forest has turned to gold.

(SCHILL *wanders down to the bench in the forest. He sits.* CLAIRE's *voice is heard*)

Claire (*Offstage*). Stop. Wait here. (CLAIRE *comes in. She gazes slowly up at the trees, kicks at some leaves. Then she walks slowly down center. She stops before a tree, glances up the trunk*) Bark-borers. The old tree is dying.

Schill. Clara.

Claire. How pleasant to see you here. I was visiting my forest. May I sit by you?

Schill. Oh, yes. Please do. (*She sits next to him*) I've just been saying good-bye to my family. They've gone to the cinema. Karl has bought himself a car.

Claire. How nice.

Schill. Ottilie is taking French lessons. And a course in English literature.

Claire. You see? They're beginning to take an interest in higher things.

Schill. Listen. A finch. You hear?

Claire. Yes. It's a finch. And a cuckoo in the distance. Would you like some music?

Schill. Oh, yes. That would be very nice.

Claire. Anything special?

Schill. "Deep in the Forest."

Claire. Your favorite song. They know it.

(*She raises her hand. Offstage, the mandolin and guitar play the tune softly*)

Schill. We had a child?

Claire. Yes.

Schill. Boy or girl?

Claire. Girl.

Schill. What name did you give her?

Claire. I called her Genevieve.

Schill. That's a very pretty name.

Claire. Yes.

Schill. What was she like?

Claire. I saw her only once. When she was born. Then they took her away from me.

Schill. Her eyes?

Claire. They weren't open yet.

Schill. And her hair?

Claire. Black, I think. It's usually black at first.

Schill. Yes, of course. Where did she die, Clara?

Claire. In some family. I've forgotten their name. Meningitis, they said. The officials wrote me a letter.

Schill. Oh, I'm so very sorry, Clara.

Claire. I've told you about our child. Now tell me about myself.

Schill. About yourself?

Claire. Yes. How I was when I was seventeen in the days when you loved me.

Schill. I remember one day you waited for me in the great barn. I had to look all over the place for you. At last I found you lying in the haycart with nothing on and a long straw between your lips . . .

Claire. Yes. I was pretty in those days.

Schill. You were beautiful, Clara.

Claire. You were strong. The time you fought with those two railway men who were following me, I wiped the blood from your face with my red petticoat. (*The music ends*) They've stopped.

Schill. Tell them to play "Thoughts of Home."

Claire. They know that too.

(*The music plays*)

Schill. Here we are, Clara, sitting together in our forest for the last time.

The town council meets tonight. They will condemn me to death, and one of them will kill me. I don't know who and I don't know where. Clara, I only know that in a little while a useless life will come to an end.

(*He bows his head on her bosom. She takes him in her arms*)

Claire (*Tenderly*). I shall take you in your coffin to Capri. You will have your tomb in the park of my villa, where I can see you from my bedroom window. White marble and onyx in a grove of green cypress. With a beautiful view of the Mediterranean.

Schill. I've always wanted to see it.

Claire. Your love for me died years ago, Anton. But my love for you would not die. It turned into something strong, like the hidden roots of the forest; something evil, like white mushrooms that grow unseen in the darkness. And slowly it reached out for your life. Now I have you. You are mine. Alone. At last, and forever, a peaceful ghost in a silent house.

(*The music ends*)

Schill. The song is over.

Claire. Adieu, Anton.

(CLAIRE *kisses* ANTON, *a long kiss. Then she rises*)

Schill. Adieu.

(*She goes.* SCHILL *remains sitting on the bench. A row of lamps descends from the flies. The* TOWNSMEN *come in from both sides, each bearing his chair. A table and chairs are set upstage, center. On both sides sit the* TOWNSMEN. *The* POLICEMAN, *in a new uniform, sits on the bench behind* SCHILL. *All the* TOWNSMEN *are in new Sunday clothes. Around them are* TECHNICIANS *of all sorts, with lights, cameras and other equipment. The* TOWNSWOMEN *are absent. They do not vote. The* BURGOMASTER *takes his place at the table, center. The* DOCTOR *and the* PASTOR *sit at the same table, at his right, and the* TEACHER *in his academic gown, at his left*)

Burgomaster (*At a sign from the* RADIO TECHNICIAN, *he pounds the floor with his wand of office*). Fellow citizens of Güllen, I call this meeting to order. The agenda: there is only one matter before us. I have the honor to announce officially that Madame Claire Zachanassian, daughter of our beloved citizen, the famous architect Siegfried Wäscher, has decided to make a gift to the town of one billion marks. Five hundred million to the town, five hundred million to be divided per capita among the citizens. After certain necessary preliminaries, a vote will be taken, and you, as citizens of Güllen, will signify your will by a show of hands. Has anyone any objection to this mode of procedure? The pastor? (*Silence*) The police? (*Silence*) The town health official? (*Silence*) The Rector of Güllen High School? (*Silence*) The political opposition? (*Silence*) I shall then proceed to the vote—(*The* TEACHER *rises. The* BURGOMASTER *turns in surprise and irritation*) You wish to speak?

Teacher. Yes.

Burgomaster. Very well.

(*He takes his seat. The* TEACHER *advances. The movie camera starts running*)

Teacher. Fellow townsmen. (*The*

PHOTOGRAPHER *flashes a bulb in his face*) Fellow townsmen. We all know that by means of this gift, Madame Claire Zachanassian intends to attain a certain object. What is this object? To enrich the town of her youth, yes. But more than that, she desires by means of this gift to re-establish justice among us. This desire expressed by our benefactress raises an all-important question. Is it true that our community harbors in its soul such a burden of guilt?

Burgomaster. Yes! True!

Second Man. Crimes are concealed among us.

Third Man (*He jumps up*). Sins!

Fourth Man (*He jumps up also*). Perjuries.

Painter. Justice!

Townsmen. Justice! Justice!

Teacher. Citizens of Güllen, this, then, is the simple fact of the case. We have participated in an injustice. I thoroughly recognize the material advantages which this gift opens to us —I do not overlook the fact that it is poverty which is the root of all this bitterness and evil. Nevertheless, there is no question here of money.

Townsmen. No! No!

Teacher. Here there is no question of our prosperity as a community, or our well-being as individuals— The question is—must be—whether or not we wish to live according to the principles of justice, those principles ˌfor which our forefathers lived and fought and for which they died, those principles which form the soul of our Western culture.

Townsmen. Hear! Hear!

(*Applause*)

Teacher (*Desperately, realizing that*

he is fighting a losing battle, and on the verge of hysteria). Wealth has meaning only when benevolence comes of it, but only he who hungers for grace will receive grace. Do you feel this hunger, my fellow citizens, this hunger of the spirit, or do you feel only that other profane hunger, the hunger of the body? That is the question which I, as Rector of your high school, now propound to you. Only if you can no longer tolerate the presence of evil among you, only if you can in no circumstances endure a world in which injustice exists, are you worthy to receive Madame Zachanassian's billion and fulfill the condition bound up with this gift. If not—(*Wild applause. He gestures desperately for silence*) If not, then God have mercy on us!

(*The* TOWNSMEN *crowd around him, ambiguously, in a mood somewhat between threat and congratulation. He takes his seat, utterly crushed, exhausted by his effort. The* BURGO-MASTER *advances and takes charge once again. Order is restored*)

Burgomaster. Anton Schill—(*The* PO-LICEMAN *gives* SCHILL *a shove.* SCHILL *gets up*) Anton Schill, it is through you that this gift is offered to the town. Are you willing that this offer should be accepted?

(SCHILL *mumbles something*)

Radio Reporter (*Steps to his side*). You'll have to speak up a little, Herr Schill.

Schill. Yes.

Burgomaster. Will you respect our decision in the matter before us?

Schill. I will respect your decision.

Burgomaster. Then I proceed to the vote. All those who are in accord with the terms on which this gift is offered will signify the same by raising their right hands. (*After a moment, the* POLICEMAN *raises his hand. Then one by one the others. Last of all, very slowly, the* TEACHER) All against? The offer is accepted. I now solemnly call upon you, fellow townsmen, to declare in the face of all the world that you take this action, not out of love for worldly gain . . .

Townsmen (*In chorus*). Not out of love for worldly gain . . .

Burgomaster. But out of love for the right.

Townsmen. But out of love for the right.

Burgomaster (*Holds up his hand, as if taking an oath*). We join together, now, as brothers . . .

Townsmen (*Hold up their hands*). We join together, now, as brothers . . .

Burgomaster. To purify our town of guilt . . .

Townsmen. To purify our town of guilt . . .

Burgomaster. And to reaffirm our faith . . .

Townsmen. And to reaffirm our faith . . .

Burgomaster. In the eternal power of justice.

Townsmen. In the eternal power of justice.

(*The lights go off suddenly*)

Schill (*A scream*). Oh, God!

Voice. I'm sorry, Herr Burgomaster. We seem to have blown a fuse. (*The lights go on*) Ah—there we are. Would you mind doing that last bit again?

Burgomaster. Again?

The Cameraman (*Walks forward*). Yes, for the newsreel.

Burgomaster. Oh, the newsreel. Certainly.

The Cameraman. Ready now? Right.

Burgomaster. And to reaffirm our faith . . .

Townsmen. And to reaffirm our faith . . .

Burgomaster. In the eternal power of justice.

Townsmen. In the eternal power of justice.

The Cameraman (*To his* ASSISTANT). It was better before, when he screamed "Oh, God."

(*The* ASSISTANT *shrugs*)

Burgomaster. Fellow citizens of Güllen, I declare this meeting adjourned. The ladies and gentlemen of the press will find refreshments served downstairs, with the compliments of the town council. The exits lead directly to the restaurant.

The Cameraman. Thank you.

(*The* NEWSMEN *go off with alacrity. The* TOWNSMEN *remain on the stage.* SCHILL *gets up*)

Policeman (*Pushes* SCHILL *down*). Sit down.

Schill. Is it to be now?

Policeman. Naturally, now.

Schill. I thought it might be best to have it at my house.

Policeman. It will be here.

Burgomaster. Lower the lights. (*The lights dim*) Are they all gone?

Voice. All gone.

Burgomaster. The gallery?

Second Voice. Empty.

Burgomaster. Lock the doors.

The Voice. Locked here.

Second Voice. Locked here.

Burgomaster. Form a lane. (*The men form a lane. At the end stands the* ATHLETE *in elegant white slacks, a red scarf around his singlet*) Pastor. Will you be so good?

(*The* PASTOR *walks slowly to* SCHILL)

Pastor. Anton Schill, your heavy hour has come.

Schill. May I have a cigarette?

Pastor. Cigarette, Burgomaster.

Burgomaster. Of course, With pleasure. And a good one.

(*He gives his case to the* PASTOR, *who offers it to* SCHILL. *The* POLICEMAN *lights the cigarette. The* PASTOR *returns the case*)

Pastor. In the words of the prophet Amos—

Schill. Please—

(*He shakes his head*)

Pastor. You're no longer afraid?

Schill. No. I'm not afraid.

Pastor. I will pray for you.

Schill. Pray for us all.

(*The* PASTOR *bows his head*)

Burgomaster. Anton Schill, stand up!

(SCHILL *hesitates*)

Policeman. Stand up, you swine!

Burgomaster. Schultz, please.

Policeman. I'm sorry. I was carried away. (SCHILL *gives the cigarette to the* POLICEMAN. *Then he walks slowly to the center of the stage and turns his back on the audience*) Enter the lane.

(SCHILL *hesitates a moment. He goes slowly into the lane of silent men. The* ATHLETE *stares at him from the opposite end.* SCHILL *looks in turn at the hard faces of those who surround him, and sinks slowly to his knees. The lane contracts silently into a knot as the men close in and crouch over. Complete silence. The knot of men pulls back slowly, coming down-*

stage. Then it opens. Only the Doctor is left in the center of the stage,
kneeling by the corpse, over which
the Teacher's gown has been spread.
The Doctor rises and takes off his
stethoscope)

Pastor. Is it all over?
Doctor. Heart failure.
Burgomaster. Died of joy.
All. Died of joy.

(The Townsmen turn their backs on
the corpse and at once light cigarettes. A cloud of smoke rises over
them. From the left comes Claire
Zachanassian, dressed in black, followed by Bobby. She sees the corpse.
Then she walks slowly to center stage
and looks down at the body of
Schill)

Claire. Uncover him. (Bobby uncovers
Schill's face. She stares at it a long
moment. She sighs) Cover his face.

(Bobby covers it. Claire goes out, up
center. Bobby takes the check from
his wallet, holds it out peremptorily
to the Burgomaster, who walks over
from the knot of silent men. He holds
out his hand for the check. The lights
fade. At once the warning bell is
heard, and the scene dissolves into
the setting of the railway station. The
gradual transformation of the shabby
town into a thing of elegance and
beauty is now accomplished. The
railway station glitters with neon
lights and is surrounded with garlands, bright posters and flags. The
Townsfolk, men and women, now in
brand new clothes, form themselves
into a group in front of the station.
The sound of the approaching train
grows louder. The train stops)

Station Master. Güllen-Rome Express.
All aboard, please. (The church bells
start pealing. Men appear with
trunks and boxes, a procession which
duplicates that of the lady's arrival,
but in inverse order. Then come the
Two Blind Men, then Bobby, and
Mike and Max carrying the coffin.
Lastly Claire. She is dressed in
modish black. Her head is high, her
face as impassive as that of an ancient idol. The procession crosses the
stage and goes off. The people bow
in silence as the coffin passes. When
Claire and her retinue have boarded
the train, the Station Master blows
a long blast) 'Bo—ard!

(He holds up his paddle. The train
starts and moves off slowly, picking
up speed. The crowd turns slowly,
gazing after the departing train in
complete silence. The train sounds
fade)

The curtain falls slowly

Krapp's Last Tape

SAMUEL BECKETT

INTRODUCTION

Samuel Beckett, the most original and influential playwright in the second half of the twentieth century, was born at Foxrock, near Dublin, Ireland, on Good Friday, April 13, 1906. His father, William Beckett, was a quantity surveyor in the building industry; his mother, Mary Roe Beckett, had been a nurse in a Dublin hospital. Their two sons, Frank and Samuel, were brought up in a comfortable, middle-class, Protestant home, and were sent to the Portora Royal School in Enniskillen, County Fermanagh, Ireland, where Oscar Wilde had been a pupil. Even as a child, Samuel was inclined to be serious. Looking back on his childhood he once said, "I had little talent for happiness." At another time, he put it punningly, "I was born grave." But at school, Samuel, like his brother, was an all-around athlete, and an excellent scholar as well. At Trinity College, Dublin, he continued to take an active part in sports, while majoring in Italian and French. As a student of its language, Beckett became interested in France and in 1926 went on a bicycle tour of the Loire. In 1927 he was awarded a Bachelor of Arts degree with first-class honors in modern literature. For a short time he taught at Campbell College in Belfast. Then in 1928 he became a teacher at the École Normale Supérieure in Paris and remained there until 1930.

Paris won Beckett's heart. At Sylvia Beach's avant-garde bookshop he met many literary figures, and through a friend was introduced to James Joyce. Beckett helped to translate into French the *Anna Livia Plurabelle* episode from *Finnegans Wake*, published a critical article about the book, and occasionally acted as reader to Joyce, whose eyesight was failing. From Joyce, Beckett learned to use parody, satire, irony, and puns in works of serious import. Beckett's humor is characteristically Irish in the tradition of Jonathan Swift, Bernard Shaw, and James Joyce. But comparing his technique with that of Joyce, Beckett has said, "The difference between Joyce and myself is that Joyce was a synthesizer. He tried to pack the whole world into a book, in as much detail as possible, and I am an analyzer, I try to take as much of the detail away as possible."

At the age of twenty-three, in his essay dealing with *Finnegans Wake*, Beckett said that though readers might find a work difficult to comprehend, it was the duty of the artist to express his view of life as he saw it. Beckett was soon to follow this practice in his own writing. In 1929 he won a prize for a long, almost incomprehensible poem called *Whoroscope*, which dealt with the philosopher

Descartes meditating on the subject of time and the transiency of life. At this time also he published an essay on Marcel Proust, which, like his poem, dealt with the passage of time and its corollary, memory. In this essay, Beckett says, "The artistic tendency is not expansive, but a contraction. And art is the apotheosis of solitude." At age twenty-three, apparently, he had chosen the form and content for his life and work.

In 1931 he returned to Dublin and took a Master of Arts degree at Trinity College, then joined the faculty as a teacher of French. Not finding teaching congenial, he resigned from the college in 1932 and left Ireland. He never again lived in that country, but made annual visits to his mother until her death in 1950.

In 1933 Beckett's father died and left him a small annuity. For the next four years he traveled in England, France, and Germany, doing odd jobs and rubbing elbows with tramps and wanderers. In 1937 he settled permanently in Paris, where he wrote and published short stories, poems, and a novel, *Murphy* (1938). When the Germans occupied Paris during World War II, Beckett became a member of the underground resistance movement; but by 1942 the Gestapo was on his trail and he had to flee with his French-born wife, Suzanne, to the Unoccupied Zone. For the next three years, in the south of France, he eked out a living as an agricultural laborer and spent his evenings writing his novel, *Watt*.

He returned to Paris in 1945 and began to write in French; he was trying for a stark, stripped, economical prose and found that he was able to achieve it in that language. There is something trance-like in the way Beckett works. When he writes, he goes into a state of "absence" from which he emerges barely knowing what he has done. This may help to explain how, during the next five years, in an amazing burst of creativity, Beckett was able to produce in rapid succession four novels, two plays, two books of short stories, and a book of criticism. These included the trilogy of novels: *Molloy, Malone Dies,* and *The Unnamable;* and the play, *Waiting for Godot*—all avant-garde works, unconventional in the extreme in both form and content. The novels brought their author to the attention of the literary world, but did not earn a great deal of money. In addition to being difficult to read, the subject matter did not recommend itself to the general public as it dealt with human suffering, the futility and sordidness of life, disgust at bourgeois ideals, pity for the down-and-out misfits of society, helpless old age, and death.

Then with the success of *Waiting for Godot*, Beckett achieved international fame and financial security. The play appeared first in book form in 1952, and the following year was produced in Paris by Roger Blin at the little Théâtre de Babylone on the Boulevard Raspail. It was presented in London in 1955, in New York in 1960, and has since been translated into more than twenty languages and performed in some twenty-five countries. The play is performed on a stage which is bare except for a dead-looking tree; two tramps are waiting for a nebulous figure, Godot, whom they have never seen and who in fact never arrives. One of the most unusual productions of *Waiting for Godot* took place in 1957 when a company of actors from the San Francisco Actors' Workshop, under the direction of Herbert Blau, presented it at the San Quentin penitentiary for an audience of fourteen hundred convicts, who had no difficulty in understanding the play's meaning. A prisoner realizes as clearly as do the characters in the play that life means waiting, killing time, hoping for some relief, which apparently will never come. Beckett's characteristic view of life is dark and dispiriting, but it reflects accurately the feelings of a great many people. As an agnostic, Beckett refuses to be taken in by or to settle for any comforting illusions. Without conventional characters, plot, or dialogue, *Waiting for Godot* still manages to generate profound emotions and theatrical excitement. It is Beckett's best-known work and one of the finest of all contemporary plays.

Endgame (1957), his next work for the theatre, also proved to be a notable success, although it is more brutal, bitter, and enigmatic than *Godot*, with characters who appear to be close to death and annihilation. When *Endgame* was produced at the Royal Court Theatre in London on October 28, 1958, it shared the bill with a one-acter called *Krapp's Last Tape*, a small masterpiece for a single actor and a tape-recorder.

Beckett was now writing furiously for radio, television, and the stage, and his plays were becoming shorter, sparser, and more enigmatic as he went on. Limiting himself at first to fewer than half a dozen characters, he eventually reduced the number to two, to one, and finally to a face, a mouth—and voices. From the late fifties to the early seventies, he composed more than a dozen dramatic works, among them *All That Fall* (1957), *Embers* (1959), *Happy Days* (1961), *Play* (1963), *Eh Joe* (1965), *Not I* (1972), and *That Time* (1975). During the same period he wrote many prose works and the scenario for a movie called *Film* which starred Buster Keaton. It should be noted that the movie has no dialogue and no traditional plot but is done entirely in pantomime. Beckett's plays might have served admirably for the talents of Laurel and Hardy and Charlie Chaplin, as well as for those of Buster Keaton.

To be present at the shooting of *Film* in 1964, Beckett made his only trip to New York. A reporter described the playwright, who was then 58, as tall, slim, and lithe, with a long, lined face, topped by brows that wrinkled as he talked in his musical tenor voice. Beckett's eyes are light blue and he wears steel-rimmed spectacles; failing sight makes it difficult for him to read for sustained periods. He is energetic in his movements, and a rapid walker. One report quotes Beckett as saying, "A frightful experience, New York!" But another states that he very much enjoyed Greenwich Village, the Bowery, and Harlem—all of which he visited before returning to his "beloved Paris."

Samuel Beckett's work has received international recognition not only in publications and productions but also in prizes. In 1959 he won the Italia Prize for his short radio play *Embers*; in 1961 he shared the International Publishers' (Formentor) Prize with the Argentinian author, Jorge Luis Borges; and in 1969 the Swedish Academy awarded Beckett the Nobel Prize for Literature. The author, who cherishes his privacy, arranged for his French publisher, Jerome Lindon, to accept the prize for him at the ceremony in Stockholm. Beckett's work has had a noticeable influence on such contemporary playwrights as Robert Pinget, Edward Albee, Tom Stoppard, and Harold Pinter, who has called Beckett "the greatest artist of our time."

Beckett and his wife make their home in France, dividing their time between their apartment in Paris and their house in the country. Beckett contends that though he lives in Paris he is a fervent Irish patriot and republican, and feels that if he lived in Dublin he would just be sitting around in a pub. He continues to write and to translate his own plays—he is equally at home in French and English; but he has said that with each work the task becomes more difficult, each word seeming to him "an unnecessary stain on silence and nothingness."

As a writer of the avant-garde, and more particularly of the Theatre of the Absurd, Samuel Beckett does not encumber his plays with the traditional elements of the drama—development of character, cause and effect in plot, and discursive, logical dialogue. He relies instead on fantasy and dream logic expressed in visual images and accompanied by language as spare and rhythmic as lyric poetry. Beckett does not make direct statements but offers hints and suggestions in order to create in the audience a response not unlike that evoked by abstract painting. And though his themes are related to philosophy, psychology, and metaphysics, he presents them in the style of vaudeville, music hall, and circus.

Throughout his career, from his early essay on Proust to his most recent plays, Beckett has been preoccupied with the problems of being, the identity of the self, and the reclamation of time through the power of memory. In *Krapp's Last Tape* we have an excellent example of the manner in which he enables a man to review significant episodes from his past. By the clever use of a tape-recorder, a mechanical memory with supernatural power, Beckett resurrects his protagonist as a young man and in middle age, and enables him, when he is on the verge of senility, to confront those past selves. This decrepit bachelor sneers at his thirty-nine-year-old self, and joins him in contemptuous laughter at what he was at twenty-seven.

Krapp is a disillusioned old recluse whose life—as a writer, a lover, a human being—has been a failure. His appearance suggests that he is either an alcoholic or a clown. We see him in his dingy room sitting at a table on which there are a tape-recorder and several boxes containing recorded tapes. He heaves a great sigh and looks at his watch—time, his life, is passing. He goes into the darkness at the rear of the stage, has a drink, and returns to the table with a ledger which contains a record of his various tapes.

From the ledger he reads aloud a description of some of the material on Spool Five in Box Three: "Mother at rest at last," "Memorable equinox," "Farewell to love." These items appear to be related: The death of his mother in the autumn brings on a spiritual crisis in March, and during an affair that summer comes the realization that he is through with love. This is the tape Krapp wants to hear; it deals with the crucial year of his life. He rummages among the boxes of tapes on the table and finally finds what he is looking for. He switches on the machine and listens intently to the strong voice of a self-absorbed, pompous man—himself—recording on his thirty-ninth birthday, and saying that he had reached "the crest of the wave" and had "celebrated that awful occasion" in a local pub. He was glad, however, to get back to his "den." Isolated and self-centered, he has turned the

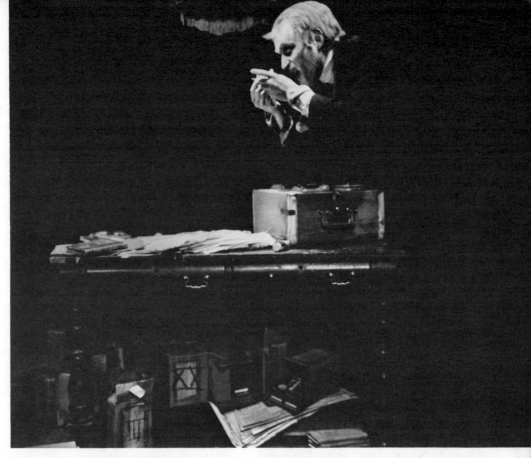

Donald Davis, peeling a banana, in the role of Krapp, which he created for the American premiere (1960). (Frederick Eberstadt)

room into a prison cell and, at seventy no different from what he was at thirty-nine, sits alone in a circle of light, surrounded by darkness.

The voice continues. The thirty-nine-year-old self has just been listening to a birthday recording he made ten or twelve years before and speaks contemptuously of himself at that time as "that young whelp," with his ridiculous aspirations and resolutions about cutting down on drink and sex. He had then been living "off and on" with a woman, considered it a hopeless business, and felt that he was well out of it. He has a good laugh at himself at twenty-seven, in which the old man joins, but when the voice asks, "What remains of all that misery?" Krapp broods.

Krapp switches off the tape at this point and goes into the darkness for two or three drinks, then returns to the machine singing, "Now the day is over . . .," a song which suggests approaching death. He resumes listening. The voice is recalling the day of his mother's death. He is sitting on a bench outside her house, watching the passers-by, among them a nursemaid wheeling a big black hooded perambulator that has a funereal look. This striking image resembles Beckett's remark, "I was born grave," as well as a line from *Waiting for Godot*: "They give birth astride of a grave, the light gleams an instant, then it's night once more."

It was a year of profound spiritual gloom, says the thirty-nine-year-old voice, until a memorable night in March—the equinox—when he had a vision, a revelation he is about to explain, but Old Krapp is bored and impatient and cuts him off. He winds the tape forward until he reaches the section he especially wants to hear: He is making love to a girl in a boat which is drifting down the stream. He listens to the tape a while, then switches off the machine and broods; it was a frightening experience, the surrender of his ego. He goes into the darkness to drink. He comes back a little unsteadily, takes a fresh tape from the drawer—Krapp's last tape, presumably—and starts to record the events of the year just past. But he begins by sneering at "that stupid bastard I took myself for thirty years ago," then he broods about the eyes of the girl in the boat. He had broken with her lest she should "take his mind off his homework"—his writing, his vision, himself.

There is little to record for the past year. It has been unproductive, empty. He asks, "What's a year now? The sour cud and the iron stool." Only seventeen copies of his book have been sold. He has gone out to the park once or twice and has sat there alone. He has re-read a book called *Effie*—possibly one of his own—and wept; it is about a girl with whom he thinks he could have been happy. A more recent woman, Fanny, a "bony old ghost of a whore," has come in a couple of times and has marvelled at his ability to perform at his age. He has gone to Vespers once, but went to sleep and fell off the pew. Even in his rejection of religion, Krapp is made to play the clown. He thinks it is time for him to finish his booze and go to bed. There he can lie awake and recall scenes from the past—"All that old misery. Once wasn't enough for you."

He rips the new tape off the machine, throws it aside, and returns to the other. He prefers to let his mind dwell on the girl in the boat, and listens again to the love scene, this time allowing the tape to run on to the finish. He was saying, at thirty-nine, "Perhaps my best years are gone. When there was a chance of happiness. But I wouldn't want them back. Not with the fire in me now. No, I wouldn't want them back." Krapp remains motionless, lost in revery, while the tape runs on in silence. Krapp will die as he has lived, alone. Beckett told Martin Held, who acted the part of Krapp in the Berlin production of the play, "The character is eaten up by dreams. But without sentimentality. There's no resignation in him. It's the end. He sees very clearly that he's through with his work, with love, and with religion."

Beckett is much occupied in the play with the symbolism of dark and light which represent the sense and the spirit. The light signifies birth, creation, salvation: the dark, sin, death, and damnation. The incompatibility of the spiritual and sensual sides of Krapp's nature is rendered theatrically by a separation of light and dark, and he moves to and fro between them. Related to the dark and the light are the colors black and white, which appear to have a similar significance: Krapp wears black trousers and a black vest, a white shirt and white shoes; the nursemaids are in starched white uniforms and wheel black perambulators; and a little white dog plays with a black ball. In his notes for the Berlin production of the play, Beckett says, "Note that if the giving of the black ball to the white dog represents the sacrifice of sense to spirit, the form here too is that of a mingling." One of the dominant colors in the world of Beckett is grey.

Steeped in a sense of uprootedness, nostalgia, impotence, and despair, *Krapp's Last Tape* nevertheless satisfies the spectator by providing him with an uncanny insight into the life of a self-defeating, alienated man. And the play will continue to have meaning for twentieth-century man so long as he is afflicted with an over-powering sense of boredom and frustration. Beckett's play is a mirror that clearly reflects his audiences' features.

THE PRODUCTION RECORD

In 1958, while Beckett was listening to a radio broadcast of selections from his works being read by Patrick Magee, he conceived the idea of writing a play spe-cially for the actor whose rich Irish inflections impressed him. "The Magee Mono-logue" was the working title of the play that became *Krapp's Last Tape.* On Octo-ber 28 of that year the new piece was presented for the first time at the Royal Court Theatre in London, appropriately starring Magee, and directed by Donald McWhinnie.

The American premiere of the work was presented, on a double bill with Albee's *Zoo Story,* under the auspices of Richard Barr, H. B. Lutz, and Harry Joe Brown, Jr., at the Provincetown Playhouse in New York, on January 14, 1960; it was acted by Donald Davis, was directed by Alan Schneider, and had scenery by William Ritman. Robert Brustein, writing in the *New Republic* (2/22/60), spoke enthusiastically of the play as Beckett's "best dramatic poem about the old age of the world," and called it flawless, economical, haunting, and harrowing.

On March 22, 1960, the play was put on at the Récamier Théâtre in Paris under Roger Blin's direction with R. J. Chauffard as Krapp. The critic M. Gautier made much of the play's "melancholy beauty."

Krapp's Last Tape has been presented innumerable times both here and abroad; in New York City alone, in its various revivals, it has rung up about nine hundred performances. In 1961 it was being done simultaneously by professional companies in New York, Washington, D.C., Los Angeles, and San Francisco. And in that same year Beckett collaborated with the Rumanian-born composer Marcel Mihalovici, who provided a musical score for an operatic version of the play.

On October 5, 1969, what has been called by some the "definitive" production of the play, was presented at the Workshop of the Schiller Theatre in Berlin, acted by Martin Held and directed by Beckett. In an interview with Ronald Hayman (*The Times,* London, 4/25/70), Held said that many of Beckett's char-acters seemed to have a strong connection with the playwright himself. Held had observed that one of the fingers on Beckett's right hand was stiff, and he decided to crook the knuckles of one of his own fingers during the performance. But being afraid of offending Beckett, he groped his way very gradually, doing it a bit more obviously each day until Beckett noticed the mimicry and said "Good!"

Beckett has also directed two productions of the play in Paris, the last one in

April, 1975, at the Petit Théâtre d'Orsay, with Pierre Chabert as Krapp. In an article written for the French review *Aesthétique*, Chabert spoke of the playwright's
methods as a director: "I must underline the extraordinary and minute care with
which Beckett stages this work, his perpetual search for a special intonation, a
special way of making a word emerge, accentuating or swallowing one of the syllables, making a pause precede or follow it, or perhaps making the voice drop
after a verb in order to suggest the action which has been described; for example,
in the story of the boat: 'I bent over her to get [her eyes] in the shadow and they
opened. (*Pause. Low.*) Let me in. (*Pause.*)'—the voice drops and the phrase is
drawn out. . . . Beckett was very insistent on this point: the necessity of finding
the right way to deliver certain words or certain phrases." As an artist Beckett is
meticulous.

New productions of *Krapp's Last Tape* continue to be offered in schools and
colleges as well as in professional stage and television productions around the
world.

AVANT-GARDE AND ABSURDIST THEATER

The playwright whose ideas and technical innovations are in advance of his
time, as Ibsen's were, is called avant-garde until audiences catch up with his
thinking; but the absurdist playwright never completely joins the ranks of the
conventional—is always accounted avant-garde—because his concepts, characters,
dialogue, and form remain incongruous, ridiculous, illogical, and a departure from
accepted reasoning and propriety. And yet the absurdist dramatist is, not unlike
Ibsen, a social commentator, who consciously employs unusual techniques in
order to impress his personal vision of life upon the theatregoing public in as
forceful, as startling, a manner as possible.

Alfred Jarry (1873–1907), the earliest master of what we now call absurdist
drama, made his appearance in the last decade of the nineteenth century. At
fifteen, Jarry wrote a puppet play that satirized the stupidity and cowardice of
one of his teachers, whom he used as a symbol for the bourgeoisie. Out of this
work grew a series of plays dealing with the exploits of a gross character called
Ubu—a stupid, bestial monster—who represented the animal nature in man. In
Jarry's masterpiece, *Ubu Roi* (1896), Ubu makes himself King of Poland, kills and
tortures the citizens, or drives them out of the country—foreshadowing Hitler.
Jarry's dialogue was wild, extravagant, and obscene; and the scenery and costumes designed for his play resembled caricatures of a comic strip. *Ubu Roi* had
only two performances but left an indelible impression on those who saw it. The
play had no immediate successors, but Eugene Ionesco has become Jarry's most
important disciple.

At the turn of the century, August Strindberg, in his dream plays, introduced
theatricalist techniques to the stage and established the principles of expressionism and surrealism, before those terms were known. Although *A Dream Play* and
The Ghost Sonata were more widely attended than the Ubu plays, the general
public could neither understand nor accept those "strange" works, and would not
for another dozen years.

It was World War I, and the feelings of confusion, neuroticism, and despair it engendered, that provided the impetus for absurdist theater. Many fixed ideas were revised, and a number of sensitive souls were shocked into the belief that not only God, but reason too, was dead. The social upheaval created by the war, which had had an unsettling effect on the general population, was felt most strongly by sensitive dramatists and directors. They knew that a play reflected the world and that if the world was shattered, then looking at the stage would be like facing a broken mirror. The image would have to be absurd! This accounts for the many strange, unusual, startling "absurdist" techniques—anti-intellectual, abstract, eclectic, symbolic—adopted by theater artists in the 1920s. Most of the plays were called "tragicomic farces" and were filled with a bitter, black humor.

The generation of directors that came after Stanislavsky felt liberated by the Russian Revolution and mounted plays in a variety of non-naturalistic styles. Vsevolod Meyerhold was the most creative of the experimentalists; he attempted to mirror the mechanistic world in his sets and in the movement of his actors. In a constructivist setting, a complex arrangement of pipes and platforms, his actors performed in a highly stylized and mechanical way. Meyerhold's directorial ideas were based on the art of improvisation. A script was merely a springboard for his conceptions, and the actors were his puppets. At his school each day's work began with the practice of "biomechanics"—exercises intended to train the actor's body, tone up his nervous system, sharpen his reflexes, and develop his energy and control. Meyerhold felt that the most important subjects for the actor to master were athletics, acrobatics, and music. Ideas similar to Meyerhold's were later expressed by Antonin Artaud, Jerzy Grotowski, and other theatricalist directors. One of Meyerhold's students, Nikolai Okhlopkov, founded the Realistic Theatre in Moscow and abolished the fixed stage; this was an early attempt to force actors and audience to mingle in what is currently called an environment.

Erwin Piscator, who helped to found the Proletarian Theatre in Berlin, drew inspiration from the work of the Soviet directors. Piscator rejected realism with its presentation of characters as unique individuals who would arouse the empathy of the audience; and adopted instead the methods of Meyerhold, which turned the actors into puppets and acrobats and the scenery into bare scaffolds, the better to portray collective man in an age of machines. To these principles Piscator added the ideas of the Soviet "agitprop" (agitation and propaganda) theaters, which presented plays in documentary form, in order to indoctrinate the masses as well as entertain them. What Piscator wound up with was Epic Theatre, the name he gave to the historical plays he produced by mixing live actors with films, charts and graphs, slides, music, song, dance, and narrators. By these methods Piscator achieved an "alienation effect," which constantly reminded the audience that it was watching a play and not reality, and thus prevented the spectators from *feeling* for the characters and started them *thinking* about their social, economic, and political problems. Epic theatre—also called "total theater" and "multimedia" —was adopted by Bertolt Brecht, who elaborated the theory and produced many plays in that style.

Another strain of absurdist theater was introduced by dadaism, an avant-garde movement among poets and artists in Zurich, Switzerland, that Tristan Tzara brought to Paris where it blossomed for a while. Dadaism was dedicated to the illogical and irrational in art as a true reflection of contemporary life. By the use of automatic writing (that is, putting down ideas that came into the mind regardless of logic or intelligibility), the dadaists claimed to be expressing their inmost feelings in the truest possible way. Yvan Goll, an expressionist-dadaist playwright, said, "The monotony and stupidity of human beings are so enormous that they can be adequately represented only by enormities. Let the new drama be an enormity." Goll's statement expresses one of the aims of the Theatre of the Absurd.

The surrealists opposed and succeeded the dadaists, and went even further in attempting to embarrass and frighten the bourgeoisie by depicting in various genres an insane world in the process of disintegration. In the mid-twenties, André Breton, the leader of the Surrealists, spoke of liberating the mind from all rational control and of producing works of art in a dreamlike condition. It was at this time in Germany that Strindbergian dramaturgy had its greatest vogue; the appeal of expressionism was mainly to the emotions through the use of pictorial and poetic effects—lyrical dialogue, music, lighting, choral speaking, non-naturalistic scenery, and fantasy costumes.

Expressionism also had a profound effect on the actor-director-poet, Antonin Artaud (1896–1948). Artaud began as a surrealist but withdrew from that camp and became a seminal figure in absurdist drama—not so much as a result of his theatrical productions as of his theoretical writings. Artaud was the founder of the Théâtre Alfred Jarry, and mounted several notable absurdist productions, which caused enormous scandals and received a great deal of notoriety. Artaud drew his company of young performers from among the students of Charles Dullin, of whom he himself was one, and put on such works as Strindberg's *Dream Play*. It was Artaud's practice as a director to use the text of a play as a goad to his imagination and inspiration, and to improvise as he went along. In his estimation, the creativity of the director was the most important element of the production; he sought for movement and speech that was anarchistic and unusual. No two performances were alike. In one of his manifestoes, Artaud, and his associate Robert Aron, wrote: "A production that repeats itself every evening according to rites that are always the same, always identical to themselves, can no longer win our approval. In the theatre we wish to create, Chance will be our god. We are not afraid of failure, of catastrophe. . . . The director who obeys no rules but follows his own inspiration will or will not make the happy find that is necessary for us." These words have had a strong influence on many contemporary absurdist directors.

Artaud's primary aim was to arouse the emotions of the audience by a return to myth and magic, which expose the dark and violent side of man's nature and produce a Theatre of Cruelty. As Artaud conceived it, the theatre was not an escape from life, but a reattachment to it—fearful as life was. He wrote: "If there is still one hellish, truly accursed thing in our time, it is our artistic dallying with forms, instead of being like victims burnt at the stake, signaling through the flames." These words, written during World War II, were an urgent plea that the theater reflect the facts of current life—the slaughter, devastation, and suffering that had become the commonplaces of the world.

After Auschwitz and Hiroshima, men have seemed to grow cold, callous, and withdrawn, sensible only of feelings of nausea, anxiety, and boredom; common reactions have been violence, escape, or apathy, with people viewing murder as a spectator sport, using sex and drugs as a way out, or hiding behind dark glasses. It is no wonder that the violent, the grotesque, and the irrational have provided the subject matter for absurdist drama. In today's theater, realism is no longer considered adequate for an in-depth portrayal of the absurdity, horror, and mean-inglessness of our lives, computerization having reduced the individual to a hole in an IBM card. And so in the plays of Eugene Ionesco, Jean Genet, and Samuel Beckett, as well as in those of such younger writers as Robert Wilson and Sam Shepard, we see a reflection of the despairing, volatile, and fragmented nature of our culture. Plot no longer consists of cause and effect, development of character, and logical, syllogistic dialogue; instead, the "plot" of the avant-garde play is circular and inconclusive, the characters are types and symbols, the dialogue is repetitive, obscure, or ridiculous. The absurdist playwright presents his personal visions in poetic images.

"The Theater of the Absurd," says Martin Esslin, "is concerned essentially with the evocation of concrete poetic images designed to communicate to the audience the sense of perplexity that their authors feel when confronted with the human condition, we must judge the success or failure of these works by the degree to which they succeed in communicating this mixture of poetry and grotesque, tragi-comic horror. And this in turn will depend on the quality and power of the poetic images evoked."

Having entered the Space Age, the horrors of nuclear threats, of growing crime, of official misconduct, seem unspeakable; while astounding technological advances in transplantation of organs of the body, and transportation to distant planets, leave us speechless. This state of affairs helps to account, perhaps, for the development of nonverbal drama, which often entirely eliminates the interchange of speech and relies heavily on music, chants, shouts, sound, gesture, and move-ment (mime, dance, and acrobatics). Performances of this sort have been var-iously called happenings, events, pieces, and so on. Many contemporary directors look with scorn upon the traditional playhouse, seeing it as an antiquated build-ing where classical and conventional modern texts can only be recited in a routine and stultifying manner. For their productions they want no stage, no sharp line of demarcation between the actor and the audience. The actor must be able to move freely around the spectator, speak to him directly, touch him, and startle him by frequent surprise effects. The primary intention is to create a physi-cal and emotional response in the audience. The place of performance is now quite often not an "old-fashioned" theater, but a location chosen for its availability or suitability; it may be a large room, a converted garage, an art gallery, a street, a park, the subway, or any other "environment" where spectators can gather. And if no one happens to be around to catch the performance, the players themselves, according to the view of one avant-garde director, constitute the audience.

Today's innovative directors, the disciples of Jarry, Meyerhold, and Artaud, are enjoying an unprecedented eminence in the theater. Very often they substitute their own aims and concepts for those of the playwright, not hesitating to mutilate the text in order to demonstrate their own creativity. Yet such men as Jerzy Grotowski, Peter Brook, Joseph Chaikin, Tom O'Horgan, and Andrei Serban have created impressive productions while leaving their personal imprint on the plays they have staged.

"It seems sensible to look upon the avant-garde theater," says Leonard C. Pronko, "not as the answer to all the ills of modern drama, but as another adventure in the theater, a new effort to revitalize a theater largely dominated for over sixty years by realism, naturalism, and the thesis play: a return to primitive sources, a search for new techniques, a challenge to contemporary drama to examine itself, to seek new frontiers. . . . Whether the avant-garde drama survives in its present form for many years or not, it will have played an important role in renewing western drama at mid-twentieth century. And we may be sure that, within another generation or two, a new courageous and outrageous drama will spring up to replace it, rebelling against whatever new conventions it may have created."

DIRECTING *Krapp's Last Tape*
An Interview with Alan Schneider

While talking with a friend at the Zurich Schauspielhaus in the summer of 1954, Alan Schneider heard the name of Samuel Beckett for the first time. *Waiting for Godot* had been produced at the Schauspielhaus, and his friend suggested that Schneider look up the play when he got to Paris. A few weeks later Schneider discovered that *Godot* was being done at the Théâtre de Babylone, a small, off-beat house on the Left Bank. Schneider attended the play and found a handful of people in the audience. Beckett was then totally unknown to the theatregoing public. On his second visit, the following night, Schneider encountered only a few more inquisitive souls. But the play held him spellbound; he was mystified and totally captivated. He made every effort—by notes, by phone, and through friends—to get in touch with the playwright, to no avail. Beckett could not be reached and Schneider returned to America.

In 1955, when he had practically given up on the play, he was approached by producer Michael Myerberg, who had obtained the American rights to *Godot*. Thornton Wilder had recommended Schneider to Myerberg as the perfect director for the play, and Myerberg hired him. Schneider was soon on his way to Europe, and this time made contact with Beckett; they "hit it off," began to see each other, and eventually went together several times to see the production of *Godot*, which was then playing in London and which Beckett thought was "Ahl wrahng!" The playwright and the director held many discussions about the play.

Schneider returned to the United States and, after encountering innumerable obstacles, managed to get the play on at the Coconut Grove Theatre in Miami,

Florida. Advertised by an enterprising publicity man as "the laugh sensation of two continents," the play promptly "failed." Schneider was disheartened because he felt he had let Beckett down, but the playwright, nothing daunted, entrusted him with his next play, *Endgame*, which opened at the Cherry Lane Theatre in New York and proved to be a notable success.

The critics have not always been kind to Beckett, and that was particularly true at the beginning of his career as a dramatist. Commenting wryly about Beckett's detractors, Schneider has said: "They begin by saluting Play A as 'awful.' When Play B comes along, that too is awful, and not nearly as good as A was. Play C is then dismissed as being awful, worse than B, which though good is not a patch on A, which in the interval has become a masterpiece." This retrospective appreciation continues, while Schneider's devotion to Beckett and his work is unwavering, and their collaboration and friendship persist to the present time.

In 1957, Beckett's television play, *All That Fall*, was aired on the BBC Third Programme. Beckett attended the tapings and was fascinated by the possibility of using a tape-recorder for dramatic purposes. He had in mind a play for the actor Patrick Magee. Beckett borrowed a machine from the BBC and played around with it while writing *Krapp's Last Tape*. He sent the completed script to Schneider, who was the first one to see it, and who promptly boarded the *Queen Mary*, heading for Paris. There he would hold lengthy discussions with the playwright about the new piece.

Schneider makes it clear that Beckett never "explains" his work; he expects his plays to speak for themselves. Beckett is primarily and uniquely a poet. "His meanings exist," says Schneider, "not to be pinned down, but to be felt, glimpsed, sensed, experienced."

To Schneider, *Krapp's Last Tape* is "a portrait of the artist as an old man." The play, says the director, is a metaphor for the life of a creative writer, who, instead of recording his thoughts and experiences in a journal, puts them on a tape-recorder. Krapp has noted what he considered important at various stages of his life. He gave up human relationships in order to be a writer, and playing back his youthful voice is for him like communing with a stranger. In his old age, as an unrecognized artist who has sold only seventeen copies of his book in the last year, he is ready to give up his intellectual pursuits and settle for old memories.

When he is ready to record the events of the recent past, Krapp's notes don't seem very impressive or important to him and he discards them, but the more distant and durable memories—gathering holly at Christmas and listening to Sunday morning church bells—come unbidden from the depths of his psyche. Tyrone Guthrie, the director, once told Schneider, "We have to struggle for our second-rate ideas, but first-rate ones come to us spontaneously."

"It was extremely difficult to find a producer for *Krapp's Last Tape*," Schneider recalls. "And no actor was interested in playing it either. I offered the part to literally dozens of actors, among them Eli Wallach, Michael Strong, and Hume Cronyn. All of them turned it down for various and sundry reasons: They had never heard of Beckett, they didn't understand the play, they couldn't see themselves in the part, they had prior commitments. Producers had similar reactions, and I couldn't find a theater that would house it. Finally I turned to Barney Rosset, Beckett's American publisher, who knew the manager of a nightclub called The Five Spot, located somewhere in the neighborhood of the Bowery. It was our wild idea to put the play on as part of the club's entertainment. We would use a back room and stop the floor-show five times during the night, and in those five spots offer the play. The manager agreed at first to our idea, but eventually reneged." Thinking back on the incident, Schneider says he is very glad that that production never took place.

Schneider then learned that Richard Barr, a producer who came from Washington, D.C., had acquired the rights to Edward Albee's one-act play *The Zoo Story.* He asked Barr to read the Beckett play and, if he liked it, to consider doing the two one-acters on a double bill. Barr agreed, was enthusiastic about *Krapp's Last Tape,* and started to look for a theater. He booked the Provincetown Playhouse in Greenwich Village. For the role of Krapp, Barr suggested Donald Davis, a Canadian actor, who was also known to Schneider as he had directed a television production of *Oedipus the King* in which Davis had played Tiresias. Davis agreed to play Krapp. Schneider had really wanted an older man for the part, but he knew that Davis, a first-rate actor, would be able to portray old age and had, besides, a rich and flexible voice that would work well on tape.

When he started rehearsals for *Krapp's Last Tape,* Schneider was also rehearsing *The Cherry Orchard* at the Arena Stage in Washington, D.C. Schneider would rehearse the Chekhov play at the theater until four in the afternoon and then go to Barr's mother's apartment and work on the Beckett play with Barr and Davis until ten or eleven at night.

"The first thing we worked on was the tape," says Schneider. "We wanted a perfect recording for the production, but that entailed a great deal of effort. We were trying to capture the character, timbre, and tempo of the voice of a thirty-nine-year-old man as it would resemble and differ from the voice of the same man at seventy. So we had Davis read the lines over and over, with varying pitches and inflections, and made about ninety tapes before we were satisfied. Then we had to decide whether the actor would handle the tape himself during the performance, or just pretend he was doing so, while the stage manager, off-stage, would run the actual sound.

Davis expressed a wish to work the tape-recorder himself, and proved to be perfect at the task. Colored leaders were inserted into the tape to indicate the various cuts, and Davis, who had a quick eye, never missed a cue. (One celebrated actor, who later appeared in the play, got so tangled up in the tape that the performance had to be called off.) When Hume Cronyn acted the part in the Forum Theatre production—he won an Obie (Off-Broadway Award) for it—he found that running the machine distracted him and interfered with his characterization, and preferred to have the stage manager deal with the sound. During the performance Cronyn ran a blank tape back and forth, just stopping it anywhere, while the stage manager, who had to be alert and precise in picking up the cues, played the actual tape."

With the tape completed to his satisfaction, Schneider was able to move ahead with the rest of the play. His aim was to strive for believability and the emotional involvement of the audience. "The necessary intertwining of comic and serious tones in Chekhov is matched by a parallel necessity in Beckett," says Schneider, "though framed in a more formal and less naturalistic pattern. *Krapp* to me has always seemed almost Chekhovian in its blend of emotional colors. . . . In fact, every Beckett play possesses its own specific tonality, its special texture; that which distinguishes it from anyone else's work. Almost any page of Beckett can be immediately identified as his, because of his particular vision of the universe and of mortal man's frail fate in it. But also because of his specific technique of organizing and orchestrating the formal elements involved; the sparseness and simplicity of his language, juxtaposed against its passages of poetic musicality; the balance and tension of its various rhythms and sounds and images; his repetitions. The constant interplay of parallel and opposing ideas and themes; counterpoint, auditory and visual. . . . It is only through constant attention to both Beckettian "texture" and to the "local situation" (who the characters are as human beings and what their human situation is) that his plays can be presented faithfully."

About the opening business with the bananas, Schneider says, "It may have phallic connotations, suggest a circus clown or an ape, but it is really the only oral satisfaction the old codger has." As to his constantly checking the time: "Krapp looks at his watch at regular intervals not just because he is bored or wants to know what time it is, but to see how long it has been since he had his last drink. Then he goes for another one." And the end of the play, with the old man listening repeatedly to his favorite portion of the tape, represents a kind of post-mortem existence which is barren except for the recurrent reminder of "the emotional warmth of his former sexual relations."

When asked if the play works well in any type of theater, Schneider said, "The type of theater—proscenium, thrust stage, or round—is not as important as its size. This is a very intimate play and the theater should be small so that the audience can be close to the actor and, in effect, share the same space. The audience should be able to hear and see everything, and since the actions and reactions are subtle and are performed in an area surrounded by darkness, great concentration is necessary. It is easier to achieve the required darkness on a proscenium or thrust stage than in the round; but the play will work satisfactorily in the latter type of theater if the actor is seated in one corner of the playing area, with his back to an aisle, and the rest of the stage is left in darkness." Light and darkness are important in this play, as Beckett has indicated in his notes.

While Beckett himself was directing *Krapp's Last Tape* in Germany, he made several alterations in the text. He called for a small curtained-off room with a light in it at the rear of the stage. From that room, at the beginning of the play, Krapp brings on the tape-recorder and the boxes containing the tapes. "I stick very closely to the author's text," says Schneider, "so most of the productions of *Krapp* I've directed have had no back room. But after Beckett revised the script, I introduced the new material into the production when I did it with Cronyn at the Forum. For that occasion—the Beckett Festival at Lincoln Center—I asked Beckett if he had a companion piece for Jessica Tandy (Mrs. Cronyn) to be presented along wih *Krapp,* and he obliged with the stunning one-acter *Not I.*"

Alan Schneider has made a television version of *Krapp's Last Tape*, starring the late Jack MacGowran, one of Beckett's favorite actors, but it has not as yet been released. With his recent production of two new Beckett works, *Footfalls* and *That Time*, Schneider remains, indisputably, the Irish playwright's "authorized" American director.

Krapp's Last Tape AT THE PROVINCETOWN*
A Review by Brooks Atkinson

When Samuel Beckett's *Krapp's Last Tape* opened in a double bill at the Provincetown Playhouse on January 14, everyone appeared to be pleased. To judge by random comments, everyone has been pleased since.

Since Mr. Beckett's previous dramas, *Waiting for Godot* and *Endgame*, did not please everybody, the success of the current play is gratifying. He has met with "public acceptance"—a cant phrase now popular in the trade marts.

Krapp's Last Tape may be more popular than its predecessors because it is short and because it is simple to understand. All that happens is that a rancid, decomposing old man listens to a tape-recording of scenes from his jubilant youth. The drama consists in the visual contrast between his wretched old age and the images of romance evoked by the tape recording.

If there is any symbolism in this sketch of misery and hopelessness, it is more intelligible than the obscure symbolism of the long plays. It is part of the common experience of life. It is also grimly comic. Mr. Beckett's molelike view of life always has a mirthless irony. He assumes that life is a grotesque practical joke that the universe plays on everybody.

Half the credit for the success of *Krapp's Last Tape* belongs to Alan Schneider, who has staged it with just the right mingling of mystery, dreariness, and sullen humor, and to Donald Davis, who plays the sole character provided in the script. Mr. Davis, from Toronto, is an actor who has had classical experience at the Stratford Shakespearean Festival in Ontario. Although the part of Krapp is scarcely a classical role, Mr. Davis gives him a dimension beyond the surface of life and portrays character in terms of motion and mood rather than dialogue. Everything he does as he blunders through the clutter of the setting is significant and amusing.

Since *Krapp's Last Tape* is short, simple, and pungent, its success requires no esoteric explanation. But perhaps there is a further reason. Mr. Beckett's world of nothingness is no longer strange. In large measure it has won "public acceptance."

To some people it seemed to be a private joke when *Waiting for Godot* confronted them in 1956. Since the symbolism was impossible to ravel out, some theatergoers regarded that odd drama as a fake. But the grisly power of *Endgame*, added to the meaningful torpor of *Waiting for Godot*, indicates that Mr. Beckett is a serious writer. He also has written several novels, *Watt* and *Malone Dies* among them, that communicate the same sense of absurdity, futility, and weariness.

Mr. Beckett's characters do not rebel against the hopelessness of their environ-

* From *The New York Times*, January 31, 1960. Reprinted by permission.

ment. They are resigned to their position as counters in an apathetic game played at their expense by a force that is not concerned about them. Nothingness is a positive force in their lives.

"What distressed Watt," Mr. Beckett wrote in *Watt* in 1946, "was not so much that he did not know what had happened, for he did not care what had happened, as that nothing had happened, a thing that was nothing had happened."

Although we are under no compulsion to accept this view of life as definitive, we have to accept it as a rational point of view because a serious writer believes it and has supported it ably in plays and novels. We do not have to regard Picasso's distortions of face and figure as definitive portraits of people, but we have abundant evidence throughout his long career that Picasso is a serious painter who sees things in life that escape most of us. In the final analysis, the burden of proof is on Beckett and Picasso. But we have to be ready to consider the proof when they provide it.

One more thing has to be said. If life is nothingness, why does Mr. Beckett go to the trouble to write about it? It would be so much easier to let go. This is the familiar paradox involved in literary professions of futility. *Krapp's Last Tape*, as well as Mr. Beckett's other plays, prove one thing: Art is not nothingness in his view. He believes in art. Through art he contributes ideas to the community. There is always one step that he refuses to take: the final step into nothingness.

The act of writing is in itself a declaration of faith in something. In the center of a meaningless universe Mr. Beckett still wants to be heard. To this extent he—unlike his characters—resists the surly indifference of the barren world he writes about.

A Solo Performance
An Interview with Hume Cronyn

Hume Cronyn, winner of an Obie [Off-Broadway] Award for his portrayal of Krapp in the 1972 production of the play, was one of the first actors to be offered the role when Alan Schneider was casting the original American production in 1959. Cronyn was forced to turn down the part at that time because of other commitments. About a dozen years later, however, the play came again to Cronyn's attention and he approached Schneider with the idea of getting up a production. Schneider was well acquainted with Beckett and his work, and would be a valuable member of the team. Because of the brevity of *Krapp's Last Tape*, another short play was needed to fill out the evening, and it was hoped that Beckett could supply one that would be suitable for Jessica Tandy (Mrs. Cronyn). Tandy, accompanied by Schneider and Barney Rosset, went to Paris, called on Beckett, and came back triumphant with *Not I*, a short play for one woman, eminently suited to Tandy's virtuosity, which would have its world premiere on a double bill with *Krapp*.

"Then began a search for a theater," said Cronyn. "We found a house on the East Side, somewhere in the Seventies, but when the owner read the script of *Not*

I, he backed out. He couldn't make head or tail of the play. Then I approached Jules Irving, who was the Artistic Director at that time of the theaters at Lincoln Center. I had known Irving when he was a student at Stanford University and I was an artist-in-residence there. Irving offered us the Forum Theatre at Lincoln Center, where we put on a festival of four of Beckett's plays.

"I have enormous respect and admiration for Beckett. But if the director and actor are true to his plays, they find themselves in a straitjacket. Beckett visualizes a performance down to the comma and period, and expects his plays to be done on stage precisely as he sees them in his mind. I mention this because of a slight contretemps that occurred between Beckett and me when the play got under way.

"I am a reasonably disciplined actor and always respectful of the text. In the script there is a stage direction, 'Krapp curses . . .' and a few lines further on, 'Krapp curses louder. . . .' But Beckett didn't provide the curses. I discussed this with Schneider, who was directing the play, and we agreed that the first time I would mutter, 'Balls . . . rubbish!' and the second time, the same words slightly louder. At one of the previews of the play, Harold Pinter was in the audience; he knew the text of *Krapp* word for word, and is a friend of Beckett's. After the performance, someone reported to me that Pinter had said that I should not have ad-libbed, and certainly should not have used an obscenity. I was sufficiently upset to call Schneider and warn him to be prepared for trouble. I said I expected he would be hearing from Beckett. Sure enough, we were just about to open when Schneider got a letter from the playwright saying, 'Please have him desist.' That made me angry and I wrote to Beckett, 'You have not provided the curses. What do you want me to say?' I received a steely, polite note in response, 'I'll make suggestions to Alan.' The upshot was that we went on with 'balls' and 'rubbish.'

"The first time I look over a play, I respond to the situations and to the characters as they're caught in the situations. Later on, I begin to see what may have to be erased. I always go through a process of collecting far more material than I can use. Then I try to retain what is essential. Once I get into a part, I find myself thinking about it all the time. It can become a kind of nightmare. Some actors have a tendency to get too absorbed in the details of what they do in a part, and that often makes the thing become mechanical. I try not to get trapped by the peripheral elements. I try to be guided by the questions, 'What's basic here? Is it true? Can I make it simpler?' In a naturalistic play, however, details are important.

"*Krapp's Last Tape* is one of Beckett's most naturalistic plays. When I acted it I didn't pay much attention to the symbolism of light and darkness, or any of the other symbols. The actor's problem is to make that old man's emotional base a true one. I had to find a way to relate the experiences and emotional memories of Krapp to my own, and yet to make them real in Krapp's terms, not in my own, so that I could fill this monologue with the vitality of actuality. The actor must start with himself and then be absorbed by the character. That is something the actor must do with every play. The symbolism is interesting intellectually, but is not really of applicable value to the actor.

"One of the tragedies of Krapp, as a person, is that he made the tapes instead of

Hume Cronyn, winner of an Obie (Off-Broadway) Award for his portrayal of Krapp at the Lincoln Center Forum Theater, 1972. (Martha Swope)

recording his thoughts in a journal, despite the fact that he is a writer. Krapp, it seems to me, was a lazy man, self-centered, self-indulgent. His fantasies, instead of feeding a creative drive, were ends in themselves. There is an analogy in this play to the plays of Strindberg, where the interplay comes not from a tape-recorder but from a husband and wife. A similar sexual conflict, however, is going on.

"I consider *Krapp's Last Tape* a relatively simple play, but an important one. The subject might very well have been dealt with by a conventional writer. The play did present some technical difficulties. The real hazard of playing alone, for instance, was the requirement of working with a tape-recorder and expecting precise cues, although the tapes were actually run by a stage manager. Absolute synchronization is required, and all through the performance I worried about that until it gave me what Mike Nichols calls 'a clenched head.'

"Albee, Story, Pinter, and many other contemporary playwrights are indebted to Beckett. He has, in fact, been the most influential playwright in the second half of this century, and one of the two or three most poetic dramatists of the last hundred years. I have come to love his work."

Krapp's Last Tape

First presented at the Royal Court Theatre, London, October 28, 1958. The part of Krapp was played by Patrick Magee.

A late evening in the future.

KRAPP's *den.*

Front centre a small table, the two drawers of which open towards audience.

Sitting at the table, facing front, i.e. across from the drawers, a wearish old man: Krapp.

Rusty black narrow trousers too short for him. Rusty black sleeveless waistcoat, four capacious pockets. Heavy silver watch and chain. Grimy white shirt open at neck, no collar. Surprising pair of dirty white boots, size ten at least, very narrow and pointed.

White face. Purple nose. Disordered grey hair. Unshaven.

Very near-sighted (but unspectacled). Hard of hearing.

Cracked voice. Distinctive intonation.

Laborious walk.

On the table a tape-recorder with microphone and a number of cardboard boxes containing reels of recorded tapes.

Table and immediately adjacent area in strong white light. Rest of stage in darkness.

KRAPP *remains a moment motionless, heaves a great sigh, looks at his watch, fumbles in his pockets, takes out an envelope, puts it back, fumbles, takes out a small bunch of keys, raises it to his eyes, chooses a key, gets up and moves to front of table. He stoops, unlocks first drawer, peers into it, feels about inside it, takes out a reel of tape, peers at it, puts it back, locks drawer, unlocks second drawer, peers into it, feels about inside it, takes out a large banana, peers at it, locks drawer, puts keys back in his pocket. He turns, advances to edge of stage, halts, strokes banana, peels it, drops skin at his feet, puts end of banana in his mouth and remains motionless, staring vacuously before him. Finally he bites off the end, turns aside and begins pacing to and fro at edge of stage, in the light, i.e. not more than four or five paces either way, meditatively eating banana. He treads on skin, slips, nearly falls, recovers himself, stoops and peers at skin and finally pushes it, still stooping, with his foot over the edge of stage into pit. He resumes his pacing, finishes banana, returns to table, sits down, remains a moment motionless, heaves a great sigh, takes keys from his pockets, raises them to his eyes, chooses key, gets up and moves to front of table, unlocks second drawer, takes out a second large banana, peers at it, locks drawer, puts back keys in his pocket, turns, advances to edge of stage, halts, strokes banana, peels it, tosses skin into pit, puts end of banana in his mouth and remains motionless, staring vacuously before him. Finally he has an idea, puts banana in his waistcoat pocket, the end emerging, and goes with all the speed he can muster backstage into darkness. Ten seconds. Loud pop of cork. Fifteen seconds. He comes back into light carrying an old ledger and sits down at table. He lays ledger on table, wipes his mouth, wipes his hands on the front of his waistcoat, brings them smartly together and rubs them.*

Krapp (*Briskly*). Ah! (*He bends over ledger, turns the pages, finds the entry he wants, reads.*) Box . . . threee . . . spool . . . five. (*He raises his head and stares front. With relish.*) Spool! (*Pause.*) Spooool! (*Happy smile. Pause. He bends over table, starts peering and poking at the boxes.*) Box . . . thrree . . . thrree . . . four . . . two . . . (*with surprise*) nine! good God! . . . seven . . . ah! the little rascal! (*He takes up box, peers at it.*) Box thrree. (*He lays it on table, opens it and peers at spools inside.*) Spool . . . (*he peers at ledger*) . . . five . . . (*he peers at spools*) . . . five . . . five . . . ah! the little scoundrel! (*He takes out a spool, peers at it.*) Spool five. (*He lays it on table, closes box three, puts it back with the others, takes up the spool.*) Box thrree, spool five. (*He bends over the machine, looks up. With relish.*) Spooool! (*Happy smile. He bends, loads spool on machine, rubs his hands.*) Ah! (*He peers at ledger, reads entry at foot of page.*) Mother at rest at last . . . Hm . . . The black ball . . . (*He raises his head, stares blankly front. Puzzled.*) Black ball? . . . (*He peers again at ledger, reads.*)

The dark nurse . . . (*He raises his head, broods, peers again at ledger, reads.*) Slight improvement in bowel condition . . . Hm . . . Memorable . . . what? (*He peers closer.*) Equinox, memorable equinox. (*He raises his head, stares blankly front. Puzzled.*) Memorable equinox? . . . (*Pause. He shrugs his shoulders, peers again at ledger, reads.*) Farewell to— (*he turns the page*)—love.

(*He raises his head, broods, bends over machine, switches on and assumes listening posture, i.e. leaning forward, elbows on table, hand cupping ear towards machine, face front.*)

Tape (*Strong voice, rather pompous, clearly* KRAPP'S *at a much earlier time*). Thirty-nine today, sound as a —(*Settling himself more comfortably he knocks one of the boxes off the table, curses, switches off, sweeps boxes and ledger violently to the ground, winds tape back to beginning, switches on, resumes posture.*) Thirty-nine today, sound as a bell, apart from my old weakness, and intellectually I have now every reason to suspect at the . . . (*hesitates*) . . .

crest of the wave—or thereabouts. Celebrated the awful occasion, as in recent years, quietly at the Winehouse. Not a soul. Sat before the fire with closed eyes, separating the grain from the husks. Jotted down a few notes, on the back of an envelope. Good to be back in my den, in my old rags. Have just eaten I regret to say three bananas and only with difficulty refrained from a fourth. Fatal things for a man with my condition. (*Vehemently.*) Cut 'em out! (*Pause.*) The new light above my table is a great improvement. With all this darkness round me I feel less alone. (*Pause.*) In a way. (*Pause.*) I love to get up and move about in it, then back here to . . . (*hesitates*) . . . me. (*Pause.*) Krapp.

(*Pause.*)

The grain, now what I wonder do I mean by that, I mean . . . (*hesitates*) . . . I suppose I mean those things worth having when all the dust has —when all *my* dust has settled. I close my eyes and try to imagine them.

(*Pause.* KRAPP *closes his eyes briefly.*)

Extraordinary silence this evening, I strain my ears and do not hear a sound. Old Miss McGlome always sings at this hour. But not tonight. Songs of her girlhood, she says. Hard to think of her as a girl. Wonderful woman though. Connaught, I fancy. (*Pause.*) Shall I sing when I am her age, if I ever am? No. (*Pause.*) Did I sing as a boy? No. (*Pause.*) Did I ever sing? No.

(*Pause.*)

Just been listening to an old year, passages at random. I did not check in the book, but it must be at least ten or twelve years ago. At that time I think I was still living on and off with Bianca in Kedar Street. Well out of that, Jesus yes! Hopeless business. (*Pause.*) Not much about her, apart from a tribute to her eyes. Very warm. I suddenly saw them again. (*Pause.*) Incomparable! (*Pause.*) Ah well . . . (*Pause.*) These old P.M.s are gruesome, but I often find them— (KRAPP *switches off, broods, switches on*)—a help before embarking on a new . . . (*hesitates*) . . . retrospect. Hard to believe I was ever that young whelp. The voice! Jesus! And the aspirations! (*Brief laugh in which* KRAPP *joins.*) And the resolutions! (*Brief laugh in which* KRAPP *joins.*) To drink less, in particular. (*Brief laugh of* KRAPP *alone.*) Statistics. Seventeen hundred hours, out of the preceding eight thousand odd, consumed on licensed premises alone. More than 20%, say 40% of his waking life. (*Pause.*) Plans for a less . . . (*hesitates*) . . . engrossing sexual life. Last illness of his father. Flagging pursuit of happiness. Unattainable laxation. Sneers at what he calls his youth and thanks to God that it's over. (*Pause.*) False ring there. (*Pause.*) Shadows of the opus . . . magnum. Closing with a—(*brief laugh*)—yelp to Providence. (*Prolonged laugh in which* KRAPP *joins.*) What remains of all that misery? A girl in a shabby green coat, on a railway-station platform? No?

(*Pause.*)

When I look—

(KRAPP *switches off, broods, looks at his watch, gets up, goes backstage into darkness. Ten seconds. Pop of cork. Ten seconds. Second cork. Ten seconds. Third cork. Ten seconds. Brief burst of quavering song.*)

Krapp (*Sings*).
> Now the day is over,
> Night is drawing nigh-igh,
> Shadows—

(*Fit of coughing. He comes back into light, sits down, wipes his mouth, switches on, resumes his listening posture.*)

Tape.—back on the year that is gone, with what I hope is perhaps a glint of the old eye to come, there is of course the house on the canal where mother lay a-dying, in the late autumn, after her long viduity. (*Krapp gives a start*), and the—(*Krapp switches off, winds back tape a little, bends his ear closer to machine, switches on*)—a-dying, after her long viduity, and the—

(*Krapp switches off, raises his head, stares blankly before him. His lips move in the syllables of "viduity." No sound. He gets up, goes backstage into darkness, comes back with an enormous dictionary, lays it on table, sits down and looks up the word.*)

Krapp (*Reading from dictionary*). State—or condition of being—or remaining—a widow—or widower. (*Looks up. Puzzled.*) Being—or remaining? . . . (*Pause. He peers again at dictionary. Reading.*) "Deep weeds of viduity" . . . Also of an animal, especially a bird . . . the vidua or weaver-bird . . . Black plumage of male . . . (*He looks up. With relish.*) The vidua-bird!

(*Pause. He closes dictionary, switches on, resumes listening posture.*)

Tape.—bench by the weir from where I could see her window. There I sat, in the biting wind, wishing she were gone. (*Pause.*) Hardly a soul, just a few regulars, nursemaids, infants, old men, dogs. I got to know them quite well—oh by appearance of course I mean! One dark young beauty I recollect particularly, all white and starch, incomparable bosom, with a big black hooded perambulator, most funereal thing. Whenever I looked in her direction she had her eyes on me. And yet when I was bold enough to speak to her—not having been introduced—she threatened to call a policeman. As if I had designs on her virtue! (*Laugh. Pause.*) The face she had! The eyes! Like . . . (*hesitates*) . . . chrysolite! (*Pause.*) Ah well . . . (*Pause.*) I was there when—(*Krapp switches off, broods, switches on again*)—the blind went down, one of those dirty brown roller affairs, throwing a ball for a little white dog, as chance would have it. I happened to look up and there it was. All over and done with, at last. I sat on for a few moments with the ball in my hand and the dog yelping and pawing at me. (*Pause.*) Moments. Her moments. My moments. (*Pause.*) The dog's moments. (*Pause.*) In the end I held it out to him and he took it in his mouth, gently, gently. A small, old, black, hard, solid rubber ball. (*Pause.*) I shall feel it, in my hand, until my dying day. (*Pause.*) I might have kept it. (*Pause.*) But I gave it to the dog.

(*Pause.*)

Ah well . . .

(*Pause.*)

Spiritually a year of profound gloom and indigence until that memorable night in March, at the end of the jetty, in the howling wind, never to be forgotten, when suddenly I saw the whole thing. The vision, at last. This I fancy is what I have chiefly to record this evening, against the day when my work will be done and perhaps no place left in my memory, warm or cold, for the miracle that . . . (*hesitates*) . . . for the fire that set it alight. What I suddenly saw then was this, that the belief I had been going on all my life, namely—(KRAPP *switches off impatiently, winds tape forward, switches on again*)—great granite rocks the foam flying up in the light of the lighthouse and the wind-gauge spinning like a propellor, clear to me at last that the dark I have always struggled to keep under is in reality my most—(KRAPP *curses, switches off, winds tape forward, switches on again*)—unshatterable association until my dissolution of storm and night with the light of the understanding and the fire —(KRAPP *curses louder, switches off, winds tape forward, switches on again*)— my face in her breasts and my hand on her. We lay there without moving. But under us all moved, and moved us, gently, up and down, and from side to side.

(*Pause.*)

Past midnight. Never knew such silence. The earth might be uninhabited.

(*Pause.*)

Here I end—

(KRAPP *switches off, winds tape back, switches on again.*)

—upper lake, with the punt, bathed off the bank, then pushed out into the stream and drifted. She lay stretched out on the floorboards with her hands under her head and her eyes closed. Sun blazing down, bit of a breeze, water nice and lively. I noticed a scratch on her thigh and asked her how she came by it. Picking gooseberries, she said. I said again I thought it was hopeless and no good going on, and she agreed, without opening her eyes. (*Pause.*) I asked her to look at me and after a few moments—(*pause*)—after a few moments she did, but the eyes just slits, because of the glare. I bent over her to get them in the shadow and they opened. (*Pause. Low.*) Let me in. (*Pause.*) We drifted in among the flags and stuck. The way they went down, sighing, before the stem! (*Pause.*) I lay down across her with my face in her breasts and my hand on her. We lay there without moving. But under us all moved, and moved us, gently, up and down, and from side to side.

(*Pause.*)

Past midnight. Never knew—

(KRAPP *switches off, broods. Finally he fumbles in his pockets, encounters the banana, takes it out, peers at it, puts it back, fumbles, brings out the envelope, fumbles, puts back envelope, looks at his watch, gets up and goes backstage into darkness. Ten seconds. Sound of bottle against glass, then brief siphon. Ten seconds. Bottle against glass alone. Ten seconds. He comes back a little unsteadily into light, goes to front of table, takes out keys, raises them to his eyes, chooses key, unlocks first drawer, peers into it, feels about in-*

side, takes out reel, peers at it, locks drawer, puts keys back in his pocket, goes and sits down, takes reel off machine, lays it on dictionary, loads virgin reel on machine, takes envelope from his pocket, consults back of it, lays it on table, switches on, clears his throat and begins to record.)

Krapp. Just been listening to that stupid bastard I took myself for thirty years ago, hard to believe I was ever as bad as that. Thank God that's all done with anyway. (*Pause.*) The eyes she had! (*Broods, realizes he is recording silence, switches off, broods. Finally.*) Everything there, everything, all the—(*Realizes this is not being recorded, switches on.*) Everything there, everything on this old muckball, all the light and dark and famine and feasting of . . . (*hesitates*) . . . the ages! (*In a shout.*) Yes! (*Pause.*) Let that go! Jesus! Take his mind off his homework! Jesus! (*Pause. Weary.*) Ah well, maybe he was right. (*Pause.*) Maybe he was right. (*Broods. Realizes. Switches off. Consults envelope.*) Pah! (*Crumples it and throws it away. Broods. Switches on.*) Nothing to say, not a squeak. What's a year now? The sour cud and the iron stool. (*Pause.*) Revelled in the word spool. (*With relish.*) Spooool! Happiest moment of the past half million. (*Pause.*) Seventeen copies sold, of which eleven at trade price to free circulating libraries beyond the seas. Getting known. (*Pause.*) One pound six and something, eight I have little doubt. (*Pause.*) Crawled out once or twice, before the summer was cold. Sat shivering in the park, drowned in dreams and burning to be gone. Not a soul. (*Pause.*) Last

fancies. (*Vehemently.*) Keep 'em under! (*Pause.*) Scalded the eyes out of me reading *Effie* again, a page a day, with tears again. Effie . . . (*Pause.*) Could have been happy with her, up there on the Baltic, and the pines, and the dunes. (*Pause.*) Could I? (*Pause.*) And she? (*Pause.*) Pah! (*Pause.*) Fanny came in a couple of times. Bony old ghost of a whore. Couldn't do much, but I suppose better than a kick in the crutch. The last time wasn't so bad. How do you manage it, she said, at your age? I told her I'd been saving up for her all my life. (*Pause.*) Went to Vespers once, like when I was in short trousers. (*Pause. Sings.*)

Now the day is over,
Night is drawing nigh-igh,
Shadows—(*coughing, then almost inaudible*)—of the evening
Steal across the sky.

(*Gasping.*) Went to sleep and fell off the pew. (*Pause.*) Sometimes wondered in the night if a last effort mightn't—(*Pause.*) Ah finish your booze now and get to your bed. Go on with this drivel in the morning. Or leave it at that. (*Pause.*) Leave it at that. (*Pause.*) Lie propped up in the dark—and wander. Be again in the dingle on a Christmas Eve, gathering holly, the red-berried. (*Pause.*) Be again on Croghan on a Sunday morning, in the haze, with the bitch, stop and listen to the bells. (*Pause.*) And so on. (*Pause.*) Be again, be again. (*Pause.*) All that old misery. (*Pause.*) Once wasn't enough for you. (*Pause.*) Lie down across her.

(*Long pause. He suddenly bends over machine, switches off, wrenches off tape, throws it away, puts on the other, winds it forward to the pas-*

sage he wants, switches on, listens staring front.)

Tape.—gooseberries, she said. I said again I thought it was hopeless and no good going on, and she agreed, without opening her eyes. (*Pause.*) I asked her to look at me and after a few moments—(*pause*)—after a few moments she did, but the eyes just slits, because of the glare. I bent over her to get them in the shadow and they opened. (*Pause. Low.*) Let me in. (*Pause.*) We drifted in among the flags and stuck. The way they went down, sighing, before the stem! (*Pause.*) I lay down across her with my face in her breasts and my hand on her. We lay there without moving. But under us all moved, and moved us, gently, up and down, and from side to side.

(*Pause.* KRAPP's *lips move. No sound.*)

Past midnight. Never knew such silence. The earth might be uninhabited.

(*Pause.*)

Here I end this reel. Box—(*pause*)— three, spool—(*pause*)—five. (*Pause.*) Perhaps my best years are gone. When there was a chance of happiness. But I wouldn't want them back.

Samuel Beckett, author of the play. (Jerry Bauer—Grove Press)

Not with the fire in me now. No, I wouldn't want them back.

(KRAPP *motionless staring before him. The tape runs on in silence.*)

CURTAIN